MW00815368

NOVELL OBJECTIVE

30.	Describe guidelines for planning file system rights.	
31.	Describe and set the directory and file attributes that can be used to regulate access to files.	Chapter 4
32.	Based on a scenario, create and implement a file system security plan that appropriately grants directory and file rights to Container, Group, and User objects, and sets directory IRFs.	Chapter 4
33.	Describe the types of login scripts and explain how they coordinate at login.	Chapter 5
34.	Design login scripts for containers, user groups, and users.	Chapter 5
35.	Use the MAP command to map network drives from a login script.	Chapter 5
36.	Create, execute, and debug a login script.	Chapter 5
37.	Define NDS security and how it differs from file system security.	Chapter 4
38.	Control access to an object in the NDS tree.	Chapter 4
39.	Determine rights granted to NDS objects through NDS rights inheritance.	Chapter 4
40.	Block an object's inherited rights to other NDS objects using an Inherited Rights Filter (IRF).	Chapter 4
41.	Determine an object's effective rights to other objects in the NDS tree.	Chapter 4
42.	Explain guidelines and considerations for implementing NDS security.	Chapter 4
43.	Troubleshoot NDS security problems using NetWare Administrator.	Chapter 4
44.	Describe the benefits of Z.E.N.works.	Chapter 5
45.	Explain the benefits of using NAL.	Chapter 5
46.	Explain the components of NAL.	Chapter 5
47.	Distribute applications using NAL and snAppShot.	Chapter 5
48.	Manage applications with NAL	Chapter 5
49.	Explain the benefits of using Z.E.N.works to manage workstations.	Chapter 5
50.	Create policy packages and configure policies in NDS.	Chapter 5
51.	Register workstations in NDS and import them into the NDS tree using NetWare Administrator.	Chapter 5
52.	Use policies to configure desktop environment throughout the network.	Chapter 5
53.	Establish remote control access to workstations on the network.	Chapter 5
54.	Configure and use the Help Requester application.	Chapter 5
55.	Identify NDS planning guidelines to follow in sample Directory structures.	Chapter 4
56.	Set user context to provide users with access to needed resources.	Chapter 5
57.	Create shortcuts to access and manage network resources.	Chapter 5
58.	Identify the actions to take and the rights needed to grant a user access to NDS resources.	Chapter 4
59.	Create login scripts that identify resources in a multicontext environment.	Chapter 5
60.	Define console command and NetWare Loadable Module (NLM).	Chapter 8
61.	Perform a basic NetWare 5 server installation.	Chapter 7
62.	Customize a NetWare 5 server installation.	Chapter 7

NetWare 5 Advanced Administration (Test 50-640) Objectives Index

NOVELL OBJECTIVE	COVERED IN
1. Choose an upgrade method and a protocol.	Chapter 7
2. Use the Installation Program to upgrade a 4.1x server to NetWare 5.	Chapter 7
3. Use the Novell Upgrade Wizard to migrate a NetWare 3.1x or NetWare 4.1x server to NetWare 5.	Chapter 7
4. Describe the function of a NetWare server and its interface and identify the server components.	Chapter 8
5. Execute server console commands and navigate the server console using hot keys.	Chapter 8
6. Load and unload NetWare Loadable Modules (NLMs).	Chapter 8
7. Identify and describe server configuration files.	Chapter 8
8. Customize the server by editing the appropriate configuration files.	Chapter 8
9. Create server script files to automate the execution of console commands.	Chapter 8
10. Describe remote console management; use various utilities to remotely manage the console.	Chapter 8
11. Describe security strategies for a NetWare server; implement console security.	Chapter 8
12. Load support for Java applications on the NetWare 5 server.	Chapter 8
13. Launch Java programs and applets from the NetWare GUI.	Chapter 8
14. Manage NetWare from the server using ConsoleOne.	Chapter 8
15. Set up network printing hardware by bringing up a print server on a NetWare 4 server and connecting a printer to the network through a NetWare server or DOS workstation.	Chapter 9
16. Regulate who can do any of the following: print to a print queue, manage print jobs in the print queue, be notified by a printer when a problem occurs, view the status of the print server, or manage the print server.	Chapter 9
17. Manage the flow of print jobs into and out of a print queue by managing the status of the print queue.	Chapter 9
18. Manage print jobs in a print queue by pausing, rushing, delaying, and deleting print jobs in the print queue.	Chapter 9
19. Describe how to customize print jobs using print job configurations, printer definitions, and printer forms.	Chapter 9
20. Identify guidelines for planning and creating custom volumes in the network file system.	Chapter 1
21. List the system-created directories; describe their contents and function.	Chapter 1
22. List suggested directories for organizing the file system.	Chapter 1
23. Identify the strengths and weaknesses of sample directory structures.	Chapter 1
24. Design and create a directory structure based on a given scenario.	Chapter 1
25. Identify the advantages, disadvantages, and storage concepts of the Novell Storage Services (NSS) file system.	Chapter 1
26. Create a Novell Storage Services (NSS) volume on your server.	Chapter 1
27. Describe NetWare 5 memory allocation and configure the server for memory deallocation and garbage collection.	Chapter 11

NOVELL OBJECTIVE	COVERED IN
28. Define virtual memory and configure a NetWare 5 server to use virtual memory.	Chapter 11
29. Create an application and adjust the CPU time allocated to it.	Chapter 11
30. Interpret the MONITOR Statistics screen.	Chapter 11
31. Monitor and modify file and directory cache performance.	Chapter 11
32. View and modify server buffer and packet parameters.	Chapter 11
33. Define and enable block suballocation.	Chapter 11
34. List the steps to enable file compression.	Chapter 11
35. Enable and manage the Packet Burst protocol.	Chapter 11
36. Enable and manage Large Internet Packets (LIPs).	Chapter 11
37. Identify and define the various backup strategies.	Chapter 1
38. Back up a NetWare server's Directory and file system, and a workstation's file system with Nwback32.	Chapter 1
39. Restore a NetWare server's Directory and file system, and a workstation's file system with Nwback32.	Chapter 1
40. Install DNS and DHCP services.	Chapter 12
41. Configure and start DHCP services.	Chapter 12
42. Import a DHCP database.	Chapter 12
43. Configure and start DNS services.	Chapter 12
44. Import a DNS database.	Chapter 12
45. Explain the services provided by the Netscape FastTrack Server for NetWare.	Chapter 13
46. Install the Netscape FastTrack Server for NetWare.	Chapter 13
47. Use the Administration Server to configure the Netscape FastTrack Server for NetWare.	Chapter 13
48. Troubleshoot and tune the Netscape FastTrack Server for NetWare.	Chapter 13
49. Explain the services provided by Novell FTP Services.	Chapter 13
50. Install and configure Novell FTP Services.	Chapter 13
51. Use Novell FTP Services to transfer binary and text files.	Chapter 13
52. Troubleshoot basic Novell FTP Services problems.	Chapter 13
53. List the default rights assigned when creating a Directory and objects.	Chapter 14
54. Explain the guidelines and considerations for implementing NDS security in a multicontext environment.	Chapter 14
55. Identify the difference between centralized and distributed NDS management.	Chapter 14
56. Determine the administrative roles needed in your organization and identify the NDS objects and rights assignments that support those roles.	Chapter 14
57. Create container administrators by implementing the appropriate NDS rights.	Chapter 14
58. Explain NDS replication.	Chapter 15
59. Identify preventive maintenance procedures for the NDS database.	Chapter 15
60. Troubleshoot NDS database inconsistencies.	Chapter 15

NOVELL OBJECTIVE	COVERED IN
61. Explain NDS database repair procedures that can be accomplished in NDS Manager, including creating a new master replica, repairing a local database, sending and receiving updates, repairing network addresses, and repairing server IDs.	Chapter 15
62. Identify the procedure for recovering NDS from a failed server or volume.	Chapter 15
63. Identify the capabilities and requirements of NIAS Remote Access.	Chapter 16
64. Evaluate the current network and user environment.	Chapter 16
65. Select an appropriate data transmission technology.	Chapter 16
66. Design a secure remote access solution.	Chapter 16
67. Design optimal performance in a remote access solution.	Chapter 16
68. Configure NIAS remote access software on the server.	Chapter 16
69. Configure Windows 95 or Windows NT clients for remote access.	Chapter 16
70. Connect remotely to a server using a modem-equipped Windows client.	Chapter 16
71. Explain the concept of Remote Authentication.	Chapter 16
72. Identify networking solutions offered by Novell.	Chapter 17
73. Explain the benefits of securing your network with BorderManager.	Chapter 17
74. List the components of a firewall.	Chapter 17
75. Identify the components of BorderManager.	Chapter 17
76. Explain the benefits of placing Windows NT domains into NDS.	Chapter 17
77. Explain the purpose of the components of NDS for NT.	Chapter 17
78. Describe how GroupWise integrates with NetWare.	Chapter 17
79. List the basic components of a GroupWise system and describe the function of each component.	Chapter 17
80. Explain how GroupWise components work together to provide GroupWise messaging services.	Chapter 17
81. Describe the major features of ManageWise.	Chapter 17
82. Identify the components of ManageWise.	Chapter 17

NDS Design and Implementation (Test 50-634) Objectives Index

NOVELL OBJECTIVE	COVERED IN
1. Describe why careful NDS design is important to the success of a network.	Chapter 18
2. Explain the roles needed to complete an NDS design.	Chapter 18
3. Explain the major tasks and functions involved in an NDS design cycle.	Chapter 18
4. Identify the importance of creating an effective naming standards document.	Chapter 18
5. Identify design rules when designing the upper layers of an NDS tree.	Chapter 18
6. Identify key issues when drafting the lower layers of an NDS tree.	Chapter 18
7. Finalize the design of the lower layers of an NDS tree.	Chapter 18
8. Explain NDS partitioning and replication.	Chapter 20
9. Determine a partition and replica strategy.	Chapter 20
10. Explain time synchronization.	Chapter 20
11. Explain how NetWare communicates time across the network.	Chapter 20
12. Plan a time synchronization strategy for a network.	Chapter 20
13. Completing a user's accessibility needs analysis document.	Chapter 19
14. Completing an accessibility guidelines document.	Chapter 19
15. Completing an administrative strategies document.	Chapter 19
16. Merge NDS trees.	Chapter 21
17. Create, modify, and manage partitions and replicas.	Chapter 21
18. Create or modify upper and lower levels of the NDS tree.	Chapter 21
19. Implement a user environment plan.	Chapter 21

The exam objectives listed above were current at the time of this book's printing. Objectives are subject to change at any time without prior notice and at Novell's sole discretion. Please visit Novell's web site (www.novell.com) for the most current exam objectives.

NetWare 5 CNA/CNE:
Administration and Design
Study Guide

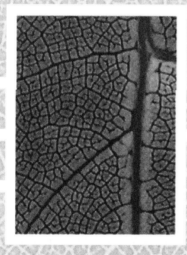

NetWare® 5 CNA(SM)/CNE®: Administration and Design Study Guide

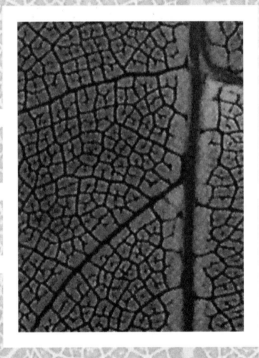

Michael G. Moncur
John Hales
Nestor Reyes
with James Chellis

San Francisco • Paris • Düsseldorf • Soest • London

Associate Publisher: Guy Hart-Davis
Contracts and Licensing Manager: Kristine O'Callaghan
Acquisitions & Developmental Editors: Bonnie Bills, Neil Edde
Editor: Vivian Jaquette
Project Editor: Michael Anderson
Technical Editor: Brian Horakh
Book Designers: Patrick Dintino, Bill Gibson
Graphic Illustrator: Tony Jonick
Electronic Publishing Specialist: Bill Gibson
Production Coordinator: Shannon Murphy
Indexer: Matthew Spence
Cover Designer: Archer Design
Cover Photographer: The Image Bank

I dedicate this book to my wife, Carin.

—*J.H.*

I'd like to dedicate this book to my wife, Susan.

—*N.R.*

Acknowledgments

I would like to thank Bonnie Bills, Michael Anderson, Bill Gibson, and Shannon Murphy from Sybex for their help in putting this book together, Vivian Jaquette for her tremendous effort in editing this book, and Brian Horakh for his technical suggestions. I would also like to express my appreciation for my coauthor and friend, Nestor Reyes, and his wife, Susan. Last, but certainly not least, I would like to thank my wife, Carin, and children, Robert, Ashley, Brianna, and Andrew, for allowing me the time to work on this book and for their love and support.

—J.H.

I am very grateful to my wife, Susan, for her unconditional support. I am also grateful for the love and support of our kids, Alberto, Liana, and Andres Reyes; Will and James Smith; and our parents, Aura and Ulpiano Reyes and Ernest and Pat Hilliard. A special mention to our brothers and sisters, Julio, Rene, Pete, Kathy, Lupita, Gisela, and Yaritza. I'd also like to thank John Hales, Bonnie Bills, Michael Anderson, Vivian Jaquette, Brian Horakh, Bill Gibson, Shannon Murphy, and Senoria Bilbo-Brown for their incredible patience and dedication to the project.

—N.R.

Contents at a Glance

Table of Contents

Chapter 17   **Integrating Other Novell Services**   **535**

Table of Procedures

Introduction

With over 81 million users and 4 million servers worldwide, NetWare is by far the most popular server operating system in the world. According to a report released by International Data Corporation (IDC) in June 1998, NetWare servers comprise 38 percent of all servers out there, while the various Unix operating systems together rank second at 21 percent, Windows NT Server third at 16 percent, OS/2 fourth at 11 percent, and several others comprising the last 14 percent. Clearly, there is a demand for professionals capable of managing NetWare. With the release of NetWare 5, the need for professional NetWare administrators trained in Novell's latest product has risen again, offering new opportunities for network administrators and those wishing to enter the field.

Why You Should Buy This Book

So you're standing in the bookstore with this book in your hand. Should you buy it?

YES—if you just want to learn to work with Novell's latest and greatest operating system. Building on your basic understanding of previous versions of NetWare, this book will quickly and directly update your knowledge and skills.

or

YES—if you are a CNE and want to upgrade your certification to the most current level. *This book gives you an affordable, efficient means of learning NetWare 5 and preparing for the CNE certification upgrade exam.*

or

YES—if you are with a training company, because this book offers the best alternative to the more expensive Novell Education training manuals.

What Subjects Are Covered in This Book?

The short answer to this question is, the information you need to know to pass the CNE update test and much more. To be more specific, the information presented in this book can help you in two distinct areas:

- The realm of Novell Education, with its unique perspective on how things work and what you should know about networking

- The real world, where tough demands on your time and energy require you to focus on only the most important information

This book contains not only the information you need to pass the CNE update test, but also information that will enable you to implement actual networks under real-world conditions. We know that you don't want materials that will be of little use to you once you've taken the tests, so we've packed this book with information that will genuinely help you administrate NetWare networks.

The following key topics are covered in this book:

- Understanding NetWare 5's new features and components

- Upgrading a NetWare 3.*x* or 4.*x* server to NetWare 5

- Using the Java console and ConsoleOne to manage the NetWare 5 server

- Migrating NetWare from IPX to TCP/IP

- Choosing and configuring the right protocol for your NetWare 5 servers and clients

- Installing and configuring DNS and DHCP services

- Implementing and managing Novell Distributed Print Services (NDPS)

- Creating and managing NSS (Novell Storage Services) volumes on a NetWare 5 server

- Installing Z.E.N.works

- Managing workstations with Z.E.N.works

- Installing, configuring, and using Netscape FastTrack Server for NetWare

- Installing, configuring, and using NIAS remote access services

How Do I Update My CNE to NetWare 5?

If you are a CNE and considering updating your certification, there are two possibilities:

Option 1   If you are a NetWare 4 or intraNetWare CNE, pass the following exam:

50-638: NetWare 4.11 to NetWare 5 Update

Option 2 If you are a NetWare 3, GroupWise, or Classic CNE, pass the following exam:

50-640: NetWare 5 Advanced Administration

If you don't already have a CNE-4 and would like to study for the NetWare 5 CNE program from scratch, we recommend these Sybex titles: *NetWare 5 CNE: Update to NetWare 5 Study Guide*; *NetWare 5 CNE: Core Technologies Study Guide*; and *NetWare 5 CNE: Integrating Windows NT Study Guide*.

Novell's tests are administered by Sylvan Prometric and VUE, which are independent testing companies. At the time of publication, registration for each test was $95. For more information on testing, you can reach Sylvan at 1-800-RED-EXAM and VUE at 1-800-511-8123. You can also register for tests online:

Sylvan Prometric:

`http://www.prometric.com/`

VUE:

`http://www.vue.com/novell/`

How to Use This Book

This is the best way to prepare for the test:

- Study a chapter carefully, making sure that you fully understand the information.

- Consider setting up a practice network to help you work through the procedures and to review concepts as you study for the tests.

- Answer the practice questions at the back of the chapter. (Answers are given in Appendix A.)

- Notice which questions you did not answer correctly, and study those sections of the book again.

- Review the practice questions until you have mastered the appropriate material.

- Study the next chapter, and repeat the process above.

- Once you have read all of the chapters, go to the Sybex Web page at http://www.sybex.com. Go to Catalog ➤ Browse by Category ➤ Certification, and then select CNE/CNA. Find the title of this book, and click that link. This will take you to a page where you can access the most recent updates to this book, as well as take an online test, "The Sybex CNA EdgeTest for NetWare 5."

- If you prefer to learn in a classroom setting, you have many options. Both Novell-authorized and independent training are widely available.

- If you have access to a NetWare 5 network on which you may practice, use this to your advantage as you study. (Of course, if you are practicing on a network used by others, be sure you do not try anything that may influence their data in any way.)

- This book contains a lot of information. To learn all of it, you will need to study regularly and with discipline. Try to set aside time every day to study, and select a comfortable and quiet place in which to do it. If you work hard, you will be surprised at how quickly you learn this material. Good luck!

Obtaining a Demo Copy of NetWare 5

At the time of publication, Novell was offering a three-user demo of Net-Ware 5, with no expiration date, for only $15 dollars plus shipping. (This is a full version of the NetWare 5 operating system, but it includes licenses for only three clients.) This can be an excellent support tool in your efforts to become skilled with NetWare 5.

The worldwide demo price is only $15 plus shipping. Orders take approximately two weeks to arrive.

To order:

In the United States, call 1-800-395-7135, Monday through Friday, 7 A.M.–5 P.M. Pacific Time.

In Latin America and Asia/Pacific regions, call 925-463-7391, Monday through Friday, 6 A.M.–5 P.M. Pacific Time.

In Europe, the Middle East, and Africa, call 353-1-8037035.

Conventions Used in This Book

Where possible, we have tried to make things clearer and more accessible by including Notes, Tips, and Warnings based on our personal experiences in the field of networking. Each has a special margin icon and is set off in special type.

Notes provide you with helpful asides, reminders, and bits of information that deserve special attention.

Tips provide you with information that will make the current task easier. Tips include shortcuts and alternative ways to perform a task.

Warnings can help you avert a possible disaster. Warnings will help you avoid making mistakes that could require a tremendous effort to correct.

How to Contact the Authors

If you have questions or comments about the content of this book, you can contact these authors:

John Hales:

JHales@compuserve.com

Nestor Reyes:

nreyes@earthlink.net

PART

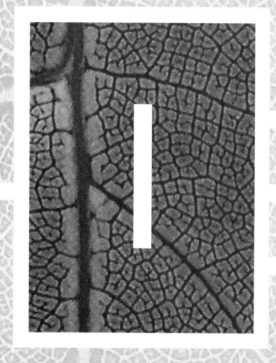

I

Introduction to
NetWare 5

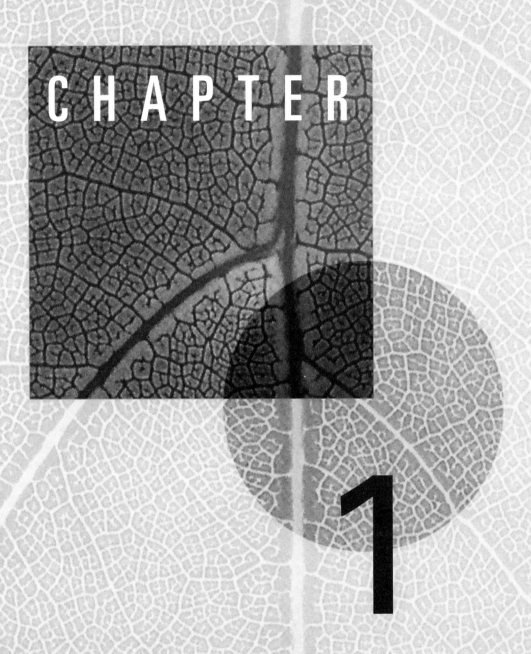

CHAPTER

1

What's New in NetWare 5?

Roadmap

This chapter summarizes the new features that were introduced with NetWare 5, which cover the CNA and CNE core requirements "NetWare 5 Administration," "NetWare 5 Advanced Administration," and "NetWare 5 Design and Implementation."

Topics Covered

- Novell Directory Services
- New Server Features
- Client Features
- NetWare 5 Support for TCP/IP
- Security Features

Skills You'll Learn

- List and describe the latest features in NDS
- List and describe the latest features for the server and the client
- Install and use the online documentation
- Explain how NetWare 5 supports TCP/IP
- List and describe the newest security features

Each version of NetWare is better than the one before, and NetWare 5 is no exception. The latest version of NetWare includes improvements in many areas, which are described in this chapter. If you're familiar with previous versions of NetWare, this chapter will give you a tour of the many new features introduced with NetWare 5. If you're new to NetWare, this is a good place to start learning about its capabilities. In the chapters that follow, you'll find in-depth information about the features introduced here.

Novell Directory Services

NetWare 5 has made some major improvements to NDS. The new NDS schema extensions and snap-ins make managing network resources a much easier task. Here are the latest improvements in NDS, with chapter references for topics covered in more detail later in the book:

WAN Traffic Manager   This new tool, implemented as a snap-in for NetWare Administrator, is used to control the WAN bandwidth. These are the three components of WAN Traffic Manager:

- WTM.NLM

- WAN traffic policies

- NWADMN32 snap-ins

(Chapter 21)

Catalog Services   Installed by default on your NetWare 5 server, Catalog Services allows contextless logins for users. The service stores NDS information in an index environment, enabling users to log in to the tree without knowing their current context. (Context is explained in Chapter 2.) This also enables administrators to get a quick "snapshot" of a particular section of the tree, allowing them to search specific areas rather than the entire Directory database. See the Novell online documentation for more information on Catalog Services.

LDAP v3   LDAP v3 (Lightweight Directory Access Protocol) is an ITU standard directory access protocol. It allows a client to query a X.500-based directory database regardless of the platform the database is on (for example, ADSI or NDS), from an intranet or Internet connection. See the Novell online documentation for more information. (Chapter 2)

ADSI   ADSI (Active Directory Services Interface) provides an open interface for accessing multiple directory services. NDS is compatible with ADSI implementation.

DS Diagnostics   Also known as DSDIAG.NLM, DS Diagnostics is used to diagnose or find problems in NDS. This utility lets you know the current configuration and health of your NDS tree.

Transitive Synchronization   This feature allows replica synchronization across multiple protocols. (Chapters 15 and 20)

For more information on the new NetWare 5 features, see Novell's online documentation and the Novell Web site (http://www.novell.com).

New Server Features

Let's go over the new server-specific features implemented with NetWare 5. The NetWare 5 operating system is greatly improved over previous versions of NetWare. These improvements include expanded multiprocessor support, including load balancing, and virtual memory for better software support.

Novell has also made a giant leap toward supporting open systems architecture by making its core protocol, NCP, independent from the IPX/SPX protocol stack. This means that NetWare can use a TCP/IP stack natively, as opposed to using tunneling, when sending packets on a TCP/IP network. Now NetWare can seamlessly integrate with the Internet, which is a goal of many companies.

These are some of the new server features (covered in more detail in Chapters 7, 8, and 11):

- Load balancing

- Memory protection

- Scheduling

- Preemptive multitasking

- Multi-Processor Kernel (MPK)

- Virtual memory

- Complete Java support

These services give the core operating system the ability to control system resources, which ensures optimization.

Application Support

NetWare 5 brings enhanced application support with its improved memory management architecture. NetWare now supports true Java-based programming. It introduces a true Java Virtual Machine, and supports both Java class and applets. Another new feature is support for the Java-based NetWare GUI, which supports Java applications written to standard interfaces. Examples of these are ConsoleOne and the DNS/DHCP Management Console. By providing Java compatibility, Novell makes it possible for developers to implement their own applications with NetWare 5 servers.

Improved memory management, including virtual memory, provides better application support as well. When an application requires more memory than is physically available, the operating system creates temporary memory that extends actual RAM in the system.

The kernel monitors and allocates resources as necessary to processes. All these new features combine to provide enhanced performance in all situations. You will find more information on the topics covered in this section in Chapters 8 and 11.

Installation Improvements

NetWare 5's upgraded Novell Installation Services (NIS) make installation much easier. You now get help from two installation wizards:

Install Wizard   Use this wizard to quickly upgrade NetWare 3.*x* or 4.*x* servers to NetWare 5.

Upgrade Wizard   Use this wizard to move data and users from a NetWare 3.*x* server to a new server running NetWare 5.

Both upgrade methods convert bindery data into NDS data and migrate and upgrade files. The wizards are covered in detail in Chapter 7, "Upgrading to NetWare 5."

New Management Features

Several new server management tools were introduced with NetWare 5, and SERVMAN was incorporated into the MONITOR utility. ConsoleOne is a Java-based graphical management tool that allows you to do basic server and NDS administration tasks. Developers can also add customized objects to ConsoleOne. You can access the local server or a remote server console screen through ConsoleOne using one of two utilities, Console Manager and RConsoleJ. You can use Console Manager and RConsoleJ to access a remote server console from a workstation.

ConsoleOne gives you access to NDS trees and makes it easy to manage, delete, and create new objects. You can also manage object properties and values. You can customize ConsoleOne with shortcuts so that you can quickly access applets, files, or folders. This information is covered in Chapters 3 and 8.

Time Synchronization Features

The newest feature in time synchronization is the Network Time Protocol, also called NTP Services. This new protocol is used to coordinate time in an IP or mixed IP/IPX environment. The IPX-based servers can only be secondary time servers in a mixed IP and IP/IPX environment. IP-based servers can be set to one of two modes, server (to act as a reference time server) or peer (to act as a primary time server). This subject is covered in Chapter 20.

Hardware Changes

Not surprisingly, all these new features mean that NetWare 5 requires more memory than previous versions. The minimum requirement is 64MB of RAM, but if you plan to run ConsoleOne (the new Java-based console utility), you'll need at least 128MB of RAM.

In addition to requiring more memory, NetWare 5 requires a better processor than previous versions; you'll need a Pentium or better. As you can tell, you are going to need to upgrade (or even replace) some of your systems.

The minimum required disk space is now 230MB, and 1GB is recommended for optimal performance. We suggest going with the optimal performance requirement, or even a larger hard drive, since the prices have dropped so dramatically.

Some other hardware you'll need is a high-speed bus, an SVGA video card and monitor, high-speed network and disk controller cards, and a CD-ROM drive to use for installations. More information on hardware requirements is found in Chapter 7.

File System Improvements

NetWare 5's new file system feature is Novell Storage Services (NSS). NSS is a 64-bit file system, an upgrade from the 32-bit file systems of NetWare 3.*x* and 4.*x*. Here are a few added benefits of the NSS file system:

Maximum file size   8 terabytes (TB).

Memory required 1MB or less for any size volume.

Maximum number of files per volume 16 trillion files per volume.

Volume limitation 256 volumes (total of traditional and NSS volumes). There is no limit on segments per volume, and the maximum total volume size is 8TB.

To learn more about these and other benefits of NSS, see Chapter 10.

Storage Management Services

NetWare 5 includes a group of NLMs (NetWare Loadable Modules) that provide SMS-compliant backup and restore functions. This group is called NetWare Backup/Restore services, or Enhanced SBACKUP. You'll need to load SBCON on the host server to provide the NetWare Backup/Restore services. NWBACK32 is run at the workstation and used to choose the type of backup or restore job you want done and submit your request to the host server.

Utility Improvements

Quite a few new utilities were introduced with the release of NetWare 5. Here are some of the newest management utilities available, with references to the chapters where they are covered in detail:

DNS/DHCP Management Console This allows the user to create and configure DNS and DHCP objects, see address additions, see audit trails made by the server, see deletions, import DNS and DHCP data to NDS, and see any rejections. You'll find information on this subject in Chapter 12.

Enhanced SBACKUP Also called NetWare Backup/Restore, Enhanced SBACKUP is composed of new server- and client-based utilities that support NetWare SMS services. These services are discussed in Chapter 10.

NWADMN32 This is the newest version of NetWare Administrator, covered in Chapters 3, 4, 9, and 14.

Z.E.N.works Z.E.N.works, short for Zero Effort Networks, is a management tool used to manage applications and workstations. For more information on this subject, see Chapter 5.

NIAS remote access server NIAS (NetWare Internet Access Server) remote access server provides users with remote access to your network via dial-in services. At the same time, it provides modem pooling for dial-out services for network clients. NIAS is covered in Chapter 16.

Oracle 8 for NetWare

NetWare 5 ships with a copy of Oracle 8 for NetWare. This provides you with a database solution and also demonstrates NetWare's increased capabilities as an application server.

Oracle 8 for NetWare comes with a five-user license, and is tightly integrated with NetWare and NDS. This means that you can manage the access to and functionality of any Oracle 8 server from NDS, making the process seamless to the users on your network.

Oracle 8 incorporates Oracle's newest advancements in client/server databases. Combined with NetWare 5's increased capabilities in software support and processor management, this makes for a complete network solution.

Printing Features

Novell Distributed Print Services (NDPS) is now included as part of your server bundle, and becomes your default print system upon installation. The new NDPS allows you to print to a network printer whether it's attached to the server, to a workstation, or directly to the network. Several components interact to provide NetWare 5 printing services, including Printer Agents (PAs), Managers, Brokers, and Gateways.

The main improvements that NDPS offers are fault tolerance, Windows 98 support, remote printer management, LPR/LPD on IP, JetDirect on IP, Xerox gateway, customizable server install, and SMTP notification of printer events.

Printers can be configured to be either Public or Controlled Access. Printer objects are created with NDS (except for Public Access printers) and maintained with NetWare Administrator (NWADMN32). You'll find more on NDPS in Chapter 6.

Online Documentation Features

Novell's online documentation has replaced DynaText. This HTML-based documentation includes an enhanced search engine and runs as a plug-in to Netscape Communicator 4.01. You can access the documentation through any browser, but you can only access the search engine services through Netscape Communicator 4.01.

The online documentation comes on a CD-ROM that is bundled in your NetWare 5 package. To install the documentation on a Windows 95/98 or Windows NT workstation, follow the directions in Procedure 1.1. (Note that the installation takes approximately one hour to complete.)

PROCEDURE 1.1

Installing Novell Online Documentation on a Windows Workstation

To install the online documentation on your Windows 95/98 or NT workstation, follow these steps:

1. Boot up your workstation. Put the online documentation CD-ROM into the CD-ROM drive and wait for the install program to auto-execute.

2. You should now see the install screen, which looks like this:

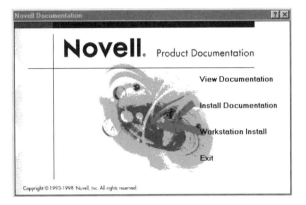

3. Select the Install Online Documentation option.

4. You will now be prompted for the directory that you want to install the documentation into. You can use the default settings or choose your own location.

5. You will be prompted to install the search engine. Choose Yes or No to indicate whether you want it installed or not. If you want to do any searches of the Novell documentation, you will have to have this search engine installed, so we suggest choosing Yes.

6. The install program will now search for Netscape Communicator 4.01. If it's not already installed on your workstation, you will be prompted to install it. Again, we recommend choosing Yes, because you can't use the search engine unless Netscape Communicator is installed on your workstation.

7. Click the Next button until you are prompted to install the Acrobat reader. Here again you will want to choose Yes, because the reader is used to display and print the Acrobat forms available on the Web pages.

8. Once the search engine has finished installing, it is added to Netscape Communicator as a plug-in.

9. You will now need to reboot your system so that the services will be available.

10. Once you have rebooted, you will see a Netscape Navigator icon on your Desktop. Double-click it.

11. Click the Bookmarks button to open the Bookmarks menu (shown below). From here you can open the online documentation, as described in the following section.

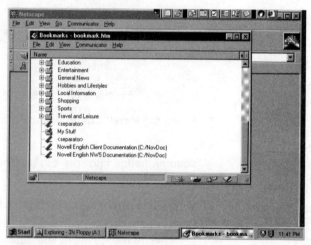

As with all of the NetWare 5 improvements, the new online documentation is friendlier to work with. Using Netscape Communicator and Novell's HTML-based online documentation makes the information easy to use and easy to read. To get started, choose the Novell English NW5 Documentation option from the Bookmarks menu. You'll see a Contents screen for the Novell online documentation, as shown in Figure 1.1.

FIGURE 1.1

The opening screen of
Novell's online
documentation

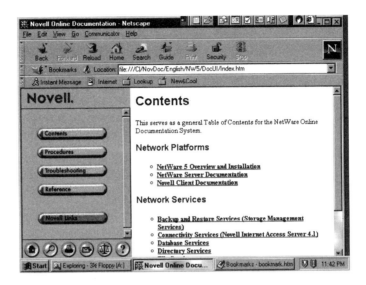

As you can see, it's like looking at a Web site. When you click any of the buttons on the left side of the screen, they open up the specified topic area on the right side of the screen. If you've surfed on the Web, you will have no problem using this tool. You'll find the search engine button in the bottom-left corner of the screen; choose the icon in the shape of a magnifying glass.

The Novell online documentation is HTML-based and has to be read with a Web browser. The preferred browser is Netscape, which comes with the documentation program, but you can use any browser you wish.

Client Improvements

The Novell Client offers new features such as Z.E.N.works and NDPS. The most significant feature is the IP-only and Compatibility Mode support for the new NetWare Client 32. This frees the client from any constraints imposed by IPX while still maintaining backward compatibility. See Chapters 2 and 5 for more information on the Novell Client.

The Automatic Client Upgrade (ACU) feature of Novell Client makes upgrading simple. See the Novell online documentation for more information.

NetWare 5 Support for TCP/IP

The NetWare 5 operating system and Novell Directory Services (NDS) now feature full native support for TCP/IP, which means that the core operating system and the clients can optionally communicate with each other using only TCP/IP as the communication protocol stack. This provides many advantages for NetWare 5.

In an increasingly Internet-aware market, supporting TCP/IP natively allows NetWare to fully integrate with the Internet and company intranets. With these new TCP/IP services and features, you no longer need to support multiple protocols (IPX/SPX and TCP/IP), as previous versions of NetWare required.

All the NetWare services available in previous versions are available over TCP/IP. The new services added to support TCP/IP are tightly integrated with NDS for ease of management, using common management interfaces. Domain Name Services (DNS) was also integrated into NDS to support domain name resolution. The following sections discuss the components and features that enable native support for TCP/IP.

Server TCP/IP Components

When you install NetWare 5, it defaults to a TCP/IP-only configuration, but you can select the protocol you need (IPX or IP). Therefore, you need to plan ahead to decide which protocol is best suited for your network. In this section we'll give you an overview of some new components that make native TCP/IP support possible for NetWare 5. The following are the new features that support TCP/IP:

NCPIP.NLM This NLM provides the core operating system with native TCP/IP support. (NLMs, or NetWare Loadable Modules, will be discussed in Chapter 8.) This enables NCP (NetWare Core Protocol) packets to communicate over TCP or UDP packets. This file is located in SYS:SYSTEM.

Service Location Protocol (SLP)   SLP provides discovery and registration of services over TCP/IP. This provides the same services as SAPs (Service Advertising Protocols) did for IPX/SPX-based networks. But SLP is much more efficient than SAPs, and it is integrated into NDS. SLP will be discussed in greater detail later in this chapter.

Domain Name System (DNS)   DNS is an Internet standard protocol used to map computer names (host names) with IP addresses. This protocol is integrated into NDS. (Chapter 12)

Dynamic Host Configuration Protocol (DHCP)   DHCP is a standard Internet protocol that provides TCP/IP configuration information to DHCP clients. This service is managed through NDS. See Chapter 12 for more information.

World Wide Web Services (WWW)   Netscape FastTrack Server for NetWare, developed by Novonyx (a joint venture between NetWare and Netscape recently absorbed by Novell), provides WWW Services for an intranet or the Internet. This service is managed by NDS. Chapter 13 covers this topic in more detail.

File Transfer Protocol (FTP)   NetWare servers can be configured to provide FTP services. See Chapter 13 for more information.

Application support over TCP/IP   Both Novell and third-party applications are supported over a pure IP (TCP/IP-only) network. Novell allows third-party application support through the Transport Layer Interface (TLI) or BSD 4.3 Sockets Interface. See Chapter 8 for more information.

Pure IP support for NetWare clients   New for NetWare clients is the support for a TCP/IP-only network. Novell has implemented changes that removed dependencies to IPX from the NetWare Core Protocol (NCP). This feature is only available for clients that support TCP/IP natively, such as Windows 95 and Windows NT.

The most striking benefit of NetWare 5 is that it gives network administrators the ability to implement a single protocol over their networks with NetWare 5 servers. If you have an existing IPX-based network, you can implement a coexisting, or migration, strategy with TCP/IP.

Compatibility with Existing IPX Networks

NetWare 5 maintains compatibility with existing IPX networks, used by previous versions of NetWare. While NetWare defaults to a pure IP protocol, you have the option of using IPX also. Every network should be designed in the manner that best supports the company's goals. This includes selecting the transport protocol best suited to your particular situation.

In today's networks, you will find two predominant protocol stacks: IPX/SPX and TCP/IP. Each has its advantages and disadvantages, but with the increased interest in the Internet throughout the business world, TCP/IP has become a more sought-after protocol. This means that you may be faced with having to migrate your network (if you had an IPX-based network) to TCP/IP.

You may have to maintain compatibility with IPX if you have existing applications that require it. In that case, you'll use the Compatibility Mode (discussed later in this section). You may also decide that you want to migrate your network in stages; if so, you will need to support both protocols for some time. And in very few instances, you will decide to implement TCP/IP from the get-go, but you will still have to provide backward compatibility. The great news is that NetWare 5 supports any of these options.

The following sections will discuss the new features that support coexistence with, or migration from, IPX to pure IP networks.

Choosing a Protocol Configuration

As mentioned earlier, NetWare 5 lets you choose the protocol(s) that best suits your network needs. There are three possible server and client configurations:

- IP only (including Compatibility Mode)

- IPX only

- IP and IPX

Server or Client with IP Only   This configuration will only allow the NetWare 5 server to communicate with clients and services that use the TCP/IP stack. The IPX stack is loaded as well, but it is not bound to the network card. IP-only servers and clients can execute IPX-based applications using Compatibility Mode (loaded by default), but you will need to install the Migration Agent (gateway) to connect to IPX-based servers and clients. (The Migration Agent will be discussed later in this chapter.)

Server or Client with IPX Only   IPX-only servers and clients can communicate with previous versions of servers and clients without any special configurations. Although both IPX and TCP/IP stacks may be loaded, only the IPX stack is bound to the network card. If you are using NetWare/IP, both the IP and IPX stacks should be loaded. The servers establish connections to clients and other servers using only the IPX stack—or, in the case of NetWare/IP, they use an IPX packet inside an IP packet (called *IP tunneling*). To communicate with IP-based NetWare 5 servers, the IPX only servers and clients will need to use a Migration Agent (gateway).

Server or Client with Both IPX and IP   Servers and clients installed with both protocols have the capability to communicate with either protocol. The NCP packets can be transported over TCP/IP or IPX. This allows the servers and clients to execute IPX-based applications and to communicate with pre-existing IPX- or IP-based clients. These servers and clients can communicate with IP-based servers through a Migration Agent (also referred to as a *Migration Gateway*). A client configured with both IP and IPX is not guaranteed to establish a connection with an IP-only server unless you use a Migration Agent. The same thing is true of applications that use bindery information.

Compatibility Mode

In all the protocol configuration options covered earlier, you can always execute IPX-based applications or connect to IPX-based servers and clients. This capability is provided by a feature called Compatibility Mode. All the Compatibility Mode server components are integrated into the SCMD.NLM module. There are three main components that make up Compatibility Mode (SLP, which provides SAP encapsulation for Compatibility Mode, is discussed later):

- Compatibility Mode Driver

- Migration Agent

- Bindery Agent

Compatibility Mode Driver   The Compatibility Mode Driver (CMD) is loaded by default when the IP-only protocol option is installed. This enables the server or client to execute applications that require IPX. The server views the Compatibility Mode Driver as a network adapter card and, if bound to both IP and IPX, it acts as an internal router for the server. This allows the server to route IPX packets to itself, a capability that is used when the server is executing IPX-based applications. Also, if the CMD is loaded with the Gateway option (/g), it provides communication between the IP and IPX worlds. In this scenario, you need to bind IP and IPX to the network adapters before loading SCMD with the gateway option.

NetWare only uses these services when needed. If they are not needed, the CMDs are idle. For the CMDs to communicate with IPX-based applications or IP-based systems, SLP must be implemented across the network. This means that the CMDs are dependent on the services provided by SLP. At least one Migration Agent must be used to connect an IP-only segment with an IPX-only segment.

See the Novell online documentation for information on CMD configuration options.

Migration Agent   You need to install the Migration Agent to enable communication between an IP-based network and an IPX-based one. You will need at least one server configured with both IP and IPX, and the CMD loaded with the gateway option on the server console:

SCMD /G

This server would have to be connected to both networks, and would be responsible for routing requests between each network. For example, an IPX-based client would connect to an IP-based server by establishing a connection with the server that has the Migration Agent installed. The IP-based server would respond to IPX-based calls using the CMD it has, and connect to the client using a server with the Migration Agent. Figure 1.2 illustrates how this process works.

FIGURE 1.2

An IPX client connecting to an IP-based server through a NetWare server running Migration Agent

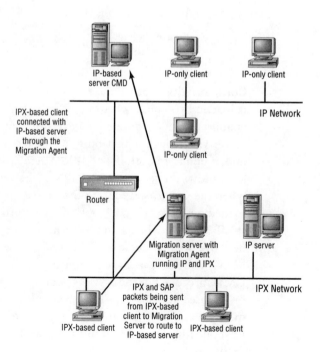

Bindery Agent   The final component of Compatibility Mode is the Bindery Agent, which provides compatibility with Bindery Services. This allows a client to access services on an existing 2.*x* or 3.*x* server or application that requires Bindery Services. To enable the Bindery Agent, you will need to create an Organizational Unit (named Bindery, for example), under the Organization object. On the server where you are enabling the Bindery Agent, make sure there is a read/write replica of the partition that contains the Bindery container object. Then set the bindery context with a command such as this:

```
SET BINDERY CONTEXT=.Bindery.Organization object name
```

Once the bindery context is set, load BINDGATE.NLM on the console. Clients attached to this server can now make bindery requests to NetWare 2.*x* and 3.*x* servers.

IPX-to-IP Migration

You may want to consider your options before migrating your network to IP only. For smaller networks, or even medium-sized ones, IPX is still a viable solution. The administration costs for an IP network are considerably higher than those for an IPX network, which takes much less configuration and administration. You can configure proxies to access the Internet if you want to provide IP services without configuring IP on the clients. But before converting your whole network to IP, you should carefully consider the costs involved, including labor and capital.

In some cases, it makes sense to migrate to an all-IP network, especially if you are supporting both protocols already. You can reduce the costs associated with running both. NetWare 5 enables you to manage both protocols and related services from a central Directory service. This allows you to manage diverse clients. It will also support you through a phased migration from one protocol platform to another.

These new features, discussed in this chapter and later in the book, provide the components for this transition:

- Migration Agent
- Protocol-independent client and server software
- Protocol-independent NDS
- Service Location Protocol (SLP)
- DNS
- DHCP

All of these components provide the vehicle for the migration. Later in the chapter you will learn about the new NDS features. Right now, let's discuss a new feature that is critical to the support of NetWare services in a native IP environment, SLP.

Service Locator Protocol (SLP)   SLP is a standard Internet protocol used for the discovery and registration of services over an IP network. (See RFC 2165 at http://www.internic.org.) SLP is not a name resolution protocol like DNS, but a service locator for clients, much like the SAP protocol was for IPX clients in previous versions of NetWare. The main purpose for SLP is to discover infrastructure services like NDS, DHCP, DNS, and NDPS. A second objective is to import SAP packets when running Compatibility Mode with IPX-based services.

One of SLP's advantages over SAP is that it registers its information with NDS, and therefore does not need to broadcast across networks as SAP does. The client only needs to query NDS for services rather than using the entire network.

Basic components include the SLP user agent (on the client), SLP Directory Agents, and the SLP service agents (on the servers). SLP uses multicast to connect an SLP user agent with several SLP service agents. For non-local service agents (on a separate network), you can use DHCP to help user agents access those service agents. An optional method to multicast, and one that is more appropriate for a large network, is to have multiple SLP Directory Agents (DAs) scattered across your network. The SLP DAs will then replicate information between each other. Both options have costs and benefits associated with them.

SLP is critical to a NetWare 5 implementation or migration to IP, since it provides the services that SAP did in previous versions of NetWare. You need to become more familiar with this topic, but an in-depth discussion of it is beyond the scope of this book.

Visit the Novell support site (http://support.novell.com) to learn more about this new protocol.

Migration Strategies   There are several migration paths you can take based on your network's current scenario. There are also migration paths you can take based on the company's goals for connectivity. In each case, you will start with an IPX-based network, or one using NetWare/IP.

First, consider which goal you want to achieve: Do you want to provide Internet connectivity or do you want to cut administrative costs? Then you need to consider whether to migrate the entire network at the same time or to do it gradually, by segments and phases.

Remember, planning is essential to a successful migration. Fortunately, NetWare's new features were designed with compatibility in mind.

Security Features

NetWare 5 restricts access to the console screen with the use of a screen saver. You can run SCRSAVER.NLM from the server console to display a screen saver. To return to the console screen, just press any key on the keyboard; you'll be prompted for a username and password. This feature prevents unauthorized users from accessing the server console.

The console agents RCONAG6.NLM and REMOTE.NLM require that a password be assigned when you load them. You can generate encrypted passwords using RCONAG6.NLM or REMOTE.NLM, further restricting access to the server console via a workstation. For more information on these new security features, see Chapter 8.

Although they are beyond the scope of this book, you should be familiar with the following new securities features of NetWare 5 as well:

Secure Authentication Services (SAS)   This service facilitates logins and authentication of applications. See Novell's online documentation and support Web site for more information.

Public Key Infrastructure Services (PKIS)   PKIS allows the NetWare 5 administrator to manage certificates and keys for the Secure Socket Layer (SSL) for LDAP servers within NDS.

Novell International Cryptographic Infrastructure (NICI)   Novell provides cryptographic services through security features such as integrity, authentication, confidentiality, and non-repudiation.

Audit   Auditing is a key element in network security. New audit features in NetWare 5 include multiple auditor capability, SSL connections, distributed and replicated audit records, and exportable audit data.

Memory Protection Features

Memory protection for the kernel is provided with NetWare 5. You can load modules or applications into a protected memory area, thus protecting the operating system from a module that crashes. This keeps the operating system from crashing every time you have ill-behaved or corrupted NLMs. Chapter 11 discusses memory protection in more detail.

Review

NetWare 5 offers many upgrades from NetWare 3.*x* and 4.*x*, including a variety of new components. These include features that increase the speed of the network, improve communication, and provide additional services and resources.

Among the important new features are pure IP support, which is incorporated into NetWare 5 servers and clients. The new snap-ins in NDS allow you to administrate other products from within the NDS tree; these snap-ins include NDS for NT, GroupWise, and ManageWise, just to name a few. Other new features we discussed in this chapter were Z.E.N.works, WWW Services, HTML-based online documentation, and NIAS remote access server.

NetWare 5 also includes more application support than previous versions. NetWare 5 is fully compliant with Java implementations, and it introduces a true Java Virtual Machine, which supports both Java class and applets. A new Java-based GUI and several Java-based applications are included with NetWare 5. The most important examples are ConsoleOne and the DNS/DHCP Management Console. Developers can also implement their own Java applications with NetWare 5 servers.

NDS Features

Novell's Directory Services was already perhaps the best network database on the market, and now they've improved it even more. Here are just a few of the latest improvements to NDS:

- WAN Traffic Manager
- Z.E.N.works

- Snap-ins for DNS/DHCP, Enhanced SBACKUP, Windows NT, GroupWise 5, ManageWise, NIAS, and Oracle 8

- Catalog Services

- LDAP v3

- DS Diagnostics

- Transitive synchronization

Server Features

NetWare 5 also includes several improvements to the server software itself, summarized here:

- The simplified installation process lets you use default settings. Two installation wizards—Install Wizard and Upgrade Wizard—make installing or upgrading to NetWare a much easier task.

- The MONITOR and ConsoleOne utilities make it easier to manage server settings.

- Time synchronization allows multiple servers to keep the same time. The newest feature is NTP (Network Time Protocol), which is used to coordinate time in an IP-only or mixed IP/IPX environment.

- The core operating system, or kernel, provides these services: load balancing, memory protection, scheduling, preemptive multitasking, the Multi-Processor Kernel, and virtual memory.

- SMS (Storage Management Services), the NetWare backup system, can now back up NDS more effectively. Backup/Restore Services are provided through Enhanced SBACKUP.

- Novell Storage Services (NSS) is a 64-bit file system that provides more advanced functionality than the 32-bit file systems that came with NetWare 3.*x* and 4.*x*.

- By working with snap-ins, NetWare Administrator (NWADMN32) provides additional features for managing network objects. Snap-ins are available for Z.E.N.works, DNS/DHCP Services, WAN Traffic Manager, GroupWise 5, ManageWise, Enhanced SBACKUP, Windows NT, Oracle 8, NIAS, NDPS, and Netscape FastTrack Server.

- The new DNS/DHCP Management Console makes it easier to manage and configure DNS and DHCP objects.

- You can use ConsoleOne, a Java-based utility, to manage the server. There is a version that runs on the workstation and one that runs on the server.

- Z.E.N.works, a management tool, helps you manage applications and workstations.

- Viewable with a Web browser and equipped with a search engine, the new online documentation makes it easy to find information on any NetWare topic.

Client Support

NetWare 5 provides Novell Client software, which is available for all Microsoft Windows, OS/2, and Macintosh workstations. The Novell Client offers new features such as Z.E.N.works and NDPS (Novell Distributed Print Services).

TCP/IP

Network communication is done through protocols, which are sets of rules that the server uses to transmit data between devices. These are some of the most common protocols:

- TCP (Transport Control Protocol)

- IP (Internet Protocol)

- IPX (Internetwork Packet Exchange)

One key advantage of NetWare 5 is that you can choose either to have an IP-only network or to use both TCP/IP. For many companies that use the Internet, the IP-only option becomes a big advantage. By using a single protocol (IP only), you can considerably reduce the costs of managing and maintaining a multiprotocol network.

NetWare 5 is now completely Internet-ready and it still provides excellent security. These are some of the new additions that are part of NetWare 5 support for TCP/IP:

- Netscape FastTrack Server

- DNS/DHCP Services

- Service Locator Protocol

- Compatibility Mode

- Migration Agent

Security Features

Network security has become a more important issue in recent years. Many networks have Internet gateways, and company networks are often set up so that mobile user can access resources from remote workstations. This has created a new pastime for hackers, who like to break into as many networks as possible. As you can imagine, security has become an increasingly important factor for network administrators.

NetWare has always provided very strong security measures, and its security features continue to improve. These are some of the latest advancements:

- Novell Directory Service security controls access to NDS objects.

- File system security controls access to disk files and directories.

- Auditing features allow you to monitor use of the network and its resources.

- Memory protection for the server protects against corruption.

- The SECURE CONSOLE command removes DOS from memory and disables loading NLMs from any directory other than SYS.

- The SCRSAVER.NLM module locks the server console.

CNE Practice Test Questions

1. The MONITOR utility:

   A. Allows you to create and delete users

   B. Allows you to set server parameters

   C. Installs a new NetWare 5 server

   D. Allows management of NDS

2. Network time synchronization:

   A. Applies to workstations only

   B. Applies to workstations and servers

   C. Is used by older versions of NetWare

   D. Sets the server's time from the workstation

3. NetWare 5 supports an IP-only implementation.

   A. True

   B. False

4. Which protocol takes priority in time synchronization across IP and IPX?

   A. NTP

   B. NSS

   C. SLP

   D. NDS

5. The protocol that provides the discovery of services and its registration over an IP network is called:

   A. Service Advertising Protocol

   B. Service Locator Protocol

   C. Novell Services Protocol

   D. Novell Directory Services

6. Remote access services for NetWare 5 is provided by:

   A. RAS server

   B. NIAS

   C. BorderManager

   D. DHCP

7. NetWare Peripheral Architecture (NPA):

   A. Is a new method of using disk drivers

   B. Controls all peripherals on the network

   C. Allows expanded access to printers

   D. Allows the server to use legacy peripherals

8. The online documentation provided with NetWare 5 is called:

   A. Novell online documentation

   B. DynaText

   C. Netscape

   D. ElectroText

9. The two main types of security in NetWare 5 are:

   A. MHS security and NLS security

   B. Hardware security and software security

   C. NDS security and file system security

   D. NDPS security and NCP security

10. The memory protection feature:

   A. Protects the server's memory from errant users

   B. Protects the server's core operating system files from errant NLMs

   C. Protects workstation memory from NLM access

   D. Protects workstation memory from power outages

11. The client software for DOS workstations is:

   A. The NetWare DOS Controller

   B. Novell DOS

   C. The NetWare DOS Requester

   D. Diverse client software

12. SCRSAVER.NLM locks the server console.

   A. True

   B. False

13. _____ provides additional addressable memory space than physically available in RAM, by allocating disk space reserved for this purpose.

   A. Protected memory

   B. CACHE

   C. Compression

   D. Virtual memory

14. _____ provides time synchronization in an IP-only or IP/IPX-based network.

   A. SAP

   B. NTP

   C. SNMP

   D. RIP

15. _____ provides the capability for contextless logins.

   A. DHCP services

   B. DNS services

   C. Catalog services

   D. Remote Access services

PART

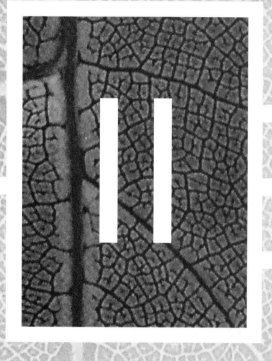

II

NetWare 5
Administration

CHAPTER

2

NetWare 5 Networking
Fundamentals

Roadmap

This chapter begins the coverage of the NetWare 5 CNA and the NetWare 5 CNE core requirement "Administration for NetWare 5." It focuses primarily on the basic fundamentals of NetWare.

Topics Covered

- How NDS Organizes the Network
- Connecting to the Network
- The NetWare File System

Skills You'll Learn

- Describe the purpose and components of NDS
- Describe the components of the Novell Client
- Install and configure the Novell Client
- Describe the components of the file system and list the tools used in managing volumes, directories, and files
- Explain when and how to use both network and search drives

N etWare 5 is a complicated system, and there is a lot to learn on your way to becoming a network administrator. To begin with, we're going to look at the two fundamental parts of NetWare 5 and how they are managed. These parts are Novell Directory Services (NDS), which keeps track of the network's resources, and the NetWare file system, which stores data and applications. In between the discussions of these parts, we'll explore another basic of networking: connecting to the network from a workstation.

How NDS Organizes the Network

NetWare 5 manages the network's resources through Novell Directory Services, or NDS. Information about each resource—users, groups, printers, servers, and other items—is organized into a single database: the NDS *Directory*. That's not to say that the database resides on a single server or that the entire database is on every server. In fact, while that is possible, in most installations of NetWare 4 and 5 the database will be split into chunks, called partitions, and then the data is placed where it is needed in a process called replication. These are advanced topics that will be addressed in Chapter 15. This database works for the entire network (potentially even on non-NetWare servers), rather than for just one particular server.

We will spend a lot of time talking about NDS in this chapter, because NDS is at the heart of the NetWare 5 network. Once you understand NDS, you will have no trouble understanding most other aspects of the network and servers.

X500 Standard

To distinguish it from a directory on a disk, the NDS Directory is written with a capital *D*.

What Does NDS Do for the Network?

NDS provides many benefits to your network. They include the following:

Ease of administration   Users and other NDS objects can be managed from NetWare Administrator, a friendly Microsoft Windows-based program. Some objects may also be managed from ConsoleOne, a Java-based tool that can be run from a workstation or even from the server. ConsoleOne will be discussed in Chapter 3. By providing a single point of administration, NetWare reduces the amount of effort required to manage a network.

Organization   You can bring order to the chaos of network administration by dividing the objects in the Directory into manageable sections.

Increased security   Security can be applied to any NDS object.

Scalability and interoperability   These are fancy words meaning that NDS can work with networks of any size and can interface with other types of networks.

✳ **Fault tolerance** The Directory can be stored on multiple servers. Thus, if an accident should befall one of the servers, the data will still be intact on the others, and, even more important from a user perspective, still transparently accessible by all clients.

✳ **Single point of authentication** Once authenticated to NDS, users never need to enter a password when accessing any NDS resources.

Let's take a closer look at each of these benefits.

Ease of Administration

NetWare 3 uses the *bindery* to keep track of each server's resources. The bindery is a simple, flat database—a simple list of resources, similar to the white pages in a phone book. When you attempt to access a resource, the server must read entries from the bindery until it stumbles upon the one you need.

Each server keeps its own bindery, and there is no connection between the binderies on the servers. If you want to access a resource, you need to log in to the server where it's located. If you need resources on two servers, you need to log in to each one. Worse, you must have an account on each server, with the appropriate rights to each resource you want to access. (The need to set up and manage all these user accounts may explain the sour mood exhibited by many NetWare 3 network administrators.)

Because NetWare 3 and earlier versions keep a separate list of resources for each server, they have what is called a *server-centric organization*. This means that each server is the center of its own little world. It may be connected to other servers, but it doesn't cooperate with them very well. This server-centric organization is illustrated in Figure 2.1.

NetWare 5, on the other hand, uses a *network-centric* system. Each server on the network is part of a single, unified network. The network has only one list of resources. The resources may be on different servers, but the Directory lists all of them, and you can access them all. This network-centric organization is shown in Figure 2.2.

In a network-centric system, you can access any resource just by knowing its name and where it fits into the Directory tree. If someone moves it to a different server, you may not even notice the difference. Best of all, you only need to create one account for each user. You can then give the users access to whichever resources they need, no matter where they are in the network.

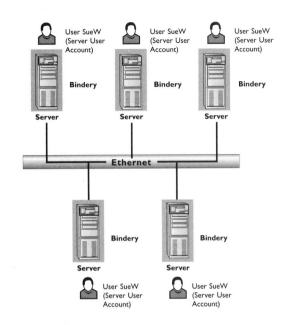

FIGURE 2.1

A server-centric organization keeps a separate list of resources at each server.

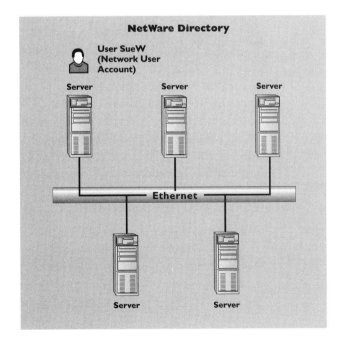

FIGURE 2.2

A network-centric organization provides a global list of resources.

NDS allows very versatile methods of administration. You can give a single, all-powerful administrator access to manage all of the objects in the network, or you can divide the Directory tree and assign an administrator for each branch. You can even create very specific administrators who only possess certain permissions to modify the directory. For example, some might have exciting titles such as "Phone Number Correctness Verifier" or "Terminated Employee Account Remover."

Organization

NDS stores information about each object in the Directory tree. The Directory tree is organized like an inverted tree. You can create separate limbs (called Organizational Units) of the tree for each department, location, or workgroup within the company. This makes it easy to organize users and other objects into logical groups, rather than one big messy bindery for each server.

Increased Security

NDS offers improved security by providing encrypted, single-login authentication. All this means is that the user logs in once for the entire network. The authentication, or password-checking, process uses *encrypted* versions of passwords, so it is virtually impossible to "snoop" on people's passwords by looking at the data on the network cable.

The tree-like structure of NDS allows you to manage sophisticated security features using a simple graphical interface. Because you can control the entire network from a single workstation, you can easily monitor the network and make sure everything is secure, without flying to other locations or taking someone else's word for it. Note that to actually monitor individual workstations, you need at least Z.E.N.works (for a basic level of monitoring) or Novell's full-fledged monitoring program, ManageWise.

Scalability and Interoperability

Although they're buzzwords in the computer industry and are thrown around constantly by computer magazines, *scalability* and *interoperability* do have meanings, and they do benefit your network.

Scalability means that NDS is constructed in a *modular* fashion (another buzzword). You can easily expand the network to include more resources and services. You can add users more easily with additive licensing (discussed in Chapter 3). Novell's Application Program Interface (API) allows programmers to make their own improvements and to add or modify objects in NDS.

Interoperability means that NDS is backward-compatible with previous Novell products, such as the bindery of NetWare 2 and NetWare 3. You can even manage these objects from within NDS. NDS is based on the X.500 (also known as DAP, or the Directory Access Protocol) standard, an international specification for network directories. NDS borrows much of its structure from the X.500 specification. It is also compatible with other directories via the cross-platform standard known as LDAP (Lightweight Directory Access Protocol), a scaled-down version of DAP.

Fault Tolerance

NDS is a *distributed database*. This means that copies of the database, or portions of it, can be stored on several servers throughout the network (see Chapters 15 and 20 for more information on this). Thus, with multiple servers, the safety of your NDS data doesn't depend on one particular server. If a server goes down, a replica (another copy) of the database on another server can take over. When the server is restored, the Directory information can once again be copied to that server.

WARNING   Fault tolerance applies to NDS data; it doesn't protect the data on your servers. Be sure to make regular backups. Many backup packages allow you to back up NDS data, which is a vitally important idea. You can never be too safe.

Single Point of Authentication

One of the core concepts of NDS is that you no longer log in to individual servers, but rather to the network. One key aspect of this, from the user's perspective, is that the user needs to know only one name and password to access any resource (that he or she has been given rights to) on the entire network. There is only one point when the user is asked for a username and password; thereafter, authentication to all of the servers that a user requests resources from is handled in the background by NDS.

How the Directory Is Organized

In NDS, every resource on a network is represented by a record in the Directory database. This record is called an *object*. Objects exist for each type of resource, such as User objects, Printer objects, Server objects, and so on.

There are three basic types of objects in the Directory database:

- The [Root] object
- Container objects
- Leaf objects

A sampling of these objects is illustrated in Figure 2.3, and they are explained in the following sections.

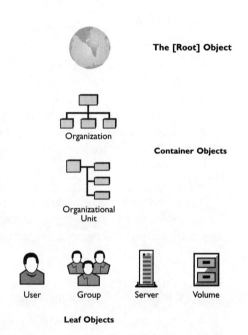

FIGURE 2.3

NDS is organized into a [Root] object, container objects, and leaf objects.

The [Root] Object

As you might guess from its name, the *[Root] object* is at the top of the Directory's upside-down tree structure. There is only one [Root] object in the Directory. It is created when the NDS tree is first created (when the first server in the tree is installed). You can't delete, rename, or move this object. The [Root] object is always referred to with brackets around its name.

Container Objects

A container object doesn't represent a network resource directly. Instead, it's used to organize other objects, much like file folders organize information in a file cabinet. Container objects can hold leaf objects (users and printers, for example) or other containers. By creating a logical hierarchy of containers, you can manage resources in a very organized fashion.

The [Root] object is the ultimate container object; it contains every single object (indirectly) in the Directory tree. The other kinds of container objects are Country, Locality, Organization, and Organizational Unit objects.

Country If you use them, Country objects may only be placed directly under the [Root] object. Country objects let you divide a multinational corporation into sections for each country. The name of the Country object must be a valid two-character abbreviation.

The Country object is included as part of the X.500 standard, and that's where the two-letter abbreviations come from. For example, US represents the United States, FR is France, DE is Germany, and CH is Switzerland. Some of these abbreviations may seem odd, but they should be obvious if you happen to speak every language. (If you do, you could probably find a more lucrative job than as a network administrator.)

> **NOTE** Although the Country object is available in NDS, Novell doesn't recommend its use in most situations. It was included for compatibility with the X.500 standard.

Know this

Locality The Locality object is new in NetWare 5. It is used for regions, states, and so on. In fact, Locality objects come in two flavors: generic locality and state or province. You can use this object to separate sites into various locations (such as Los Angeles or San Diego) or states, such as California or Oregon. This object is not widely used, as Organizational Units have been around since the dawn of NDS and are completely flexible for any purpose.

Organization The Organization object is used to divide the network into big pieces, such as a company, a university, or a department. The Directory tree must have at least one Organization object. Since most networks do not need to use Country objects, the Organization object is usually the first object beneath the [Root] object.

Some large corporations and government agencies might require multiple Organization objects, but the vast majority of companies use a single Organization object to hold the entire Directory tree. You can subdivide the Organization object with Organizational Units, or create leaf objects directly under the Organization if you wish.

Organizational Unit   The Organizational Unit object is where the network really gets organized. You can use several levels of Organizational Units to further divide the tree into categories. For example, one company could have different Organizational Units to represent its Accounting, Research, Marketing, and Customer Service departments, as illustrated in Figure 2.4.

FIGURE 2.4

Organizational Unit objects can be used to further divide the network's resources.

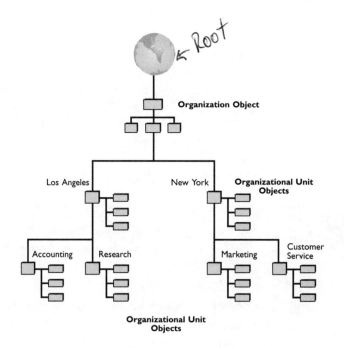

(handwritten: ← Root)

Organization Object

Los Angeles   New York   **Organizational Unit Objects**

Accounting   Research   Marketing   Customer Service

Organizational Unit Objects

Leaf Objects

Leaf objects are the leaves of the Directory tree. They can't contain other objects. Leaf objects represent the network resources. They must be placed (with a few exceptions) within either Organization or Organizational Unit objects. About 20 types of leaf objects are available. Most of these objects are covered in Chapter 3. For those that aren't, a chapter reference is given. These are some of the common leaf objects:

User   The User object represents a user on the network.

Group   You can organize users into logical groups, called Group objects, so that they share the same rights.

(handwritten in margin: User Name & Last name for login)

(handwritten: like security needs in these groups)

Organizational Role   This is an assignment that is given to a user. For example, an Organizational Role called "backup administrator" might be used for the person who runs a tape backup. You would assign the user who currently does the job to the Organizational Role. This would give that user whatever rights are needed to back up the server. If a different user were assigned to the task, you would simply switch that user to the Organizational Role.

NetWare Server   This object represents a NetWare server.

Volume   A Volume object represents a disk volume on a server. By browsing objects under a Volume object, you can look at the files and directories on the volume. However, even though you can browse directories and files from NetWare Administrator, they are not actually stored in NDS.

Profile   You can use a Profile object to group users who require a similar login script. This object will be briefly explained in Chapter 3, with a detailed explanation of login scripts to come in Chapter 5.

Printer, Print Queue, Print Server   These are used for queue-based network printing and will be explained in Chapter 9. These objects are here for compatibility with previous versions of NetWare, but have been superseded with the following Novell Distributed Print Services (NDPS) objects: Printer Agent, NDPS Broker, and NDPS Manager. NDPS is explained in Chapter 6.

Application   This is used by Z.E.N.works (Zero Effort Networks) to provide users with access to applications and to distribute them. Z.E.N.works is explained in Chapter 5.

Properties and Values

Each type of object in NDS has a list of *properties*. These are pieces of information that are specific to a particular type of object. For example, a User object has properties such as Login Name, Full Name, Title, and Telephone Number. The information stored in a property is called the *value* of the property. For example, the value of the Title property might be "Vice President."

Not all properties make sense for all objects. It's unlikely that a Printer object will have a telephone number. Because of this, NDS has a different list of properties for each type of object. However, the same types of objects have the same properties available. For example, all User objects have the same list of properties (Full Name, Title, Login Script), and all Printer objects have the same properties list (Administrator, type of printer).

For each type of object, certain properties are *required*. For example, the required properties for a User object are Login Name and Last Name. Other properties of the User object, such as Telephone Number and Title, are optional. Nonetheless, you may find it useful to fill these out in order to identify and catalog the objects in your network.

Some properties can hold more than one value. For example, the Telephone Number property for a User object can hold multiple numbers for each user. This type of property is called a *multivalued* property. The majority of properties are the opposite; they are *single-value* properties, which can have only one value.

NetWare 5 includes utilities that let you work with properties and their values. The NLIST utility, for example, allows you to search for objects with a certain property value or to list certain properties, such as all users and their phone numbers.

It will be easier to search for resources on your network if you keep property values consistent. In planning your network, you should decide which properties you will use for different objects and how to format their values. This is part of the NDS planning procedure, which you'll learn about in Chapter 18.

The types of objects you can create and the list of properties for each one of them are defined in the *NDS schema*. This defines the basic structure of NDS and is installed on the server with NDS. Novell provides an API that allows programmers to write applications which, when run by the network administrator, can *extend* the NDS schema. This makes it possible to add specialized types of objects or new properties for existing objects.

Referring to NDS Objects

You can access any object in the Directory if you know its name and its location in the tree. The next sections describe the different types of syntax you can use to refer to NDS objects and how to determine the name for each object.

Object Names

Each object in a Directory tree has an *object name*. NetWare 5 has a specific terminology for object naming. The object name is usually the most obvious name for the object; a user's object name is the login name, and a server's object name is the server name. The object name is also referred to as the object's *common name.*

The common name isn't enough to identify an object uniquely. NDS allows you to create Users or other objects with identical object names, as long as they are in different container objects. To completely identify the object, you also need to know where it is in the tree.

Understanding Context

An object's *context* is a description of the object's location in the tree. The context is the name of the object's parent container, the container object's parent, and so on all the way to [Root]. A context is described with a list of container objects, beginning with the *furthest* one from [Root]. For example, if the Organizational Unit IDAHO is under the Organization WESTERN in the Country US, the context for any leaf object under IDAHO is

IDAHO.WESTERN.US

NDS keeps track of your *current context*, or default context. This is usually the context that contains your User object. When you access a resource without specifying its full location, NetWare will look for it in the current context.

Distinguished Names

By combining an object's common name with its context, you can determine its *distinguished name,* or DN. Since this name includes the name and location of the object, it is a unique name for the object. Although two objects can have the same common name, each will have a unique distinguished name.

Although it is possible for two objects to share the same common name, it is good practice not to do this. This topic will be explored in more detail in Chapter 18.

Distinguished names begin with a period and also use a period between each object's name. For example, if the User object JOHN is in the Organizational Unit MARKETING, which is in the Organization ABC, John's distinguished name is

.JOHN.MARKETING.ABC

Relative Distinguished Names

To avoid specifying all of the container objects over an object, you can use a *relative distinguished name,* or RDN. The RDN relies on your current context, and starts there instead of at [Root] to look for the object.

If you leave off the first period in a name, it is an RDN. The simplest example of using an RDN is when you access an object that is in your current context. For example, as shown in Figure 2.5, if your current context is .ACCT.PHILCO (the ACCT Organizational Unit under the PHILCO Organization) and you want to access a printer called PRINTER1 in the same context, you can simply specify its name as

PRINTER1

When an object is outside your current context, you can still use an RDN. Enter a period at the end of the RDN to move up a level in the Directory tree. For example, again referring to Figure 2.5, if you are in the .ACCT.PHILCO context and you wish to access a printer called PRINTER2 in the MKTG.PHILCO context, the RDN is

PRINTER2.MKTG.

FIGURE 2.5

Some examples of relative distinguished names (RDNs)

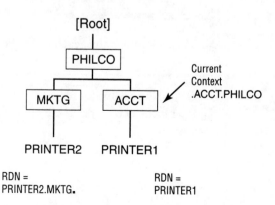

Typeless Names and Typeful Names

RDN (handwritten annotation)

So far, we've been using *typeless names*. They include the names of objects but not the types of objects. For instance, in the distinguished name .SUE.PR.ACCT.WNC, we know that SUE is a common name, but we don't say whether PR, ACCT, and WNC are Organizations or Organizational Units. We can make an educated guess, and NetWare can too. These typeless names can be used in almost any situation where NetWare asks for an object's name.

Nevertheless, a more formal method of naming is possible: *typeful naming*. As the name implies, this kind of name includes the type for each object. The object types can include the following:

C	Country
L or S	Locality
O	Organization
OU	Organizational Unit
CN	Common Name (for leaf objects)

To make the typeful name, add the object type and an equal sign to each object. The typeful name for the user SUE mentioned above would be

Know this (handwritten annotation)

.CN=SUE.OU=PR.OU=ACCT.O=WNC

You should understand typeful names, because you will need to use them on rare occasions. For the vast majority of NDS tasks, however, the typeless name works fine, and it is much easier to type. Typeful names are important for compatibility with X.500.

Connecting to the Network

To access the network, you will need to establish a connection to a Directory tree through a server. This is accomplished by running *client software* at the workstation. Because DOS and Windows workstations are the most common clients, we refer to that type in the following discussion.

A workstation normally works as a stand-alone machine. The operating system provides access to the workstation's own resources, such as its disk drives and local printers. You can install network client software on the workstation to provide access to network resources as if they were actually local. Once the client software is running, network drives can act just like local disk drives, and network printers can act just like local printers. This allows any software—even applications that were never intended to run on a network—to be used with network resources.

The current client software for DOS, Windows 3.*x*, Windows 95/98, and Windows NT is called the Novell Client (formerly Client 32). Client 32 was introduced in 1996 to replace the client software used by previous versions of NetWare (the NetWare Shell [NetX] and the NetWare DOS Requester [VLMs]). It was renamed the Novell Client with the release of NetWare 5, but is still often referred to as Client 32, because it is a change in name only, not in the underlying architecture. The Novell Client provides the following benefits:

- Support for NDS and the bindery (allowing access to Netware 3, 4, and 5 servers).

- Background authentication through NDS.

- Support for Packet Burst Protocol and Large Internet Packets (LIP).

- Full 32-bit support for Windows 95/98 and Windows NT, including login scripts and a graphical login utility.

- In Windows 95/98 and Windows NT, you can configure client parameters with a simple graphical interface, rather than modifying a configuration file.

Microsoft includes a client for Novell networks with Windows 95/98 and Windows NT; however, they do not fully support NDS. For all of these features, you will need to install the Novell Client.

The Novell Client requirements vary depending on the platform. Each system's requirements are summarized in the chart below.

Operating System	Requirements
DOS 5.0 or later (optionally with either Windows 3.1 or Windows for Workgroups)	A 386 or better processor RAM: 8MB Hard drive space available: 15MB For DOS and Windows 3.1, a memory manager such as EMM386
Windows 95/98	A 386 or better processor (486 recommended) RAM: 8MB (16MB recommended) Hard drive space available: 14MB (for typical installation, maximum 28MB for a full installation) For Windows 95 only: Service Pack 1 or OSR 2
Windows NT Workstation 4	Service Pack 3 or later

In addition, a network card is required for all platforms. You should also have the driver software that was provided with the card, although a driver may be included with NetWare or Windows. Of course, the network card should be connected to the network cable.

We'll look at the components of the Novell Client in detail after a discussion of the underlying network protocols.

Network Protocols

Your workstation communicates with the NetWare server through the use of *communication protocols*. A protocol is a set of rules for moving data across the network. In a sense, the protocol is the "language" used for communication on the network, and the client and the server must speak the same language. The most common protocols that can be used for NetWare workstation connections are IPX and TCP/IP.

The IPX Protocol

The IPX (Internetwork Packet Exchange) protocol was the standard protocol for NetWare networks until version 5 and is included with NetWare 5 as well. IPX divides data into *packets*. These packets contain the data that is to be transmitted, along with addressing information that determines the computer that the packet should be sent to. There are three main addresses used for NetWare networks:

- The *IPX external network number* is set on all servers in a network. Multiple servers in the same physical network use the same number. This number is used to route data across multiple physical networks. This is sometimes also called a cable or segment address. It must be the same for all servers on the same segment and different from all servers on different segments. (Note that if a server has multiple network cards installed, it may be on several different external networks at the same time.)

- The *IPX internal network number* is set at each server. This number is used to locate the server on the network, and it must be unique.

- Each workstation has a *network address*, similar to the internal network number of the server. This address is used to locate a specific workstation on the network. Network addresses are usually set in hardware in the network card (sometimes these addresses are called MAC addresses) and they usually cannot be changed.

The TCP/IP Protocol Suite

The TCP/IP (Transmission Control Protocol/Internet Protocol) suite of protocols are the ones used on the Internet and thus in more and more companies as well. This protocol also has address issues and is not as easy to set up as IPX, but allows for connectivity with the Internet, Unix computers, and other computers running TCP/IP. TCP/IP also breaks down data into packets, much like IPX, and, as with IPX, each packet contains addressing information and data. There are three primary components needed to make this protocol suite work:

- An *IP address* is the address used to uniquely identify you on the network. No two computers can have the same IP address and function properly. It is made up of four numbers between 0 and 255, separated by periods. Do **NOT** make these up unless you know what you are doing and understand the ramifications of your actions. An example of an IP address is: 167.64.75.34

- A *subnet mask* is used to determine if the destination computer is on the same subnet (or segment) as you are, or if it needs to be routed to the destination. A typical subnet mask is 255.255.255.0

and this ⟶ ⚡

- A *default gateway* (or *default router*) is used to send all packets destined for any subnet but its own. While technically optional, it will be found on all but the smallest networks.

The ODI Specification

To create a User object you need Last & First name (Ø password)

ODI (Open Data-link Interface) is a specification used with both the TCP/IP and the IPX protocols for DOS and Windows workstations on the network. ODI allows workstations or servers to use multiple protocols with one or more network cards. Each workstation or server can use a combination of protocols on the same network card. This allows your workstation to communicate with the NetWare 5 network and other systems, such as a mainframe computer or Internet connection, concurrently.

In addition, the ODI specification provides a modular way of installing network drivers. When a network adapter is replaced, only one piece of client software—the LAN card driver—needs to be changed. With the release of NetWare 5, ODI drivers are optional on Windows 95/98 and NT computers. They will be used if they are already installed, but otherwise the native NDIS (Network Driver Interface Specification) drivers will be used instead.

Components of the Novell Client

Like most complex software, the Novell Client actually includes several different components. Data passes through each of these components as it is sent from and received by a node on the network. There are three primary software components of the Novell Client:

Know these ⟶

- LAN card driver—ODI or NDIS
- Protocol(s)—TCP/IP and/or IPX
- The Novell Client

All of these components are loaded automatically by the Novell Client installation program. We will examine each component in detail in the following sections.

Network Card Driver

The LAN driver is the software that communicates with the network card. After the data is sent across the network and received by the network card, this program converts it into a standard format that the NetWare client software understands. The type of LAN driver used for NetWare 5 is an ODI driver (for DOS and Windows 3.*x*) or an NDIS driver (for Windows 95/98 and Windows NT).

The LAN driver is the only part of the client software that is not guaranteed to come with NetWare 5. Although NetWare provides ODI drivers for common network cards, and Windows comes with many common NDIS drivers, you should use the most current driver provided by the manufacturer of the network card. That driver should be included on a disk that came with the card, or you should be able to download it from the vendor's Web site. The Novell Client ODI-based LAN drivers have the extension .LAN. For example, the ODI driver for an NE-2000 card is CNE2000.LAN. NDIS drivers will typically be found in either a Windows 95/98 subdirectory or a Windows NT subdirectory and have the extension .SYS. The NE-2000 card referred to above is named NE2000.SYS.

The TCP/IP or IPX Protocols

The IPX and TCP/IP portions of the client handle the communication protocols. Packets are created and passed on to the LAN drivers for processing by the network card.

The Novell Client

The final layer of communication is provided by the Novell Client module. This module is responsible for communications with the operating system and application software on the workstation. The Novell Client allows applications to use network resources, such as files and printers, as if they were local to the workstation.

Installing the Novell Client

The Novell Client can be installed from disks, a CD-ROM, or over the network. For instructions on installing it on the Windows 95/98 platform, refer to Procedure 2.1. For other platforms, refer to the online documentation.

PROCEDURE 2.1

Installing the Novell Client on a Windows 95/98 Computer

To install the Novell Client on a Windows 95/98 computer, do the following:

1. Insert the NetWare 5 Novell Client Software CD or the first Novell Client diskette, or map a path to the installation directory on the network. (Mapping network drives is explained later in this chapter.)

2. Run the SETUP program. For the CD installation, this will begin automatically when you insert the CD or you double-click on the CD name
under Explorer or My Computer. You can start this program manually
by running D:\WINSETUP.EXE. (Replace *D* with the letter of your CD-
ROM drive. If this has been copied to a network path, browse to that
location and run WINSETUP.EXE.)

3. A dialog box will appear asking you to choose the desired language.
Click on your selection to proceed.

4. A screen will appear asking you to choose which client you want
installed and/or to install Z.E.N.works (see Chapter 5 for more information). We will discuss only the Windows 95/98 client here, but the
others are similar.

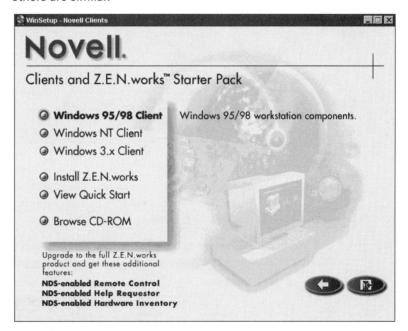

5. The next choice you need to make is what you want to install. You can
choose the client itself, the documentation for the client, Netscape
Navigator 4.04 (to view the client documentation), Win2NCS (for
remote access; for more information, refer to Chapter 16), or Java (to
install the run-time environment for Java applets). We will discuss
only the Client option at this point.

PROCEDURE 2.1 (CONTINUED)

6. You are now presented with a license agreement for the Novell Client. Click Yes to agree to the terms of the license and continue.

7. The main Novell Client installation dialog box is now displayed, as shown here. If you want to install the default components, choose Typical and then click Install to begin the installation process. If you want more control over what is installed, choose Custom and then click Next. For a detailed discussion of the Custom options, either click Help during the installation process or refer to the online documentation.

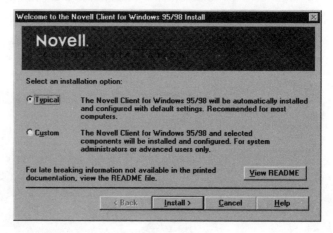

8. The installation program will now install the files for the Novell Client, and remove any previously installed Novell or Microsoft client software. You may be required to insert your Windows 95/98 CD-ROM during this procedure.

9. At this point, the program will recommend that you configure the Client. Click Yes to set the preferred (or default) context, tree, and/or server.

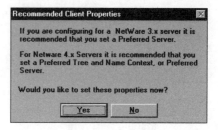

10. The Novell NetWare Client Properties dialog box appears; in it you may customize the client. At this point, you should enter the name context and preferred server or tree. If you clicked No in Step 9 or need to change any settings later, simply go to Control Panel ➤ Network, and then choose Novell NetWare Client and click Properties.

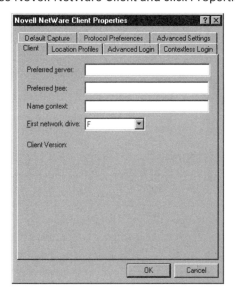

11. The installation process will copy some more files and then the final dialog box will appear, giving you the option to either click Reboot to restart the computer with the Novell Client or Close to return to Windows 95/98, in which case you will need to manually reboot to use the newly installed client.

Login and Logout

On a DOS workstation, once the client software is loaded, you can log in to the network by using the LOGIN command followed by your username (either as a distinguished name or as a relative distinguished name). You must first switch to a network drive. For example, to switch to network drive

F and log in as user SUE (assuming the correct context has already been configured), use the commands:

```
F:
LOGIN SUE
```

If the correct context hadn't been already set or you wanted to log in as a different user in a different context, you could use the user's distinguished name or a relative distinguished name. For example, if the user's current context was set to .CorpHQ.MyCo and you wanted to login as the user ASHLEY in the .FieldOffice.MyCo context, you could type

```
F:
LOGIN .ASHLEY.FieldOffice.MyCo
```

You could also use this command:

```
F:
LOGIN ASHLEY.FieldOffice.
```

The LOGIN program is called LOGIN.EXE, and it is located in the LOGIN directory on the server. This directory is the only one you can access when you are not logged in. Once you type the LOGIN command, NetWare will verify that the user specified exists, and if so, you will be asked to enter your password. If you type the password correctly, you will be allowed access to the network. If you are using a graphical version of login (in other words, a Windows version), the login utility is actually stored on the user's hard drive when the Novell Client is installed. Before you can log in, you will need an account on the network, which means that a User object must be created in NDS. This process is explained in Chapter 3.

The opposite of LOGIN is LOGOUT. The LOGOUT command disconnects you from the network.

In Windows 3.1, Windows 95/98, or Windows NT, you can select the NetWare Login icon in the Start menu or Program Manager to log in. Depending on the installation of the Novell Client, this dialog box may be displayed automatically when you start the computer. You can also log out from Windows 95/98 and Windows NT by choosing Start ➤ Shut down and then choosing Shut down, Restart, or Close all programs and log on as a different user. If you choose Close all programs, you will be returned to the Login dialog box, where you can start again.

Know this ↓

Always try to update/upgrade on Thursday's

if it doesn't work then you can find help on software.

The NetWare File System

NetWare's *file system* is the system that manages disk storage on the network. NetWare uses files and directories similar to those used by DOS. In fact, the NetWare file system is specifically designed to be compatible with DOS clients, as well as Windows 95/98, Windows NT, and OS/2 clients.

Components of the File System

The NetWare file system organizes disk access into several components. These include volumes, directories and subdirectories, and files. The next sections describe each of the components.

Volumes

A *volume* is the major unit of storage in a NetWare server. This is similar to a disk drive (or more accurately, a partition) under DOS. However, a NetWare volume isn't necessarily a single disk drive. There is a sophisticated relationship between disks and volumes. A single disk drive can be divided into multiple volumes. In addition, a volume can span more than one disk drive.

[handwritten note: NLM: network loadable module]

A volume is located on a NetWare server. Each server can have many separate volumes. NDS uses a Volume object to represent the volume. Volume objects are automatically given a name that combines the name of the server and the name of the volume. For example, the VOL1 volume on file server CENTRAL has the NDS common name of CENTRAL_VOL1. This allows several servers to have volumes with the same name, even if they reside in the same NDS container.

When you install NetWare 5, at least one volume must be created: the SYS volume. This volume contains the NetWare operating system files for the server's use. Each server must have a SYS volume. If you delete or rename the SYS volume, the server will become confused and refuse to start properly.

[handwritten note: Test server: use before putting on PDC use alternate server to test software]

Directories and Subdirectories

A volume is divided into directories. These allow you to organize the file system in the same way that container objects organize the NDS tree. The structure of file system directories is similar to the NDS Directory or the directories that you are already using on your hard drive. One very important note before we begin: *The NDS Directory and the file system are two completely, totally separate entities and must not be confused.*

Each file system directory can contain other directories or subdirectories. When you install a NetWare server, several directories are created automatically on the SYS volume:

SYSTEM   Contains NetWare server utilities, configuration files, and NLMs (described in detail in Chapter 8). Most tasks performed on the file server use the SYSTEM directory.

PUBLIC   Contains utilities that run from a workstation. By default, all users in the same container as the server or any subcontainers of the server's container have access to PUBLIC. There are subdirectories for various operating systems, such as Windows 95 and Windows NT.

MAIL   Used to store configuration files for each user. Bindery-based clients use this directory mainly for access to the server. There may or may not be any files or directories in this directory.

LOGIN   Contains the LOGIN.EXE utility and other files essential for the DOS login process. By default, this is the one directory users can access before logging in.

ETC   Contains sample files for configuring TCP/IP and interoperating with Unix.

DELETED.SAV   Contains deleted files *from deleted directories* before they are permanently removed. This is a hidden directory.

NOVDOCS   Created only if you choose to install the online documentation, this will contain the documentation in HTML format.

JAVA   Contains the support files for the JAVA-based interface on the server. It acts like an extension to the SYSTEM directory for support of JAVA functionality.

NETBASIC and PERL   Contain the support files that allow the server to process NetBasic and Perl scripts on Web pages.

NDPS   Exists if NDPS has been installed on the server and contains all the files, drivers, utilities, and so on to enable NDPS (Novell Distributed Print Services, covered in Chapter 6) to fully function.

A subdirectory is simply a directory inside another directory. The terms *directory* and *subdirectory* are often used interchangeably.

When you refer to a directory on a NetWare volume, the NetWare standard syntax uses a colon between the volume name and the directory, and either a backslash (\) or a forward slash (/) between directory and subdirectory names. For example, the SYSTEM directory on the SYS volume is referred to as SYS:SYSTEM. To refer to the DATA subdirectory under the PUBLIC directory on the VOL1 volume, use this syntax:

```
VOL1:PUBLIC\DATA
```

Since you can access multiple servers at the same time, you can specify the server name as well. Include the server name before the volume name, and use a backslash between the server name and the volume. To illustrate this syntax, consider this example: the CHECKS subdirectory under the AP subdirectory under the DATA directory on the VOL5 volume on the QED server would be written as

```
QED\VOL5:DATA\AP\CHECKS
```

If you are using Windows 95/98 or Windows NT, the format may be slightly different, depending on where the path is needed. If you use Microsoft utilities to accomplish tasks, such as mapping a drive, you need to use the Microsoft standard method, which is called the Universal Naming Convention (UNC). In this syntax, the server name is preceded by two backslash (\\) characters, followed by the volume name, followed by another backslash, followed by the desired path, again separating directories and subdirectories with backslash characters. To enter the same path to the CHECKS directory referred to in the previous example, you would type

```
\\QED\VOL5\DATA\AP\CHECKS
```

You can also map a drive using the volume object instead of the physical server and volume names. Using the previous example, the same path could be written with the volume object (assuming the volume object is in the current context) as follows:

```
QED_VOL5:DATA\AP\CHECKS
```

One final option that I want to discuss here is mapping a root drive. A *root drive* (sometimes called a fake root) is a mapped drive to a path that to the user appears as if it is the root of the volume. This can be handy with program directories or home directories. For example, if you map a root drive to drive P: for the directory location described above, when the user goes to that drive they will see at a command prompt P:>, whereas if you mapped it with any of the other commands, the user would see P:\DATA\AP\CHECKS>.

Files

At last we come to a really useful item. The whole point of the file system is to store and manage files. A file can contain an application program, a word processing or spreadsheet document, a database, a graphic image—any item that can be stored on a disk.

NetWare 5 supports both the DOS filename format to store files and the long filename format used by Windows 95/98 and Windows NT. In the DOS format, each file has an eight-character name and a three-character *extension*. The extension is usually used to specify the type of file, such as TXT for a text file or EXE for a program. Filenames are usually written in all uppercase letters, but the file system is not case-sensitive; you can type names uppercase or lowercase. In the long filename format, you may have filenames that are up to 255 characters long, including multiple spaces and periods. These files also usually have an extension associated with them. The extension is the characters after the last period, and is typically, although not always, three characters long, for compatibility with DOS applications.

Using Command-Line Utilities

NetWare includes a wide variety of utilities. These are programs that you can use to manage the server and network resources.

Some of the utilities that you can use to manage the file system are *command-line* utilities. This means that they don't present you with a menu or ask you questions. You must specify all of the parameters for the command after the name of the command itself. You can run these utilities on any DOS workstation (or Windows 3.1, Windows 95/98, or Windows NT workstation via a command prompt window) attached to the network.

Since the NetWare file system acts just like a DOS file system, you can also use any DOS or Windows utility to manage files on the server. However, most of these utilities don't fully support the additional features of NetWare's file system, such as security and file attributes.

You can display a list of available options for just about any NetWare utility by typing the name of the utility followed by /?. For example, type **NDIR /?** to see a list of the options for the NDIR utility.

The following are two command-line utilities that you might find useful for managing your network file system:

NDIR You are probably familiar with the DIR command in DOS. This is probably the most commonly used command. Its function is to list all of the files in a directory. The NDIR command is a special NetWare version. In addition to the list of files, the NDIR listing includes NetWare-specific information, such as the name of the owner of the file. Typing NDIR by itself will list all the files in the current directory. Advanced options allow you to view only certain files or to search an entire volume for a file.

NLIST When you need to see a list of items, you can use this utility. NLIST is a general-purpose utility for listing any NDS object. The NLIST VOLUME command lists Volume objects that are available in the Directory tree. You can also use the /D option to display additional information about a specific volume.

Using Network and Search Drives

As we mentioned before, DOS doesn't really understand networks. The network client software adds networking capabilities to DOS, but it still isn't tightly integrated with NetWare. Most DOS applications don't allow you to refer to NetWare volumes by their volume names. This is where *mapped drives* come in. While it is true that Windows 95/98 and Windows NT offer far more advanced integration of the network with the local computer, the ability to refer to a long path by a drive letter is a very useful shortcut. For example, if you tell users to store their files in SERVER1\DATA:USERS\JQPUBLIC, you will invariably get them saving files all over the volume (and probably other places as well) and then asking you to find them. It is much simpler to tell the users to store their files on the H drive (for home directory) instead.

DOS, Windows 95/98, and Windows NT use drive letters to refer to the physical drives on the workstation. Typically, drives A and B are floppy drives, and the workstation hard drive is usually the C drive. If your workstation has several drives and/or partitions, they will use additional letters. The remaining letters are available for the two types of mapped drives: network drives and search drives.

Mapping Network Drives

When you map a network drive, you basically assign a drive letter, or *drive pointer,* to a certain volume and directory. Think of this as a convenient shortcut to referring to a network directory.

[Handwritten margin notes:]
F: Login drive
G: Dept drive
U: Home directory
H: Apps
P: App specific

You use the MAP command to map network drives. The MAP command line includes the drive letter to be used, an equal sign, and the network volume and directory to map the drive to. For example, the following command maps drive G to the PUBLIC directory on the SYS volume, on the APP server:

```
MAP G:=APP/SYS:PUBLIC
```

By default, NetWare maps the first available drive (usually F:) to the SYS: volume. Before you log in, the LOGIN directory will be the only accessible directory on that drive.

The MAP command is useful in login scripts (discussed in chapter 5) and is often used there. If you are using Windows 95/98 or Windows NT, you can also map drives through Windows Explorer or Network Neighborhood. To do so with Network Neighborhood, simply navigate (by double-clicking) to the desired directory, right-click on it, and choose Map Network Drive, or for a Novell-enhanced version of this dialog box, choose Novell Map Network Drive. All you need to do at that point is choose a drive letter and indicate whether you want that drive to automatically be remapped again for you when you log in next, and then click OK.

Mapping Search Drives

NetWare uses a second kind of drive mapping called a *search drive*. Search drives point to directory paths that will be searched when you type a command name at a DOS prompt. For example, the MAP command itself is in the SYS:PUBLIC directory. A search drive that points to this directory allows MAP to be found when you type the command, no matter which directory you are in at the time. This concept is the same as the DOS PATH statement, and in fact actually modifies the PATH.

Search drives are assigned both a number and a letter. The MAP command refers to them by number. You can map up to 16 search drives, numbered S1 through S16. When you type a command, NetWare looks for the command file name in each of the search drives, beginning with S1. The first match that it finds is executed. One key bit of information to note is that this is only for commands typed at a DOS prompt. It has no effect for program items (in Windows 3.1) or shortcuts in the Start menu in Windows 95/98 or Windows NT.

For example, the command to map the S1 search drive to the APP/SYS:PUBLIC directory is:

```
MAP S1:=APP/SYS:PUBLIC
```

This will replace whatever S1 was (like C:\WINDOWS). Typically, you'll use the MAP INS command instead. This will insert the chosen directory into the path. Using the above example, the command would be

```
MAP INS S1:=APP/SYS:PUBLIC
```

Backing Up the File System

System directory & databases

Of course, no matter how well you organize and manage your file system, there is always a risk of losing data due to hard drive crashes, user error, and other problems. While there's no sure way to prevent these types of problems, you can make sure that the data is safe by keeping a backup copy (or better yet, several backup copies). Along with disk storage, your network should include a backup device—typically a tape drive. We'll start this section with a technical explanation of how NetWare 5 supports backups; we'll then explore the different types of backups and their advantages.

> Although we're focusing on the NetWare 5 file system here, NetWare 5 provides you with the capability to back up NetWare 3.1*x* and 4.*x* servers, client workstations, and the NDS database.

Understanding SMS

NetWare 5 includes built-in support for backup utilities through a system called SMS, or Storage Management Services. SMS is not a backup program; rather, it is a system that allows backup software to work with the operating system to allow simple backups of data. SMS includes the following components:

- The backup engine, called the *storage management engine,* is the actual backup application. Novell provides a simple application called Enhanced SBACKUP. It offers a new interface and a few more advanced capabilities than previous versions of NetWare. New in NetWare 5 is a GUI (graphical user interface) backup program that can be run on a Windows 95/98 or Windows NT workstation, called NWBACK32. It is a simple, graphical way to set up the backup process. Also new in NetWare 5 is the ability to schedule when you want the backups to be done.

- *Target Service Agents* (*TSAs*) are components that allow a particular device—or target—to be backed up.

TSAs are available for a wide variety of systems:

- TSA500.NLM supports backups of NetWare 4.11 and 5 server volumes. (New in NetWare 5)

- TSADOSP.NLM supports backups of the DOS partition(s) on the NetWare server. (New in NetWare 5)

- TSA312.NLM supports NetWare 3.12 server volume backups.

- TSA311.NLM supports NetWare 3.11 server volume backups.

- TSANDS.NLM supports backup and restore of the NDS database.

- W95TSA.EXE is the executable client for Windows 95/98 workstations.

- NT TSA (which is made up of TSAMain.exe [the Windows NT service that interacts with the TSAPROXY.NLM] and TSAPrefs.exe [for configuration of the service]) is the client portion for Windows NT workstation backup.

- TSAPROXY.NLM is called a host TSA and supports backup of OS/2, Unix, Windows 95/98, Windows NT, and Macintosh workstations. Again, you must also load a workstation version of the TSA.

When you install the client software, you have the option of installing the workstation TSA component. You can also install it at any time by running the client software installation program.

The Enhanced SBACKUP Utility

NetWare 5 includes a simple server-based backup application as well as the Windows 95/98 and Windows NT GUI-based version. While not the best possible backup software, it can support all types of backups supported by SMS. SBCON runs on the server console, or you may use NWBACK32 at the workstation. To use it, you'll need a tape drive or other backup device attached to the server. If your tape device is attached to a workstation, you will need to use third-party backup software (which may or may not be able to back up NDS, retain rights assigned to files and directories, and so forth). For more information on how to use SMS and/or Enhanced SBACKUP, refer to the online documentation.

You will find a discussion of backup strategies in Chapter 10.

Review

In this chapter, we presented an overview of three fundamental areas of NetWare 5:

- Novell Directory Services (NDS)
- Connecting to the Network
- The NetWare file system

Novell Directory Services

NetWare 5 manages the network's resources through Novell Directory Services, or NDS. Information about each of these resources is organized into a single database: the Novell Directory. This database works for the entire network, rather than one particular server.

NDS offers many benefits, including ease of administration; a more manageable organization of resources; increased security, scalability, and interoperability, and fault tolerance.

In NDS, every resource on a network is represented by a record in the Directory database. This record is called an object. Objects exist for each type of resource. There are three basic types of objects in the Directory database:

- The [Root] object
- Container objects (Country, Locality, Organization, and Organizational Unit)
- Leaf objects (User, Printer, Group, and so on)

Each type of object in NDS has a list of properties. These are pieces of information that are stored about a specific type of object. The information stored in a property is called the value of the property. There is a separate list of properties for each type of NDS object. The list of properties is called the Directory schema, and it can be extended.

NDS Object Naming

The following guidelines are used in naming NDS objects:

- Each object in an NDS tree has an object name. The object name is also referred to as the object's common name.

- An object's context is a description of the object's location in the tree.

- An object's distinguished name (DN) is its common name combined with its context.

- A relative distinguished name (RDN) provides a path to the object from the current context.

Client Connections

The client software runs on the workstation and establishes a connection to a server. The client software for DOS, Windows, Windows 95/98, and Windows NT is called the Novell Client, which replaces the NetWare DOS Requester and the NetWare shell, used by previous versions of NetWare.

The workstation communicates with the server through the use of communication protocols. The most common protocols used for NetWare workstation connections are IPX (Internetwork Packet Exchange) and TCP/IP (Transmission Control Protocol/Internet Protocol).

ODI (Open Data-link Interface) is a specification used with DOS workstations on the network. ODI allows workstations or servers to use multiple protocols on the same network. It also provides a modular way of installing network drivers. The equivalent specification for Windows 95/98 and Windows NT is Microsoft's NDIS (Network Driver Interface Specification).

The Novell Client is composed of several key items:

LAN card driver   This is the software that communicates with the network card. After the data is sent across the network and received by the network card, this program converts it into a standard format that the Novell Client software understands. The type of LAN driver used for NetWare 5 is either an ODI driver (which has the extension .LAN) or an NDIS driver (which has the extension .SYS).

Protocols   Normally you'll use IPX and/or TCP/IP, but you can load other protocols, such as AppleTalk, along with (or instead of) TCP/IP and/or IPX.

The Novell Client   This is the actual client software, responsible for communications with the operating system and application software on the workstation.

From a DOS workstation that has the client software loaded, you can log in to the network by using the LOGIN command followed by your username (either in RDN or DN format), after you switch to a network drive. The LOGIN program (LOGIN.EXE) is located in the LOGIN directory on the server. This directory is the only one you can access when you are not logged in. To disconnect from the network, use the LOGOUT command.

To do the same thing from a Windows 95/98 or Windows NT computer, you will enter the same information (name, password, and possibly context) in the Login dialog box. On these operating systems, the login program is stored on the user's local hard drive. To log out, simply choose Start ➤ Shut down and then choose Shut down, Restart, or Close all programs and log on as a different user.

The File System

NetWare's file system manages disk storage on the network. NetWare uses files and directories, similar to those used by DOS. Components of the file system include the following:

- Volumes are the major unit of NetWare disk storage.

- Directories and subdirectories divide the volumes and provide organization.

- Files store data or applications within directories.

In order to access a NetWare volume from DOS, you map a drive. You can map drives from other clients as well (as a shortcut to a network path) or use UNC (Universal Naming Convention) syntax instead for Windows 95/98 and Windows NT workstations. Mapped drives include the following:

- Network drives are used to access volumes and directories.

- Search drives provide a list of possible locations for executable commands.

You should also back up your file system and other data. NetWare 5 supports backups with the Storage Management System, or SMS. SMS includes two main components:

- TSAs (target service agents) allow various devices (targets) to be backed up.

- A backup engine, such as Novell's Enhanced SBACKUP utility, performs the actual backup.

CNE Practice Test Questions

1. Novell Directory Services (NDS):

    A. Stores information for each network resource

    B. Uses a tree-like structure

    C. Refers to each resource as an object

    D. All of the above

2. Which of the following is *not* a benefit of NDS?

    A. Better organization of resources

    B. Fault tolerance

    C. An efficient file system

    D. Increased security

3. The type of organization NDS uses is:

    A. Server-centric

    B. Network-centric

    C. Noncentralized

    D. Resource-centric

4. The three basic types of NDS objects are:

    A. Container, Leaf, [Root]

    B. Properties, Values, Objects

    C. Organization, Organizational Unit, Country

    D. Typeless, typeful, distinguished

5. The [Root] object:

    A. Can be located anywhere in the Directory

    B. Is at the top of the NDS tree and can't be modified

    C. Can be deleted when it is no longer needed

    D. All of the above

6. Container objects include:

    A. Country, Group, Organization

    B. Organization, [Root], Group

    C. Country, Organization, Organizational Unit

    D. Organization and Group

7. Leaf objects include:

    A. User, Group, Organization

    B. User, Printer, Resource

    C. User, Group, Profile

    D. All container objects, plus User

8. NDS properties:

    A. Are the same for all objects

    B. Are used by container objects only

    C. Are all optional

    D. Can be assigned values

9. An object's name along with its full context is:

    A. Its distinguished name

    B. Its relative distinguished name

    C. Its common name

    D. Its context name

10. An object's context is:

   A. Any object in the same container

   B. The container object it resides in and the container's container and so on up to the [Root]

   C. Its common name

   D. The name of the Directory tree

11. A relative distinguished name:

   A. Begins at the [Root] object

   B. Begins at the current context

   C. Begins with the first Organization object

   D. Uses the default system context (DSC)

12. Which is an example of a *typeless* name?

   A. CN=FRED.OU=ACCT.O=ORION

   B. CN=FRED

   C. FRED.ACCT.ORION

   D. CN=FRED.ACCT.O=ORION

13. The protocol(s) usually used with NetWare is/are:

   A. VLM

   B. IPXODI

   C. IPX

   D. TCP/IP

   E. Answers A and B

   F. Answers C and D

14. Until you log in, the only files you can access on the network are:

   A. LOGIN.EXE and client software

   B. All files in the PUBLIC directory

   C. All files in the LOGIN directory

   D. All files on the SYS: volume

15. Which is the correct order of a NetWare server's file system organization?

   A. Directory, file, volume

   B. Volume, directory, file

   C. File, volume, directory

   D. File, directory, NDS

16. The NDIR utility:

   A. Must be used in place of the DOS DIR command

   B. Lists files in the current directory

   C. Lists information about NDS objects

   D. All of the above

17. The NLIST utility:

   A. Can be used to list volumes or other NDS objects

   B. Displays a list of files in the current directory

   C. Is another name for NDIR

   D. Was used in NetWare 3

18. Which is the correct syntax to map drive F: to the SYS:PUBLIC directory?

A. `MAP F: SYS\PUBLIC`

B. `MAP SYS:PUBLIC /D=F`

C. `MAP SYS:PUBLIC=F:`

D. `MAP F:=SYS:PUBLIC`

CHAPTER

3

How to Manage Container and Leaf Objects

Roadmap

This chapter covers several of the management tools used with the NDS tree, many of the common leaf objects, and licensing, all topics that are found in the CNA and CNE core requirement "NetWare 5 Administration."

Topics Covered

- Using NetWare Administrator, UIMPORT, and ConsoleOne
- Common Leaf Objects
- Licensing Objects

Skills You'll Learn

- Describe how to use NetWare Administrator
- Explain how to manage multiple users with template objects and UIMPORT
- Describe the features of the new utility, ConsoleOne, and how to use it to create users
- Explain the purpose of many of the common leaf objects and list when to use them
- Explain what licensing is and the objects associated with it in the NDS tree
- Describe how to assign licenses to objects

N DS allows you to easily manage all of the users, servers, and other objects on your network from a single database, the NDS Directory. This chapter explains how to manage the objects in your Directory tree using several utilities provided with NetWare 5:

- NetWare Administrator (NWADMN32.EXE) is a Windows-based utility that allows you to browse through the objects in the tree and create, modify, and delete them. This utility also includes additional features to manage the file system and its security.

- UIMPORT is a utility for creating multiple users automatically. We will also look at other methods of creating and managing multiple users, since you will probably use User objects more than any other NDS object.

- ConsoleOne is a new Java-based utility in NetWare 5 that allows you to manage the network from either a workstation or the server itself. The server offers some additional options not available with the workstation implementation for managing local resources, but both allow you to manage, albeit in a limited manner, objects in the tree.

You should become familiar with these utilities, because you will use them extensively in your career as a network administrator, and because you'll need a basic knowledge of them for the CNE tests. In particular, you will use a simulator of NetWare Administrator to answer many questions. This chapter provides an overview of each utility and how to use it to create and manage NDS objects.

The second section describes the NDS objects you will use most often. These objects form the basis for the tree and the reason that servers exist. They include users, servers, and volumes as basic objects—in other words, objects that you may already be familiar with, at least conceptually. Many other objects, including profiles and groups, will aid you in managing the tree in a simple manner.

The final section of the chapter deals with licensing issues. We will discuss the objects that are created in the tree, how to assign licenses to users, and when you run out of them, how you add additional licenses.

Using NetWare Administrator

NetWare Administrator is probably the most important utility in NetWare 5. You can manage almost every aspect of the network with NetWare Administrator. This includes users, security, printing, and even the file system. As a network administrator, you'll spend a lot of time using NetWare Administrator.

Since it is a Windows 95/98-based utility, you need a 32-bit version of Windows to run it. To run NetWare Administrator for Windows 95/98 or Windows NT, use the filename NWADMN32.EXE (in SYS:PUBLIC\ WIN32). There are a couple of issues to be aware of on these platforms.

First, be sure you are running the Win32 version, not the Windows 95 version (NWADMN95.EXE) in the WIN95 subdirectory or the NT version in the WINNT subdirectory. Second, you need to use the Novell Client for Windows 95/98 or Windows NT, not other client software, such as the Microsoft client included with Windows 95/98, which will not access NDS correctly.

There is currently no version of NetWare Administrator for Macintosh, OS/2, or Unix workstations. There also isn't a version for DOS or Windows 3.*x.* For this reason, you'll need at least one Windows 95/98 or Windows NT machine on your network. You can still use the NetWare 4.11 version on Windows 3.*x* computers, but you won't be able to manage NetWare 5-specific objects, such as Z.E.N.works-related objects and NDPS objects.

Running NetWare Administrator

Here are the steps to get started with NetWare Administrator:

1. Be sure you are running the correct client software (in other words, the Novell Client) and that you are logged in to the network.

2. Choose Run from the Windows 95/98 or Windows NT Start menu.

3. Type the name of the program to run, **NWADMN32.EXE**. Because NetWare Administrator is in a subdirectory of the PUBLIC directory, you will need to specify the correct path, even if you have a search drive mapped to PUBLIC.

Since you will be running NetWare Administrator frequently, you may wish to create a shortcut or Start menu entry for it in Windows. In fact, we highly recommend that you place it at your fingertips for easy access.

When NetWare Administrator starts, you will see a representation of the Directory tree and a Windows menu bar, as shown in the example in Figure 3.1.

We will now take a guided tour of the options that NetWare Administrator makes available. If you have access to a NetWare 5 server, you might find it useful to try things out on your own Directory tree as you read.

The Object Menu

The Object menu, shown in Figure 3.2, allows you to create, rename, or delete an object; modify properties; and control object rights. Before you select an option from this menu, highlight the object or objects that you want to affect.

F I G U R E   3.1

NetWare Administrator
is the most important
utility in NetWare 5.

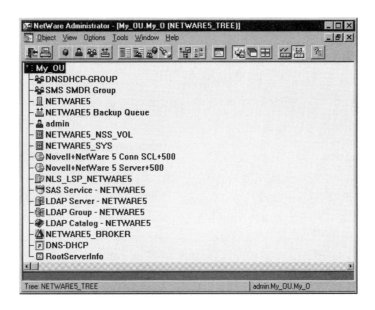

F I G U R E   3.2

The Object menu
allows you to perform
functions related to
objects.

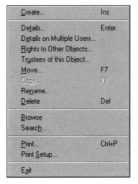

Instead of using the Object menu, you can click the right mouse button
("right-click") after highlighting the object. You will see a pop-up menu
listing common commands that can be performed on that type of object.
You can also double-click an object name to go directly to the Details
option of a leaf object or to expand a container object.

Creating an Object

The Create option allows you to create a new NDS object. Before selecting this option, highlight the container object that will hold the new object. The new object will be created in this container. After you select the Create option, NetWare Administrator presents a list of object types, as shown in Figure 3.3. Choose the type of object you wish to create and click OK.

FIGURE 3.3

The New Object menu lets you select the type of object you wish to create.

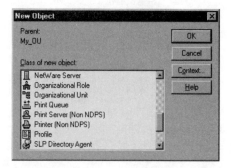

Another dialog box appears, presenting some properties for you to fill in. The properties listed will depend on the type of object you are creating. For example, when you are creating a User object, the Create User dialog box asks you to specify the Login Name and Last Name properties, as shown in Figure 3.4. These are the values you are required to specify to create the object.

FIGURE 3.4

You are required to enter certain properties to create an object; other options simplify the process.

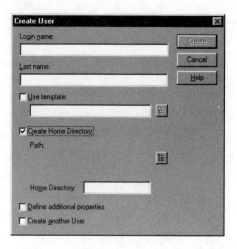

There are also four checkboxes in the Create User dialog box, which you can use to set additional options:

Use Template   Copies the default settings for a new User object from a Template object. Template objects are explained later in this chapter.

Create Home Directory   Sets up a home directory for the user and allows you to specify its location (the server, volume, and directory).

Define Additional Properties   Brings up the Details dialog box, which allows you to set values for the other properties of the object.

Create Another User   Returns you to the Create User dialog box after creating the user, so that you can create another user immediately.

Viewing Property Values

The Details option on the Object menu allows you to view all of the properties of an object and specify or change their values. For example, when you highlight a User object and select Details, you will see a dialog box like the one shown in Figure 3.5.

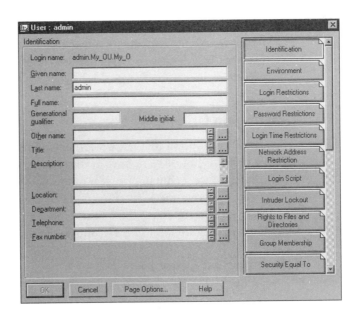

FIGURE 3.5

Choosing the Details option produces a dialog box that allows you to change properties of an object.

Properties are divided into categories. The categories and properties displayed depend on the type of object that is being modified. Use the buttons along the right side of the dialog box to select a category. You can then fill in the values of properties or change existing values.

Moving a Leaf Object

The Move option on the Object menu allows you to move a leaf object from one container to another. Highlight the leaf object you wish to move and then select the Move option. Next, you will see the Move dialog box, shown in Figure 3.6. Navigate through the Directory to find the destination container object, and then select OK.

FIGURE 3.6

Select the container object into which to move the leaf object.

 Although you can select the Move option for a container object, you won't be allowed to move container objects using this menu option. You must use the NDS Manager utility, described in Chapter 21, to move container objects.

Deleting an Object

The Delete option on the Object menu allows you to delete an object. You can use this option to remove any leaf object or empty container object (you cannot delete a container object unless you first delete all of the objects within the container). After selecting Delete, you are prompted to confirm that you wish to delete the object. One note of caution: There is no way to undo this action after you've confirmed the deletion.

Renaming an Object

The Rename option on the Object menu allows you to change an object's common name. After selecting Rename, type the new name for the object.

The Rename dialog box also contains two options that you can control with checkboxes:

Save Old Name   Adds the object's old name to the object's Other Names property. This allows you to track an object after renaming it.

Create Alias in Place of Renamed Container   For container objects, check this box to create an Alias object with the old name of the container. This allows users to continue using the old name to refer to the object. Alias objects are discussed later in this chapter.

Searching for an Object

The Search option on the Object menu allows you to search the Directory tree for objects with certain property values. The options in the Search dialog box, shown in Figure 3.7, allow you to set specific parameters for the search.

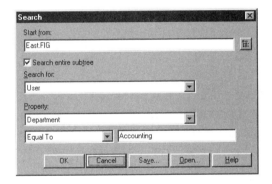

These parameters work as follows:

Start From   Allows you to specify a container object where the search will begin. If the Search Entire Subtree box is checked, NetWare Administrator will search all the objects in all of the child containers (and their child containers, and so on) of the container as well; otherwise, the search will be confined to a single container. The button to the right of the Start From text box (known as the Browse button) allows you to select a container from a graphical display of your Directory tree.

Search For   Allows you to specify the type of object that will be searched for, such as User, Printer, or Server.

Property   Gives you a choice of properties to search for. The list of properties to choose from here depends on the type of object you have selected.

Beneath the Property option are two boxes that allow you to specify a condition for the search. In the box on the left, you can choose whether to find properties that are Equal To or Not Equal To a value, or Present or Not Present. Enter the value to search for to the right of the condition. This will be used with the Equal To or Not Equal To option for matching objects. For example, the options shown in Figure 3.7 specify a search for User objects with a value of Accounting in the Department property.

The Save button allows you to save the search parameters to a file. After you save the search parameters, you can later load those parameters using the Open button in the Search dialog box. In this way, you can keep a library of frequently used search criteria and quickly perform specific searches.

After the search is completed, you are presented with a list of objects that meet the criteria you selected. You can then perform any of the operations described in this chapter on those objects.

Printing the Directory Tree

The Print option on the Object menu allows you to print the listing of objects in the current context. You can use the Print Setup option on the Object menu to change options related to printing or to change the printer to be used.

The View Menu

NetWare Administrator's View menu, shown in Figure 3.8, provides several options that allow you to control the way in which NDS objects are displayed. These include setting the current context, choosing objects to include, sorting objects, and expanding or collapsing the display.

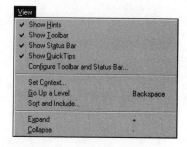

FIGURE 3.8

The View menu allows you to control the way in which NDS objects are viewed.

Choosing a Context

The Set Context option on the View menu allows you to change the current context. You can select any container object, or even other trees. This object will be the first shown in the NetWare Administrator window. The Set Context dialog box is shown in Figure 3.9.

FIGURE 3.9

The Set Context option allows you to view objects in a different context and/or tree.

You can type the name of a container object in the Context area, or click the button to the right of the Context text box to browse through the Directory tree and select a container object as the context.

Selectively Viewing and Sorting Objects

The Sort and Include option on the View menu allows you to specify which types of NDS objects are displayed in the NetWare Administrator window. The Browser Sort and Include dialog box, shown in Figure 3.10, lists all of the possible object types. Highlight the names in the Available Classes list that you wish to include in the display and move them to the Included Classes list by clicking on the left arrow button. By default, all types are included. You can exclude those types you don't want to see by selecting them in the Included Classes list and clicking on the right arrow button.

FIGURE 3.10

The Sort and Include option allows you to limit your display to certain types of objects.

Object types are listed in the order in which they will be displayed. To change this order, highlight an object type and use the up and down arrow buttons on the left side of the dialog box to move the object up or down in the list.

After making your desired changes, click the OK button. The settings you have chosen will be used next time you run NetWare Administrator and stay as set until you change them again, if Save Changes on Exit (found in the Options menu and discussed later in the chapter) is checked.

The sort options only change the order in which you view NDS objects. They don't affect the NDS database itself.

Expanding and Collapsing Container Objects

The Expand and Collapse options on the View menu allow you to control whether objects under a container object are displayed. Highlight a container object before selecting these commands. The Expand command displays all objects under the container. The Collapse command displays only the container object.

If you make changes to the Include or Sort settings, you must re-expand the containers in the display before the settings will take effect. A quick way to do this is to highlight the object at the top of the display (usually [Root]) and select Collapse, then select Expand.

You can also double-click a container object to expand it. Double-click again to collapse the display.

The Options Menu

NetWare Administrator's Options menu, shown in Figure 3.11, allows you to set several options related to the behavior of the program. Selecting each of the options toggles the option's status. A checkmark is displayed to the left of each activated option.

FIGURE 3.11

The Options menu allows you to control the behavior of Net-Ware Administrator.

Save Settings on Exit   Controls whether settings, including window sizes, current context, and view settings, are saved as the default when you exit the program.

Confirm on Delete   Controls whether the confirmation dialog box is displayed when you delete an object. If this option is turned off, the object will be deleted immediately when you select Delete.

Get Alias Trustees and **Get Aliased Object Trustees**   Control how the Trustees of This Object command works with Alias objects (described later in this chapter). You can choose to see the trustee list of either the original object or the Alias object itself. Only one of these options can be selected.

The Tools Menu

NetWare Administrator's Tools menu provides options to open new NetWare Administrator windows and start other programs. The Tools menu, an example of which is shown in Figure 3.12, is also extensible, meaning that depending on the options you have installed, the menu may change.

FIGURE 3.12

The Tools menu provides quick access to some useful windows and utilities.

Not all of these options may be on your Tools menu, depending on the options you have installed, but some of the standard options include:

Internet Connections   Allows you to quickly go to your favorite Internet sites.

NDS Browser   Opens a new NetWare Administrator window, with the selected container object at the top. This allows you to examine objects within the container in a separate window or to manage multiple NDS trees at the same time.

Salvage   Provides a method of restoring deleted files. The Salvage window, shown in Figure 3.13, lists the deleted files and allows you to salvage (restore) or purge (permanently remove) them. You must select a volume or directory first for the Salvage button to be selectable.

FIGURE 3.13

The Salvage option allows you to restore deleted files.

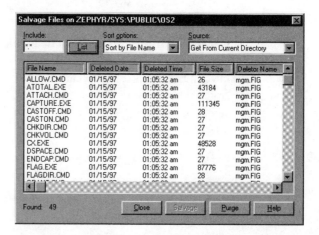

Remote Console   Runs the Remote Console (RConsole) utility in a window. (The first screen you see will remind you that RConsole is not always reliable when it's run under Windows.) This utility is discussed in Chapter 8.

Pure IP Remote Console   Similar to the Remote Console option just discussed, but this option is used for connecting to servers that support TCP/IP, whereas the Remote Console option is for servers using IPX.

Install License   Allows you to manage application and NetWare licenses using NLS (NetWare Licensing Services). Non-NLS-aware applications can also be tracked by choosing from the submenu, Metered Application. More information on licensing is available later in this chapter.

Print Services Quick Setup (Non-NDPS)   Lets you quickly set up printers and other important objects for queue-based printing. See Chapter 9 for details on this feature.

NDPS Public Access Printers and **NDPS Remote Printer Management**
Allow you to quickly manage NDPS printers. More information on NDPS is found in Chapter 6.

Creating and Managing Multiple Users

No matter what type of organization the network serves, chances are that many of your users have similar characteristics. For example, all of the users you create in the EAST Organizational Unit might have the same Location property: Eastern Branch. In the following sections we'll introduce three ways of dealing with multiple users simultaneously:

- You can define a Template object to create users with similar characteristics.

- You can modify multiple users at the same time using NetWare Administrator.

- The UIMPORT utility allows you to create users through an automated process.

Creating Users with Templates

Often when you create a user, you'll use a similar set of properties. You can easily create more than one user with similar properties using a *Template*. This is a special type of object that is used to assign default properties for new User objects you create. The users remain associated with the Template, and you can later use it to modify their properties.

You can create as many Template objects as you need. To create a Template, choose Template from the list of object types after choosing the Create option. You can then specify properties for the Template. The properties of the Template object are similar to those of a User object, as shown in Figure 3.14.

To create a user with the Template property values, follow the usual procedure for creating objects but check the Use Template box in the Create User dialog box, and then specify the Template to use. Any users you create become associated with the Template object, and appear in its Members of Template property. You can modify all of the member users of a Template, as described in the next section.

Modifying the Template's properties does not have an effect on existing users, whether they are members of the Template or not. This only affects new users created after the change. To modify the existing members of a Template, use the Details on Multiple Users option, described below.

FIGURE 3.14

Property values entered for the Template object can be copied to new User objects you create.

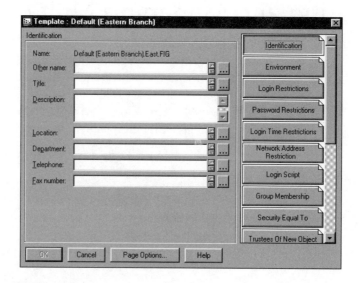

Managing Multiple Users

The Details on Multiple Users option, which is on the Object menu shown in Figure 3.2, allows you to modify any number of users at the same time. You begin either by specifying certain users or by choosing an object associated with the desired users. Do one of the following:

- To select multiple users, hold down the Ctrl key and click them, or press Shift and click to select a contiguous range of users.

- Highlight an Organization, Organizational Unit, Group, or Template object to modify all of the users currently associated with or contained in (as appropriate) the object.

Once you've made your selection, choose the Details on Multiple Users option from the Object menu. A modified version of the User object properties dialog box is displayed. Any properties you change in this dialog box will affect all of the users you selected.

Changing properties for a large number of users may take some time. NetWare Administrator will warn you of this and allow you to abort the process.

Creating Users with UIMPORT

Suppose you need to create users automatically on a regular basis, or you want to create users based on a database of users you already have in an application. You can use the DOS-based UIMPORT utility to create users based on a database file. We'll look at this process in detail in the following sections.

Creating the Database File

First, you'll need a database of user information. The database can include as much or as little information as you need. You can create this database using a database or spreadsheet program. You may already have a database you wish to use, such as a listing of mainframe users or a payroll database.

In order to use the database with UIMPORT, you will need to export it to an ASCII file. Follow your application's instructions to create a comma-delimited ASCII file. Other file formats can be used, but you will need to modify the control file. For example, a file that includes last names, first names, department names, and phone numbers might look like this:

```
JQPUBLIC, JANE Q.,ACCOUNTING, 555-1234
JDOE, JOHN, MARKETING, 555-1235
HJTILLMAN, HENRY J., COMPUTER ROOM, 555-1255
```

Creating the Control File

After you have set up a comma-delimited database (or a database in another format, if you modify some control file parameters), you need to create a *control file*. This is an ASCII file that specifies the fields used in the database file and the method of importing them. You can also specify the NDS context for the new users in this file. If you don't specify the context, users will be created in your current context.

Here's a simple example of a control file that would work with the data file example above:

```
Import control
    Name context=.acct.abc_inc
    Create home directory=n
FieldNames
    Last name
    Given name
    Department
    Telephone
```

There are many other keywords you can use in control files. For details on the syntax, see the Novell documentation. Here are some highlights:

- Use the IMPORT MODE=R option in the Import control section to delete users instead of creating them.

- Use the keyword Skip in the Fields section to skip one of the fields in the data file.

If you chose to create a database file that was not comma-delimited, refer to the online documentation for the parameters that must be specified.

Performing the Import

Once you have a valid database file and control file, you're ready to perform the import. Copy both files to the same directory. Start a DOS session, and switch to that directory. For example, if you have a control file called USERS.CTL and a data file called USERS.DAT, you can simply type **UIMPORT** followed by the control filename and data filename:

```
UIMPORT USERS.CTL USERS.DAT
```

You will be notified of any errors while UIMPORT processes the files. Once the users have been created, you can easily define additional properties using the method described in "Managing Multiple Users," earlier in this chapter.

Creating Users with ConsoleOne

ConsoleOne is NetWare's latest management tool. It can be run from either a workstation or the server itself, although with fewer options on the workstation. It is not a full-featured management tool, at least not yet. In fact, Novell says that it is a "proof of concept," meaning that they proved with this tool that network management can be done with an application written in Java. This allows, at least in theory, network management to be done from any platform supporting Java, such as OS/2, Macintosh, or even Unix. While it's still under development, ConsoleOne is the future direction of NetWare's administration utility, and so you should begin to get familiar with it now. Updates will be available on the Novell Web site (`http://www.novell.com`) as the product is upgraded and becomes more fully functional.

In this section, we will focus on how to set up support for Java on your workstation, how to start ConsoleOne, and how to create users with it. You'll find more details on ConsoleOne in Chapter 8.

To install support for Java on your computer, run the WINSETUP.EXE program again, just as you did when installing the Novell Client initially. (The installation process is described in Chapter 2.) After choosing your language and platform, at the screen where you choose to install the client, choose the Java option. You will be asked to confirm that you want to install support for Java, and after you affirm that you do, it will install itself. If you don't install Java first, the initial splash screen for ConsoleOne will appear, but nothing else will happen.

To use ConsoleOne, simply run the CONSOLE1.EXE program found in SYS:PUBLIC\MGMT. The Java support files will load, a splash screen will appear letting you know that it is loading, and then you will see the screen shown in Figure 3.15. To reiterate, if the Java support files are not installed first, the splash screen will appear and stay on the screen indefinitely, but ConsoleOne will not start.

F I G U R E 3.15

ConsoleOne's opening screen

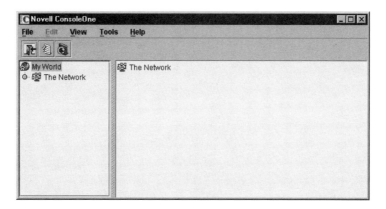

For details on creating a user object with ConsoleOne, refer to Procedure 3.1.

PROCEDURE 3.1

Creating a User Object with ConsoleOne

To create a new user, open ConsoleOne and follow these steps:

1. Browse to the desired container and either choose File ➢ New ➢ User or right-click the container and choose New ➢ User. Then click the Create User icon.

PROCEDURE 3.1 (CONTINUED)

2. Fill in the New User dialog box, which is an abbreviated form of NetWare Administrator's Create User dialog box. You will need to fill in the Login Name and Last Name fields and you may optionally choose either Create Another User or Define Additional Properties, as described above. When you are finished, click Create and the user is created.

To modify the properties of an existing user, either right-click the user name and choose Properties, or choose File ➤ Properties. A dialog box such as the one shown in Figure 3.16 will then appear.

FIGURE 3.16

Modifying the properties of a user

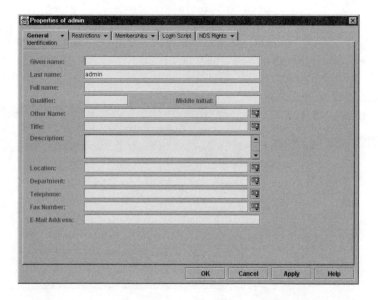

As noted previously, the current version of ConsoleOne is a "proof of concept"; therefore it doesn't, at this point, offer all the functionality of NetWare Administrator. We will, however, briefly discuss how to move around in the product.

As you may notice in Figure 3.16, there are not as many tabs as you are accustomed to seeing in NetWare Administrator. The tabs are all there, but they are organized into groups. For example, to view the Environment tab, click the tab labeled General and, from the menu that will then pop up, choose Environment. You will know that additional tabs are available within a given tab if there is a downward-pointing triangle to the right of the tab name. Explore this interface, as it is probably the way more interfaces will be designed in the future. When you have finished, click OK.

Refer to Table 3.1 for a list of how the tabs are grouped.

T A B L E   3.1:   Tab Organization for the User Object in ConsoleOne

ConsoleOne Tab Name	NetWare Administrator Tabs Contained on This Tab
General	Identification
	Environment
	Postal Address
	See Also
Restrictions	Password Restrictions
	Login Restrictions
	Time Restrictions
	Address Restrictions
	Intruder Lockout
	Account Balance
Memberships	Group Membership
	Security Equal To
	Security Equal To Me
Login Script	Login Script
NDS Rights	Trustees of this Object
	Inherited Rights Filters
	Effective Rights

Using Leaf Objects

Now that you know how to manage the objects in the Directory, we'll take a look at the types of leaf objects available for your Directory tree.

There are actually about 25 leaf objects available in NDS. The actual number will vary, depending on the options you have installed. The following list describes the functions of the most common ones, the same ones you'll need to understand for the Administration test:

User Represents a user on the network.

Group Represents a set of users who share the same rights.

Organizational Role Represents a role, or job, assigned to one or more users.

NetWare Server Represents a NetWare server.

Volume Represents a volume on a server.

Alias Serves as a pointer (or shortcut, to use Windows 95/98 terminology) to another object in the Directory.

Profile Provides a way to assign a common login script and file rights to a group of users.

Directory Map Points to a directory in the file system.

Template Allows you to quickly and easily create users.

You can create some of these objects with NetWare Administrator or ConsoleOne. Others are created automatically and can't be changed, but you can examine and modify some of their properties.

In the next sections, we'll take a closer look at each of these objects.

The NDS container objects (Country, Locality, Organization, and Organizational Unit) are described in Chapter 2.

User Objects

Each user who needs to access the network must have a User object. When you create the User object, you specify the login name and last name for the user. After that, the user is ready to log in to the network. If necessary, you can give the user rights to files, directories, or other NDS objects and/or set any properties necessary.

As explained earlier in the chapter, you can create any number of Template objects, which can be used to create or manage multiple users.

Group Objects

When you create multiple users in a container object, they form a *natural group;* that is, they are automatically given rights based on the rights you give to their container object. The Group object lets you do the same thing for any number of User objects, whether they're in the same container or not. This presents two possibilities:

- You can choose only some of the users in a container.

- You can choose users from multiple containers.

You can create a Group object in any container. After you create it, you can add users to it by using the Member List property of the Group object. These users are called the *members* of the group. A User object can be a member of any number of groups.

The Group object is used for security and also is useful in login scripts (to assign drive mappings, display special messages, and so on). Any member of a group will receive the same rights that the Group object has.

Organizational Role Objects

The Organizational Role object is similar to a group. It is usually used to assign a role, or job, to a particular user. This user is called the *occupant* of the Organizational Role. An Organizational Role can have more than one occupant.

Using Organizational Roles makes it easier to manage a network in a changing company. If you assign rights to users individually, you will need to do so any time a new person takes the job. Thanks to the Organizational Role object, the process is simple. You can just add a new occupant to the Organizational Role and remove the old one.

Organizational Roles are also important because they allow you to assign administrators—users who have the right to manage an area of the Directory tree or file system. The various types of administrators you can set up for your network are explained in Chapter 14.

The NetWare Server Object

The Server object is used to represent a server on the network. You can create this type of object under rare circumstances; normally it is automatically created when a server is installed. You should not need to change the properties of the Server object.

The Volume Object

When you install the server, a Volume object is automatically created for each disk volume on the server. Like the Server object, the Volume object should not be deleted unless the volume is no longer in existence.

Although the Volume object is not a container object, you can "expand" it like a container object in NetWare Administrator. Under the Volume object you will find a list of directories on the volume. You can browse through the directories of the file system in the same way that you can view NDS objects. This is how you control security in the file system. You can also do routine file management tasks, such as creating new directories and deleting and renaming files.

Be careful here: The volume object is an NDS object, but the volume itself and the files on it are not.

Alias Objects

You've seen the word *alias* on Wanted posters, and the Alias NDS object has a similar purpose: It's another name for an object. Whereas a criminal uses an alias to avoid being found, however, NDS aliases are usually used to help users find the object. Another analogy often used for alias objects is that they are like shortcuts in Windows 95/98 and Windows NT 4, in that they provide a pointer to the original object.

You can create an Alias object yourself. The main reason to do this is to make a resource in one container, such as a printer, available to users in another container. For example, users in the ACCT Organizational Unit might need to access a printer in the MKTG Organizational Unit. You can create an Alias object for the printer in the ACCT container. To the users, it's just another available printer. They can access it without specifying a different container.

In addition, NDS Manager (covered in Chapter 21) can automatically create Alias objects to help users find a container that has been moved. When you move an object using the Object menu, you can check the box labeled "Create an alias for this container object." The same capability (to automatically create an alias) is available in NetWare Administrator when you rename a container. You can check the box labeled "Create alias in place of renamed container." This will create a pointer from the old object to the new object.

Profile Objects

 Each user in NDS can have a login script, which is a series of commands that are executed each time the user logs in. The Profile object is essentially a login script. Assigning users to a Profile object provides an easy way to give them all the same login script. A user can have only one Profile object assigned to him or her.

Profile objects and their use with login scripts are discussed in more detail in Chapter 5.

Directory Map Objects

 The Directory Map object is a special object that points to a directory in the file system. This allows you to simplify MAP commands and makes it easier to maintain the system when an application or data directory is moved.

When you create a Directory Map object, you set the Directory Path property to the path that the Directory Map object will point to. You will need to find the Volume object in the NDS tree first.

As an example, suppose you create a Directory Map called WP to point to the directory that you use for word processing files, SYS:APPS\WP. Users who wish to map a drive to that directory could simply type a MAP command like this (assuming the user and the directory map object are in the same context):

```
MAP F:=WP
```

A more important benefit of using a Directory Map object is that it can save you work when you reorganize your directories. For example, suppose that you moved word processing files to a different volume to make more space available on the SYS volume. The new location is VOL2:APPS\WP. Rather than changing all the login scripts to point to the new directory, and telling everyone about the change, you can simply point the Directory Map to the new location. Once you've done that, users could use the same MAP command to reach the new directory.

If you still use DOS applications, Directory Map objects can be a great help when you change software versions. If, however, you are using Windows applications, which modify .INI files and/or the registry and which place .DLL files all over the hard drive, they are not nearly as useful.

Templates

 As described in the section above on Managing Multiple Users, Templates can aid in the creation of new users. They make the job of user creation much faster, and since you have less typing to do, there's less chance of errors. They also allow you to modify every object based on the template quickly and easily if something changes, such as the department's name or location.

Licensing

NetWare lets you keep track of licensed products through the Novell Licensing Service (NLS). It stores this information in NDS, which makes it easy to manage and provides you with a central point of administration.

You need to have the Novell Licensing Service installed in order to run NetWare 5 servers. NetWare 5 installs NLS by default at installation, but if you want to upgrade existing NetWare 4.11 servers to NetWare 5, you'll need to set up NLS on the 4.11 servers prior to installing NetWare 5. Run SETUPNLS.NLM on the NetWare 4.11 server to install NLS and extend the schema. NLS also requires that at least one server in each partition have a read/write replica with NLS installed.

In this section you will learn about NLS components, NLS objects, and the management tools that are available.

Novell Licensing Service Components

To understand how the Novell Licensing Service works, first you need to know about the components that make up the service. There are three basic components that make up NLS:

NLS Client   The NLS client is an NLS-enabled or Z.E.N.works-configured software package that will request a license before it executes. If a valid license cannot be presented, the software will not run. This ensures that users cannot use software beyond their licensing limitations, protecting your company from liability.

License Service Provider (LSP)   This is a NetWare server running the NLSLSP NLM. Its function is to respond to NLS client requests. When an NLS client requests an available license, the LSP scans the NDS tree for a License Container object that represents the software for an available license (License Containers are discussed below). This LSP scans the tree until either an available license is found or the LSP has contacted all License Container objects. You need at least one LSP per tree.

Licensing Objects   There are two licensing objects that are configured for NLS, the Licensing Container object and the License Certificate object. The following sections discuss these two objects and their functions.

License Container Objects

License Container objects are special-purpose container objects. Like any other container object, they hold leaf objects, but unlike most other containers, they can only contain License Certificate objects. Each product gets its own container, but there may be multiple certificates in any container.

By default, NetWare creates two of these License Containers to keep track of licenses for the operating system itself, which describe the type of license and license connections. They are Novell+NetWare 5 Conn SCL+500 and Novell+NetWare 5 Server+500. The names of the containers were derived by taking the following three components and concatenating them with plus (+) signs:

- Publisher

- Product

- Version

Hence, you can see that the information for the two default objects is as follows:

Publisher   Novell

Product   NetWare 5 Conn SCL (user connection licenses) and NetWare 5 Server (licenses for the operating system itself)

Version   5.00 (It is simpler to leave off the period, because NDS attaches special meaning to the period character. If you choose to use it in objects you create, it will appear like this: 5\.00.)

The License Container and License Certificate objects installed by default are shown here:

Novell+NetWare 5 Conn SCL+500
  └ SN:300003667
Novell+NetWare 5 Server+500
  └ SN:300003667

License Certificate Objects

The reason that License Container objects exist is to hold License Certificate objects. By default, a server base connection certificate is installed in the Novell+NetWare 5 Server+500 container. The certificate typically supports one server. User licenses are stored in the Novell+NetWare 5 Conn SCL+500 container. There is one license certificate installed, but if you display the details for the certificate, you can see how many user licenses that certificate supports. This information is summarized on the General tab, as shown in Figure 3.17. More detailed information on the certificate can be found on the Policy Information tab of the certificate, as illustrated in Figure 3.18. You cannot modify the properties of license certificates that relate to the license itself. You can, however, create what Novell calls a metered certificate for any product that doesn't support NLS, and for those products you can specify all of the details. Information on metered certificates, the objects involved, and where to place them in the tree can be found in the online documentation.

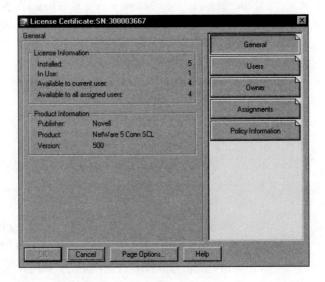

FIGURE 3.17

The License Certificate object's Details screen, with the General tab selected

There are a couple of concepts you need to understand in order to manage License Certificate objects, namely how to assign ownership of the object and how to assign users who can use the license.

F I G U R E   3.18

The License Certificate
object's Details screen,
with the Policy Infor-
mation tab selected

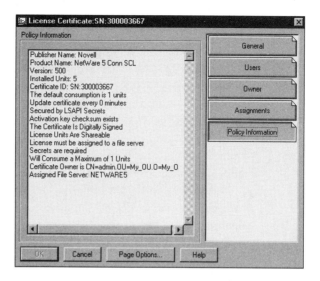

Assigning Ownership

The owner of the license has several special abilities, which will be covered shortly. First, however, we need to discuss who is the owner by default, and how to become the owner. The owner of a license certificate is, by default, the user who created the certificate. The user who creates them is, therefore, usually Admin or another administrator.

The owner of a certificate is the only person who can assign another owner. The owner is also the user who assigns other users who may use the certificate. The current information on ownership can be found under the Owner tab of the Details page for the certificate.

Assigning Users

By default, no objects are assigned to the certificate. This means that anyone can use the certificate. Once you assign an object (or objects) here, however, only that object can use the certificate. Novell doesn't recommend assigning specific users to the certificate. Instead, if you choose to assign licenses at all, you will want to assign the certificate to a group or container, allowing all of the users in the group or container to use the certificate. This allows you to control who can use what license. This might be useful if, for example, different departments purchased their own licenses to keep one department from poaching licenses from another. You can assign objects by opening the Details page for the certificate, clicking the Assignments tab, and filling in the appropriate information.

Novell Licensing Service Administration Tools

There are two tools you can use for the administration of licenses. One is a stand-alone tool called NLSMAN32.EXE and the other is a snap-in (NLSADMN32) for NetWare Administrator that incorporates the functionality of NLSMAN32.EXE. These tools, for Windows 95/98 and Windows NT-based computers, allow you to view the licenses that are installed anywhere in the tree. You can view which licenses were installed, their usage over time, and so on. This is a great analysis tool. You can do everything from both tools except generate reports, which you can't do from NLSADMN32 (NetWare Administrator).

To use the stand-alone tool, run SYS:PUBLIC\WIN32\NLSMAN32.EXE, or open it from NetWare Administrator by selecting Tools ➢ NLS. The opening screen for NLSMAN32 will be displayed, as shown in Figure 3.19. You are asked, as you can see, to choose the context to begin searching for License Containers in, if you want to search subcontainers as well, and if you want to walk the tree or use a license catalog to find the License Containers.

F I G U R E 3.19

The main screen for the NLSMAN32 license administration tool

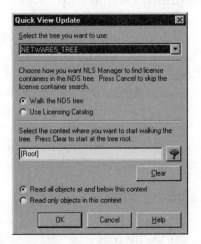

Once NLS has searched the selected container(s), you will be shown the NLS Manager quick view screen. This view sorts all of the license containers in the selected context(s) by product, so you can quickly tell which licenses you have and where they are. This view is illustrated in Figure 3.20. To analyze the data, select a License Container or certificate and click on the Create Report button or choose Actions ➢ Create License Usage Report. For more information on this, refer to the online documentation.

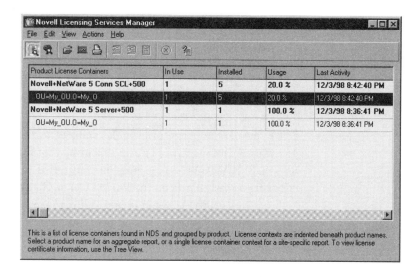

FIGURE 3.20

The NLS Manager screen shows which licenses you have and where they are kept.

Review

NDS allows you to manage all of the users, servers, and other objects on your network from a single Directory tree. In this chapter, you learned the details of managing objects using two utilities: NetWare Administrator (a Windows-based utility) and ConsoleOne (a Java-based utility). This chapter also provided descriptions of the commonly used NDS objects.

NetWare Administrator

With NetWare Administrator you can browse through the objects in the tree and manage them. You can run NetWare Administrator by choosing Run from the Windows 95/98 or Windows NT Start menu. NetWare Administrator's menus offer these options for managing and viewing information about your network:

- The Object menu allows you to create, rename, or delete an object; modify properties; and control object rights.

- The View menu allows you to control the way in which NDS objects are displayed, including setting the current context, choosing objects to include, sorting objects, and expanding or collapsing the display.

- The Options menu allows you to set several options related to the behavior of the NetWare Administrator program.

- The Tools menu provides options to open new NetWare Administrator windows and start other programs.

ConsoleOne

The ConsoleOne program provides some of the same functionality as the NetWare Administrator. To run this utility, execute Console1.EXE in SYS:PUBLIC\MGMT. You must have installed Java (which you can do by choosing to install it from the Novell Client CD) before this utility will run.

From this utility, you can create and manage a few of the basic objects, such as users and groups. This utility is still in development, so it is not fully functional at this point.

Commonly Used Leaf Objects

The leaf objects you will use most often include the following:

- User objects, which represent users on the network. You must create a User object for anyone who needs to log in to the network.

- Group objects, which allow you to organize users into logical groups that share the same rights.

- Organizational Role objects, which simplify assignments or "jobs" given to a user. You can change the occupant of the Organizational Role to give the rights to a new user.

- NetWare Server objects, which represent a NetWare server. It is created automatically when the server is installed.

- Volume objects, which represent volumes on a server. This object is created automatically when the server containing the volume is installed.

- Alias objects, which act as a pointer to another object in the Directory. This is used to make an object accessible to users in a different container and as a pointer from the old name or location of an object to the new one.

- Profile objects, which you can use to give several users the same login script.

- Directory Map objects, which point to a directory in the file system. This object allows MAP commands to be simplified and makes it easy to move directories without updating MAP commands in login scripts.

- Template objects, which allow you to create and modify multiple users quickly and more accurately.

Licensing

The objects involved with licensing include both container and leaf objects. The container object is called a License Container and the leaf object is a License Certificate. The License Container object will be created automatically when a new product is installed or a new server is installed. One or more License Certificates are usually associated with each License Container. You can control who can use the license by assigning objects that are allowed to use the license on the Assignments page of the Details dialog box for the certificate. Set the owner using the Owner page.

License usage can be tracked using the Novell Licensing Services Manager. You can view information on historical usage, see trends, and so on with this product. It is a Windows 95/98 and Windows NT product, and is found in the following path: SYS:PUBLIC\WIN32\NLSMAN32.EXE.

CNE Practice Test Questions

1. The two utilities used to manage NDS objects are:

   A. NetWare Administrator and NWADMN32

   B. ConsoleOne and NetWare Administrator

   C. SYSCON and NETADMIN

   D. NDSADMIN and NWMANAGE

2. The Create function in NetWare Administrator is found on:

   A. The File menu

   B. The Function menu

   C. The Actions menu

   D. The Object menu

3. The required properties when creating a User object are:

   A. Login name and address

   B. First name and last name

   C. Login name and last name

   D. Network address and first name

4. A Template object:

   A. Is created for each user

   B. Specifies defaults for new User objects

   C. Lets you classify the context for new users created with this Template

   D. Lets you control access rights for groups

5. The menu item used to display property values in NetWare Administrator is:

   A. Properties

   B. Values

   C. Attributes

   D. Details

6. The Move option can move which types of objects?

   A. User, Server, and Group

   B. Container objects only

C. Leaf objects only

D. User objects only

7. ConsoleOne can be used to manage:

A. User objects only

B. Only some basic NDS objects

C. All NDS objects

D. Bindery objects

8. The Group object can group users:

A. In the same container only

B. In different containers only

C. In the same or different containers

D. In the [Root] container only

9. To assign a user to an Organizational Role, you use the:

A. User's Role property

B. Organizational Role's Member property

C. User's Profile property

D. Organizational Role's Occupant property

10. The NetWare Server object:

A. Can be created when you wish to install a new server

B. Is created automatically when the server is installed

C. Is deleted automatically when the server is removed

D. Can be used to add logins to the server

11.   The Alias object:

   A. Represents, or points to, another object

   B. Is created whenever an object is deleted

   C. Can be used instead of the User object

   (D.) All of the above

12.   Which is a correct MAP command for the Directory Map DATA?

   A. `MAP F:=DATA:`

   (B.) `MAP F:=DATA.MAP`

   C. `MAP F:=DATA`

   (D.) `MAP F: DATA /DM`

13.   Which objects are associated with the Novell Licensing Service (NLS)? (Choose all that apply.)

   (A.) License Certificate

   B. License Type

   C. License Template

   D. License Container

CHAPTER

4

How to Use NetWare Security

Roadmap

This chapter covers security systems in NetWare, including login, file system, and NDS security, which is a section of the NetWare 5 CNA and the NetWare 5 CNE core requirement "Administration for NetWare 5."

Topics Covered

- Restricting User Access to the Network
- Detecting Intruders
- File System Rights vs. File Attributes
- Assigning File System Rights and Attributes
- Rights Inheritance and Inherited Rights Filters (IRFs)
- NDS Object Rights vs. NDS Property Rights
- Assigning NDS Rights
- Calculating Effective Rights for the File System and for NDS
- Maximizing Efficiency While Providing Security

Skills You'll Learn

- Describe how to use NetWare Administrator to assign and view rights and attributes for files and directories
- Describe how to use NetWare Administrator to assign and view NDS object and property rights
- Describe how rights are combined with IRFs to calculate effective rights
- List several strategies for maximizing productivity and security
- Explain the capabilities of NetWare to keep unauthorized users from logging in to the network

These days we can't have enough security—we have locks, car alarms, home alarms, even personal alarms. These safety measures are also necessary in networking. The security features of NetWare 5 allow you to control who can access what on the network. You can make the network as secure—or insecure—as you want it to be.

NetWare 5 provides several types of security, summarized here:

Login security   Allows users to connect to the network using passwords. It includes restrictions on when users can log in and from where, among others.

File system security   Controls access to the file system.

NDS security   Controls access to NDS objects.

Server security   Controls access to the file server itself. We'll examine this type of security in Chapter 8.

Network printing security   Controls access to network printers. We'll examine printing with NDPS (Novell Distributed Print Services) in Chapter 6 and with queue-based printing systems in Chapter 9.

All of these types of security have their uses. We'll begin this chapter with a look at login security and then introduce the concept of trustees, which are used in both file system and NDS security. We'll then examine file system security and NDS security in detail.

Using Login Security

The first type of security a user encounters when accessing the network is *login security*. Although a workstation is connected to the network, users have virtually no access to the network's resources until they successfully log in. We examined the login process and the LOGIN command in Chapter 2.

You define a user's login name and password as part of configuring the User object. We looked at the basics of creating a User object in Chapter 3. Here we will examine the technical side of the login process and take a look at the properties of the User object that affect login security.

The Login Process

From a user's point of view, the login process is simple, but behind the scenes, it's actually quite complex. While NetWare 3 and earlier versions required a separate login for each server on the network, NetWare 4 and 5 use NDS to allow you to use a single login to access the entire Directory tree, and all servers within it. The process that NetWare uses to accomplish this is called *authentication*.

When you enter your username and password, NetWare does not send the password across the network for authentication; this would be a security risk. Instead, the username, password, workstation, and other vital details are encrypted to form a unique *user code*. The same process is performed at the authenticating server, and if the codes match, the user is given access.

Along with preventing password snooping, this process also ensures that accurate information is being received, and that the workstation, network address, and other data have not been tampered with. This ensures that the login process is secure—provided users choose effective passwords and don't reveal them.

Restricting User Access

Several of the property categories of a User object are labeled as *restrictions*. These are various categories of items you can control to keep the network secure. For example, you can restrict the number of logins a user can have open at the same time, the workstations the user can log in from, and/or the time of day the user is allowed to log in. The following categories of restrictions are available:

Login Restrictions   Allows you to disable the account entirely, make it expire on a certain date, or limit the number of concurrent logins for the user. Figure 4.1 shows this property page displayed in the NetWare Administrator utility.

Password Restrictions   Includes a variety of options dealing with passwords. You can specify whether the user can change passwords, how often the user will be required to change the password (if ever), and how many grace logins are allowed (in other words, the number of logins allowed with an expired password before a password change becomes mandatory). You can also specify how long the password must be (minimum) and whether the new password must be unique (which in NetWare means different from any of the last eight passwords used). This property page is shown in Figure 4.2.

FIGURE 4.1

The Login Restrictions page allows you to control account expiration and other features.

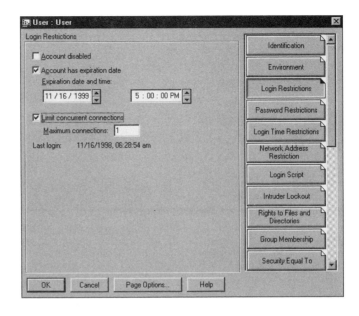

FIGURE 4.2

The Password Restrictions page allows you to control the user's password features.

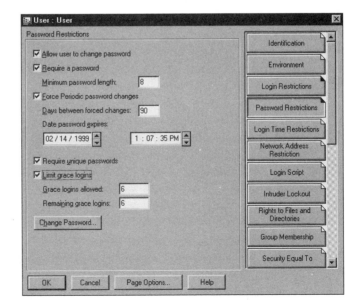

Login Time Restrictions Controls the times and days of the week the user is allowed access to the network. In the example shown in Figure 4.3, the user's access has been restricted to Monday through Friday from 8 A.M. to 5 P.M. If the end of the allowed time is reached and the user hasn't logged off, he or she will be given a five-minute warning, after which he or she will be thrown off, losing any unsaved data.

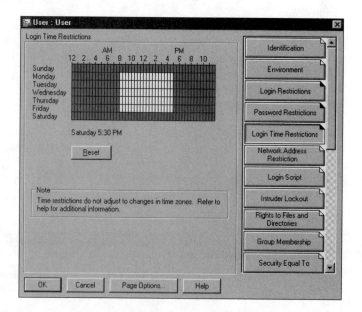

FIGURE 4.3
The Login Time Restrictions page allows you to specify the days and times the user can log in.

Network Address Restrictions Allows you to create a list of workstation addresses the user is allowed access from. This allows you to limit the user to a single workstation or a particular group of workstations. This restriction can be done by IP or IPX address, hardware (MAC) address, and so on.

Detecting Intruders

NetWare uses the term *intruder* to refer to anyone who attempts to log in using an invalid password, and the system is able to quickly lock the account when such an intruder is detected. Of course, users occasionally make mistakes, so you can configure the system to be as lenient as you desire. You can control this feature from the Intruder Detection property tab of an Organization or Organizational Unit object. These properties are shown in Figure 4.4.

FIGURE 4.4

Intruder Detection options allow you to control what happens when an invalid password is used.

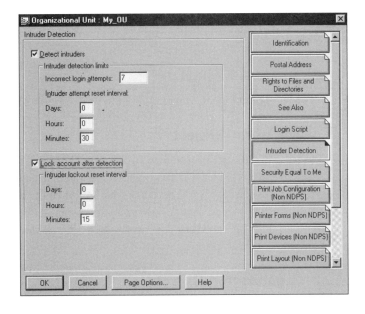

You can specify the number of incorrect login attempts (and the time period for those attempts) that will be allowed before the account is locked. In the example shown in Figure 4.4, the administrator has decided that 7 failed attempts within 30 minutes constitutes an intruder. You can also specify a reset interval, which will unlock the account if a certain time elapses after the intruder detection. If a user's account is locked and is not reset automatically, you can unlock it from the Intruder Lockout property category of the User object.

Trustees

File system security and NDS security have many similarities. One of the most important of these is *trustees*. A trustee is, simply, anyone who has rights to a file, directory, or NDS object—anyone or *anything*, to be precise. With both file system and NDS security, almost any object can be a trustee—in other words, almost any object can be given rights to any other object.

The following types of objects are often used as trustees in either system:

- The [Root] object
- Organization objects

- Organizational Unit objects
- Organizational Role and Group objects
- User objects
- The [Public] trustee

These objects are explained in the sections that follow.

The [Root] Object

Rights can be assigned to the [Root] object. This can be dangerous because *all* users in the Directory tree are given any rights assigned to the [Root] object. For small networks, assigning rights to the [Root] object can be an easy way to assign rights to publicly available files, such as those in the PUBLIC subdirectory, and to NDS objects that everyone needs access to, like a certain printer.

Organization Objects

Since an Organization object is usually a major division of the Directory tree, the warning given about the [Root] object applies here. Rights should only be assigned to an Organization object when files need to be made available to the entire Organization or NDS rights to a certain object (such as a Directory Map object) need to be accessible by all users in the Organization.

Organizational Unit Objects

The Organizational Unit object is the most common place to assign file system and NDS rights—and the most convenient. Since these containers are usually specific to a particular department or class of users, rights assigned here can be given to logical groups of users. This is where the advantages of a well-designed Directory tree become obvious.

Organizational Role and Group Objects

Organizational Role objects or Group objects can be used when files or objects are not needed by all members of a container and/or by users in multiple containers. This allows you to keep tight control over who can access these objects and files. This may be useful for applications that you want to restrict to a specific set of users. When using this method, be sure to add the users to the Group or Organizational Role object.

User Objects

Rights can also be assigned to a User object. In a well-designed network, you should rarely have to use user rights, because assigning rights to the previously discussed objects allows easy maintenance without having to assign rights to each user. Assigning rights to a User object can be useful, however, when only a certain user should have access to a file, directory, or object, such as the user's home directory, or when an administrator should only have rights to a portion of the tree.

The [Public] Trustee

The [Public] trustee object does not represent an actual object in the Directory tree. Instead, it provides a method of assigning rights to all users attached to the network—*even those who are not logged in*. Obviously, it would be dangerous to assign many rights to this trustee. You should use this method only for special cases. NetWare 5 assigns a minimal set of rights to this trustee to enable users to log in.

Using File System Security

First, we'll look at file system security, which is the most common kind of security used in NetWare 5. By controlling access to the file system, you can protect data from users who should not access it. In addition, you can give users access to the directories and files they need, while keeping those files safe.

File System Rights

A trustee can have several different types of rights to a file or directory. These rights specify which actions the trustee can perform on that file or in that directory.

If you are assigned rights (through any of the above objects) to a file or directory, these rights are called *explicit rights* or *trustee rights*. The other type of rights are *inherited rights*, which we discuss in the next section.

These are the available file system rights:

Read [R]   Read data from an existing file.

Write [W]   Write data to an existing file.

Create [C]   Create a new file or subdirectory.

Erase [E]   Delete existing files or directories.

Modify [M]   Rename and change *attributes* of files.

File Scan [F]   List the contents of a directory.

Access Control [A]   Control the *rights* of other objects to access files or directories.

Supervisor [S]   Users with the Supervisor right are automatically granted all other rights.

Inherited Rights

If an object is a trustee of a directory, the rights are *inherited* in the subdirectories of that directory. In other words, by default, the rights granted at one level of the tree flow down that tree. The Inherited Rights Filter (IRF) controls which rights can be inherited. The IRF cannot be used to grant rights; it can only block or allow rights that were given in a parent directory.

The IRF is simply a list of the rights a user or other trustee can inherit for that directory or file. If a right is included in the IRF, it can be inherited. If you leave a right out of the IRF, it means no user can inherit that right for that directory. The default IRF includes all the rights, so everything flows down.

The IRF will not allow you to filter out the Supervisor right in the file system. This is why administrators (such as the default user, Admin) have all rights to all directories. However, an IRF can filter the Supervisor right in NDS. This will be explained in more detail later in the chapter, in the section on NDS security.

Effective Rights

Your rights in a directory begin with the rights granted explicitly to you or an object (such as an Organizational Role) you are associated with, or those inherited from a parent directory. The inherited rights (and *only* the inherited rights, not the explicit rights) are then filtered by the IRF. The end result is called your *effective rights* for that file or directory. This is what NetWare actually looks at when controlling user access. We like to think of the difference between explicit and inherited rights before and after, respectively, the IRF, as similar to the difference between gross income (everything coming in) and net profit (what you actually have left over after taxes and other expenses).

For example, in Figure 4.5, user RALPH has been given the rights RWMF in the DATA directory. He inherits the same rights in the AP directory because the IRF allows all of those rights [RWCEMF]. In the AR directory, however, his rights are limited to R and F by the IRF. Although the C right is included in the IRF, user RALPH does not receive this right because he did not have it in the DATA directory. The analogy that we like to use here is, just as the IRS allows you to inherit $600,000 tax-free (the IRF), if your benefactor only had $500, you can only get $500 (effective rights).

FIGURE 4.5

Effective rights are the actions a trustee can perform in a file or directory.

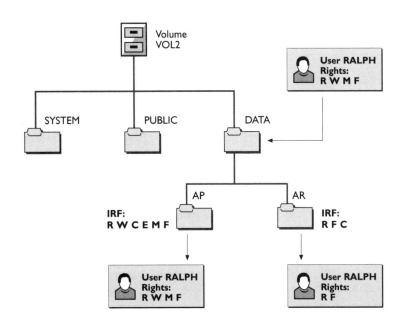

File Attributes

Another layer of file system security is *attribute security*. Attributes are options that can be applied to a file or directory to give it certain behaviors. An example is the Hidden attribute, which hides a file from the directory listing. Some attributes are set by the user or system administrator; others are set automatically by NetWare to indicate a condition. The latter are called *status flags*. For example, the Archive Needed attribute indicates that the file has changed since the last backup. These are the available file and directory attributes (not all attributes can be used in both places):

A (Archive Needed)   NetWare sets this attribute automatically when a file is changed. Backup programs use this to determine which files need to be backed up. This is a status flag.

Cc (Can't Compress)   This attribute is set by NetWare to indicate that no significant amount of space would be saved by compression. This is a status flag.

Ci (Copy Inhibit)   Stops users from copying the file (Macintosh users only).

Co (Compressed)   Indicates that the file is already compressed. This is a status flag.

Dc (Don't Compress)   Prevents file or directory contents from being compressed. This can be a file or directory attribute.

Di (Delete Inhibit)   Prevents a file or directory from being deleted; over-rides the Erase right. This can be a file or directory attribute.

Dm (Don't Migrate)   Prevents file or directory contents from being migrated to an optical jukebox, tape, or other high-capacity storage. This can be a file or directory attribute.

Ds (Don't Suballocate)   Causes the file to be written in whole blocks, regardless of whether block suballocation is enabled.

H (Hidden)   Prevents a file or directory from being shown in the directory listing. This affects DOS programs only; Windows 95/98, Windows NT, and NetWare utilities can display hidden files if requested and the user has the File Scan right. This can be a file or directory attribute.

Ic (Immediate Compress)   Causes the file, or all files in the directory, to be compressed immediately when written. This can be a file or directory attribute.

M (Migrated)   Indicates files that have been migrated to high-capacity storage. This is a status flag.

N (Normal)   This is not an actual file attribute but is used by the FLAG command to assign a default set of attributes (Shareable, Read/Write). This can be a file or directory attribute.

P (Purge)   Causes the file to be purged (erased) immediately when deleted. The file cannot be salvaged (undeleted) later if this attribute is set. This can be a file or directory attribute.

Ri (Rename Inhibit)   Prevents the user from renaming the file or directory; overrides the Modify right (although anyone with the Modify right can turn off Rename Inhibit). This can be a file or directory attribute.

Ro (Read Only)   Prevents users from writing to, renaming, or erasing the file. This automatically sets the Ri (Rename Inhibit) and Di (Delete Inhibit) attributes. This combination of attributes overrides the Write, Erase, and Modify rights.

Rw (Read/Write)   Allows both reading and writing to the file. This attribute is set when the Ro (Read Only) attribute is cleared; it also automatically clears Di (Delete Inhibit) and Ri (Rename Inhibit).

Sh (Shareable)   Allows multiple users to access the file at the same time. This attribute is typically set only for Read Only files.

Sy (System)   Indicates files used by the system. This attribute is typically set for core operating system files. This can be a file or directory attribute.

T (Transactional)   Indicates that the file is a file protected by the Transaction Tracking System. This feature can be used only with applications that support TTS.

X (Execute Only)   Prevents the file from being modified, erased, copied, or even backed up. Once set, this attribute cannot be removed by anyone, so only those with the Supervisor right can set it.

Managing File System Security

All of the rights and attributes mentioned above can be managed with the NetWare Administrator utility. Note that you cannot make changes to security unless you have the correct rights. If possible, log in as the user Admin or an equivalent to follow along with the examples in this chapter.

Browsing the File System

In order to control file system security, you can browse the hierarchy of files and directories from within the NetWare Administrator utility. You can browse a volume in two ways:

- Double-click the name of a volume. This expands the listing to display the names of files and directories under the root directory of the volume, as shown in Figure 4.6.

FIGURE 4.6

Double-click a volume
name to view the
contents of the volume
in the main NDS
window.

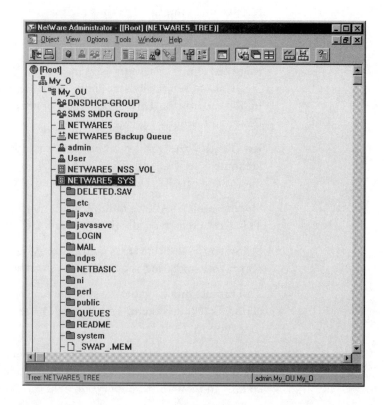

- Click the volume name once to highlight it. Select Tools from the menu bar, then Browse. This opens a new window that shows only the volume and its contents.

After you open the volume for display, you can navigate through the directories. Double-clicking a directory name opens that directory. If you select a file or directory, the Object menu includes options that allow you to perform file operations such as copying, moving, renaming, and deleting. In addition, the Details option on the Object menu allows you to view the attributes and trustees of the file or directory and to make changes.

You can also manage files using the Windows *drag-and-drop* feature in NetWare Administrator. If you drag a file into a directory, you can move or copy the file. This feature is similar to dragging and dropping in Windows Explorer (or File Manager, in earlier versions of Windows). The advantage of doing it here is that the file's trustees can also be copied.

Assigning Trustee Rights

You can assign trustees in several ways:

- Add users as trustees to a *file* using the NetWare Administrator utility or the FILER utility.

- Add file and directory trustee rights to an *object* using NetWare Administrator.

Assigning Trustees to a File or Directory

To assign trustees to a file or directory in NetWare Administrator, follow the steps listed in Procedure 4.1. (See the online documentation for information on using the FILER utility to accomplish this task.)

PROCEDURE 4.1

Assigning Trustees to a File or Directory

Assigning trustees to files and directories is simple with NetWare Administrator. With the volume expanded to show the desired level of detail, follow these steps:

1. Click the file or directory name to highlight it.

2. Select Object ➢ Details. The Details screen for the file appears.

3. Click the Trustees of this Directory button, located along the right side of the Details screen, to display the trustees information for a directory, as shown on this screen:

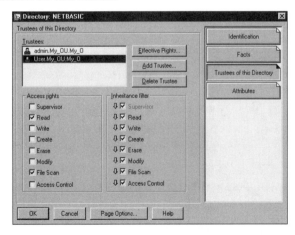

PROCEDURE 4.1 (CONTINUED)

4. If trustees are already assigned to the directory, they will be listed. If you select one of these, the rights for that user in the directory will be shown.

5. You can add or remove rights by clicking the checkboxes next to the names of the rights.

6. To add a new trustee, click the Add Trustee button. This presents the Select Object dialog box, which allows you to select a user, group, or another object. The Select Object dialog box looks like this:

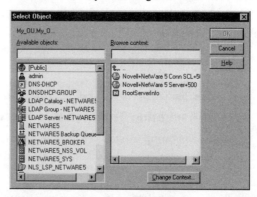

7. After you have added a trustee, you can assign rights by clicking the checkboxes. The Read and File Scan rights are granted by default.

8. Click the OK button to save your changes. The rights are immediately assigned and usable by the trustee.

NetWare Administrator provides a shortcut for accessing the Details option. After selecting the file or directory, right-click your mouse to display a pop-up menu. The Details option is listed first. Depending on the type of object you selected, there will be different options available on this menu. For files only, you can also double-click the filename to open the Details page.

Assigning File Rights to an Object

An alternate method of adding trustee rights is to start with the user. This method also works with other objects, such as groups or containers. Follow the steps listed in Procedure 4.2.

PROCEDURE 4.2

Assigning File System Rights to an Object

You can assign any file system rights desired to many types of objects, including User, Group, Organizational Role, Organizational Unit, and Organization. To do so, follow these steps:

1. Navigate through the NDS tree and highlight the object you want to add as a trustee.

2. Select Object ➤ Details. The Details screen for the object appears.

3. Click the Rights to Files and Directories tab.

4. Select which volumes are to be displayed. The simplest way to do this is by using the Find button. This allows you to quickly find all volumes in the tree or a portion thereof, depending on the context you choose. The default is to search the current container only. All directories and files that the object has rights to are displayed, as shown in this example:

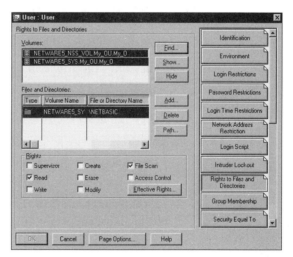

5. To add an object as a trustee to another directory or file, click the Add button. You'll see the Select Object dialog box, which allows you to select volumes, files, and/or directories.

6. After a file or directory has been added to the list, simply highlight it and NetWare Administrator will display the rights that the trustee has. By default, Read and File Scan are assigned.

7. Click the checkboxes to add or remove rights as needed.

8. Click OK to save your changes. The rights are immediately assigned and usable by the new trustee.

Modifying the Inherited Rights Filter (IRF)

You can view and modify an IRF for a directory by using the Details screen, which is the same screen that displays the trustees for that directory. To display this screen, select the directory, choose the Details option (from the Object menu or the pop-up menu that appears when you right-click the object name), and then click the Trustees of this Directory button.

In the Inheritance Filter list, you can change the inheritance status for each right by clicking its checkbox. A downward-pointing arrow icon to the left of the checkbox indicates that the right is allowed to flow into this directory. If the arrow has a line beneath it, it is blocked from flowing into this directory.

Remember the following things about IRFs:

- They only affect *inherited* rights, not explicit rights.

- They affect everyone.

- They can never increase an object's effective rights, only reduce them.

- The Supervisory *file system* right *cannot* be blocked. In other words, you cannot deselect this checkbox.

- An explicit granting of rights will override the rights inherited from above and is not affected by IRF.

Displaying Effective Rights

An Effective Rights button appears in both an object's Rights to Files and Directories screen and on the directory's Trustees screen. Click this button to view the current effective rights for the object in that directory. Rights that the user has are displayed in black, while those that the user does not have are grayed out. Figure 4.7 shows the Effective Rights dialog box.

FIGURE 4.7

A user's effective rights can be displayed for any file or directory.

The effective rights in this dialog box are updated whenever you make a change; the user doesn't have to log in or out to display the current effective rights. However, when you make a change to a user's rights, you must save the changes with the OK button before the Effective Rights dialog box will reflect those changes.

By viewing the Effective Rights dialog box, you can easily determine whether you have assigned rights correctly. It is a good idea to check the resulting effective rights after you make changes, because of the interaction between explicit and inherited rights for the many objects that may be given them.

You can calculate effective rights by hand using the diagram shown in Figure 4.8.

FIGURE 4.8

Use this diagram to manually calculate effective rights for a user.

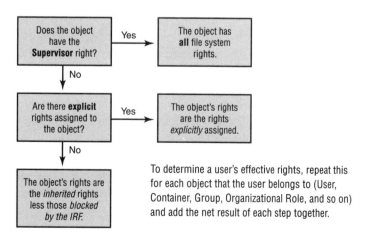

Modifying File Attributes

Modifying file and directory attributes is very simple with the NetWare Administrator. Follow the steps outlined in Procedure 4.3 to assign the attributes desired.

PROCEDURE 4.3

Assigning Attributes to Files and Directories

To modify file attributes using the NetWare Administrator program, follow these steps:

1. Click the file or directory to highlight it.

2. Select Object ➢ Details to open the Details screen for the selected object.

3. Click the Attributes button on the right side of the screen to see the current attributes for the file, as shown in this example:

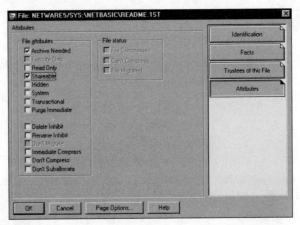

4. You can add or remove attributes by clicking the checkboxes next to the attribute names.

5. Select the OK button to save your changes. The changes take effect immediately.

The list of attributes is dynamic. If an option is not available for the current file or directory, the item is grayed out in the dialog box, and you cannot select it. In addition, some selections are made automatically. For example, selecting the Read Only attribute automatically selects the Delete Inhibit and Rename Inhibit attributes.

Planning File System Rights to Maximize Security and Efficiency

To maximize the security of the directory structure and minimize the time you must spend administering file system security issues, you should plan rights from the root of each volume down and use Group, Organizational Role, and container objects as much as possible.

Planning Rights from the Root Down

The idea behind this strategy is to make appropriate rights assignments and then block those assignments as necessary with an IRF. As you do so, keep in mind the following principles:

- Less access should be granted near the top of the tree and more further down the tree (in general, the structure for rights should resemble a triangle, with the root at the top).

- Grant rights to directories and then individual files if necessary. Avoid file assignments except as necessary, as they can be time-consuming.

- Grant as few rights as you can to as small a group as possible near the root of the volume, as the rights will flow down to all subdirectories below the point where the assignment was made.

- Remember, as you assign rights and block them with IRFs, that the Supervisor right cannot be blocked by an IRF.

Utilizing Groups, Organizational Roles, and Containers

When you assign rights to trustees, you should assign them to objects that encompass multiple users. For example, assign rights first to containers (which probably contain the largest number of users associated with this object), then to groups and Organizational Roles, and finally to users. To minimize the amount of time you must spend administering the file system and make your directory structure as secure as possible, make assignments to individual users as infrequently as possible (with the obvious exception of home directories).

Using NDS Security

While file system security allows you to control access to volumes, files, and directories on a server, NDS security is used to control access to objects in the Directory—users, groups, printers, and entire organizations. You can control users' ability to modify and add objects and to view or modify their properties. With an understanding of NDS security, you can assign users the rights they need in the Directory while maintaining a secure network.

Login Security

NDS provides *login security* for the network. (This security was provided by the bindery in NetWare 2 and 3.) Login security is handled by a password for each user object. The workstation software sends this password to NDS in an encrypted form, so there is no way of reading these passwords from elsewhere in the network.

Although NDS provides incredibly sophisticated levels of security, none of them will be effective if your users use simple passwords or no passwords at all. You should require passwords on the network and advise users not to use common words or names. (You would be amazed how many users on the average network use their own or their children's names for passwords.) This policy ensures that there are no weaknesses in network security.

Trustee Rights

Like the file system, NDS security assigns rights through the use of trustees. The trustees of an object are called *object trustees*. An object trustee is any object that has been given rights to the object. The list of trustees for an object is called the *Access Control List*, or *ACL*. Each object has a property containing the ACL.

While the file system has one list of rights that a trustee can receive, NDS security provides two categories of rights: object rights and property rights.

Object Rights

Object rights are the tasks that a trustee can perform on an object. There are four types of object rights (six for containers):

Supervisor   The trustee is granted all of the object rights listed below, as well as the Supervisor property right to All Properties. (Property rights will be discussed in just a moment.) Unlike the Supervisor right in the file system, the NDS Supervisor right *can be blocked* by the Inherited Rights Filter (IRF).

Browse   The trustee can see the object in the Directory tree. If the Browse right is not granted, the object is not shown in the list.

Create   The trustee can create child objects under the container object. This right is available only for container objects.

Delete   The trustee can delete the object from the Directory.

Rename   The trustee can change the name of the object.

Inheritable   This right, which applies only to container objects, allows the object rights you choose to be inherited by objects in that container, just as normal rights are. This is a new feature in NetWare 5. In previous versions of NetWare, object rights were always inheritable.

Property Rights

Property rights allow a trustee to perform certain tasks on the object's properties. This allows the trustee to read or modify the property values. There are five types of property rights (six for containers), which are different from the types of object rights:

Supervisor   The trustee is given all of the property rights listed below. Once again, this right can be blocked by the IRF. Remember, trustees with the Supervisor object right are automatically given supervisory rights to all properties of the object.

Compare   The trustee is allowed to compare the property's values to a given value. This allows the trustee to search for a certain value but not to look at the value itself.

Read   The trustee can read the values of the property. The Compare right is automatically implied (and granted).

Write   The trustee can modify, add, or remove values of the property. Be very careful when assigning this right to the ACL property of any object, because this will allow the trustee to modify the NDS rights of any object that this object is a trustee of. This right implies the Add Self right as well.

WARNING   Be especially careful when assigning this right to a trustee for the ACL of a server object, as the trustee will have the Supervisor file system right to all volumes on the server. This is the only case in which NDS rights give file system rights.

Add Self   The trustee is allowed to add or remove itself as a value of the property. For example, a user that is granted the Add Self right for a group can add himself or herself to the group. The Write right automatically grants the Add Self property.

Inheritable   This right, which applies only to container objects, allows the All Properties or Selected Property rights you choose to be inherited by objects in that container, just as normal rights are. This is a new (and long-awaited) feature in NetWare 5. This allows you to designate a user to be responsible for changing addresses and phone numbers, for example (by giving that user the Write right to those properties), without giving them any administrative control over NDS or having to assign those rights to each object individually.

Property rights can be granted in two ways: All Properties or Selected Properties. If All Properties is selected, the same list of rights is granted to each of the properties of the object.

WARNING   You should think twice (or even three times) before assigning rights to All Properties of an object, especially when granting the Write right. This can be a security risk. It is usually better to assign rights to only the properties that the trustee needs to access.

When granting Selected Properties, you are allowed to select or deselect each of the property rights for each property of the object. This allows you to fine-tune security and allow access only to what is needed. Because of the security risks involved in using the All Properties option, you should use Selected Properties for all users except administrators.

An object trustee can have both All Properties rights and Selected Properties rights for the same object, if the All Properties rights were inherited from a parent object. In this case, Selected Properties rights override the All Properties rights for that property if there are any conflicts. For example, you could give a trustee the Supervisor right to All Properties for a parent object and then use Selected Properties to limit rights to certain properties of one of its child objects. Rights without a Selected Properties assignment follow the All Properties assignment.

One of the object properties that can be selected is the Object Trustees property. This property contains the trustee list, which is the ACL (Access Control List) itself. If a user is given Supervisor or Write rights to this property, the user can add and delete trustees and modify the NDS rights of the object. To avoid this security risk, don't assign the Write or Supervisor rights to this property or to All Properties. To reiterate the note above, if the Write or Supervisor right is given to a *server object*, the object will have the Supervisor file system right to *all volumes* on the server.

Inherited Rights in NDS

Like the file system, NDS uses a system of *inherited rights*. When an object trustee is given rights to a container object, the trustee also receives the same rights for all children of the object. Inheritance affects both object rights and property rights.

Object and Property Rights Inheritance

Object rights are inherited in the same fashion as file system rights if the Inheritable object right is also selected. When a trustee is given object rights for an object, the rights are inherited by each child object as well. The trustee receives rights for these objects also, unless the rights are blocked by an IRF, don't apply for that object (for example, the Create right for a leaf object), or the Inheritable object right wasn't granted.

Property rights can be inherited in the same manner as object rights.

Blocking Inherited Rights

When a trustee is given rights to a container object, the rights flow down the Directory tree until they are blocked. You can block inherited rights in two ways: with a new trustee assignment or with the IRF.

Explicit Assignments   You can block the rights a trustee can inherit for a particular object by giving the trustee a new explicit assignment to the object, just as in the file system. For example, in Figure 4.9, user RON is given full rights [SBCDR] to the entire NHA_CO Organization. However, RON has been given a new explicit assignment of Browse and Rename only [BR] for the ORLANDO Organizational Unit. While RON receives full rights in the TAMPA Organizational Unit (inherited from NHA_CO), his rights in ORLANDO are limited to [BR] by the new trustee assignment.

FIGURE 4.9

Inherited rights can be
blocked with a new
explicit assignment.

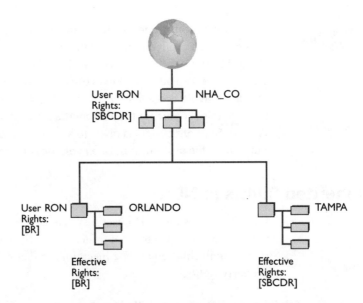

A new trustee assignment can be used to block rights, as in the example shown, or to grant additional rights. The new trustee assignment replaces the rights that would have been inherited. The trustee assignment is also called an *explicit assignment*. Because an explicit assignment blocks inherited rights, you do not need to consider inherited rights if an explicit assignment has been granted.

The Inherited Rights Filter (IRF) Each NDS object has an IRF for object rights. The IRF is a list of the rights that a user can inherit for the object. For example, in Figure 4.10, user JANS has been given the [BCDR] rights to the ACCTG Organizational Unit. She inherits these same rights in the AP Organizational Unit, which has the default IRF. The IRF for the PR Organizational Unit has been set to [SBR], so JANS' rights in PR are limited to [BR].

Each object also has an IRF for property rights. Like the rights themselves, the IRF can be set for All Properties or Selected Properties. You can also set an IRF for All Properties and set different IRFs for certain Selected Properties.

Remember, the IRF cannot give a user additional rights; it can be used only to filter (block) rights that a user would otherwise inherit. Also, the IRF affects only inherited rights; it doesn't block security equivalence, which is described in the next section.

The Inherited Rights
Filter can be used to
block inherited rights.

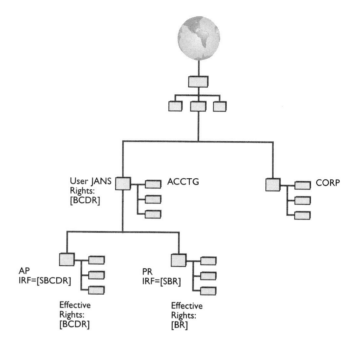

Security Equivalence

In several situations in NDS, a trustee automatically receives all of the rights
given to another trustee. This is referred to as *security equivalence.* By understanding these equivalences, you can easily grant rights to users and make
sure that unnecessary rights are not granted. There are two types of security
equivalence: implied and explicit.

Implied Security Equivalence

When rights are given to a container object, all objects within the container
receive the same rights through security equivalence. If one of these objects
is a container object, the objects underneath it also receive the rights. This is
referred to as implied security equivalence or container security equivalence.

In the example shown in Figure 4.11, giving a trustee assignment to the
ACCTG Organization would give the same rights to the PAYABLES and
BILLING Organizational Units and all leaf objects under them. Giving a
trustee assignment to the [Root] object would give the same rights to all
objects in the entire tree.

FIGURE 4.11

In implied security
equivalence, rights
given to a container
are passed on to
objects within the
container.

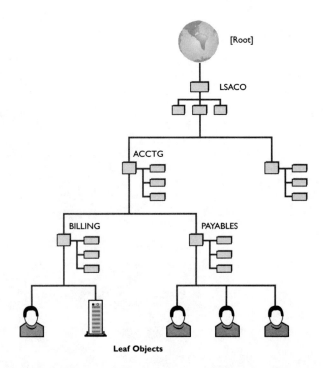

Because rights flow from container objects to their children, you may be tempted to describe this process as "inheritance." However, this is not how *inheritance* is defined in NetWare. *Inheritance* means that rights given to a trustee for a container object are given to the same trustee for the object's children.

It is important to understand the difference between inheritance and implied security equivalence, because the IRF does not affect security equivalences. This distinction can be one of the most difficult concepts to master in NDS security. You can avoid confusion by remembering the following concepts:

- An object inherits the trustee rights assigned to its parent objects. These rights can be blocked by the IRF.

- A trustee is security equivalent to all of its parent objects. These rights cannot be blocked by the IRF.

These concepts are further illustrated in Figure 4.12. Look at this Directory tree carefully, and read the following statements about the objects in the Directory.

FIGURE 4.12

This Directory tree shows examples of both inherited rights and implied security equivalence.

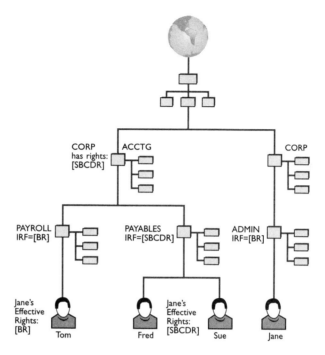

- The CORP Organizational Unit has been given full rights to the ACCTG Organizational Unit. (CORP is a trustee of ACCTG.)

- The ADMIN and PAYROLL Organizational Units both have an IRF of [BR] (Browse and Rename only).

- Jane receives full rights [SBCDR] to objects in the ACCTG Organizational Unit. This is because Jane has an implied security equivalence to the CORP container object. The IRF given to the ADMIN Organizational Unit does not affect Jane's rights.

- Jane inherits full rights to all objects in the PAYABLES organizational unit, including the User objects Fred and Sue.

- Jane's rights to the User object Tom are limited to Browse and Rename only [BR] by the IRF of the PAYROLL Organizational Unit.

Explicit Security Equivalence

A second, much simpler type of security equivalence is also available: *explicit security equivalence*. This is a security equivalence that is specifically given to a user. You can assign explicit security equivalences in three ways:

- Each user has a Security Equal To property. You can add users or other objects to this list, and the user receives the rights given to those objects.

- If a user is assigned to the membership list of a Group object, the user becomes security equivalent to the Group object.

- If a user is an occupant of an Organizational Role object, the user becomes security equivalent to the Organizational Role object.

All explicit security equivalences are listed in the user's Security Equal To property. Security equivalences that the user receives through an Organizational Role or Group membership are automatically added to this list.

Security equivalences cannot be combined or "nested." For example, if the user John is made security equivalent to another user, Wendy, and Wendy is made security equivalent to the Admin user, John does not become security equivalent to Admin and does not receive administrative rights. He receives only those rights given to (or inherited by) Wendy's User object.

Security equivalence is *not* the recommended method to make backup administrators. If the first user is deleted, then the second has no rights either. You should always make a second Admin user by assigning that user the same rights as Admin, [S] object rights to [Root].

Calculating Effective Rights

A user's effective rights are the tasks the user can actually perform on the object. As you have learned, there are many factors that affect a user's rights to an object in the Directory:

- Rights given directly to the user (explicit trustee assignments)

- Inherited rights from rights the user has been given to objects higher in the Directory tree

- The Inherited Rights Filter or an explicit assignment, which can override inherited rights

- Rights received from containers the user resides in through implied security equivalence

- Security equivalences to Group or Organizational Role objects

Luckily, the NetWare Administrator utility provides a simple method for displaying a user's effective rights to an object. If you find it necessary to calculate effective rights manually, you can do so by following these steps:

1. Start with any explicit rights given to the user for the object.

2. If there are no explicit rights, calculate the inherited rights—any rights given to the user for parent objects minus those blocked by the IRF.

3. Add any rights given to the user's security equivalents for the object. These include group memberships, organizational roles, or members of the user's Security Equivalent To property.

This is the same process that was illustrated in Figure 4.8 previously, with the exception that the Supervisor object and property rights can be blocked with an IRF.

Using NetWare Administrator to Control NDS Security

You can use the NetWare Administrator utility to manage the following aspects of NDS security:

- Viewing trustee rights

- Adding a trustee

- Changing object and property rights

- Modifying the IRF

- Displaying effective rights

These topics will be discussed in the following sections.

Viewing a Trustee's Rights

NetWare Administrator provides two ways to view trustee rights. Both of these options are accessed from the Object menu:

Trustees of This Object This option allows you to view a list of trustees for the object you have selected, as shown in Figure 4.13. You can then select a trustee to view detailed information.

F I G U R E 4.13

The Trustees of this Object option allows you to view an object's trustee list.

Rights to Other Objects This option allows you to view a list of objects that the selected object is a trustee of. First, enter a context to search in. You can then select an object from the list to view the trustee's rights to the object, as shown in Figure 4.14.

F I G U R E 4.14

The Rights to Other Objects option allows you to list a trustee's rights.

Each of these screens includes all of the possible rights for the object. A checkbox next to the option displays whether the right is granted and allows you to grant or revoke the right.

These techniques allow you to view and change explicit rights only. To view a user's effective rights, see the "Displaying Effective Rights" section later in this chapter.

Adding a Trustee

You can add a trustee in two ways. Procedures 4.4 and 4.5 describe the two methods.

PROCEDURE 4.4

Adding Trustees to an Object

To add a trustee to an object, follow these steps:

1. Browse through the Directory tree to find the object, and then highlight it.

2. Select Object ➢ Trustees of This Object. (Alternatively, you can simply right-click the object.)

3. Click the Add Trustee button to access the Select Object dialog box.

4. Find the object that will become a trustee in the Select Object dialog box, and then click the OK button. The trustee is now added to the list. You can change the trustee's rights as described in the next section, "Changing Object and Property Rights."

The method described in Procedure 4.4 works well when you want to set up the security for an object or otherwise make several changes to an object's trustees. On the other hand, the method discussed in Procedure 4.5 works well when you want a trustee to have rights to several other objects, such as when a new user or group is created.

PROCEDURE 4.5

Adding Objects to a Trustee

To make an object the trustee of one or more objects, do the following:

1. Browse through the Directory tree to find the object that will become a trustee and then highlight it.

2. Select Object ➤ Rights to Other Objects.

3. Click the Add Assignment button to access the Select Object dialog box.

4. Select the object or objects that the trustee will have rights to, and then click OK. The object is (or multiple objects are) added to the list of objects the trustee has rights to. To change these rights, follow the steps outlined in the next section, "Changing Object and Property Rights."

Changing Object and Property Rights

While either the Rights to Other Objects or Trustees of this Object dialog box is displayed, you can change the object rights given to the trustee. Simply highlight the trustee or object, and click the checkbox next to each type of right to grant it (by checking the box) or revoke it (by unchecking the box).

You can also change property rights within either of these dialog boxes. You can assign rights for All Properties by selecting All Properties and then checking or unchecking the box next to each property right.

To assign rights to selected properties, click the Selected Properties button. You are presented with a list of properties, which varies depending on the type of object. Select the property to change rights for, and check or uncheck the boxes as appropriate.

A checkmark is displayed to the left of each property for which you have changed the rights (relative to the All Properties setting). Properties without a checkmark have not been changed in Selected Properties and will default to the setting for All Properties.

Modifying the IRF

The IRF can be changed from within the Trustees of this Object dialog box. Procedure 4.6 outlines the process for making modifications to the IRF.

PROCEDURE 4.6

Modifying the IRF of an Object

Follow these steps to change the IRF for an object:

1. Browse through the Directory tree to find the object, and then highlight it.

2. Select Object ➤ Trustees of this Object.

3. Click the Inherited Rights Filter button. The Inherited Rights Filter dialog box is displayed, as shown here:

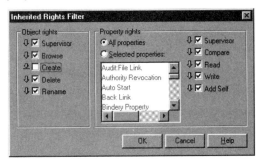

4. To change the IRF for object rights, use the checkboxes on the left. A checked box means the right can be inherited; an unchecked box means the right is blocked. An arrow or blocked arrow to the left of the checkbox indicates this visually as well.

5. To change the IRF for All Properties, click the All Properties button, and then check or uncheck the box for any property right.

6. To change the IRF for Selected Properties, click the Selected Properties button, and then select the property to be changed. Check or uncheck the appropriate boxes. Note that there is no indication that the All Properties IRF has been overridden for any property; you must select and view each property. Fortunately, this capability is rarely used. When you click OK, the assignment is made and takes effect immediately.

Displaying Effective Rights

An Effective Rights button appears in both the Trustees of this Object and Rights to Other Objects dialog boxes. The behavior of the Effective Rights button will vary depending on whether it was selected from the Rights to Other Objects or Trustees of this Object dialog box. In the former case, it will display the effective rights that the object you selected has to any other object (before you've made changes in the Rights to Other Objects dialog box). In the latter case, it will show any object's effective rights to the object you selected when choosing Trustees of this Object. In either case, rights that the user has been granted are displayed in black. Those that the user does not have are grayed out. Figure 4.15 shows an example of the Effective Rights dialog box.

FIGURE 4.15

Displaying a trustee's effective rights for an object

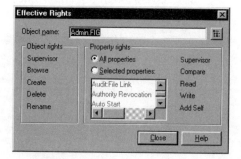

If you have made changes to a trustee's rights, you must save the changes with the OK button before the Effective Rights display can reflect those changes.

By viewing the Effective Rights display, you can easily check to determine whether you have assigned rights correctly. It is a good idea to check that the effective rights are those you intended after you make changes, because the interaction between explicit and inherited rights and the many objects that can give an object rights may affect the final outcome.

Review

The security features of NetWare 5 are used to control which users and other NDS objects have access to files, directories, and objects.

Several types of security can be controlled by NetWare 5:

- Login security allows users to connect to the network using passwords.

- File system security controls access to the file system.

- NDS security controls access to NDS objects.

- Server security controls access to the file server itself.

- Network Printing security controls access to network printers.

Login Security

Login security is the first type of security a user encounters when accessing the network. A User object must be created for each user, and the properties of this object can control and restrict logins to that account:

- Authentication is the basic process that controls logins, and it allows a single login to access multiple servers.

- User account restrictions allow you to restrict when and where the user can log in.

- Intruder Detection counts incorrect login attempts, and locks out accounts that may have been compromised.

Trustees

Much of NetWare 5 security centers around trustees. A trustee is any object that has been assigned rights to a file, directory, or NDS object. With both file system and NDS security, any object can be a trustee—in other words, any object can be given rights to any other object.

The following types of objects are commonly used as trustees in the file system or in NDS:

- The [Root] object

- Organization objects

- Organizational Unit objects

- Organizational Role and Group objects

- User objects

- The [Public] trustee

File System Security

The available file system rights are as follows:

Read [R]   Read data from an existing file.

Write [W]   Write data to an existing file.

Create [C]   Create a new file or subdirectory.

Erase [E]   Delete existing files or directories.

Modify [M]   Rename and change attributes of files and directories.

File Scan [F]   List the contents of a directory.

Access Control [A]   Control the rights of other objects to access files or directories.

Supervisor   Users with the Supervisor right are automatically granted all other rights. This right cannot be blocked with an IRF.

NDS Security

While file system security allows you to control access to volumes, files, and directories on a server, NDS security is used to control access to objects in the Directory—users, groups, printers, and entire organizations. You can control users' ability to modify and add objects and to view or modify their properties. With an understanding of NDS security, you can assign users the rights they need in the Directory while maintaining a secure network.

Like the file system, NDS security assigns rights through the use of trustees. The trustees of an object are called object trustees. An object trustee is any user (or other object) that has been given rights to the object. The list of trustees for an object is called the Access Control List, or ACL. Each object has a property containing the ACL.

While the file system has a single category of rights that a trustee can receive, NDS security provides two categories of rights: object rights and property rights.

Object rights give the trustee the ability to perform certain operations on an object. Here are the six types of object rights:

Supervisor   The trustee is granted all of the object rights listed below. In addition, the user has the Supervisor property right to All Properties. Unlike the Supervisor right in the file system, the NDS Supervisor right can be blocked by the Inherited Rights Filter (IRF).

Browse   The trustee can see the object in the Directory tree. If the Browse right is not granted, the object is not shown in the list.

Create   The trustee can create child objects under the selected container. This right is available only for container objects.

Delete   The trustee can delete the object from the Directory.

Rename   The trustee can change the name of the object.

Inheritable   The trustee can inherit the selected rights to the objects below this container. This right is available only for container objects.

Property rights allow a trustee to manipulate the object's properties. This allows the trustee to read or modify the property values. There are six types of property rights, which are different from the types of object rights:

Supervisor   The trustee is given all of the property rights listed below. Once again, this right can be blocked by the IRF. Trustees with the Supervisor object right are automatically given supervisory rights to all properties of the object.

Compare   The trustee is allowed to compare the property's values to a given value. This allows the trustee to search for a certain value but not to look at the value itself.

Read   The trustee can read the values of the property. The Compare right is automatically implied.

Write   The trustee can modify, add, or remove values of the property.

Add Self   The trustee is allowed to add or remove itself as a value of the property. For example, a user that is granted the Add Self right for a group can add himself or herself to the group. The Write right implies the Add Self property right.

Inheritable   The trustee can inherit the selected property rights for the objects in the container. This right only applies to container objects and will not be displayed for leaf objects.

Property rights can be granted in two ways: All Properties or Selected Properties. If All Properties is selected, the same list of rights is granted to each of the properties of the object.

NDS Inheritance

Like the file system, NDS uses a system of inherited rights. When an object trustee is given rights to a container object, the trustee also receives the same rights for all children of the object. Inheritance affects both object rights and property rights.

Object rights are inherited in the same fashion as file system rights. When a trustee is given object rights for an object, the rights are inherited by child objects—the trustee receives rights for these objects also, unless the rights are blocked.

Property rights can be inherited in the same manner as object rights, with one exception: Only rights given with the All Properties option are always inheritable. If a trustee is given rights to Selected Properties of an object, those rights cannot be inherited by child objects unless the Inheritable property right is also granted. The issue of inheritance only really applies to container objects, since leaf objects contain no objects beneath them to inherit rights.

When a trustee is given rights to a container object, the rights flow down the Directory tree until they are blocked. You can block inherited rights in two ways: with a new trustee assignment or with the Inherited Rights Filter (IRF).

Security Equivalence in NDS

There are several situations in NDS in which a trustee automatically receives all of the rights given to another trustee, which is referred to as security equivalence. There are two types of security equivalence:

- Implied security equivalence means that an object receives rights given to its parent containers.

- Explicit security equivalence is given with the Security Equal To property, group membership, or Organizational Role occupancy.

Effective Rights in NDS

A user's effective rights are the tasks the user can actually perform on the object. If you find it necessary to calculate effective rights manually, you can do so by following these steps:

1. Start with any explicit rights given to the user for the object.

2. If there are no explicit rights, calculate the inherited rights—any rights given to the user for parent objects minus those blocked by the IRF.

3. Add any rights given to the user's security equivalents for the object. These include group memberships, organizational roles, or members of the user's Security Equivalent To property.

CNE Practice Test Questions

1. The two types of NetWare 5 trustee rights are:

   A. File system security and NDS security

   B. File system security and object rights

   C. Trustee rights and object rights

   D. All Properties and Selected Properties

2. Which of the following cannot be a trustee?

   A. Organization

   B. User

   C. Organizational Role

   D. File

3. The File Scan right:

   A. Allows you to copy files

   B. Allows you to list files in a directory

   C. Allows you to read the contents of files

   D. Allows you to search for a file

4. The IRF affects:

A. Security equivalence

B. Inherited rights

C. Explicit assignments

D. All of the above

5. File attributes:

A. Are always set by NetWare itself

B. Are always set by the user

C. Cannot be changed

D. Give a file certain behaviors

6. You can manage file system security with:

A. NetWare Administrator

B. NETADMIN

C. SYSCON

D. SECURE

7. The IRF lists:

A. Rights to be blocked

B. Rights to be granted

C. Rights allowed to be inherited

D. Rights that cannot be inherited

8. The list of trustees for an object is stored in:

A. The Object Trustees property, also known as the ACL

B. The Trustee database

C. The Trustee file

D. Both A and B

E. Both A and C

9. The two types of rights in NDS are:

   A. Object rights and file rights

   B. Object rights and property rights

   C. All Properties and Selected Properties

   D. Object rights and the IRF

10. Inherited rights can be blocked with:

    A. The IRF

    B. An explicit assignment

    C. Both A and B

    D. None of the above

11. Explicit security equivalences can be granted with:

    A. Container occupancy

    B. Group, Organizational Role, Security Equal To

    C. Group, container occupancy

    D. All of the above

12. Which of the following does *not* have an impact on effective NDS rights?

    A. Explicit rights

    B. Inherited rights

    C. Rights given to child objects

    D. Rights given to parent objects

13. The [Public] trustee:

A. Assigns rights to all users when logged in

B. Assigns rights to anyone attached to the network

C. Assigns rights to Admin only

D. Assigns rights to the file system only

CHAPTER

5

Managing Login Scripts and Workstations with Z.E.N.works

Roadmap

This chapter covers login scripts and Z.E.N.works, including both its workstation and application management capabilities. These topics are a part of the NetWare 5 CNA and CNE core requirement "Administration for NetWare 5."

Topics Covered

- Login Scripts
- Z.E.N.works
- Application Launcher
- Workstation Management with Z.E.N.works

Skills You'll Learn

- Explain when to use each type of login script
- List the common commands and variables used in login scripts
- Describe how Z.E.N.works can help you manage applications with the Application Launcher
- List the components of and objects needed for the Application Launcher
- Explain what Policy Packages are as they relate to workstation management
- Describe the process of remotely controlling workstations

As a network administrator, you should remember one maxim: The easier things are for users, the fewer questions you'll have to answer. You'll learn several ways to make life easier for users in this chapter:

- Using login scripts, you can set up drive mappings and other defaults for the user, so that he or she doesn't have to manually set up drives and/or printers.

- The Application Launcher lets you define lists of applications a user can run and gives the user a simple way of accessing them. It also allows you to set up applications for individual computers easily.

- Workstation Policies allow you to specify what a user can and can't do at his or her own workstation. For example, you could restrict a user's ability to view the Network Neighborhood in Windows 95/98 and Windows NT.

- Remote control of users' workstations can be a valuable asset in troubleshooting from a remote location or helping a user with a problem.

If you're careful about setting up these options, you can make the network friendly and accessible to users—even those who fear computers. In addition, even the most computer-literate user appreciates not having to type the same complicated commands each time he or she logs in or accesses an application. In addition, you can make your life as an administrator much easier by simplifying the application distribution process, controlling what users can and can't do with their local computers, and remotely troubleshooting problems.

Using Login Scripts

A *login script* is a list of commands that NetWare executes each time the user logs in. You can use login scripts to set defaults for the user—such as drive mappings, search drive mappings, printer configurations, and variable settings—and to execute commands, such as starting the Application Launcher.

You can create and edit login scripts using the NetWare Administrator utility. Each of the objects we'll talk about below—users, containers, and profiles—have a Login Script property, which you can use to enter login script commands.

Login Script Types

There are four types of login scripts: user, container, profile, and default. When a user logs in, NetWare checks for each of these and executes them. Login scripts are always executed in the same order:

1. **Container** login script for the user's immediate parent container (if found).

2. **Profile** login script (if assigned).

3. **User** login script (if defined).

or

4. **Default** login script. (If NetWare doesn't find a user login script, it executes the commands in the default login script instead.)

Each of the types of login script has its own purpose. You can provide a complete configuration for your users with a minimum of maintenance by taking advantage of each of these types of scripts. The sections below explain each of the login script types. One quick note, though, before we go on: If there is a conflict between the various login scripts (for example the container, profile, and user login scripts all map drive G), the last one to execute will prevail.

NetWare 3 had a *system login script,* which was executed for any user who logged in to the server. There is no system login script in NetWare 5, because you don't log in to each server individually, but rather to the network as a whole. You can use container login scripts for the same purpose, but if user objects are in several different containers, you will need to provide a container login script for each of those containers.

Container Login Scripts

You can create a *container login script* for any Organization or Organizational Unit object. This script is the first script executed for users in the container. You can use this login script for drive mappings, printer settings, and other options that are needed by all users in the container.

NetWare executes only one container login script—for the user's parent container. For example, in Figure 5.1, user JOHNM has the distinguished name JOHNM.AP.ACCT.AQP_CO. Although JOHNM is in the containers AP, ACCT, and AQP_CO (as far as security equivalencies are concerned), only the login script for AP is executed because AP is JOHNM's parent container. If the AP Organizational Unit has no login script, no container login script is executed.

To edit the container login script, you use NetWare Administrator. The login script is stored in the container object's Login Script property. The container script can only be edited by a user with the Write right to this property, usually the ADMIN user or a container administrator.

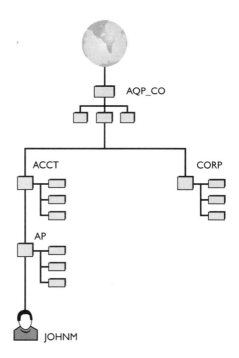

Profile Login Scripts

The Profile object is a special NDS object you can use to assign the same login script to several users. You can use a *profile login script* to execute a certain set of drive mappings or other commands for certain users in the Directory, whether a subset of users in a container or users in multiple containers.

To set up a profile login script, open NetWare Administrator and follow these steps:

1. Create a Profile object. You can place this object in any container, but the logical place for it is in the same container as the users who need it.

2. Edit the Profile object's Login Script property, and insert the desired commands.

3. For each user who will execute the profile login script, make his or her User object a trustee of the Profile object. At a minimum, the User object must have the Browse [B] right to the object itself and the Read [R] right for the Profile object's Login Script property.

4. Each User object has a Profile property. Edit each User object's Profile property, and select the Profile object you have created. You can select only one Profile object per user.

User Login Scripts

The final login script to execute is the *user login script*. You can use a user login script to execute specific commands for a particular user. One important use for the user login script is to override certain commands in the container login script.

Each user has a Login Script property. You edit this property using NetWare Administrator to create or modify the user's login script. To keep your life simple, you want as few user login scripts as possible. You should also be aware that, by default, any user can edit his or her own login script.

The Default Login Script

The *default login script* is built into the LOGIN utility. You cannot edit it. The default script is executed when a user has no user login script. The default login script provides a basic set of search and drive mappings—for example, a search mapping for the PUBLIC directory.

The default login script allows users to log in to a new system without having to create a login script. If you are using container or profile login scripts, the default login script may cause conflicts or duplicate mappings. You can prevent conflicts with a special login script command: NO_ DEFAULT. If you include this command in the container or profile login script, it prevents the execution of the default login script.

The following are the commands executed by the default login script. You will learn what each command means later in this chapter.

```
MAP DISPLAY OFF
MAP ERRORS OFF
MAP *1=SYS:
MAP *1=SYS:%LOGIN_NAME
IF "%1"="ADMIN" THEN MAP *1:=SYS:SYSTEM
MAP INS S1:=SYS:PUBLIC
MAP INS S2:=SYS:PUBLIC\%MACHINE\%OS\%OS_VERSION
MAP DISPLAY ON
MAP
```

Login Script Variables

Login script variables let you include changing information in a login script. You can use login script variables anywhere in the login script; NetWare substitutes the current value of that item. Use the percent (%) sign at the beginning of each variable name to indicate that it is a variable. Variables may be uppercase or lowercase, but since some commands require them to be uppercase, it's best to use uppercase all of the time.

Listed below are the most common login script variables. The full list of variables can be found in the online documentation.

MACHINE   Specifies the type of computer being used; typically IBM_PC.

OS   Specifies the type of operating system, which can be MSDOS, WIN95, WINNT, and so on. (Windows 98 displays as WIN95.)

OS_VERSION   Specifies the DOS version, such as 6.22, V4.00 (Windows 95), or V4.10 (Windows 98).

STATION   Represents the connection number of the workstation. Since no two computers may share the same connection number at the same time, it can be used to guarantee uniqueness.

LOGIN_NAME   Gives the login name of the user.

GREETING_TIME   Specifies a time of day—MORNING, AFTERNOON, or EVENING.

MEMBER OF *Group*   Usually used with the IF command (see below) to make some drive mappings, display messages, and so on conditional.

PASSWORD_EXPIRES   The number of days before the user's password expires; can be used to warn a user of an impending forced change so the user can think of a good password.

PLATFORM   The version of Windows (or other operating system) that the client is using. Windows choices include WIN (for 3.1), W95, or WNT.

WINVER   The version of Windows running on the client, for example 4.00.950a (for the original version of Windows 95) or 4.10.1998 (for Windows 98).

There are also variables for the day of the week, month, year, time, and so on. In addition, any property value may also be used; see the online documentation for more details.

Login Script Commands

Each login script is a sequence of *login script commands*. Each type of login script uses the same set of commands. Although some of these commands are the same as NetWare commands, most are specific to login scripts. The most important login script commands are explained in the following sections. For a complete list of commands, refer to the online documentation.

MAP

MAP is probably the most commonly used login script command. You can use this command to assign drive letters as network drives and search drives, just as you would with the MAP command-line utility.

In addition to the usual MAP commands, you can use two additional commands in login scripts: MAP DISPLAY and MAP ERRORS. Both of these have a single parameter, On or Off. The functions of these commands are as follows:

MAP DISPLAY   Controls whether NetWare displays each drive, and what it is mapped to, as each drive is mapped when the user logs in. The default is On.

MAP ERRORS   Controls whether NetWare displays map error messages as it executes the login script. These errors are usually caused by an invalid path or by a MAP command for a path the user does not have rights to. The default is On.

IF, THEN, and ELSE

You can use the IF command to execute a command or set of commands *conditionally*. The IF command is followed by a condition, the keyword THEN, and then a command or list of commands to be executed if the condition is met. Here is a simple IF command:

```
IF MEMBER OF "PAYABLES" THEN MAP N:=SYS:DATA\AP
```

In this example, the MAP command for drive N will be executed only if the user is a member of the PAYABLES group.

You can use two keywords to specify more complex conditions:

- The ELSE keyword specifies commands to be executed when the IF condition is not met.

- The END keyword ends a complex IF statement. It must be used if the IF statement uses more than one line.

Here is a more complicated example of an IF command:

```
IF %LOGIN_NAME = "ADMIN" THEN
  MAP F:=SYS:SYSTEM
  MAP J:=VOL1:TOOLS\ADMIN
ELSE
  MAP F:=SYS:HOME\%LOGIN_NAME
  MAP J:=VOL1:TOOLS\PUBLIC
END
```

In this example, drives F and J are mapped to certain directories for the Admin user and to different directories for all other users. The indentation is not required, but it is good programming style and will help you see the logic employed if you need to modify the script in the future.

The condition in the IF statement uses login script variables. NetWare sets these variables when running the login script. You can use them to test individual information for the user or workstation. You can also use these variables with the WRITE command, described below.

You can use a login script variable, MEMBER OF *GROUP*, to perform actions based on group membership. The first example in this section uses this method. You can use IF NOT MEMBER OF to perform actions if the user is not a member of the specified group.

INCLUDE

The INCLUDE command allows you to include another login script within the current script. The other script can be a script belonging to another container or profile object or a DOS text file containing login script commands. Here are some examples:

INCLUDE .OU=VIP.O=My_Co   Runs the login script for the VIP Organizational Unit.

INCLUDE SYS:PUBLIC\LOGIN1.TXT   Executes commands from a text file.

NetWare executes the commands in the other login script or file as if they were included in the current login script. If the login script or file ends with the EXIT command (described below), all login script processing ends; otherwise, the current script continues with the commands after the INCLUDE command. To successfully execute the script, the user must have at least the File

Scan and Read rights if a file is used; if a container login script is used, the user must have at least Browse object rights to the object and the Read property right to the Login Script property of the object.

CONTEXT

You can use the CONTEXT command to set the current Directory context for the user. For example, the following command sets the context to the AP Organizational Unit under the main ZYX_CO Organization:

```
CONTEXT .AP.ZYX_CO
```

WRITE

You can use the WRITE command to display a message to the user. Login script variables let you display specific information for the user. For example, the following WRITE command is typically used to greet users:

```
WRITE "Good %GREETING_TIME, %FULL_NAME."
```

This displays a message such as "Good Morning, Bob Smith."
Another example displays the current time:

```
WRITE "The time is %HOUR:%MINUTE:%SECOND %AM_PM."
```

This displays a message such as "The time is 11:30:23 AM."
By taking advantage of the WRITE command, you can advise users of conditions that may affect their use of the network, such as planned maintenance.

DISPLAY and FDISPLAY

You can use these commands to display the contents of a text file when the user logs in. FDISPLAY uses a *filtered* format to display the file, removing printer codes and unprintable characters; DISPLAY writes the file to the screen in raw format. Here is an example of the FDISPLAY command:

```
FDISPLAY SYS:PUBLIC\NEWS.TXT
```

This command simply displays the NEWS.TXT file to the user during the login process.

You can use the display commands to display information, such as system news or warnings about system problems. You can also combine them with the IF command to display detailed error messages. For example, you might use the FDISPLAY command below to explain a printer error to the user:

```
#CAPTURE L=1 Q=LASER1_QUEUE
IF NOT ERROR_LEVEL = 0 THEN FDISPLAY SYS:PUBLIC\PRTERROR.TXT
```

In this example, if the CAPTURE command fails, the PRTERROR.TXT file is displayed. This file could give instructions on correcting the problem or tell users who to call for help.

REM or REMARK

These commands allow you to insert a comment in the login script. A semicolon (;) or asterisk (*) can also be used to indicate a comment. The following are all comments:

```
REM The following commands set up drive mappings
***Be sure to include the user's mappings here***
;Don't try this at home
```

You should document each of your login scripts, and include such things as when it was created or last updated and by whom, what various sections are for, and so on, so that maintenance is much easier when changes are required.

COMSPEC

You can use the COMSPEC command to specify the location of the COMMAND.COM file. DOS uses this file to run the command interpreter. Some DOS programs unload COMMAND.COM and reload it when they finish. If this is not specified correctly, the workstation displays the error message "Unable to Load COMMAND" and will need to be rebooted.

You must use COMSPEC if your users are using a version of DOS loaded on a network volume/drive. If they run DOS from their individual workstations only, this command is not needed and should not be used. Also, this command is for DOS users only.

PAUSE

The PAUSE command simply stops the login script until you press a key. This command can be useful in debugging login scripts; by including PAUSE in strategic places, you can view messages that otherwise would have scrolled off the screen.

FIRE PHASERS

The FIRE PHASERS command will cause the computer to beep. If your client is running Windows and has a sound card and speakers installed, you can optionally include a sound file to be used instead of the default PHASERS .WAV file. This command is often used with the WRITE and DISPLAY commands mentioned previously to attract the user's attention to the message. It is also useful for your remote help desk staff to have an audio confirmation that the login process was completed successfully.

LASTLOGINTIME

The LASTLOGINTIME command will display the time that the user last logged in. This can be used (with some user education) as a basic security measure. If each user checks the time and verifies that they logged in about then, reporting any instance that they didn't log in at the time specified, you'll know when to investigate potential hacking into your system.

NO_DEFAULT

This command prevents the default login script from running. If you don't want the default login script to run and you don't have user login scripts in place, put this command in either a container or profile login script.

DOS Commands

You can also use any DOS command in your login scripts. Precede each DOS command with a number sign (#). DOS commands are most commonly used with the CAPTURE command to control network printing. You can use any DOS command, with the following restrictions:

- You should execute only DOS commands that return immediately, such as CAPTURE. If you wish to execute a menu or other program and end the login script, use the EXIT command. If you are in Windows and want the program to run and also to continue executing the login script, use the @ command instead (described below).

- You don't need to use a number sign with the MAP command. There is a login script version of MAP.

- You can't use the SET command to set DOS variables in a login script. You should use the DOS SET login script command instead.

- The DOS commands referred to here are *external commands*, meaning that they are contained in separate program files. Internal DOS commands, such as DIR and batch files, cannot be used unless you execute a copy of COMMAND.COM.

Using the Novell Client on the network client, Windows 3.*x*, Windows 95/98, and Windows NT can also run login scripts. However, using DOS commands in this fashion may not work the way you expect on these platforms.

Using EXIT with Login Scripts

You can use the EXIT command to end all login script processing. You can also include a command that executes at the DOS prompt after the user logs in. One use for EXIT is to run a menu, as mentioned in the previous section.

Because the EXIT command ends the login script, it should either be the last command in the script or be placed inside an IF...THEN statement. In addition to ending the current script, the EXIT command prevents any further scripts from executing. Thus, if the EXIT command is included in the container login script, it prevents the profile and user login scripts from executing. If you include EXIT in the profile login script, it prevents the user login script from executing.

You can use the EXIT command by itself or follow it with a command in quotation marks, such as in this example, which would automatically exit the login script and execute a menu at the end of the login script:

```
EXIT "NMENU ACCT"
```

DOS executes the command after the login script has finished. NetWare actually places the command in the keyboard buffer, so DOS believes the user typed it. The size of the keyboard buffer limits the command to 14 characters. This trick works only under DOS. You can also use EXIT to execute a command in Windows, with the added advantage that you are not limited to 14 characters.

If you are executing a DOS program that will stay running, such as a menuing program, you should run it with the EXIT command. Although you can execute DOS commands anywhere in the script with the # prefix, the LOGIN.EXE program remains in memory while they execute. This means that the login script can't be modified, memory and other resources are consumed, and so on. By passing commands to DOS using the keyboard buffer, EXIT executes the command after the LOGIN program has finished.

By default, users have the rights to edit their own user login scripts. You can add the EXIT command at the end of the container or profile login script if you wish to prevent user login scripts from executing.

Running Programs from a Login Script on a Windows Client

If you want to run a program and keep the login script processing, you can use the @ command just like you would use the # on a DOS client. The advantage of using @ is that the program is loaded and the login script continues, so other login scripts could execute and/or other programs could be loaded. For more information on the @ command versus the # command, refer to the online documentation.

Benefits and Features of Z.E.N.works

Z.E.N.works stands for Zero Effort Networks, and while they aren't truly zero effort (which is a good thing, or there would be no need for system administrators), Z.E.N.works can make life much easier for us. There are two versions of Z.E.N.works— the Starter Pack, which comes free with NetWare 5 on the Client CD, and the full version, which must be purchased as a separate component. The full product encompasses all of the functionality in the Starter Pack and gives you additional features. Let's look at the features of each.

The Starter Pack allows you to manage applications and the workstation. Specifically, you can manage and distribute any application, manage roaming profiles for Windows 95/98 and Windows NT, and even update the Novell Client and other software automatically.

The full version offers all of the starter pack's functionality and adds the following features: remote control of workstations, a Help Requester application to make it easier for users to ask for help with problems, and the ability to keep a hardware inventory of each computer in NDS for troubleshooting and maintenance.

There are more details on the various features later in the chapter, but let's begin by discussing the application management capabilities.

Using Application Launcher

NetWare Application Manager (NAM) and its companion, NetWare Application Launcher (NAL), have been improved and upgraded with NetWare 5 and the Z.E.N.works Starter Pack. (Z.E.N.works is also available for NetWare 4.11.) In addition to making NAL and NAM part of Z.E.N.works, Novell also renamed the combination to simply Application Launcher. Users can run the front end, either Application Launcher (AL) or Application Explorer (AE), under Windows 3.*x*, Windows 95/98, or Windows NT to access the applications.

The AL and AE windows display icons and allow the user to double-click an icon to start an application. If this sounds familiar, that's because it's very similar to what you can do with a folder on the Desktop (Windows 95/98 and Windows NT 4) or in a Program Manager group (Windows 3.*x* and Windows NT). So why use Application Launcher? There are some definite advantages:

- You can define an application's icon once to make the application available to a large group of users.

- Users can use a nearly identical interface to launch applications, whether they are using Windows 3.1, Windows 95/98, or Windows NT.

- You can assign the same list of applications to multiple users easily.

- You can use AL (but not AE) as the Windows shell, allowing you much more control over the features a user can access.

- Once you've set things up, you can add an icon to a user's Start menu without walking to their workstation, and users can't inadvertently delete icons.

- If a user deletes a component of the application (for example, a .DLL file), AL or AE can automatically reinstall the missing or damaged component.

- You can automatically upgrade software without involving users.

- Software upgrades can be either pushed (forced on the user) or pulled (requested by the user) at your discretion.

The Z.E.N.works Application Launcher consists of three components for administrators and two for users. The administrator's components are the Application Launcher snap-in to NetWare Administrator and Application objects, often created through the third component, snAppShot. The components on the user's end are Application Launcher (AL) and/or Application Explorer (AE). We'll look at these components in the following sections.

The Application Launcher can only be used on Windows workstations.

Creating and Managing Application Objects

Let's begin by looking at the administrator's components. First we'll look at the Application Launcher snap-in for NetWare Administrator, then we'll see how to use it to create and manage Application objects.

The snap-in is installed when you install Z.E.N.works, either the full product or the Starter Pack. After the snap-in is installed, you can create and manage Application objects with NetWare Administrator and snAppShot.

Unlike some previous versions of NAL, there is now only one type of Application object. We will describe the process of creating applications, setting their properties, and configuring them for users in the following sections. snAppShot will be covered below in the section entitled "Creating a Complex Application Using snAppShot."

Creating an Application Object

Let's begin by defining what an Application object is. An *Application object* details all of the changes an application makes to a workstation when it is installed. An Application object contains all of the .INI file changes, registry additions and deletions, changes to text files (including AUTOEXEC.BAT and CONFIG.SYS), and other important information about the object. However, an Application object does not contain the actual files that make up the application. You only need to create an Application object once for each application, although you may copy the object and make modifications to it if you have similar needs for other copies of the application (for example, on different servers).

To create an Application object, simply choose an NDS container for the Application object to reside in and choose Create from the Object menu. The most convenient approach is to use the same container that contains the users who need access to the application. Novell's recommendation is similar: Place the Application objects (and the related application files) as close to the user as possible, and certainly not on the other side of a WAN link. (We will discuss tree design in Chapters 18 and 20.)

After you select the container, choose Object ➤ Create, and then click Application. A wizard will appear, as illustrated in Figure 5.2.

FIGURE 5.2

The Create Application
Object Wizard

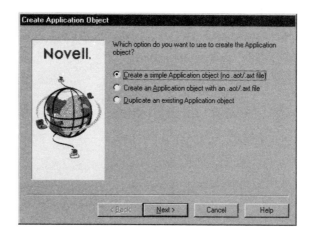

The steps that you need to do next depend on the choice made here. As Figure 5.2 shows, there are three choices that can be made here. The first is to create a simple application, such as a DOS application that doesn't change AUTOEXEC.BAT or CONFIG.SYS or a Windows 3.1 program that doesn't make any .INI file changes.

The second choice is to create a complex application, such as a Windows 3.1 program (with .INI file updates) or a Windows 95/98 or Windows NT program with registry updates. This requires the creation of .AOT or .AXT files, created by snAppShot. This is the method normally used when the application is installed by a setup program.

The third choice is to duplicate an existing object, such as when you want to create applications that are almost identical, but may have different installation paths. The third method simply entails modifying the properties of an existing Application object. We will discuss the properties of Application objects in a later section. First, however, let's look at the process of creating an Application object using either of the first two methods.

Creating a Simple Application   As mentioned above, this is the easiest type of object to create and is used for the simplest Applications. From the dialog box shown in Figure 5.2, choose Create a Simple Application Object (no .AOT/.AXT file) and click Next. All you need to create the object is an object name and a path to the program. This dialog box is shown in Figure 5.3.

FIGURE 5.3

Creating a simple
Application object

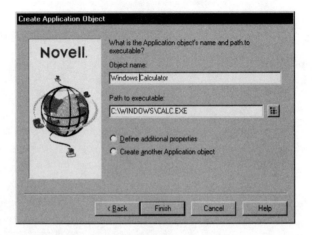

You can click the small Browse button to the right of the Path field to look through NDS and the file system to find the application. Be sure to specify the executable program name. In the example shown in Figure 5.3, we created an object named Windows Calculator and set the path to C:\WINDOWS\ CALC.EXE. Optionally, you may click the Define Additional Properties button if you wish to further configure the Application object, or click the Create Another Application Object button if you wish to create a second Application object. In any case, when you are finished, click Finish.

That's all there is to creating a simple application, but no one can use the Application object until you set some of the properties described below in the section entitled "Managing Application Properties."

Creating a Complex Application Using snAppShot   In previous versions of the NetWare Application Manager, creating a complex application was a complicated task. With the new Z.E.N.works Application Launcher, the Create Application Object Wizard, and snAppShot, the process is greatly simplified. Even though the task is much easier, there are still many steps and potential pitfalls. The simplest way to understand the process is with an example. For our example, we will install the compression software WinZip; of course, the process we describe works for any application. You can download WinZip from http://www.winzip.com if you would like to follow along. We downloaded WinZip 7.0 SR-1 for this demonstration and will use it in all the example screens as well. Ready? Let's begin.

PROCEDURE 5.1

Installing a Complex Application

To install a complex application (one that involves changes to .INI files, the registry, and so on), follow these steps:

1. First you need to create the appropriate .AOT file. To create the .AOT file with snAppShot, run SYS:PUBLIC\SNAPSHOT\SNAPSHOT.EXE. The opening snAppShot dialog box will appear:

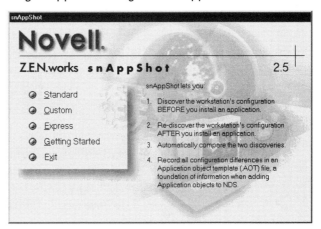

2. Choose which method you wish to use to install the new application. Normally you will choose Standard, as we will in this procedure, and click Next. The dialog box shown below will appear:

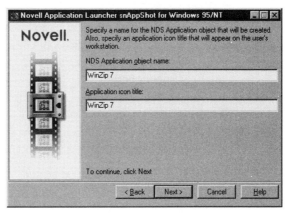

PROCEDURE 5.1 (CONTINUED)

3. Next you specify the name of the NDS object that you will create and the name the user will see when he or she goes to run the application. Our example uses the name WinZip 7 in both cases, but you can use any name you wish. After you have entered both names, click Next, and the dialog box shown below will appear:

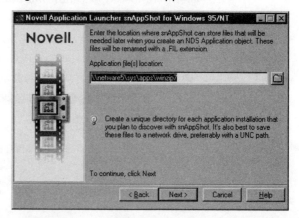

4. You must choose where to keep the files that snAppShot will create (they will have a .FIL extension). Novell (and we) strongly recommend a network path (so that all users can get to it later). In particular, you should not choose a mapped drive (like F:\APPS\WINZIP7), but rather the UNC path to the location (in this example, we chose \\NETWARE5\SYS\APPS\WINZIP7). That way drive mappings, which may vary from computer to computer, aren't a factor when the user installs or runs the application later. When you are finished, click Next.

5. If the directory you chose in Step 4 doesn't exist, a dialog box will appear asking if you want to create it. Assuming you spelled everything correctly and mean the directory that you typed, choose Yes. A dialog box prompting you for the location of the .AOT files will appear, as shown here.

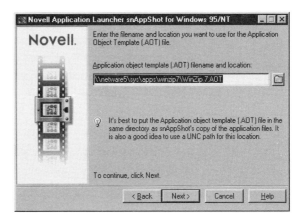

6. Enter the filename and location where you wish the .AOT files to be stored. The default is the same directory where the .FIL files will be. This is where Novell recommends that you keep them. When you are finished, click Next.

7. snAppShot will then ask which drives to scan for changes. You should always include the drive you are installing the application on, the drive with the Windows system files, and your C drive (for changes to AUTOEXEC.BAT and CONFIG.SYS). Add and/or remove drives as necessary. When you have finished, click Next, and the Settings Summary dialog box shown below will appear.

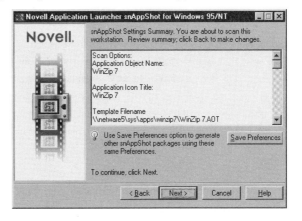

PROCEDURE 5.1 (CONTINUED)

8. Review the summary information provided. If you need to make any changes, click Back until you get to the appropriate dialog box and then make any needed corrections. If you added drives, wanted other files and/or directories included or excluded, or in other ways customized the settings that snAppShot uses by default, you can save these settings for future use with the Save Preferences option. (The saved file will have an .INI extension.) When you have finished, click Next.

9. snAppShot will proceed to analyze your computer for the "before" picture and will save this for comparison with the "after" picture it will take later. When it has finished, you will see the dialog box shown here:

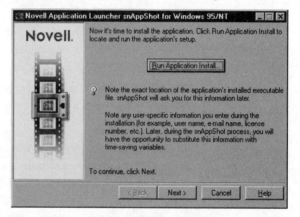

10. Click the Run Application Install button to install your desired application. snAppShot will let you navigate to the setup program for your application program. For the WinZip example, we navigated to WINZIP70.EXE. The installation program then executes. Install it as you would any other application. If you want to run it from the network, install it on a mapped drive (be sure that this drive was scanned in Step 7); otherwise, install it on your local hard drive. We chose for this example to install the application in the default location, C:\PROGRAM FILES\WINZIP.

11. After the installation program has finished and you have exited the application if necessary (as it was for WinZip), return to the snApp-Shot program. You will see a dialog box reminding you that snAppShot is waiting for the application to be installed. Click Next and you'll see the dialog box shown here.

12. Enter the location where you installed the application if you want your users to have the program installed in the same location. Usually you will want to specify this location, as .INI files and registry entries will refer to this location. Since we installed the example application in the C:\PROGRAM FILES\WINZIP directory, we entered that here. When you have finished, click Next, and the dialog box shown below will appear.

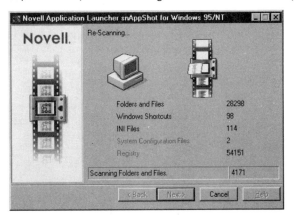

13. After it has finished generating the "after" picture, snAppShot will generate the actual template needed for the Application object. You will see the progress window shown here.

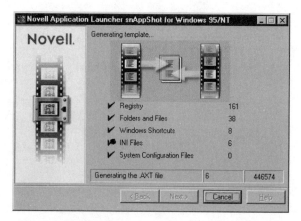

14. When snAppShot has finished, it will display a Completion Summary screen (shown below) and tell you what to do next (described in the next few steps) and how to customize the object. You may want to print this out for future reference as you customize the object, especially the first few times you create an Application object this way. When you have finished reading the information, click Finish.

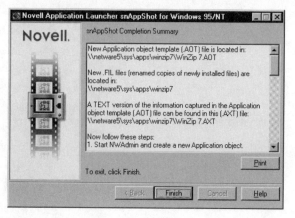

15. Congratulations! You have completed snAppShot and are now ready to create the Application object in NDS. To do so, start NetWare Administrator and navigate to the container where you would like to create the new object, and then choose Object ➣ Create and select Application. This will display the dialog box shown earlier in this chapter in Figure 5.2.

16. Choose Create an Application Object with an .AOT/.AXT File and then click Next.

17. A dialog box will appear asking for the path to the .AOT or .AXT file. Fill it in with the path noted above (in this example, that would be \\NETWARE5\SYS\APPS\WINZIP7) and click Next. The dialog box shown below will appear.

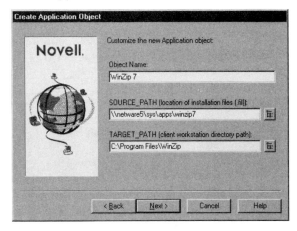

18. With this dialog box you can customize any of the settings made during the snAppShot procedure, but normally the defaults here will be fine. Make any desired changes and click Next.

19. The final screen will appear, summarizing your choices and allowing you to choose either Display Details After Creation (of the newly created object) or Create Another Application Object. In most cases, you will want to verify that the object is set up correctly, so you can select Display Details After Creation and then click Finish. In a few seconds, the settings will be imported and the process is over. You have created an Application object using snAppShot. Remember, however, that no one can use the application yet. That is the focus of the next section, "Managing Application Properties."

Managing Application Properties

You have now successfully created an Application object. However, before users can access the application, you need to define some of its properties. Select the object and choose Object ≻ Details to display the Details dialog box shown in Figure 5.4. If you choose either the Define Additional Properties (simple application) or Display Details After Creation (complex application) option on the final summary screen, this dialog box will be displayed automatically.

FIGURE 5.4

The Details dialog box includes various properties of the Application object.

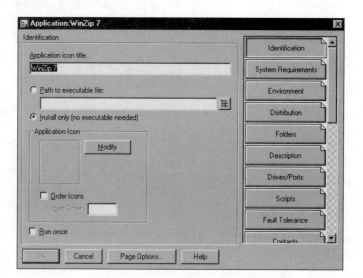

On the right side of the screen are numerous buttons that lead to property pages for the Application object. These are the most important property pages and their functions:

Identification   Includes the application's name and path. You can change the icon used for the application here. You can also specify that this application will only run once, meaning that after it is run, it will not appear again in the list. This is useful if you are installing an application and don't want to run the installation program over and over.

System Requirements   Shown in Figure 5.5, this property page allows you to specify the requirements that must be met before the application icon can be displayed for the user. You can set operating system and version and hardware requirements, including minimum RAM, processor, and free hard drive space.

F I G U R E   5.5

The System Require-
ments page for the
Application object

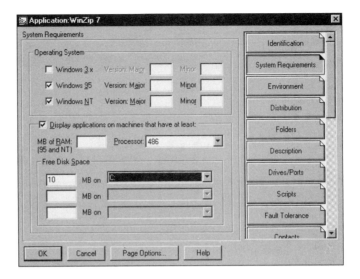

Environment   Allows you to specify command-line parameters for the application. You can also specify a working directory; this directory will be set as the current directory before the application starts. The Run Minimized option specifies to run the program as an icon, and the Clean Up Network Resources option specifies whether drives and printers are disconnected after the user exits the application. For 16-bit Windows programs running on Windows NT, you can also choose whether the WOW session should be shared or separate.

Drives/Ports   Shown in Figure 5.6, this property page allows you to specify drive mappings and printer port captures for the application. These will be set up before the application starts and disconnected when it exits if you enable the Clean Up Network Resources option on the Environment property page.

Description   A text field you can use to describe the application. Users running AL or AE can view the description by right-clicking the icon.

Scripts   Allows you to define two lists of commands. The first is executed before the application is started, and the second is executed after the user exits the application. You can use these scripts to set up any special configuration needed for the application. They both use the same commands as login scripts, described earlier in this chapter.

FIGURE 5.6

The Drives/Ports property page allows you to specify drive mappings and printer capture settings for the application.

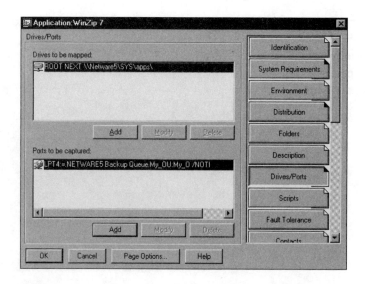

Fault Tolerance   Allows you to enable load balancing and/or fault tolerance. Load balancing allows you to associate multiple Application objects with a primary object (the one you assign to other objects, such as users, groups, or containers, to grant access to the application). Then, if the primary Application object is unavailable, another is chosen from the list at random, and if that one is unavailable, another is chosen at random, and so on until either there are no more Application objects left or the application runs. This property is used primarily in a LAN environment where there are several servers to choose from. Fault tolerance operates on the same principle, except that successive Application objects are not chosen at random, but rather in the order you specify. This property is typically selected when the application is used across a WAN link. If you enable both properties, all load balancing objects are checked before moving on to the fault tolerance objects.

Contacts   A list of users who are responsible for the application. These users can be notified when other users experience a problem with the application.

Associations   Shown in Figure 5.7, this page allows you to set a list of users, groups, or containers that will be given access to the application. An application cannot be used by anyone until associations have been set up.

F I G U R E 5.7

The Associations property page allows you to specify sets of users who can access the application.

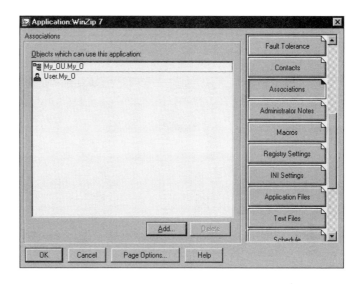

Administrator Notes   This is the place for you to keep notes on the application, such as who installed it, what service packs have been applied, and by whom, and so on. It is not accessible by end users.

Macros, Registry Settings, INI Settings, Application Files, and Text Files   These pages allow you even greater control over how the application is installed. They also let you see the exact changes made to the registry, various .INI files, and/or text-based configuration files, such as AUTOEXEC.BAT and CONFIG.SYS.

Schedule   Allows you to specify when users can use this application (the default setting is Always).

Termination   Allows you to specify a message and what will happen when the user's allotted time for using the application expires.

Application Site List   This wonderful feature allows you to give mobile users (who travel from office to office in your company) access to applications based on the closest available server, as opposed to always using the same server, possibly across WAN links.

File Rights   This is a favorite new feature and one long sought-after by administrators. It allows you to associate any necessary file system rights to use the application with the *application* instead of the user, group, container, and so on. In the past, rights were given to users; thus when they changed positions, their rights had to be taken away and granted to new users. Also, users were associated with applications, but until file system rights were in place, they still couldn't use the associated application. This solves both problems. The File Rights property page is displayed in Figure 5.8.

F I G U R E   5.8

The File Rights page allows you to associate needed file rights with the application.

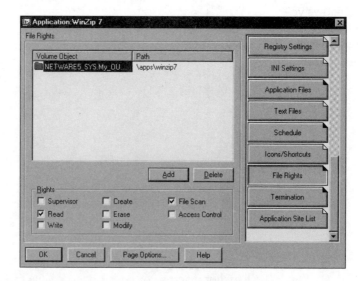

User and Container Properties for Applications

There are also one or two pages (depending on the object type) on User, Organization, Organizational Unit, and Group objects that are used to configure applications and settings for that user or set of users:

Applications   Shown in Figure 5.9, this page allows you to set a list of applications the user (or users in the container or group) has access to. You can add applications here as an alternative to adding users to the application's Associations property. This is also an easy way to view the list of applications a user has access to. You can also specify where this icon will appear: Desktop, Start menu, System Tray, and/or AE and AL.

Launcher Configuration   Shown in Figure 5.10, this page includes a variety of settings for Application Launcher. You can specify whether the user can exit AL and AE or log out only, whether window positions are saved, and whether the user inherits applications from parent containers, among many other settings. This property is available for User objects and Container objects only, not for Group objects. You can view effective rights here as well.

F I G U R E   5.9

The Applications property page allows you to configure access to applications.

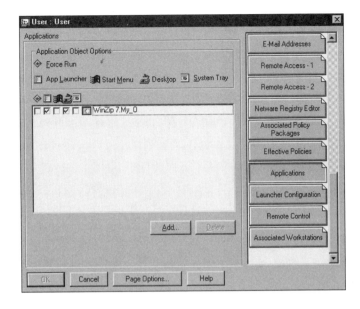

F I G U R E   5.10

The Launcher Configuration page allows you to configure Application Launcher settings for a user or container.

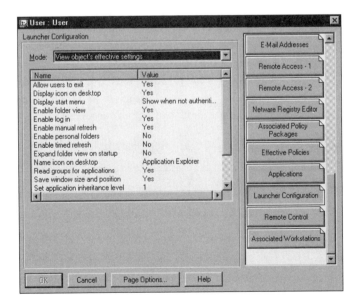

At this point you should also assign whatever file system rights are necessary for the user to run the application if you didn't associate them with the Application object. See Chapter 4 for details about file system security.

Installing and Using Application Launcher and Application Explorer

Once you've created Application objects, you still need to configure the workstations to run Application Launcher. You can do this in a few different ways:

- Allow the user to run AL and/or AE from an icon.

- Configure AL or AE to start automatically along with the standard Windows Explorer or Program Manager shell.

- Configure AL to be the shell in place of Windows Explorer or Program Manager.

We'll look at each of these approaches in the sections below. For a description of how AL works from the user's point of view, see the "Launching Applications with AL or AE" section later in this chapter. First, however, it is important to understand Application Launcher and Application Explorer.

Application Launcher and Application Explorer

What are the features and benefits of Application Launcher (AL) and Application Explorer (AE) and when should you use either? Let's begin with a quick overview of each. AL is available on all Windows platforms, from Windows 3.1 through Windows NT. AE, on the other hand, is a 32-bit application designed only for use with Windows 95/98 and Windows NT 4.0. AL and AE each have their place, and each has features that make it better suited for a particular environment than the other. Table 5.1 summarizes some of the differences.

T A B L E   5.1:   Application Launcher vs. Application Explorer

Feature	Effect	Application Launcher	Application Explorer
Shell (Windows Explorer or Program Manager)	Replaces the shell	Yes	No
	Enhances the shell	No	Yes

T A B L E 5.1: Application Launcher vs. Application Explorer *(continued)*

Feature	Options	Application Launcher	Application Explorer
Icon locations	Application Launcher	Yes	Yes
	Start menu	No	Yes
	System tray	No	Yes
	Desktop	No	Yes

Setting Up an Icon for AL or AE

The simplest, least secure, and least automated (from the user's viewpoint) approach is to allow the user to run AL or AE from an icon. The user will still have access to other items in the Start menu, Windows Explorer, or Program Manager, and can choose to run AL or AE only when needed. This is useful if you are not using AL or AE for all applications, or if users run some applications from their local disk drives. The disadvantage of this approach is that you have little control over what users do with the application; they can even delete the AL or AE icon.

To add an icon for AL in Windows 3.1 or Windows NT 3, follow these steps:

1. Choose a Program Manager group to contain the icon and highlight it.

2. From the Program Manager, select File ➤ New.

3. Select Program Item as the type to create.

4. Enter a description of the program and the location of the AL application. In most cases, this is F:\PUBLIC\NAL.EXE. Be sure to use a drive letter mapped to the SYS volume. You do *not* need to specify a working directory. Click OK when you are done.

To add a Start menu entry for AL or AE in Windows 95/98 or Windows NT 4, follow these steps:

1. From the Start menu, choose Settings ➤ Taskbar.

2. Choose the Start Menu Programs tab.

3. Click the Add button, and then enter the location of AL, usually F:\PUBLIC\NAL.EXE, or the location of AE, usually F:\PUBLIC\NALEXPLD.EXE. Click Next.

4. Select a menu folder to place the new entry in (typically Novell), and then click Next.

5. Enter a name for the program and click Finish.

Starting AL or AE Automatically

You can also configure AL or AE to start automatically. The user will still be able to access the Start menu, Windows Explorer, or Program Manager, but the Application Launcher or Application Explorer window will be displayed immediately. This approach has the same security disadvantage as the approach described above, but it is useful when security is not an issue and automation is important. To start AL or AE automatically, you can take two approaches.

The first approach is based on the local workstation. Begin by creating an icon as described in the previous section. Then move the icon to the StartUp folder (under the Programs menu in Windows 95/98 and Windows NT 4) or the Startup Program Manager group (in Windows 3.1 and Windows NT 3). AL or AE will be launched when Windows starts.

The second approach is a little bit safer, in that the user can't delete the icon for it, but it will still start automatically. To do this, you will modify container, profile, or user login scripts as appropriate. If you want to use AL, add the following line to the appropriate login script:

```
@\\servername\sys\public\nal.exe
```

If you want to use AE instead, your login script might be a little bit more complicated. If you only have Windows 95/98 and Windows NT 4 clients, add the following line to the appropriate login script:

```
@\\servername\sys\public\nalexpld.exe
```

If you have other platforms on the network, however, be sure to add conditional logic to make sure the user is running one of the supported platforms. Refer to the login script sections above ("Login Script Variables" and "Login Script Commands") or the online documentation for more information.

Using AL as the Windows Shell

A more secure approach is to use AL as the Windows shell, replacing Program Manager or Windows Explorer. This allows you total control over what the user can access, and prevents the user from adding or deleting icons. There are disadvantages, though: The user must use AL and they may not be familiar with AL's interface. Users will be unable to access applications on local hard drives that don't already have an Application object set up.

Before you can set up AL as the shell, you will need to copy several files to the workstation's hard drive. You will find these files in the SYS:PUBLIC directory (or subdirectories thereof) on the server. You'll also need to edit the SYSTEM.INI file in the C:\WINDOWS directory for all versions of Windows except Windows NT. For Windows NT, you will need to edit the registry to make the change. This process is not complicated, but there are many variations depending on the client installed (VLM or the Novell Client) and the version of Windows you are using, so we won't discuss all the specifics here, but rather refer you to the online documentation.

In any case, once the modifications described above have been made, the next time you restart the workstation, AL will be launched instead of the usual shell. If you need to change it back, simply replace the SHELL entry in the SYSTEM.INI file or edit the registry (as appropriate) and return it to the previous value.

If AL is configured as the shell, the workstation will become completely useless when the network is down or disconnected. If this is an issue, you should run AL automatically, as described in the previous section.

Launching Applications with AL or AE

Now that you're familiar with the process of configuring Application objects and installing AL and AE, here's a look at how Application Launcher works from the user's point of view. To run AL or AE from a workstation, use the icon you created above or simply run the program, usually F:\PUBLIC\NAL .EXE (for AL) or F:\PUBLIC\NALEXPLD.EXE (for AE).

Let's begin with an overview (from the user's perspective) of AL before turning to AE. The main AL screen is shown in Figure 5.11. As you can see, icons are displayed for each of the applications available to the user. The most important function, of course, is that the user can double-click an icon to run it. There are a few other options available from the AL menu.

FIGURE 5.11

AL displays icons for each Application object the user has access to.

File ➤ Open   Starts the currently selected application. You can also get to this option by right-clicking the icon.

File ➤ Verify   Checks that all of the application is installed, and updates any components that may be missing, if needed. After verification, the program will be executed. You can also access this option by right-clicking the icon.

File ➤ Properties   Displays some of the application's properties, such as the user to contact, time restrictions, and the description. You cannot modify the properties from within AL, however. Also available by right-clicking the icon.

File ➤ Exit   Exits AL, if the user is allowed to do so.

File ➤ Login   Allows you to log in if you haven't already done so or if you want to log in as someone else. The administrator can configure whether or not the user is allowed to do this.

The View menu   Allows you to choose between formats for the display, and to refresh the display. The Refresh option is useful if an application has recently been added or modified.

The Help menu   Provides access to a simple online help system that describes the functions of AL.

The AE options are similar, with some exceptions described here. The first is the interface. Figure 5.12 shows the AE interface when you first open the application. Opening the folder for the desired tree exposes a list of objects that you belong to, such as your user account, containers, and groups, which have applications associated with them. This is illustrated in Figure 5.13. Opening these folders displays the icons for the programs.

FIGURE 5.12

The opening screen
for Application
Explorer

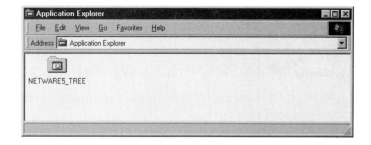

FIGURE 5.13

The second level of
folders in Application
Explorer

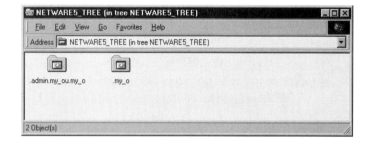

Managing Workstations with Z.E.N.works

Although the Starter Pack does provide some useful features, described previously, to use Z.E.N.works to its fullest potential you need to purchase the full product. The features described in the following sections on remote control and the Help Requester system are only available with the full product. The section on Policy Packages applies to both the Starter Pack and the full product. Let's begin with workstation policies.

Workstation Policies

You may want to take advantage of the Help Requester or remote control features described above. But you can't. Yes, we know you bought and installed the full version of Z.E.N.works and you have even installed the Z.E.N.works client on your workstations, but you still can't. Why? Because your workstations must be registered with NDS and then imported into the

NDS tree as Workstation objects. So, you ask, how is that done? Well, there are two separate, but related, tasks to accomplish. The first is registration and the second is importing the workstations into the tree.

Registering and Importing Workstations

Registering workstations is easy. In fact, it has probably happened on most of your workstations. There are only two requirements (plus the appropriate NDS rights) that must be met for this to take place (assuming the desktop management features of the Z.E.N.works client were installed):

- The Z.E.N.works client must be installed on each workstation to be registered.

- A user must log on at each workstation to complete the process.

As for the NDS rights, the user needs the Read and Write property rights to the WM:RegisteredWorkstation property. This right is usually granted to [Root] and all containers below it when Z.E.N.works is installed, but if that wasn't done at installation—or more likely, if new containers have been added since then—this assignment can be made with WSRIGHTS.EXE, which is in the SYS:PUBLIC\WIN32 directory.

If you didn't install the desktop management features of the Z.E.N.works client, you will either need to create an application for Application Launcher to run or add some commands to a login script. For help with either of these techniques, refer to the online documentation.

You can see the workstations that have been registered with NDS by selecting the container where the user object that logged in is located and choosing Object ➤ Details, and then displaying the Workstation Registration page, shown in Figure 5.14.

In addition to the fields that you can see in Figure 5.14 (User, Computer, and IPX address), the following fields are also registered: IP address, host name (for TCP/IP; the field is called DNS), CPU, OS, and the server that authenticated the client.

Once the workstation is registered, the next step is to import the workstation into the tree and make it a *Workstation* (not Computer) object. This cannot happen until a Policy Package exists for the user (or a group or container the user belongs to) and the Workstation Import Policy has been enabled. This is because the name of the NDS object is defined as part of this policy. The specific steps to create a Policy Package will be discussed in the

FIGURE 5.14

Viewing registered
workstations

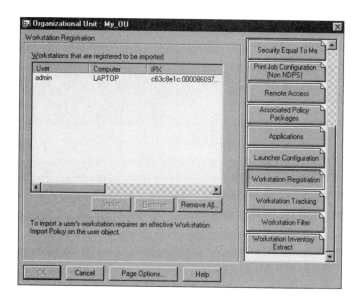

next section; for now you just need to know that it must exist and be set up correctly. The policy doesn't need to be in the same container as the user; any parent container of the user will work. For better performance, Novell recommends placing this in the user's container or at least in a partition that is on the LAN, not across the WAN.

Once the Policy Package has been set up, you can import a workstation. To do so, choose Tools ➤ Import Workstations and the dialog box shown in Figure 5.15 will appear. Here you can specify what context you want to look in, and whether you want to include subcontainers. After you click OK, Z.E.N.works will search for workstations to be imported, import them, and then display the results screen shown in Figure 5.16.

FIGURE 5.15

The Import Work-
stations dialog box

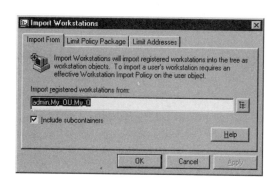

F I G U R E   5.16

The results of import-
ing workstations into
the tree

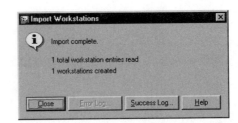

The end result of the operation is one or more Workstation objects. The screen displays the Workstation object and its common name, which in this case is the combination of the computer (NetBIOS) name and IPX address.

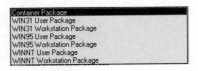

The initial importing is now complete. Remember, however, that work-station importing is an ongoing process. New workstations will be added and others will leave, and all need to be added to (or removed from) NDS.

The Types of Policy Packages Available

To create a Policy Package object, simply choose the container where you want the object to be created, select Object ➤ Create, and then choose Policy Package. After you click OK, the Create Policy Package dialog box appears. One of the things you must choose is the package type, as shown in Figure 5.17. Notice that there are seven types of policies that can be created: Container Package, WIN31 User Package, WIN31 Workstation Package, WIN95 User Package, WIN95 Workstation Package, WINNT User Package, and WINNT Workstation Package. The Windows 95 packages are used for Windows 98 as well. There are more policies available as you move from Windows 3.1 to Windows 95/98 to Windows NT, and therefore you have more control.

F I G U R E   5.17

The types of Policy
Packages that can be
created

```
Container Package
WIN31 User Package
WIN31 Workstation Package
WIN95 User Package
WIN95 Workstation Package
WINNT User Package
WINNT Workstation Package
```

Choose the appropriate package type (Container, User, or Workstation) and platform (WIN31, WIN95, or WINNT), give the package a name, and click Create. You might want to check the Define Additional Properties box before clicking Create, because by default a package is useless. Why? There are two reasons: All of the policies are unchecked (and therefore not enforced), and the package is not associated with any objects. You must do both for a policy to take effect. If you forget to associate the package with any objects, you will get a warning dialog box reminding you that you must associate the package with at least one object for it to be used.

Before we look at the specifics of a policy and how it is created, let's examine the three basic Policy Package types.

Container Policies

This type of policy can only be associated with containers and is fundamentally different than the other policies that will be discussed below. This policy directs how and where NDS searches for policies for a user in calculating the effective policies in effect for a user. The default is to search first for policies associated with the user, then those associated with any groups the user belongs to, and finally those associated with the user's parent container, and its parent, and so on, all the way to [Root]. While this strategy is the most comprehensive and will work in many situations, you may choose to change the default setting for the following reasons:

Better security   By restricting the search location, you can control how far up the tree to search. For example, if your tree has global users (like administrators) at the top of the tree and you have Policy Packages associated with the top-level containers for them, you wouldn't necessarily want these policies to be in effect for your users further down in the tree. Simply limit how many parent containers will be searched.

You don't want to use the default search order   You may want, for example, to search containers before searching groups for policies or to not search groups at all.

Better use of bandwidth   If NetWare searches the entire tree up to [Root], it make take some bandwidth to search all of the parent containers, particularly if the replicas holding all of the various parent containers are not on your local server. This is especially true if NetWare must cross WAN links to find information on remote servers.

To create a Container Policy Package, follow the steps outlined in Procedure 5.2. (For other Policy Package types, follow the same procedure but change the type specified in Step 3.)

PROCEDURE 5.2

Creating a Container Policy Package

To create a Container Policy Package, follow these steps:

1. Choose the container where you want to create the Policy Package. Select Object ≻ Create, and then select Policy Package from the list of available objects.

2. Click OK, and the Create Policy Package dialog box will appear, as shown here:

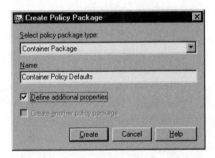

3. From the Select Policy Package Type drop-down list, choose Container Package, and enter a name for your new package in the Name field.

4. If you wish to set the policies when you create the object (our preference), check the Define Additional Properties box. Click Create and the Policy Package object is created. Now you can modify the desired properties.

After you have created the Container Policy Package object, choose Object ≻ Details to set up the desired policy. (This step will not be necessary if you checked the Define Additional Properties box in Step 4). From the Container Package: Container Policy Defaults dialog box, simply check the Search Policy box to enable the policy. Like all policies, it is not checked by default. After checking the box, you can click on Details and change the search order and/or the containers to be searched for policies. Remember to associate this policy with at least one object, and click OK when you are finished.

User Policies

We briefly mentioned user policies above, in the context of setting the policy to enable workstation importing. In this section we'll briefly describe the process of creating this object and the associated policy, as well as list some of the policies that can be enforced.

The process for creating a user policy is almost identical with that for creating a container policy, described in Procedure 5.2 above. The only difference is that you choose to create a user policy package instead of a container policy in Step 3. As discussed previously and illustrated in Figure 5.17, there are three types of user policies that can be created: WIN31 User Package, WIN95 User Package, and WINNT User Package. There are multiple packages available because each platform allows different restrictions to be placed on users, depending on the capabilities of the platform. We will discuss the Windows 95/98 package because it will probably be the most widely used package, but the others are similar and the process for making changes is the same.

After you have created the object and displayed its properties, you will see the dialog box shown in Figure 5.18.

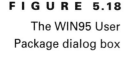

FIGURE 5.18

The WIN95 User
Package dialog box

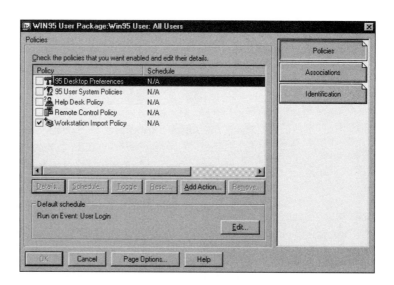

To enable a user to register the information necessary so that you may import the workstation, you must enable the Workstation Import Policy for the user (or one of the groups he or she belongs to, or a parent container). Procedure 5.3 describes the process. Other policies can also be enabled in a similar manner.

Enabling the Workstation Import Policy for a Windows 95/98 User

To enable the Workstation Import Policy to create NDS objects for workstations, follow these steps:

1. Select the object you created for this purpose and go to Object ➢ Details. (The process for creating the object was outlined in Procedure 5.2.)

2. Check the box next to Workstation Import Policy and then, with the policy still selected, click Details. The Workstation Location dialog box shown below will appear.

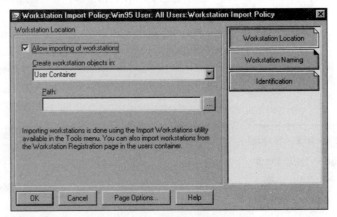

3. Check the Allow Importing of Workstations box and select a location in which to create the workstation object. Novell recommends that you choose User Container (in other words, the same container as the user is in), but you can select other locations here as well.

4. Click on the Workstation Naming button to specify how the workstation will be named when it is imported into NDS. The default is Computer and Network Address, with IPX the preferred network address. You can name the workstations anything you like by clicking on Add and choosing other parameters from the Add Name Field dialog box. You can also reorder the parameters by selecting them and clicking on the up or down arrow. The Workstation Naming page and the Add Name Field dialog box are shown below.

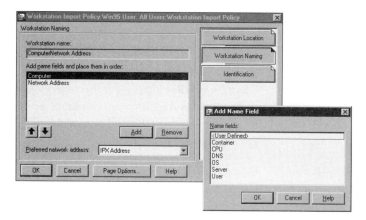

5. Click OK as needed to get back to the main dialog box for this object and select the Associations page. Then select the desired object(s).

6. Click OK when you are finished to complete the process. Once you have associated the package with at least one object and set at least one policy, the package is useful.

Remember that this policy must be associated with an object for it to be useful. In the process outlined in Procedure 5.3, the purpose of the policy is to allow all users to register the information necessary so that the administrator can import their computers. Therefore, as you saw in the screens shown, we named the policy All Users. Notice that we also added the type of package to the name, as each package type is platform-specific and we want to be able to see what we have created. This is a practice that works well in general. As its name implies, this policy is for all users, so we would associate it with the top-level Organization object.

The other important piece to setting policies is scheduling when they will be run. User policies default to being run each time the user logs in, but they can be scheduled to run when various events occur or at specified times. Events include when a user logs in or out, when the system is shut down, or when a screen saver is active, and there are various other options that only apply to Windows NT. You can also choose to run events Daily, Weekly, Monthly, or Yearly, by clicking on the appropriate selection.

Table 5.2 briefly reviews the purpose and effect of each policy in the WIN95 package.

T A B L E 5.2:   Windows 95 User Policies

Policy	Purpose
95 Desktop Preferences	Controls the desktop appearance and related settings for the user. Covers things such as wallpaper, screen saver, and color scheme, as well as options found in the Mouse, Sound, Accessibility Options, and Keyboard Control Panel applets.
95 User System Policies	Controls what the user can and can't do with his or her own computer. Covers things such as removing Find, Run, and taskbar settings from the Start menu, disabling the ability to shut down the workstation, hiding Network Neighborhood and/or icons on the desktop, and so forth. Essentially, these are the options that can be found in the Windows 95/98 or Windows NT System Policy Editor.
Help Desk Policy	Allows you to specify who should be contacted when problems arise, and how they should be contacted. Enables the user to use the Help Requester program and specifies what e-mail system to use, among other options.
Remote Control Policy	Allows you to specify if this user's workstation can be controlled remotely, and if so, if the user should be asked for permission and/or notified that remote control is about to take place. More information on this is given below in the section on remote control.
Workstation Import Policy	Allows the user to register his or her workstation's information with NDS so you can import it, as described above.

For more information on any of the options in this section or in Table 5.2, refer to the online documentation. The best source for this is the help file, which you can find in NetWare Administrator or open manually; the path and filename are SYS:PUBLIC\WIN32\NLS\ENGLISH\DMPOLICY.HLP.

Workstation Policies

Workstation policies are similar to user policies, except that they control workstations settings on a per-computer instead of a per-user basis. They are created in the same manner as other policy packages (as described in

Procedure 5.2) and modified like user policies (as described in Procedure 5.3). Table 5.3 summarizes the workstation policies for a Windows 95/98 computer and the purpose of each. The other two platforms are similar, with Windows NT having a few more options and Windows 3.1 providing fewer options.

T A B L E 5.3: Windows 95 Workstation Policies

Policy	Purpose
95 Computer Printer	Use to add or modify the installed printers list and the options for the printers, such as the default printer, and various NetWare options, such as banner pages and form feeds. You can also choose the appropriate driver for the printer here.
95 Computer System Policies	Lets you specify per-computer settings, such as access control method (share or user level), logon banner, and minimum password length for the Windows password. Many of these settings can also be controlled with System Policy Editor for Windows 95/98 or Windows NT.
95 RAS Configuration	Allows you to configure Dial-Up Networking (DUN) phonebook entries.
Novell Client Configuration	Allows you to control the configuration of the Novell Client, such as the tree, context, first network drive, protocols used, and services, including the TSA for backups.
Remote Control Policy	Lets you decide whether or not to enable remote control for this workstation and parameters for taking control. More information on this is provided below in the section on remote control.
Restrict Login	Allows you to specify either where login is allowed from or workstations where login is disallowed.
Workstation Inventory	Allows you to enable and set the schedule for the workstation, updating its configuration information for its associated NDS workstation object.

As for scheduling, most of the events default to running at login, but, as with user policies, this schedule can be modified as described in the user policy section.

For more information on any of the options in this section or in Table 5.3, refer to the online documentation. The best source for this is the help file, as described above.

Remote Control of Workstations

Remote control of workstations is possible only with the full Z.E.N.works product. Before this can take place, the target workstation must have been registered with, and then imported to, NDS. The target workstation must also have the remote control application installed and operating. You can do this manually, through a login script, or automatically via the normal scheduling service of Z.E.N.works. The remote control program is named WUSER.EXE, and it is normally found on your local hard drive in the C:\NOVELL\ZENRC directory.

In addition to installing and running the application, you must make sure a policy exists that allows remote control. This can be done on a per-user or per-computer basis through the policies discussed in the last section. If both workstation and user policies are in effect, the effective policy will vary, depending on the particular property in question. For more information on conflicting settings, view the online documentation.

The third set of requirements that must be met are that the user taking control must have the following effective rights: the Write right to the DM:Remote Control property and the Read right to the WM:Network Address property. These rights can be granted individually, inherited from above, or added to the desired trustee by adding it to the Operators page for the workstation.

Once all the prerequisites have been met, you can take over a remote workstation by selecting it in NDS and either choosing Tools ➤ Remote Control Workstation, or by opening Object ➤ Details and choosing the Remote Control page, and then clicking on the Remote Control button. If you have set up everything correctly, a window similar to Figure 5.19 will appear.

You now have complete control over the desktop and can do anything on the remote computer, just as though you were sitting at it. You can help a user with a problem, change system settings, and so on. This is a wonderful and very powerful tool. Before we conclude this section on remote control, let's briefly review the icons in the top-right corner of the window. Described in order from left to right, these icons allow you to display the Start menu; switch between applications (like pressing Alt+Tab on the remote workstation); display the Task Manager (Windows 95/98) or NT

F I G U R E   5.19

Open a remote control
window to use a
remote desktop.

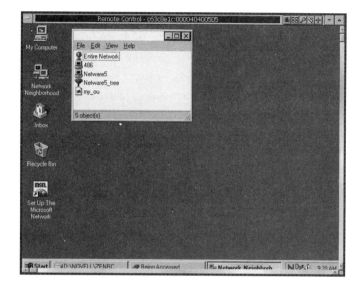

Security dialog box (Windows NT) (like pressing Ctrl+Alt+Del on the
remote workstation); pass through keys to the remote system (so that your
local system doesn't interpret them); and navigate to portions of the remote
desktop that don't fit in the window on your desktop.

The Help Requester

The purpose of this tool is to allow users to communicate with you or your
support staff when they have problems. To enable this feature, you need to
install Z.E.N.works (the full version) and create a policy that allows the user
to use the Help Requester application (see the preceding section for more
information on policies). The program the user runs is SYS:PUBLIC\
HLPREQ32.EXE for Windows 95/98 and Windows NT or SYS:PUBLIC\
HLPREQ16.EXE for Windows 3.1. You can have this program ready for the
user automatically by adding it to a login script or by using the Application
Launcher (described above).

When the application runs, the user sees the screen shown in Figure 5.20.
From here, the user can click on the Mail button to send an e-mail about the
problem or the Call button to call for technical support. He or she can also
get help on how to use the program and information that may be helpful
about the workstation's setup. Users can see information about who is

logged in, as well as their own telephone number and location (in case someone needs to come out and solve the problem or a return phone call is needed). Probably the most useful screen is shown when the user clicks on the Call button, as seen in the bottom half of Figure 5.20.

FIGURE 5.20

The main Help Requester window, shown with the Call window open

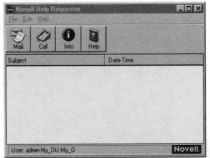
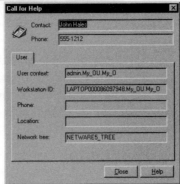

As you can see in Figure 5.20, from here the user can tell the support personnel who he or she is logged in as, context and tree information, and so forth, as well as viewing the person and phone number to call for support. If the user has sent e-mail for support, the list of messages that have been sent will be displayed here as well.

Workstation Inventory

Workstation inventory is a simple but powerful feature also only available with the full Z.E.N.works product. With this tool installed and properly set up (through a workstation policy), the workstation will automatically update its corresponding workstation object in NDS with its current configuration. To access this information, select the workstation, display the details for it, and go to the Workstation Inventory page. You will see a summary screen such as the one shown in Figure 5.21.

The Workstation
Inventory summary
screen displays work-
station details.

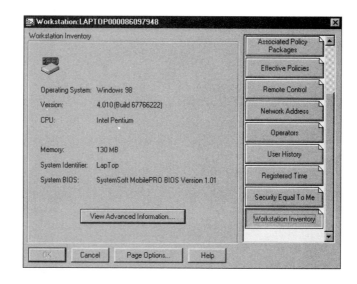

By clicking on the View Advanced Information button, the administrator
can learn much more about the hardware configuration of the selected computer. Some of the more useful details that can be displayed include drives
installed, the bus or buses installed, services and devices installed, the hardware configuration (including I/O ports, DMA, IRQs, and memory addresses
used), and information on the display (including monitor type, video BIOS,
and driver settings such as resolution and color depth). The adapter information screen is shown in Figure 5.22.

F I G U R E   5.22

The Display Adapter
tab is accessible
through the Work-
station dialog box.

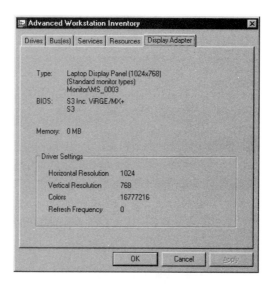

As you can see, Z.E.N.works is a very powerful product, even in the Starter Pack version. The full version offers many more time-saving features to make you even more productive. Novell continues to enhance and upgrade this product. For the latest information, go to `http://www.novell.com` and search for Z.E.N.works.

Review

This chapter covered two major systems that affect the user's environment:

- Login scripts can set up drive mappings and other defaults for the user, so that he or she doesn't have to type DOS commands to set up drives or printers.

- Z.E.N.works lets you define lists of applications a user can run, and gives the user a simple way of accessing them through Application Launcher. Z.E.N.works also supports container, user, and workstation Policy Packages to control what a user can and can't do and to set up his or her environment. The full Z.E.N.works product also gives you remote control capability, a Help Requester application, and workstation inventory capabilities.

Login Scripts

There are four types of login scripts: user, container, profile, and default. Login scripts are always executed in the same order:

1. Container login script for the user's parent container (if found)

2. Profile login script (if assigned)

3. User login script (if found)

4. Default login script (if no user script is found)

Each of these can be used for a specific purpose:

- You can create a container login script for any Organization or Organizational Unit object. This script is the first script executed for users in the container.

- You can use a profile login script to execute a certain set of drive mappings or other commands for certain users in the Directory, whether or not they are in the same container.

- You can set up user login scripts to execute specific commands for a particular user.

- The default login script is built into the LOGIN utility. You cannot edit it. The default script is executed when a user has no user login script.

The login script is composed of login script commands such as these:

MAP   Used for mapping network drives and search drives.

IF, THEN, and ELSE   Used for conditional actions.

INCLUDE   Calls other files or scripts for use in this script as well.

CONTEXT   Sets the current context.

WRITE   Displays a message to the user.

DISPLAY and FDISPLAY   Displays an entire file.

EXIT   Ends a script.

In addition, you can use any external DOS command or program preceded with the # sign. Windows programs can be preceded with an @ symbol.

Login script variables let you customize and control login script execution.

Application Launcher

Application Launcher is a system that allows users convenient access to applications, and it allows you to manage these applications through NDS. Application Launcher consists of two types of components, summarized in the following lists and reviewed in more detail below.

You set up and use these administrative components:

- Application Launcher snap-in to NetWare Administrator

- Application objects

- snAppShot

Your end users work with these components:

- Application Launcher (AL)

- Application Explorer (AE)

Administrative Components

The Application Launcher snap-in to NetWare Administrator allows you to create and manage Application objects through NetWare Administrator.

snAppShot is the tool used to create complex applications by taking a "before" picture of a computer, having you install the application, and then taking an "after" picture and comparing the two. It can detect new or changed files, .INI file changes, registry changes, and changes to text files such as AUTOEXEC.BAT. It creates .AOT and .AXT files that can be used to create Application objects.

Application objects are created for applications in NetWare Administrator in the same way that other types of objects are created. There is only one type of Application object, but it can be configured with many properties.

End-User Components

The user can run either Application Launcher (AL) or Application Explorer (AE) as the shell to provide applications. AE runs only on Windows 95/98 and Windows NT 4, whereas AL runs on all Windows platforms. You can choose to run the applications (AL and AE) from an icon, automatically from the StartUp group, or from a login script. Application Launcher can also replace the standard Windows shell. Once AL or AE is started, you can double-click an icon to launch the application.

Managing Workstations with Z.E.N.works

The full Z.E.N.works product allows you to remotely control workstations for troubleshooting, training users to do various tasks, and so forth. The full product also allows you to give the users the Help Requester application, giving them simple, easy access to technical support via phone or e-mail. The workstation inventory component can be a great aid to troubleshooting because it lets you see the hardware configuration of a computer through the workstation's associated NDS object. This capability also requires the full Z.E.N.works product.

Both the full version and the Starter Pack of Z.E.N.works give you the ability to set policies that affect what a user can and can't do and how workstations are configured. Policy Package objects are very powerful tools that allow you to control the user environment.

CNE Practice Test Questions

1. Which is the correct order for login script execution?

    A. User, container, default, profile

    B. Container, user, profile or default

    C. Container, profile, user or default

    D. Container, default, user or profile

2. The container login script is executed:

    A. For each container the user is in

    B. For the user's parent container

    C. For the profile container only

    D. For the [Root] container only

3. Which is a properly formatted MAP command for a login script?

    A. `MAP F:=SYS:APPS`

    B. `#MAP F:=SYS:APPS`

    C. `MAP F=SYS:APPS`

    D. `MAP F:=SYS`

4. The INCLUDE command:

    A. Exits the login script and starts another

    B. Executes another script, then returns

    C. Adds commands to a login script

    D. Adds a login script to the Profile object

5. Which of the following is *not* a valid comment?

    A. `REM Do not change this script`

    B. `***Do not change this script***`

    C. `# Do not change this script`

    D. `;Do not change this script`

6. To use a DOS command in a login script:

    A. Include the name of the command only

    B. Include # and the name of the command

    C. Include a semicolon (;) and the name of the command

    D. Place the command in an INCLUDE file

7. Two of the components of Application Launcher are:

    A. NAL and NAM

    B. AL and NMENU

    C. AE and Application objects

    D. AE and Windows 3.1

8. AL runs under which operating systems?

    A. Windows 95

    B. Windows 3.1

    C. Windows NT

    D. All of the above

9. Application objects for complex applications are created using which of the following tools?

   A. snAppShot

   B. NetWare Administrator

   C. APCONFIG

   D. Both A and B

10. To give a user access to an application, modify:

   A. The User object's Application property

   B. The Application object's Association property

   C. Either A or B

   D. None of the above

11. What kind of Policy Packages can be created?

   A. Container

   B. Workstation

   C. User

   D. All of the above

12. User policies are *not* available for which operating systems?

   A. Windows 95

   B. Windows 3.*x*

   C. DOS

   D. Windows NT

13. What do you have to do before you can take control of a remote workstation?

A. Register the workstation

B. Import the workstation

C. Both A and B

D. None of the above

CHAPTER

6

How Printing Works

Roadmap

This chapter covers the components of NDPS (Novell Distributed Print Services) and how to configure them and the clients that use NDPS. This information is a part of the CNA and CNE core requirement "NetWare 5 Administration."

Topics Covered

- Components of NDPS
- Using NetWare Administrator to Set Up NDPS
- Controlling Access to Printers
- Managing Print Jobs
- Configuring Client Access to Printing
- Scheduling the NDPS Implementation

Skills You'll Learn

- List the components of NDPS and the purpose of each one
- Describe the process of setting up NDPS using NetWare Administrator
- Describe how access to printers can be controlled with NDPS
- List the ways print jobs can be managed with NDPS
- Explain how to configure clients to use NDPS

P rinting is one of the fundamental services a network provides. With the new version of NDPS (Novell Distributed Print Services) version 2, introduced with NetWare 5, you can print to a network printer, whether it's attached to the server, to a workstation, or directly to the network. NetWare manages print jobs and sends them to the printer one at a time, in an orderly manner. With NDPS and the appropriate client, even the old issue of printer drivers is resolved, as the appropriate driver will automatically be installed when the client needs to use the printer.

Of course, there's more to printing than just users and a printer. The next section introduces the components of the NetWare 5 printing services.

Components of NetWare 5 Printing

Several components interact to provide NetWare 5 printing services: Printer Agents (PA), Managers, Brokers, and gateways. Printers can be configured to be either Public or Controlled Access printers. You create these objects under NDS (except for Public Access Printers) and maintain them from within the NetWare Administrator utility. The components of NetWare 5 printing are shown in Figure 6.1 and are described in the following sections.

FIGURE 6.1

Several components interact to provide network printing services.

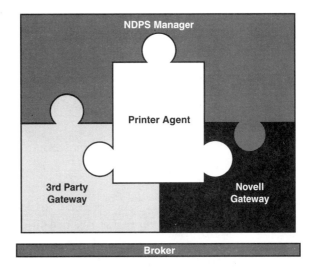

For more information than is found here, you can refer to two excellent sources for help. Both can be found on the online documentation CD. The first is in the documentation itself. You can get to the NDPS quick reference card by navigating to the Novell online documentation home page, then clicking on the following icons or links: Contents ➢ Print Services ➢ NDPS Quick Reference Card. The second good source on the CD is a multimedia introduction to NDPS; view it by executing \NOVDOCS\NDPSVIEW\NDPS.EXE. We highly recommend that you go through this introduction for help in getting started with NDPS.

Printer Agents

Printer Agents (PAs) are the central component of NDPS. The PA handles the functions that were previously done by the Printer, Print Queue, and Print Server objects in queue-based printing. (While queue-based printing still exists, it is now primarily for compatibility with older servers and clients and with non-Windows clients. Queue-based printing is discussed in Chapter 9.)

With NDPS, there must be one *Printer Agent (PA)* for every physical printer. There are never multiple PAs for a single printer, nor are there multiple printers controlled by a single PA. These are the primary functions of a PA:

- Managing the printing process, including all of the print jobs.

- Responding to requests from clients on the status of print jobs and the capabilities of the printer, such as the ability to duplex, print in color, and so on.

- Producing notifications for various events that may occur, such as completion of the print job, printer errors, and so on. The list of those to be notified for various events can be customized.

- Allowing you to print to any kind of printer, from a humble dot-matrix to a full-color document production system.

Printer agents can be any of the following:

- Software that runs on a server and represents a physical printer connected to any of the following:

  - A server

  - A workstation

  - A printer that is attached directly to the network, such as with an HP JetDirect card

- Software that is built into a printer that is directly connected to the network

Printer Agents can be configured in two different modes:

Public Access   These printers, which are immediately available to all users on the network as soon as they are created, do not support security or event notification. They are not represented by objects in the NDS tree. More information on this type of printer is found later in this chapter.

Controlled Access   These printers must be configured with various properties, including who is allowed to use the printer. Event notification is fully supported. Printers of this type are represented as objects in the NDS tree, as described below.

NDPS Manager

The *NDPS Manager* is the component of NDPS that allows you to create and manage PAs. You create an NDPS Manager just as you would any other object in the NDS tree. One NDPS Manager can manage any number of PAs. You need to create the NDPS Manager before you can create any PAs; you will need to create one (NDPS Manager) per server that will support NDPS.

On the server, the NDPSM.NLM utility provides the NDPS Manager's functionality. You can load this NLM manually, or it will automatically load when you create a PA on the server. Any given server can support a maximum of one NDPS Manager. If you have a printer physically attached to a server, it (the server) must run the NDPS Manager software.

Gateways

Gateways are the third component of NDPS. Gateways link the NDPS system to printers that are not NDPS-aware, or in other words to printers that don't have NDPS support built into them. There are three gateways that ship with NetWare 5: HP's gateway for JetDirect cards, Xerox's gateway for interfacing with Xerox printers, and the Novell Printer Gateway, which can interface with any kind of printer. (NDPS was developed as a joint venture between the three companies.) Novell's gateway is a generic gateway for any type of printer, and so it has more limited functionality than the third-party gateways, which are specific to a particular manufacturer's line of printers.

Gateways offer as much functionality as the manufacturer desires. For example, a gateway could even automatically create a PA whenever one of the manufacturer's network-connected printers is plugged into the network, without any intervention on your part.

Gateways provide the following benefits and capabilities to NDPS-aware clients:

- Printing to Unix and Macintosh printers

- Printing to queue-based printers

- Sending print jobs to printers that don't natively understand NDPS

- Interrogating the printer for its capabilities and current status (offline, online, and so on)

- Managing the printer (in conjunction with the PA and NDPS Manager)

The Novell gateway, as mentioned previously, is the generic interface to any printer. It supports both local (attached to the server directly) and remote (connected to a client workstation) printers. It supports non-NDPS-aware clients that print to queues, so that when they print to a queue, the information is retrieved from the queue and sent to the appropriate printer. This gateway supports both IPX and IP (in NDPS 2.0, the version that ships with NetWare 5). There are two subcomponents that make this gateway work:

- Print Device Subsystem (PDS)

- Port Handler (PH)

These two components are discussed in the next sections.

Print Device Subsystem

The *Print Device Subsystem (PDS)* allows the gateway to query a printer and get printer-specific information, such as whether the printer has the ability to print in color. This information is then stored in a database and can be referred to as needed in the future. This component automatically loads when a PA is created that uses the Novell Printer Gateway.

Port Handler

The *Port Handler (PH)* is the component that makes the gateway generic, not specific to any particular protocol or interface. It does this by abstracting the physical hardware or protocol information from the PDS. It supports the following communication methods:

- Serial port

- Parallel port

- Queue-based printers (such as older JetDirect cards that acted as a print server)

- Remote printers over the following protocols:

  - RP (Remote Printer) mode over IPX

  - LPR over TCP/IP

NDPS Broker

The purpose of the *NDPS Broker* is to support the gateway and the NDPS Manager, as illustrated previously in Figure 6.1. As you can see in the figure, the broker underlies both components. The Broker provides three services to NDPS:

- Service Registry Service (SRS)
- Event Notification Service (ENS)
- Resource Management Service (RMS)

The role each of these services plays will be discussed in the following sections. As Brokers can play a support role for a potentially large number of NDPS Managers, NDPS by default will not create a new Broker unless an existing Broker can't be found within three hops (routers) from the current server.

Service Registry Service (SRS)

The purpose of the *Service Registry Service (SRS)* is to make the Public Access printer mode possible. It allows these printers to register with the SRS; then, when an administrator or user wants information on that printer or wants to use it, SRS provides a central location for obtaining the information or making the use possible. The SRS maintains the following information, among other things, about each Public Access printer:

- Name
- Type
- Address on the network
- Manufacturer
- Model

Before SRS, printers frequently advertised their existence through SAP (Service Advertising Protocol) via broadcasts. This wasn't a problem when there were few network-connected printers on the network. As the number grew, however, more and more bandwidth was consumed with these broadcasts.

Enter SRS. Now, when a client needs to access a Public Access printer, instead of listening to SAP broadcasts, it will consult with SRS. What if there are multiple registries on the network? No problem; they automatically synchronize their information with each other, so all Public Access printers networkwide can be utilized.

The SRS also keeps track of the ENS and RMS systems available on the network.

Event Notification Service (ENS)

Event Notification Service (ENS), as its name implies, handles notifying users of various events. You configure the ENS to send notification to the appropriate person (or file). For example, a user may get a message such as "job completed" or "add paper," but an administrator may get a "toner low" message. Notification can take place via any of the following methods:

- Pop-up boxes, which appear on the appropriate workstations when an event occurs. This method is always available.

- E-mail, sent from GroupWise (discussed in Chapter 17), MHS (Message Handling Service) or SMTP (Simple Mail Transport Protocol), if any of those systems are installed.

- Log file, wherein the messages are written to a file that a user can examine later. This method is always available. This may be useful for such things as "toner low" messages, allowing the administrator to check the log daily or weekly for such messages and then handle all of the toner issues at once.

The ENS is also extensible, meaning that other mechanisms, such as paging, could be added if a third-party vendor were to create the ability.

Resource Management Service (RMS)

The *Resource Management Service (RMS)* keeps track of all the resources needed by NDPS clients and printers, as well as anything else that may request them. These are the resources that RMS tracks:

- *Banner pages,* pages that print before each print job and list the owner of the job, among other details. These pages are customizable, to the point that you can add logos or even photographs.

- Printer drivers for Windows 3.*x*, Windows 95/98, and Windows NT 4. Other drivers can be installed if a driver doesn't ship with NetWare 5.

- *Novell Printer Definition (NPD) files,* which contain a list of capabilities specific printers have. These files are necessary because many printers do not have the capability to dynamically provide this information to NDPS when they are queried for it.

RMS also offers these benefits:

- A simplified way to distribute and update resources.

- The ability to automatically download printer drivers on Windows clients.

- The ability to implement plug-and-print, which means that you can simply plug a printer into the network and print to it with no further configuration necessary. (Nonetheless, further configuration may be desirable, for greater control and to enable advanced capabilities, such as event notification.)

Public Access Printers

Public Access printers are not represented in the NDS tree with individual objects, but each has an associated PA. Public Access printers have their disadvantages, offering no control over who can use them and no support for event notification, but they do make possible the concept of plug-and-print.

Controlled Access Printers

Controlled Access printers, on the other hand, do allow you to control who can use the printer. There are many options available for configuring security and event notification. Controlled Access printers do have associated objects in the NDS tree. This mode can be set for a new printer, or you can convert a Public Access printer into a Controlled Access printer.

The default security settings allow any user in the container where the printer is created (and in any of its subcontainers) to use the printer, but no one else has access except for the user who creates the printer.

Setting Up NDPS with NetWare Administrator

Now that you know the components that must exist to properly set up NDPS, it is time to learn how to set them up. As you have probably guessed by now, each object is created and managed through NetWare Administrator. In the next few sections, we will discuss the process of creating the NDPS Manager object and Printer Agents for both Controlled Access and Public Access printers.

Creating the NDPS Manager

Before you can create PAs, you must have an NDPS Manager in place. As you may recall from the discussion above, the NDPS Manager can control any number of Printer Agents. Hence, the NDPS Manager must exist first.

The user that creates this object must have at least the Create NDS right, as well as the following file system rights to the volume on which you will store the information needed by the NDPS Manager: Read, Create, and File Scan. The steps for creating a new Manager are covered in Procedure 6.1.

PROCEDURE 6.1

Creating an NDPS Manager

NDPS Managers can control any number of Printer Agents. They are, however, limited to a maximum of one per server. To create the NDPS Manager, follow these steps:

1. Open NetWare Administrator and select the container in which you want to create the object.

2. Go to Object ➤ Create, and then choose NDPS Manager from the list of options. The Create NDPS Manager Object dialog box will appear, as shown here:

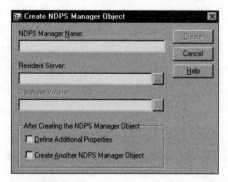

3. Enter a name for the NDPS Manager and the server to which it will be assigned. The specified server needs to have NDPS already installed on it. (See Chapter 7 for more information on how to do this.) It will only be usable on the specified server.

4. Specify the volume on that server where you want to store the files that the NDPS Manager requires. Novell states that 3 to5 MB should typically be sufficient. Notice also that, by default, all of the spooled print jobs will be stored on this volume, unless you specify a different volume for each Printer Agent. Be sure there is sufficient space on the volume for the print jobs or modify the PAs to use another volume.

5. Click Create when you are finished and an NDPS Manager object will be created.

That's all there is to creating an NDPS Manager. You are now almost ready to move on to creating PAs. Before you can create PAs, however, you need to load the NDPSM.NLM on the appropriate server. You can manually do this at the server, using the Browse button if necessary to find the context of the NDPS Manager, or you can automate this process by placing this statement and the context of the NDPS Manager in AUTOEXEC.NCF. For more information on console commands and AUTOEXEC.NCF, refer to Chapter 8.

Creating Printer Agents

Printer Agents (PAs) can be configured in two different manners, namely to represent Public Access or Controlled Access printers. Novell recommends creating Controlled Access printers, because they can fully exploit the capabilities of NDPS. The following sections cover the process of creating both types of PAs. Remember that PAs are assigned to specific NDPS Managers.

Public Access Printers

Public Access printers are available to all users on the network and don't support event notification. They can be converted at any time to Controlled Access printers, as discussed below. This type of printer can be created in one of three ways: automatically by some third-party gateways when a new printer is added to the network; through the NDPS Manager object in NetWare Administrator; or through NDPSM.NLM at the server console. Procedure 6.2 presents the second method for creating Public Access printers, using NetWare Administrator.

PROCEDURE 6.2

Creating a Public Access Printer

To create a Public Access printer using NetWare Administrator, follow these steps:

1. Double-click the name of the NDPS Manager that you want to manage this printer to display its Details dialog box.

PROCEDURE 6.2 (CONTINUED)

2. Select the Printer Agent List page. A dialog box will be displayed, as shown here:

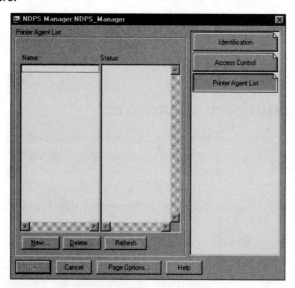

3. Click the New button. The Create Printer Agent dialog box will appear, as shown here:

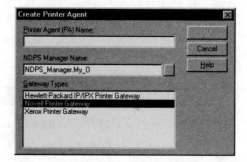

4. Enter a name for this PA. The NDPS Manager Name field will automatically be filled in.

5. Choose a gateway type. Depending on the gateway you select, you will be shown varying dialog boxes. Fill them in as appropriate. The three standard gateways will be described in more detail later in this chapter.

That's all there is to creating a Printer Agent for a Public Access printer. Remember, Novell recommends that you convert Public Access printers to Controlled Access to utilize all of the features that NDPS offers.

Controlled Access Printers

Controlled Access printers can fully exploit the features of NDPS. To create this type of printer, you will create an object in NDS and then configure it. We will begin by explaining how to create a new Controlled Access printer in Procedure 6.3.

PROCEDURE 6.3

Creating a New Controlled Access Printer

To create a new Controlled Access printer, follow these steps:

1. Select the container in which you want the new Controlled Access printer to be created.

2. Choose Object ➢ Create, and then choose NDPS Printer from the list of options. The Create NDPS Printer dialog box appears, as shown here:

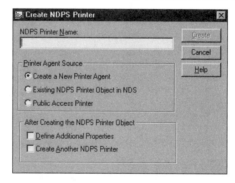

3. Enter a name for the NDPS Printer object.

4. Choose the Create a New Printer Agent option in the Printer Agent Source section of the dialog box.

5. Click Create. The Create Printer Agent dialog box appears, as shown previously in Procedure 6.2. Enter the name of the new PA, choose the NDPS Manager you want to manage this printer, and choose the desired gateway type. The steps for configuring each gateway are covered below.

Procedure 6.4 outlines the steps for converting a Public Access printer to Controlled Access mode.

PROCEDURE 6.4

Converting a Public Access Printer to a Controlled Access Printer

If you have already created some Public Access printers and now want them to be Controlled Access printers to take full advantage of the features that NDPS offers, follow these steps:

1. Select the container in which you want the new Controlled Access printer to be created.

2. Choose Object ➢ Create, and the choose NDPS Printer from the list of options. The Create NDPS Printer dialog box appears, as shown above in Procedure 6.3, Step 2.

3. Enter a name for the NDPS Printer object. Select the Public Access Printer option in the Printer Agent Source section of the dialog box, and then click Create.

4. A warning dialog box will appear, as shown below. This is to remind you that all of the clients that are using the old Public Access printer will have to reinstall the printer as a Controlled Access printer.

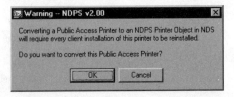

5. Click OK to proceed. The Select Printer Agent dialog box will appear, as shown here:

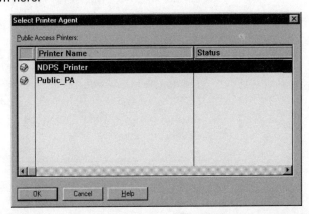

6. Select the name of the Public Access printer you wish to convert, and then choose OK to complete the conversion.

That's all there is to creating a Public Access printer or converting one to a Controlled Access printer. You may want to go back and configure access controls and/or notification settings on the printer. Remember, by default, only the container it was created in (and any subcontainers) can use a Controlled Access printer. Changing the default settings will be covered in detail below, in the section on setting up access control.

Using the Novell Printer Gateway

To use the Novell Printer Gateway in configuring either of the two types of printers, follow the steps in Procedure 6.5. (This procedure covers only the configuration of the gateway, not the process of creating the printer type.)

PROCEDURE 6.5

Configuring the Novell Printer Gateway

To configure the Novell Printer Gateway, follow these steps:

1. After you have created a PA, you will be prompted for the gateway type. This occurs in Step 5 of Procedure 6.3 (for creating a Controlled Access printer) and Step 5 of Procedure 6.2 (for creating a Public Access printer) above. Choose the Novell Printer Gateway option. The first of the configuration dialog boxes will be displayed, as shown here:

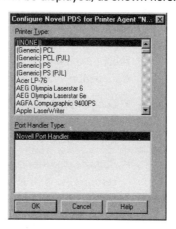

PROCEDURE 6.5 (CONTINUED)

2. Choose the appropriate model from the Printer Type list. If your printer is not in this list, either choose the closest generic type or update the list of Novell Printer Definition (NPD) files through the Resource Management Service. For information on how to do this, refer to the online documentation.

3. Choose the appropriate Port Handler Type from the list of available options. The Novell Port Handler is for printers that are physically connected to the file server, those that are attached to workstations, or those that get print jobs from queues.

4. Click OK. The Configure Port Handler dialog box will appear, as shown here:

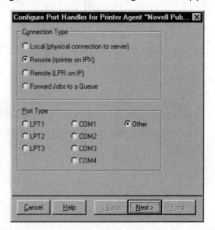

5. You must also select the appropriate port type in the bottom half of the dialog box (LPT1 through LPT3, COM1 through COM4, or Other). In this dialog box, you can choose one of four Connection Type options for the printer. Depending on the Connection Type you choose, another dialog box or two will appear. The following list outlines the next steps for each Connection Type:

   ▪ Local (Physical Connection to Server) is for those printers that are directly connected to the file server. If you choose this option, proceed to Step 6.

   ▪ Remote (rprinter on IPX) is for printers that are connected to workstations via NPRINTER.EXE or to servers via NPRINTER.NLM, or for printers that are directly connected to the network, but which are operating in remote printer mode. If you choose this option, the dialog box shown below will be displayed. Because this mode is used to emulate a print server in the queue-based print system, you must specify the SAP name (the equivalent of the PSERVER name) and printer number. The printer number will be 0 unless you specify multiple PAs to use the same SAP name. You can also set address restrictions to limit where the printer will accept jobs from. (By default, there are no restrictions.) Proceed to Step 7.

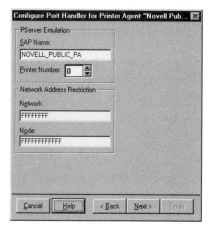

- Remote (LPR on IP) is for IP-based printers directly connected to the network or printers attached to computers running LPD (Line Printer Daemon, similar to PSERVER). If you choose this option, the dialog box shown below will be displayed. You will need to specify either a host address (IP) or a host name (such as printer1.sybex.com), and a Printer Name, if the host requires one. Proceed to Step 7.

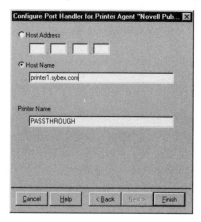

PROCEDURE 6.5 (CONTINUED)

- Forward Jobs to a Queue sends jobs to a print queue to be processed by the legacy queue-based system (described in Chapter 9). If you choose this option, the dialog box shown below will be displayed. In this case, you will need to select the queue and a user who is allowed to use the queue. As the Caution message in the dialog box warns, if there is a password on that user's account, you will have to enter the password at the server console every time this PA starts. To simplify this process, we recommend that you create a User object without a password especially for this purpose, giving it rights to use the queue only. Proceed to Step 7.

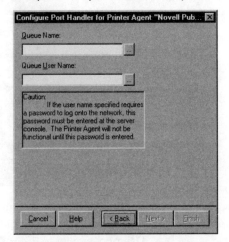

6. When you click the Next button to continue, you will see the dialog box shown below. Select a controller type—Auto Select (the type we and Novell strongly recommend), Compatible (for output only), or 1284 ECP (for ports that are so configured)—and choose Interrupt or Polled mode.

PROCEDURE 6.5 (CONTINUED)

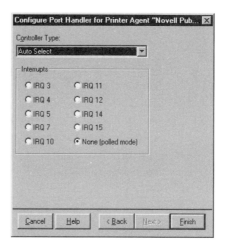

7. Click Finish after you have completed the configuration. Novell will now load the PA. When this is finished, the Select Printer Drivers dialog box will appear:

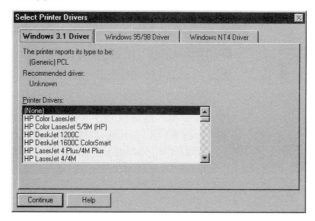

PROCEDURE 6.5 (CONTINUED)

8. Select the appropriate printer driver for each of your client platforms, namely Windows 3.1, Windows 95/98, and/or Windows NT 4. Based on the printer selection you made in Step 1, a recommended driver will be presented. If you chose a generic printer, there won't be a recommended driver; check with your printer's documentation to see what type of printer it emulates. You can also choose None, which will require the user at each workstation to pick and properly install the correct driver. When you click Continue, you will be presented with a dialog box summarizing your choices. If everything is correct, click OK to complete the process.

Using the Hewlett-Packard IP/IPX Printer Gateway

To use the Hewlett-Packard IP/IPX Printer Gateway to configure a JetDirect card (internal or external), follow the steps in Procedure 6.6. (This procedure covers only the configuration of the gateway, not the entire creation process.)

PROCEDURE 6.6

Configuring the Hewlett-Packard IP/IPX Printer Gateway

To configure the Hewlett-Packard IP/IPX Printer Gateway, follow these steps:

1. After you have created a PA, you will be prompted for the gateway type. This occurs in Step 5 of Procedure 6.3 (for creating a Controlled Access printer) and Step 5 of Procedure 6.2 (for creating a Public Access printer) above. Choose the Hewlett-Packard IP/IPX Printer Gateway option. A configuration dialog box will be displayed, as shown here.

PROCEDURE 6.6 (CONTINUED)

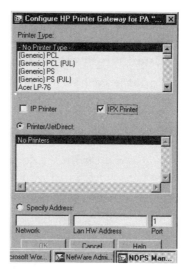

2. Select the appropriate printer type.

3. Choose the type of connection that the JetDirect card is configured for, either IP or IPX, and a list of cards will appear. If the desired card is not listed and you know the hardware address, you can enter it and the network it's on instead. If you have an internal card or an external box with only one port, the port will be 1; otherwise, enter the appropriate number.

4. Click OK when you are finished. You may be prompted for printer driver information; if so, choose the appropriate drivers as described in Procedure 6.5, Steps 7 and 8.

Since the Hewlett-Packard IP/IPX Gateway is specific to HP JetDirect cards, the process is far simpler than the one for configuring the generic Novell Printer Gateway, described above.

Using the Xerox Printer Gateway

To use the Xerox Printer Gateway to configure either of the two types of printers, follow the steps in Procedure 6.7. (This procedure covers only the configuration of the gateway, not the entire process of creating the printer type.) Xerox printers require that a queue-based printing system be in place. The Xerox Setup Wizard automates the transition to NDPS for you, and it will also create the old queue-based objects for the printer. (More information on queue-based printing is in Chapter 9.)

PROCEDURE 6.7

Configuring the Xerox Printer Gateway

To configure the Xerox Printer Gateway, follow these steps:

1. After you have created a PA, you will be prompted for the gateway type. This occurs in Step 5 of Procedure 6.3 (for creating a Controlled Access printer) and Step 5 of Procedure 6.2 (for creating a Public Access printer) above. Choose the Xerox Printer Gateway option. The opening screen of the Xerox Setup Wizard will be displayed, as shown here:

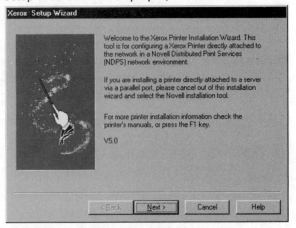

2. Click Next after reading the introductory screen.

3. Select the desired printer from the list that appears next. (This list is generated via SAP over IPX.) Click Next.

4. Choose a new name for the printer or accept the default, which is the same name as the print server. You must also specify the name of the queue that this printer will service. Click Next when you have finished.

5. Verify that all of the information is correct. Click Next to proceed or Back to return to a previous screen and make corrections.

6. The wizard will now create the necessary queue-based objects, completing the configuration process.

Setting Up Access Control on Controlled Access Printers

Once a Controlled Access printer is created, you may want to configure who can use the printer. As mentioned previously, the default is that the printer may be used by everyone in the container where the object is created (and therefore in any of its subcontainers), along with the user who created it. To set up access control, you need to understand three important roles. The three access roles that are used in NDPS are Manager, Operator, and User. Each of these three roles has mutually exclusive capabilities, but NDPS makes sure that you don't do anything stupid like making a user the manager of a printer without giving him or her the ability to print to the printer. Let's begin by discussing what each role allows the associated trustee to do.

The purpose of the Manager role is to handle the Printer object as a whole and the way the printer is set up. This role is usually filled by administrators. The Manager can do any of the following:

- Change the properties of the NDPS Printer object

- Add and delete other Managers, Operators, and Users

- Configure notification

- Create, change, and delete printer configurations

The next key NDPS role is Operator. These are the people responsible for the day-to-day operation of the printer. Operators can do the following:

- Control all options on the Printer Control tab of the printer

- Pause, restart, and reinitialize printers

- Perform any type of job maintenance, such as copying, moving, deleting, and reordering print jobs

- Set printer and spooling defaults

The final NDPS role is User. This role is for those who need to be able to print to the printer. They can do the following:

- Send print jobs to the printer

- Manage print jobs that they have sent to be printed

Once you understand each of these roles, assigning objects to the appropriate role is simple. To do so, open the Details dialog box of the desired NDPS Printer, choose the Access Control page, and then select the desired role. The NDPS Printer dialog box, shown in Figure 6.2, will be displayed. Using the Add and Delete buttons, you can add new objects to any of the roles or remove objects from roles previously assigned to them. You can also specify notification information for the selected object.

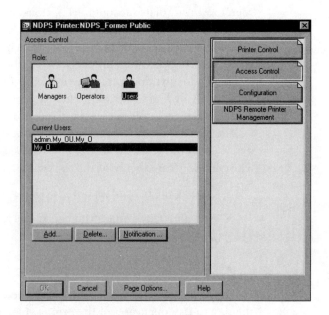

Controlling Job Properties

Once you have set up the printer the way you desire and users start using the printer, occasionally someone will need to fix problems, change the order of print jobs, and so on. Remember, however, that only Operators can perform all of these functions for any document; users can only modify the documents they have sent to the printer.

Operator tasks can all be accomplished from the Printer Control tab of the desired printer. Any of the tasks related to print jobs are accessed by clicking on the Jobs button and choosing Job List. Many other functions can be accomplished from this screen as well. Refer to the online documentation for more information. Figure 6.3 shows the screen that displays when you click the Printer Control page for an HP printer, while a generic page for most other printers is shown in Figure 6.4. As you can see, the button functions are almost the same.

FIGURE 6.3

The Printer Control page of an HP printer with the Jobs menu pulled down

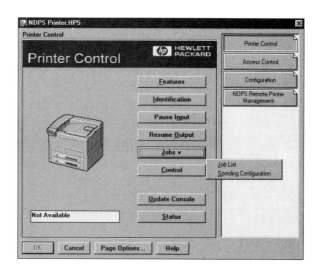

FIGURE 6.4

The Printer Control page of a generic NetWare printer with the Jobs menu pulled down

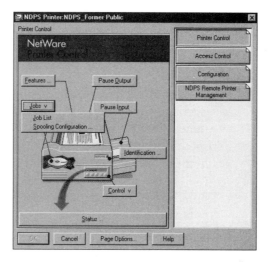

To do any print job management, pull down the Jobs menu and select Job List. The dialog box shown in Figure 6.5 will appear.

FIGURE 6.5

The Job List dialog box with the Job Options menu displayed

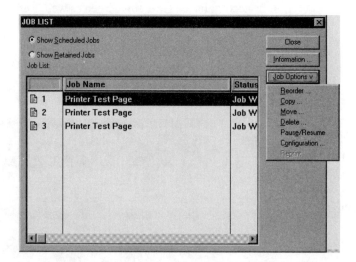

From here, pull down the Job Options menu and choose whichever task you need to perform. These are the common tasks (and their associated dialog boxes):

Reorder   Choose the new position in the list by changing the Job Position.

Copy or **Move**   This dialog box is shown below. Choose the appropriate option to copy or move this print job to another printer managed by the same NDPS Manager. Since the print output is already formatted for a specific printer, the printer that you are moving or copying to should be of the same type, or you will get garbage for output. These options allow you to get a job out in a hurry on another printer. The original job will print when this printer becomes available if you chose Copy; it will come out only on the new printer if you chose Move.

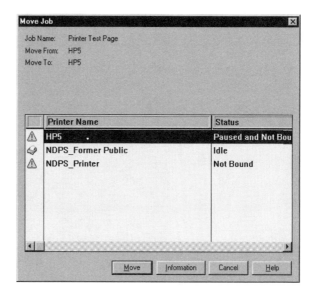

Delete   This allows you to delete a job that you don't want to be printed. A dialog box will prompt you to confirm that you are deleting the right job or jobs.

Configuration   Use this option to control the various settings for the selected print job. There are four tabs in the Job Configuration dialog box:

General   This tab, shown below, lists the number of copies you requested, the maximum number that can be requested (as set by the administrator), the priority of the job and the maximum priority (again set by the administrator), the banner selected, and the medium (paper type) chosen.

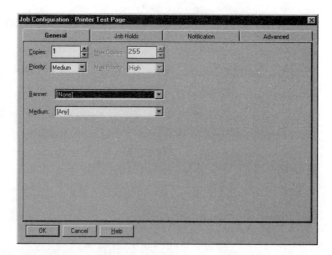

Job Holds   This tab lists any holds that have been placed by either the user or an operator on the job (for an indefinite period of time), a time the job should be held until, if the printer should be paused before or after printing this job (for example to change paper types), and the desired amount of time the job should be retained for later use.

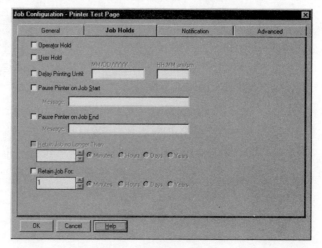

Notification   Select this tab to choose the way you want to be notified when various conditions exist and to set the conditions for notification. The following screen shows some of the conditions that can generate notification.

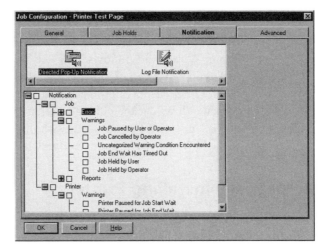

Advanced   This tab lists various statistics about the print job, such as how big it is and when it was sent, as well as details like the name of the document and the current state of the job.

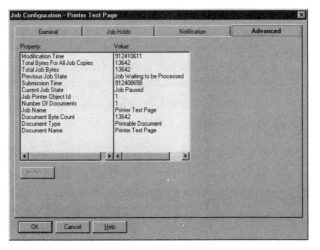

Configuring Clients to Use NDPS

Now that you know how to install and configure NDPS, there is only one more piece of the puzzle that must be in place before you can use the system. That piece is client access. In this section, we will look at the three ways that clients can be configured to use NDPS: automatically, by having NDPS install the printer(s) (called a *push* install); manually, by running the Novell Print Manager (called a *pull* install); and manually, by using the Add Printer Wizard in Windows 95/98 or Windows NT 4.

As you may recall, to fully utilize NDPS you must have a Windows-based client. Other clients can utilize some components on a limited basis. In addition, Windows clients will require that the Novell Client or Client 32 (version 2.2 or higher) be installed, with the NDPS option selected. Installation of the Novell Client was covered in Chapter 2.

Automatically Installing Printers

Once you have created a printer and selected the appropriate printer drivers, you can have NDPS automatically create the printer for a user and download the appropriate drivers. You may also set this printer to be the default printer if you wish. This can be accomplished two ways, from the Printer Agent side or from the container side. To set this up from the printer side, refer to Procedure 6.8.

PROCEDURE 6.8

Configuring NDPS to Automatically Install a Printer for a User (from the Printer Agent Side)

To have NDPS automatically install a printer for a user from the Printer Agent side, follow these steps:

1. Select the Printer Agent that you want to install and display its Details page.

2. Select the NDPS Remote Printer Management tab. The dialog box shown here will appear:

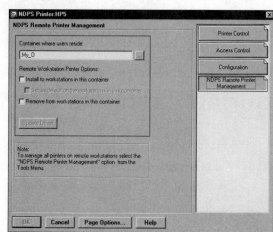

PROCEDURE 6.8 (CONTINUED)

3. Choose the appropriate option in the Container Where Users Reside field. This should be the container in which you want the printer installed and in which the remote printer management information is stored.

4. Check either the box labeled "Install to workstations in this container" or "Remove from workstations in this container" (they are mutually exclusive). If you choose the Install option, you may also check the box to set this printer as the user's default printer and/or automatically update the driver, if you recently installed a new driver, by clicking the Update Driver button. These settings will take effect automatically the next time the user logs in.

5. Click OK when you are finished. This completes the configuration for automatic installation.

Procedure 6.9 explains how to set up NDPS from the container side.

PROCEDURE 6.9

Configuring NDPS to Automatically Install a Printer for a User (from the Container Side)

To have NDPS automatically install a printer for a user from the container side, follow these steps:

1. Select the container that you want to have the printer installed in and display its Details page.

2. Select the NDPS Remote Printer Management tab. This dialog box will appear:

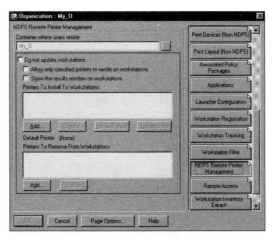

3. Check the box labeled "Allow only specified printers to reside on workstations" if you want to allow only the listed printers to be used. The next time the user logs on, any printers not on the list will be deleted.

4. Check the box labeled "Show the results window on workstations" if you want users to be notified anytime their printing setup is modified.

5. Add printers to install to or to remove from users' workstations by clicking the appropriate Add button. You will be presented with a list of printers to select from. You can also click the Browse button to select any other Printer Agent.

6. You can set a printer to be the default printer using the Set As Default button and/or update the printer driver by clicking the Update Driver button.

7. Remove printers you no longer want in either list by pressing the appropriate Delete button.

8. Click OK when you are finished. This completes the configuration for automatic installation.

Manually Installing Printers with Novell Printer Manager

Novell Printer Manager enables users to manage their own printing environment. With this tool, users can do all of the following tasks (and more):

- Create new printers on their computer

- View the list of print jobs on a printer and get real-time information on the status of those jobs

- Change the order of print jobs

- Pause, resume, and delete print jobs

- Submit print jobs with a hold, so that they will print later (for example, after normal business hours)

To use the Novell Printer Manager, execute SYS:PUBLIC\NWPMW16.EXE for clients running Windows 3.1 or SYS:PUBLIC\WIN32\NWPMW32.EXE for clients running Windows 95/98 or Windows NT 4. The main window will be displayed, as shown in Figure 6.6. From here you can view all of the NDPS printers you have installed, install new ones, and so on.

FIGURE 6.6

The Novell Printer
Manager window

Because we are concentrating on printer installation in this section, we will only look at that portion of the program. Most of the other options are self-explanatory, or they have been explained previously in the "Controlling Job Properties" section. To install a new printer, follow the steps outlined in Procedure 6.10.

PROCEDURE 6.10

Installing a New Printer Using the Novell Printer Manager

To install a new printer with the Novell Printer Manager (NWPMW16 or NWPMW32), follow these steps:

1. Open the Novell Printer Manager and choose Printer ➢ New. The following dialog box will appear:

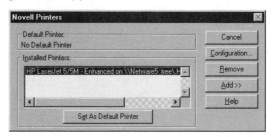

PROCEDURE 6.10 (CONTINUED)

2. Click the Add button and the dialog box will expand, as shown here:

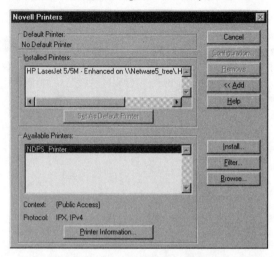

3. In this dialog box, you can view the printers that are available to you in your current context. To view printers in another context, click Browse.

4. The best reason to install printers this way is the Filter button. Click it and this dialog box will appear:

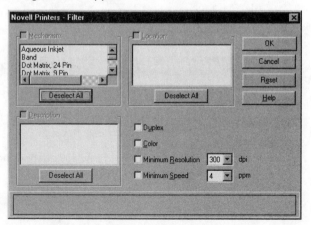

5. Select any criteria you wish and click OK. NDPS will search through all of the Public Access and Controlled Access printers in your current context for printers that meet the criteria you enter. Any matches will be displayed in the Available Printers list.

PROCEDURE 6.10 (CONTINUED)

6. Select the desired printer and click Install. You will be prompted to confirm the printer name, to select whether you want to use this printer as the default printer, and to select the configuration you wish. Click OK and the printer will automatically show up in your list of installed printers. That's all there is to it. Those who have used previous versions of NetWare will appreciate this much simpler installation procedure.

As you can see, this is a fairly straightforward process for users, and it offers them the ability to search for printers with specific features. The downside is that this is another application to learn and use. If Novell Printer Manager is something you think you might want to use widely, consider making an application icon for it and distributing it with Z.E.N.works, as discussed in Chapter 5.

Installing Printers Manually with the Add Printer Wizard

If you have users who are running Windows 95/98 or Windows NT 4, they can use the tool they may be most familiar with to install new printers, an install wizard. All the user has to do is choose the Add Printer Wizard (from the Start ➤ Settings ➤ Printers menu), choose to install a network printer, and browse for the NDPS printer of their choice. The printer will be automatically installed for them.

Review

In this chapter we covered the basics of NDPS (Novell Distributed Print Services). We began by reviewing the NDPS components and then turned to implementation details for both the Printer objects in NetWare Administrator and for clients.

NDPS Components

NDPS is made up of four primary components, the Printer Agent (PA), the NDPS Manager, the NDPS Broker, and gateways. Let's briefly review the purpose of each.

Printer Agent

The PA is at the core of NDPS. It does the jobs that were formerly accomplished by the Print Queue, Print Server, and Printer objects in queue-based printing. The PA is the primary interface between the user, the printer, and NDPS. It manages the printing process, replies to requests for information on print jobs or printer features, and generates event notification. There is a one-to-one relationship between printers and printer agents. There can never be more than one PA per printer or more than one printer per PA.

NDPS Manager

The NDPS Manager manages any number of PAs on a single server. There can never be more than one NDPS Manager per server. This object is responsible for the creation and management of PAs.

Gateways

NDPS gateways allow information to flow between NDPS and the printer. They allow for interoperability between queue-based systems and NDPS, and between non–NDPS-aware clients and the NDPS architecture. There are three gateways that ship with NDPS—manufacturer-specific gateways from HP and Xerox, and the Novell Printer Gateway, which can interface with any kind of printer.

Broker

The Broker component supports the rest of the NDPS system. You don't need many Brokers in a network; in fact, a new Broker is not installed by default unless one can't be found within three hops. The NDPS Broker provides three primary services, the Service Registry Service (SRS), Event Notification Service (ENS), and the Resource Management Service (RMS).

The SRS is responsible for maintaining the list of Public Access printers (PAPs) on the network. When a new PAP comes online, it registers with the SRS. When clients are looking for a printer, the SRS provides the list of PAPs.

The ENS is responsible for all notifications that need to be sent, whether to job owners or others, such as the administrator. Notifications can be sent when events occur, such as a print job finishing or a printer running low on toner. Notifications can be sent via a pop-up window or e-mail, or through log files.

The RMS tracks all of the resources that are needed by various components of NDPS, including printers, clients, and the system itself. These things include printer drivers and banner page information.

Printer Types: Public Access and Controlled Access Printers

The NDPS system includes two types of printers, Public Access and Controlled Access. Public Access printers are available to everyone on the network, but don't support access control or event notification. Controlled Access printers support both features and are represented by objects in the NDS tree. Novell recommends that you use Controlled Access printers as much as possible, since they fully support NDPS.

Creating Objects in NetWare Administrator

The first thing you will need to set up for NDPS is an NDPS Manager. This is created like any other object in NDS. Simply specify the name, the server with which it will be associated, and the volume on that server that you want to use for its storage needs, including print job storage needs by default. This service is run by executing NDPSM.NLM on the server you specified, which should be placed in that server's AUTOEXEC.NCF.

To create a Public Access printer, open the NDPS Manager, select the Printer Agent List page, and click New. Next, specify the Printer Agent's name and the gateway type. Configure the gateway as needed and install the appropriate printer drivers for your platforms, and you are done.

To create a Controlled Access printer, go to the container in which you want to create the NDPS Printer object, select Object ➤ Create, and then choose the NDPS Printer option. You can create a new Printer Agent or convert an existing Public Access printer to a Controlled Access printer. Give your new or converted printer a name and a PA name, and then select the appropriate gateway. Configure the gateway as appropriate and install the correct printer drivers, and the process is complete.

Setting Up Access Control on Controlled Access Printers and Printing Management

Access control on Controlled Access printers is handled through three roles, the Manager, the Operator, and the User. The Manager is the one who creates and configures the printer's properties and assigns others as Operators and Users. Operators handle the day-to-day printing tasks, such as moving and copying print jobs, pausing the printer, and so on. Users can print and manage the documents they print. All of the configuration options you need are on the Access Control page of the Details page for each Controlled Access printer.

Most of the printing management tasks, such as copying and moving print jobs, reordering print jobs, and so on, are handled on the Printer Control page of the Details page for each Controlled Access printer. Operators can do any of the tasks listed on this tab; users can only manage their own print jobs.

Setting Up Clients to Use NDPS

You can configure Windows-based clients to use NDPS printers automatically or manually. The automatic way, often referred to as a push installation, is to choose the container or printer in question and then specify what you want installed on the user's computer. You can even automatically update drivers.

You can manually update and control printers through the Novell Printer Manager. If your clients are running Windows 95/98 or Windows NT 4, they can also use the Add Printer Wizard. The advantage of the wizard is that users may already be familiar with this kind of tool. The advantage of the Novell Printer Manager is that you can search for printers that meet certain criteria.

CNE Practice Test Questions

1. What are the major components in NDPS Printing?

   A. Print Server, Print Queue, Printer

   B. Manager, Printer Agent, Gateway, Broker

   C. Manager, Printer Agent, Print Queue

   D. Gateway, Broker, Printer

2. What is the main responsibility of the NDPS Manager?

   A. Manage Printer Agents

   B. Manage printers

   C. Manage print queues

   D. None of the above

3. Which gateway ships with NDPS?

   A. Novell

   B. Xerox

   C. Hewlett-Packard

   D. All of the above

4. Which type(s) of printer can be created?

   A. Public Access

   B. Controlled Access

   C. Both of the above

   D. There is only one type of printer, simply called a printer

5. Which of the following is (or are) represented by an object in NDS? (Choose all correct answers.)

   A. Public Access printer

   B. Controlled Access printer

   C. Manager

   D. Broker

   E. Gateway

6. The NDPS Manager Printer Agent List page lists:

   A. Public Access PAs

   B. Controlled Access PAs

   C. Both of the above

7. A Public Access printer is created with:

   A. NDPS Manager

   B. NetWare Administrator, as an object in the NDS tree

   C. Novell Printer Manager

   D. PCONSOLE

8. A new Controlled Access printer is created with:

   A. NDPS Manager

   B. NetWare Administrator, as an object in the NDS tree

   C. Novell Printer Manager

   D. PCONSOLE

9. Printers can be automatically installed on workstations by the administrator through:

   A. The NDPS Remote Printer Management page of printers or containers

   B. NDPS Manager

   C. Novell Printer Manager

   D. The Add Printer Wizard

10. Printers can be manually installed on workstations by the user through (choose all that apply):

   A. The Add Printer Wizard

   B. NDPS Manager

   C. Novell Printer Manager

   D. PCONSOLE

   E. Printers can't be installed by users

PART

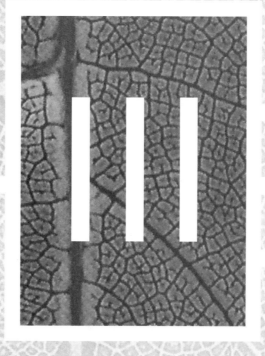

III

NetWare 5
Advanced
Administration

CHAPTER

7

Upgrading to NetWare 5

Roadmap

This chapter covers system requirements and methods available to upgrade to NetWare 5, which is a section of the CNE core requirement "NetWare 5 Advanced Administration."

Topics Covered

- Upgrading to NetWare 5

- Planning the Upgrade

- Performing the Upgrade

Skills You'll Learn

- Determine whether the existing server hardware meets the requirements for NetWare 5

- Know when to use IP only or IP/IPX protocol

- Prepare for the upgrade to NetWare 5

- List and describe the tools available for upgrading to NetWare 5

- Determine which upgrade tool is appropriate for different situations

In this chapter you will learn how to upgrade an existing NetWare 3.*x* or 4.*x* server to NetWare 5, including the system requirements and special needs you'll need to be aware of before upgrading. Based on these requirements, you will have to choose between doing a same-server upgrade or a server-to-server migration. You'll also have to choose a protocol, based on current implementation, to perform the upgrade. Finally, you will need to determine the appropriate utility with which to perform the upgrade.

Novell has made considerable efforts to make the upgrade to NetWare 5 as seamless and painless as possible. You will see that there have been considerable improvements from previous versions of upgrade and install utilities.

Here's the most important tip for a successful upgrade to NetWare 5: Make a backup first. To be completely safe, make two backups, and restore a few files to test the backup. This may sound paranoid, but there are many steps involved in the upgrade process, and many things can go wrong. Ninety-five percent of the time, everything works fine—but it isn't easy to explain to the CEO of the company that you're in "the other five percent." Play it safe.

Upgrading to NetWare 5

You can upgrade some existing NetWare 3.*x* and 4.*x* servers to NetWare 5 without purchasing additional hardware. However, NetWare 5 is a more sophisticated operating system and requires more resources to run efficiently. You may need to upgrade the processor, install additional RAM, or add more disk storage space in order to achieve optimum performance.

Hardware Requirements

Table 7.1 summarizes the hardware requirements for NetWare 3.*x*, 4.*x*, and NetWare 5. Minimum requirements are given, along with suggested hardware for optimal performance in a simple network. You should determine the requirements of your own server using the information given in the following sections.

T A B L E 7.1:   Hardware Requirements for NetWare 3.*x*, 4.*x*, and 5

Operating System	RAM (Minimum/ Optimal)	Disk Storage (Minimum/Optimal)	Processor (Minimum/ Optimal)
NetWare 3.*x*	4MB/8MB	50MB/ 500MB	386/486
NetWare 4.*x*	20MB/32MB	90MB/ 500MB–1GB	386/486, Pentium, or Pentium Pro
NetWare 5	64MB/ 128MB	230MB/ 1GB	Pentium 200MHz/ Pentium Pro 200MHz or higher

If you do have to buy a new server, don't write off the old server completely. If it's not too old, it will probably make a fine workstation. Be sure the upgrade is a success before you reformat that hard drive, though.

Do You Need More Memory?

NetWare 5 definitely requires more memory than any previous version. Your NetWare 3.*x* server may have run just fine with 8MB, but you'll need at least 64MB for an efficient NetWare 5 server. If you are planning to use Java applications, including ConsoleOne, you will need a minimum of 128MB.

Be sure that you also have plenty of room for additional memory. If you add a disk drive, additional software, or additional users to the network, you'll need it.

Do You Need More Disk Storage?

Disk storage requirements have changed considerably between previous versions of NetWare and NetWare 5. You'll need a minimum of 30MB for the DOS partition, and 50MB is recommended. The SYS volume requires a minimum of 200MB, but 500MB to 1GB is recommended. Altogether, you'll need a minimum 230MB of disk storage.

If your existing server doesn't meet the DOS partition requirements, then an across-the-wire (server-to-server) migration is the upgrade method for you.

Do You Need a Faster CPU?

NetWare 5 puts a higher load on the processor (CPU) than previous versions. A 386 might suffice for NetWare 3.*x* networks of up to 30 or 40 users, but for NetWare 5 you will definitely need a Pentium 200MHz for that many users. Since they're fairly low priced, you might even consider starting with a Pentium Pro with a speed of 200MHz or higher. You will need the power of a good processor to run version 5.

This is the category where you should think seriously about purchasing an entirely new machine. There are very few machines that can be upgraded to a higher processor without great expense and inconvenience. In addition, a new machine comes with parts that were intended to work together, and are new and unlikely to fail—or if they do fail, at least they'll be under warranty.

What About New Hardware?

After considering the requirements discussed in the above sections, you may discover that your machine needs quite a bit of help. In many cases, the best idea is to buy an entirely new machine to serve as the NetWare 5 server. If your budget supports it, a new machine can provide you with improved speed, reliability, compatibility, and expandability.

As a final benefit, a new machine will allow you to perform a server-to-server upgrade or across-the-wire migration to upgrade the server. A *server-to-server* upgrade transmits data across the network to create a copy of the old server's setup on the new server. This method doesn't make any changes to your existing server, and if something goes wrong, you can quickly bring the old server back online.

In addition to the hardware you'll need to run NetWare 5, you will want to have the following hardware included in your new system:

- A high-speed bus—EISA or the more recent PCI. VESA local bus is another alternative, but is not well supported by network card manufacturers.

- Network cards that support the bus you've chosen.

- Disk controllers that support the high-speed bus, and fast disk drives. Be sure to verify that the disk controller has HAM support, because NetWare 5 does not support the older .DSK format.

- A CD-ROM drive. Unless you have another server with a CD-ROM drive on the same network, you'll need this for installing the server and for occasional maintenance.

Planning the Upgrade

Upgrading your network to NetWare 5 is definitely not something that you should do spontaneously. In order to upgrade successfully, you must plan the process carefully. This includes choosing the best method for your upgrade and preparing hardware, software, and users for the transition.

Choosing an Upgrade Strategy

The first consideration when upgrading is the type of upgrade you will use. There are two methods of upgrading:

- Install Wizard: Use this method to quickly upgrade NetWare 3.1*x* or 4.*x* servers to NetWare 5. This is also known as an *in-place upgrade*.

- Upgrade Wizard: Use this method to move data and users from a NetWare 3.*x* server to a new server running NetWare 5. This method is also called a *server-to-server* upgrade or an *across-the-wire migration*.

In practice, you'll usually use the Install Wizard program for upgrades on the same server and the Upgrade Wizard if you are upgrading an existing 3.*x* server to a new server. Let's take a closer look at these methods.

The Install Wizard is used for new installs, as well as upgrades. There is no "custom" or "simple" install option in NetWare 5. The customization is done at the end of the installation process, when you will be able to set a custom server ID, select sub-components, and so on.

Which upgrade method should you use? That depends on whether you want to use the existing hardware, or more importantly, if you *can* use the existing hardware. In most cases, because of the increased resources required by NetWare 5, you will need to do a server-to-server upgrade.

Preparing for the Upgrade

Before performing an upgrade, you must prepare for it. Aside from choosing which method to apply, there are other considerations. If you are upgrading a 4.*x* server, you will need to do the following:

- Upgrade DS.NLM on the 4.*x* servers when installing into an existing tree. The minimum DS.NLM required for Novell 4 servers is 5.15, and for IntranetWare 4.11 servers, the minimum DS.NLM is version 5.99a.

Directory Services · Network Loaded Module

DS.NLM version 6 is now available online at http://support.novell.com. Although the minimum required version is 5.99a, it's generally a good idea to use the newest version of the DS.NLM on the server.

- Upgrade ROLLCALL.NLM. When installing NetWare 5 into an existing tree, the 4.11 servers need to be upgraded to ROLLCALL .NLM version 4.10. (This version is available in NetWare's support pack 5.)

- Schedule a time for the upgrade. Estimate how many hours of downtime you'll need, then double that number. Be sure that all users are informed of the upgrade time, and that they are logged out when you begin.

- Schedule your upgrade at a time of day when you can reach Novell technical support, your Novell reseller, or a qualified consultant (unless you're *really* confident). *Thursday Evening*

- Make a backup. Then hide it, and make another one. Nobody has ever regretted making too many backups.

- Delete all unneeded files from the server.

- If you are upgrading from NetWare 3.1*x*, run the BINDFIX utility twice on the NetWare 3.1*x* server. BINDFIX is similar to NetWare 5's DSREPAIR, and is used to repair problems in the bindery. The first run will repair any problems with the bindery; the second will ensure that you have a backup copy of the bindery files. If BINDFIX reports any errors, consult the NetWare 3.1*x* documentation.

Like Scandisk

- If you are upgrading from an earlier version of NetWare 4.*x*, run the DSREPAIR utility and be sure there are no errors in the NDS database.

- To perform the upgrade using the Upgrade Wizard, you will need to install the latest client software in at least one workstation. This workstation will be used to run the Upgrade Wizard for the upgrade to a new NetWare 5 server.

Copy the CD-ROM drivers to the DOS partitions prior to installing NetWare 5 (unless you plan to boot from the CD-ROM).

Upgrading to an existing tree is the most complicated scenario. You will need to make sure all existing servers are upgraded to the latest NetWare support pack for the operating system you are running. Document the hardware settings on your system and plan for any customization ahead of time. Finally, perform at least two backups of any server being upgraded.

When upgrading an existing tree to NetWare 5, always start with the servers that hold the master replica of the [Root] partition. For more information on installing NetWare 5 in a mixed environment, check the Novell Web site (`http://support.novell.com`) for document #2943193 on installing version 5 servers into a mixed 4.10/4.11 environment.

Choosing a Protocol

192.168.41.x 59

In a move to support standard protocols, be a more open network operating system, and be easily integrated with intranet and Internet resources, NetWare 5 defaults to a *pure IP* installation. If your current NetWare installation is on an IPX-based network, you will have to select IPX on your new server for compatibility with your old system. Whether your plans are to migrate to an IP network or just to access resources in an intranet or Internet environment, you have the option to select various protocol combinations. By selecting both IP and IPX during the upgrade, you'll make it easier for your network to work with both protocols.

For more information on IP/IPX compatibility and migration, consult the IPXTOIP.HTM file on your NetWare 5 CD.

Performing the Upgrade

Now you're ready to begin the actual upgrade process. Before you start, read all of the instructions given below, as well as those given in the NetWare manuals, very carefully. Make sure you have a good backup of all the data and bindery information on the server, and that you have chosen the best upgrade method for your particular needs.

Upgrading with the Install Wizard

This is the easiest method of upgrading. All you have to do is run the install program from the NetWare 5 installation CD-ROM. This method works only for systems that already have NetWare 3.*x* and 4.*x*. All of the previous version's files and settings—users, trustee rights, and all other information—are converted to NetWare 5 format.

Since no data is copied over the network, this is the fastest method of upgrading. In fact, if all goes smoothly, you could be done within half an hour. However, there are some disadvantages to consider:

- Once you've started the upgrade, there's no turning back. If something goes wrong, you'll need to either resolve the problem or reinstall the old NetWare version and restore a backup. If you are upgrading from a version of NetWare 3.*x* supplied on floppy disks, you might be busy for quite a while.

- The server must be brought completely down before you can begin the upgrade, causing user downtime.

- This method won't work if you're replacing the NetWare 3.1*x* server with a new machine, or if you need to change the partition sizes on the hard disk. Be sure your existing machine can handle NetWare 5 before you begin.

Most importantly, keep a backup of the old server, and be sure you know where the disks or CD-ROM for the old NetWare version are, in case you have to revert to the old system.

PROCEDURE 7.1

Upgrading Using Install Wizard

To begin the Install Wizard upgrade, follow these steps:

1. Bring the server down.

2. Insert the NetWare 5 CD-ROM into the drive.

3. Load the drivers to access the CD-ROM drive from DOS. Boot from the CD-ROM or establish a mapped drive to a network drive where the NetWare 5 install files are stored. If you are booting from the CD-ROM, skip to Step 7.

4. Change to the CD-ROM drive letter or mapped network drive.

5. At the DOS prompt, type **INSTALL** and press Enter.

6. You will be led through several installation phases, starting with a DOS phase, and given menus and prompts to choose from. Select the appropriate upgrade option for your system (3.x or 4.x).

7. Select video, mouse, and other drivers (hard drive and LAN cards) as appropriate for your system.

8. You are shown the existing NetWare partition and volumes.

9. Once the volume is mounted and files are copied, you will begin the graphical phase of the installation, which uses the NetWare 5 GUI for Java applications. The first screen looks like this:

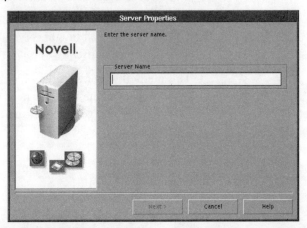

10. Continuing through the graphical phase, you will review installed volumes and drivers and selected protocols, as seen in the following screen:

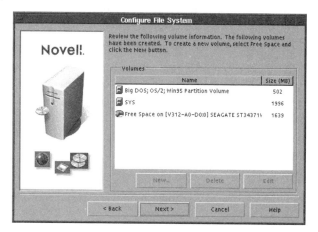

11. The next screen will prompt you to configure NDS. You will be asked for the license disk after the NDS upgrade. Install the license.

12. You will be asked at the next screen to select additional products that you want installed.

13. Once you have completed the upgrade, you will be given the opportunity to customize the installation using a Summary screen like the one shown here:

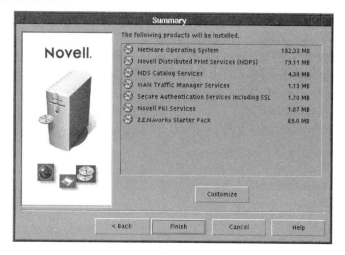

14. Once you have completed the installation, you need to down the server and restart your system.

You still have some things to consider after the upgrade to a NetWare 5 server. Post-upgrade issues will be discussed in the following sections.

After the upgrade, test the server. Be sure all of the old applications work. You will also want to install the new client software on all workstations to take advantage of NDS. Chapter 2 gives instructions for installing this software.

The installation places all of your former bindery objects (users, groups, and so on) in a single Organizational Unit object, which you specify during the installation. This object will be set as the bindery context automatically. If your network is large and complex, you will probably want to reorganize with Organizational Units after you've made sure the upgrade was a success.

Upgrading with the Upgrade Wizard

If you're replacing your old NetWare 3.x server with a new NetWare 5 server, this is the only way to go. With the Upgrade Wizard method, you install a new NetWare 5 server on a new machine, then add it to the network. Running the Upgrade Wizard from a workstation, you copy all data, users, and trustee assignments from the old server to the new server. Once you're sure the new server is operational, you can bring the old server down and start using the new one. This process is illustrated in Figure 7.1.

FIGURE 7.1

Upgrading a 3.x server using the Upgrade Wizard to perform an across-the-wire migration

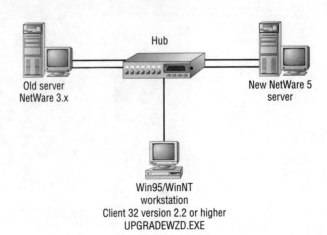

The Upgrade Wizard method is much safer than the Install Wizard method. Here are some additional advantages:

- Since you're keeping the old server intact, you can put it back online at a moment's notice.

- There are always two copies of the data, so there is less risk of data loss (but make a backup anyway).

- You can actually migrate data from multiple volumes on the old server to a single volume on the new NetWare 5 server. In addition, you can migrate multiple NetWare 3.x servers to the same NetWare 5 server. This allows you to easily reconfigure the network for efficiency, if the new server can handle the load.

The Upgrade Wizard has one principal disadvantage: It's *slow*. The process can take anywhere from half an hour to four or five hours. The actual time will depend on the speed of the servers (both the new one *and* the old one) and the speed of communication over the network. Be prepared to spend the better part of a day completing this process—or a night, if the company doesn't want users to spend a day without network access. You'll also need to keep users off the old server during the Upgrade Wizard process. Figure 7.2 illustrates the startup dialog box for the Upgrade Wizard.

FIGURE 7.2

The Upgrade Wizard Startup screen

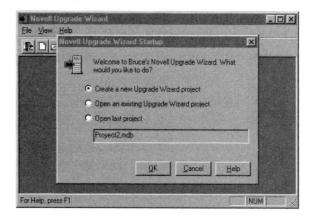

PROCEDURE 7.2

Preparing to Use the Upgrade Wizard

Do the following before you start the Upgrade Wizard:

1. Install Client 32 version 2.2 or higher for Windows 95 and version 4.11 or higher for NT workstations.

2. Install NetWare Administrator on the designated workstation.

3. Install the Novell Upgrade Wizard on the designated workstation. You will find the installation file on the NetWare CD-ROM under this path:

   `\PRODUCTS\UPGRDWZD\UPGRDWZD.EXE`

4. Decide where in the existing tree the NetWare 5 server will be located.

5. You need to log in as the Admin or as a user with supervisor rights to the tree and attach to the NetWare 3.x server as a user with equivalent supervisor rights.

6. Copy updated NLMs on the NetWare 3.x server, which are located on the default installation path for the Upgrade Wizard under this path:

   `C:\Program_Files\Novell\Upgrade\Products\NW3x\`

7. Down the 3.x server and reboot. This will load the new NLMs you copied in Step 7. (It's also possible to reload specific NLMs without downing the server. See the Upgrade Wizard documentation.)

8. Make sure all name space modules are loaded on the NetWare 3.x servers that are in use.

9. Determine what you are going to upgrade—files, binderies, or both. In most cases, you will upgrade the entire server.

10. You will also need to make sure that TSA312 is loaded on the NetWare 3.x server and TSA500 is loaded on the NetWare 5 server.

Completing this procedure allows the Upgrade Wizard to communicate with the 3.x and 5 servers during the upgrade. As you will see in the following sections, the Upgrade Wizard will abort if it can't communicate with both servers.

Once both servers and the workstation are prepared as described in Procedure 7.2, you can launch the Upgrade Wizard from the Start menu of the designated workstation, as shown in Figure 7.3.

FIGURE 7.3

Launching the
Upgrade Wizard

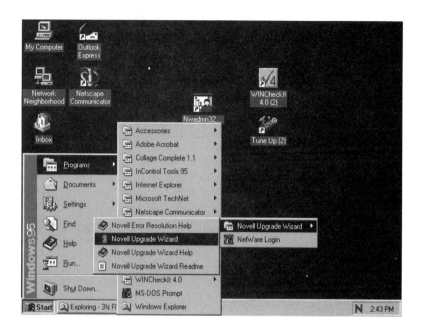

PROCEDURE 7.3

Using the Upgrade Wizard

When using the Upgrade Wizard, you will go through the several phases, described in the following steps:

1. In the project creation phase, you select the source server and target tree. A window screen displays two windowpanes. The left windowpane displays the 3.x servers, and the right windowpane displays the NDS tree, as shown in the following example screen.

PROCEDURE 7.3 (CONTINUED)

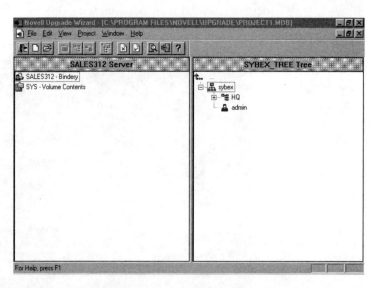

2. In the object selection phase, you select the 3.*x* server volumes and bindery information you are going to migrate and then drag those objects to the intended location in the tree. Drag volumes to the target server and bindery objects to the target context. The two screens that follow show examples of volume and bindery selection.

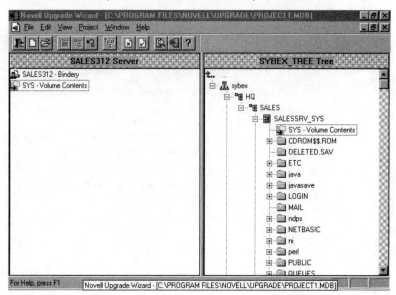

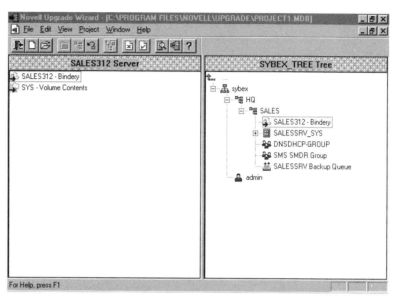

3. Next comes the verify phase, when you verify that the selected objects can migrate to the target locations. Start the process by choosing Project ➣ Verify Project. Any inconsistencies or duplicate objects will be detected in this phase. A sample result of the Verify Project function is shown here:

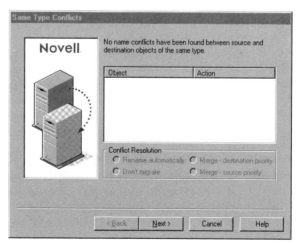

4. The final step is the migration phase, when you launch the actual migration of the objects selected to their target destinations in the tree and new server. Do this by choosing Project ➤ Start Migration. The progress of the migration will be displayed, as shown here:

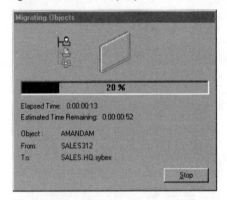

Once you have upgraded and migrated the NetWare 3.*x* server, you need to modify any configuration files that were in place in the old server to comply with NetWare 5 settings and commands.

 Refer to the online documentation for the Upgrade Wizard to learn more about post-upgrade issues.

Review

Using the Install Wizard and Upgrade Wizard utilities provided with NetWare 5, you can easily upgrade an existing NetWare 3.*x* or 4.*x* server to NetWare 5 without losing any data, users, or rights that you have set up.

Hardware Requirements

Depending on the amount of additional hardware you'll need to support a NetWare 5 server, you may wish to consider a new machine. If you keep the existing machine, make sure it meets these guidelines:

- Memory: NetWare 5 requires a minimum of 64MB RAM.

- Disk storage: You should have at least 230MB free (200MB for SYS, 30MB for DOS)

- Processor: Your processor should be a Pentium-based system.

- Other hardware: Other necessities include a high-speed bus, high-speed network and disk controller cards, and a CD-ROM drive.

Upgrade Utilities

The first thing to consider when upgrading is what type of upgrade you will use. There are two methods of upgrading:

- Install Wizard: This method works for NetWare 3.*x* and NetWare 4.*x* servers and is the easiest way to upgrade. Simply run the Install Wizard from the NetWare 5 installation CD-ROM. Users, trustee rights, and all other information are converted to NetWare 5 format.

- Upgrade Wizard: With this method, you install a new NetWare 5 server on a new machine, then add it to the network. You then use the Upgrade Wizard utility to copy all data, users, and trustee assignments from the old server to the new server. Once you're sure the new server is operational, you can bring the old server down and start using the new one.

In practice, you'll usually use the Install Wizard for upgrades to the same server and the Upgrade Wizard if you are upgrading to a new server.

Practice Test Questions

1. Which item is *not* likely to need upgrading when you move to NetWare 5?

A. The processor (CPU)

B. Memory (RAM)

C. Disk storage

D. Network cabling

2. Will a NetWare 5 server require more or less memory than a NetWare 3.*x* server?

A. Less

B. More

C. It requires the same amount of memory

D. It depends on the server

3. Which upgrade is the most likely to require an entirely new machine?

A. Memory

B. Disk storage

C. CPU

D. Network card

4. The minimum disk space for Netware 5 is approximately how much more than required for Netware 3.*x*?

A. 180MB

B. 100MB

C. 75MB

D. 32MB

5. Which component does not affect the performance of the NetWare 5 server?

  A. Memory

  (B) Floppy disk drive

  C. Network card

  D. Disk controller

6. What speed of CPU do you need for NetWare 5?

  (A) Pentium class

  B. 486 or higher

  C. 386 or higher

  D. 286 or higher

7. Which software wizard is used for an across-the-wire migration?

  A. Install Wizard

  (B) Upgrade Wizard

8. If you were going to do a fresh install of NetWare 5 on a new machine, which wizard would you use?

  (A) Install Wizard

  B. Upgrade Wizard

9. All of the following should be considered when planning an upgrade, *except*:

  A. Hardware

  (B) Size of the server room

  C. Software

  D. Preparing users for transition

10. When installing NetWare 5 into an existing tree, you need to do which of the following to the 4.11 servers?

    A. Upgrade the DOS.NLM

    B. Upgrade the ROLLCALL.NLM

    C. Upgrade the NW32.NLM

    D. Upgrade the INSTALL.NLM

11. When should you use DSRepair?

    A. When you want to repair a volume

    B. When upgrading from a version of NetWare 4.*x*

    C. When you find errors in the bindery

    D. When you want to use the BINDFIX

12. NetWare 5 defaults to a pure IP installation:

    A. True

    B. False

13. Which is the fastest method of upgrading?

    A. Install Wizard

    B. Upgrade Wizard

14. Using the Install Wizard involves each of the following *except:*

    A. Upgrading NDS

    B. Installing the license

    C. Selecting disk and network drivers

    D. Unloading the NLMs

15. To prepare a Windows 95 or Windows NT workstation to run the Upgrade Wizard, you need to do all of the following *except:*

   A. Install Client 32 version 2.2 or higher

   B. Update NLMs on the NetWare 3.*x* server

   C. Install NetWare Administrator on the workstation

   D. Reorganize the Organizational Units

16. Which software wizard allows for the safest installation of NetWare 5?

   A. Install Wizard

   B. Upgrade Wizard

17. All of the following are steps in creating an upgrade project, *except:*

   A. Launching the Upgrade Wizard

   B. Selecting protocols that you will need

   C. Choosing a project name

   D. Clicking on Create a New Upgrade Project

18. Which phase is *not* included in the Upgrade Wizard?

   A. Project creation

   B. Migration

   C. Verify

   D. Backup

CHAPTER

8

Using the Server Console

Roadmap

This chapter covers the NetWare server, its components, and the console interface, which is part of the CNE core requirement "NetWare 5 Advanced Administration."

Topics Covered

- What's in a NetWare 5 Server?
- NetWare 5 Console Commands
- Managing Server Configuration Files
- Using the NetWare GUI
- What Is ConsoleOne?
- Remote Access to the Server
- Securing the Server Console

Skills You'll Learn

- Identify NetWare 5 server components and the console interface
- Manage the server console and utilities
- Describe server NLMs and use them
- List and describe server configuration files
- Identify and use the NetWare GUI
- Describe NetWare Java support and enable it
- List ways to access the server remotely
- Protect the server console from intruders

The NetWare 5 server doesn't work like a regular PC. Since it runs NetWare 5, it's a completely different system. None of the DOS commands you might be familiar with work on the server, but there are special commands that do.

In this chapter we'll take a look at the components of a NetWare 5 server and the types of commands and utilities that you can use on the server. In addition, you will learn how to edit the server's configuration files, access the server from a workstation on the network, and prevent unauthorized access to the server.

What's in a NetWare 5 Server?

A NetWare server is any computer that runs the NetWare operating system. NetWare can run on any PC-compatible computer with a Pentium or better processor. You should also have sufficient RAM and disk storage space (discussed in Chapter 7).

The software that runs on the NetWare 5 server includes the core operating system—the kernel—and loadable modules. Let's take a look at each of these in detail.

Operating System Overview

The NetWare operating system provides the basic services of a network. The *kernel* is the core of the operating system. These are some key services provided by the core OS in NetWare 5:

- When multiprocessors are available, the kernel is able to distribute the load intelligently among multiprocessors. This is called *load balancing*.

- Memory protection is provided for NetWare 5. Applications can run in a separate memory area from the kernel, thus protecting the kernel from corrupted applications that could crash it.

- The administrator can prioritize applications through scheduling, ensuring that critical business applications have adequate processor time.

- NetWare 5 supports *preemptive multitasking*. This allows the kernel to take over the processor at any time, improving application system support.

- The Multi-Processor Kernel (MPK) can detect whether your system has one or multiple processors on the motherboard. (The maximum number of processors that NetWare 5 supports for a single system is 32.)

- Virtual memory supports applications that need to address more memory than is available through physical RAM. Additional RAM is created from freed hard disk space, which provides better support for applications and improves their performance. This process is transparent to the application.

These services ensure that the operating system controls system resources, optimizing their use. With multiple processors, the kernel can distribute the workload. The memory management and virtual memory features allow for better application support. All in all, you have a kernel that monitors and allocates resources as necessary to services.

NetWare Loadable Modules (NLMs)

Along with the core OS, the server can run NetWare Loadable Modules, or NLMs. These are programs that run on the NetWare server. The NetWare operating system allows NLMs to integrate fully with the system; what this means is that NLMs and the OS share the same memory and can perform some of the same functions.

Because NLMs provide some of the services of NetWare, it is called a *modular* network operating system. This has some advantages over a fixed system:

- Because NLMs can be loaded and unloaded, you can load only the ones you need. This allows you to save memory for needed services.

- Third parties can also develop NLMs. You can find NLM virus software, backup software, and many other applications.

Many NLMs are provided with NetWare 5 itself; these fit into four categories, described in the following sections.

Disk Drivers

Disk drivers provide an interface to the disk hardware on the server. In order to access the disk, the NetWare core operating system sends messages to the disk driver. Disk devices have two drivers associated with them, which usually have .CDM and .HAM file extensions. The new disk driver standard is called NPA (NetWare Peripheral Architecture). Drivers that use this standard actually consist of two files, with two different extensions:

- A Common Device Module, or CDM, which controls the device

- A Hardware Access Module, or HAM, which controls the host bus adapter

LAN Drivers

Just as disk drivers connect NetWare with the disk drive devices in the server, LAN drivers provide an interface to LAN cards in the server. You can load a module for each card in the server and unload them when they are not needed. LAN driver modules have a .LAN extension.

Name Space Modules

NetWare 5 provides a full set of features that allow access to non-DOS computers, including the Macintosh and OS/2. Both of these operating systems allow long filenames instead of the typical DOS eight-character name. In order to fully support long filenames, NetWare uses *name space modules*. These modules have the extension .NAM.

If you are using an OS that allows extended filenames, you should add the proper name space. Once the name space is added to the volume, the name space NLM is auto-loaded for that OS when you start the server.

Utility NLMs

The final category of NLMs includes utilities that perform a wide variety of functions. These have the extension .NLM. Utility NLMs, some included with NetWare 5 and others that are available separately, provide the following functions:

- Network printing (PSERVER)

- Novell Directory Services (NDS)

- Backup and restore

- Storage Management Services (SMS)

- Remote server console access

- File system

- Authentication
- Network printing
- Security
- Server monitoring
- Power supply monitoring
- Network management
- Communications
- Routing
- Media management
- Java Virtual Machine
- Data migration

NetWare 5 Console Commands

You will use the server console as the interface to access server-based utilities and to manage the server. In this section we will discuss commands and utilities you can use from the server console.

Server Console Commands

You're probably familiar with the DOS prompt—the prompt where you enter a command on a DOS workstation. The NetWare file server console has a similar prompt where you can enter NetWare *console commands*. These can be used to perform a wide variety of functions, maintain the server, and load and unload NLMs.

The file server prompt is referred to as the *colon prompt* because it always ends with a colon. The prompt is usually the name of the file server. For example, if you accessed the console of a server called TRIFFID, the prompt would appear as

TRIFFID:

If you're looking at a screen that doesn't display the colon prompt, you can use the Alt+Esc key combination to switch screens until you see the colon prompt. The next sections explain the available console commands, which you'll need to understand in order to manage the server.

BROADCAST

The BROADCAST command allows you to send a message to users on the network. To use this command, specify a message to be sent and a user to send it to. The keyword ALL can be used to send the message to all users who are currently attached to the network.

The main purpose of BROADCAST is to let users know about conditions that might affect their use of the network. Here's a command that would send a message to all users:

```
BROADCAST "The system will be going down at 9:00" TO ALL
```

The console command SEND serves the same function as BROADCAST.

CLEAR STATION

This command allows you to force a user off the network. Because the powerful MONITOR utility allows you to do the same thing, you may not use this command as often. CLEAR STATION can be used to free a workstation that is hung, but it does not close files correctly, and data may be lost. Use it as a last resort.

CLS

This command simply clears the screen on the file server—useful if you wish to hide the commands you've typed from prying eyes or if you just like to be tidy. Be aware, however, that CLS only clears the screen, not the keyboard buffers. You (or someone you didn't intend) can still use the up-arrow (↑) key to view and execute previous commands.

CONFIG

CONFIG displays a summary of how the server is connected to the network. This command can be useful in determining what network cards are installed and how long the server has been running. The output of the CONFIG command is shown in Figure 8.1.

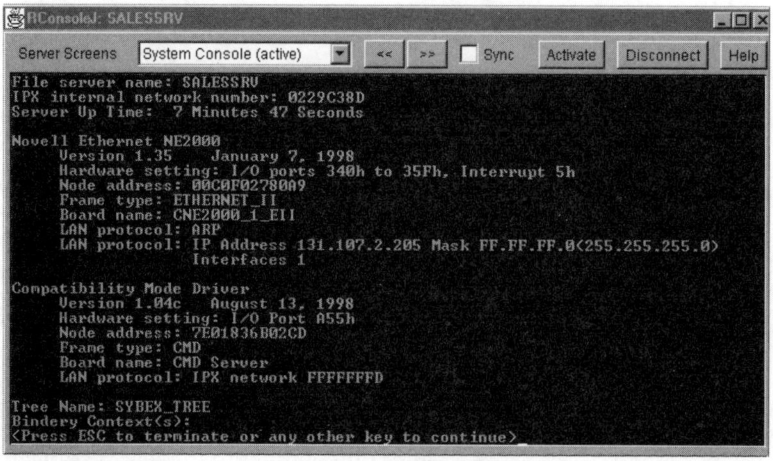

FIGURE 8.1

The CONFIG command displays a summary of the server's configuration.

```
RConsoleJ: SALESSRV                                              _ □ ×

Server Screens   System Console (active)  ▼   << | >> | □ Sync | Activate | Disconnect | Help

File server name: SALESSRV
IPX internal network number: 0229C38D
Server Up Time:   7 Minutes 47 Seconds

Novell Ethernet NE2000
    Version 1.35    January 7, 1998
    Hardware setting: I/O ports 340h to 35Fh, Interrupt 5h
    Node address: 00C0F02780A9
    Frame type: ETHERNET_II
    Board name: CNE2000_1_EII
    LAN protocol: ARP
    LAN protocol: IP Address 131.107.2.205 Mask FF.FF.FF.0(255.255.255.0)
              Interfaces 1

Compatibility Mode Driver
    Version 1.04c   August 13, 1998
    Hardware setting: I/O Port A55h
    Node address: 7E01836B02CD
    Frame type: CMD
    Board name: CMD Server
    LAN protocol: IPX network FFFFFFFD

Tree Name: SYBEX_TREE
Bindery Context(s):
<Press ESC to terminate or any other key to continue>
```

DISABLE LOGIN

The DISABLE LOGIN command prevents users from logging in. It does not affect users who are already logged in, only those who try to log in after you type the command. If you're feeling mischievous, you might enjoy doing this every now and then just to cause a stir; otherwise, the best use for this command is when the server is having a problem and you need to take it down. You can use the DISABLE LOGIN command to stop users from logging in and use CLEAR STATION or the MONITOR utility to take care of those who are already logged in.

DISMOUNT

This command dismounts a volume, making it inaccessible to users. This is the opposite of the MOUNT command. A volume must be mounted before it can be accessed.

DISPLAY NETWORKS

This command displays a list of internal network numbers that NetWare can detect on the server and other servers it is communicating with. This can be useful for configuring communication between servers.

DISPLAY SERVERS

This command displays an internal list table of known servers that can be seen across the network from the current server. (This does not necessarily mean those servers are accessible.) If you are on a multiserver network, this is a way to verify that the network connection is still intact and communication is working. An example of the list of servers is shown in Figure 8.2.

F I G U R E 8.2

The DISPLAY SERVERS command lists known servers.

```
SERVER1:display servers
   MGM_____  0   MGM_____  0   SERVER1    0   SERVER1    0
There are 4 known servers
SERVER1:
```

DOWN

This is probably the most drastic server command—but you'll use it more often than most others. The DOWN command is used to take the server down. If any users are on the network, they are sent a message saying that the server is going down. NetWare then checks for open files; if any files are open, it asks you whether to close all files before bringing the server down. Type **Y** for yes. (If you don't close all files, you could lose data when the server goes down.) Once all the files have been closed, the system dismounts all volumes and exits to the DOS prompt. You should always use the DOWN command before powering off the server so that any data in the cache buffers is written to disk.

HELP

HELP may be the most useful command of all. It allows you to display instructions for any server command. For example, the following command displays a list of options for the BROADCAST command:

    HELP BROADCAST

The output of this HELP command is shown in Figure 8.3.

```
SERVER1:help broadcast
BROADCAST "message" [[TO] username|connection_number] [[and|,] username|
            connection_number...]
 Send a message to all users logged in or attached to a file server or to a
 list of users or connection numbers.
 Example:  broadcast "Please delete unneeded files to free disk space"

SERVER1:
```

LOAD

LOAD is a commonly used command. It allows you to load an NLM both in protected and unprotected memory mode. After the NLM loads, you may see a screen provided by that utility.

A complementary command, UNLOAD, allows you to remove an NLM from memory.

To load NLMs in protected memory, use the LOAD PROTECTED command, which takes the following syntax:

LOAD PROTECTED *NLM name*

In NetWare 5 you can load an NLM without the LOAD command. You can simply type the name of the NLM and then press Enter.

MOUNT

The MOUNT command is used to mount a disk volume. MOUNT is not necessary in most circumstances—NetWare automatically mounts all available volumes when the server starts. You may need to use this command, or its complement DISMOUNT, if you wish to mount or remove a disk volume while the server is up.

MODULES (or M)

MODULES is another command that applies to NLMs. You can simply type the letter M instead of the word MODULES and it will do the same thing. This command lists all of the NLMs that are currently in the server's memory. This is a way to diagnose a problem with software. An example of the output of this command is shown in Figure 8.4.

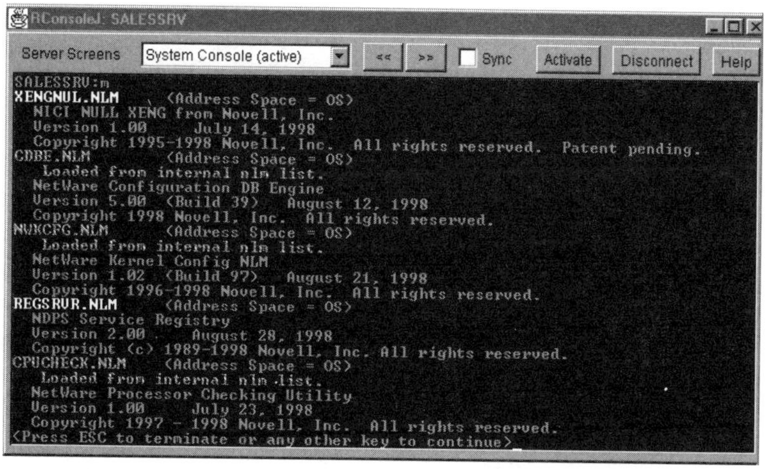

FIGURE 8.4

The MODULES command displays a list of NLMs that are currently in memory.

RESTART SERVER

Use the command RESTART SERVER when you need to bring the server down and back up quickly. You might need to do this if you have installed new software or made a change to the server configuration files.

SET

SET allows you to modify parameters that affect the server's performance. For example, the following command controls whether file compression will be performed:

```
SET File Compression = OFF
```

There are literally hundreds of SET commands for different purposes—worse, you have to spell them correctly. Luckily, the MONITOR command has a Server Parameters option that you can use for viewing and modifying parameters.

TIME

The TIME command returns the date and time; in addition, it tells you the time synchronization status of the server. The output of the TIME command is shown in Figure 8.5.

F I G U R E 8.5

The TIME command displays the server's time and synchroniza-tion information.

UNLOAD

UNLOAD lets you remove an NLM from memory; execution of the NLM stops immediately. Since a poorly written NLM may crash when you unload it, be careful using this command.

NetWare 5 NLM Utilities

Next we'll take a look at some of the most important NLMs included with NetWare 5. These provide a variety of services for managing the server, installing software, and setting parameters.

EDIT

This NLM is useful for editing files on the server, and is similar to a workstation-based editor. You can also create additional .NCF files using the EDIT.NLM utility. To use this utility, type **EDIT** followed by the name of the file, including the path. If you don't specify a path, the SYS:SYSTEM directory on the server will be the assumed path. For example, this command edits the AUTOEXEC.NCF file in the SYSTEM directory:

```
EDIT AUTOEXEC.NCF
```

INETCFG

This utility is loaded at the server console and provides a convenient menu for setting up network boards, protocols, and bindings. It can be used to configure protocols (such as AppleTalk or TCP/IP) on the server, to edit the AUTOEXEC.NCF, and to manage the MPR (Multi-Protocol Router).

When you first start INETCFG, you will be presented with a screen that will ask you to move LOAD and BIND commands out of the AUTOEXEC.NCF file. Click Yes to make modifications to the server's AUTOEXEC.NCF file that are required for routing and using INETCFG options.

The LOAD and BIND commands in the AUTOEXEC.NCF file are moved into a new file, INITSYS.NCF. This is the file that INETCFG makes changes to. This provides a convenient separation of commands and makes the AUTOEXEC.NCF file smaller and easier to manage.

INETCFG also adds the following commands to the AUTOEXEC .NCF file:

- LOAD CONLOG allows server console messages to be logged to a file to help in debugging.

- INITSYS.NCF executes the commands in the INITSYS.NCF file.

- UNLOAD CONLOG deactivates console logging. If this is not done, the log file can become quite large. You can control the maximum size of the log with a SET command. Unloading CONLOG also ensures that the log file is written and will not be lost if the server crashes.

After you have moved commands to the INITSYS.NCF file using INETCFG, you should not add LOAD or BIND commands to the AUTOEXEC.NCF file or try to modify them in this file. You should make the changes using the INETCFG utility. These changes will be written to the INITSYS.NCF file automatically.

NWCONFIG

The NWCONFIG loadable module is used to change installation parameters and to upgrade or install additional software. You can access this module at any time by typing **LOAD NWCONFIG** at the server console. The main NWCONFIG menu is shown in Figure 8.6.

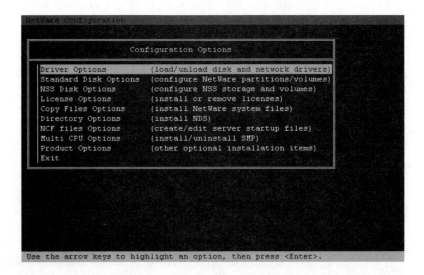

Using the NWCONFIG menu, you can change the following parameters:

Driver Options   Allows you to load and unload network and disk drivers.

Standard Disk Options   Lets you set up partitions and volumes on a disk and use the mirroring features.

NSS Disk Options   Allows you to set up NSS storage and volumes.

License Options   Used to add or change server licenses. The licenses are kept on a license diskette provided with NetWare. You can add additional licenses in any combination or delete installed licenses.

Copy Files Options   Used to copy files into the SYSTEM and PUBLIC directories on a new server.

Directory Options   Allows you to install or remove NDS.

NCF Files Options   Lets you create or edit the AUTOEXEC.NCF and STARTUP.NCF files.

Multi CPU Options   Allows you to install and configure SMP (Symmetric Multiprocessing) for support of multiple-processor computers.

Product Options   Used to add or remove optional products.

NWCONFIG replaces the INSTALL NLM used in previous versions of NetWare.

MONITOR

The MONITOR NLM is probably the most widely used NetWare utility. It is loaded on the server, usually in the AUTOEXEC.NCF file. The MONITOR screen, shown in Figure 8.7, provides a dynamic display of information about the server. If you watch these numbers carefully, you can be sure your server is running smoothly.

FIGURE 8.7

MONITOR provides statistics that let you know how the server is running.

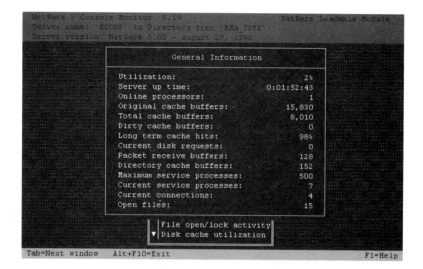

Along with the information displayed at the top of the screen, MONITOR has a menu that you can use to display specific categories of information. Most of these include running statistics that are updated as server conditions change. The MONITOR menu offers these options:

Connections   Lets you see who is logged into the server. You can view specific information about a user in the list. Pressing the Delete key when a user's name is highlighted logs the user out by force.

Storage Devices   Displays information about disks on the server and the volumes on them.

LAN/WAN Information   Displays network numbers, LAN driver information, and statistics for each LAN or WAN.

Loaded Modules   Lists the NLMs loaded on the server.

File Open/Lock Activity   Displays information about open files on a volume.

Disk Cache Utilization   Displays statistics about cache buffers and lets you determine which applications are using them.

Virtual Memory   Lets you view virtual memory parameters.

System Resources   Displays statistics about resources used by each module.

Server Parameters   Allows you to view and change SET parameters. This replaces the SERVMAN utility that existed in previous versions of Net-Ware. You can view the server parameters by selecting that option on the main menu of the MONITOR utility, as shown in Figure 8.8.

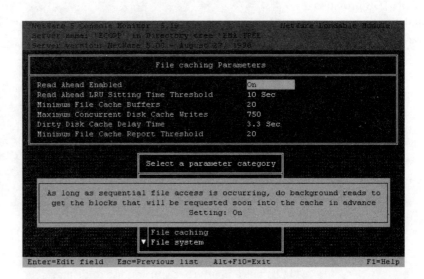

FIGURE 8.8

Selecting the server parameters option from the MONITOR utility main menu

Managing Server Configuration Files

You can customize the NetWare 5 environment, like any other operating system, to suit your company's needs. NetWare 5's configuration files let you set up your network to start services automatically, and parameters can be modified from their default settings at boot time.

Similar to DOS .BAT (batch) files, these configuration files are text files that execute a sequence of commands when they are run. These files have an .NCF extension, which stands for NetWare Command File. The following configuration files are created when you install NetWare 5:

- STARTUP.NCF loads device drivers needed to bring up the server.

- AUTOEXEC.NCF executes commands after the server starts.

Most of the commands described in this chapter can be used within these files, and they can be modified using the EDIT, INETCFG, or NWCONFIG utilities described earlier in this chapter. You can also create additional .NCF files and execute them at startup or use server console commands to perform a task, or various tasks.

You will note a # character in front of some lines in the .NCF files. These characters indicate a remark of some kind. Most such remarks provide documentation for the command in the next line, but some remarks are used to deactivate the command that follows. Removing the remark makes the command active.

We'll take a closer look at AUTOEXEC.NCF and STARTUP.NCF in the following sections.

See the "Utilities Reference Manual" section of the online documentation for more information on the EDIT NLM and creating .NCF files.

The STARTUP.NCF File

The STARTUP.NCF file contains commands that the server processes immediately after it starts. Only certain types of commands can be placed in this file; it is usually used for disk drivers and memory allocation settings. If you need to execute other commands, you should use the AUTOEXEC.NCF file, described in the next section.

NetWare can't access the NetWare partition until a disk driver is loaded, so the STARTUP.NCF file is located on the DOS partition, in the same directory as the SERVER.EXE program. STARTUP.NCF usually contains just one command, which loads a disk driver. Here's an example command for loading the IDE disk driver:

```
LOAD IDEATA.HAM PORT=2f8 INT=A
LOAD IDE.CDM
```

After the disk driver is successfully loaded, NetWare can access the NetWare partition. The SYS volume is automatically mounted after the disk driver loads. The next file, AUTOEXEC.NCF, is located on this volume.

As mentioned before, STARTUP.NCF is created at installation, and it is executed when SERVER.EXE is loaded. If you suspect a problem with the STARTUP.NCF file, you can bypass it by executing SERVER.EXE with the option –NS, such as

```
C:\NWSERVER\SERVER.EXE -NS
```

This will allow you to load each STARTUP.NCF command individually and check for errors. The -NS option will make SERVER.EXE override the STARTUP.NCF and AUTOEXEC.NCF files. Thus when the server finishes booting up, no drivers are loaded and the server prompt is displayed. You can then load each driver individually, allowing you to identify which driver is corrupted.

The AUTOEXEC.NCF File

The AUTOEXEC.NCF file is read when the server starts and after the SYS volume has been mounted. This file is located in the SYS:SYSTEM directory. The commands in this file are executed after those in STARTUP.NCF. You can add just about any of the commands described earlier in this chapter to this file.

The most important uses for this file are to specify the file server's name and internal network number and to load and bind the network drivers. You can also use it to specify the server's time zone and time synchronization information. Here's an example of a simple AUTOEXEC.NCF file:

```
SET TIME ZONE = MST7MDT
SET DAYLIGHT SAVINGS TIME OFFSET = 1:00:00
SET START OF DAYLIGHT SAVINGS TIME = (APRIL SUNDAY FIRST
2:00 AM)
SET END OF DAYLIGHT SAVINGS TIME = (OCTOBER SUNDAY LAST
2:00 AM)
SET DEFAULT TIME SERVER TYPE = SINGLE
SET BINDERY CONTEXT = .OU=GROUP1.O=WEST
FILE SERVER NAME WEST_23
IPX INTERNAL NET 44998
LOAD NE2000 PORT=300 INT=5 FRAME=ETHERNET_802.2
BIND IPX TO NE2000 NET=99
```

The file in this example was created automatically when a server was installed; it includes the basics needed to run the server. You may need to add commands to this file when you install additional software on the server or if you wish to modify settings.

Go to the "NetWare Server Operating System Manual" in the online documentation for more information on .NCF files.

Using the NetWare GUI

NetWare 5 provides a user-friendly environment with the introduction of its graphical user interface (GUI). The NetWare 5 GUI runs on top of X-Windows and acts as an interface to access Java-based applications. The NetWare GUI supports Java applications written to Java AWT (Abstract Windowing Toolkit) and Java Foundation classes. This allows developers to create Java applications independent of the NetWare GUI, allowing the Java applications to run on other interfaces. To support Java applications using the NetWare 5 GUI, your NetWare server platform must meet the following requirements:

- 48MB of RAM

- PS/2 or serial mouse

- VGA or VESA video support

It is highly recommended by Novell that you have no less than 64MB of RAM; 128MB of RAM is preferable. Novell also recommends that you have at least a Pentium 200MHz processor.

Java Applications Supported by NetWare 5

NetWare 5 supports both Java classes and Java applets. Java classes are complete applications and Java applets are short functions that run on a Java-compatible browser. The JAVA.NLM is a part of the JavaSoft Java Virtual Machine (JVM) interpreter for Java classes. Once JAVA.NLM is loaded, you can run Java applications.

Make sure that the long name space module is added on the volume where the Java applications reside.

Java Applications and NetWare 5 GUI

The NetWare 5 GUI is pre-configured with Java programs and applets, but it is not intended to be a full-feature desktop environment.

The NetWare GUI allows you to add other Java programs and configure settings and properties relating to the video card and mouse of the server. The most important Java application is ConsoleOne, which is a management interface. We will discuss this application in greater detail in the next section.

What Is ConsoleOne?

NetWare 5 comes with a server graphical utility, written in Java, which allows you to do basic server and NDS administration tasks. This is called ConsoleOne. Developers can add customized objects to ConsoleOne, allowing vendors to take advantage of it.

You can use ConsoleOne to edit server configuration files, access local and remote server consoles, and manage the local file system and Directory services. It can be started from the server console with either of the following commands:

```
:C1START.NCF
```

or

```
:STARTX.NCF
```

The first command will auto-load the Java Virtual Machine and the GUI before loading ConsoleOne. The second command allows ConsoleOne to be started from the NetWare 5 GUI as a menu option.

When ConsoleOne loads, it will display a toolbar, menu bar, and two windowpanes, as shown in Figure 8.9.

The left windowpane of ConsoleOne allows you to navigate from object to object, and the right windowpane displays the properties and values of the objects. To access properties and values, use the menu bar or toolbar at the top of the display. Your menu and toolbar options will vary depending on the object that is highlighted.

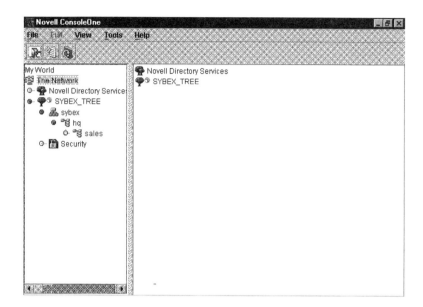

Access Remote or Local Server Consoles

You can access the local server or a remote server console screen through
ConsoleOne using one of two utilities—Console Manager or RConsoleJ. In
order for you to gain access to local or remote servers using these tools, your
target server must have the agent RCONAG6.NLM loaded. The RConsole
RCONAG6 agent can be accessed through a TCP or SPX port configured
during the loading of the agent. The auto-loading of this agent is remarked
out in the AUTOEXEC.NCF by default at installation. The Console Manager's main screen, which can be accessed through ConsoleOne, is shown in
Figure 8.10.

Access NDS Objects

ConsoleOne gives you access to NDS trees, allowing you to manage objects,
delete objects, and create new objects. You can also manage object properties and values. Figure 8.11 shows NDS objects as seen on a ConsoleOne
screen.

FIGURE 8.10

Console Manager

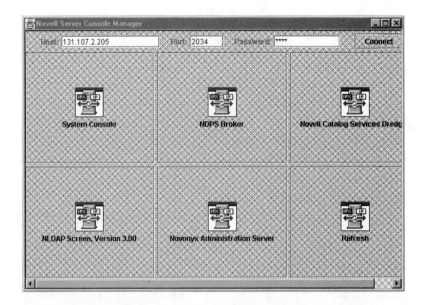

FIGURE 8.11

NDS objects in
ConsoleOne

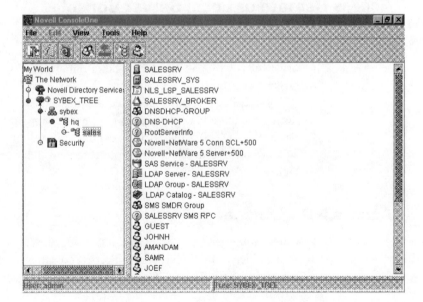

Access Files and Folders

Administrators can add shortcuts to resources on the ConsoleOne interface, allowing you to access files, folders, and applets more quickly. A *shortcut* is a text file that specifies a file, folder, or applet to be added to the ConsoleOne interface.

By default ConsoleOne includes several shortcuts. You can access frequently used configuration files by going to MyServer ➤ Configuration Files object. You will then be able to select the files you want to view.

Remote Access to the Server

In most cases, network managers will place servers in secure locations that provide restricted access, to protect the server. This makes it difficult to be in front of the server when you want to execute administrative tasks, but you can still do the work if you have remote access.

NetWare 5 provides remote access capabilities, and in this section you will learn how to identify and use them.

RConsoleJ or RConsole

You can use RConsoleJ (written in Java) or the traditional RConsole to access the server console from a workstation. To access a target server's console from a workstation, you have to prepare the server and the workstation for remote access, as follows:

1. To use RConsoleJ on the workstation, it is preferable to have TCP/IP as your default protocol in the server and workstation.

2. Load RCONAG6.NLM on the target server.

3. On the workstation, execute this command: SYS:PUBLIC\RCONJ.EXE.

In addition to the command line, you can also run RConsoleJ for NetWare Administrator using the menu bar. Go to Tools ➤ Pure IP Remote Console. You will then have text access to the target server's console.

To use RConsole, you will have to determine if you are going to access the server via a network connection over IPX or through a modem. If you are going to use a modem, follow the steps in Procedure 8.1.

Accessing the Server with a Modem

To access the server console with a modem, do the following on the target server:

1. Install a modem on the server and the workstation. Remember to record the phone number for both locations.

2. On the target server console, load REMOTE.NLM. You will be prompted for a password.

3. Load AIO.NLM and RS232.NLM. These NLMs initiate communications with the server and allow access to REMOTE.NLM.

If you will be accessing the server console using a LAN connection over IPX, do the steps in Procedure 8.2.

Using RConsole over a LAN Connection

To use RConsole over a LAN connection, do the following on the target server:

1. Load REMOTE.NLM. You will be prompted for a password.

2. Load RSPX.NLM. This sets communication to REMOTE.NLM over IPX/SPX.

3. Once the server is configured, you can run RCONSOLE.EXE from the workstation.

4. Execute RCONSOLE.EXE from the command line:

   SYS:PUBLIC\RCONSOLE.EXE

5. From NetWare Administrator, select Tools ➤ RConsole.

6. A DOS text utility window appears on the screen with two menu options.

7. If you are connecting to the server via a modem, select ASYNC. If you are connecting via a LAN connection, select SPX.

PROCEDURE 8.2 (CONTINUED)

8. A screen showing available servers is displayed. Select the server you want to access.

9. The server's console pops up on your monitor. You can now perform any console function, including using a command line or an NLM utility.

RConsole Shortcut Keys

When running RConsole from your workstation, you can use the following shortcuts and keys to navigate the screens and activate the RConsole menu screen:

- Pressing Alt+F1 will activate the Options menu.

- Pressing Alt+F2 will display an Exit menu option screen.

- Press Alt+F3 or F4 and you will change console screens.

- Press Alt+F5 and the workstation's network and MAC address will appear.

- When you invoke the Options menu by pressing Alt+F1, you have the option to go back to the workstation's operating system, exiting temporarily from the remote session. Pressing Esc returns you to the remote session.

Securing the Server Console

Securing the network from unauthorized access is a key task for the network administrator. You have learned about the many utilities and services NetWare provides to secure the Directory, software, and file systems on a NetWare 5 server and its clients. One aspect of network security that is often overlooked is the physical security of the server itself. A server that is accessible to the public is very vulnerable to damage.

Consider locking up the server in a cabinet specially designed for servers and then locking the cabinet in a room with restricted access. Locking up the server keeps unauthorized individuals from playing with the server console. Other steps you can take to protect your network are covered in the following sections.

SCRSAVER.NLM

You can further protect the server console by entering **SECURE CONSOLE** on the console screen. This command disables NLM loading from any directory other than SYS:SYSTEM, and it prevents intruders from changing the server time and date.

NetWare 5 further restricts access to the console screen with the use of a screen saver. You can run SCRSAVER.NLM from the server console and a screen saver appears. To return to the console screen, just press any key on the keyboard to display a prompt for a username and password. Only authorized users can access the server console.

Password Encryption

The console agents RCONAG6.NLM and REMOTE.NLM require that a password be assigned when you load them. You can generate encrypted passwords using RCONAG6.NLM or REMOTE.NLM, further restricting access to the server console via a workstation. To add password encryption to RCONAG6.NLM, follow Procedure 8.3.

PROCEDURE 8.3

Generating Encrypted Passwords with RCONAG6.NLM

To generate an encrypted password with RCONAG6.NLM, do the following:

1. From the server console, load

   :RCONAG6 ENCRYPT

2. You are asked for a password.

3. Provide a TCP port number.

4. Provide an SPX port number.

5. The command you will use with the encrypted password is displayed, and you are asked if you want to place the command line in the following file:

   SYS: \SYSTEM\LDRCONAG.NCF

6. Click Yes if you want to use the file. Use this .NCF file to load RCONAG6 with an encrypted password.

PROCEDURE 8.3 (CONTINUED)

7. Enter the following command to use an encrypted password from the server console (of course, you will replace the words *encrypted password* with your encrypted password):

   `:RCONAG6 -E encrypted password TCP port SPX port`

8. To view the help file, execute this command:

   `:RCONAG6 /?`

   You have now set up an encrypted password to use with RCONAG6, adding more security to your server console.

Physical security is, by far, the most important factor in network security. If someone can walk up and access your file server without being watched, he or she can do damage no matter how secure your network is.

Review

The NetWare 5 server doesn't work like a regular PC. Since it runs NetWare 5, it's a completely different system. A NetWare server is any computer that runs the NetWare operating system. NetWare can run on any PC-compatible computer with a Pentium or better processor plus sufficient RAM and disk storage space.

The software that runs on the NetWare 5 server includes the operating system—NetWare itself—and loadable modules. The following services are provided by the operating system itself, the core operating system:

- Multi-Processor Kernel (MPK)

- Memory protection for the kernel

- Virtual memory for application support

- Load balancing between multiple processors

- Scheduling processor time for applications

- Preemption multitasking

Along with the core OS, the server can run NetWare Loadable Modules, or NLMs. NLMs are programs that run on the NetWare server. The NetWare operating system allows NLMs to integrate fully with the system. What this means is that NLMs and the OS share the same memory and can perform some of the same functions.

These are a few types of NLMs:

- Disk drivers to interface with disk drives

- LAN drivers to interface with LAN cards

- Name space modules to provide extended file-naming services

- Utilities to perform server management functions

The NetWare file server console has a prompt where you can enter NetWare console commands. These can be used to perform a wide variety of functions, maintain the server, and load and unload NLMs. The file server prompt is referred to as the colon prompt, because it always ends with a colon. If a screen that doesn't display the colon prompt is visible, you can press Alt+Esc to switch screens until you see the colon prompt.

Here are some console commands you'll use frequently:

- BROADCAST for sending messages to users

- CLEAR STATION for disconnecting a user

- CLS to clear the server's screen

- CONFIG to display configuration information

- DISABLE LOGIN to prevent user logins

- DISPLAY NETWORKS to display available networks

- DISPLAY SERVERS to display available servers

- HELP to display instructions

- LOAD and UNLOAD to control NLMs

- MODULES to display module information

- MOUNT and DISMOUNT to control disk volumes

- RESTART SERVER to bring the server back up

- SET to change server parameters

- TIME to display time and synchronization information

The final category of server utilities are NLMs. The following NLMs were introduced in this chapter:

- NWCONFIG, for installing and configuring services and products

- INETCFG, for installing LAN cards, configuring the multiprotocol router, and modifying AUTOEXEC.NCF

- MONITOR, for watching file system statistics

The server uses two configuration files that automate the loading of services and applications and set server parameters. These are AUTOEXEC.NCF and STARTUP.NCF. You can use NWCONFIG, INETCFG, or the EDIT NLM to modify these two files.

NetWare 5 incorporates a GUI based on X-Windows. Java applications are supported through the NetWare 5 GUI, and are written to support it. The NetWare 5 GUI includes several Java applications and you can add others.

ConsoleOne, a Java-based application, provides a GUI interface to manage NetWare servers, files and directories, configuration files, and NDS directories. This is a new feature for NetWare 5. You should anticipate heavier processor and memory loads when using this utility.

NetWare 5 provides remote access to the server console through the RConsole and RConsoleJ utilities. These provide you with the capability to manage servers from a central location.

You should include the physical security of your server as part of your overall security strategy. NetWare provides you with utilities to secure the server console, but you should also consider hooking up the server in a secure, restricted location.

CNE Practice Test Questions

1. Commands you can use at the server console include:

   A. DOS commands

   B. NLMs and console commands

   C. NLMs only

   D. DOS or NLM commands

2. The kernel provides all of the following services *except:*

   A. Load balancing for multiple operating systems

   B. Scheduling processor time for applications

   C. Memory protection for the kernel

   D. Multi-Processor Kernel (MPK)

3. NLMs come from:

   A. Novell

   B. Third parties

   C. Both of the above

   D. None of the above

4. The two parts of an NPA disk driver are:

   A. NPA and CDA

   B. HAM and CAM

   C. HAM and CDM

   D. NPA and HDM

5. LAN driver modules have the extension:

   A. .NLM

   B. .DRV

   C. .LAN

   D. .MOD

6. The command to display configuration information is:

   A. DISPLAY CONFIG

   B. MODULES

   C. CONFIG

   D. VERSION

7. The command used to prevent logins is:

  A. SET LOGIN = NO

  B. DISABLE LOGIN

  C. LOGIN OFF

  D. SECURE CONSOLE

8. The command needed to bring down the server is:

  A. DOWN

  B. RESTART

  C. DISMOUNT

  D. UNLOAD

9. The key or key combination used to switch screens in RCONSOLE is:

  A. F3 or F4

  B. Alt+Esc

  C. Ctrl+Esc

  D. Alt+F3 and Alt+F4

10. The two modules you must load to enable remote access with RConsole are:

  A. REMOTE and MONITOR

  B. REMOTE and ACCESS

  C. RSPX and REMOTE

  D. RSPX and RCONSOLE

11. Utility NLMs can provide the following functions:

  A. Server monitoring

  B. Upgrading system files

  C. Network management

  D. A, B, and C

  E. B and C

  F. A and C

12. Which are the two configuration files installed with NetWare 5?

   A. STARTUP.NCF and AUTOEXEC.NCF

   B. RConsoleJ and RConsole

   C. NWCONFIG and CONFIG

   D. All of the above

   E. None of the above

13. What new server console interface provides a user-friendly environment in NetWare 5?

   A. Java applets

   B. NetWare 5 GUI

   C. Java AWT

   D. Java Foundation classes

14. Which of these describes ConsoleOne?

   A. It is a server graphical utility.

   B. It allows you to do basic server and NDS administration.

   C. Its main screen has a toolbar, a menu bar, and two windowpanes.

   D. You can use it to edit server configuration files.

   E. All of the above

   F. A, C, and D

15. What is the *new* feature in NetWare 5 to lock the server console?

   A. SECURE CONSOLE

   B. LOCK CONSOLE

   C. LOCK SCREEN

   D. SCRSAVER.NLM

16. Which NLMs can generate encrypted passwords?

   A. PASSWORD.NLM and NETWORK.NLM

   B. RCONAG6.NLM and REMOTE.NLM

   C. RSPX.NLM and REMOTE.NLM

   D. EDIT and NWCONFIG

17. When you type the M command at the server console, it does which of the following?

   A. Loads modules currently loaded

   B. Unloads modules currently loaded

   C. Lists modules currently loaded

   D. Removes modules from the server's memory

18. NWCONFIG is used to do which of the following?

   A. Configure NWADMIN

   B. Install and configure SMP

   C. Configure NetWare NDS

   D. None of the above

19. What options does MONITOR offer?

   A. Disk cache utilization

   B. Storage devices

   C. LAN/WAN information

   D. File open/lock activity

   E. All of the above

   F. None of the above

CHAPTER

9

Queue-Based Printing

Roadmap

This chapter covers components and administration of queue-based printing, which is part of the CNE core requirement "NetWare 5 Advanced Administration."

Topics Covered

- Components of NetWare 5 Queue-Based Printing

- Managing Printing with NetWare Administrator

- Creating Forms and Configuring Print Jobs with NetWare Administrator

Skills You'll Learn

- List and describe the components of queue-based printing

- Set up and configure components of queue-based printing with NetWare Administrator

- Set up printing administrators to regulate who can print, manage print jobs, and manage the print server

- Create forms and configure your print jobs

P rinting is one of the fundamental services a network provides. Although NDPS (discussed in Chapter 6) is NetWare's preferred printing method, NetWare continues to support queue-based printing for backward compatibility purposes. Queue-based printing services allow you to print to a network printer, whether it's attached to the server or to a workstation. NetWare manages print jobs and sends them to the printer one at a time, in an orderly manner. The next section introduces the components of the NetWare 5 queue-based printing services.

Components of NetWare 5 Queue-Based Printing

Several components interact to provide NetWare 5 queue-based printing services: print servers, print queues, and printers. You can create these objects under NDS and maintain them from within the NetWare Administrator (NWADMN32) utility. Additional components include the CAPTURE utility and the port driver (NPTWIN95.EXE, NPRINTER .EXE, or NPRINTER.NLM), which complete the interface between the workstation and the printer. The components of NetWare 5 queue-based printing are shown in Figure 9.1 and are described in the following sections.

FIGURE 9.1

Several components interact to provide network printing services.

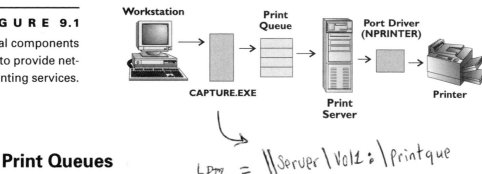

Print Queues

In order to print to a printer on the network, you must first send the data to a *print queue*. The print queue stores each set of data, or *print job*, that it receives. The jobs are then sent, one at a time, to the print server (described next). Print queues serve two main purposes:

- To allow you to continue working while the printer prints. Your workstation quickly sends the job to the print queue, and printing is performed by NetWare, without using your workstation.

- To allow multi-user printing. Many users can add jobs to the queue, and they are printed in the order received. Each print job is completed before another job starts.

NetWare 5 stores all print queue information in the properties of the Print Queue object. This includes identification information for the print queue and information for each of the print jobs. The print jobs themselves are stored on a file server volume. The process of selecting a volume is described later in this chapter.

Print Servers

The *print server* accepts print jobs from print queues and sends them to the appropriate printer. In NetWare 3.1*x*, print servers were limited to 16 printers; in NetWare 4 this limit was increased to 256. This allows you to easily use a single print server for the entire network.

You create the Print Server object in NDS. The properties of the Print Server object provide identification information and define the list of printers the server can send jobs to.

Along with the NDS object, you must run the print server software (PSERVER.NLM) on a server. This is the program that actually controls the printing process.

Printers

You must create a Printer object to represent each network printer. The properties of the Printer object identify the printer and list the print queues that the printer accepts jobs from. Other properties define the type of printer and how it is accessed. Printers can be attached to a server, to a workstation, or directly to the network. Printer types are described in the following sections.

Printers Attached to the Server

Printers can be connected directly to a printer port on a server. This is the simplest method to configure and use. Before you configure a printer in this way, note the following:

- You must have an available port (serial or parallel) on the server for each printer. A typical machine has 1 to 3 parallel ports and 2 serial ports.

- The printer usually needs to be located near the server. The limit for an IEEE 1284 parallel printer cable is 25 feet. Serial devices have a range of 50 feet.

- Unlike NetWare 3.1*x*, in NetWare 5 you do not need to load PSERVER .NLM on the same server the printer is attached to. However, you must run NPRINTER.NLM to drive the printer. NPRINTER.NLM is described later in this section.

Remote (Workstation) Printers

Printers can also be attached to workstations. These printers are referred to as workstation printers or *remote printers*. The print server sends each job to the workstation, and the workstation sends it to the printer. Workstation printers can run under DOS, Windows 3.1, Windows 95/98, and Windows NT. We'll look at the specifics for DOS, Windows 3.1, and Windows 95 in the following sections. If you're running Windows 98 or Windows NT, we recommend using the default NDPS printing system, covered in Chapter 6.

Configuring DOS Workstation Printers   In order to use a workstation printer on a DOS or Windows 3.1 workstation, you run the NPRINTER.EXE program on the workstation. This replaces the RPRINTER program used in NetWare 3.1*x*. NPRINTER is faster and much more reliable than RPRINTER. You can run up to seven copies of NPRINTER on your workstation to drive multiple printers. A workstation can have a maximum of three parallel and four serial printers.

Since NPRINTER is a TSR (terminate and stay resident) program, you can continue to use the workstation while the network printers are being used. You must leave the workstation turned on in order to make the printer available to network users. Remote printing has the following disadvantages:

- The workstation can be slowed down if a printer is used heavily or if multiple printers are supported.

- If the workstation crashes or is turned off, the printer is unavailable to network users.

- A small amount of memory (approximately 10KB) is used for each remote printer on the workstation.

You can run Windows 3.1 on a workstation that supports remote printers. In order to do this, you must run NPRINTER for each printer before starting Windows. NPRINTER is more reliable under Windows than RPRINTER, but some Windows applications can cause instability even with NPRINTER.

To use NPRINTER, specify the printer name on the command line. For example, the following command might be used to remotely attach the Check_Printer Printer object:

```
NPRINTER .Check_Printer.ABC_INC
```

WARNING   If you use a workstation printer as a network printer, be sure to use the CAPTURE command on the workstation to send jobs to the queue. If the user prints to the printer locally, network print jobs can be interrupted, and the workstation may crash.

Configuring Windows 95 Workstation Printers   Windows 95 includes a utility called NPRINTER Manager that makes it convenient to set up a workstation printer. Use Procedure 9.1 to set up and configure a workstation printer with Windows 95.

PROCEDURE 9.1

Configuring Windows 95 Workstation Printers

Follow these steps to set up a remote printer:

1. Run the NPRINTER Manager file, NPTWIN95.EXE, located in the SYS:PUBLIC\WIN95 directory.

2. Select an NDS Printer object for the printer. You can also select a bindery-based printer.

3. Select the Activate When NPRINTER Manager Loads option to automatically start the printer each time you load NPRINTER Manager; otherwise, you will have to specify the printer each time.

4. The printer is now active. You must leave NPRINTER Manager running to drive the printer.

In order to run NPRINTER Manager automatically when you start Windows 95, you may wish to add NPTWIN95.EXE to the Programs ➤ StartUp folder on the Start menu.

Directly Connected Network Printers

A final type of printer is attached directly to the network. This capability is built into many high-end printers, and many others can be attached to the network with an add-on card. Hardware devices are also available to connect the network to one or more printers. Directly connected printers are a very efficient way to manage printing.

Directly connected printers can be configured in one of two modes:

- In *remote mode,* the printer acts as a remote (workstation) printer. Instead of running NPRINTER.EXE on a workstation, the hardware device handles these functions. This configuration is better than having a workstation printer, because this way no workstation is slowed by printing.

- In *queue server mode,* the printer acts as a separate print server. Jobs are sent directly from the print queue to the printer. This may be the best arrangement for some networks, because the load on the server is insignificant.

To determine which mode to use, consult the documentation for your printer or network interface. Most network printers also include an installation program that can create the needed bindery or NDS objects and configure the printer.

Legacy printers (not NDS-aware) that were developed for NetWare 3.1*x* can be used on NetWare 5 networks with no problems.

Redirecting Printers with CAPTURE

Some applications (such as WordPerfect for DOS) support network printing directly. You can select a network queue to print to rather than a local printer. However, many applications do not provide this support. You can use the CAPTURE command-line utility to print to network printers from these applications.

CAPTURE is a TSR (terminate and stay resident) program that allows you to *redirect* printing to a network printer. You specify a local printer port (usually LPT1, LPT2, or LPT3) with the CAPTURE command. After the CAPTURE command is executed, any printing that your workstation sends to this port is redirected to the network queue you specified.

A basic CAPTURE command specifies the local port to redirect and the network queue to redirect to. The following command redirects the workstation's LPT1 port to a print queue called WEST41_Q:

```
CAPTURE /L=1 /Q=WEST41_Q
```

NetWare 5 allows you to specify a printer name without knowing which queue it is attached to. This command captures the LPT2 port to a printer called PRINTER5:

```
CAPTURE /L=2 /P=PRINTER5
```

Even if you specify a printer to capture to, a print queue is used. NetWare finds the first available print queue serviced by the printer you specify. Since NetWare must search for a queue, you can improve performance by specifying the queue name rather than the printer name.

You can use other CAPTURE options to control the printing process. Use forward slashes (/) or spaces to separate the parameters. This list summarizes the CAPTURE options:

AU (Autoendcap) or NA (No Autoendcap)   Allows jobs to be sent as soon as the application exits or signals that it is finished sending the job to the printer. Not all applications support this option. Autoendcap is enabled by default. You can use the NA option to deactivate it.

B=*text* (Banner) or NB (No Banner)   Specifies whether a banner is printed before the job. The *banner* is a page that describes the job and the user that sent it and can be used to send printouts to the appropriate person. If you specify the B option, follow it with text to be included at the bottom of the banner, such as B=ACCOUNTING.

C=*number* (Copies)   Specifies the number of copies to be printed.

CR=*filename* (Create file)   Allows you to redirect printing to a file instead of a printer. The file can later be sent to a printer.

D (Details)   Displays details about a captured port. Use the L option (described below) to specify the port.

EC (End Capture)   Ends capturing to the port. This option replaces the ENDCAP command used in previous versions of NetWare. Any job that is currently being sent is completed. There are three options for EC:

- EC L=*port* ends capturing for the specified port. If no port is specified, LPT1 is assumed.

- EC ALL ends capturing for all ports.

- ECCA ends capturing and cancels the current job. Nothing is sent to the print queue.

F=*number or name* (Form)   Allows you to specify a form to be used with print jobs. Forms are defined with the NetWare Administrator and are described later in this chapter.

FF (Form Feed) or NFF (No Form Feed)   Specifies whether a *form feed* character is sent to the printer after the print job is completed. This option ensures that printing for the next job starts at the top of a page.

Most applications send a form feed by default. Using the FF option unnecessarily results in blank pages being printed between jobs.

/? or /H (Help)   Displays a list of options for the CAPTURE command.

HOLD (Hold job)   Specifies that print jobs are to be *held* in the print queue and not printed. You can later release the jobs using NWADMN32.

J=*name* (Specify job)   Selects a *print job configuration* to be used. A print job configuration contains options similar to CAPTURE options, and its name can be used with no other options. You can create print job configurations using the NWADMN32.

K (Keep)   Tells CAPTURE to keep your print job even if the capture is not ended correctly. A capture may not end correctly if your workstation is disconnected or turned off while a job is being printed. Without this option, the job is discarded when this happens. With the Keep option, the job is sent to the queue.

L=*number* or LPT*n* (Local port)   Specifies the logical port number to redirect to the queue. You can use numbers from 1 to 9, as described below. The options L=2 and LPT2 both select the LPT2 port for redirection.

NAM=*name* (Banner name)   Specifies a name to be included at the top of the banner. This defaults to the user's login name. This option also activates the Banner option.

NOTI (Notify) or NNOTI (No Notify)   Specifies whether users are notified when the print job has finished printing. If notify is enabled, users receive a message on their screen or in a pop-up window (under Windows) when the job has completed.

P=*name* (Printer) or Q=*name* (Queue)   Specifies a printer or queue for the port to be redirected to. Only one of these options can be used.

S=*name* (Server)   Specifies a server name for the queue. This is used for bindery-based queues only.

SH (Show)   Displays the current CAPTURE parameters for each port.

T=*number* (**Tab spacing**) or **NT** (**No tab conversion**)   Specifies the number of spaces to use in place of tab characters in the document. Use the NT option if print jobs don't require conversion.

TI=*number* (**Timeout**)   Specifies a timeout in seconds to be used to end a print job. If the specified number of seconds elapses with no data having been sent to the printer, the job is considered finished and sent to the print queue.

When you use CAPTURE, data is sent to a print job in the specified queue. There are three ways that you can end the job and send it to the printer:

- Use the EC option to discontinue CAPTURE and send the job to the printer.

- Set a timeout with the TI option. If the specified number of seconds elapses with no printing having occurred, NetWare assumes that the job is finished and sends it. The port remains captured for future jobs.

- Set the AU (Autoendcap) option. This allows NetWare to detect when an application exits or is finished with the printer. If the application supports it, this option is the fastest method. If you set both the AU and Timeout options, the Timeout covers the applications that don't support the AU option.

The Port Driver (NPRINTER)

Before data is sent to the printer, it is sent to the *port driver*. The port driver receives data from the print server and transmits it to the printer. NPRINTER can be run in one of three ways:

- For a printer connected to a server, load NPRINTER.NLM on the server. If the printer is attached to the same server that the print server (PSERVER.NLM) is running on, NPRINTER is loaded automatically for the printer. You can also attach the printer to a different server and load NPRINTER.NLM manually on that server.

- For remote (workstation) printers, run the NPRINTER.EXE program, described earlier in this chapter.

- With directly connected network printers, you do not need to run NPRINTER. The NPRINTER software is built into the printer or interface.

Managing Printing with NetWare Administrator

Because printing services have been integrated into NDS, you can use the NetWare Administrator utility to manage all aspects of printing. This includes creating the objects required for printing, configuring them, and managing print jobs in print queues.

Creating Objects

You can use NetWare Administrator to create the objects required for printing. The properties of these objects control how they interact and define the devices used for printing. In order to enable printing with NDS, you must create a Print Server object and at least one Printer and Print Queue object.

These objects can be created anywhere in the Directory tree. However, in order to provide easy access, it is best to create all of the objects in the context where the users who use the printers are located, or as close to it as possible. You can create the objects in any order.

Creating the Print Server

You must create a Print Server object for each server that runs PSERVER.NLM and for directly connected network printers that use queue server mode. Since each print server can provide access for up to 256 printers, you typically need only one Print Server object for the entire network. Refer to Procedure 9.2 for instructions on making Print Server objects.

PROCEDURE 9.2

Creating a Print Server Object

To create a Print Server object, follow these steps:

1. Start NetWare Administrator and navigate through the Directory tree to the desired context. Highlight the context in which you want to create the Print Server object.

2. Right-click and select Create from the Object menu.

3. Select Print Server as the type of object.

PROCEDURE 9.2 (CONTINUED)

4. Enter the Print Server name in the Create Print Server dialog box, shown in the screen below. The Print Server object is now ready for use. You can change its properties by selecting Details from the Object menu.

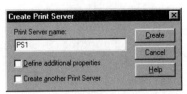

The properties of the Print Server object are used to identify the print server and to specify parameters. Several pages (categories) of properties are available. These are described in the sections below.

Identification This page specifies information about the Print Server object. The Identification information includes the name, network address, status, and other information. You enter this information in the Identification property page, which is shown in Figure 9.2. Most of these properties are optional. You can use the Change Password button to choose a password for the print server; this password will be required when PSERVER.NLM is loaded at the server. The status of the print server is also shown in the Identification properties page. If the print server is running, you can disable it with the Unload button.

Assignments This page lists the printers that have been assigned to the server. After you create the Printer object, you can use the Add button to add the printer to the list. Only printers in this list can receive jobs from the print server. The Assignments property page is shown in Figure 9.3.

Users On this page, you specify which users can send jobs to printers in the print server. You can add specific users to this list or choose groups or container objects to provide access to multiple users.

Operator You can use this page to specify one or more users who have Operator privileges on the print server. These users can unload the print server and perform other control functions. This list can include individual users; you can also use an Organizational Role object here to assign a print server operator.

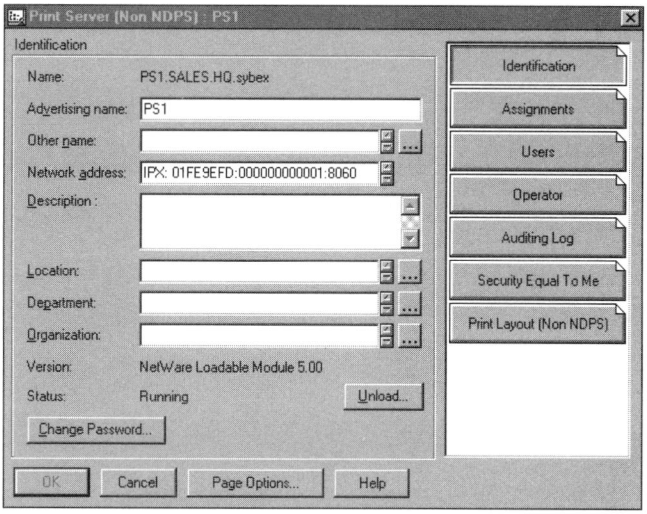

FIGURE 9.2

The Identification property page specifies information about the Print Server object.

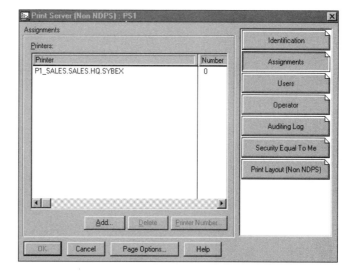

FIGURE 9.3

The Assignments property page lists the printers that have been assigned to the print server.

Auditing Log   This page, shown in Figure 9.4, provides a powerful auditing feature for printing. If this is enabled, a log is maintained of the print server's activities. Each print job is added to the log, and the information in the log specifies whether printing was successful, which printer the job went to, and how long it took to print the job. To activate the auditing feature, use the Enable Auditing button. The text on this button changes to Disable Auditing, and then the button can be used to stop the auditing process.

F I G U R E 9.4

The Auditing Log page allows you to audit printing.

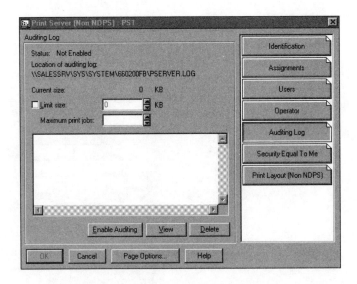

Print Layout (Non NDPS)   The Print Layout page allows you to view the configuration of the print server graphically. This is a powerful feature that you can use to determine how printing has been configured and to troubleshoot printing problems. The Print Layout property page is shown in Figure 9.5.

F I G U R E 9.5

The Print Layout property page provides an illustration of how the components of printing interact.

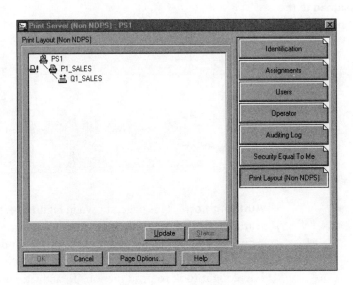

The print server, print queues, and printers are shown with lines between them to define their relationship. You can watch for two indicators of printer problems:

- An icon with a red exclamation mark is displayed to the left of objects that are not functioning. This means that the print server is not running, the printer is not connected, or the print queue is not accepting jobs.

- A dashed line is displayed instead of a solid line if the connection is a temporary one that will not be reestablished the next time the print server is loaded.

Creating Print Queues

You must create at least one print queue for each non-NDPS printer on the network. Multiple printers can also service print queues, and multiple queues can be routed to a single printer. In addition to NetWare 5 print queues, you can define a Print Queue object that sends print jobs to a queue on a bindery-based server. This makes it easy to integrate bindery and NDS printing. Refer to Procedure 9.3 for details on setting up a Print Queue object.

PROCEDURE 9.3

Creating a Print Queue Object

To create a Print Queue object, follow these steps:

1. Start NetWare Administrator and navigate through the Directory tree to the desired context. Highlight the context in which to create the print queue. For ease of access, it should be located in the same context as the users who use this queue.

2. Go to Object ➣ Create.

3. Select Print Queue as the type of object to create. You will be presented with the Create Print Queue dialog box, shown here:

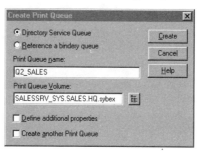

4. Select whether this print queue is an NDS queue or if it will reference a bindery queue.

5. Select a name for the print queue. For bindery queues, enter the name as it appears on the bindery server.

6. Select a volume to store print queue entries on. For NDS queues, this can be any volume; for bindery queues, this should be the SYS volume on the bindery server.

7. Click the Create button. You've now created a Print Queue object with your desired settings.

After the Print Queue object is created, highlight it and select Details from the Object menu to define its properties. The properties are discussed in the sections below.

Identifying the Print Queue   The Identification property page, shown in Figure 9.6, allows you to view and change identifying information for the print queue.

FIGURE 9.6

The Identification property page shows information about the print queue and allows you to control it.

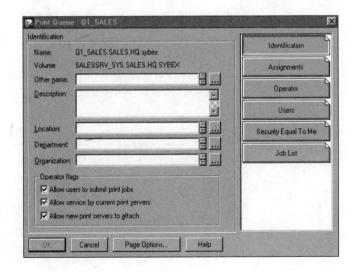

In addition, three checkboxes in the Operator Flags section of the page allow you to control the print queue's behavior:

Allow users to submit print jobs   Controls whether users can add jobs to the print queue. If this option is turned off, users receive an error message when they attempt to print to a port that has been redirected to the queue.

Allow service by current print servers   Controls whether the print servers print entries in the queue. If you turn off this option, entries are added to the queue but are not printed until it is turned back on.

Allow new print servers to attach   Controls whether new print servers can be attached to the print queue. If you turn this option off, all current print servers continue to print, but new ones are not able to attach.

Viewing Queue Assignments   The Assignments property page allows you to view the objects that have been assigned to this print queue. These include print servers that are authorized to obtain entries from the queue and printers that are set up to print jobs from the queue.

The properties on the Print Queue object's Assignments page are for your information only and cannot be changed. Changes are made from the Assignments property pages of the Print Server and Printer object dialog boxes.

Queue Users and Operators   The Users property page allows you to specify a list of users who can submit jobs to the print queue. Use the Add button to add to this list. You can add individual users, but it is more common to add multiple users by using group objects or container objects.

The Operator property page allows you to specify users who can control print jobs in the queue, as described in the next section. You can include individual users in the list or use an Organizational Role object to assign a print queue operator.

Managing Print Jobs   The final page of properties for the Print Queue object is the Job List property page. This lists each of the print jobs that have been submitted to the queue and shows their sequence. This screen is shown in Figure 9.7.

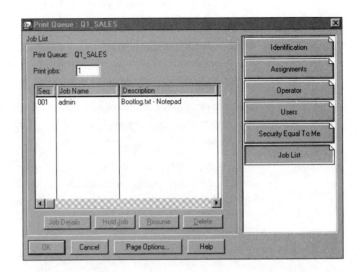

You can use the Job List property page to view the jobs that have been sent to the printer. In addition, you can manage the jobs with the following functions:

Job Details   Displays complete information about the highlighted job. This screen is shown in Figure 9.8. You can modify certain information, such as the job description, and place the job on hold if desired.

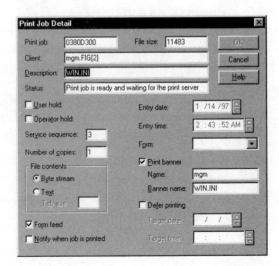

Hold Job   Allows you to place a job on hold; the job is not printed until released.

Resume   Allows a held job to be printed.

Delete   Removes an entry from the queue.

Creating Printer Objects

The Printer object is the final object required for network printing. You must create a Printer object to represent each printer on the network. Follow the directions given in Procedure 9.4.

PROCEDURE 9.4

Creating a Printer Object

You can create a Printer object by following these steps:

1. Start NetWare Administrator and navigate through the Directory tree to the desired context. Highlight the context you wish to place the Printer object in.

2. Go to Object ≻ Create.

3. Select Printer as the type of object to create.

4. Enter a name for the printer, and click the Create button. You've now created a Printer object.

After the Printer object is created, you can modify its properties by using the Details option from the Object menu. The properties of the Printer object allow you to identify the printer, specify how it is connected to the network, and specify print queues to print from. These properties are described in the sections below.

Selecting Printer Assignments   The Assignments property page, shown in Figure 9.9, allows you to assign Print Queue objects to be serviced by the printer. Use the Add button to add more queues. The Priority box allows you to change a queue's priority, and the Delete button allows you to remove a print queue from the list.

The Default Print Queue option allows you to specify a print queue to be used when a user includes the P option in the CAPTURE command to specify the printer's name rather than specifying a print queue.

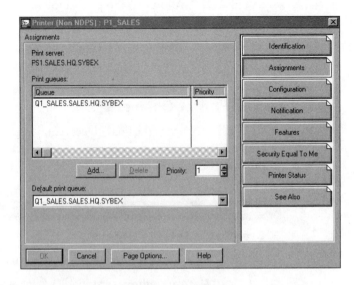

Configuring Printers   The Configuration property page, shown in Figure 9.10, allows you to configure the printer. This controls the type of port the printer is connected to, the communication parameters, and other settings.

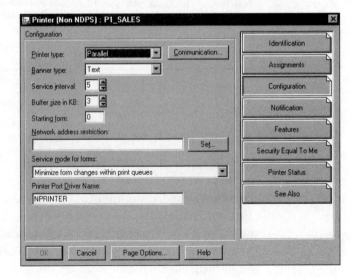

These are some of the available options on this screen:

Printer type   Allows you to specify the type of port, parallel or serial, the printer is attached to. You can also specify Unix or AppleTalk printers.

Communication button   Allows you to view parameters specific to the type of port used. The Parallel Communication screen for a parallel printer is shown in Figure 9.11. Use this screen to set the physical port the printer is attached to, the type of communication, and other settings.

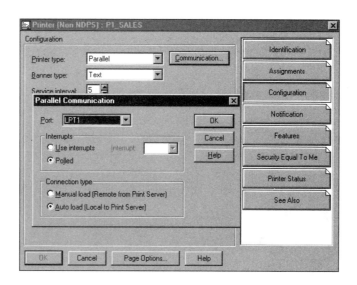

Banner type   Specifies whether the banner used for the printer is in text (ASCII) or PostScript format. The PostScript format can be used on compatible printers only.

Service interval   Controls how often the printer checks for new jobs in the print queue. The default is 5 seconds.

Buffer size in KB   Controls the size of the buffer used to store data before it is sent to the printer. This can range from 3KB to 20KB. The buffer is stored in the RAM of the server or workstation that runs NPRINTER.

Starting form   Selects the default type of form for the printer.

Network address restriction   Allows you to select a certain list of network addresses that the printer can use.

Service mode for forms   Specifies how form changes are managed.

Printer port driver name   Displays the remote printer utility that will attach to the network printer, whether it's attached to the workstation, to the server, or directly on the network.

Other Printer Properties   The remaining pages of printer properties allow you to identify the printer, provide notification for printer errors, and display printer status:

Identification   Allows you to define a name and other information for the printer. Most of this information is optional.

Notification   Lets you choose users to be notified when an error occurs at the printer.

See Also   Allows you to reference other objects that are related to the Printer object. This is for your information only and is not used by NetWare.

Printer Status   Displays the current printer status and information about the job that is currently printing.

Using Quick Setup

In NetWare 5, you will use the Quick Setup option in NWADMN32 for configuring print properties and creating NDS print objects. Quick Setup makes it easy to create the necessary objects for printing—Print Server, Print Queue, and Printer—all at the same time. Refer to Procedure 9.5 for detailed instructions.

PROCEDURE 9.5

Using the Quick Setup Option

To access the Quick Setup option, follow these steps:

1. Open NetWare Administrator and select the desired container to hold the new objects.

2. Choose Print Services Quick Setup (Non-NDPS) from the NWADMN32 tools menu.

3. You are presented with a set of options you can select for the new objects, as shown here:

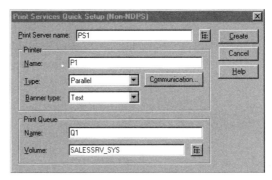

4. Specify the basic information for the printer, print queue, and print server.

5. If you already have a print server running, you can select it; otherwise, a new server will be created.

6. When finished, click the Create button. Within a few moments, all of the objects you need will be created.

Creating Forms and Configuring Print Jobs with NetWare Administrator

You can also control form definitions and print job configurations using the NetWare Administrator utility. The printer form information is stored as an attribute of each container object, and that information affects leaf objects in that container.

You can create print job configurations using the NetWare Administrator utility as follows:

- Each user has a Print Job Configurations property that can be used to define configurations specific to the user.

- Each Organization or Organizational Unit object also has a Print Job Configurations property. This allows you to define job configurations that can be used by any user in the container.

Review

Printing is a fundamental service of NetWare 5. Although NDPS (discussed in Chapter 6) is the preferred printing method, NetWare continues to support queue-based printing. Queue-based printing allows users to print to a network printer, whether it's attached to the server or to a workstation, in an orderly manner. Queue-based printing is handled by several components, described in the following section.

Queue-Based Printing

Queue-based printing uses the following components to carry out print jobs:

- In order to use a printer on the network, you must first send the data to a *print queue*. The print queue stores each set of data, or *print job*, that it receives. The jobs are then sent, one at a time, to the print server.

- The *print server* accepts print jobs from print queues and sends them to the appropriate printer. In NetWare 3.1x, print servers were limited to 16 printers; with NetWare 4 this limit was increased to 256. This allows you to easily use a single print server for the entire network. You create the Print Server object in NDS. The properties of the Print Server object provide identification information and define the list of printers the server can send jobs to.

- You must create a Printer object to represent each network printer. The properties of the Printer object identify the printer and list the print queues that the printer can accept jobs from. Other properties define the type of printer and how it is accessed. Printers can be attached to a server, to a workstation, or directly to the network.

- CAPTURE is a TSR (terminate and stay resident) program that allows you to *redirect* printing to a network printer. You specify a local printer port (usually LPT1, LPT2, or LPT3) with the CAPTURE command. After the CAPTURE command is executed, any printing that your workstation sends to this port is redirected to the network queue you specified.

- Before data is sent to the printer, it is sent to the *port driver*. The port driver receives data from the print server and transmits it to the printer. The port driver is also called NPRINTER and is run by NPTWIN95.EXE, NPRINTER.EXE, or NPRINTER.NLM.

Using NetWare Administrator to Manage Printing

To manage printing, use NetWare Administrator. The Print Server, Print Queue, and Printer objects can be configured and managed from within this utility.

CNE Practice Test Questions

1. The NDS objects used for printing are:

  A. Print server, print queue, port driver

  B. Print server, print queue, printer

  C. Printer, print server, port driver

  D. CAPTURE, printer, print server

2. The number of printers controlled by a NetWare 5 print server:

  A. Is limited only by the server's memory

  B. Is limited to 16 printers

  C. Is limited to 256 printers

  D. Is limited to 3 parallel printers and 2 serial printers

3. There are three basic types of network printer:

  A. Workstation, server, queue

  B. Workstation, server, directly connected

  C. NDS, bindery, workstation

  D. Dot matrix, laser, daisy wheel

4. Which is the correct CAPTURE command to capture the LPT2 port to the CHECKS queue, assuming the queue is in the users' local context?

   A. CAPTURE J=2 P=CHECKS

   B. CAPTURE L=1 B=2 Q=CHECKS

   C. CAPTURE LPT2 P=CHECK_PRINTER

   D. CAPTURE L=2 Q=CHECKS

5. The Print Server object:

   A. Is not used in NetWare 5

   B. Moves jobs from the print queue to the printer

   C. Moves jobs from the print queue to the port driver

   D. Stores a list of jobs to be printed

6. To configure a workstation printer, you use the _____ program.

   A. RPRINTER

   B. REMOTE

   C. WPRINTER

   D. NPRINTER

7. Which is the order in which components are used when a print job is processed?

   A. CAPTURE, print queue, printer

   B. CAPTURE, print queue, print server, port driver, printer

   C. CAPTURE, port driver, print server, print queue, printer

   D. Port driver, CAPTURE, print queue, print server, printer

8. CAPTURE can use which LPT ports?

   A. LPT 1 through 3

   B. LPT 1 through 5

   C. Only those you have the hardware for

   D. LPT 1 through 9

9. The Print Server object:

   A. Is created automatically when the printer is installed

   B. Needs to be created for each printer

   C. Can handle up to 256 printers

   D. Is not needed for most printers

10. You can stop and continue a print job with which NWADMN32 functions?

    A. Pause and play

    B. Pause and resume

    C. Hold and resume

    D. Hold and unhold

11. The number of printers on the network is limited by:

    A. The print server

    B. The number of ports on the server

    C. The number of queues

    D. Disk storage available

12. You can use the CAPTURE command to send a print job to:

    A. A printer or a print server

    B. A printer only

    C. A printer or a queue

    D. A printer or NPRINTER

CHAPTER

10

Planning the NetWare File System

Roadmap

This chapter covers the NetWare file system, the NSS file system, and NetWare Backup/Restore services, which is a section of the CNE core requirement "NetWare 5 Advanced Administration."

Topics Covered

- Components of the NetWare File System

- Planning the NetWare File System

- The NSS File System

- Backing up Servers and Workstations

Skills You'll Learn

- List and describe the components of the NetWare file system

- Plan and design custom file system configurations

- List and describe system-created directories

- List and describe suggested directories

- Describe and plan an NSS file system

- Set up an NSS volume

- Describe components for SMS

- Back up a NetWare file system with SMS

- Describe backup strategies

In this chapter you are going to learn about the structure of the NetWare file system and planning considerations. We will cover issues regarding system-created and administrator-defined volumes and directories. This is very important, because you are going to define your file system security based on the design of the file system. A well-designed file system will be easier to secure.

Novell introduced a new file system with NetWare 5, called NSS (NetWare Storage Services). You will learn how to install it and some points to consider before implementing this file system.

You will learn about NetWare's Storage Management Services (SMS), Novell's backup system. Whether you use Novell's solution or one from a third party (such as ARCServe), you will need to have a backup strategy in place to protect the file system and to have the data you need to recover from a crash.

Components of the File System

In this section you will learn about the components of the NetWare file system. You need to understand the NetWare file system in order to design and implement a file structure that ensures security while meeting the needs of users.

When you install a NetWare 5 server, you create one or more volumes, which are the largest file storage units in the NetWare 5 file system. Volumes are further divided into directories and subdirectories. One of the most important aspects of configuring the network is the assignment of directories for data and program files.

When you install applications on the network or provide a location for data files, keep the following issues in mind:

Accessibility   Keep the directory structure simple so that the users can find files easily.

Security   Position the directories so that it will be easy to make security assignments for them. Take advantage of the fact that child directories inherit rights from parent directories. For example, you can create a single directory for spreadsheet data and then subdivide the directory for particular projects. Giving a user access to the data directory allows him or her access to all of the projects.

Backups   A useful strategy is to separate program and data files. This makes it easy to perform backups because the files you need to back up— the data files—are always in the same place.

Volumes

Volumes are the root of a NetWare file system. When a NetWare server is installed, a NetWare partition is created on the free space available on the drive. This NetWare partition holds storage units called volumes, introduced in Chapter 2. The SYS volume is created by default, and it stores system-related directories and files. At installation you will need to decide if you are going to use the SYS volume for all data storage or if you are going to create multiple volumes, including the SYS volume, to separate the user data from system data. Think of volumes as you would think of a file cabinet; they are meant to store information in a logical manner so that the data can be retrieved easily.

Directories

Directories are used to break a volume into logical subcategories. The root of a non-NSS volume is limited to 512 entries, so you should be careful when creating a large number of directories off the root of the volume.

You should look at directories as the drawers in the file cabinet. To further subdivide a directory, you can use subdirectories as you would folders in a file cabinet. Directories and subdirectories allow you to organize data in greater detail. Keep in mind that the more complicated your directory structure, the harder it will be to find files.

Files

Files are the most basic storage units of a file system. They contain critical information and are what you ultimately want to protect. Files should be stored in directories; avoid saving files on the root of a volume. Create directory names that reflect the type of files to be held in each directory. An example of a logical file structure is shown in Figure 10.1.

F I G U R E   10.1

A sample NetWare file structure

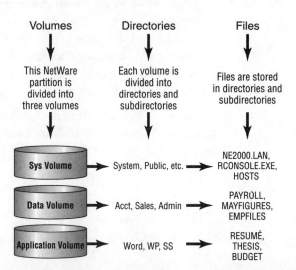

Planning the File System

Planning the file system is an important part of your overall NetWare implementation. In this section, you will be given some guidelines that will help you develop a practical file system. By building your network with the proper design, you will ensure that your users have access to data and applications on the file server, and at the same time provide security and protection for valuable resources on the server.

The following sections cover system-created volumes and directories, and you will be given suggestions on how to design or create a file system that fits your users' needs. You will also learn how to provide security for directories and files.

System-Created Directories

When you install a NetWare file server, a SYS volume is created with system-created directories, as shown in Figure 10.2.

FIGURE 10.2

The system-created directory structure on a file server

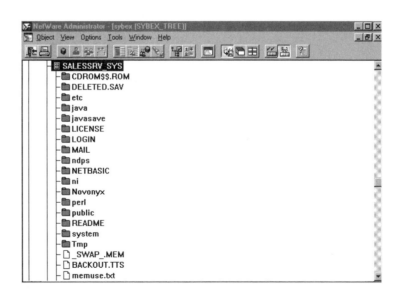

System-created directories allow for the operation of the server. You will find that each directory supports different functions, some at the server and others at the administrative level. These are the system-created directories and their functions:

CDROM$$.ROM   When you mount a CD-ROM volume, the index of the information on the CD-ROM is stored in this directory. You should make sure you have enough free space to store this information.

DELETED.SAV   All volumes contain this hidden directory. When directories are deleted, the files they contained are stored in this directory.

ETC   Contains TCP/IP configuration and related files.

JAVA   Stores Java support files.

JAVASAVE   Contains other Java-related files.

License   Contains server license files.

Login   Stores files that allow users to login. This is the only directory available to users before they log in.

Mail   This directory is used for backward compatibility to Bindery Services.

NDPS   Contains files supporting Novell Directory Distributed Printing Services (NDPS).

NETBASIC   Stores NETBASIC support files.

NI   Contains NetWare installation files.

Perl   Holds Perl-related files.

Public   Stores the NetWare client files, utilities, and commands that are available to users and administrators.

Readme   Contains documents relating to NetWare topics.

SYSTEM   Stores NetWare operating system files, NLMs, server console utilities, and commands.

You should not delete any of these directories, since loss of any system directory could cause the server to crash. It is highly recommended that you dedicate the SYS volume to only the system-created directories. In doing so, you ensure protection for the system directories by allowing only administrators access to them. By keeping user data and applications in a separate volume, you can restrict access to the SYS volume, avoiding harmful mistakes by users.

Suggested Directory Structures

When creating your file system structure, strive for ease of administration and user access. There is no single "right" way to design a file system, but you should follow these guidelines before you plan and implement your file system:

- Use the SYS volume for server system directories and files only.

- Create additional volumes for user data and applications.

- If the printing levels require it, create a separate volume to hold print queues.

- Consider adding name space modules to volumes to support the various desktop platforms your users will be using.

- Decide on naming conventions for volumes and directories that reflect their purpose.

Additional information on planning and creating NetWare volumes is provided in the CNE course on "Service and Support." You can also go to the Novell Web site (http://www.novell.com) for additional information on this subject.

After you have decided on the number of volumes you will create and the naming convention you will use, consider the following suggestions when designing a directory structure:

- Designate a directory to hold user or private directories, which will hold users' own files and users' Z.E.N.works profile directories.

- Create Z.E.N.works default profile directories.

- Add directories to hold applications in a common location for easy access and administration.

- Create directories for shared data storage, so that common groups of users can access data in a secure manner.

Refer to Figure 10.3 for an example of an organized directory structure.

FIGURE 10.3

Sample file system
organized into
directories

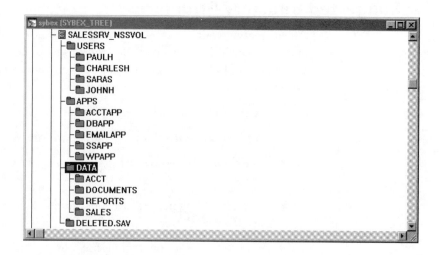

FIGURE 10.3

Sample file system
organized into
directories

The NSS File System

NetWare 5 offers an optional storage access system, Novell Storage Services (NSS). NSS is a new technology developed by Novell to provide quick and unlimited access to storage devices. NSS is independent of the operating system, yet it is compatible with NetWare 5 and the NetWare file system. NSS is not limited by FAT file system constraints as previous versions of NetWare were. In this section, you will learn about the considerations and setup procedures for the NSS file system.

Considerations

There are advantages and disadvantages to consider before implementing an NSS file system. Among the considerations are its advantages over previous NetWare file systems:

- Files created in an NSS volume can have a much greater capacity, up to 8 terabytes instead of the 2GB file size limitation NetWare volumes had previously.

- You can access and store an almost unlimited number of files on an NSS volume.

- NSS volumes load very quickly and require much less server memory and fewer resources.

- NSS volumes can be repaired in the same amount of time it would normally take to mount them without errors.

- NSS also provides improved support for CD-ROM files, detecting and then mounting them as read-only volumes.

You can find more information on the support for CD-ROMs at the Novell Web site (http://www.novell.com). Go to the section on utilities within the reference area of the site.

Before implementing NSS, you should also consider its disadvantages:

- NSS can't create a SYS volume, because NSS doesn't support TTS.

- This system does not support many fault tolerance features of traditional NetWare partitions.

- NSS doesn't support disk suballocation, file compression, or file migration.

NSS may support these features in the future, but at the time this book was being published, there was no support for them.

You need to balance the advantages with the disadvantages to decide whether NSS is appropriate for your needs. If you are managing large databases, NSS is probably the best file system for you.

Setting Up the NSS File System

Before setting up an NSS file system, you need to be familiar with the following concepts:

- An NSS *provider* finds free space and registers it as usable. This usable free space can be found within NetWare volumes and on IBM-formatted free space. There are two providers included with NetWare:

  - NSS Media Manager (MMPRV) is responsible for finding free space in IBM-formatted partitions and file systems.

  - NSS File Provider (NWPRV) finds free space on existing NetWare volumes.

- An NSS component called a *consumer* arranges registered free space into deposit objects, which represent a store of free space. The consumer sets input and output paths to the stored data. It also registers the free space so that other consumers or traditional file systems can't use the space.

- A *storage group* represents a group of deposit objects as a single storage device, which is made into an NSS volume. You can then mount the NSS volume just as you would a traditional volume.

To set up an NSS file system, first you need to decide which available or preexisting storage space you want to use. Once you have decided how much space you want to make available for NSS, you can begin to set it up as described in Procedure 10.1.

PROCEDURE 10.1

Setting Up an NSS File System

To create NSS components, follow these steps:

1. Load NSS.NLM from the server console.

2. Select NSS providers and consumers.

3. Create an NSS storage group.

4. Create an NSS volume and mount it.

5. Type **volumes** on the server console to display all volumes on the server. You now have an NSS volume available to use as a file system, as well as the SYS volume and any additional volumes you may have created.

You can find valuable information on NSS at the Novell Web site (http://www.novell.com). Look under the section on network services for the Net-Ware 5 pages.

Backing Up Servers and Workstations

The main focus of a network administrator is to guarantee users fast and secure access to their data and applications. To do this, you need to ensure the reliability and performance of the systems you manage. No network is foolproof. Plan for a disaster, from simple data loss to complete system loss. You must implement a backup strategy to protect your users from loss of data due to a system failure.

In the following sections you will learn about Novell's backup solution, called SMS (Storage Management System). NetWare SMS can back up file systems, NDS directories, and workstations, as part of Novell's complete solutions strategy. We will also discuss backup strategies for ongoing backups.

Storage Management Services (SMS)

Of course, no matter how well you organize and manage your file system, there is always a risk of losing data due to hard drive crashes, user error, and other problems. While there's no sure way to prevent these types of problems, you can make sure that the data is safe by keeping a backup copy. Along with disk storage, your network should include a backup device—typically a tape drive. We'll start this section with a technical explanation of how NetWare 5 supports backups; we'll then explore the different types of backups and their advantages.

NetWare 5 also lets you back up NetWare 3.1*x* servers, client workstations, and the NDS database.

Understanding SMS

NetWare 5 includes built-in support for backup utilities. This system is called SMS, or Storage Management Services. SMS is not a backup program; rather, it is a system that allows backup software to work with the operating system to allow simple backups of data. SMS includes NetWare Backup/Restore and

Target Service Agents, described below. *NetWare Backup/Restore* is a group of NLMs and executables that provide the backup engine and the user interfaces. These are some of its components and their functions:

SBCON.NLM   Loads the Enhanced SBACKUP (Backup/Restore) on the host server.

QMAN.NLM   Manages the print queue.

SBSC.NLM   Holds the SBACKUP Communication Module, which is auto-loaded with QMAN.

SMSDI.NLM   Holds the Storage Management Services Device Interface, which is also auto-loaded with QMAN.

SMDR.NLM   Contains the Storage Management Data Requestor, which is responsible for requesting data from the target and sending it to the tape storage device on the host server.

NWBACK32.EXE   Runs at the workstation. You can choose the type of backup or restore job you want done and submit it to the host server, which has NetWare Backup/Restore running on it.

Target Service Agents (TSAs) are components that allow a particular device—or target—to be backed up. TSAs are available for a wide variety of systems:

TSA500.NLM   Supports backups of NetWare 5 server volumes and NSS volumes.

TSA410.NLM   Supports backups of NetWare 4 server volumes.

TSA312.NLM   Supports NetWare 3.12 server volume backups.

TSA311.NLM   Supports NetWare 3.11 server volume backups.

TSANDS.NLM   Supports backup and restore of the NDS database.

TSADOS.NLM   Is a TSA that runs on the server and supports backup of DOS workstations. You must also load the TSA executable file on the workstation.

TSAPROXY.NLM   Is a TSA that runs on the server and supports backup of OS/2, Unix, Windows 95, Windows NT, and Macintosh workstations. Again, you must also load a workstation version of the TSA.

When you install client software for DOS, OS/2, Windows 95, Windows NT, or Macintosh, you have the option of installing the workstation TSA component. You can also install it at any time by running the client software installation program.

NetWare Backup/Restore

NetWare 5 includes a group of NLMs that provide the backup and restore functions; this group is called NetWare Backup/Restore (Enhanced SBACKUP).

NetWare Backup/Restore runs on the server; to use it, you'll need a tape drive or other backup device attached to the server. If your tape device is attached to a workstation, you will need to use third-party backup software. NetWare Backup/Restore doesn't support tape devices attached to a workstation. Use Procedure 10.2 to run NetWare Backup/Restore.

PROCEDURE 10.2

Backing Up Data Using NetWare Backup/Restore

To run NetWare Backup/Restore, follow these steps:

1. Load the following at the server console prompt:

   - Any tape device drivers supported by NetWare.

   - QMAN.NLM, the queue manager. This also auto-loads SMDR and SMSDI, which are supporting NLMs.

   - The target NLMs: TSA500, TSANDS, and so on.

   - SBCON.NLM for the user interface.

2. On a Windows 95 workstation, run SYS:\Public\NWBACK32.EXE. You'll now have access to the NetWare Backup/Restore services. The first screen shown below displays the Quick Access menu of backup and restore options. The screen that follows shows an example of a Restore Configuration window, in which you would configure what you wanted to restore and where you wanted it restored.

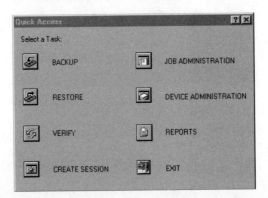

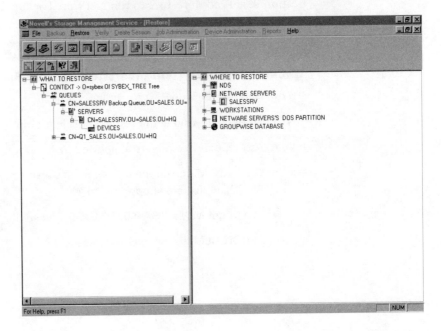

NetWare Backup/Restore must run at the host server. You can configure and submit backup and/or restore jobs from SBCON.NLM at the server console or from NWBACK32 on a Windows 95 workstation.

While using SBCON.NLM at a host server to submit backup and/or restore jobs, you will see some of the menu screens shown below.

The main menu of NetWare Backup/Restore services gives you these options:

Select the type of job you wish to do from the Job Administration menu:

The Restore Options menu displays some of your Backup/Restore choices:

Specify backup details using the Backup Options menu:

You can find more information on NetWare Backup/Restore services on the Novell Web site (http://www.novell.com).

Choosing a Backup Strategy

Unlike many utilities, a backup program isn't very useful if you only run it occasionally. Instead, you should have a *backup strategy*. This strategy determines when you make backups, which type of backups you make, and the tapes you back up to. In the following sections, we will look at the types of backups and tape rotation you can include in your strategy.

Full Backup

A full backup is the simplest type of backup, and the safest. It includes all the data on a volume or workstation. For servers with relatively small amounts of data storage, a regular full backup is the best solution. There are several advantages to this strategy:

- All files are available on each backup tape if you need to restore them.
- A minimum of configuration is required to run the backup.

There are disadvantages, however:

- The backup and restore process can be very slow with large amounts of data.
- If you have a large amount of data, a single backup tape may not be enough to hold a full backup.

Incremental Backup

An incremental backup strategy begins with a full backup at regular intervals—perhaps once a week. Backups that take place between the full backup store only the files that have changed *since the previous backup*.

For example, if you make a full backup on Monday, Tuesday's backup includes only the files changed since Monday, Wednesday's backup includes only the files changed since Tuesday, and so on. This system has a few advantages:

- Incremental backups are the quickest strategy to execute (but restore times will be longer, as we'll explain below).
- The latest changes are always available on the most recent tape.

However, there are some significant disadvantages to this strategy:

- Restoring a group of files can be time-consuming, because they may be located on several different tapes.

- If you must restore all files, you will need all of the incremental tapes, along with the last full backup tape; if any tape is damaged or missing, you will not have an up-to-date backup of some files.

Differential Backup

The differential backup strategy is popular because it offers the best of both worlds; it is something of a compromise between the full and incremental strategies. In this system, again, you make a full backup regularly. Between full backups, you make differential backups, which include the information changed *since the full backup*.

For example, if you make a full backup on Monday, Tuesday's backup includes all files changed since Monday. Wednesday's backup also includes all files changed since Monday, and so on. The advantages of this strategy are clear:

- Backups are reasonably fast because a large amount of data usually remains unchanged.

- To restore a file, or even all files, you need a maximum of two tapes (or sets of tapes, if your backup spans several tapes): the last full backup and the last incremental backup.

As you might have guessed, each successive differential backup will be larger and more time-consuming than the one before. For a successful differential backup strategy, you should schedule full backups frequently enough so that the differential backups don't become inconvenient. This will depend on your users and how often data is changed on your volumes.

Tape Rotation

With any backup method, you need a number of tapes—a minimum of one for the regular full backup and one for each day for incremental backups or one for differential backups. However, you should add additional tapes to provide a regularly archived backup.

In deciding on a tape-rotation scheme, realize that backups have two purposes for most companies. While they are obviously useful in case of data loss or system problems, they can also be handy for accounting and auditing purposes.

For example, a company may need to run a report on the data from the end of the previous month or year. The company might have five tapes, labeled MON through FRI. FRI is used for a full backup, and MON through THU for differential backups. To keep an archive, the company might have four FRI tapes and use FRI1 one week, FRI2 the next week, and so on. This ensures that backups are available for the previous four weeks, along with the current backup. Many companies takes this one step further and make a month-ending tape that is rotated once a year.

The last, and one of the most important, principles related to backups is to keep at least one copy of the data off-site, such as in a safe deposit box. Some companies use the week-ending or month-ending tape for this purpose. No matter which strategy you choose, be sure to keep copies off-site. All of the backups in the world are of no value if they are destroyed in an earthquake, flood, hurricane, fire, or other disaster—along with your network.

Review

In this chapter you learned that when the server is installed, a default volume (SYS) and default system directories are created. You should also consider creating additional volumes and directories that suit your needs. Keep in mind that ease of administration and convenient user access to data and applications are key elements in implementing a good file system.

The NetWare File System

NetWare's file system manages disk storage on the network. NetWare uses files and directories similar to those used by DOS. The file system is organized like this:

- Volumes are the major unit of NetWare disk storage.

- Directories and subdirectories divide the volume.

- Files store the data or applications within a directory.

NSS File System

NSS is a NetWare 5 optional storage access system that provides almost unlimited storage capabilities and much quicker access than previous NetWare file systems. With the advantages and disadvantages that come with NSS, you should ensure that NSS is right for your needs.

Storage Management Services (SMS)

You should choose a backup strategy for the file system to ensure a constant and consistent backup of all your critical data. NetWare 5 supports backups with the Storage Management System, or SMS. These three components work together in SMS to provide you with a backup and restore process:

- TSAs (Target Service Agents) allow various devices (targets) to be backed up.

- A backup engine, such as Novell's Backup/Restore (Enhanced SBACKUP) utility, performs the actual backup.

- A tape backup device that is supported by NetWare copies your system information from the hard disk to a tape.

Your backup strategy should specify the types of backups used:

- A full backup backs up all data in each backup cycle.

- An incremental backup backs up data since the last full or incremental backup.

- A differential backup backs up data since the last full backup.

CNE Practice Test Questions

1. Which backup strategy requires the most time for backing up data?

    A. Incremental

    B. Differential

    C. Full

    D. Partial

2. Which backup strategy requires the most time if you need to restore a full volume?

    A. Incremental

    B. Differential

    C. Full

    D. Partial

3. What are the components of a NetWare file system?

　　A. Cabinets, drawers, and folders

　　B. Volumes, directories, and files

　　C. Data, applications, and groups

　　D. Users, groups, and administrators

4. All of the NLMs provide backup functionality *except*:

　　A. QMAN.NLM

　　B. SBCON.NLM

　　C. NWBACK32.NLM

　　D. SBSC.NLM

5. What are the three concepts to be familiar with in an NSS file system?

　　A. Enhanced SBACKUP, TSA, and tape backup device

　　B. Provider, consumer, and storage groups

　　C. Full, incremental, and differential backups

　　D. Print, storage, and user services

6. Which is not a feature of an NSS file system?

　　A. An almost unlimited number of files on the NSS volume

　　B. Suballocation and file compression

　　C. Improved CD-ROM support

　　D. Less server memory and resources

7. What is a good reason to create another volume besides the SYS volume?

    A. To provide additional volumes for user data and applications

    B. To protect your server system directories and files by having only those on the SYS

    C. To have a separate volume to hold print queues if printing levels require it

    D. All of the above

8. SMS can back up the following:

    A. Unix servers

    B. Windows 95 workstations

    C. Macintosh workstations

    D. All of the above

9. All of the following are TSAs *except*:

    A. TSA500

    B. TSANDS

    C. TSAPROXY

    D. TSA400

10. What priorities should you follow as a guideline when designing a file system?

    A. Security, ease of administration, and user access

    B. Large SYS volume, no shared directories, and departmental printers

    C. Naming conventions, configuration of mail, and file migration

    D. Login security, printer at every workstation, and Backup/Restore

11. You should create directories for which of the following to make administration of the file system easier?

A. Print server

B. Shared data storage

C. Common groups of users

D. Applications in common location

E. A, C, D

F. B, C, D

12. Planning the NetWare file system is an important part of your overall NetWare design.

A. True

B. False

CHAPTER

11

Server and Network Optimization

Roadmap

This chapter covers the NetWare 5 memory model and how it allows network administrators to monitor and optimize server and network performance, which is a section of the CNE core requirement "NetWare 5 Advanced Administration."

Topics Covered

- Memory and CPU Performance
- Disk Optimization
- Network Performance

Skills You'll Learn

- Describe the NetWare 5 memory model
- Define virtual memory and protected memory
- Describe how NetWare 5 improves application support
- Explain how to improve server performance
- List ways to improve disk performance
- Explain ways to improve network performance

In this chapter you will learn the basics of monitoring and optimizing NetWare 5 server and network performance. NetWare 5 is stable enough that it can run for months at a time without a problem. Nonetheless, it is important to monitor server and network performance so that you can correct problems before they become severe. You will also learn how to use various settings to optimize and streamline your network for maximum performance.

Optimizing and Monitoring Server Performance

In this section, we'll take a look at the things you can do to run your server at its best possible speed and to keep it running smoothly, with no crashes. You can use the MONITOR utility and SET command to view and modify system parameters, which can improve performance. The areas on the server that can be improved include memory, CPU, disk access, and the network interface.

Optimizing Memory

The server's memory is used to store the NetWare 5 operating system, device drivers, NLMs, and buffers for disk and network communication. Because memory is so important to server performance, NetWare 5 uses sophisticated memory management techniques. By understanding how memory is managed and how it affects server and network performance, you can keep both running smoothly.

Memory Allocation

Memory allocation is the process that NetWare uses to assign memory needed by the system or applications. NetWare 5 assigns memory in 4KB blocks, or *pages*. The memory manager assigns, or *allocates*, the pages of memory needed by an application. The pages can be located in several different areas of memory, but they appear as a single block of memory to the application.

NLMs or system programs are assigned an *allocation pool* when they are loaded. The allocation pool is based on an estimate of the amount of memory the application requires. As the application requests memory pages, NetWare assigns them from this pool. When the application frees the memory, it is returned to the pool. Memory is assigned efficiently, because each application uses its own memory pool.

Memory Deallocation   When an NLM no longer needs memory, it turns the memory over to the system. This process is called *deallocation*. When memory is deallocated, it is simply marked as unused. However, the memory is not available to other applications immediately; first it must be picked up during the garbage collection process described in the next section.

Garbage Collection Garbage collection is a process that runs periodically (every 5 minutes by default) on the server. This process finds areas of memory that have been deallocated and returns them to the main memory pool so that they can be used by other applications. You can use SET commands to control how often garbage collection is performed and improve its efficiency.

Monitoring Memory Usage

The System Resources option in the MONITOR utility allows you to view the server's total available and used memory. In addition, you can highlight the name of a system module and press Enter to view detailed memory information about that module. The Server Memory Statistics screen is shown in Figure 11.1.

FIGURE 11.1

The MONITOR utility's Server Memory Statistics screen displays information about memory usage.

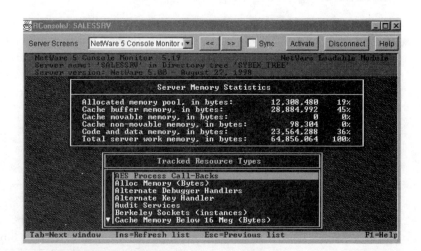

SET Commands for Memory Management

You can use several SET commands to control the allocation and use of memory. You can also place these commands in the server's STARTUP.NCF file. Here's an example of a SET command:

```
SET GARBAGE COLLECTION INTERVAL = 25
```

Most servers can run efficiently with no change to the default memory settings. Be sure that you understand what the settings mean before you change them. If a new setting does not solve your problem or improve system speed, change it back to the default.

These SET commands can affect memory performance:

SET Garbage Collection Interval   Controls how often the garbage collection process is performed. This value is given in minutes and can range from 1 to 60. The default is every 5 minutes.

SET Auto Restart After Abend   Controls whether the server will reboot automatically when an abend (server crash) occurs. This command can help you keep the network up and running, but it may also prevent you from finding out when a crash occurs. This setting is Off by default.

This is an example of a SET command that cannot be typed at the console but must be added to the STARTUP.NCF file:

SET Reserved Buffers Below 16 Megabytes   Reserves buffer space in the lower 16MB of memory for device drivers that are limited to that area. You can set this value between 8 and 300; it defaults to 16.

Figure 11.2 shows the main option menu for the SET command.

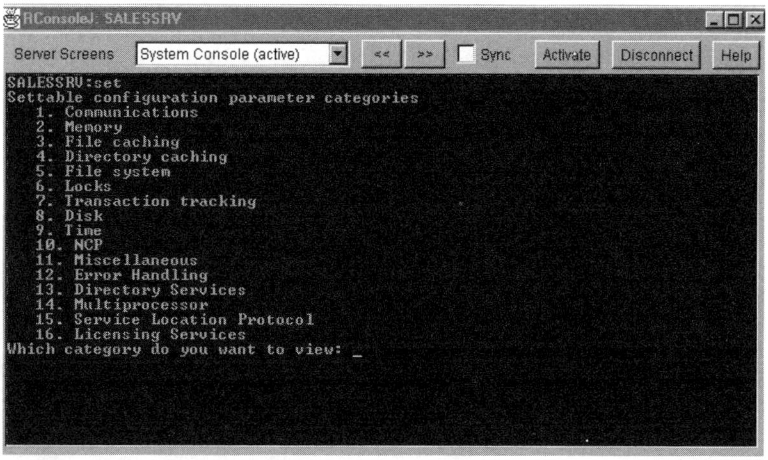

FIGURE 11.2

The main options menu for the SET command

Optimizing CPU Performance

The type and speed of the server's CPU can dramatically affect system performance. If your server is running slowly, you can use the SPEED command or the MONITOR utility to determine the cause of the problem.

First, type **SPEED** at the server console to verify that your CPU is running at its normal speed. SPEED calculates a number based on CPU performance; this should be approximately 90 for a 386, 900 for a 486, and 3,000 or more for a Pentium-based machine. If your server displays an unusually low number, check the Turbo or Speed switch on the server, and be sure it is set to the highest speed. For a NetWare 5 server, the speed should be 3,000 or more, since NetWare 5 requires a Pentium or above for the CPU.

If your CPU is running normally but your system is still slow, you should check to see if an application has enough threads assigned to it. You can also see if the application is using a lot of CPU resources. Most NLMs use between 2 and 10 percent of system resources. If an NLM is using a higher percentage, unload it or configure it differently. Of course, if you are running an intense application such as a backup program or database, you can expect its utilization to be high. You can see which applications are using up the most time on your CPU by working through Procedure 11.1.

PROCEDURE 11.1

Monitoring the Busiest Threads

To see which applications are using the most CPU time, follow these steps:

1. At the server console, type **MONITOR** and press Enter.

2. Go to Kernel ➤ Applications ➤ Application Group, pressing Enter after each menu selection.

3. Press F4, and the screen will display a list of system applications like the one shown below. You will see which applications are taking up the most time in your CPU.

4. Now you know which applications are using too much memory, so you can reconfigure or remove the worst culprits. To return to the server console prompt, press Esc at each screen until you're all the way out.

Virtual Memory

Virtual memory (VM) has been incorporated into NetWare 5's memory management process to use physical RAM for maximum efficiency. *Virtual memory* allows an application to address memory space larger than the amount the server has in physical RAM. This is accomplished through the use of swap files.

A *swap file* is a file on the hard drive that simulates RAM, expanding as needed. A swap file is created on the SYS volume by default, with a minimum size of 2MB; since the file can grow, you need to be careful that you do not run out of space in the SYS volume.

You can also create swap files in another volume; doing so allows you to remove the swap file from the SYS volume, preserving more space there. You must be careful when adding a swap file to another volume, however. You need to add the file commands to the AUTOEXEC.NCF file to delete the swap file from the SYS volume, and then create the swap file in the desired volume.

WARNING

When you reboot the server, it will automatically put the swap file back in the SYS volume unless you enter commands in the AUTOEXEC.NCF.

As part of the virtual memory system, NetWare monitors application codes, which will be explained in more detail below. Codes that are inactive for a period of time are moved to the swap file on SYS or another volume where you've created a swap file. When the code is needed, it is moved from the swap file to the server's physical RAM.

The default setting for a swap file is as follows (values are in MB):

```
MIN = 2
MAX = Free volume space
MIN FREE = 5
```

Note that the minimum free space of 5MB is what would be left on the volume when the swap file grows to full capacity. To change virtual memory parameters, use Procedure 11.2 on the server console.

PROCEDURE 11.2

Changing the Virtual Memory Parameters

To view the virtual memory parameters, follow these steps:

1. At the server console type, **MONITOR !H** and then press Enter.

PROCEDURE 11.2 (CONTINUED)

2. The monitor screen will be displayed. Select Server Parameters ➢ Memory, pressing Enter after each menu selection.

3. As you scroll down the menu, you will see a variety of virtual memory set parameters. Select one you would like to change and make the appropriate revision.

4. All of your parameter changes will be saved automatically. Press Esc to exit this screen or Yes to exit to the monitor.

The MONITOR !H command displays hidden set parameters. These should only be displayed and viewed by an administrator.

You will use the SWAP console command to add swap files to volumes, or to delete them. Enter this HELP command at the server console to list all the swap commands available to you:

HELP SWAP

You will be presented with information on using the SWAP command, as shown in Figure 11.3.

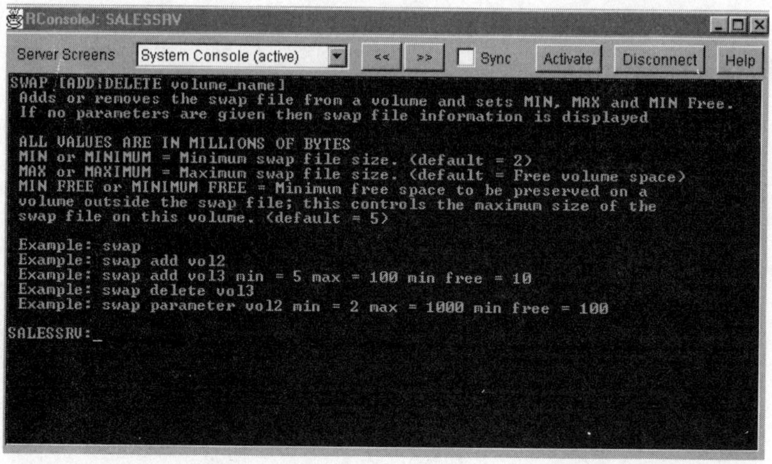

FIGURE 11.3

The Help screen for using the SWAP command

```
RConsoleJ: SALESSRV                                        _ □ ×
Server Screens  System Console (active) ▼  << >> □ Sync  Activate  Disconnect  Help

SWAP [ADD|DELETE volume_name]
 Adds or removes the swap file from a volume and sets MIN, MAX and MIN Free.
 If no parameters are given then swap file information is displayed

ALL VALUES ARE IN MILLIONS OF BYTES
MIN or MINIMUM = Minimum swap file size. (default = 2)
MAX or MAXIMUM = Maximum swap file size. (default = Free volume space)
MIN FREE or MINIMUM FREE = Minimum free space to be preserved on a
volume outside the swap file; this controls the maximum size of the
swap file on this volume. (default = 5)

Example: swap
Example: swap add vol2
Example: swap add vol3 min = 5 max = 100 min free = 10
Example: swap delete vol3
Example: swap parameter vol2 min = 2 max = 1000 min free = 100

SALESSRV:_
```

Applications and Threads

NetWare 5 allocates CPU time to all applications that are running off the server. An administrator can allocate more CPU time to business-critical applications, allowing them to finish before other applications use the resources. This is a welcome addition with NetWare 5.

Applications are composed of many *threads*, which are each a path of code, like an *If statement routine*. An If statement is built into a program to define how to proceed once the individual using the program enters data. These codes have a beginning and an end, but the end can include numerous different paths or endings, each with its own thread.

NetWare 5 uses application groups to gather a number of threads and ensure that they have appropriate time on the processor. An administrator can create an application group and assign this group more threads so it can have additional processor time. The more threads that are assigned to an application, the more processor time the application gets. A NetWare 5 server's CPU can suspend threads from one application that is not in use at the time and allow threads from another application waiting in line to run. The system can then allow the threads that were suspended to start back up where they left off.

Share value of an application can be adjusted once the application is loaded. *Share value* is the amount of CPU time an application has relative to the amount that other applications have. You can adjust this by using the MONITOR utility and going to Kernel ➤ Application. From here you can check which applications are running, along with their share values. The default share value is 100. To change an application's share value, press F3 and enter the new value.

The NetWare Application group is the only application that is created by default when you install a NetWare 5 server. Some applications are created when programs load their NLMs. Other programs don't create applications, and these are assigned to the NetWare Application group by default.

Protected Memory

In NetWare 5, *protected memory* (an area of memory that is shielded from the operating system to protect it from injury or damage) can be used to protect the core operating system from crashing because of corrupt NLMs. Areas of *protected memory* are also called *protected address spaces*. The NetWare operating system can't run in this area; it runs in an area called *OS address space* or the *kernel address space*. You can load one or more NLMs into protected address spaces using the commands in Table 11.1.

T A B L E 11.1: Commands for Protected Address Spaces

Server Console Command	Results
MODULES	Lists the NLMs that are loaded, along with the name of the address space they are in.
PROTECTION	Lists all the address spaces on the system and the NLMs that reside in them.
LOAD PROTECTED *Module_Name*	Loads the NLM that you specify into a new protected space.
RESTART *Module_Name*	Loads the NLM you specify into a new protected space, with Restart enabled. This means that if the NLM ends abnormally (abends), the system will shut down and restart the space, reloading the NLM into that space.
LOAD ADDRESS SPACE=*Address_Space_Name* *Module_Name*	Loads the specified NLM(s) into the protected space. This command allows you to load more than one NLM into the same protected space.
PROTECT NCF_*Filename*	Designates a new protected space with the same name as the .NCF filename. This is where you will load all the NLMs listed in .NCF files.
UNLOAD ADDRESS SPACE=*Address_Space_Name* *Module_Name*	Unloads a specified NLM from the address space, but the address space remains.
UNLOAD ADDRESS SPACE=*Address_Space_Name*	Unloads all the NLMs in a particular address space and removes the address space at the same time.
UNLOAD KILL ADDRESS SPACE=*Address_Space_Name*	Allows you to remove the address space without first removing the NLMs within it. The NLMs are then returned to the system.

SYSCALLS (the common name for the NetWare Operating System Call and Marshalling Library) is an NLM that intercepts corrupted calls and blocks them from passing calls to the core operating system, thus protecting the operating system. Together, SYSCALLS and memory protection act as the interface between the server and the protected address spaces. To load SYSCALLS, use this server console command:

SYSCALLS

When SYSCALLS is loaded, the screen displays a list of NLMs for which calls to the system are filtered.

Optimizing Disk Performance

The speed of disk access on the NetWare volumes affects the overall performance of the server and the network. NetWare 5 provides sophisticated *cache* mechanisms that move frequently accessed information from the disk to the server's RAM for faster access. You can optimize these mechanisms to streamline performance. In addition, the file compression and block suballocation features allow the server to store more information on available disk space; these features will be described in more detail later in this section.

Monitoring Cache Buffers

A NetWare server always sets a certain amount of RAM aside for *cache buffers*, the place where memory blocks are first transferred after they are read from the disk. If the same information is needed again, it can be read from RAM rather than the disk drive. Blocks written to the disk are also written to the cache, and blocks in the same area are written all at once. This provides a dramatic improvement in disk speed.

You can view cache statistics by using the Cache Utilization option in the MONITOR utility. This Cache Utilization Statistics screen, shown in Figure 11.4, provides several pieces of information about the performance of the cache. Many of these concern cache hits. A *cache hit* occurs when the information required is found in the cache, and the disk does not need to be accessed.

If the server is running smoothly, the short-term and long-term cache hit percentages should be 90 percent or higher. When these numbers are low, the server runs slowly. Applications that read many files with little repetition, such as backups, will cause a low cache hit percentage; this is nothing to worry about.

F I G U R E   11.4

The Cache Utilization
Statistics screen
provides information
about the disk cache.

Optimizing Cache Buffers

The simplest solution to cache problems is to add more RAM to the server.
You can also use the following SET commands to optimize the cache process:

SET Dirty Disk Cache Delay Time   Specifies how long the server waits
after a write request before it is written to the disk. (A *dirty* disk cache, or
buffer, contains information that needs to be written to the hard disk.)
This value can range from .1 second to 10 seconds and defaults to 3.3 seconds. You can set this to a higher value if users frequently write to the
disk. This may improve access speed.

SET Maximum Concurrent Disk Cache Writes   Specifies the amount of
write requests the server can perform at one time from the dirty disk cache
buffers. The default is 750.

SET Minimum File Cache Buffers   Controls the minimum number of
cache buffers that are available. When NLMs are loaded, they take memory
away from cache buffers. You can set this parameter to make sure some
buffers are always available. This value defaults to 20 and can be set as high
as 2,000.

SET Minimum File Cache Report Threshold   Sets a threshold for warnings about low cache buffers. It can be set between 0 and 2,000 and
defaults to 20. When the amount of available cache buffers decreases
below the set amount, a warning is displayed on the server console.

SET Read Ahead Enabled   Can be set to On or Off. This parameter controls whether the server reads ahead when reading from the disk. This means that extra blocks are read into the cache, assuming that they will be requested next. The default is On. This setting improves disk access speed in most cases.

SET Read Ahead LRU Sitting Time Threshold   Controls the read-ahead process. Reading ahead writes over the least recently used (LRU) areas of the cache. These areas must be sitting, or unused, for the set amount of seconds before they are overwritten. The sitting time can range from 0 seconds to 1 hour; the default time is 10 seconds.

Block Suballocation

When NetWare writes data to a disk, it uses increments called *blocks*. The disk drive is divided into blocks of equal size. NetWare 5 chooses an optimum block size based on the size of the drive and the server's RAM.

How Suballocation Works

Suballocation divides the blocks used for disk storage into portions as small as 512 bytes, allowing more efficient use of disk space. Block suballocation uses two types of blocks on the volume: normal blocks and suballocated blocks. A file always begins at the boundary between two blocks. Whole blocks are used for as much of the file as possible. If a partial block is left at the end of the file, the block is suballocated. The remaining suballocation units (512-byte fragments) of the block can be used for suballocated portions of other files. This eliminates the waste of space caused by very small files and by files that use a fractional block. Normal blocks and suballocated blocks are illustrated in Figure 11.5.

Controlling Suballocation with File Attributes

To use some files efficiently, you should avoid using suballocation. Files that are added to frequently, such as Oracle 8 database files, should not be suballocated. You can turn off suballocation for a file using the DS (Don't Suballocate) file attribute. To set this attribute, use the FLAG command with this syntax:

```
FLAG filename DS
```

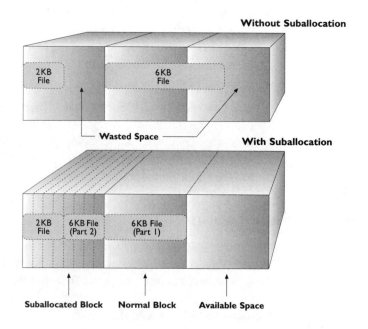

FIGURE 11.5

Block suballocation uses normal blocks and suballocated blocks to optimize disk storage.

 A free copy of Oracle 8, a database program, ships with NetWare 5. This is a five-user licensed version. You'll find further support for Oracle on the Oracle CD.

Disabling Block Suballocation

You can disable block suballocation for a volume when the volume is created. By default, block suballocation is set to On. You can disable suballocation using Procedure 11.3. (Note that once suballocation is enabled, you cannot disable it without reformatting the volume.)

PROCEDURE 11.3

Steps to Disable Suballocation on a Volume

Follow these steps to disable suballocation on a new volume:

1. Start the NWCONFIG module by typing **NWCONFIG** at the server console.

2. Select Standard Disk Options ➢ NetWare Volume Options.

3. Highlight the name of the volume for which you want to block sub-allocation and press Enter. The status of the volume will be displayed, as shown here:

4. Use the down-arrow key to move down to the Block Suballocation field. Highlight the field and press Enter.

5. Press Enter to toggle the suballocation setting from On to Off.

6. Press Esc to exit and save the changes. You've now disabled block suballocation on the volume.

File Compression

The NetWare 5 file compression feature allows files that are not currently in use to be compressed. This can dramatically improve the amount of disk storage available on your server while keeping the files available for easy access.

NetWare checks for files that have not been accessed for several days. When such a file is found, it is compressed into a temporary file. If the compression process is successful and the compressed file is significantly smaller, the original file is deleted, and the compressed file is put in its place.

You can use file attributes to disable compression for specific files or directories and to determine whether a file is compressed. These attributes are described in more detail in Chapter 4.

How Does Compression Work?

You might expect that the only way to make a file smaller is to remove some of the data; fortunately, this is not how NetWare does it. It uses several systems that allow a small number of bytes to represent a larger amount. You may be familiar with compression software such as PKZIP and LHARC, which use similar techniques.

Let's consider a simple example. Imagine a file that contains the character *A* 400 times in a row. The normal file would store all 400 *A*s, each in its own byte, for a total of 400 bytes. The compressed file would simply store a code that means "Insert 400 *A*s here." Thus, the 400-byte file would be reduced to 3 or 4 bytes yet still retain all of its content.

In practice, few files compress quite that well. Different types of files will undergo different amounts of compression:

- Simple text files will compress to about one-quarter of their original size. (Of course, files containing only a single character will compress even better, but you probably don't have any of those.)

- Binary files (such as executable files or some word processor documents) will compress a bit, but the benefit is not great.

- Some graphic files (such as uncompressed TIFF and Microsoft Power-Point) will compress well—often to as little as one-tenth of their original size.

- Many graphic formats (including GIF and JPEG) include built-in compression, so they won't compress any further.

When Does Compression Happen?

You may have experience with on-the-fly file compression systems, such as Stac Electronics' Sticker and the DriveSpace program provided with some versions of MS-DOS. These compression programs usually have one thing in common: They slow down your system. As a file is written to the disk, it must be compressed, and compression takes a heavy toll on the CPU.

NetWare file compression works a little differently. Rather than compressing every file as it is written, NetWare periodically scans the disk and looks for files that nobody has accessed for a while. By default, this time period is seven days, but you can change it to anything from 1 to 10,000. The server compresses the files that have been unused during the specified time period. This will still slow down the server, but NetWare is smart enough to wait until everyone has gone home to do its compression work. The time defaults to 6 A.M., but you can set it to a more convenient time for your company.

When a user tries to access one of these compressed files, the server uncompresses it, and then allows it to be accessed as usual. The file remains uncompressed until it has not been touched again for seven days.

Activating File Compression

NetWare 5 enables file compression by default; however, if you have upgraded to NetWare 5 from a previous version of NetWare, you must activate the feature manually. Once activated, you cannot disable file compression without recreating the volume; however, you can disable compression for directories and files. As a network administrator, you have full control over the compression feature. You can choose which files and directories will be compressed and which should never be compressed. You can also set some directories or files to be instantly compressed when written.

You can also use a SET command to disable compression on the server. Follow the steps in Procedure 11.4 to enable file compression.

PROCEDURE 11.4

Enabling File Compression

Follow these steps to enable file compression:

1. Start the NWCONFIG utility by typing **NWCONFIG** at the server console.

2. Go to Standard Disk Options ➤ NetWare Volume Options.

3. Highlight the desired volume, and press Enter. The Volume Information screen will be displayed, as shown here:

4. Use the down-arrow key to move to the File Compression field. Highlight it and press Enter.

5. Use the Enter key to toggle the file compression setting from Off to On.

6. Press Esc to exit and save the changes. You've now enabled file compression.

Disadvantages of File Compression

Although NetWare's file compression feature eliminates the problems of most compressed file systems, there are some disadvantages to using compression. You should take these factors into account when deciding whether to activate file compression on your server:

Speed of access   When a user requests a file that has been compressed, a delay occurs as the server uncompresses the file. In most networks this won't happen very often, but if your users frequently access files that no one has used for more than seven days, the network may slow to a creeping halt. Depending on the file size and the server speed, decompression can take from 30 seconds to as long as 10 minutes. You can avoid this delay by turning off compression on these files. Using a SET parameter, you can also change the amount of time that should NetWare wait before compressing the files.

Backups   Files backed up from a compressed volume should be restored onto a volume that also has compression enabled, to ensure that space is available. In addition, unless the backup system supports compression, files are restored in an uncompressed state, and NetWare compresses them after seven days. Thus, restoring an entire volume could require a much greater amount of disk space than the original volume needed.

Compression is enabled permanently   Once you enable compression on a volume, you cannot turn it off and uncompress the files without re-creating the volume (which erases all the data on the volume). You can, however, disable compression for individual files and directories. You can also disable compression with a SET command, described in the next section.

Server performance   On a heavily used server, compression and decompression can happen constantly, which can slow your server. However, this slowing is minimal and well worth the increase in available storage.

Controlling File Compression with SET Commands

You can optimize the file compression process with a variety of SET parameters. These allow you to enable or disable compression, control how often compression is performed, and fine-tune the compression process.

The SET commands listed below can be typed at the server console, or you can add them to the server's STARTUP.NCF or AUTOEXEC.NCF file to permanently set the parameter.

SET Compression Daily Check Stop Hour   Specifies an hour (in military time) when the server stops checking for files that are ready to compress. You can use this setting, along with the Check Starting Hour setting described below, to ensure that the compression process happens at a time when few users are on the network. The default setting is 6 (6 A.M.).

SET Compression Daily Check Starting Hour   Sets the time that the server begins checking for files to compress. The default setting is 0 (midnight).

SET Minimum Compression Percentage Gain   Controls the level of compression that is required in order to keep the file compressed. For example, if this value is 10 percent, the file must be at least 10 percent smaller; otherwise, the original, uncompressed version of the file is kept. The default is 20 percent.

SET Enable File Compression   Can be set to On or Off, which controls whether the compression process will occur. The default setting is On. If you set this to Off, there may still be compressed files on the server, but no additional files will be compressed.

SET Maximum Concurrent Compressions   Specifies the number of volumes that can be compressing files at the same time. This defaults to 2. Larger values may slow the server considerably.

SET Convert Compressed to Uncompressed Option   Can be set to 0, 1, or 2. This parameter controls what is done with a file after it is accessed and subsequently uncompressed. Option 0 keeps the file compressed, option 1 keeps it compressed after the first access only, and option 2 leaves the file uncompressed. The default is 1.

SET Decompress Percent Disk Space Free to Allow Commit   This is quite possibly the longest SET command available, but understanding its purpose is simple. It specifies the percentage of the volume's space that must be available before a file is uncompressed. This parameter prevents uncompressed files from filling up the volume. The default is 10 percent.

SET Decompress Free Space Warning Interval   Controls how often a warning is displayed when there is not enough free space to uncompress a file. This parameter can be set to a value in minutes or to 0 to disable the warnings. The default is 31 minutes, 18.5 seconds. Settings can range from 0 seconds to over 29 days.

SET Deleted File Compression Option   Controls whether compression is performed on deleted files. (The deleted files are still available for salvage through the NetWare Administrator utility.) The setting can be 0, 1, or 2. Option 0 never compresses deleted files; option 1 compresses them one day after deletion; and option 2 compresses files immediately after they are deleted. The default is 1.

SET Allow Unowned Files to Be Extended   Controls whether an unowned file can be extended. This parameter can be set in the STARTUP.NCF file. The default setting is On.

SET Days Untouched before Compression   Controls how many days a file must remain untouched before it is compressed. The default is 14 days.

File Attributes for File Compression

Several of the new NetWare 5 file attributes are related to file compression. Some of the most frequently used attributes are described below. File attributes are explained in detail in Chapter 4.

Ic (Immediate Compress)   Can be used to specify that a file (or directory of files) should be compressed immediately each time it is written to. This type of compression happens regardless of the time of day and may slow the server.

Dc (Don't Compress)   Can be used to prevent files or directories from being compressed. This can be used on a file that needs to be accessed quickly or one that must be updated frequently.

Cc (Can't Compress)   Set automatically by the server. This attribute indicates that the file has been left uncompressed because the savings in disk space would be insufficient if it were compressed.

Data Migration

Many companies need extremely large amounts of disk storage. One area where much space is needed is in *imaging* applications. Imaging tries to replace filing cabinets full of paper by scanning documents and storing them as graphic files. These files are typically stored on an optical storage device, or *jukebox*. A jukebox has a very high storage capacity and stores data in a permanent form, which is less likely to be lost in the event of a device failure or system crash. These systems require time-consuming procedures to move old data onto the jukebox.

The name *jukebox* isn't a coincidence; these systems often work in the same way as the kind that plays music. A bank of optical disks is set up so that a mechanical arm can move the appropriate disk into the drive. A jukebox system is expensive, but at least you won't need to insert a quarter each time you want to use it.

The *data migration* features give you the best of both worlds: You can migrate data to the jukebox, yet still keep it accessible to your users. Files that aren't in use can be moved to the jukebox automatically. These files still appear to be on the NetWare volume. When a user chooses to access one of these files, it is *demigrated*, or copied back to the NetWare volume. The only effect a user might notice when accessing a migrated file is a slight delay (typically less than a minute) while the file is retrieved from the jukebox.

There are three strategies that NetWare employs when implementing data migration: online, nearline, and offline. *Online* refers to data on a fixed drive. *Nearline* refers to data on an attached disk subsystem, typically an optical jukebox. (This data is transferred with the migration feature. The directory entries are kept on the fixed disk FAT tables for quick access.) *Offline* storage is used for archiving data or backing up data, and is not easily accessed.

Data migration is performed by a NetWare service called the *High-Capacity Storage System (HCSS)*. You can enable or disable migration for each of the disk volumes on your server.

NetWare Peripheral Architecture (NPA)

NetWare uses software *device drivers* to access storage devices on the Net-Ware server. The device driver provides an interface between the NetWare operating system and file storage devices, such as disk drives and tape drives. *NetWare Peripheral Architecture (NPA)* is a standard for device drivers. In

NPA, the disk driver is separated into two modules that work together to provide access to the disk or other device:

- The *Host Adapter Module (HAM)* provides the interface between NetWare and the host adapter, or drive controller card. This could be a SCSI, an IDE, or another type of controller.

- The *Custom Device Module (CDM)* provides the interface to the hardware devices (disk drives) attached to the host adapter. If several different types of disk drives are attached to the same host adapter, you can use a separate CDM for each one.

NPA provides two advantages to the traditional disk driver architecture: scalability and modularity. *Scalability* means that you can load only the particular modules that you need, saving memory and CPU resources. *Modularity* makes it easier to make hardware changes in the system. If you change the hardware configuration of the server, you will only need to replace one driver (either the HAM or CDM). NetWare 5 does not support .DSK drivers.

Disk Controller Considerations

The speed of disk access on the server depends heavily on the type of drive and controller used. The main types of disk drive are IDE (Integrated Drive Electronics) and SCSI (Small Computer Systems Interface). While IDE drives are most commonly used in PCs, SCSI devices are better suited for NetWare servers. SCSI is a reliable, intelligent protocol and allows multiple drives—up to 16 with the latest SCSI-2 devices.

High-end SCSI controllers include such features as a built-in cache, bus mastering, and PCI or VESA local bus interfaces. By taking advantage of these devices, you can streamline disk performance on your network.

Using Turbo FAT Indexing

The File Allocation Table (FAT) keeps track of each file on the volume and lists the blocks that the file occupies. Randomly accessed files that are added to frequently can be spread across many different blocks on the disk, which can slow access.

To alleviate this, NetWare includes turbo FAT indexing. When a file is randomly accessed and has more than 64 FAT entries, a turbo FAT is created for the file. This is an index of the location of blocks for that file only. Because the file has its own index, it can be quickly accessed.

The turbo FAT is loaded into memory when the file is accessed. A single SET parameter, SET Turbo FAT Re-Use Wait Time, controls how long the turbo FAT is kept in memory, in case the file is accessed again. This value defaults to about 5 minutes.

Optimizing Network Performance

In this section, you'll learn how important it is to optimize your network to achieve maximum speed and performance. You can use packet and buffer settings and the Packet Burst Protocol to streamline communication between the server and clients. NetWare 5 also supports Large Internet Packets, which can improve communication between multiple servers in an enterprise network. We'll discuss each of these optimization techniques in the following sections.

Measuring against a Baseline

The most important thing you can do to optimize network performance is to determine a baseline for the network. A *baseline* is a measure of performance speed when the network is running smoothly. Establishing a baseline allows you to quickly determine if the network is running too slow. You can do this with the use of a network monitoring tool such as ManageWise, discussed in Chapter 17.

In addition to monitoring system performance, follow these tips:

- Use bridges and filters to keep data from being sent unnecessarily.

- If much routing is needed, consider using a dedicated router rather than your server.

- Try to use consistent protocols throughout as much of the network as possible.

Packets and Buffers

All communication between the server and clients is divided into *packets*, set amounts of bytes that are transmitted at the same time. Each packet includes a header that identifies the destination and source of the packet and the data itself. Figure 11.6 illustrates packet transmission. The size of the packets and the buffers used to transfer them can be changed to improve performance, as described in the following sections.

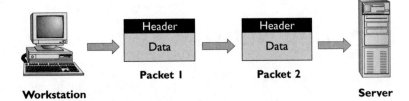

FIGURE 11.6

Data sent between the server and clients is divided into packets.

Changing Packet Size

The size of packets depends on the software and hardware used and on the topology of the network. Default packet sizes are 1,514 bytes for Ethernet and 4,202 bytes for ARCnet and Token Ring.

You can modify the packet size used with the Maximum Physical Receive Packet Size parameter, but not with the SET command at the server console. Instead, use MONITOR, or change the STARTUP.NCF file manually. The change takes effect when the server is restarted.

You can use different packet sizes only if your network interface cards and drivers support them; consult their documentation for more information. If your network uses a router, you must consider the packet size that it supports; see the section called "Using Large Internet Packets (LIP)" later in this chapter for more details.

Packet Receive Buffers

NetWare reserves an area of memory for *packet receive buffers*. These buffers are used as an intermediate area to hold each packet as it is transferred between the server and other servers or clients. To ensure efficient communication, make sure that a sufficient number of packet receive buffers are available.

The main screen of the MONITOR utility displays the current amount of available packet receive buffers. NetWare allocates additional packet receive buffers when needed. You can control the minimum and maximum amounts by using the SET commands for packet receive buffers:

SET Maximum Packet Receive Buffers   Sets the maximum amount of buffers that can be allocated. This parameter defaults to 500. If the MONITOR statistics show that the maximum number of buffers is being used, you should increase this number. A good range is 700 to 1000.

SET Minimum Packet Receive Buffers   Sets the minimum amount of buffers. NetWare allocates this amount when the server is started. This allows the server to run at optimal speeds immediately. The default setting is 128. If the server is slow after you start it, you can increase this number.

SET Maximum Service Processes   Allows you to control the maximum number of communications that can be processed at the same time. By increasing this number, you reduce the need for additional packet receive buffers. The default is 40.

SET Minimum Service Processes   Sets the number of server processes assigned to the server at startup. The default is 10. In a large network, you will want to set this parameter to a higher number to support a large number of requests.

SET New Packet Receive Buffer Wait Time   Lets you set the amount of time that NetWare waits when additional buffers are needed without allocating them. This prevents the number of buffers from being increased by a brief period of high usage. This value ranges from .1 second to 20 seconds and defaults to the minimum .1 second setting.

Monitoring Network Interface Cards (NICs)

You can use MONITOR to display statistics for the Network Interface Cards (NICs) in the server. Access this information through the LAN/WAN Information option. The type of statistics with which you are provided depends on the NIC and driver software used on the server. The statistics include packets sent and received, errors, and other information. An example statistics screen is shown in Figure 11.7.

For example, the Total Packets Received and Total Packets Transmitted statistics (provided for NE2000 cards) indicate the number of packets that the card transmitted and received since the server was loaded. If there is a big difference between these numbers (thousands of packets), this can indicate that there is a problem with communication between the server and the network. You can resolve this, but you will need to analyze the network to determine the cause of the problem.

FIGURE 11.7

You can see statistics on the Network Interface Cards by using the MONITOR utility.

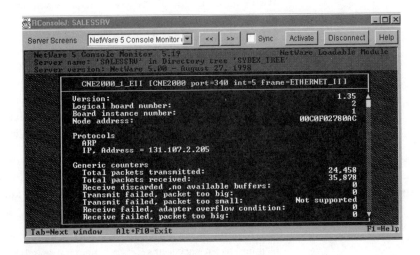

Using Packet Burst Protocol

Protocols are the languages that the server uses to communicate across the network. The IPX protocol sends data across the network, divided into *packets*. Packets are a specific size and contain a certain amount of information. Packets are sent using a *handshaking* process. In this process, after each packet is sent successfully, the other machine sends back an acknowledgment. The sender waits until it receives this acknowledgment before sending the next packet. This requires two-way communication for each packet. Two-way communication can be particularly slow when a WAN link is involved, because each acknowledgment must be sent across the WAN before the next packet can be sent.

Using Packet Burst Protocol, multiple packets can be sent without individual acknowledgments. This protocol allows much faster transfers of large files. Up to 64KB can be sent in a single *burst*, or group of packets. Packet bursts can improve performance across the network between 10 and 300 percent, depending on the server and the way it is used. Packet Burst Protocol is illustrated in Figure 11.8.

How Packet Burst Works

The client (using the NetWare DOS Requester) and the server negotiate to determine the size of the packet bursts, also called *window size*. The server may also use a delay, called the *burst gap time*, to ensure that packets are sent slowly enough for the client to keep up. These parameters are set automatically.

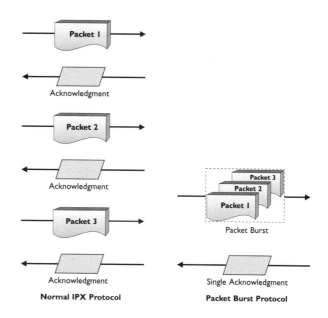

Once Packet Burst Protocol is enabled, the client sends a single request
and receives an entire burst of packets. After the packets are received, it
sends an acknowledgment. The acknowledgment specifies which packets
were received correctly. If any packets were not received, they are sent again
individually; there is no need to resend the entire packet burst. This error-
correction process is illustrated in Figure 11.9.

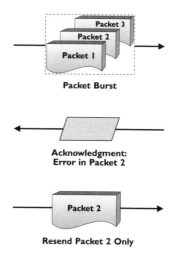

Enabling and Optimizing Packet Burst Protocol

Packet Burst Protocol is automatically enabled on the NetWare 5 server. The NetWare DOS Requester provided with NetWare 5 also enables it automatically on the client. If clients are still using the NetWare shell, you must upgrade them in order to take advantage of Packet Burst Protocol, which requires the NetWare DOS Requester.

When a workstation establishes a connection with a server, the client and server negotiate to determine whether packet burst can be used. If a client is used that does not support packet bursts, the normal NetWare protocols are used instead. The DOS Requester also supports servers that do not use packet burst; in fact, a client connected to two servers might use packet burst with one and not the other.

To disable Packet Burst Protocol for individual clients, set the PB BUFFERS parameter in the DOS Requester section of the NET.CFG file. This value can range from 0 to 10. Setting it to 0 disables packet burst entirely. Higher values can be used to increase the number of packets that can be sent from the workstation at one time.

Higher values for the PB BUFFERS parameter do not always increase performance. If this value is set too high, performance can actually decrease, because more memory is required. Low numbers such as 2 or 3 provide acceptable performance.

Using Large Internet Packets (LIP)

NetWare's Large Internet Packet feature provides another method of improving the speed of communication on the network. As explained earlier in this chapter, packet sizes can be changed to improve communication. The client and server negotiate to determine the packet size. Ethernet and Token Ring topologies allow larger packet sizes to be used.

When a NetWare server is used as a router, however, the packet size of routed packets is limited to 512 bytes. This causes all communication through the router to be limited to smaller packets. By using the Large Internet Packet feature, you can avoid this limitation and allow full-size packets to be routed. The use of routers with and without Large Internet Packets is shown in Figure 11.10.

LIP can be used in conjunction with Packet Burst Protocol for maximum performance. This allows several large packets to be sent across the network with a single acknowledgment. Using LIP with Packet Burst Protocol eliminates the bottlenecks associated with normal network communication and offers a streamlined alternative.

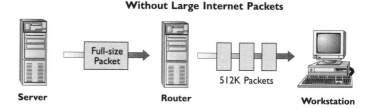

FIGURE 11.10

Large Internet Packets allow more efficient use of a router.

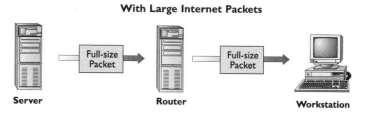

Enabling LIP

Large Internet Packets are enabled by default at the NetWare 5 server and the client using the NetWare DOS Requester. You must also ensure that the correct packet size is set for the router.

The SET Maximum Physical Receive Packet Size parameter can change the allowable packet size on each server that acts as a router. This parameter can range from 618 to 24,682. The default value of 4,202 is sufficient to allow LIP for Ethernet or Token Ring protocols.

Review

In this chapter, you've learned that it is important for network efficiency that your servers run at their best at all times. When there is a bottleneck in one area of the network, it affects the whole network. It is important to a company's workflow to optimize the network, memory, CPU, and disk performance. Understanding what the statistics mean on your server helps you to tune and configure your system for its best performance. This also helps you catch problems before they become major disasters.

Optimizing and Monitoring Server Performance

It is important to monitor server and network performance in order to detect problems before they become severe. You can monitor and optimize your server and network using the SET command and MONITOR utility. The major areas that affect performance are memory and CPU, disk access, and network communication.

Optimizing Memory Performance

NetWare 5 uses sophisticated memory management techniques. Memory is divided into 4KB blocks called pages. These pages are allocated, or made available, for each NLM or other application that requires memory. These pages may not reside in a single area of memory, but the application sees them as one block.

When an NLM or system program starts, it is given an allocation pool of memory based on an estimate of the memory it will require while running. When the application requests memory, it is taken from this pool and returned to it when the memory is no longer in use. Because each application uses its own memory pool, memory can be managed easily.

When an application no longer needs an area of memory, it is returned to the system, or deallocated. A periodic garbage collection process finds these areas of memory and returns them to the main memory pool, allowing them to be used by other applications.

Optimizing CPU Performance

The CPU speed and type of the server can also affect system performance. You can use the SPEED command to determine whether your server is operating at the optimum speed. In addition, the Kernel ➤ Application screen in the MONITOR utility shows you if a particular NLM is using a large part of the CPU's resources.

Virtual Memory

Virtual memory is part of NetWare 5's memory management system. It allows an application to address memory larger than physical RAM by using swap files on the hard drive to simulate RAM. By moving code between physical RAM and page files, virtual memory uses the system's physical RAM more efficiently. Applications can load all their code in virtual memory, improving performance.

Protected Memory

NetWare 5 provides an area for NLMs to run without sending corrupted calls to the core operating system, which is called protected memory. This feature keeps your server from crashing due to corrupted applications or NLMs.

Optimizing Disk Performance

The speed of disk access on NetWare volumes also affects the speed of the server and the network. Areas relating to disk access include cache buffers, disk controllers, turbo FAT indexing, file compression, and block suballocation.

NetWare sets aside a certain amount of RAM as cache buffers, which are used to hold information from the disk drive and to avoid using the disk quite as much. You can view statistics relating to cache buffers in MON-ITOR; several SET commands allow you to optimize their use.

Suballocation and Compression

The block suballocation feature of NetWare 5 divides the blocks used for disk storage into portions as small as 512 bytes, allowing for more efficient use of disk space. This eliminates the waste of space caused by very small files and by files that use a fractional block. Block suballocation is enabled individually for each volume and can be changed only when the volume is created. It can also be controlled for individual files and directories using file attributes.

The file compression feature allows files that are not currently in use to be compressed. When a file has not been accessed for several days, it is compressed into a temporary file. If the compressed file is significantly smaller, it replaces the original file.

File compression is enabled by default for each volume. You cannot change the setting without creating the volume again. You can use file attributes to disable compression for individual files and directories or to specify files or directories to be compressed each time they are written to. You can also use a SET command to prevent any files from being compressed.

Other Factors

The disk controller and drive type used affect disk performance. IDE drives are commonly used, but SCSI drives are more suited to a NetWare server. High-end 32-bit (PCI or VESA local bus) disk controllers should be used whenever possible for optimum performance.

The turbo FAT indexing feature provides an extra index for files that use more than 64 different areas of the disk. This makes access to the file more efficient. The turbo FAT is kept in the server's RAM while the file is being accessed. Only randomly accessed files can be indexed with the turbo FAT.

Optimizing Network Performance

The final category of server performance is network communication. You can monitor and optimize several factors in order to improve communication:

- The packet size is negotiated between the client and server; larger packets can improve performance.

- The number of packet receive buffers is controlled by SET commands that control the amount of RAM used to hold packets. You can use MONITOR to determine the correct settings.

- MONITOR allows you to check statistics for the server's NIC (Network Interface Card). These statistics provide information about the amount of use, errors that have occurred, and performance limitations.

- The Packet Burst Protocol allows several packets to be sent with a single acknowledgment. This improves communication speeds, especially over WAN links. Packet burst is enabled by default.

- A NetWare server used as a router is typically limited to 512-byte packets. The Large Internet Packet (LIP) feature allows packets to be passed through the router without limiting their size. This improves speed and can be used in combination with Packet Burst Protocol for maximum efficiency. LIP is enabled by default.

CNE Practice Test Questions

1. Which statement is true of memory allocation?

    A. Each NLM is given an allocation pool to draw memory from.

    B. Memory is allocated in 4KB pages.

    C. Memory is deallocated when it is no longer needed.

    D. All of the above.

2. The garbage collection process:

    A. Returns deallocated memory to the memory pool

    B. Deallocates unused areas of memory

    C. Takes memory away from NLMs that are not currently processing

    D. All of the above

3. The term *cache hit* means:

    A. Cache was successfully read instead of the disk

    B. Information is in the cache waiting to be written

    C. Data in the cache may be damaged

    D. Cache memory has run out

4. Block suballocation:

    A. Allows blocks of different sizes to be used

    B. Divides blocks into 4KB sections

    C. Divides blocks into 512-byte sections

    D. Compresses files that are not in use

5. File compression:

    A. Compresses all files

    B. Compresses files not in use

    C. Compresses files in the cache

    D. Allows you to compress files manually

6. Which areas of server performance can be optimized?

    A. CPU, memory, video

    B. CPU, memory, disk, network

    C. Network, NIC, LIP

    D. Cache, disk, router

7. For an efficient server, the Long-Term Cache Hits statistic should be:

   A. Above 50 percent

   B. Below 10 percent

   C. Above 90 percent

   D. Below 90 percent

8. Packet sizes on the network:

   A. Are typically 1,514 bytes for Ethernet

   B. Can be restricted with the STARTUP.NCF file

   C. Are negotiated between the client and server

   D. All of the above

9. The Large Internet Packets feature:

   A. Allows integration between NetWare and the Internet

   B. Allows large packets to be used between the client and server

   C. Allows packets to pass through a router without limiting their size

   D. All of the above

10. The System Resource option in MONITOR allows you to do which of the following?

   A. View the server's total allocated memory

   B. View the list of resources you can add to the server

   C. View a list of hardware resources you have installed on the server

   D. View all the SET commands for the system resources

11. What is the server console command to list all the SET commands?

   A. SET HELP

   B. HELP SET

C. SET

D. SET COMMANDS

12. What is the command you would use to list all the SWAP commands?

A. SWAP HELP

B. HELP SWAP

C. SWAP

D. SWAP COMMANDS

13. What is a thread?

A. An NLM

B. A portion of the CPU

C. An application

D. A path of code

14. What utility can you use to verify that the CPU is running at its proper speed?

A. SET

B. SPEED

C. NWCONFIG

D. CPU

15. What does SYSCALLS do?

A. Tracks the calls the core operating system is receiving

B. Calls the core operating system

C. Intercepts corrupted calls and blocks them from passing calls to the core operating system

D. Sends applications to the CPU

16. What is the NetWare Application group?

    A. The newest Novell software used for Java programming

    B. A group created by default when you install NetWare 5

    C. An application developed by Novell to be used with NetWare Administrator

    D. An application used for garbage collection

17. What is the MONITOR !H command used for?

    A. To display hidden set parameters

    B. To display HELP commands

    C. To display hot spots in the CPU

    D. To display hard drive settings

18. What utility can you use to enable suballocation on a volume?

    A. SET

    B. SPEED

    C. NWCONFIG

    D. CPU

CHAPTER

12

DNS/DHCP Services

Roadmap

This chapter covers DNS/DHCP Services concepts, planning, and configuration, which is a section of the CNE core requirement "NetWare 5 Advanced Administration."

Topics Covered

- DNS/DHCP Services Overview
- Installing DNS/DHCP Services
- Configuring DNS/DHCP Services

Skills You'll Learn

- Describe DNS/DHCP Services
- Install and use DNS/DHCP Services
- Install and use DNS/DHCP Management Console
- Configure and start DNS Services
- Configure and start DHCP Services

In this chapter you will learn how to describe, install, and configure DNS/DHCP Services. We will also cover DNS/DHCP's integration with NetWare Directory Services. You can take advantage of the Domain Name System (DNS) and Dynamic Host Configuration Protocol (DHCP) to administrate the network.

You will need to plan and configure DNS/DHCP Services, which can require a lot of up-front work on the administrator's part. NetWare 5 incorporates the administration of DNS and DHCP through DNS/DHCP Services. These services are also integrated into NDS for ease of administration.

DNS/DHCP Services Overview

NetWare 5 supports standards-compliant Domain Name Services (DNS) and Dynamic Host Configuration Protocol (DHCP). It also integrates these protocols with Novell Directory Services, allowing for centralized and secure management of the DNS/DHCP Services.

DNS is a client/server protocol that provides name resolution services across an intranet or the Internet. *DHCP* provides IP addressing and configuration services to DHCP client computers. This service greatly reduces the administration of an IP-only network by automating the assignment of IP configurations to computers on your network.

Domain Name Services (DNS)

DNS resolves a host name (a computer name) to an IP address. This allows a user to find a server or host using a common name instead of the IP address, which is a set of numbers that is difficult to understand and generally hard to remember. Here is an example of a DNS entry in a DNS server:

IP Address	Resource Record	Host Domain Name
131.107.2.85	A	SALESHOST.SYBEX.COM

These three fields form the DNS entry. The IP Address field gives the unique address assigned to the host. The Resource Record field identifies the type of record; in the example above, the letter *A* indicates that this is a host record. The Host Domain Name field holds the name given by the administrator to the host. The following sections will give more details on these fields.

DNS is composed of two components, the hierarchy and the name service. The hierarchy provides the naming convention and rules. The naming service provides the mapping between the IP address and the host name.

Dynamic Host Configuration Protocol (DHCP)

DHCP assigns IP configurations to DHCP clients, including a unique IP address, a subnet mask, and additional parameters as needed.

DHCP can assign IP addresses in three ways:

- It can assign permanent IP addresses.

- It can assign IP addresses dynamically with time (lease) limits.

- It allows the administrator to enter a specific IP address for a computer.

Administrating with NetWare Administrator

Integrating DNS/DHCP Services with NDS requires extending the NDS schema, which adds the appropriate objects. NetWare Administrator needs to have DNS/DHCP snap-ins to view the new DNS and DHCP objects. Although you can see the new objects, they cannot be managed from NetWare Administrator. In order to manage and configure these objects, you need to use the DNS/DHCP Management Console.

Administrating with DNS/DHCP Management Console

NetWare 5 includes a Management Console to administrate DNS/DHCP Services. This is a new Java-based utility that runs on Windows 95/98 or Windows NT. This utility can run independently of NetWare Administrator or you can run it from the Tools menu of NetWare Administrator. The DNS/DHCP Management Console allows the administrator to do the following:

- Create DNS and DHCP objects and configure them

- See audit trails made by the server

- View address additions and deletions

- Import DNS and DHCP data to NDS

- See any rejections

Installing DNS/DHCP Services

To take advantage of DNS/DHCP Services, you first need to install them. This involves two steps:

- Extending the NDS schema and copying related NLMs to the SYS:SYSTEM directory

- Installing the DNS/DHCP Management Console and snap-ins

Extending the NDS Schema

You can use the NetWare GUI or DNIPINST.NLM to extend the schema and copy related NLMs. When you install DNS/DHCP Services on you NetWare 5 server, the schema extension allows NDS to add the new DNS and DHCP objects and places them in the Directory Services. Procedure 12.1 explains how to extend the schema and copy related NLMs to SYS:SYSTEM using DNIPINST.NLM.

PROCEDURE 12.1

Installing DNS/DHCP Services Using DNIPINST.NLM

To install DNS/DHCP Services, follow these steps:

1. Insert the operating system install CD-ROM. At the server console command line, type **LOAD CDROM** and press Enter.

2. On the server console, type **DNIPINST** and press Enter. You will be prompted to log in to NDS at this time. You will need to use an administrative account.

3. After you log in, a list of default objects to be created is displayed. Press Enter to accept the default list.

4. You have now installed the DNS/DHCP Services. This procedure extended the NDS schema, copied files to the SYS:SYSTEM directory, and created three default objects. A screen confirming that the services were installed properly will be displayed, as shown here:

```
            Novell DNS/DHCP Services Setup
  Novell DNS/DHCP Services NDS schema extensions were
  added successfully. You can now use the Java-based
  DNS/DHCP Management Console to configure the system.
              <Press ENTER to continue>
```

If you are planning to use the DNS/DHCP Services, we strongly recommend that you identify the server you will use beforehand. That way you can install the services during the installation of the server.

The extension of the schema creates three objects by default. These are the DNS/DHCP Group object, the DNS/DHCP Locator object, and the Root-ServerInfo Zone object. Figure 12.1 shows the default DNS/DHCP objects added to an NDS tree.

FIGURE 12.1

The default DNS/DHCP objects appear in your NDS tree after you install DNS/DHCP Services.

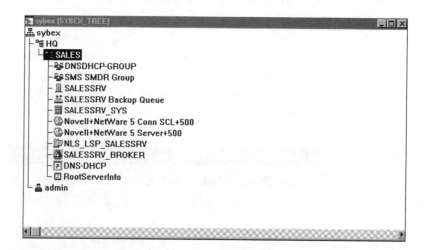

DNS/DHCP Group Object

The DNS/DHCP Group object is automatically a trustee of all DNS/DHCP objects, and any member of this group has access to properties associated with DNS/DHCP objects. A typical member is a DNS/DHCP Locator object.

DNS/DHCP Locator Object

The DNS/DHCP Locator object maintains global default information on the location of DNS/DHCP resources such as DNS zones, IP addresses, and servers in the tree. After it's run once, the DNS/DHCP Management Console can display all resources without searching the tree, because the DNS/DHCP Locator object keeps the information. This object is not configurable; therefore, it is not displayed in the DNS/DHCP Management Console.

RootServerInfo Zone Object

The RootServerInfo Zone object maintains information on Internet root domain servers. These servers are located throughout the Internet and resolve the names of root domains (.com, .edu, .net, and so on). When a local DNS server cannot resolve a domain name, it forwards the request to the root domain name server that the RootServerInfo Zone object is pointing to.

Installing DNS/DHCP Management Console and Snap-Ins

Now that you've extended the NDS schema and the default objects have been created in NDS, you will need to install the DNS/DHCP Management Console and the snap-ins to manage these objects and to configure DNS/DHCP Services. You will also use the Management Console to create and administrate DNS and DHCP objects.

DNS and DHCP Objects

DNS/DHCP Services uses a set of NDS objects, which are added when the schema is extended. When you add the snap-ins, these objects are made available to the DNS/DHCP Management Console, so they can be created, administrated, and configured in NDS. You will learn more about the DNS and DHCP objects later in this chapter.

These are the DNS objects you will need to create:

- DNS Name Server object
- DNS Zone object
- Resource Record Set object
- Resource Record object

You will also need to create these DHCP objects:

- DHCP Server object
- Subnet Address Range object
- IP Address object
- Subnet Pool object
- Subnet object

Installing the DNS/DHCP Management Console and Snap-Ins

You will need to prepare a Windows 95 or Windows NT workstation before you install the DNS/DHCP Management Console. Make sure that you have a minimum of 48MB of RAM; 64MB is recommended. You will also need 8.5MB of free space on the workstation.

PROCEDURE 12.2

Installing the DNS/DHCP Management Console

To install the DNS/DHCP Management Console, follow these steps:

1. Log in to the network on your Window 95 or Windows NT workstation, with a user object that has supervisor rights.

2. Select the path to the NetWare DNS/DHCP Management Console install utility, SYS:PUBLIC\DNSDHCP\SETUP.EXE, and then press Enter.

3. Follow the prompts in the Setup Wizard. An example Setup Wizard screen is shown here:

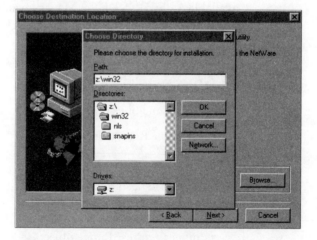

4. When installing the snap-ins, select the target directory where NWADMN32 is located, SYS:PUBLIC\WIN32.

5. When you have completed the prompts in the Setup Wizard, you have installed the DNS/DHCP Management Console. You must reboot your workstation before you can begin using it, however.

Configuring DNS/DHCP Services

This section will cover creating and configuring both the DNS and DHCP objects needed to implement the services and ways to manage them. You will use DNS/DHCP Management Console to create and configure the objects.

Let's take a trip back in memory lane. Can you remember when one or two individuals kept a log of which IP addresses were in use and what addresses were available? Paper trails and spreadsheets of IP addresses were commonplace. Administrators of this information needed to assign you an IP address, or you were unable to set up your computer. Now, DHCP automates the administration of IP addresses for you, and DNS tables help you with the resolution of host names to IP addresses.

Configuring and Starting DNS

With traditional DNS services, you had to do some planning to configure properly. Based on your network's load, number of domains, and number of users, you determined how many master and secondary name servers you wanted to configure. By placing the right number of DNS servers, you ensured proper load balancing for quicker name address resolution. Now the master and secondary name servers ensure redundancy of the DNS database.

The *master name servers* allow you to add or delete DNS records, and update the SOA serial numbers. The *secondary name servers* provide redundancy for the master DNS servers. DNS data is then replicated between the master and secondary name servers. They both resolve addresses to name requests from clients. You can distribute the load among the name servers to enhance performance without impacting the network with too much DNS database replication.

NetWare 5 DNS services store all DNS records in NDS, and they are replicated throughout the tree. That means you can strategically select NetWare 5 servers to be DNS servers based on their location, to get a better response time. NetWare servers designated as DNS servers then retrieve DNS information from the NDS. This ensures that DNS data is replicated efficiently through NDS.

DNS Zones

DNS information is stored in zones. Zone information is stored in NDS as Zone objects. A *zone* contains DNS information pertaining to a domain name, and is managed and replicated throughout the Directory services.

There are three Zone objects you can create: a standard DNS zone, an IN-ADDR.ARPA zone, and an IP6.INT zone. All DNS zones must be configured as primary or secondary DNS zones.

If you select a NetWare server to support a *primary DNS Zone object*, it can do the following for you:

- Resolve host names to IP addresses by querying the NDS tree

- Add or delete DNS records

- Update the SOA serial number

If you select a NetWare server to support a *secondary DNS Zone object*, it can do the following:

- Receive DNS information from a primary DNS zone not stored in the NDS tree

- Place DNS information in the NDS tree, which NDS distributes throughout the tree

DNS Objects

DNS objects are NDS objects formed when the NDS schema is extended and are used to administer and control DNS services. There are four objects you need to configure before you can run DNS services:

- DNS Server objects

- DNS Zone objects

- Resource Records objects

- Resource Records Set objects

We will walk through the configuration procedure for each object in the following sections. In addition, you will need to start the DNS services from the server console after the objects are configured and to configure your clients to use DNS.

DNS Server Objects   The *DNS Server object* is responsible for resolving DNS requests. It contains information on zones such as Resource Records, DNS server IP addresses (for the purpose of forwarding requests not resolved locally), and related information. Use Procedure 12.3 to configure a DNS Server object.

PROCEDURE 12.3

Configuring DNS Server Objects

To configure DNS Server objects, follow these steps:

1. From the DNS/DHCP Management Console, select the DNS Service tab.

2. Click the Create button on the toolbar.

3. Highlight and click the DNS Server option, as shown below. Then click OK.

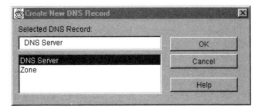

4. You are prompted to designate a server to be your DNS server. Choose the appropriate server and then click OK.

5. Enter your company's domain name and press Enter.

6. Click Create. With this procedure you have created the DNS Server object, and now you can create the Zone objects.

DNS Zone Objects   A *DNS Zone object* is a container object in the NDS tree. It stores the data for a single DNS zone, which can be a primary or secondary zone. DNS Zone objects contain the Resource Records needed to resolve DNS requests from clients. Use Procedure 12.4 to configure a DNS zone.

PROCEDURE 12.4

Configuring DNS Zones

To configure DNS zones, follow these steps:

1. From the DNS/DHCP Management Console, select the DNS Service tab.

2. Select All Zones Object.

3. Click the Create button on the toolbar.

4. Select DNS Zone and then click OK.

5. Select the NDS context you want to establish the zone in and then click OK.

6. Enter the domain name and choose the type of DNS zone you want and then press Enter. (If you choose a secondary zone, it will be active after you start DNS services on the NetWare server.)

7. Assign a DNS server or servers to the zone, and then press Enter.

8. Click Create to create the new zone and then click OK.

9. The new Zone object will be displayed in the left window of the DNS/DHCP Management Console. Select the new Zone object and the Details window will appear in the right window.

10. You will now have to enter Resource Records in the new primary zone you just created. You will learn how to create Resource Records in Procedure 12.5.

DNS Resource Records Objects A *Resource Record object (RR)* maps a host name to an IP address. DNS servers need this information to resolve DNS clients' requests. Resource Records are entered in the respective zones. When a Resource Record object is created, a *Resource Record Set object* is created by default, which holds the DNS Resource Record objects.

Resource Records cannot be modified. If you want to make changes, you will have to delete the record and create it again. Here are the most important types of Resource Records and their functions:

Address (A) records Map standard host names to IP addresses

Canonical Name (CNAME) records Map aliases to standard host names

Start of Authority (SOA) records   Identifies the DNS server's zone of authority

Name Server (NS) records   Map domain names to DNS servers

Pointer (PTR) records   Map IP addresses to host names (known as *reverse lookup*)

Mail Exchange (MX) records   Map SMTP addresses to domain names.

PROCEDURE 12.5

Creating Resource Record Objects

To create Resource Record objects, follow these steps:

1. From the DNS/DHCP Management Console, select the DNS Service tab.

2. Select a DNS Zone object.

3. Click the Create button on the toolbar.

4. Select Resource Record and click OK.

5. Enter a domain name in the Domain Name field.

6. Select the Resource Record type you wish to create. Using the information you gathered during the planning phase—IP address, host name, and a registered domain name if your network is to be accessible from the Internet—fill in the fields of the Create Resource Record dialog box, shown here:

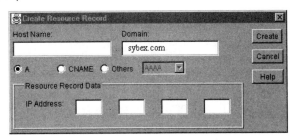

7. After you've entered the Resource Record information, click the Create button to create this Resource Record object.

8. You are now ready to start DNS Services on the DNS server. To do so, type NAMED at the server console command line.

Configuring Clients to Use DNS Services

Once you have created the DNS Server object and the DNS Zone objects, and entered Resource Records in the zones, you will need to configure the clients to use DNS Services. To navigate to the DNS Configuration dialog box on a Windows 95 workstation, go to Control Panel ➤ Network ➤ TCP/IP Properties and then click the DNS Configuration tab. An example is shown in Figure 12.2.

FIGURE 12.2

The DNS Configuration dialog box on a Windows 95 workstation

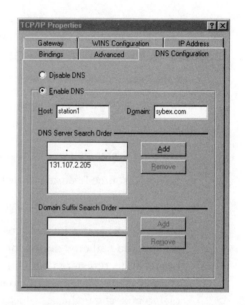

Configuring and Starting DHCP

In this section you will learn how to create and configure DHCP objects and how to configure the client and start the service. Planning and designing your network involves assigning IP addresses and a subnet mask. You can assign this information manually, host by host, or use DHCP Services to do it automatically.

DHCP Objects

DHCP objects are NDS objects used to administer and control DHCP services. They are added automatically to the NDS when the NDS schema is extended. To configure and start DHCP Services, you will need to create and configure the following DHCP objects:

- DHCP Server object

- Subnet object

- Subnet Address Range object

- IP Address object

- Subnet Pool object

After using the DNS/DHCP Management Console to create and configure DHCP objects, you will start DHCP Services and set up the clients as DHCP clients.

The *DHCP Server object* is responsible for supplying IP configuration information to DHCP clients. The DHCP Server object obtains its information from DHCP data stored in the Subnet object and Subnet Pool object.

The *Subnet object* contains Subnet Address Range and IP Address objects, which have a range of available IP addresses to assign to clients. The *Subnet Pool object* contains a set of Subnet Address Range objects that can support multiple subnets on a single physical network.

The following sections will walk you through the process of creating and configuring each of the DHCP objects.

DHCP Server Objects

You'll need to create DHCP Server objects to make DHCP available to your network. Use Procedure 12.6 to set up a DHCP Server object.

PROCEDURE 12.6

Creating and Configuring DHCP Server Objects

To create and configure DHCP server objects, follow these steps:

1. From the DNS/DHCP Management Console, select the DHCP Service tab.

2. Click the Create button on the toolbar.

PROCEDURE 12.6 (CONTINUED)

3. Select DHCP Server as the type of object to create, as shown on the screen below, and click OK.

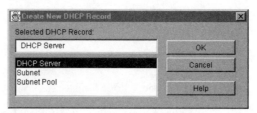

4. You have now created a DHCP Server object. Now select the server in the tree that you wish to be the DHCP server.

Once you have created the DHCP Server object, you can configure more information in the Details window of the object, such as audit trails, audit logs, audit alerts, mobile user options, and synchronization wait time. To check whether an IP address is already in use before you assign it to a client, you can configure the DHCP server to ping the address first.

Subnet Objects   A *Subnet object* represents an IP subnet assigned to a physical network segment. You can configure the IP address and range of the subnet. The Subnet object can be created in a container object such as Locality, Organization, or Organizational Unit (covered in Chapter 2) to reflect that container's location in the physical network. Follow Procedure 12.7 to create a DHCP Subnet object.

PROCEDURE 12.7

Creating a DHCP Subnet Object

To create a DHCP Subnet object, follow these steps:

1. From the DNS/DHCP Management Console, select the DHCP Service tab.

2. Click the Create button on the toolbar.

3. The Create New DHCP Record dialog box will be displayed. Select the Subnet option as shown on the screen below and then click OK.

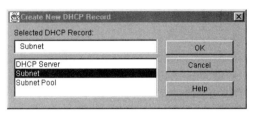

4. Configure the Subnet object by entering the information on the subnet's range of IP addresses and the subnet mask to be used.

Before you attempt to design an IP network, we strongly suggest reading up on the subject. TCP/IP is a very complex protocol to configure and maintain. Visit the Novell Web site (http://www.novell.com) and check some of their white papers on TCP/IP. The Sybex Web site (http://www.sybex.com) also provides useful reference material.

The Subnet object and its properties must be unique within the NDS tree. The configuration of a Subnet object will fail if there is a duplicate entry when you create the object.

Once you have created the Subnet object, you can configure the following settings in the Subnet Object Details window:

- DNS zone for dynamic updates
- Domain name
- Subnet pool reference
- Default DHCP server

DHCP Subnet Address Range Object and IP Address Object   You can configure DHCP for dynamic addressing with the *Subnet Address Range object* or for manual addressing with the *IP Address object*. Follow Procedure 12.8 to set up the appropriate object for the type of addressing you wish to do.

PROCEDURE 12.8

Creating a Subnet Address Range Object or an IP Address Object

To create a Subnet Address Range object or an IP Address object, follow these steps:

1. From the DNS/DHCP Management Console, select the DHCP tab. Then select the Subnet object where you will configure the range of addresses.

2. On the toolbar, click the Create button.

3. The Create New DHCP Record dialog box will be displayed, as shown below. Select the Subnet Address Range object (if you will be configuring with dynamic addressing) or the IP Address object (if you will be configuring with manual addressing).

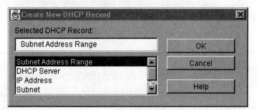

Subnet Pool Object   Many TCP/IP protocol stacks allow you to configure more than one subnet in a single network segment. The Subnet Pool object can assign IP addresses to multiple subnets in a single physical segment. You can also configure this object using the DNS/DHCP Management Console.

Additional DHCP Options   You can configure additional DHCP options, both global or for a specific subnet, to further facilitate the administration of your IP network. These options include DNS servers, default gateways, the preferred server, and the NDS context. The Global Preferences page of the DHCP Service provides a DHCP Options Table you can use to choose configuration options, as shown in Figure 12.3. For more information on using this table, see the Novell online documentation.

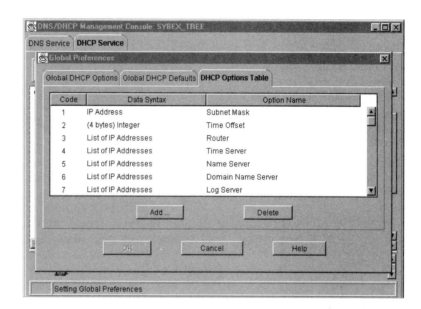

Starting DHCP Services and Configuring Clients

After you have configured DHCP Services, you need to start the services. Enter the following command at the server console:

DHCPSRVR

Figure 12.4 demonstrates the proper configuration settings for Windows 95 and 98 workstations. Most clients support DHCP (OS/2, Macintosh, Windows NT, et cetera); refer to your system manual for information on setting up specific platforms.

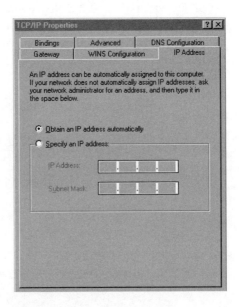

Review

In this chapter, you learned that NetWare 5 uses the standards-compliant TCP/IP protocols DNS and DHCP. DNS uses a name-to-address resolution protocol, and DHCP is used for centralized administration and distribution of IP addresses. DHCP can also be used to configure additional TCP/IP information. You also learned that clients need to be configured to use DNS/DHCP Services.

DNS/DHCP Services offer these benefits:

- Simplify administration of IP addressing

- Automate updating host names with updated IP addresses

- Allow you to customize and configure IP addressing with the DNS/ DHCP Management Console

DNS/DHCP Services

DNS/DHCP Services are integrated with NetWare Directory Services. You learned that you need to install DNS/DHCP Services, create and configure their respective objects, and configure and start the services. All the information related to DNS/DHCP Services is stored in NDS. This allows for secure and centralized administration of the services. DNS/DHCP Services are managed with the DNS/DHCP Management Console.

These are the two protocols used in DNS/DHCP Services:

- DNS (Domain Name System), which is a client/server protocol that provides name resolution services across an intranet or the Internet

- DHCP (Dynamic Host Configuration Protocol), which provides IP addressing and configuration services to DHCP client computers

Installing DNS/DHCP Services

When you install DNS/DHCP Services, the NDS schema is extended and new objects are created. Files related to DNS/DHCP Services are copied to the SYS:SYSTEM directory on the server. These three objects are created by default and provide the foundation for administrating the services:

- DNS/DHCP Group object

- DNS/DHCP Locator object

- RootServerInfo Zone object

You will also need to install the DNS/DHCP Management Console and snap-ins. The Management Console is the administrative tool, and the snap-ins allow you to view the new objects in NetWare Andministrator and the DNS/DHCP Management Console.

Configuring DNS/DHCP Services

After installing DNS/DHCP Services, you will need to configure them. You will create a series of objects to store DNS and DHCP information. NDS distributes the information to the respective clients, using DNS and DHCP servers.

These are the DNS objects you'll need to create and configure:

- DNS Server object
- DNS Zone object
- Resource Record objects
- Resource Records Set objects

These are the DHCP objects you'll need to set up:

- DHCP Server object
- Subnet object
- Subnet Address Range object
- IP Address object
- Subnet Pool object

Once the services are configured, you will start them and prepare the workstation hosts to be DNS and/or DHCP clients.

DNS Services begin when you enter the following command on the server console:

NAMED

DHCP Services begin when you enter the following command on the server console:

DHCPSRVR

CNE Practice Test Questions

1. Which of the following is a step in installing DNS/DHCP Services?

   A. Install network cards

   B. Install server volume

   C. Extend NDS schema

   D. None of the above

2. DNS is a/an _____ name resolution protocol that maps a/an _____ address to a host _____.

   A. IP, domain, name

   B. Domain, name, IP

   C. Name, IP, domain

   D. Domain, IP, name

3. You can administrate DNS/DHCP Services using NetWare Administrator.

   A. True

   B. False

4. To start DNS Services once it has been installed and configured, enter this server console command:

   A. SERVER.EXE

   B. DNS.EXE

   C. DNSSRV

   D. NAMED

5. DNS is a client/server protocol that provides domain name resolution services across an intranet and the Internet.

   A. True

   B. False

6. DNS maps a network address to a computer name.

   A. True

   B. False

7. DNS protocol standard is composed of which *two* components:

  A. Subnet range

  B. Naming conventions

  C. Mapping between IP address and name

  D. Host names

8. DHCP provides a/an _____ with _____ configuration information.

  A. Server, IPX

  B. Client, IP

  C. Application, service

  D. Mouse, keyboard

9. Snap-ins allows you to _____ DNS/DHCP objects with NetWare Administrator.

  A. Edit

  B. Configure

  C. View

  D. Start

10. The following is a DNS object:

  A. Subnet object

  B. OU Object

  C. Resource Record object

  D. Subnet mask

11. DHCP assigns IP addresses _____.

  A. Dynamically

  B. Routinely

C. Randomly

D. Indirectly

12. DHCP allows the administrator to assign a specific address to a computer.

   A. True

   B. False

13. The DNS/DHCP Management Console allows the user to:

   A. Configure and administrate DNS objects

   B. Delete user objects

   C. Edit AUTOEXEC.NCF

   D. Install DNS/DHCP Services

14. After the NDS schema is extended, you can create and install DNS/DHCP objects with NetWare Admnistrator.

   A. True

   B. False

15. You can install DNS/DHCP Services using:

   A. NetWare 5 GUI

   B. INSTALL.NLM

   C. ConsoleOne

   D. DNS/DHCP Console

16. DHCP objects include:

   A. Subnet objects

   B. Resource Record objects

   C. Organizational objects

   D. User objects

CHAPTER

13

WWW and FTP Services

Roadmap

This chapter covers WWW and FTP Services, which is a section of the CNE core requirement "NetWare 5 Advanced Administration."

Topics Covered

- WWW Services
- The Netscape FastTrack Server
- Configuring the Web Server
- FTP Services
- Managing FTP Services
- Transferring Files with FTP
- Troubleshooting FTP Services

Skills You'll Learn

- Describe NetWare 5 WWW Services
- Install and configure the Netscape FastTrack Server for NetWare
- Administrate WWW Services
- Install, configure, and administrate FTP Services
- Transfer files between an FTP client and NetWare FTP Services
- Troubleshoot problems with FTP Services

In this chapter, you will learn about the process of installing and configuring WWW and FTP Services on a NetWare 5 server. You will also learn how to manage and troubleshoot these services.

NetWare 5 includes the Netscape FastTrack Server for NetWare as its Web server offering, providing TCP/IP standards–compliant WWW Services for intranets and the Internet. We'll look at the Netscape FastTrack Server in detail in this chapter.

Although it doesn't get as much publicity as the Web does, FTP (File Transfer Protocol) is one of the most commonly used Internet protocols. Novell FTP Services, included with NetWare 5, adds support for this protocol on a NetWare server. You can use this protocol for general-purpose file transfers over the Internet or an intranet, or even across multiple platforms. You can use FTP with a Web server to allow visitors to the Web site to download files or browse directories on your network.

WWW Services

The World Wide Web, commonly known as the Web or WWW, has become the most popular part of the Internet. The main function of NetWare's WWW Services, a client/server application, is to publish documents from a dedicated server. Web documents are written in a special code called *HTML (Hypertext Markup Language)*.

The HTML file defines how the Web page will look and what information it will contain—the text, graphics, fonts, layout, and so on. Embedded in the text are links to other Web pages, called *hyperlinks,* or simply *links*. A link contains the address, or *URL (Uniform Resource Locator),* of another Web page, represented by an underlined word in text or sometimes embedded in a graphic. When you click the underlined word or graphic link, you can see the page that the URL points to. The URL is an addressing standard for Web services. Any time you use a URL, it automatically tells the *HTTP (Hypertext Transfer Protocol)* that you are accessing a Web page. The URL can point to Web pages on the same server or on another server on the Web.

A *Web browser*, which is a client-side application, is needed to see the URL. The first widely used Web browser was introduced by Mosaic, but the two major browsers on the market today are Netscape Navigator and Microsoft Internet Explorer.

The Web has evolved from publishing simple text documents to presenting complex graphical and business-capable applications. These provide users many services and functions.

You can make Web services available to your users through the Internet or your company's intranet by using a TCP/IP network and HTTP. TCP/IP provides the transport mechanism to move data between computers, and

HTTP provides the request/response mechanism between the Web server and a client browser. The current version of HTTP is 1.1, which brings considerably enhanced performance and security.

NetWare 5 uses the Netscape FastTrack Server for NetWare 5 to provide Web services for your intranet or the Internet. The next section will cover installing, configuring, managing, and troubleshooting a Netscape FastTrack Server. The Netscape FastTrack Server uses the following NLMs for its WWW Services:

- CRON.NLM (NetWare Scheduler)
- NSHTTPD.NLM (Netscape FastTrack Server for NetWare)
- NETDB.NLM (network database access)
- CSSYSMSG.NLM (systems messages facility)
- BTRIEVE.NLM (Btrieve client/server database)
- NSLCGI.NLM (LCGI support library)
- ADMSERV.NLM (Netscape Administration Server)

Netscape FastTrack Server

The Netscape FastTrack Server is a complicated piece of software and may require a slight upgrade to the server you plan to install it on. In the following sections you will learn about the hardware and software requirements for the Netscape FastTrack Server, and how to install it.

Checking System Requirements

You should have no trouble installing the Netscape FastTrack Server on most servers that can run NetWare 4.11 or higher, but make sure your server meets all of the following system requirements:

Memory The Netscape FastTrack Server requires 64MB of RAM and, as always, the more the better.

Hard Disk Storage The Netscape FastTrack Server software requires 100MB of free hard disk space on the SYS volume. In addition, be sure you have sufficient space for the HTML documents and graphics that you'll make available on the Web server.

TCP/IP   The server needs to be configured to use TCP/IP.

Long Name Space   You'll need to ensure long name space support for the volume that will hold your Web content. (NetWare 5 supports long name space by default.)

Unique IP Address   A unique IP address must be assigned to the NetWare server.

Installing the Netscape FastTrack Server

Before installing the Netscape FastTrack Server, you will need to set up a workstation with the following features:

- The Windows 95 or Windows NT operating system
- TCP/IP as the default protocol
- Latest Novell Client software installed
- Netscape 3.*x* or higher installed
- CD-ROM device to access the installation files on CD
- NetWare 5 operating system installation CD

You will use this client workstation to install the Netscape FastTrack Server on the NetWare server.

PROCEDURE 13.1

Installing the Netscape FastTrack Server

To install the Netscape FastTrack Server, follow these steps:

1. Log in to the Directory tree.

2. Map a drive to the root of the SYS volume on the server designated for Web services. (You will need a user account that has Supervisor rights to the server.)

3. At the client workstation, put in the NetWare 5 operating system installation CD, go to the PRODUCTS\WEBSERV directory, and locate the SETUP.EXE file.

4. Double-click the SETUP.EXE file and the Install Wizard is displayed, as shown here:

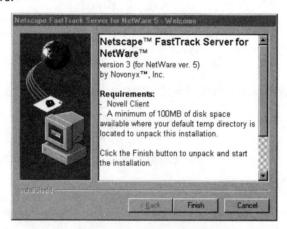

5. Click Finish. The installation files will be unpacked.

6. You will be prompted for the IP address and host name of the target Web server. Enter the appropriate information.

7. You will be prompted for the port number to use on the Netscape Fast-Track Server. Enter the port you wish to use or accept the default setting, port 80.

8. Select the account name and password for the user to manage the Web server.

9. You will be asked whether you want the Netscape FastTrack Server to start when the server is started. Click Yes.

10. The Install Wizard will now copy the files to the server. Once the files are copied, choose the option to start the Netscape FastTrack Server on the NetWare server.

11. Start your browser and connect to the Web server by host name or IP address. An example of a successful connection is shown here:

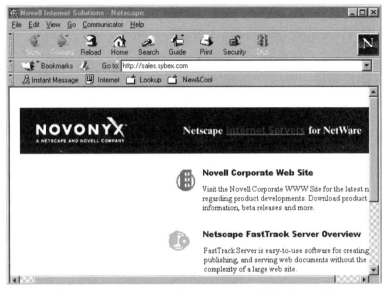

Copyright 1998 Netscape Communications Corp. Used with permission. All Rights Reserved. This electronic file or page may not be reprinted or copied without the express written permission of Netscape.

12. You will be prompted to add the startup file (NSWEB.NCF) for the FastTrack Server to AUTOEXEC.NCF. The NSWEB.NCF has all the necessary load commands to start WWW Services. With this file in the AUTOEXEC.NCF, WWW Services will start automatically when you restart the server. You've now successfully installed the Netscape FastTrack Server.

The installation adds files that can start or stop the FastTrack Server. You will need to enter the following command on the server console to start the Netscape FastTrack Server:

NSWEB

This file contains all the load commands to start the Web server. Also, a few lines are added to the AUTOEXEC.NCF file, as seen in Figure 13.1, which start the FastTrack Server when you restart the NetWare server. To shut down the FastTrack Server, enter the following command on the server console:

NSWEBDN

The file contains all the unload commands needed to stop the FastTrack Server.

FIGURE 13.1

Add commands to AUTOEXEC.NCF to load the Netscape FastTrack Server.

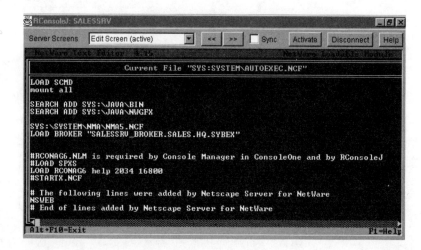

Managing Files and Directories

Of course, a Web server isn't much good if you don't have any documents to publish. We'll look at the process of publishing documents later in this chapter; in the meantime, let's take a look at the Netscape FastTrack Server, its directory structure, and the way files are stored on the Web server.

Figure 13.2 shows the directory structure created on the target server when you install the FastTrack Server.

How Web Documents Are Organized

During installation, Netscape FastTrack Server creates a directory to store Web documents and related files (SYS:\NOVONYX\SUITESPOT\DOCS). Subdirectories can also be created under this directory to organize Web content and make it available to clients.

FIGURE 13.2

The directory structure of the server after Netscape FastTrack Server has been installed

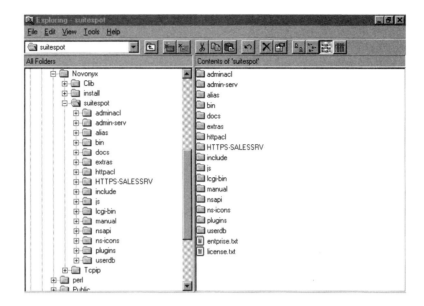

For more information on using the Netscape FastTrack Server for Net-Ware, go to these files on your intranet (using the server name and host name for your system):

- Readme file:

  `http://`*`server_hostname`*`/readme/readme.htm`

- Scripting information:

  `http://`*`server_hostname`*`/Netscape_scriptng.htm`

Configuring the Web Server

After you have installed the FastTrack Server, you will need to configure the WWW Services. You will need to spend some time planning in order to develop the Web environment that best suits your client's needs. You can configure and manage your FastTrack Server using the Administration Server and Server Manager. All run on the NetWare 5 server designated as the Web server.

The *Administration Server* is a group of NLMs that run on the Web server, providing a single interface to help you manage the FastTrack server.

The Administration Server is accessed through its own home page. The *Server Manager* is a series of forms used by the Administration Server to configure and manage the FastTrack Server. Both tools will be described in the following sections.

Administration Server

The Administration Server is accessed from a browser, but you must first run ADMSERV.NLM from the server console to enable the administration Web pages. If you add the FastTrack startup file (NSWEB.NCF) to AUTOEXEC .NCF, this NLM loads automatically when the server is started.

When you run ADMSERV.NLM, the port number for the home page of the Administration Server will be displayed; make sure you document this number. To access the Administration Server home page from a browser, type the Web site's URL, using the Web server's host name and port number:

```
http://server_hostname:admin_port_number/
```

When you enter this address, a screen like the one shown in Figure 13.3 will be displayed. This screen prompts you to log in, entering the username and password you selected when you installed the FastTrack Server. You will then gain access to the Administration Server Web pages, as shown in Figure 13.4.

FIGURE 13.3

The login screen for Administration Server

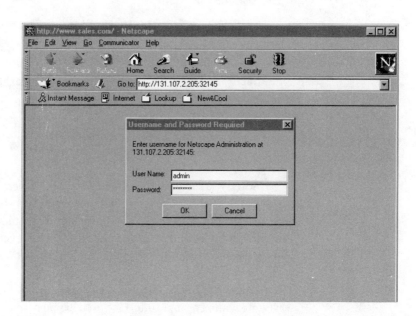

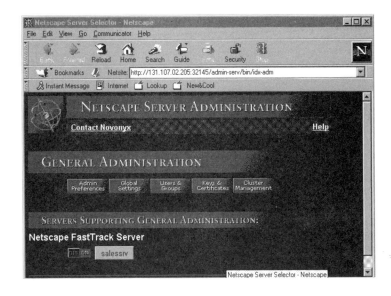

You can access the Server Manager through the Administration Server home page. At the bottom of the home page, you will see a button with your server's name on it; the example in Figure 13.4 shows the server name salessrv. Double-click the button and the Server Manager screen is displayed, as shown in Figure 13.5.

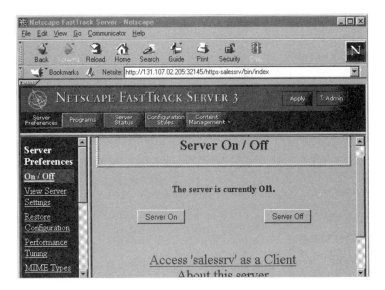

The server configuration buttons at the top of the screen can be used to configure the FastTrack Server. Selecting any of these buttons displays links associated with them on the left side of the page. Clicking on a link displays the corresponding configuration page in the main browser window.

Server Manager

The Server Manager allows you to configure the entire FastTrack Server or specific resources like a directory or a file. On some of the configuration pages, you can use wildcard characters to find a resource to configure. Figure 13.6 shows an example of a configuration page that allows the use of wildcard characters, the Query Handler. For details on wildcard characters, see the Novell online documentation.

FIGURE 13.6

Configuration pages such as the Query Handler allow the use of wildcards.

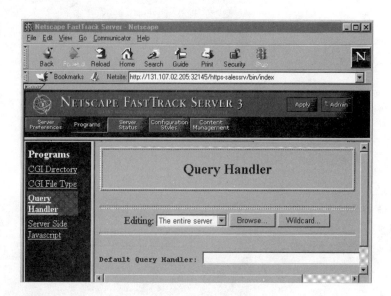

After making changes on the FastTrack Server or a particular resource, you must save and apply the changes. To return to the Administration Server home page, click the Admin button located in the upper-right corner, as shown in Figure 13.6.

Managing Web Server Security

After you install the FastTrack Server, default rights are assigned to the directories. All users receive read and file scan rights to the directories, including documents, and users are given full rights to logs and sample directories.

If you are making your Web site accessible to the Internet or you don't want anyone modifying the site, leave the default rights. This is especially true if you allow anonymous users to access the Web site. An *anonymous user* is anyone who accesses your Web site without a specific user account.

Changing Web Server Settings

The Netscape FastTrack Server will most likely meet your needs without modification. However, if it is heavily used, you may need to change its configuration to optimize performance. To do this, you will need to use the Administration Server and Server Manager.

These are some of the configuration options you can change:

- Basic server parameters

- Directories in the document tree

- Document preferences

- Access to the Web site

We will discuss ways to modify these parameters in the following sections.

Modifying Basic Server Parameters

The Server Manager can start and stop the Netscape FastTrack Server. You will need to do this when you make changes to the FastTrack Server and they need to be activated. To start or stop the FastTrack Server, just click the On or Off button at the bottom of the Administration Server home page, as seen in Figure 13.4.

You can also change the server port number from the default port 80 to improve security. To configure the port number on the FastTrack Server, access the Server Manager, as described earlier in this chapter. Select the Server Preferences tab, and then in the left frame, click the Network Settings link. The Network Settings page will be displayed in the main frame of the screen. Replace the default port number with the desired number, entering it in the Server Port field shown in Figure 13.7.

It's a good idea to change the default port number, because port 80 is a standard number for HTTP. Changing the port number forces hackers to guess which number you used, making it more difficult for them to break into your Web site.

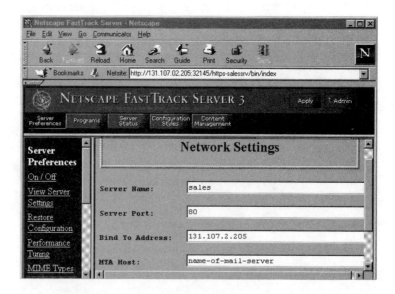

Once you have changed the server's port number, you will need to use the new number when accessing the Web site. Use your machine's host name and port address in the following format:

```
http://host_name:new_port_number
```

Modifying Directories in the Document Tree

By default, Web documents are stored in this directory:

SYS:\NOVONYX\SUITESPOT\DOCS

This is the root directory of the home page. To modify this default directory, go to Server Manager ➤ Content Management ➤ Primary Document Directory. If you want to move all your documents to another directory, change the document root directory to a new location and enter the new directory in the Primary Directory field, as shown in Figure 13.8.

You can also use the Server Manager to create additional directories to store Web documents. Procedure 13.2 describes how to add another directory to your Netscape FastTrack Server.

F I G U R E 13.8

Use the Primary
Document Directory
screen to modify the
default directory.

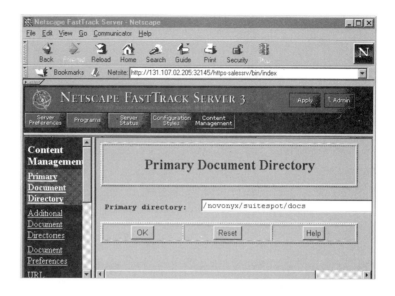

PROCEDURE 13.2

Adding a Directory to the Netscape FastTrack Server

To add another directory, follow these steps:

1. Go to the Server Manager home page and select the Content Management button.

2. In the left frame, click the Additional Document Directories link. You will see the screen shown here:

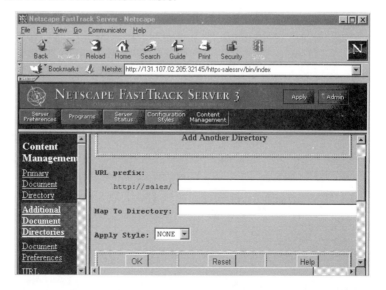

3. The main window displays a form in which to enter the URL prefix (this is the address you will use from the browser to access the new directory). Enter your desired prefix.

4. Enter your desired path in the Map to Directory field (this is the path to the directory on your server).

5. Click OK to apply your changes.

This procedure creates links to directories that contain information or documents that run on your Web server. This gives you flexibility and increased storage capacity.

Configuring Document Preferences

With the FastTrack Server, you can predetermine how the Web server responds to document requests made from browsers. The following sections describe different ways you can configure the FastTrack Server to give a standard response to browser requests.

Index Filenames

When a user requests access to your Web site by entering your domain name as the URL, not specifying a filename, you can specify which file will be displayed as the home page. A *home page* is the "front page" of your Web site, the first screen you want users to see when they access your Web site. The default files that will be displayed are index.html and home.html. If you specify more than one filename to be the default home page, the server will look in the primary document directory of the Web site for the files, in the order in which the filenames appear, until it finds one. These files are what a user sees as your Web site's home page.

Directory Indexing

The Netscape FastTrack Server automatically creates an index of the files and subdirectories your document directory holds. Typically when a user accesses your Web site a predetermined index file is displayed, but if one is not present the server will display the index file it created when the server indexed the document directory. This index file displays the contents of the DOCS directory.

Server Home Page

By default the server uses the index.html file as your Web site's home page. You can select a different file to be the home page through the Server Manager if you prefer. From the Server Manager, click the Content Management button and then click the Document Preferences link in the left window. The right window displays the Document Preferences screen, shown in Figure 13.9, where you can change the default index filenames, directory indexing, and home page settings.

FIGURE 13.9

Use the Document Preferences page in the Server Manager to modify default home page settings.

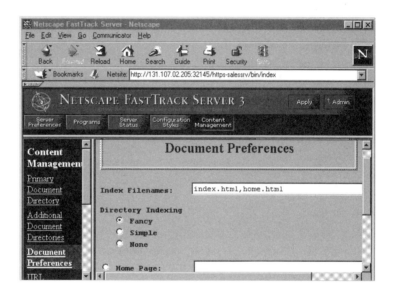

Restricting Access

By default, anyone can access the Netscape FastTrack Server Web site you create on your server. If your Web site is meant to be public, then this default setting is fine. On the other hand, if your Web site is for internal use only, you need to restrict access to it, which you can do by binding the FastTrack Server to NDS. Using NDS, you can create users and groups to set access restrictions to the Web site.

WARNING

Once you enable NDS authentication, everybody who requests access to one of your Web pages will be prompted to enter a password, regardless of whether the document is secure or not. If you want to be able to differentiate documents that require authentication and documents that do not, you must use LDAP authentication.

Procedure 13.3 walks you through the steps for binding the FastTrack Server to NDS, thus restricting access.

PROCEDURE 13.3

Binding the Netscape FastTrack Server to NDS

To bind the FastTrack server to NDS, follow these steps:

1. Start Administration Server and then select the Global Settings tab.

2. In the left window, select Configure Directory Services.

3. In the right window, specify that the FastTrack Server use NDS.

4. You will also be prompted to enter a context. Do so and then click OK.

5. Click Save to save your changes and exit Administration Server. You will need to restart the Administration Server and the FastTrack Server before the changes will be implemented. This procedure enables NDS to control access to the Web server, granting access only to those with authenticated user accounts.

The next step to restrict access to your Web site is to make trustee assignments to the Web contents, directories, and files. When a user tries to access the Web site, he or she will be prompted to enter a login name and password. The login name has to be an NDS user account with access rights to the Web site, or the login request will be denied.

Use Procedure 13.4 to carry out the second phase in restricting access to your Web site.

PROCEDURE 13.4

Creating Access Restrictions for the Netscape FastTrack Server

After you have bound the Netscape FastTrack Server to NDS, restrict access to it by following these steps:

1. Start NetWare Administrator and then navigate through the tree to the desired context.

2. Create a group for the users who will be given access to the Web site.

3. Assign trustee rights to the group on the document directory of the Web site, granting the group at least read and file scan rights.

PROCEDURE 13.4 (CONTINUED)

4. Add members to the group, and make sure you include yourself so that you can verify your success in the next step. (For information on adding user accounts to a group, see Chapter 3).

5. Test the restrictions you've set by attempting to access the Web site using a browser. First use an invalid account to make sure the restrictions deny access, and then enter valid account information to make ensure that valid users can enter. If you've set up the restrictions properly, only members of your Web Users Group object will be able to access the Web site.

Web Server Troubleshooting

The Netscape FastTrack Server will work well in its default configuration under most circumstances. If the server is getting heavy traffic and performance is disappointing, there are a few settings you can change to improve speed. We'll look at these settings in this section, as well as how the content of Web pages can affect the server's performance.

You can affect the server's performance by doing the following to your FastTrack Server:

- Tune server performance with the FastTrack Server Manager. Use this tool to manage and adjust the settings for concurrent requests, simultaneous connections, and other settings that affect the server's performance.

- Modify the Maximum Packet Receive Buffers setting, which controls the amount of memory set aside for incoming network packets.

- Modify the Maximum Physical Receive Packet Size setting, which controls the maximum size for incoming network packets.

- Regulate Web server content. Sometimes problems with server performance are not caused by the server but by the number of large files and complex programs—images, multimedia, Java, imagemaps, and CGI programs—that users must download when they access your Web pages. You might need to regulate and tune this area as well.

These adjustments are explained in detail in the following sections.

Tuning Server Performance with the Server Manager

The Server Manager can manage the following settings, which can affect the Netscape FastTrack Server performance:

Maximum Number of Simultaneous Requests   This parameter controls how many concurrent requests the server can respond to. The default is 48. Since every network is different, we recommend that you closely monitor your Web servers for performance and adjust the parameter as needed. Always keep in mind that an increase in this parameter adds load to the server.

Domain Name System Lookups   This parameter is Off by default. If you suspect slow response from the server, you may want to check whether this feature's setting has been changed to On. If it has, then turning the setting back to Off can improve performance.

Listen-Queue Size   This is a socket-level parameter that indicates how many simultaneous connections the socket can accept. The default is 100. You should be careful when changing this parameter. Again, we recommend that you monitor the performance of the server and adjust this parameter as needed. The main purpose for this setting is to avoid overloading the server with too many connections.

HTTP Persistent Connection Timeout   Persistent connections are a feature of HTTP 1.1. In previous versions of HTTP, a lot of unnecessary overhead was created, because browsers accessing a Web site had to establish a new connection for each Web page being downloaded. With HTTP 1.1, when a client connects to the FastTrack Server and establishes a Web connection, the connection can be maintained for a preset period of time so that all the pages of a Web site can download on the same connection. This reduces overhead and improves performance. Setting the timeout properly ensures a persistent connection for the right amount of time without overloading the server. Because every network is unique, there is no one ideal setting for this parameter, but with good monitoring and analysis you can determine the right setting for your purposes.

PROCEDURE 13.5

Using the Server Manager to Tune Server Performance

To improve server performance using the Server Manager, follow these steps:

1. Start the FastTrack Server Manager and then click the Server Preferences button at the top of the screen.

2. In the left window, click the Performance Tuning link.

3. The right window displays the Performance Tuning screen shown below. Adjust the default settings to reconfigure the parameters discussed in the previous sections. After you've entered the new settings, click Apply. You will need to restart the FastTrack Server to activate the new settings.

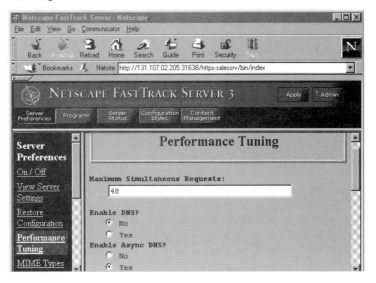

Modify Maximum Packet Receive Buffers

The Maximum Packet Receive Buffers setting controls the amount of memory set aside as a buffer for packets. This value can range from 50 to about 4 billion, and defaults to 100. Larger numbers use more memory.

You may wish to change this setting to a higher number if you have a large amount of Web traffic and have memory to spare. To change the setting, add a command like the following to your STARTUP.NCF file:

```
SET Maximum Packet Receive Buffers = 2000
```

NOTE

This parameter and the Maximum Physical Receive Packet Size parameter (explained below) can only be changed in the STARTUP.NCF file, since memory for buffers is allocated when the server starts.

Modify Maximum Physical Receive Packet Size

The final parameter you may need to change is Maximum Physical Receive Packet Size. This parameter controls the amount of memory set aside as a buffer for each packet. Since different network topologies use different packet sizes, this parameter should be set to accommodate the largest packet size used by your network.

The list below shows the default maximum packet sizes for common network topologies. Unless you are using a different topology, you should not need to change this parameter:

Topology	Maximum Packet Size
Ethernet	1514
Token Ring	4202
ARCnet	512

If you do need to change this parameter, you must do so in the STARTUP.NCF file. Add a line like the following:

```
SET Maximum Physical Receive Packet Size = 4202
```

Regulating Web Server Content

If users are complaining about slow performance when accessing your Web site, changing the above parameters may help. However, it's possible that the problem lies in the content of your Web pages.

Since most Web content is created on a local network, it's easy to forget that the majority of Web users are accessing your site with modems with typical speeds of 33.6K baud. Be especially wary of the following items when creating pages for a public access Web site:

Images Full-color image files can be quite large. In addition, a page with a large number of images will require several threads to load, slowing down the server. You can speed up the server by reducing the number of images where possible. Also, when saving images, set the quality to 256 colors or less, rather than full color, to reduce their size. You may also want to offer text-only versions of the Web pages.

Multimedia Audio and video clips are usually many times larger than image files. Keep these to a minimum, or at least warn users that downloading them may take some time. Audio files can be reduced in size by converting them to a lower-quality format (such as 8-bit rather than 16-bit).

Java   Complex Java applets tend to require a large amount of download time, and may take several minutes to start over a modem connection. You may want to weigh the benefits a Java applet brings to your Web page against the cost in performance. Monitor the performance of browsers downloading the applets to ensure acceptability by the users.

CGI programs   Although CGI programs aren't transmitted to clients, the user has to wait while the program executes. Complex programs can delay this response, as well as putting a heavy load on the server's processor. To ensure that the use of CGIs or ISAPI filters does not overload your server, monitor server performance and adjust your pages accordingly.

Imagemaps   Clickable images also require a bit of processing at the server. You can use client-side rather than server-side maps to improve the server's performance.

FTP Services

*F*TP Services is a powerful tool used to transfer files among dissimilar operating systems. For example, a Unix client can communicate and transfer a file to a NetWare server. NetWare uses two NLMs to provide FTP Services and the NFS name space to support Unix naming conventions and security. These are the two modules:

FTPSERV.NLM   This module provides FTP Services on a NetWare server.

INETD.NLM   This module activates FTPSERV.NLM when an FTP client makes a request. This saves resources on the server when FTP Services is not being used, since this module is much easier on the server.

Before you can install FTP Services, make sure you have the required hardware (including a CD-ROM drive) and software loaded. The FTP server requires TCP/IP to run. Secondly, you need to load NFS name space support by loading the NFS.NAM file, and then entering the command **ADD NAME SPACE NFS TO** *volume_name* on the server console, using the name of the volume where FTP documents are going to be stored.

PROCEDURE 13.6

Installing an FTP Server

To install an FTP server, follow these steps:

1. On the NetWare 5 server designated to be the FTP server, insert the NetWare 5 operating system CD-ROM in the drive.

2. Enter **CDINST** at the console prompt to load non-NSS CD-ROM support.

3. Enter **CD MOUNT NETWARE5** at the console prompt to mount the volume from the CD-ROM on the server. (If you have NSS installed, the CD-ROM will mount automatically.)

4. Enter **NWCONFIG** to install FTP on the server.

5. From the NWCONFIG menu, select Product Options.

6. From the Product Options menu, select Install a Product Not Listed.

7. You will be prompted to select a path to the installation files. Press F3 to choose the installation path, and type the path to the NWUXPS directory on the CD-ROM: **NETWARE5:\PRODUCTS\NWUXPS**

8. The FTP Services installation program now prompts you for the path to your server boot files. Enter the path to the directory on the DOS partition where SERVER.EXE is stored, usually C:\NWSERVER.

9. Next, you are asked whether to install the FTP Services online documentation. Choose Yes or No. After the installation is completed, the UNICON utility is launched. You can choose which services to run and configure them from within this utility, described in the next section.

Managing FTP Services

The main utility for configuring FTP Services is *UNICON*. You can use this utility to manage all aspects of FTP Services, as well as the other services supported. These will be described later in the chapter.

To launch the UNICON utility, enter **UNICON** at the server console. You will be prompted to enter the username and password for the Admin account. After you do, you will be presented with a menu of options. In the following sections, we'll discuss these options and how to configure them.

UNICON Options

After you launch the UNICON utility, you will see the main menu show in Figure 13.10.

Use these menu options to configure FTP Services:

Change Current Server   Allows you to manage FTP and other services for a different server on the network.

View Server Profile   Displays a list of information about the server and the services running on it.

Manage Global Objects   Allows you to manage users and groups for FTP access.

Manage Services   Displays a list of services currently running. You can select each service to access a menu of options specific to that service.

Start/Stop Services   Allows you to start and stop various FTP services. This option is explained in detail in the next section.

Configure Error Reporting   Allows you to choose a log file that will store error messages relating to the various services.

Perform File Operations   Allows you to perform simple file maintenance operations.

Starting or Stopping Services

The Start/Stop Services option displays a list of services that are currently running. By default, the only service running is DNS or NIS. If the FTP services were running, you would see them displayed here. The available services include the following:

DNS Server (Domain Name Service)   Provides identification for domain names.

NIS Server (Network Information Service)   This is an alternate protocol for domain management, and can be used instead of DNS.

FTP Server (File Transfer Protocol)   Allows users to transfer files via FTP.

NetWare-to-Unix Print Gateway   Allows clients on the NetWare network to print to Unix machines.

Unix-to-NetWare Print Server   Allows clients on a Unix network to print to NetWare printers.

These services are collectively called Novell Unix Services.

To start a service that is not currently running, press the Insert key and choose the service from the list. To stop a currently running service, highlight its entry and press Delete.

Managing the FTP Server

To manage the FTP server, go to the UNICON main menu ➤ Manage Services ➤ FTP Server. Select from the following options:

View Current FTP Sessions   Displays a list of users who are currently connected to the FTP server, along with the files they are accessing.

Set Parameters   Allows you to set various parameters for the FTP server. These options are described in detail in the next section.

View FTP Log File   Displays the FTP log file, which logs all FTP accesses.

View Intruder Log File   Displays a separate log of failed logins to the FTP server. These may have been caused by an intruder attempting to hack your server, or simply by valid users entering the wrong password.

Restrict FTP Access   Allows you to edit a file that can restrict access to certain users or domains.

Clear Log Files   Resets both of the log files.

Setting FTP Parameters

The Set Parameters option in the FTP Administration menu (covered in the previous section) allows you to configure settings for the FTP server. The FTP Server Parameters screen is shown in Figure 13.11.

FIGURE 13.11

The FTP Server Parameters screen allows you to configure FTP server settings.

Use the FTP Server Parameters screen to adjust the following settings:

Maximum Number of Sessions   Controls the maximum number of users that can be simultaneously connected to FTP. Depending on the speed of your server and the number of users, you may need to adjust this parameter to limit connections. The default is 16.

Maximum Session Length   Sets the maximum length of a single FTP session. Modifying this setting can be useful, ensuring that users log out and make a session available to another user within a reasonable length of time.

Idle Time Before FTP Server Unloads   Sets the amount of time a connection can be open with no FTP access before the server automatically unloads.

Anonymous User Access   Lets you choose whether anonymous (guest) access is allowed. Your decision on whether to allow anonymous access will depend on the security level you want and the purpose of the FTP site. Anonymous FTP is explained in the next section.

Default User's Home Directory   Sets the default directory users will be in when first connected to the FTP server.

Anonymous User's Home Directory This directory and its subdirectories are made accessible to anonymous users.

Default Name Space Sets whether the FTP server accepts DOS filenames or long filenames. You must have the long name space module loaded in order to use non-DOS filenames.

Intruder Detection Enables intruder detection when set to Yes. This disables the FTP server temporarily after a certain number of unsuccessful login attempts are made.

Number of Unsuccessful Attempts Sets the number of unsuccessful login attempts that will be permitted before the user account is locked out.

Detection Reset Interval Controls the amount of time after an intruder is detected before other users regain access to the FTP server.

Log Level Controls how much detail is included in log entries.

Configuring the FTP Server

Once you've installed the FTP server, there are a few tasks you'll need to perform to configure the server for your needs. By default, when you install the FTP server no one has access to the FTP site. You need to decide who will be given access to the server and what they can do on it, which will depend on the purpose of the site and the type of files users can download. To implement your decisions, follow the instructions in the sections below.

Setting Up Anonymous FTP

Anonymous FTP is the most common type of FTP access. It allows you to make files publicly available over the Internet or to all users on your network. This is not a good option if you are providing sensitive files for download. Use Procedure 13.8 to set up anonymous FTP on your server.

PROCEDURE 13.7

Configuring Anonymous FTP

To configure anonymous FTP, follow these steps:

1. Load UNICON from the server console and then go to Manage Services ➤ FTP Server ➤ Server Parameters. In the FTP Server Parameters screen, set Anonymous User Access to Yes.

2. Create a directory for anonymous FTP on the server from a client workstation.

3. Assign the directory to the Anonymous User's Home Directory field in Server Parameters ➤ Anonymous FTP.

4. Place the files you are going to make available for downloads in the directory you created for the Anonymous account. This can be done from a client connected to the server with access to the directory. Be sure to set rights to the files, as described later in this section. Because allowing anonymous FTP access opens your site to potential security risks, make sure you set proper restrictions to protect your documents.

Managing FTP Users

In addition to allowing access to anonymous users, you can configure your FTP server to allow wider access to users with passwords, as described in Procedure 13.8.

This procedure allows you to improve security on your FTP server by restricting access to the server based on individual user needs. A combined approach is generally used so that guests can get access to certain files via anonymous FTP and your users can use their network accounts for fuller access. This allows for a more secure environment.

Creating an FTP User

To create an FTP user, follow these steps:

1. From the UNICON main menu, go to Manage Global Objects ➤ Manage Users ➤ User Filtering Options.

2. From the User Filtering Options menu, select By NetWare Name. (This option allows you to view the user list by NDS User object name and context.)

3. Press Enter to show the list of FTP users. (The only user at this point is Guest.)

4. Press Insert to create a new user. Choose Unix as the user type.

PROCEDURE 13.8 (CONTINUED)

5. Enter a name for the user. Use the user's NetWare login name, if applicable. Repeat this process for every user account you wish to create.

6. Press Esc to return to the user list.

7. Highlight the Username option and press Enter.

8. You are now shown a list of NDS users. If the FTP user corresponds to an NDS user, choose that username here. The same rights assigned to the NDS user account on the file system will now be available to the new FTP/Unix user.

9. Press Esc to return to the UNICON main menu. You have now created a user account for the FTP server. This user account corresponds to an NDS account and the rights associated with it.

Transferring Files with FTP

Once you have installed and properly configured the FTP server, you should test it using an FTP client. You'll need a properly configured workstation and FTP client software. Luckily, FTP client software is easy to find—this function is included in most Web browsers, and an FTP command is built into Windows 95. In addition, many free and commercial FTP clients are available on the Internet.

Client Requirements

Before using FTP software on a workstation, be sure it is configured correctly:

- TCP/IP should be installed and configured.

- The IP address, subnet mask, and other settings should be set correctly, as discussed in Chapter 12.

- For NetWare clients, the Novell Client should be installed and configured to use TCP/IP.

Using a Web Browser

You can easily use FTP from a Web browser. To do this, you'll need to use a URL to refer to the server. This consists of the protocol (FTP), the host name, the directory name, and the filename. FTP uses the Unix filename format, so use forward slashes to divide the file.

For example, the file SYS:\PUBLIC\SALES.DOC on the local FTP server FileServ would have this URL:

```
ftp://FileServ/sys/public/sales.doc
```

or, if you want to enter with a user account rather than as an anonymous user:

```
ftp://user_name:password@FileServ/sys/public/sales.doc
```

On the Internet, the directory /pub/netware on the server `ftp.starlingtech` `.com` would have this URL:

```
ftp://ftp.starlingtech.com/pub/netware/
```

If you connect to an FTP server and you do not specify a directory name, the browser will display a list of the files in the home directory of the user account used to connect to the server, as shown in Figure 13.12. You can then click on a file to download it.

F I G U R E   13.12

A file listing on an FTP
server

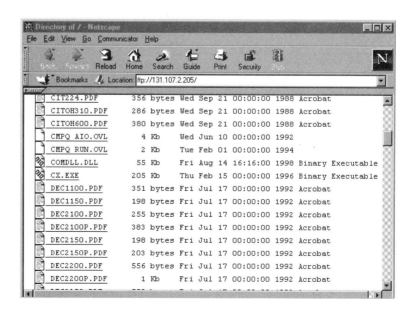

FTP filenames and directory names are case-sensitive. Be sure you use the correct case.

Using Command-Line FTP

Although not as friendly as a Web browser, command-line versions of FTP that use a consistent syntax are available for virtually every operating system. For example, you can use the FTP command from a DOS prompt under Windows 95. The following command begins an FTP session with the ftp.starlingtech.com server:

```
FTP ftp.starlingtech.com
```

Once you are connected to the FTP server, you can use FTP commands to control the FTP session. Some of the most common FTP commands are listed in Table 13.1.

T A B L E 13.1	Command	Function
Common FTP Commands	GET *filename*	Downloads a specified file from the server.
	PUT *filename*	Uploads the specified file to the server from the current directory.
	MGET *filespec*	Downloads multiple files using a wildcard.
	MPUT *filespec*	Uploads multiple files using a wildcard.
	BIN	Changes the transfer mode from text to binary. Non-text files must be transferred using binary mode.
	DIR	Displays a more detailed list of files with ownership information, size, and other details.
	LS	Displays a list of all files in the directory.

Troubleshooting FTP Services

Like most other parts of the network, FTP does not always run smoothly. In the sections below we'll look at some of the common problems you may encounter while using FTP and how to solve them.

Users Can't Connect to FTP Server

If users are unable to connect to your FTP server, check the following:

- There may be a network problem. Verify that the server is up and that there are no problems with the network wiring.

- The FTP server may not be running. Use the Start/Stop Services option on the UNICON main menu to verify that the FTP Service is started.

- The client software may not be correctly configured. If your users cannot reach *any* FTP sites, verify that FTP is configured on their workstation and that the FTP software is installed correctly.

Connection Refused by FTP Server

If users are able to connect to the FTP server, but receive an error message, check for the following:

- The FTP server may be overloaded. Check the Maximum Number of Sessions parameter and increase it if necessary.

- Access to the FTP server may be restricted. Go to the Restrict Access page from the FTP Administration menu to check whether restrictions have been set appropriately.

Users Cannot Download a File

If the user can connect to your FTP server but can't download a particular file, check that the file exists in the proper directory, and that its rights have been set to readable—both in the NetWare file system and in UNICON. If a user needs to upload a file, be sure that the directory is set to writeable.

If a download stops during a file transfer or is extremely slow, the server may be overloaded. To alleviate this problem, upgrade the server or limit the number of concurrent users by adjusting the Maximum Number of Sessions parameter.

Review

This chapter covered the WWW and FTP Services provided by Net-Ware 5. Along with the WWW Services, the Netscape FastTrack Server for NetWare is Novell's WWW implementation. Novell's FTP Services are also included with the release of NetWare 5.

WWW Services

NetWare 5 uses the Netscape FastTrack Server to provide Web services to the Internet or your company intranet. Your Web documents can be viewed with a Web client, or browser. Web servers and browsers communicate using HTTP (Hypertext Transfer Protocol).

Netscape FastTrack Server

The Netscape FastTrack Server is a complicated piece of software, and may require a slight upgrade to your machine. This chapter covered the hardware and software requirements for the Netscape FastTrack Server, as well as the installation process. You also learned how to configure, manage, and troubleshoot a Netscape FastTrack Server. The Netscape FastTrack Server uses the following NLMs to provide Web services:

- CRON.NLM (NetWare Scheduler)
- NSHTTPD.NLM (Netscape FastTrack Server for NetWare)
- NETDB.NLM (network database access)
- CSSYSMSG.NLM (systems messages facility)
- BTRIEVE.NLM (Btrieve client/server database)
- NSLCGI.NLM (LCGI support library)
- ADMSERV.NLM (Netscape Administration Server)

Configuring the Web Server

To configure the FastTrack Server, use the Administration Server. The Administration Server is accessed through its own home page. Within the Administration Server, you can access the Server Manager, which gives you numerous forms for configuring and managing the FastTrack Server.

Installing and Managing FTP Services

FTP (File Transfer Protocol) is one of the most commonly used Internet protocols. Novell FTP Services adds support for this protocol on a NetWare server. You can use this protocol for general-purpose file transfers over the Internet or an intranet—even across multiple platforms.

This chapter covered system and software requirements for installing FTP Services and the procedure for installing the FTP server.

Once installed, FTP Services is managed with the UNICON utility. This utility allows you to set parameters, create and manage FTP users, and view log files.

FTP File Transfers

FTP clients are available for virtually all operating systems. Most Web browsers include an FTP capability. You can also use command-line FTP clients, such as the one provided with Windows 95 or Windows 98.

FTP Troubleshooting

FTP errors are most often caused by the following circumstances:

- There is a problem with the network connection.
- The FTP server is not running or is not configured properly.
- Use is restricted, or the maximum number of users has been exceeded.
- Rights are set improperly for a file or directory.

In the last section of this chapter, you learned how to investigate and resolve these problems.

CNE Practice Test Questions

1. The protocol used for Web servers is:

   A. FTP

   B. SMTP

   C. HTTP

   D. TFTP

2. Web documents are typically viewed with:

A. A Web viewer

B. A Web browser

C. Any word processor

D. An HTTP server

3. The language used to create hypertext Web documents is:

A. HTTP

B. SGML

C. HTML

D. NetBasic

4. Which protocol must be installed on client machines for them to have access to the Web?

A. HTTP

B. HTML

C. TCP/IP

D. FTP

5. By default, anonymous users have which rights to Web documents?

A. Read and write

B. Read only

C. Write only

D. Read, write, and create

6. The default data directory for Web documents is:

A. SYS:WEB\DOCS

B. SYS:WEBDOCS

   C. SYS:\NOVONYX\SUITESPOT\DOCS

   D. SYS:WEB\SERVER\DOCS\HTML

7. Which configuration file is used to restrict access to documents?

   A. CONFIG.CFG

   B. ACCESS.CFG

   C. RESTRICT.CFG

   D. None of the above

8. How much RAM is required for NetWare 5 to support Web Services?

   A. 24MB

   B. 48MB

   C. 64MB

   D. 32MB

9. The Netscape FastTrack Server software itself requires how much disk storage?

   A. 50MB

   B. 70MB

   C. 90MB

   D. 100MB

10. Along with TCP/IP, which of the following is required to install Fast-Track Server?

   A. IPX protocol

   B. A unique IP address

   C. A default gateway

   D. All of the above

11. FTP is mainly used for:

   A. Logging in to remote servers

   B. Transferring files

   C. Sending files via e-mail

   D. Server management

12. You can install Novell FTP Services using:

   A. SETUP program

   B. NWCONFIG utility

   C. UNICON utility

   D. CDROM utility

13. FTP settings are managed with this utility:

   A. NWCONFIG

   B. INETCFG

   C. UNICON

   D. FTPCON

14. The FTP Service:

   A. Starts and stops automatically when needed

   B. Can be started or stopped using UNICON

   C. Can be stopped by unloading UNICON

   D. Is always running

15. Which of the following is *not* a service provided by Novell Unix Services?

   A. Unix-to-NetWare Print Server

   B. HTTP

   C. FTP Server

   D. DNS Server

16. The Maximum Number of Sessions option controls:

    A. The maximum number of sessions per user

    B. The maximum number of sessions per day

    C. The maximum number of concurrent users

    D. The maximum number of configured FTP users

17. If the FTP server is frequently overloaded, one solution is to adjust which parameter?

    A. Idle Time Before FTP Server Unloads

    B. Maximum Number of Sessions

    C. Maximum Bandwidth

    D. Intruder Detection

18. Which of the following is an example of proper FTP URL syntax?

    A. `http://ftp.starlingtech.com/pub/novell/`

    B. `ftp://ftp.starlingtech.com\pub\novell`

    C. `ftp://ftp.starlingtech.com/pub/novell/`

    D. `ftp:ftp.starlingtech.com:pub/novell`

19. Which users can log in to the FTP server?

    A. Any NDS user

    B. Users who have been given access through UNICON

    C. Administrators only

    D. Users in the FTP server's context

20. Which is the correct FTP command for downloading a file?

    A. `DOWNLOAD file1.zip`

    B. `GET file1.zip`

    C. `PUT file1.zip`

    D. `MPUT file1.zip`

21. If a user can connect to the FTP server but receives an error message, which is *not* a possible cause of the problem?

A. Access is restricted

B. FTP server is overloaded

C. Network is down

D. User is not set up correctly

CHAPTER

14

Securing the NDS Tree

Roadmap

This chapter covers NDS Advanced Security and its administration, a section of the CNE core requirement "NetWare 5 Advanced Administration."

Topics Covered

- NDS Default Rights

- Planning NDS Security

- Determining Administrative Strategy

Skills You'll Learn

- List the default rights for the Directory objects

- Understand a multicontext environment, and know the guidelines and considerations when implementing NDS security

- Understand the concepts of centralized and distributed administration

- Determine the appropriate administrative role for a given scenario

A s companies become more dependent on their networks, the issue of security and user access to network resources falls in the hands of the network administrator. Securing the NDS tree is a critical component of NetWare 5 security.

Chapter 4 covered NDS security concepts such as object and property rights, trustees, and how inheritance works. You also learned how to assign rights and how to change them through assigning new rights, or IRFs. In this chapter, you will be introduced to advanced concepts in NDS security and its administration.

Administrators need to balance two important tasks: protecting network resources against intruders and ensuring that users can access resources. This chapter helps you with both. There is only one Admin user account by default in the tree. This ensures that only those people familiar with the Admin account can carry out administrative tasks.

You will learn to assign only needed rights, by assessing whether the default rights are enough or not. Advanced concepts like mobile user needs and a multicontext environment are important to understand, because they help you to anticipate additional rights that might be needed.

Another advanced concept that can help you to administrate the tree is that of distributed management. You will learn later in this chapter about different roles you can assign without giving full rights, keeping the tree secure. This is distributed administration.

The tools you will use to control the file system and NDS security (most importantly NetWare Administrator) were introduced in Chapter 4. Refer to that chapter for information on how to perform the tasks described in this chapter.

NDS Default Rights

Default rights allow the authorized users and network administrators to access and administer new objects. From the moment you create a new Directory (or NDS tree), default rights are assigned to all Directory objects as they are created.

Being aware of what those default rights are will help you identify where your tree lacks security and implement changes accordingly. Default rights are described in the following sections.

New Tree

The following are the default rights for a new tree:

[Public]   Browse [B] and inheritable [I] object rights to [Root] object

Admin   Supervisor [S] and inheritable [I] object rights to [Root] object

When a tree is initially created, the Admin user (or object) is given supervisor and inheritable object rights to the [Root] object. The inheritable object right allows inheritance over the entire tree of the supervisor right.

The [Public] object has browse rights to the [Root], thus making the [Root] visible to all users. [Public] is also given the inheritable object right, which allows the browse right to be inherited throughout the tree.

All objects are equivalent to the [Public] trustee object; therefore any rights assigned to the [Public] trustee object are also assigned to all objects.

Container Object

The following are the default rights of the container object:

- Read [R] rights to the Login Script property of the container
- Read [R] rights to the Print Job Configuration property of the container

All container objects have equivalent rights to their parent container, and all leaf objects have equivalent rights to their container object and parent container objects. This means that all user objects can read the login script and print job configuration of their own container and the containers above them in the NDS tree.

Server Object

The following are the default rights of the server object:

- Supervisor [S] object rights to itself
- [Public] has read [R] rights to the Messaging Server property of the server object

The default rights of the server object allow the server to update its own properties and add information to itself. Users have read rights to the Messaging Server property on their server, which enables them to locate the messaging server assigned to their server. To install a server in the tree, a user has to have supervisor rights and inheritable object rights to the partition and container in which the server is to be installed.

Admin Object

The following are the default trustee rights assigned to the Admin object:

- Supervisor [S] and inheritable [I] object rights to the [Root] object

This allows the Admin user object to administrate the whole tree, provided the inheritable object right is not filtered. (Filtering NDS rights were discussed in Chapter 4.)

User Object

The following are the default rights of the User object:

- Read [R] rights to all property rights
- Read and write [RW] property rights to the user's own login script
- Read and write [RW] property rights to create and send print jobs to the (non-NDPS) printer
- The [Root] object is assigned the read [R] right to the Network Addresses and Group properties of the User object.
- The [Public] object is assigned the read [R] right to the Default Server property so that NDS can determine the default server of the User object.

Individuals on the network have their own user objects in the NDS tree. By default, NDS allows user objects to identify the network address and any group that they are a member of, determine the default server they are assigned to, and change their own login script and print job configuration.

For better control and security, create a user template and modify the read and write property rights for the login script and print job configuration to read only. This way you, as the Admin for all user objects, will be the only one who can modify these properties.

Public Object

The following are the default rights for the [Public] object:

- Browse [B] rights and inheritable [I] object rights to [Root]

WARNING When you assign rights to the [Public] trustee object, all users will obtain these rights.

Planning NDS Security

When you install NDS for the first time, a tree is formed and the Admin account is created. Supervisor object rights and inheritable object rights to the [Root] object are assigned by default to the Admin object. This makes the Admin object the only user account that is capable of managing the tree by default.

In small networks, the default rights are sufficient to manage a NetWare 5 network. Larger networks that host multicontext environments may require additional NDS rights for users needing access to network resources. Planning is critical in this process. You need to determine which resources each user needs to access and who administrates those resources.

User Access to Resources

As you saw in Chapter 4, there are some guidelines you can follow when implementing NDS security. You should give additional rights to NDS objects to allow access to network resources in multiple contexts. You will also need to give additional rights if you want to distribute administrative tasks to other users.

For most users, default NDS rights are enough to access network resources. In some instances you need to grant users additional rights. For example:

- To use a Directory Map object, users need read rights to the Path property of the object.

- To use the Profile Login Script object, users need read rights to the Login Script property or All Properties of the Profile object.

- To administrate an object's properties, users need the read and write rights to properties you want them to administrate.

There is a particular group of people who need special attention: your mobile and remote users. Assign additional NDS rights to these users only when necessary. When doing so, follow these guidelines:

- Use default NDS rights to begin with.

- Do not use the All Properties option unless necessary. Use Selected Property Rights instead, because when you assign a right to All Properties, you could be giving more rights than you intended.

- Avoid using the All Properties option with the write [W] right, for this will give the user access to the Access Control List (ACL) of the objects given rights. Assigning a user the write right to the ACL property of an object gives the user the ability to modify the trustee list of the object.

Administrative Roles

The Admin object is the only account capable of administrating the tree unless you make changes to the default settings. As a precaution to protect the Admin account, follow these guidelines:

- Assign all objects and property rights in addition to the supervisor and inheritable object rights to the Admin object at the [Root] object. This ensures that a supervisor IRF will not block access to an object, its properties, or its contents.

- Rename the Admin object. This makes it more difficult for users to identify the Admin account.

- Avoid making other user accounts equivalent to the Admin account. If the Admin account is deleted accidentally, then all accounts that are equivalent to it will revert to their own trustee assignments.

- Create and use organizational role objects for administrative tasks when possible.

- Change passwords regularly.

Determining Administrative Strategy

In a large network, it is important to determine who will administer—or control—the Directory tree and the objects within it. You can use two kinds of administration in NetWare 5: centralized administration and distributed administration. Both of these are made possible by NDS, and they are discussed in the following sections.

Centralized Administration

It is possible to use the Admin user account, or a group of administrators, to control the entire network. This is one of the benefits of NDS, and it may be the best solution for smaller organizations. NetWare 5 assigns a central administrator, the Admin user, by default. The Admin user is given the supervisor and inheritable rights to the [Root] object and inherits rights to all objects unless they are blocked.

Even if you choose to use distributed administration on your network, you should leave one user (such as the Admin account) with full rights to the entire Directory tree. This account is required to assign other administrators, move objects in the tree, create partitions, merge trees, and manage time synchronization.

A central administrator can also be used in emergencies, such as when a portion of the Directory tree is left without an administrator.

WARNING   Avoid logging in with the Admin account unless you require the rights to administer the entire Directory tree. If the Admin account is left logged in and unattended, someone could cause serious damage to the network.

Distributed Administration

One of the most important advantages of NDS security is that it allows distributed administration. You can assign separate administrators to different branches of the Directory tree, as well as a separate administrator for the server's file system. The following sections describe the types of administrators you can create.

Container Administrators

You can create an administrator who has rights to one container in the Directory tree and the objects within it. This assignment is called a *container administrator*. Since the Directory tree is often divided by locations, divisions, or workgroups, this is often the best way to distribute administrative tasks. The concept of a container administrator is illustrated in Figure 14.1.

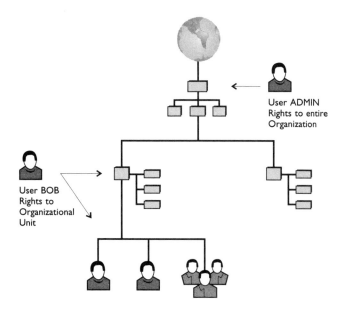

You can assign the rights for a container directly to the user who administers it. However, the Organizational Role object is a better way to create container administrators. By using an Organizational Role as the administrator, you gain the following benefits:

- If the job of container administrator is switched to a different user, you can simply make the new user the occupant of the Organizational Role object.

- If two or more users will share the job of container administration, you can assign multiple occupants to the Organizational Role.

- If some containers are too small to have their own administrator, you can assign the same user to two or more Organizational Roles.

As you can see, the Organizational Role provides a flexible, simple method of assigning container administrators. Create a container administrator using the steps in Procedure 14.1.

PROCEDURE 14.1

Creating a Container Administrator

To create a container administrator, follow these steps:

1. Create the Organizational Role object. You should create this object inside the container that it will administer. See Chapter 3 for details on creating Organizational Roles.

2. Assign the Organizational Role as a trustee of the container, and give it rights. The type of rights depends on your network security plans:

   - Assign the Organizational Role object supervisor or full rights [SBCDRI] if the Organizational Role object will control the file system also. If you give the object the supervisor right to the container, that account also inherits the supervisor right to the file system of any servers in the container.

   - Assign the browse, create, delete, rename, and inherit [BCDRI] rights separately if you wish to assign a separate administrator for the file system.

3. Assign any other rights you wish to give the Organizational Role object, such as file system rights (if they were not assigned in Step 2).

4. Make one or more users occupants of the Organizational Role object. From this point on, the users who are occupants of the Organizational Role object will be able to administrate the objects assigned to them. If a person leaves the company, all you need to do is remove that person's account from the tree, making it easier to manage administrators.

Exclusive Container Administrators

In a network for which security is very important, it may be unacceptable for the central administrator to have full rights (or any rights) to a container or file system in the tree. Because of this, you may want to make the container administrator the only administrator for the container. You can assign an *exclusive container administrator* by blocking the rights of central administrators (such as Admin) with the IRF. This allows you to maintain a highly secure network. Figure 14.2 illustrates the concept of an exclusive container administrator.

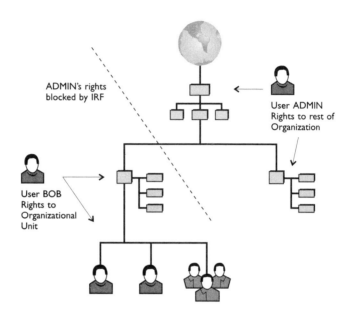

When you create an exclusive container administrator, there is no longer a central administrator. Therefore, you should take the following precautions when you set up this type of administrator:

- If the container administrator rights are assigned to an Organizational Role object, it is best to give explicit rights for the container to a second user (or Organizational Role) also. Otherwise, if the Organizational Role object is deleted, you lose control over that branch of the Directory tree. If this happens, there is no easy solution.

- Make sure that the Organizational Role object also has the supervisor right to its own object. This allows the container administrator to add other administrators. In addition, the Admin user can be added to the Organizational Role temporarily if a central administrator is required.

WARNING If you do use exclusive administrators, you should coordinate with them and reestablish a central administrator before performing operations such as moving trees. You can restore a central administrator's rights. The exclusive administrator simply needs to change the IRF to allow inheritance again.

As noted earlier, if at all possible, it is best to keep a central administrator in addition to the container administrators. A central administrator will be needed when merging Directory trees or moving objects in the tree. This user provides a solution for emergencies when the container administrator is deleted or the user who occupies the role is not available. Procedure 14.2 describes the steps for creating an exclusive container administrator.

PROCEDURE 14.2

Creating an Exclusive Container Administrator

To create an exclusive container administrator, follow these steps:

1. Create the Organizational Role object. You should create the Organizational Role within the container that it will administer.

2. Assign one or more users as occupants of the Organizational Role. It is important to do this now, because after the following steps are performed, the Admin user will no longer be able to add users to the role.

3. Assign the Organizational Role as a trustee of the container object. You should assign full rights [SBCDRI] to ensure that an IRF of an object or container does not prevent access.

4. Give the Organizational Role the supervisor right to its own object. This step ensures that the occupant of the role can add other occupants. If a central administrator is needed (such as when merging trees), the Admin user can be added to this role.

5. Change the IRF of the container so that only the browse object right and the read property right are granted. This allows other administrators to examine objects in this branch of the Directory tree, but not to control them.

PROCEDURE 14.2 (CONTINUED)

6. If Admin or another user has an explicit trustee assignment to the container, remove the assignment so that only the container administrator will have control over the container.

7. If Admin or another user has rights to the administrator Organizational Role object, remove those rights. This prevents other administrators from restricting the exclusive container administrator's rights or giving themselves rights. (If the administrator Organizational Role object is located in the container it will administer, the IRF will prevent other administrators from accessing it.)

All of these measures are implemented for the exclusive container administrator to protect it from the central administrators. If there is any back door left, this nullifies the concept of an exclusive container administrator.

WARNING

The NetWare Administrator utility does not allow you to filter the supervisor right unless you have already given this right to a container administrator. You should also assign this right to at least one other user, because if the administrator Organizational Role is deleted, you lose access to that branch of the Directory tree.

File System Administrators

You can assign a separate administrator for the file system of a server. As with other types of administrators, this assignment is best accomplished with an Organizational Role object. This type of administrator is illustrated in Figure 14.3, and the process for creating a file system administrator is described in Procedure 14.3.

F I G U R E   14.3

A file system adminis-
trator is given rights to
the file system.

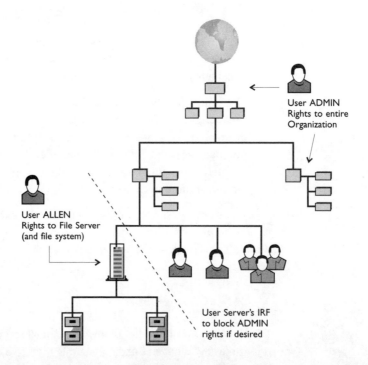

User ADMIN
Rights to entire
Organization

User ALLEN
Rights to File Server
(and file system)

User Server's IRF
to block ADMIN
rights if desired

PROCEDURE 14.3

Creating a File System Administrator

To create a File System Administrator, follow these steps:

1. Create the Organizational Role object, and add one or more users to it.

2. Make the Organizational Role a trustee of the File Server object with the supervisor right. The administrator will inherit the supervisor right for all volumes on the server. As an alternative, you can assign file system rights separately for each volume (or only one volume) on a server.

3. If you wish the administrator to be an exclusive administrator of the file system, block the rights of other administrators by removing the supervisor right from the file server's IRF. Admin (or another admin-istrator) was given rights to the file system when the server was installed. You need to remove this trustee assignment to create an exclusive file system administrator.

PROCEDURE 14.3 (CONTINUED)

The default file system administrator is the Admin account. You must make sure that the Admin account does not have inherited or trustee rights to the server object. This is the final step in securing the exclusive file system administrator from any central administrator.

If you create an exclusive file system administrator, be sure to assign the file system rights to at least one other user so that you will not lose access to the server.

Other Types of Administrators

In NetWare 3.1*x*, you could assign a variety of managers and operators. You can use Organizational Roles to duplicate these administrators in NetWare 5:

- *User account managers* and *workgroup managers*: These can be replaced with container administrators in NDS. You can use Organizational Roles to create user account managers and workgroup managers, as described in the previous sections.

- *Print queue operator*: Print Queue objects in NDS have a Print Queue Operators property. You can create a print queue operator by adding a user or Organizational Role to the list of print queue operators.

- *Print server operator*: The Print Server object has a Print Server Operators property. You can add users or an Organizational Role to the operators list to assign operators.

- *Password managers*: The Password Manager can use either a User object or Organizational Role object, but needs read and write property rights to the Password Management property of the container to be managed.

- *Print Job Operator*: The Print Job Operator can be a user object or Organizational Role object, but you have to add it to the printer operators list.

These are not the only types of administrators you can assign. The flexibility of NDS security allows you to create highly specialized types of administrators. You can create Organizational Roles that combine the roles described above or assign specific rights to suit the needs of your network.

Review

This chapter covered three aspects of NDS security:

- NDS default rights
- Planning NDS security
- Determining administrative strategy

NDS Default Rights

All NDS objects are created with default rights assigned to them. The Admin user object is assigned supervisor and inheritable object rights to the [Root] object. This gives the Admin account administrative rights to the entire tree. The [Public] trustee is assigned browse and inherited object rights, allowing all users to view the tree. In most cases the default rights are sufficient to administrate the tree, but NDS security is flexible enough to adapt to more complicated administrative structures, as explained in this chapter.

Planning NDS Security

As we have seen with default rights, sometimes the default NDS rights are not enough to provide access to network resources. In cases where users need access to profile login scripts and directory map objects, they must be granted additional rights beyond the default rights. When security and resource administration need to be delegated, then administrative roles have to be assigned and additional rights granted. You need to be familiar with the NDS object and property rights and be careful about how many rights you grant.

Administration

Two types of administration are possible in NDS: centralized administration and distributed administration. You can also use a combination of both methods. You can assign three types of administrators in the Directory:

- A container administrator has rights for all objects within a container.

- An exclusive container administrator has supervisor or All Property rights for all objects, including itself, in a container. In addition, an IRF is used to prevent other administrators from having rights to the container's objects.

- A file system administrator has rights for a server's file system. An IRF can be used to block the rights of other administrators if desired.

By using Organizational Role objects, you can also create other types of administrators to suit the needs of your network.

CNE Practice Test Questions

1. What are the two types of administration in NetWare 5?

   A. Distributed and container

   B. Centralized and distributed

   C. Centralized and decentralized

   D. Distributed and central

2. Which object is best used to assign an administrator?

   A. Organization

   B. Organizational Unit

   C. Organizational Role

   D. Group

3. Who might need additional rights?

   A. Server

   B. [Public]

   C. Remote users

   D. [Root]

4. Which of the following is *not* a network resource?

   A. File server

   B. [Public] object

   C. Network printer

   D. Network application

5. An exclusive container administrator:

   A. Shares responsibilities with other administrators

   B. Has rights for a single container only

   C. Is the only administrator for a container

   D. Cannot control the file system

6. To which property right should you change a user's login script and print job configuration property rights for better security and control?

   A. Read [R]

   B. Browse [B]

   C. Inheritable [I]

   D. Supervisor [S]

7. A container administrator can do all of the following *except:*

   A. Write and maintain login scripts

   B. Move objects

C. Create user accounts

D. Create printer objects

8. What are the two objects automatically created when you install NDS on the first server?

A. Admin and [Root]

B. [Root] and a print server object

C. [Root] and a container object

D. [Public] and an Organizational Role object

9. True or False: In most cases, the default NDS rights are sufficient for administering the network.

A. True

B. False

10. All of the following are rights *except:*

A. Browse [B]

B. Read [R]

C. Inheritable [I]

D. Configure [C]

11. The following is a right of [Public]:

A. [RW] to [Root]

B. [C] to server

C. [B] to [Root]

D. [RW] to default server for user object

12. NDS allows user objects to do which of the following:

    A. Change the rights assigned to them by the Admin

    B. Install their own server objects

    C. Identify and change another user object's login script

    D. Identify the default server to which the user object is assigned

13. The _____ is considered a _____ administrator when it is assigned rights to add user accounts.

    A. Admin, centralized

    B. Distributed, file system

    C. Organizational Role object, container

CHAPTER

15

Maintaining Novell Directory Services

This chapter covers several advanced features of NDS administration, including partitioning, replicating, and troubleshooting the NDS database. You need to manage Directory services to ensure its reliability and consistency. Users cannot access resources administrated by the Directory if it is corrupted or inaccessible. There is much more to being a network administrator than just creating users and giving them access to files and printers, as you will see in this chapter.

Partitioning and Replicating Your Directory Tree

Because the Directory can grow to include a large amount of information, Novell lets you divide it into smaller units. These units, called *partitions*, can then be replicated onto other servers. Because it can be divided and distributed across multiple servers, NDS is referred to as a *distributed database*.

Novell's terminology can be confusing. Not only are there disk directories and an NDS Directory, but also disk partitions and NDS partitions, which are two different things. In this chapter, the word *partition* is used exclusively for NDS partitions.

NDS, when distributed, appears to network users as a completely unified structure without separations. The partitions may break limbs off the Directory tree and spread them about, but to the network user, the tree still appears and functions as a single cohesive Directory.

Partitioning the Directory

In NDS, a *partition* is a branch of the Directory tree. When you install NetWare 5, a single partition, called the [Root] partition (because it starts with the [Root] object), is created. The [Root] partition includes the [Root] object and all other objects, as shown in Figure 15.1.

FIGURE 15.1

The [Root] partition is created during the installation process.

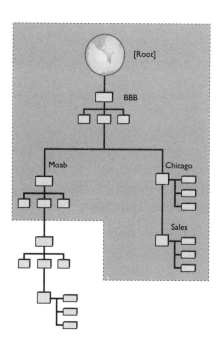

Partitions are made up of container objects, under which leaf objects are kept together as a group. Leaf objects are always kept in the same partition as the container object that holds them. The partition is named after the parent object.

Partitions are referred to as *parent* or *child* partitions, depending on their relationship to other partitions. A partition that resides above another is called the parent partition; the one below it is called the child. This relationship is illustrated in Figure 15.2.

F I G U R E   15.2

Partitions are called parent or child partitions, depending on their location.

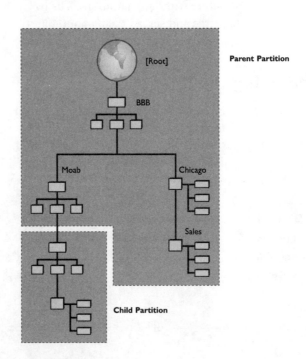

Replicating the Directory

Each partition can be copied and stored on any NetWare 5 server on your network. This is called *replication*. Replication is useful for two main reasons:

- It establishes greater fault tolerance. By storing copies of partitions on multiple servers, you can help ensure that access to your Directory will remain intact, even if a disk crashes or servers go down. Also, you will give users greater freedom to log in without being dependent on one particular server's availability to provide authentication, since a replica can fulfill this role in place of the original partition.

- It can improve network performance. If users need to use a WAN link to access Directory information, you can decrease response time and network traffic by providing a replica that they can access locally.

Types of Replicas

There are four different types of NDS replicas. Each is used for a particular purpose, as described in the following sections.

Master Replicas   NetWare 5 creates a *master replica* when a partition is defined. This replica controls all partition operations, including creating, merging, and moving partitions. The master replica also controls replica creation, deletion, and repair.

The term *replica* can be a bit confusing. Even if there is only one copy of a partition, it is still called a replica. If there is only one replica, it must be a master replica.

There can be only one master replica for each partition. When objects are changed in a master replica, the same change will be made automatically on all replicas of that partition. The server that stores the master replica of a partition must be accessible before you can split the partition (create a new partition) or join it with another partition.

Read/Write Replicas   *Read/write replicas* contain the same information as the master replica, but each partition may have multiple read/write replicas. Changes made to these replicas will also be reproduced automatically on all other replicas of the same partition. Read/write replicas, however, cannot be used when splitting or joining a partition.

If your network loses a master replica, you can change one of the read/write replicas to master replica status. Read/write replicas support the login process by providing authentication.

Read-Only Replicas   *Read-only replicas* are used on servers where reads of the partition are necessary but writes are to be prevented. Because read-only replicas do not support the authentication process, their usefulness is limited.

These replicas contain the same information as the master and read/write replicas but do not allow for alteration of objects. You can use them for searching and viewing objects.

Subordinate Reference Replicas   You do not create *subordinate reference replicas*. NDS creates these replicas automatically. Subordinate references do not contain object data; they point to a replica that does. They do not support user authentication, object management, or even object viewing.

NDS creates subordinate references on a server when a replica of a partition appears on that server without a replica of that partition's child. A subordinate reference is simply a pointer (similar to a Windows shortcut) describing the location of the child partition or its replica.

Subordinate references ensure that there is efficient access to relevant portions of the NDS database on each server. NDS will automatically remove the subordinate reference if the child partition's replica is added to the server.

Guidelines for Placing Replicas

There are many factors that you should consider when deciding where to place the replicas on your network. These are discussed in the following sections.

Strategic Placement of Replicas   To maximize fault tolerance and access to replicas without compromising network efficiency, place replicas on servers located near the users who will be using them regularly. This will allow access to replicas without unnecessary traffic across WAN links.

Novell recommends creating three or more replicas for each partition to ensure fault tolerance. Each server used for Bindery Services must contain a master or read/write replica that contains the bindery context.

Minimal Partitioning   To minimize problems with subordinate references, create as few partitions as possible. Avoid too many replicas of the [Root] partition, because this partition tends to have many child partitions. Since a child partition or a subordinate reference must accompany its replica wherever it appears, the [Root] partition can create a lot of subordinate references, which can increase network traffic unnecessarily.

While you should avoid making too many replicas of the [Root] partition, you *do* need to replicate it at least once. If you fail to replicate it at all, you are taking a dangerous risk. You need the [Root] partition to access the Directory tree.

Network Traffic Considerations   The NDS database remains consistent by transmitting any change made to an object in a partition to all replicas of that partition. This is known as *Directory synchronization*.

Directory synchronization takes place across *replica rings*. A replica ring can be technically described as the list of all the replicas a partition has. Each partition has at least one replica, the master replica, plus additional replicas (for example, a read/write replica) for redundancy and load balancing. Because Directory synchronization requires that every replica be updated to reflect any changes to any object, a considerable amount of communication is required between NetWare 5 servers. On LANs, this communication is not usually a major consideration, because most LANs have plenty of bandwidth available. The extra bandwidth needed for this communication does become a concern on WAN links, where bottlenecks can occur.

Potential Problems with Subordinate References   When you want to change a partition that has a subordinate reference, make sure the subordinate reference is accessible before you make the change. If the subordinate reference is located on the other side of an unstable connection, such as some types of WAN links, you could be creating a potential problem: the data in the subordinate reference cannot be updated to match the master.

Default Partitions and Replicas

When the first server is installed, NDS creates and stores a master replica of the [Root] partition on that server's SYS volume. The second and third servers receive a read/write replica of the [Root] partition. By default, any servers installed after that do not receive replicas. You can create additional replicas of a partition on any server in the tree at your discretion. (Since unnecessary replicas will take up bandwidth on your network, you should plan for this before you do it.)

Replicas in Merged NDS Trees

When two or more Directory trees are merged, the *source* tree servers (servers of trees that are being merged into the [Root] of another tree) that hold replicas of their [Root] partition are given a read/write replica of the new [Root] partition. They also receive subordinate references to the child partitions of the new [Root] partition.

The servers of the *target* tree (the tree whose [Root] remains as the [Root]) are given subordinate references to the uppermost partitions in the source trees if the target tree servers currently hold replicas of the [Root] partition. Figures 15.3 and 15.4 show an example of two Directory trees before and after they are merged.

F I G U R E 15.3

F I G U R E 15.3

Two separate
Directory trees
before merging

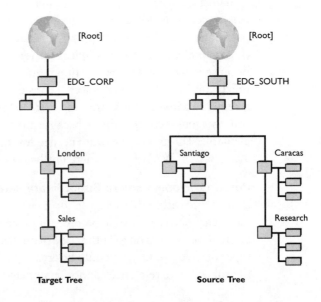

Target Tree   Source Tree

F I G U R E 15.4

When directories are
merged, the organiza-
tions are combined
under one [Root]
object.

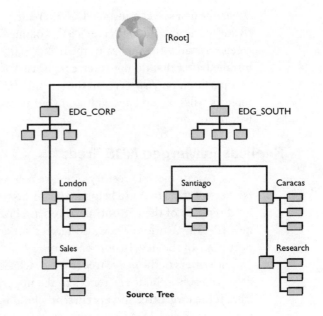

Source Tree

Managing Partitions and Replicas

Now that you understand the basics of NDS partitioning and replication, we'll take a look at the actual process of creating, deleting, and managing partitions and replicas. *NDS Manager* is the utility used for this.

NDS Manager (NDSMGR32.EXE) is a Windows-based application for managing partitions and replicas. We will examine the use of NDS Manager in the following sections.

Viewing Partitions and Replicas

When you start NDS Manager, a split window is displayed, as shown in Figure 15.5.

FIGURE 15.5

NDS Manager displays information about partitions and replicas.

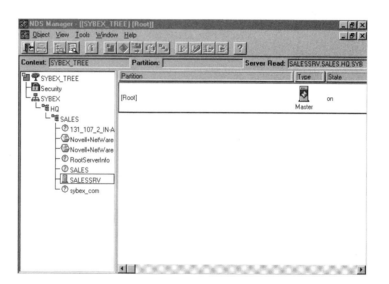

The main NDS Manager window is split into two sections:

- The left side displays the Directory tree. Only container objects and Server objects are shown. A container that is the root of a partition appears with an icon to the left of the container object's icon.

- The right side displays a list of replicas. If you have highlighted a partition's container, the replicas for that partition are listed. If you have highlighted a Server object, the replicas stored on the server are listed.

Creating (Splitting) a Partition

Creating a new partition is also called *splitting* a partition, because the process involves splitting a child container object from its parent container's partition. Use Procedure 15.1 to create a new partition.

Creating a New Partition

To create a new partition, follow these steps:

1. Start NDS Manager and highlight the container object that will be the root of the new partition.

2. From the NDS Manager menu, select Object Create Partition.

3. The Create Partition dialog box will appear, as shown below. Verify that you have chosen the correct object, and then click Yes to continue.

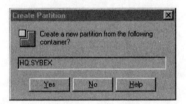

4. The new partition will now be created. Depending on the complexity of your network and the number of replicas to be made of the parent partition, this may take several minutes.

5. Create replicas of the new partition as needed. You will want to partition the tree to reduce the overall size of the Directory Services database. This helps improve performance and redundancy, as described later in this chapter.

Deleting (Merging) a Partition

The process of deleting a partition is called *merging* partitions. When you merge a partition, it is combined with its parent partition. All of the objects that were contained in the partition become child objects of the parent partition. Follow the steps in Procedure 15.2 to merge a partition.

PROCEDURE 15.2

Deleting a Partition

To delete a partition, follow these steps:

1. Start NDS Manager and highlight the container object at the root of the partition.

2. From the NDS Manager menu, select Object ➤ Partition ➤ Merge.

3. The Merge Partition dialog box will appear, as shown below. Verify that you have chosen the correct child and parent partitions, and then click Yes to continue.

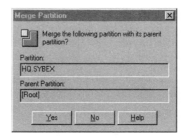

4. The partitions will now be merged. Depending on the complexity of the network and the number of replicas required, this may take several minutes. Using this procedure can reduce the number of partitions and replicas. As your company evolves and your needs change, the tree can be reconfigured very easily.

Adding a Replica

NDS Manager allows you to manage the replicas for a partition easily. Follow the steps in Procedure 15.3 to add a new replica to a server.

PROCEDURE 15.3

Adding a Replica

To add a replica of a partition, follow these steps:

1. Start NDS Manager and select the partition you want to add a replica to.

2. From the NDS Manager menu, choose Object ➤ Add Replica.

3. The Add Replica dialog box appears.

4. Choose a server to hold the new replica, and indicate whether the new replica will be read/write or read only.

5. Click OK to add the new replica. This may take several minutes. Adding replicas is an effective way to ensure redundancy on the Directory database. Placing the replicas in a strategic location improves network performance, as we discussed earlier in this chapter.

Removing a Replica

Removing a replica of a partition is also simple.

Removing a Replica

To remove a replica, follow these steps:

1. From NDS Manager, highlight and expand the partition you want to remove a replica from.

2. Highlight the server that contains the replica to be removed.

3. In the right window, right-click the replica of the partition you want to remove from the server and select Delete.

4. Click Yes to confirm the deletion. Now that you've deleted this replica, be sure to create a new replica on a different server, if needed, to keep the partition safe. As the need for replicas changes, you can reduce or increase the number of them. You need to be very careful, and plan properly, so that you don't end up with too many replicas of a partition.

Moving a Container Object

As discussed in Chapter 2, you can't move a container object using the NetWare Administrator's Move Object option. The reason is that moving a container object is considered a partitioning operation. You can easily accomplish this using the NDS Manager utility, as described in Procedure 15.5.

PROCEDURE 15.5

Moving a Container Object

To move a container object, follow these steps:

1. Using Procedure 15.1 above, split the container object you wish to move into its own partition.

2. From the NDS Manager menu, choose Object ≻ Partition ≻ Move.

3. Choose the new context for the container object.

4. Click Yes to begin the process of moving the container object. This may take several minutes. This procedure is another example of how configurable NDS is. You can easily reorganize a Directory at the Organizational Unit level, even in a large network.

Maintaining NDS

Aside from adding or deleting user accounts, supporting the network, and taking care of your users in general, you will need to consider a maintenance schedule for NDS. There are some preventive maintenance techniques you can use to ensure the best possible performance and to avoid unnecessary downtime due to crashed Directory services.

There is no way to avoid all NDS problems. In fact, if you deal with a NetWare 5 server for any length of time, you will undoubtedly need to handle several problems. However, most common NDS problems can be avoided with a bit of planning. Here are some tips to keep NDS running smoothly:

Replica Placement   Always keep at least three replicas for each partition. It can't be stressed enough that you should have replicas of a partition strategically placed throughout your network, preferably close to the users, and at each end of the WAN links. This improves response times for logins as well as redundancy. If a replica is lost, even if it's the master replica, it can be restored if another replica is available.

Regulating Partition Maintenance Rights   Use a single workstation to manage NDS partitions, such as when you are splitting partitions, merging partitions, or moving container objects. This will make it easy to keep track of the changes you have made and to avoid inconsistencies. Otherwise, conflicting messages can be received from different locations in the network, causing NDS corruption. You should also limit the number of users you allow to do maintenance functions on the tree.

Backing Up the Directory   Use your backup software to make frequent backups of the NDS database. The best frequency depends on how often changes are made in your network, but it should be at least once a week. Many backup programs will back up NDS data automatically while other data is being backed up.

Planning Server Downtime   From time to time, you will need to take the server down for maintenance. This usually will not cause a problem with NDS. Once NDS notices that the server is down, other servers that need to send updates to a replica on that server will keep trying until the server comes back up. When you bring the server up, it may take several minutes to resynchronize the replicas.

Preventing the SYS Volume from Running Out of Space   Never let any server's SYS volume run out of space. The NDS database is kept in a hidden directory on the SYS volume. If the volume runs out of space, TTS is disabled, no changes can be made to NDS, and the server loses synchronization with other replicas. To be safe, keep at least 50MB free at all times—more if you use Z.E.N.works with applications. If possible, keep space-consuming data, such as print queues, on a volume other than SYS.

Maintain NDS Standard Version   In NetWare 5 you can also use the NDS Manager to update the NDS NLM (DS.NLM) remotely, thus allowing you to centrally maintain a standard version of DS.NLM. The process is available on a tree-by-tree basis and only with NetWare servers of the same version. You cannot maintain the same DS.NLM version across NetWare server versions. All the servers in the tree have to be updated with the same version in order for the new features in NDS to be made available. Use Procedure 15.6 to maintain DS.NLM versions.

PROCEDURE 15.6

Updating NDS Versions on Multiple Servers

To view NDS version numbers in the Directory tree on multiple servers, and then select the latest version to update with, follow these steps:

1. From the NDS Manager menu, select Object ➢ Preferences ➢ NDS Update Options, and then click Entire Tree Sub-tree.

2. In the left window, select the container that contains the servers and highlight the servers you want to check on.

3. Go to Object ➢ NDS Version, and click View. This will search the entire tree for servers and display their DS.NLM version numbers.

4. Select a server that holds the most recent version of DS.NLM to be the source for distributing the file.

5. Go to Object ➢ NDS Version and click Update. The screen will display the status of the update. You might be notified about servers that weren't upgraded, for example servers that already had the latest version or that have a different OS. Click OK.

6. An NDS Version Update window appears and displays the servers in the context you selected.

7. In the Source for Version Update field, enter the server with the DS.NLM version you want to use for the update.

8. Highlight all the servers for which you want to update the DS.NLM. (Some server names may be grayed out, indicating that they can't be upgraded because either they have the same version of DS.NLM or they have a different version of NetWare.) Move these servers to the Target Servers to be Updated list by clicking the right arrow between the Servers list and the Target Servers list.

9. Click OK to perform the update. This is a very effective way to maintain a standard NDS version across your tree. Just remember that this does not work across different NetWare versions. You must be using the same version on each server you want to update.

Troubleshooting NDS

NDS is the most important feature of NetWare 5. It is also the most common source of problems with NetWare 5 servers. In the previous sections, you learned how to avoid some of the most common NDS problems. In the next sections, you will learn how to correct them when they do happen.

You should use NDS Manager or DSREPAIR (described later in this chapter) to check synchronization before performing any complicated NDS operations. You will also use these tools to perform repairs on the tree database.

Managing NDS Inconsistencies

NDS is a distributed database; each change you make to NDS begins at the replica where you make the change and is passed to each of the other servers that contain a replica. Depending on communication delays, network use, and the complexity of the change, it can take anywhere from 10 seconds to an hour or two for all replicas to receive the change.

Fortunately, NDS was designed with this in mind. The NDS database is *loosely consistent*, which means that it remains functional even if replicas do not have exactly the same information. You may notice these inconsistencies, but they do not necessarily represent a problem with NDS.

The process that NDS uses to send information between replicas is called synchronization. Two replicas are synchronized if they contain exactly the same information. In a busy network, the synchronization process is happening constantly to update the latest changes. The process is different depending on the type of change.

Simple changes, such as adding a User object or changing a property, are synchronized quickly. All that is required is to send updates to each server that has a replica of the partition where the object is located. Creating a partition is also a relatively simple task.

Complex changes include joining partitions, moving partitions, and merging Directory trees. These changes require updates to multiple partitions, and each server with a replica of any one of the partitions must be contacted to send updates. These changes can take a long time.

Symptoms of NDS Problems

Although some inconsistencies between NDS replicas are a normal occurrence, severe inconsistencies may be an indication of a corrupt NDS database or another problem. Here are the symptoms you should watch for:

- Changes made to an NDS object or its rights seem to disappear.

- An object or its properties change unexpectedly. For example, a user can no longer log in because the password is incorrect, but the user has not changed the password.

- Errors may be inconsistent. For example, a user may be able to log in successfully after several unsuccessful attempts.

- Unknown objects, shown with a question mark, appear in the Directory tree. It is normal for these objects to show up when a server has been removed or when a partitioning operation is in progress. However, if they appear without an apparent cause, there may be a problem.

If you notice any of these symptoms, or if any part of NDS seems to behave inconsistently, follow the instructions in the following sections to narrow down and correct the problem. If a corrupt Directory is left alone, it will probably become worse. Be sure to diagnose and correct the problem as soon as you notice any symptoms.

Checking NDS Synchronization

If the problems you are having with NDS are not severe, you should let the servers run for a few hours before attempting any repairs. NDS double-checks itself, and it may repair the problem automatically. Do not take any servers down, because this would prevent NDS from synchronizing and correcting errors.

If the problem still occurs, you should check the synchronization of the server. You can use the DSREPAIR and DSTRACE utilities to accomplish this, as described in the following sections.

Checking Synchronization with DSREPAIR

DSREPAIR is a versatile utility that can be used to solve many NDS problems. You can use one of the functions of DSREPAIR to check the synchronization of replicas on the network. You should do this if you suspect a problem in NDS. In addition, you should check the synchronization before performing a major operation, such as merging trees, splitting partitions, joining partitions, or moving a container object. To use this function of DSREPAIR, work through Procedure 15.7.

PROCEDURE 15.7

Checking Synchronization with DSREPAIR

To check synchronization with DSREPAIR, follow these steps:

1. Start the DSREPAIR utility by typing **LOAD DSREPAIR** at the server console.

2. Go to Advanced Options ➢ Replica and Partition Operations.

3. The list of partition replicas on the server is displayed. Select the partition for which you want to check synchronization.

4. An options menu is displayed. Select Report Synchronization Status on All Servers.

5. DSREPAIR will check the synchronization status for all replicas and display a log file. Examine the log file. If no errors appear, the replicas on that server are fully synchronized.

Using the NDS TRACE (DSTRACE) Parameter

NDS TRACE (DSTRACE) is a special SET parameter that can be used to monitor the activities of NDS. Information is displayed each time NDS replicas are synchronized. This can be helpful when you are diagnosing an NDS problem.

To start tracing NDS, enter one of these commands at the server console:

```
SET NDS TRACE TO SCREEN= ON
```

or

```
SET DSTRACE=ON
```

The Directory Services Trace screen, NDS Trace or DSTRACE, is now available for use. Press Alt+Esc at the server console to switch to this screen.

You can leave NDS TRACE running and check the screen periodically for problems. One of the most common problems will produce this message:

```
SYNC: End sync of partition name. All processed = NO.
```

If NO is displayed here, and the message keeps repeating after a few minutes, there is a serious problem with NDS. You should run the DSREPAIR utility, as described in the next section.

When you no longer need the NDS TRACE screen, type this command at the server console:

```
SET NDS TRACE TO SCREEN = OFF
```

Resolving NDS Problems

Once you have determined that there is a problem in the NDS database, you should take action to resolve it. The next sections describe three ways to do this. You should try the DSREPAIR utility first. The second option, forcing replica synchronization, provides a more drastic option. As a last resort, you can restore an NDS backup.

Using the DSREPAIR Utility

The DSREPAIR utility provides several options for repairing NDS problems. These are listed on the utility's Available Options menu, shown in Figure 15.7. The most useful of these is the first, Unattended Full Repair. When you select this option, NetWare scans the NDS database for errors. All errors found will be repaired if possible. The other options allow you to perform specific steps for troubleshooting, which may be useful if the Unattended Full Repair option fails or if you are troubleshooting a specific problem.

F I G U R E   15.6

The DSREPAIR utility can repair most NDS problems.

Before you run DSREPAIR, make a backup copy of NDS using your backup software. If the NDS database becomes corrupted further, you may lose information on all replicas. Since there may be errors in the database, do not overwrite an older backup if you have one.

After DSREPAIR has finished scanning the database, it displays a log file. This log lists the tasks that were performed and problems that were found and corrected. Examine the log carefully and make sure that any errors were repaired.

Although DSREPAIR can repair most NDS corruption, you may lose some of the information. After DSREPAIR has finished its work, use NetWare Administrator to look at the Directory tree and make sure that all its objects are intact. If there are still problems with NDS, you may need to force synchronization, as described in the following section.

You can also run most of the DSREPAIR procedures remotely using the NDSMGR32 utility.

Forcing Synchronization

If DSREPAIR is unable to repair the problems you are having with NDS, you may want to try forcing synchronization. This option will send updates from the master replica to all other replicas. Any changes waiting on those replicas will be ignored.

If you force synchronization, you may lose changes to NDS that were made at a replica other than the master. Make a backup copy of NDS before proceeding. Use Procedure 15.8 to force synchronization with the NDSMGR32 utility.

PROCEDURE 15.8

Forcing Synchronization

To force synchronization with NDSMGR32, follow these steps:

1. Start the NDSMGR32 utility, which is located in the following path: SYS:\PUBLIC\WIN32\NDSMGR32.EXE.

2. In the left window, select the partition you are having problems with.

3. In the right window, right-click the master replica.

4. Click the Send Updates button. You will be asked to confirm the choice. After you do, updates will be sent to all other replicas. This process may take several minutes, and it will cause a lot of traffic on the network.

After the forced synchronization process is completed, load DSREPAIR at the server and use the Unattended Full Repair option again. If there are still NDS errors that DSREPAIR cannot fix, you will need to restore a backup.

Removing NDS from a Server

There are some instances in which you are forced to remove NDS from a server, for example if you have a corrupted replica on the server or there are problems synchronizing with other servers in the replica ring.

In any case, to remove NDS from the server you need to load the NWCONFIG utility on the server console and then select the appropriate Directory options. You can also force the removal of NDS without using the Admin account by entering **NWCONFIG –DSREMOVE** at the server console. Once NWCONFIG loads and the menu is displayed, select Directory Services ➤ Remove Directory Services. Using the –DSREMOVE option with NWCONFIG allows you to bypass the NDS authentication to the tree, permitting you to force the removal of the Directory services from the server.

Restoring an NDS Backup

As a last resort, you can restore NDS from a backup. Assuming the backup was performed before the NDS problems began, this should permit a full recovery. Note the date of the backup. If you have made changes to NDS (such as creating users or changing rights) since that date, you must reenter them after you restore the backup.

To restore NDS, first use the NDSMGR32.EXE utility to delete all replicas of the partition. Then restore the partition data using your backup software. This will create a new master replica from which you can re-create the other replicas.

Be sure all users in the Directory tree are logged out of the network when you back up or restore NDS data. Do not bring down any servers, however.

Managing Server Downtime

At one time or another, your file server will go down. You might take it down to perform maintenance or to reset the server, or it may go down unexpectedly due to a hardware or software problem. Because NDS is constantly doing self-maintenance, you should be careful in these situations.

NDS is always checking on servers that hold replicas of partitions. If a server goes down, NDS will hold information intended for that server. It's okay if the server is down for maintenance or for a short period of time (less than 2 days); NDS can handle short periods of downtime. But if the server is down due to a crash and you are replacing it with another server, you need to remove the crashed server from the tree. The following sections discuss how to deal with unplanned downtime, as well as how to remove a server from the tree permanently.

Unplanned Downtime

A hardware or software problem can cause a server to go down unexpectedly. If this happens, diagnose the problem. If you can bring the server up within an hour or two and the hard disk containing the SYS volume is undamaged, NDS will resynchronize, and there should not be any NDS problems.

If you are going to take down the server that contains the master replica for a partition, you may need to set up another master replica. If the downtime will be brief, another master should not be required. If the server will be down for an extended period (several hours to a day or more), you should change another replica to master status. This will allow you to make changes to NDS objects in the partition without the use of the server that is down.

If you are bringing a server down for an extended period, you should first remove any replicas that are on the server. (Refer to Procedure 15.4 for instructions on removing a replica.) This way your network will not be slowed by servers trying to contact the server that is down. After you bring the server back up, you can re-create the replicas.

If you have lost the SYS volume on the server, you will need to reinstall NetWare 5 on the server.

Removing a Server Permanently

You may wish to remove a server permanently if it is no longer needed.

PROCEDURE 15.9

Removing a Server Permanently

To remove a server permanently using NDS Manager, follow these steps:

1. Remove any replicas on the server.

2. If any master replicas were stored on the server, change another server's read/write replica to master status.

3. Bring the server down.

4. Delete the Server and Volume NDS objects. To delete the Server object, you must use the NDSMGR32 utility. As we mentioned earlier in the chapter, NDS constantly checks up on the servers in the tree. Once you have removed unwanted Server and Volume objects from the tree, however, NDS will no longer monitor them.

When you remove a server, be aware that you are also removing replicas of the NDS database. Be sure you re-create the replicas on other servers to maintain fault tolerance.

Review

The advanced features of NDS covered in this chapter were partitioning, replicating, maintaining, and troubleshooting the NDS database.

NDS Partitions and Replicas

The Directory can be divided into partitions. Each partition can be replicated on one or more servers. A partition consists of a container object and the objects within it. The partition is given the name of the container. The [Root] partition is the only partition in a new NDS installation.

There are four types of replicas:

- NetWare 5 creates a master replica when a partition is defined. There is only one master replica per partition.

- Read/write replicas contain the same data as the master replica. There can be more than one of this type of replica. Changes made to a read/write replica will be copied to the master replica.

- Read-only replicas allow access to NDS data but do not allow changes.

- Subordinate references are created automatically by NetWare. These replicas point to children of a partition that are not located on the server.

Maintaining NDS

There is no way to avoid all NDS problems. In fact, if you deal with a Net-Ware 5 server for any length of time, you will undoubtedly need to handle several problems. However, most common NDS problems can be avoided with a bit of planning, as explained in this chapter. Here are some tips to keep NDS running smoothly:

- Always keep at least three replicas for each partition.

- Use your backup software to make frequent backups of the NDS database.

- Use a single workstation to manage NDS partitions.

- Never let any server's SYS volume run out of space.

- Use DSREPAIR to check synchronization before performing any complicated NDS operations.

Troubleshooting NDS

Most of the problems you will encounter with NDS deal with synchronization, the process of sending updates between replicas in the server. NDS can handle some loss of synchronization, but if a serious problem occurs, you must repair it. The following steps can help you determine if there is a problem:

- Check for symptoms of NDS problems, such as inconsistent behavior and unexpected changes to objects.

- Use DSREPAIR to check the synchronization of replicas.

- Use NDS TRACE to display messages about NDS synchronization and detect problems as they occur.

If you determine that there is a problem, you should act to fix it as soon as possible. Try the following options to repair NDS corruption:

- Use the Unattended Full Repair option of the DSREPAIR server utility to automatically fix most problems.

- If DSREPAIR is unsuccessful, try to force synchronization with the master replica using the NDSMGR32 utility.

- If the first two methods don't solve the problem, you can restore from an NDS backup.

- Removing and reinstalling NDS is also an option. If you are having synchronization problems on a particular server belonging to a tree, you can remove NDS from the server, eliminating the corrupted files. Then reinstall NDS on the server and reintegrate it into the existing tree.

Server downtime requires special consideration because of the synchronization and replication features of NDS. If you are bringing a server down for an extended period, you should remove any replicas that are on the server first. If it contains a master replica, set up another master replica on another server. If you have lost the SYS volume on a server that went down due to a hardware or software problem, you will need to reinstall NetWare 5 on the server.

CNE Practice Test Questions

1. Which factor does not need to be considered when partitioning and replicating?

   A. The size of individual partitions

   B. Naming standards

   C. Subordinate references

   D. The physical location of objects

2. An NDS backup:

   A. Includes all data on the server

   B. Can be used to install a new server if necessary

   C. Includes only the NDS database

   D. Includes NDS and file system information

3. To delete a Server object, you can use:

   A. The INETCFG utility

   B. NDS Manager

   C. NetWare Administrator

   D. The DELSERV utility

4. Which is *not* a good strategy for avoiding NDS problems?

    A. Keep at least three replicas of each partition

    B. Don't allow the SYS volume to run out of space

    C. Keep at least two master replicas

    D. Make frequent NDS backups

5. Which utility is used to check replica synchronization?

    A. NDSREPAIR

    B. DSCHECK

    C. DSREPAIR

    D. INETCFG

6. Which is the correct syntax for NDS TRACE?

    A. `SET NDS TRACE to screen= ON`

    B. `LOAD NDS TRACE`

    C. `NDS TRACE BEGIN`

    D. `TRACK ON`

7. Which option should you try first when you have found an NDS problem?

    A. Reinstall NetWare 5 on the server

    B. Use NDSMGR32 to send updates to all replicas

    C. Restore the NDS database from a backup

    D. Use DSREPAIR to check for and correct problems

8. How many replicas of each partition should you have?

    A. 2

    B. 5

    C. 3

    D. 1

9. What should you do before you remove a server from the Directory tree?

   A. Down the server

   B. Back up the server

   C. Remove all replicas from the server

   D. No preparation is necessary

10. Which utility is used to remove NDS from a server?

    A. DSREPAIR

    B. NWCONFIG

    C. INETCFG

    D. MONITOR

11. When the replica of a parent partition is placed on a server, a subordinate reference replica of the child partition is placed by NDS.

    A. True

    B. False

CHAPTER

16

NIAS Remote Access and Mobile Users

Roadmap

This chapter covers understanding, designing, and configuring remote access, which is a section of the CNE core requirement "NetWare 5 Advanced Administration."

Topics Covered

- NIAS Remote Access
- Mobile Users
- Data Transmission Choices
- Remote Access Security Issues
- Optimal Remote Access Performance Issues
- Remote Authentication Dial-In User Service (RADIUS)

Skills You'll Learn

- Design a plan for NIAS remote access
- Configure a remote workstation or laptop for NIAS remote access
- Configure a server to be an NIAS remote access server
- Describe the best choice of data transmission for your network and users
- Describe what a mobile user is and who should be one
- Design a plan to make sure that any remote access will not become a security problem with your company
- Describe different ways to help your users have optimal performance while remotely connected to the network
- Describe the RADIUS protocol and RADIUS proxy

In this chapter you'll learn why it is so important to know how to set up and configure your users so they can use NIAS remote access services, which allow you to configure your mobile users for remote access to your network.

Today we live in a generation of constant movement. Companies have employees traveling via plane, train, and car to remote locations for company business. These employees have to be able to stay in contact with the company and access the resources they need. Remote access has become the buzzword for mobile users.

What Is NIAS Remote Access?

*N*IAS *(Novell Internet Access Server)* remote access server runs on a NetWare 5 server, providing the ability to support multiple modems and give users access to network resources. You can think of NIAS remote access in very simple terms. A network server is in one location (different country, state, or city) and your mobile user is in another location. Your user needs access to the company's network via their modem, which entails connecting the modem to a phone line, then to a server modem, and finally to the NIAS remote access server. Before you can set up this kind of connection, there are some things that should be in place first:

- One or more modems connected to the NIAS remote access server

- A modem connected to the remote workstation or laptop

- Extra 5MB of RAM in the NIAS remote access server

- A login name and password for the user to access the remote network

- Remote workstation or laptop configured for remote access services

- Remote workstation or laptop and NIAS remote access server set up with some type of data communication connection between them

Figure 16.1 illustrates the difference between a LAN and NIAS remote access.

The following sections explore each of the elements that you will need to establish remote access.

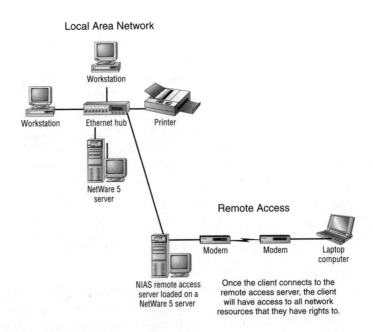

FIGURE 16.1

A local area network
and remote access via
a laptop computer

Design Your Plan of Action

There are several factors you need to consider when planning for remote access:

- Which users need remote access?

- Where are these users located, and how many are there at each location?

- Do you have enough phone lines/WAN links to handle additional network traffic and routing?

- How many NIAS remote access servers will you need?

- Where are the best locations to place NIAS remote access servers? (Consider how many remote users you'll have in each location?

- What type of services or resources will the mobile users need while attached to the network remotely?

- How many simultaneous remote access connections will you need per NIAS remote access server?

Who Needs Access?

The first question you might consider during the remote access design phase is, Who needs remote access, and why do they need it? This privilege should not be given lightly to every user who asks for it. You must determine whether they truly have a need for resources while at home or some other location. Are they a regular mobile user, or is this the only time they will need remote access? Security is always at risk when you give remote access, even though NIAS includes security measures. We will discuss remote access security later in this chapter.

Remote access allows mobile users to perform the following tasks:

- Send reports to the company via e-mail or even print to a printer on the network at a different location

- Access the resources in their files and directories on the NetWare 5 network

- Teleconference with the boss or attend a company business meeting without ever leaving home

- Print a document remotely by attaching and printing to a company printer they have rights to

- Administrate the network remotely, if they have rights as the Admin user

NIAS vs. LAN Connections

While in the planning stage of remote access, there are a few concerns you need to take into account. Not only do you need to decide who needs access, and where to place NIAS remote access servers, but what kind of connection you'll provide and how fast you will connect them. Here are the key steps:

- Select a data transmission media. Even if users connect with a 56Kbps modem, their access speed will be much slower than it is when they are attached locally to the LAN. The xDSL connections that will be described later in this section can provide much faster speeds than POTS or ISDN, but a LAN will always be much faster, with Ethernet transferring data at 10 to 100 megabits per second.

- Design an effective security plan. In most companies, this is the number one concern. Yes, it is true that it is less secure accessing the network via a voice telephone connection than by a local connection on the LAN. NIAS remote access includes some measures to increase security, which we will cover later in this chapter.

- Select locations for your NIAS remote servers. Place your NIAS servers in locations where you have large numbers of mobile users. By doing this, you cut down on the phone bills incurred when remote users access the remote access server via modem.

These points illustrate why it is very important to have a well thought-out plan of action before you start deploying the NIAS remote access servers. Your goal as administrator is to provide efficient, secure network access to remote users just as you do for other users.

Selecting a Data Transmission Media

Selecting the data transmission media of both the remote user and your NIAS remote access server is one of the key steps in designing a remote access system. Data transmission media is the physical connection by which information travels. Selecting a media determines the speed of the connection. In a LAN, the connection is usually cable, fiber optic, and so on. But for data transmission between the NIAS remote access server and remote users, your connection is provided through *telecoms* (telephone company connections). You need to choose the best data transmission media for your NIAS remote access server and your remote users. The telecom options are explained in the following sections.

ISDN ISDN stands for Integrated Services Digital Network. This is an upgrade to the old phone system that offers the speed of a digital connection, as compared to traditional analog phone lines (POTS, discussed below). *ISDN* is an evolving set of standards for a digital network that carries both voice and data communications. It requires the support of a TA (Terminal Adapter) and NT1 (Network Termination 1 device) on the client and server. The NT1 connects the server to the telecom.

An ISDN connection is more costly than traditional analog connections. It is typically billed on a per-channel basis. If you are designing a plan of action, you need to decide if the need for speed outweighs the cost of providing it. The following questions will help you decide whether ISDN service is the best solution for your company:

- Will remote users be sending or receiving voice transmissions?

- Will remote users be sending or receiving video transmissions?

- Will remote users need high digital speeds for data transmissions?

- What type of resources will remote users need to access through the NIAS remote access server?

ISDN offers two interfaces for the customer: Basic Rate Interface and Primary Rate Interface.

Basic Rate Interface (BRI) *BRI* is ISDN's basic service, which is made up of two 64Kbps bearer channels and one 16Kbps delta channel.

Bearer channels, or *B-channels,* are circuit-switched connections that carry voice and data. Each B-channel is capable of sending data at 64Kbps. Two B-channels combined through a process called bonding can deliver an aggregate throughput of 128Kbps. This is possible through your hardware and NIAS software, which supports MPPP (Multilink Point to Point Protocol).

Delta channels, or *D-channels,* use packet-switched connections and are used to control signals. For example, the D-channel can be used to hold or activate conference calling, call forwarding, and caller identification.

Primary Rate Interface (PRI) PRI is ISDN's high-speed service, which is a T1 (in North America and Japan) or E1 (in Europe) circuit with ISDN software installed on it. PRIs can be used to consolidate multiple BRI circuits into a single larger circuit, which is easier to manage and sometimes more cost-effective. A *T1* is a network communications line that has 24 64Kbps channels; with ISDN software installed, you get 23 B-channels, and one 64Kbps D-channel. An *E1* is a network communications line that has the same configuration but offers 30 B-channels and one D-channel. (Remember, a T1 operates at up to 1.544Mbps and an E1 at up to 2.048Mbps).

POTS *POTS* stands for plain old telephone service, which can be used for data communication between the remote user and the NIAS remote access server. The equipment needed by both the remote user and the NIAS remote access server is a modem and access to POTS. For basic communication between the remote user and their office, this service could provide a low-cost telecom connection. If your users need remote access to attend videoconferences or to upload or download large files and graphics, this service probably won't be suitable for your company. Once again, you need to weigh the pros and cons of each service.

In today's POTS environment you typically find 33.6Kbps and 56Kbps modems. The biggest difference between the two is that 33.6Kbps modems provide the same speed on download as well as upload. By contrast, 56Kbps modems are only effective when downloading from the server. Additional equipment is needed if you want to balance the speeds in both directions. You will need a special 56Kbps modem on the server and a digital connection, which could bring the cost up considerably.

56Kbps modems will only operate at 56K when they are dialing into an ISDN device with an integrated modem connected to a B-channel. Achieving the 56K baud rate requires that the signal only go through one digital-to-analog conversion, and only with a server running ISDN is the digital data never converted back to analog.

xDSL   *DSL (Digital Subscriber Line)* increases the speed of traditional analog telephone lines. This enables the remote user to have high-speed remote access to the NIAS remote access server over POTS. The family of DSLs is called *xDSL*, and here are several examples:

HDSL-High Speed DSL   Downloads at a rate of 1.544 Mbps and uploads at the same speed. Requires two cable pairs and provides symmetric transmission.

ADSL-Asynchronous DSL   Downloads at variable rates of up to 8.192Mbps, but upload rates are slower. Requires a splitter at the remote user's site as well as some extra installation costs.

"Splitterless" DSL   Downloads at a rate of less than 1Mbps, and upload rates are about the same. This doesn't require a splitter, which will reduce installation costs but also slow performance.

DSL uses packet-switching technology. It can be either asymmetric or symmetric. *Asymmetric DSL* allows for video on demand and Internet access at faster downstream speeds. *Symmetric DSL* allows for the same bi-directional speed.

xDSL is not available in all areas. Before you spend hours designing a remote access plan around xDSL, check with your local telephone service to make sure that option is available to you.

Designing an Effective Security Plan

Network security is probably one of the most important issues you will face when designing a remote access plan for your users. Your main objective is to protect your network data against unauthorized access. It has become a pastime for hackers to see how many network systems they can crack or break into. This is a serious problem, but the risk of break-ins can be reduced with some advance planning for remote access. (See also Chapter 17, which explains how to build NetWare firewalls.)

NDS, discussed in previous chapters, is Novell's NetWare Directory Services. The network administrator assigns rights in NDS, which allow only authorized users to access particular files and directories. This is where designing a good Directory tree is very important. Assigning too many rights, or inappropriate rights, to users can really hurt the security of your company. Unauthorized users shouldn't have access to sensitive data. Remember that network security is critical to a company's livelihood.

There are three main ways to ensure remote access security, which we'll discuss in the following sections:

- Security policies for remote access

- Demilitarized zones for remote access servers

- Effective security configurations

Security Policies for Remote Access

First you need to decide on some guidelines for remote access. Establish policies such as these: (1) Each user will be given a unique user ID and a password; (2) Users will be given rights only to the resources that they need while accessing the network remotely; and so on. To design a remote access security policy appropriate for your company, use these questions as a starting point:

- Who are the remote users? Make a list of jobs, NDS groups, resources needed, and locations they need to access.

- Who will be in charge of security in your network?

- If you discover that an intruder has been on your network, what measures will be taken?

- Will the remote passwords be encrypted? Will users use the same password as their LAN password or a different one when connected remotely?

- Are there some data files or applications that you won't grant remote access to at all?

- Will remote connections be encrypted?

- Do you want the remote server to do callbacks to remote users?

Demilitarized Zones for Remote Access Servers

Where is your most sensitive company data located? You might think about isolating it on a server that the average user wouldn't have access to, to cut down on the chance of sensitive company information being stolen or corrupted by disgruntled employees. A good way to do this is by creating a demilitarized zone. A *demilitarized zone* is an isolated area of the network that keeps unauthorized users from going beyond the NIAS.

Although creating a demilitarized zone goes beyond the scope of this book, it is important that you understand the concept. A screening router is the main component in the demilitarized zone and a basic component of most firewalls. (See the "BorderManager" section of Chapter 17 for more information on firewalls.) *Screening routers* do just as their name implies: They screen remote users and won't let unauthorized users go beyond the NIAS remote access server. NetWare 5 servers, commercial routers, or a host-based router with packet-filtering capabilities can screen and connect remote access users to the network. Figure 16.2 shows an example of a demilitarized zone.

FIGURE 16.2

Implementing a demilitarized zone for remote access servers makes them more secure.

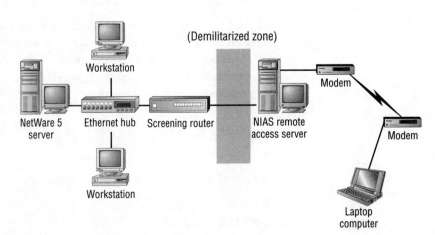

DMZs are very tricky to set up properly, and they can be implemented in several different ways. Consult a network security analyst before attempting to implement a DMZ yourself.

Effective Security Configurations

Remember that by default the NIAS remote access server offers remote users unrestricted access. That's why it is very important to develop an effective security configuration for your network, before a problem happens. Always be proactive (not *reactive*), because this will save you a lot of headaches down the line. When you are putting together your security plan, here are some things to remember:

- Set company restrictions to your NIAS remote access server, as covered earlier in this chapter.

- Design a demilitarized zone for remote access on your network. Firewalls are a big part of network security.

- Make the security administrator in your company a part of the remote access design team.

Location of NIAS Remote Servers

You'll need to take into account several cost considerations when deciding on the location of the NIAS remote servers. Here are some questions to help you find the best choice for your company:

- Will you need new servers, or do you have servers available at each site where you plan to place a NIAS remote server? A low-cost option would be to install NIAS remote access servers on existing servers, provided that they can handle the added workload.

- How many remote users are there at each location? Locate the areas where you have the most remote users and place NIAS remote access servers in those areas. Then you can minimize the expense of long-distance connections.

- Will you need to buy more hardware for the LAN because of the increased traffic remote users will bring to the network? Design your remote access plan to anticipate who needs remote access and who doesn't. Every user that is connected, whether remotely or directly on the LAN, causes increased traffic on your network. So plan your user access carefully. Make sure your network routers and WAN links can handle the extra traffic. If they can't, fix the problem before it hurts your network performance.

Optimal Remote Access Performance

Users accustomed to the speed of a fast local connection may perceive even optimal remote access performance as slow. You should consider, as part of your implementation plan, educating users on what performance to expect when dialing in to their network resources. At the same time, you should anticipate where bottlenecks may occur as users connect remotely to their network, optimizing performance. There are three areas you need to monitor and optimize for the best possible performance, as discussed in the following sections: the server, the client user, and the remote access service.

Optimizing Server Performance

NIAS remote access servers should have the recommended amount of hardware to optimize remote access. The bandwidth for connections to the NIAS remote access server should be adequate for all locations on the network.

This is where planning the appropriate data communication media is important. Your goal is to have a high-performance, low-maintenance NIAS remote access service.

Optimizing Client Performance

Servers can't complain, but remote users can—and that's exactly what they will do if remote access to your network is slow. It is normal for remote access to be slower than LAN connections, but it is still important to optimize the performance as much as possible for your users, to ensure that their work is productive.

Here are some ways to optimize performance for the remote user:

- Load the programs or resources that remote users use frequently on the remote workstation or laptop.

- Install the newest modem version in the remote workstation or laptop.

- Tell the remote user to expect slower connections so they won't be disappointed when it happens.

- Limit the login scripts for the remote user.

- Evaluate different data communication connections, keeping in mind the type of resources and needs the remote user will have when connected remotely. This should help you determine which type of connection is best suited for them.

Optimizing Remote Access Service Administration

You can manage remote users and groups through NetWare Administrator or the remote access server console. The remote access server uses the Remote Access Management Agent (RAMA), which is compatible with

SNMP (Simple Network Management Protocol), in order to be managed by ManageWise or any SNMP-based management tool.

NIAS remote access server can also provide DHCP services to clients, thus eliminating the need to manually configure and administrate IP addresses for them. DHCP, discussed in more detail in Chapter 12, provides the following services for remote users:

- An IP address while they are remotely connected

- A DNS server address and domain

- A default gateway router

Configuring NIAS Services

As discussed previously in this chapter, prior to configuring the NIAS server, you must have the right hardware and software to configure and install the services. You'll need at least the following:

- Modem for the NIAS remote access server

- Modem for each remote user that needs to have remote access

- A data communication connection, such as POTS, ISDN, or xDSL

- NIAS remote access server software

- Extra 5MB of RAM, beyond the normal requirements for your Net-Ware 5 server, to handle the extra traffic

- Windows 95 or Windows NT for the client loaded on the remote workstation or laptop

- Login and password to the network for remote user access

Configuring the NIAS Remote Access Server

Now you are ready to configure the NIAS remote access server. You'll need to do the following tasks:

- Decide which data transmission media will best support your client's needs (modem pool, ISDN, X.25, etc.).

- Install the data transmission hardware on the server and workstations. The process for this depends on which data transmission media you selected.

- Select the services you want, for example RAMA (Remote Access Management Agent) and PPPRNS (Point to Point Protocol Remote Node Services).

- Configure IP and IPX addresses for remote access.

- Configure and start up your NIAS remote access server, keeping in mind your design plan as you do so.

You will now start the process of setting up remote access services with the NIAS 4.1 remote access server (previously done with NetWare Connect).

In order to configure remote access services, you must have installed remote access services during the initial installation of the server. If you didn't do this, you can copy the files needed from the NetWare 5 operating system CD in the products/RAS directory to the respective directories on the server. To configure your NetWare 5 server for NIAS remote access services using modems, use Procedure 16.1.

PROCEDURE 16.1

Configuring Your NIAS Remote Access Server

To configure your server for NIAS remote access services using modems for communication, follow these steps:

1. Type **NIASCFG** on the server console.

2. You will be prompted to transfer files to the NETINFO.CFG file, which is managed by the INETCFG.NLM. Press Enter and all the LAN driver load commands located in the AUTOEXEC.NCF file will be transferred (discussed in Chapter 8).

3. Restart the server and run NIASCFG again. Then go to Configure NIAS ≻ Remote Access.

4. You are prompted to enter a username and password. (You need to be using an account that has Supervisor rights to the tree, such as Admin.)

5. After your login is authenticated, you are asked if you are installing synchronous devices. If you are installing a modem, click No.

6. NIAS will attempt to detect the modems. (Note: When you install multiple modems, use the same model for each to save time.)

7. You will be asked which services you want to install for Windows 95 or Windows NT workstations. Select PPPRNS (Port to Port Protocol Remote Node Services). This matches the PPP protocol on the workstations.

PROCEDURE 16.1 (CONTINUED)

8. You are prompted to select IP or IPX. Choose the protocol you want your users to use when they connect to the remote access server.

9. Select whether you want header compression or not. Also enter the range of IP addresses you made available for remote access clients. Then press Esc and click Yes a second time to save your settings.

10. A message is displayed about current connections. Press Enter to continue and the system will reinitialize.

11. You can now start the services. PPPRNS is started at this time. If you want NIAS to be managed using SNMP, select RAMA. Press Esc to complete the configuration process.

12. A message is displayed advising you that all users have access to the remote access services. Now you will want to configure password security using the Configure Security option.

As you can see, during the initial configuration of an NIAS remote access server, you are prompted for a variety of information. If you want to customize your NIAS settings, you will need to use NIASCFG and know which options to use.

For more information on configuring an NIAS remote access server, refer to the Novell online documentation.

Configuring the Client for Remote Access

In order to provide users with remote access, you need to configure their remote workstations or laptops to connect to the NIAS remote access server. After you have installed the necessary hardware, you will want to install the latest Novell Client software.

The following sections will walk you through the process of configuring Windows 95 and Windows NT for remote access.

Windows 95 Clients

To configure a Windows 95 client for remote access services on an NIAS remote access server, follow Procedure 16.2.

PROCEDURE 16.2

Configuring a Windows 95 Client for Remote Access

To configure a Windows 95 workstation as an NIAS remote access client, follow these steps:

1. Make sure that the hardware (modem) and dial-up networking are installed on your computer. (If you are not familiar with this setup, check the Windows Help files for the installation procedures.) After you have verified the above, you can start configuring dial-up networking to access your remote network with NIAS remote access server.

2. From the Windows main screen, go to My Computer ➢ Dial-Up Networking. Double-click the Make New Connection icon, and the Install Wizard begins.

3. The first screen prompts you to enter a name for the connection (give it a logical name) and to select a modem (select the previously configured modem name).

4. The next screen will prompt you to enter the phone number of the remote access server. Click Next here, and then click Finish at the next screen.

5. You have created a Dial-Up Networking icon for the remote access server. Now you need to configure its properties. Go to My Computer ➢ Dial-Up Networking.

6. Right-click the icon for the remote server dial-up network you just created.

7. From the menu that appears, select Properties. A dialog box will be displayed. Click the Server Types tab.

8. The Server Type property page is displayed. Make sure that the dial-up server type is displayed as PPP: Internet, Windows NT Server, Windows 95.

9. Check any additional boxes needed for encrypted passwords and compression.

10. Select the protocols supported through remote access. If you selected TCP/IP as the protocol setting, you will need to select TCP/IP settings.

PROCEDURE 16.2 (CONTINUED)

11. Check the boxes labeled "IP header compression," if the remote access server is configured the same way, and "Use default gateway on remote network."

12. Click OK at each window that appears until you exit the program and you are back in Windows Explorer. You are now finished configuring the Windows 95 client for remote services and are ready to connect to the NIAS remote access server.

Follow Procedure 16.3 to connect a Windows 95 client to an NIAS remote access server.

PROCEDURE 16.3

Connecting a Windows 95 Client to an NIAS Remote Access Server

To connect a Windows 95 workstation to an NIAS remote access server, follow these steps:

1. On the Windows 95 workstation, go to My Computer ➤ Dial-Up Networking.

2. Double-click the icon for the dial-up network that you configured to access your remote access server.

3. You will be prompted for your username. Enter it, including the NDS context, and your password.

4. Click Connect. The modem will dial, and when a connection is made, you will be prompted to log in to your network.

5. Once your login has been authenticated, the connection is complete. You can now go to Network Neighborhood to see the network resources available to you.

Windows NT Clients

Procedure 16.4 will walk through the steps for configuring a Windows NT workstation for remote access.

Configuring Windows NT for NIAS Remote Access Services

To configure remote access services on a Windows NT client, follow these steps:

1. On the Windows NT workstation, go to My Computer ➤ Dial-Up Networking.

2. If you haven't installed dial-up networking yet, you will be prompted to do so at this time. (If you installed dial-up networking previously, skip to Step 9.) Click Yes when you are prompted that there are no RAS-capable devices to add.

3. Click Next to detect a modem, and click Next again after NT detects a modem.

4. Enter the area code and select a tone at the prompt.

5. You are now prompted for the phone number of the remote access server. Enter the number, and click Finish.

6. You are now prompted with the Add RAS Device screen. Make sure your modem is displayed correctly. Click Continue to confirm the modem choice.

7. After NT completes the installation, you will be prompted to restart the computer. After you have restarted the NT workstation, log in once again.

8. Select My Computer ➤ Dial-Up Networking.

9. Click OK to add a new entry in the Windows NT phone book.

10. Click Next to confirm the name of the phone book.

11. Configure the dial-up networking for IP by checking the box labeled "I am calling the Internet." Also place a check next to the box labeled "The non-Windows NT server I am calling expects me to type login information after connecting, or to know TCP/IP addresses after dialing." Click Next.

12. Enter the phone number of the NIAS remote access server and Click Next.

PROCEDURE 16.4 (CONTINUED)

13. The Serial Line Protocol dialog box will be displayed. Select PPP (point to point protocol) as the type of protocol. Make sure the Login Script box is not checked. In the IP address field, enter **0.0.0.0** so that the NIAS remote access server can issue an IP address to this client.

14. Click Finish, and at the next screen click Close. You are now finished configuring the Windows NT client for remote services and are ready to connect to an NIAS remote access server.

Follow Procedure 16.5 to connect a Windows NT client to an NIAS remote access server.

PROCEDURE 16.5

Connecting a Windows NT Client to an NIAS Remote Access Server

To connect a Windows NT workstation to the NIAS remote access server, follow these steps:

1. On the Windows NT workstation, go to My Computer ➤ Dial-Up Networking.

2. Double-click the phone icon that matches the name of your remote access server.

3. You will be prompted for your username. Enter it, including the NDS context, and your password.

4. Click Connect. The modem will dial, and when a connection is made, you will be prompted to log in to your network.

5. Once you have passed the authentication process, the connection is complete. You can now double-click the Network Neighborhood icon to see which network resources are available to you.

Remote Authentication Dial-In User Service (RADIUS)

The *RADIUS (Remote Authentication Dial-In User Service)* protocol is a TCP/IP standards-based protocol that provides remote dial-in user authentication through an Internet service provider. This service is vendor independent, which means that every vendor supports this protocol. NetWare 5 supports the RADIUS protocol through BorderManager.

RADIUS Protocol

RADIUS consists of a RADIUS server that retrieves all user information from a central database (like NDS) and a RADIUS accounting server that logs information on remote dial-in users. These two components run on your network. To accept dial-ins, you need to use a proxy RADIUS that runs at your ISP, or Internet Service Provider. RADIUS provides the following services:

- Centralized administration
- Client/server environment
- Security over an Internet connection (VPN)
- Support for multiple platforms
- Customization options

RADIUS Proxy

The RADIUS proxy allows an organization to outsource its modem bank, or dial-up hardware resources, to an ISP. The RADIUS proxy is located at the ISP. Clients connecting through the Internet then access the RADIUS proxy located at the ISP, which forwards the connection request to the RADIUS server located at their company's network. Once the client is authenticated, the user is given access to your network through the BorderManager server. This process requires a dedicated connection to the Internet from the BorderManager server to the ISP.

Review

In this chapter, you learned about NIAS (NetWare Internet Access Server) remote access service and how it can benefit the mobile user. Before implementing remote access, you should design a plan to account for any security, performance, cost, and data communication issues the company might have.

As we discussed, there are different settings you can use to optimize your NIAS remote access server for remote access. These were the key concepts we discussed in this chapter:

- NIAS remote access

- Mobile users

- Data transmission media

- Remote access security issues

- Optimal remote access performance

- Remote Authentication Dial-In User Service (RADIUS)

NIAS Remote Access

NIAS remote access is a way for users to access network resources from a remote location. Before you can enable remote access, you must have the following things in place:

- Modems in the server and remote workstation or laptop

- 5MB of extra RAM in the NIAS remote access server

- Login and password for each remote user

- NIAS remote access service configured on the server and remote workstation or laptop

Designing Remote Access

Remote access should start with a well-designed plan of action. The network administration or person in charge of designing the plan has various considerations to think about. Here are just a few:

- Who needs access?

- NIAS versus LAN connections
- Selecting a data transmission media
- How to design an effective security plan
- Where to locate the NIAS remote servers

Optimal Performance

Whether your users are connected remotely or directly to your LAN, optimal performance is what you strive for. You need to educate users regarding what performance they can expect while connecting from remote locations. Even though a remote connection is slower than a local LAN connection, you need to optimize the remote access on the server and client side. You should strive for these goals:

- Optimal performance on the server
- Optimal performance on the client workstation
- Optimal performance for remote access services administration

Configuring NIAS Services

After making sure that your hardware meets the requirements for remote access connection, you must design and configure remote access. While configuring NIAS remote access services on both the server and client, take into account the plans you made during the design phase. You'll need to configure each of the following items:

- The NIAS remote access server
- Windows 95 clients
- Windows NT clients

RADIUS

The RADIUS (Remote Authentication Dial-In Services) protocol provides the following services:

- Centralized administration
- Client/server environment

- Security over an Internet connection (VPN)
- Support for multiple platforms
- Customization options

The RADIUS proxy allows an organization to outsource its modem bank, or dial-up hardware resources, to an ISP.

CNE Practice Test Questions

1. Which of the following is *not* a requirement for providing a remote user access to NIAS remote access server?

   A. Modem for the server

   B. 5MB of additional RAM on the server

   C. User account and password

   D. None of the above

2. An important question to ask when planning for remote access services is (choose all that apply):

   A. Who needs remote access?

   B. Where are the users located?

   C. What do they need access to?

   D. How many simultaneous connections do you need to support?

3. A dial-up connection is faster than a LAN connection.

   A. True

   B. False

4. Of the following dial-up connections, which presents you with the fastest service?

   A. ISDN

   B. POTS

   C. xDSL

5. Of the following dial-up connections, which is the cheapest solution?

   A. ISDN

   B. POTS

   C. xDSL

6. A consideration in the location of NIAS remote access servers is the number of remote users in a geographical area.

   A. True

   B. False

7. A critical component in optimizing performance on an NIAS is the data transmission media selected.

   A. True

   B. False

8. BRI and PRI are options within which data transmission media?

   A. POTS

   B. ISDN

   C. HDSL

   D. ADSL

9. Which of the following statements is true of a demilitarized zone?

   A. It is used for military use *only* in their networks.

   B. It makes remote connections less secure on the NIAS remote access server

   C. It isolates an area, which keeps unauthorized users from going beyond the NIAS

   D. It is a zone that you configure in the NIAS during installation.

10. Which component of the RADIUS protocol is located at the ISP?

   A. RADIUS server

   B. RADIUS accounting server

   C. RADIUS proxy

   D. None of the above

CHAPTER

17

Integrating Other Novell Services

Roadmap

This chapter briefly covers BorderManager, GroupWise, NDS for NT, and ManageWise, which are part of the CNE core requirement "NetWare 5 Advanced Administration."

Topics Covered

- Secure Access to the Internet with BorderManager
- Integrating with Windows NT Using NDS for NT
- Messaging with GroupWise 5
- Using ManageWise for Network Management

Skills You'll Learn

- List the networking solutions offered by NetWare
- Describe the services provided by BorderManager
- Describe the components of a firewall
- Describe the firewall components of BorderManager
- Describe the benefits of integrating Windows NT with NDS
- List the components of NDS for NT
- Describe the components of GroupWise and how they integrate with NDS to provide messaging services
- Describe the features and components of ManageWise

NetWare 5 comes packaged with some impressive services right out of the box. In fact, it is a complete network solution in most situations.

There are additional network services offered by NetWare that provide solutions to issues not covered in the retail package, including secure access to the Internet, integrating Windows NT with NDS, messaging services, and network management. The following sections expand on these issues briefly, describing the NetWare solutions available.

Secure Access to the Internet

If you want to monitor and control network traffic between your intranet and the Internet, BorderManager is the solution. Think of Border-Manager as the border guard for your company's network border with the Internet. In this section, you will learn about each of BorderManager's features and the relationship between them: firewalls and their components, the OSI model, and finally BorderManager and its firewall components.

Firewall Components

A firewall is a brick wall placed between buildings or houses to block a fire from spreading. In networking, the term *firewall* is used to indicate a control mechanism for inbound and outbound communication between networks. Firewalls provide added security to prevent unauthorized users from accessing the Internet (outbound access) or unauthorized people from accessing your private network from the Internet (inbound access). You can also apply firewalls to prevent interdivisional communications; for example, you may not want a user in the Sales department to have access to a resource in the Accounting department.

A firewall can be composed of a packet-filtering router, circuit gateway, or an application gateway. Most firewalls are made up of a combination of these components, providing security at all layers of the OSI (described below).

Understanding Firewalls and the OSI Model

Firewall components control network traffic much like a router does. To understand the impact a firewall has on the network, you first need to understand how network communication works.

OSI Model

The best way to understand networks is to look at the *OSI (Open Systems Interconnect)* model, which was created by the ISO (International Standards Organization), an international body that establishes network standards all vendors comply with. *Standards* are agreed-upon rules (protocols) that are established by organizations like the ISO.

The OSI model is not a protocol or an application, but a reference that specifies a group of properties divided by layers. If you've heard the adage "To understand a forest, you must first look at each tree," it applies to networking as well. To understand networking, you must look at each layer.

The OSI model divides networking into seven layers. The OSI model is presented in reverse order, starting with the seventh layer and working its way down to the first layer. The upper five layers are generally implemented with software and the lower two layers are generally implemented with hardware and software. Each layer addresses a specific set of network properties and functions, as described here:

Layer 7 – Application   Provides the network services functions, such as Directory services, file and print services (like NDPS), and so on.

Layer 6 – Presentation   Provides translation of file formats between different operating systems (for example, ODBC).

Layer 5 – Session   Coordinates communication between systems, maintaining sessions for as long as needed and performing security, logging, and administrative functions. This is also the layer responsible for encryption of data prior to transmission (for example, PKI).

Layer 4 – Transport   Provides mechanisms for multiplexing upper-layer applications; the establishment, maintenance and cleanup of virtual circuits; information flow control; and transport fault detection and recovery. Also responsible for host-to-host packet delivery and name resolution (for example TCP, Transport Control Protocol).

Layer 3 – Network   Defines protocols for forwarding data by opening and maintaining a path on the network between multiple systems to ensure that data arrives at the correct destination node. Specifies routing properties and methods between multiple network segments (for example IP, Internet Protocol).

Layer 2 – Data Link   This layer is divided into two portions, the MAC and the LLC. The LLC is a marshalling layer between the upper network layer and the physical topology. The MAC provides each computer with a unique 6-byte hexadecimal address (also called the BIA, an acronym for burned-in address) that is assigned to each card; often these numbers are represented in the form 00:00:00:00:00:00 (for example, ARP).

Layer 1 – Physical   Provides the physical elements of a network, such as cabling, adapters, and signals (for example, IEEE 802.3-Ethernet).

For more information on the OSI model, go to this helpful site: `http://www.networkstudyguides.com/osi`.

The OSI model describes the role each component or protocol has in networking. It also describes how data flows from one host to another through each layer. As you will see in the next section, firewalls have a role in several layers of the OSI model.

Firewalls

Firewalls offer control mechanisms to various layers of the OSI model. The following firewall components affect the layers of the OSI model:

Packet-Filtering Routers   Also called screening routers, *packet-filtering routers* restrict incoming packets from the Internet to your network (intranet). These routers can use source IP addresses, port numbers, and node addresses to restrict access to your internal network from the Internet. By denying access to a specific port number, IP address, or node address, a packet-filtering router can affect the data link, network, and transport layers of the OSI model.

Circuit Gateways   These are also called circuit-level proxies, and they control outbound connections from your intranet to the Internet. This component acts on behalf of the client making the request. When a user wants to access the Internet, the request is forwarded to a port on the circuit gateway. The circuit gateway then replaces the user IP address with its own, accessing the Internet for the client. This firewall component affects the session layer of the OSI model. Circuit gateways allow you to implement RFC 1597 (Address Allocation for Private Intranets); the terms *Network Address Translation (NAT), Port Address Translation (PAT),* and *IP Masquerading* may all be grouped into this category. For more information on these terms, please refer to the Novell online documentation.

Application Gateways   These application-level proxies control access to the presentation and application layer of the OSI model. Firewalls that include application gateways are considered the most secure type, because the data must actually be handled by the firewall, processed, and then sent back to the client. Sometimes other features such as caching are integrated into Application gateways; these are also called *caching proxies.*

BorderManager and Its Firewall Components

To address the need for firewalls on NetWare networks, Novell offers Border-Manager. *BorderManager* for NetWare offers a comprehensive suite of services that include routing, remote access, IP gateway, proxy cache, and Virtual Private Network (VPN) encryption software. The following components provide these services:

NIAS 4.1   This software provides routing gateway services and remote access to your network for dial-up clients. These services include Multi-protocol routing, WAN support, packet filtering, *Network Address Translators (NAT,* which translates private IP addresses to registered ones), an *IPX mapping gateway* (which translates private IPX addresses to registered IPX addresses), and inbound/outbound remote access (discussed in the previous chapter). NIAS 4.1 also provides Virtual Private Network (VPN) encryption software through its tunneling and encryption services over the Internet, eliminating the need for private lines.

HTTP Accelerator   This is used to accelerate access from the Internet to your company Web sites. In this situation, BorderManager is used as a front end to your public Web sites, reducing access to your internal network from the outside and improving response time to client requests from the Internet. You configure your DNS to point the host WWW to your BorderManager server(s). Then when a client requests a document, the BorderManager server requests it from your real Web server. After receiving the document, it keeps a copy in its cache for future reference. All subsequent requests for the same document result in faster access times. (Note: Be sure not to use Border-Manager FastCache with pages that have dynamic content or that need to be updated frequently.) Using FastCache also protects your Web servers, because they are not directly exposed to the Internet. All updates can be done in a secure network on the Web server, and then the contents are cached to the disk on the BorderManager server.

Hierarchical Proxy Cache   This is used to place multiple caches on BorderManager, to hold information from sources frequently accessed by users on both sides of your network. The objective is to make users request the BorderManager server, which in turn accelerates response time, improving your Web security and performance, rather than having user requests processed by your Web servers. This functionality is achieved through the caching services on the BorderManager server.

> For more information on BorderManager, visit the area of Novell's Web site that covers this feature (http://www.novell.com/bordermanager).

As you can see, BorderManager is a comprehensive solution for various network services and should be considered whenever you do any network planning.

Integrating Windows NT with NDS

NetWare offers another network service for managing multiple operating systems that support different applications critical to your organization. Because Windows NT is a popular workstation, NetWare offers NDS for NT (Windows NT workstation 4.0) and an NT application server (Windows NT server 4.0). NDS for NT is a suite of services that integrates Windows NT platforms and domains (equivalent to Microsoft Directory Services) into NDS. Integrating this platform into NDS allows you to administrate all your NT resources through NetWare Administrator. The following sections provide an overview of NDS for NT, its components, and its functions.

NDS for NT Overview

Networks are complex enough to manage; imagine how difficult the job would be if you had to manage multiple directory services as well. You would have to manage user accounts for NDS, Windows NT, domains, stand-alone servers, and Windows NT workstations, which all require user accounts to access their resources. (Some of you probably don't have to imagine this scenario; it is actually a very common problem in medium-sized to large companies.)

Using NDS for NT lets you avoid this situation, as well as offering the following benefits:

- All network components are managed by a single database. This means that NDS for NT will manage, through NDS, Windows NT domains, stand-alone servers, and workstations. The NDS schema is extended when NDS for NT is installed, enabling Directory services to handle requests to Windows NT domains from NT servers and workstations.

Two immediate benefits are simplified user administration (users need only one user account for all resources) and reduced administration costs (you have a single point of administration through NetWare Administrator).

- Applications that require access to a Windows NT domain can be managed through NDS, because NDS for NT incorporates the NT domain database into the Directory services database. Again, your job is simplified with a single point of administration.

- Since the NDS and domain database are integrated into one unit, users are only required to log in once to gain access to both systems. It is the objective of all network administrators to simplify logins for their users, and NDS for NT accomplishes this. A user needs only to log in to the Directory tree to access all the resources available to them, including Microsoft Windows NT. (Beware: At this point, passwords cannot be synchronized due to the lower grade of security implemented in Windows NT.)

- Through NDS, you gain management capabilities over the Windows NT domain. Giving users access across multiple domains (trust relationships) and moving user accounts from domain to domain, along with assigning access to individual objects in a multidomain environment, can be very time-consuming and complicated. With NDS for NT, Windows NT domains databases are integrated into Directory services; therefore, a single user account can be given access throughout the network, moved easily, and given security restrictions on each object on the network. With NDS for NT, you can give users access to multiple domains very easily.

For more information on NDS for NT, go to the Novell Web site (http://www.novell.com) and navigate to the Products section.

NDS for NT Components and Their Functions

This section covers the components that make up NDS for NT and their functions. In the following sections, we'll discuss these components:

- SAMSRV.DLL
- Domain Object Wizard

- Novell NDS for NT client
- NetWare Administrator
- Mailbox Manager for Exchange

SAMSRV.DLL

When NDS for NT is installed on a *Windows NT domain controller* (a domain controller holds the account database that controls access to a domain), SAMSRV.DLL is replaced with a version from NetWare, and the original file is renamed MSSAMSRV.DLL. Afterward, any calls made from a domain client are redirected to NDS through the new SAMSRV.DLL, and NDS authenticates the user account. NDS for NT must be installed on the PDC (Primary Domain Controller) and the BDCs (Backup Domain Controllers) of a Windows NT domain being integrated into NDS.

Domain Object Wizard

The Domain Object Wizard is installed when NDS for NT is installed. This graphical user interface extends the NDS schema and migrates existing Windows NT domain accounts to NDS. The Domain Object Wizard runs automatically when you reboot the Windows NT server after installing NDS for NT. To uninstall NDS for NT, you can run the Domain Object Wizard a second time, this time choosing the Uninstall option.

Novell NDS for NT Client

The Novell NDS for NT client is installed along with NDS for NT. This allows a Windows NT server running NDS for NT to access NDS from any platform it's ported to.

NetWare Administrator

NetWare Administrator (described in earlier chapters) is the graphical user interface used to manage all network resources through NDS. When NDS for NT is installed and the NDS schema is extended, new objects are created. Snap-ins make these objects available through NWADMN32.EXE.

Mailbox Manager for Exchange Snap-In

With the Mailbox Manager for Exchange snap-in, NetWare Administrator can manage Exchange server mailboxes. Adding and deleting mailboxes is done through NDS and synchronized through the Exchange server. Therefore, you can support an Exchange server environment without complicated domain structures.

Of course, you can still manage your NT domains the hard way, using User Manager for Domains.

GroupWise 5 and NetWare

GroupWise 5 provides a series of network services that enable messaging, together with some workgroup applications. This section gives an overview of GroupWise and its components.

GroupWise 5 is a messaging application that includes functions such as messaging, a calendar, scheduling, shared folders, a workflow process, and remote and Internet access. As its name implies, GroupWise 5 helps groups, departments, and project groups exchange information, saving time and operating costs.

Because it is integrated with NDS upon installation, GroupWise 5 can be administered through NetWare Administrator, allowing for a single point of administration. Using NetWare Administrator, you can configure the GroupWise system, user properties, the Message Store, system diagnostics, and client software. When the GroupWise software is installed, the NDS schema is extended with the needed information. The GroupWise administration module is also added to NetWare Administrator, allowing you to manage GroupWise.

GroupWise 5 System Components

The following sections cover these GroupWise 5 system components:

- Client
- Message Transfer System
- Administration Program
- Message Store
- Directory Store
- Document Store

The Client

The GroupWise 5 *client* is the component through which users access, create, and deliver messages. This application resides on the user's desktop and interfaces with the different GroupWise components available to it. Clients are available for Windows NT workstations and Windows 95, Windows 3.1, Macintosh, and Unix operating systems. (Unix and other platforms not listed here are supported through a product called WebAccess, which enables users to access their GroupWise client using any Web browser.)

Message Transfer System

The *Message Transfer System (MTS)* is responsible for routing messages from server to server. When a user sends mail to another user in a different location, it's the MTS that directs the message to the right server. This component includes two elements: a Message Transfer Agent and a Post Office Agent.

GroupWise 5 Administration Program

The *GroupWise Administration Program* is added as a module to NetWare Administrator. You can only access this program using NetWare Administrator. This program allows you to administrate, configure, and manage the users and components of GroupWise.

Message Store

The *Message Store* stores the messages clients send to each other. When a message is created, it is stored in the message store for later delivery; this system is called store and forward. GroupWise has both a database and a file-based Message Store. Messages that are too large to store in the database are stored as files. The Message Store is located on the NetWare server.

Directory Store

The *Directory Store* is a distributed database that provides user-addressing information to the Message Transfer Agent and the GroupWise Address Book. The *Messaging Transfer Agent* gets routing information from the Directory Store so it can deliver mail to the right user's address. The *Address Book* is populated by the Directory Store and provides users with current addressing information for each other.

The Directory Store can be accessed efficiently by other components and users. Since this is a distributed database, it needs to be synchronized through a process known as *directory synchronization*. The Directory Store is replicated by NDS throughout the tree, but the components that need directory information access the Directory directly and not through NDS.

Document Store

The *Document Store* is a shared library of documents and files used by a group of users who are associated in some way or who need to share the same information. Document management is provided through the Group-Wise library, a shared locator where documents and files are stored for the use of a group of people.

For more information, see the GroupWise pages on the Novell site (http://www.novell.com/groupwise) or visit http://www.gwmag.com (a Novell site for people who already have GroupWise installed).

Using ManageWise for Network Management

To perform network management jobs such as tracking network performance, managing inventory, analyzing traffic, and monitoring workstations and servers, you need to use an application suited to those tasks. NetWare's solution is ManageWise, a comprehensive package that provides a large array of services, including these:

- Asset inventory and management
- Server monitoring and management
- Desktop management
- Network traffic analysis and management
- Network-wide virus protection

Asset Inventory and Management

ManageWise performs the tasks of asset inventory and management through the NetExplorer component. This component allows ManageWise to track inventory of all network systems, display graphical maps of the devices on the network, inventory individual devices, and manage IP and IPX addresses. This component must run on at least one device on the network.

Server Monitoring and Management

ManageWise uses the NetWare Management Agent component to monitor every server on the network. As the administrator, you can configure settings to notify you of any problems. You can manage the servers remotely and monitor print queues. NetWare Management Agent can also monitor performance trends on the server and save the data for later analysis. This agent must be loaded on all the servers you want to monitor.

Desktop Management

ManageWise can also monitor and manage desktops remotely using Z.E.N.works (Zero Effort Networks) components. (Z.E.N.works is covered in Chapter 5.) These components must be installed in every workstation and run on the workstations and servers. Using the desktop management function and NetWare Administrator, you can monitor desktops and control them remotely from a central location.

Network Traffic Analysis and Management

To help you monitor network traffic and analyze the data you gather, ManageWise offers LANalyzer Agent Software. This agent allows ManageWise to gather traffic information on a segment-by-segment basis and helps you analyze it. It provides support for commonly used protocols and networks. The agent needs to be loaded on at least one server per network segment.

Network-Wide Virus Protection

Viruses are a constant threat to network resources. To protect against them network-wide, ManageWise installs *Virus Protect* elements on the workstations and the servers. Some of the services provided by Virus Protect include real-time scanning and protection, workstation/mobile computer protection, and self-maintenance.

Review

In this chapter, you learned about additional services NetWare offers beyond what the NetWare 5 package provides:

- Secure intranet/Internet access

- Integration with Windows NT

- Messaging services

- Network management capabilities

Secure Intranet/Internet Access

BorderManager provides a comprehensive suite of services designed to protect your network, control access to the Internet, and accelerate response to Web site requests. In this section, you learned about the following:

Firewalls Provide added security to prevent unauthorized users from accessing your company intranet (inbound access) or unauthorized network users from accessing the Internet (inbound access). We discussed three different types of firewalls:

- Packet-filtering routers

- Circuit gateways

- Application gateways

OSI model Describes the role each component or protocol has in networking and how data flows from one host to another through each layer. These are the seven layers: (7) Application, (6) Presentation, (5) Session, (4) Transport, (3) Network, (2) Data Link, and (1) Physical.

BorderManager and its firewall components Novell uses BorderManager as its solution to firewall implementation in NetWare 5 environments. You learned about these firewall components:

- NIAS 4.1

- HTTP Accelerator

- Hierarchical Proxy Cache

Integrating Windows NT with NDS

To integrate Windows NT with NetWare, Novell offers NDS for NT. NDS for NT redirects requests made by Windows NT domain clients to NDS. This produces a single directory from which you can control all your resources. Users need only a single user account to log in to both NetWare and Windows NT domains.

These are the components of NDS for Windows NT:

- SAMSRV.DLL

- Domain Object Wizard

- Novell NDS for NT client

- NetWare Administrator

- Mailbox Manager for Exchange snap-in

GroupWise 5

NetWare offers messaging services through GroupWise 5, a suite of services and databases that provides mail messaging and group-related tasks. These services enable groups of people working on the same project to share resources and keep in touch.

These are the GroupWise 5 system components:

- Client

- Message Transfer System

- Administration Program

- Message Store

- Directory Store

- Document Store

ManageWise

Network management capabilities are provided through ManageWise, a suite of applications that provides a wide scope of services. These are some of the services it provides:

- Asset inventory and management

- Server monitoring and management

- Desktop management
- Network traffic analysis and management
- Network-wide virus protection

CNE Practice Test Questions

1. Which of the following are additional network solutions offered by NetWare? (Select all that apply.)

    A. NDS for NT

    B. BorderManager

    C. GroupWise 5

    D. All of the above

2. Which network solution offers firewall services?

    A. NDS for NT

    B. BorderManager

    C. GroupWise 5

    D. ManageWise

3. Which is *not* a component of a firewall?

    A. Packet-filtering routers

    B. Circuit gateways

    C. Application gateways

    D. Application routers

4. Which layers of the OSI model do packet-filtering routers relate to? (Select two.)

    A. Application

    B. Session

    C. Network

    D. Transport

5. Which of these is a component of BorderManager?

    A. NIAS 4.1

    B. LANalyzer

    C. Z.E.N.works

    D. NetWare Administrator

6. _____ redirects requests from Windows NT domain clients to NDS.

    A. MSSAMSRV.DLL

    B. SAMSRV.DLL

    C. PROXYSRV.DLL

    D. SAMLIB.DLL

7. To manage GroupWise 5 components, first you need to load NetWare Administrator to access the GroupWise Administration module.

    A. True

    B. False

8. The Message Store routes messages between servers.

    A. True

    B. False

9. Which GroupWise component do the client and Message Transfer Services access?

   A. Directory Store

   B. Message Store

   C. Document Store

   D. All of the above

10. ManageWise can monitor network traffic as well as record, inventory, and manage network resources.

    A. True

    B. False

11. Which component of ManageWise monitors and can remotely manage workstations?

    A. NetExplorer

    B. LANalyzer

    C. Z.E.N.works

    D. NetWare Management Agent

PART

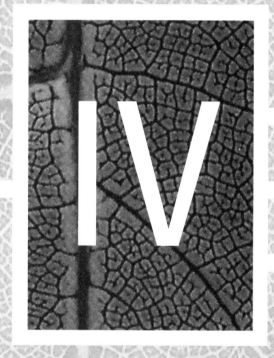

IV

NetWare 5 Design
and Implementation

CHAPTER

18

Planning Your NDS Tree

Roadmap

This chapter covers some of the basic components of designing and implementing either a new network or an upgrade to NetWare 5, a section of the CNE core requirement "NetWare 5 Design and Implementation."

Topics Covered

- Design and Implementation
- Project Roles
- Naming Standards Document
- Tree Design

Skills You'll Learn

- Explain the design and implementation process for a new NetWare 5 network, including the purpose and tasks in each of the four phases

- List the roles you will need to fill to successfully design and implement the new tree

- Define some common naming standards and why they are important, and place those standards in a naming standards document

- Explain the options available for creating the upper layers of the tree

- Describe the methods that can be used to organize the lower layers of the tree and the factors that affect the design of those layers

---

Welcome to Part IV! As you've learned in the previous parts of this book, a well-organized NDS tree provides many advantages for the network. But how does a well-organized tree come about? Creating a tree that provides maximum benefits and flexibility as the organization of the network changes is a complex process and requires a great deal of planning.

Network design and planning is so important that Novell created a separate CNE test for it. In Chapters 18 through 21, you'll learn about a range of considerations for planning and creating an effective NDS tree and network.

Planning NDS Design and Implementation

As you've learned about NetWare 5 and networking from this book, you have assumed the role of network administrator—the person responsible for planning, configuring, and maintaining a network for a single organization. Throughout Part IV of this book, we'll look at the network administration of a large network spanning multiple locations, which requires a great deal of administration and planning. You may eventually be required to plan a network of this size for your organization, or perhaps you are interested in becoming a *network consultant*, working on network projects for companies.

In this section you'll assume the role of a consultant and explore the process involved in designing and planning a complex network. We'll also look at the other people who should be involved in the process and what their roles entail.

The Design and Implementation Process

First, let's look at the process of designing and implementing NetWare 5 for a large company. There are several phases to the project:

1. In the *project approach phase,* you determine the approach you will use.

2. In the *design phase*, you design the Directory tree and create an accessibility plan. This also includes planning partitions and replication, and time synchronization.

3. In the *implementation phase,* you develop a migration strategy, create an implementation schedule, and finally implement NetWare 5 and NDS.

4. In the *ongoing analysis phase,* you manage and monitor the network and verify that it works, going through the entire design and implementation process again as needed.

We will look at each of these phases in detail in the following sections.

The Project Approach Phase

This phase focuses on a single task: preparing for NDS design. This includes the following steps:

- Assembling the project team

- Gathering information about the company and its current network (if any)

- Determining the scope of the design

- Making a preliminary schedule

We'll look at each of these tasks in detail later in this chapter.

The Design Phase

The design phase includes several important procedures. Each is listed below, along with the chapter that covers it:

- Designing the Directory tree (Chapter 18)

- Determining a partition and replica strategy (Chapter 20)

- Planning a time synchronization strategy (Chapter 20)

- Creating an accessibility plan, including providing for mobile users, security, and the file system (Chapter 19)

Depending on the size of the network, you may not need to worry about partitions and replicas or time synchronization. You will determine this when you decide upon the scope of the project, which is covered later in this section. The design phase is time-consuming and research-intensive, because the whole project depends on the issues decided during this phase.

The Implementation Phase

The implementation phase is the fun part—where the actual installation, migration, and upgrades take place. It involves three tasks, each covered in the chapters indicated:

- Developing a migration strategy (Chapter 21)

- Creating an implementation schedule (Chapter 21)

- Implementing NetWare 5 and NDS (Chapters 7, 8, 11, 14, and 21)

Of course, none of these tasks is optional. This phase is often the most time-consuming, since this is when the physical work is done, but it should be easy if you have planned well.

The Ongoing Analysis Phase

The final phase of the upgrade is an ongoing one that includes two main tasks:

- Managing NetWare 5

- Monitoring NetWare 5

These procedures aren't actually part of the design process—they happen after the design and implementation is complete. If nothing goes wrong, the client company will handle these; and you, the NetWare consultant, can go home and count your money. This is where current network use and changing conditions are evaluated to decide when it is time to redesign the network.

Starting the Design Process

In this section we'll introduce the various tasks you'll need to perform as you determine how to approach the project. This includes putting together a team, training team members, gathering information about the company, defining the scope of the project, and scheduling the project.

Organizing the Project Team

As a NetWare consultant or a company's network administrator, you aren't on your own. You should assemble a team of people for any design and implementation project. These may include your own employees, employees of the client company, and outside specialists.

Several different specialists may be required in your team. Which members you actually use will depend on the scope of the project and the resources you have available, but you should at least consider each of the roles discussed in this section and make sure that someone is taking responsibility for the function that role serves.

Among the various team members you might include in the design and implementation process, the following are considered the primary (core) roles:

- Project manager

- NDS expert

- Server administrator

- Connectivity specialist

If you have a large project, several other roles will be useful as well. Remember, one person may have more than one role. The following roles are secondary:

- Workstation specialist
- Application specialist
- Printing specialist

We'll describe the roles of each of these primary and secondary team members in the following sections.

The Project Manager

The *project manager* is usually an employee of the client company who is in charge of the network at some level. This is your contact with the company. The project manager is responsible for keeping the company's interests in mind and answering any questions you (and the team of experts) might have.

The project manager is responsible for coordinating with the NDS expert to guide the transition to NetWare 5, overseeing the design phase, and managing the implementation. Most importantly, the project manager is the one with access to the client company's money; this person is responsible for acquiring the equipment and materials needed to perform the upgrade.

As the title implies, the project manager's role includes directing the project. He or she communicates with the executives and other departments of the company, manages costs and time estimates, and organizes and schedules meetings.

The project manager is concerned with efficient network design, and with the costs involved. He or she determines the implementation timeline, evaluates software, and supports the software and the network. The project manager is also concerned with administrator and user productivity, and he or she is responsible for training both administrators and users.

The NDS Expert

The *NDS expert* is someone experienced with NDS and NetWare 5. This may be you or part of your consulting team. The NDS expert is usually in charge of the design process, acting as the team leader. The responsibilities of this role include the following:

- Leading the project team and choosing team members, and then ensuring their participation
- Creating the actual Directory tree design within the required timeline

- Planning for NDS security, partitioning and replication, and time synchronization

- Communicating with management and the project manager to determine everyone's needs, and ensuring that the network design meets them

- Coordinating login scripts with other team members

- Documenting the design, or assigning someone to do so

The Server Administrator

The *server administrator* is someone experienced with NetWare server administration. This may be the person responsible for maintaining servers at the client company. The responsibilities of this specialist include the following:

- Determining and planning the pilot installation

- Maintaining an acceptable level of network performance and testing the usability and stability of the new servers

- Implementing server upgrades and migrations in all departments

- Helping with the time synchronization strategy

- Determining where servers are to be placed and the policies and procedures for adding new servers and removing discontinued servers from the tree

- Ensuring sufficient disk space is available for the operating system as well as all applications and data stored on the server

- Keeping the migration running smoothly

- Planning for backups and disaster recovery

- Dealing with compatibility issues

The Connectivity Specialist

The *connectivity specialist* handles the physical aspects of the network—LANs, WANs, routers, and telecommunications. This person may be part of your consulting team, a specialist from the phone company, or a WAN specialist.

This specialist manages the protocols, WAN links, and other physical considerations, and aids in their planning. His or her priorities include keeping network traffic moving quickly and keeping the LAN and WAN efficient. This expert advises the other members of the team about networking issues. The person in this role also advises the NDS expert and consults with him or her on WAN links and issues affecting the tree's design. In addition, the connectivity specialist is concerned with bandwidth utilization, both current and projected after the upgrade, as well as connectivity issues with other platforms.

The Workstation Specialist

The *workstation specialist* is the lucky person who gets to upgrade each of the workstations—or to assign the task to other people. The responsibilities of this specialist include the following:

- Upgrading workstations to the latest client software, automating the process when possible.

- Scheduling the workstation upgrades.

- Determining whether memory and hardware will need to be upgraded. Testing compatibility of hardware with Novell Client.

- Watching and evaluating the performance of the new client software.

- Designing login scripts and coordinating them with the rest of the team.

- Setting up the servers to accommodate mobile users and Bindery Services.

The Applications Specialist

The *applications specialist* is responsible for maintaining and upgrading applications, whether on client machines, the network, or the servers. This specialist tests applications to ensure their compatibility with Novell Client software, stability in the new environment, and updates them as needed.

The applications specialist also works with Bindery Services and helps the other members of the team ensure that applications will not be affected by the changes.

The Printing Specialist

The *printing specialist* is the printer expert. The printing specialist is responsible for setting up and configuring printers, upgrading software and drivers as needed, and ensuring that users can access the printers in the new environment. The printing specialist should handle the parts of the migration plan that involve printers.

This specialist may also work with login scripts and Bindery Services. Responsibilities also include setting up Unix and Macintosh print services, if required by the company. This person will be testing NDPS and the issues in implementing it. He or she will probably be very grateful for NDPS, as driver issues become, in large part, a problem of the past. The printing specialist also needs to ensure that the workstation specialist installs the NDPS components when installing the client software.

Gathering Information

Once you've assembled a project team, you should gather the information needed for the upgrade and implementation of NetWare 5 and NDS. This includes the company's organizational charts, detailed diagrams of the WAN and of each LAN, and information about every resource in the network—servers, printers, workstations, and other equipment.

You should also gather information about the company's *workflow*—how the company is managed and how various tasks are performed. If the company produces a product, it is a good idea to follow the product through the stages of production.

Defining the Project Scope

By evaluating the information you gathered in the previous step, you can determine the scope of the project. This simply means assessing how big the project is and which tasks will need to be performed. Answering these questions should help you determine the scale of the project:

- Which team members will you need to complete the necessary tasks?
- Will you need to worry about time synchronization planning?
- Will you need to use partitions and replicas?
- Will you need additional servers or workstations?

Scheduling the Project

The final task is to schedule the project itself. This should be done by the entire team as a group and coordinated with representatives of the company. Unfortunately, executives often have different ideas about how fast things should happen; you may need to educate them about the difficulty of each task and the sequential tasks that must be finished for a successful outcome.

The specific steps involved in the project planning process are covered in Chapter 21.

NDS and Object Naming Reviewed

The basics of NDS were explained in Chapter 2, and some of the network design issues were introduced in Chapter 14. You should be familiar with the material in those chapters for a fundamental understanding of the design and implementation process. This section will provide you with a quick review to ensure that you understand the basic concepts of NDS, objects, properties, and naming.

NDS Concepts

A basic concept in NDS is that of an *object*. An object represents each resource on the network, and other objects are used to organize objects. The objects are placed in a tree-like structure, called the *Directory tree*. The terms used to describe objects are listed below. Note that an object can fit more than one of these descriptions:

- A *container object* is used to organize other objects. Container objects include Country, Organization, Organizational Unit, and Locality. Container objects can contain other container objects or leaf objects.

- A *leaf object* represents an actual network resource. There are a wide variety of leaf objects; the most common include User, Group, Organizational Role, Volume, and Server.

- A *parent object* is a relative term (no pun intended): A container object that holds an object is that object's parent.

- Similarly, a *child object* is one that is contained by the parent object. Leaf objects are always child objects; container objects can be both parents and children.

The following terms describe special objects:

- The *[Root] object* is at the top of the Directory tree. There is only one [Root] object per Directory tree. It cannot be deleted, moved, or renamed.

- The *[Public] trustee* is a special object that does not appear in the Directory tree. It is used to assign rights. Rights given to this object are automatically given to all objects on the network, logged in or not.

- *Admin* is a User object that maintains security. This user is created when NDS is installed. Admin begins with full rights, but these rights may be blocked. This user may also be renamed for greater security.

Be sure you understand the basics of NDS security, described in Chapter 4, and login scripts, which are covered in Chapter 5.

Object Naming and Properties

Each object has a list of *properties*, which contain information about the object. For example, the properties of a User object include login name, full name, telephone number, and login script. Each type of container and leaf object has a list of properties. The information you place in a property is called the *value* of the property. For example, the value of a User object's Last Name property might be *Smith*.

The following are the different types of names used to describe objects in the Directory tree:

- An object's *common name* is the simplest name for the object. A User object's common name is its login name.

- An object's *distinguished name (DN)* is a combination of its common name and its position in the Directory tree. The distinguished name is represented by a list of objects, beginning with the common name and ending with the container directly below [Root]. A period is used at the beginning of the name and between each component.

- An object's *relative distinguished name (RDN)* identifies the position of the object relative to the current context. Relative distinguished names do not begin with a period.

- An object's *context* is the container object that contains the object. The context is represented by the distinguished name of the parent object.

- Your *current context* is the part of the Directory tree that you are currently located in. This is not necessarily what you are looking at in NetWare Administrator. This is similar to the concept of a current directory in the file system.

- A *typeful name* includes the type of object for each component—for example, .CN=MARC.OU=ACCT.O=ABC_INC. Typeful names use these abbreviations:

  - CN= for the common name (used for all leaf objects)

  - C= for a Country object

  - O= for an Organization object

  - OU= for an Organizational Unit object

  - L= or S= for a Locality object

- A *typeless name* is a name that does not include information about object types—for example, MARC.ACCT.ABC_INC. Typeless names can be used in most cases.

Creating a Standards Document

The first step in planning a Directory tree is to write everything down. Creating a written plan helps to ensure you've asked all of the right questions and can help you explain to clients why the Directory tree was planned a certain way.

A *standards document* is a detailed document that describes how objects will be named in the Directory tree. It should include each type of object that will be used, properties that will be defined, and other considerations. These items are described in the following sections, which will provide a description of each of the items you should include in your standards document and why they are important. This chapter will also include an example document that defines all standards. Since a standards document is for your information and the client's, it has no official format, but you're welcome to use the format presented in our example. Choose a layout that works best for you and your client.

When writing your standards, use pencil or, more likely, a word processor. Nothing is ever set in stone with networking, so you should expect to make major changes to the document before you're finished implementing the network.

The Importance of Naming Standards

If you've had any experience with a poorly planned (or completely *unplanned*) network, you can probably think of a few advantages for naming standards. Typical small-company networks were started with a fresh copy of NetWare and have survived, often for years, with additions as they are needed—despite changes in the company or even in the network administrator position. Thus, you will find inconsistencies—a user named Tom Smith might have a login name of TOMS, TSMITH, TOM, SMITH, or even SHORTY or BOZO. In a small company, these inconsistencies can be an annoyance but don't cause serious problems; you can always ask Tom what his login name is.

But if you're in a huge, multinational corporation and you need to send e-mail to an employee named Tom Smith in the records department of the London branch, inconsistent names can make this task difficult. Your only hope is to spend a while on the phone, which reduces the usefulness of e-mail.

If naming standards are defined and followed, this problem doesn't occur. You can simply use your knowledge of the standard to determine the exact name of the employee. A logical name such as TSMITH.RECORDS .LONDON.ABC_INC is much easier to remember and can even be applied to new employees or locations.

We've used a User object in our example, but the benefits of naming standards apply to any object you name. A typical user may correctly name (and therefore find) other users, printers, and servers; a network administrator has the responsibility of naming every object in the Directory tree.

What to Include in the Standards Document

Your standards document should include the following:

- Naming standards for each container object and which type will be used in which situations

- Naming standards for each type of leaf object that will be used

- For each object, the list of properties that must be defined and the format for their values

- Which characters are not allowed

These items are explained in more detail in the following sections.

Object Naming Standards

The most important aspect of the standards document is the format of object names. A consistent format for these names is crucial for locating the resources in a large Directory tree. The standards document serves as a reference so a new department or new administrator won't create his or her own conflicting standards.

You should define a naming standard for any object you will use (immediately or eventually) in the Directory tree. The following sections discuss some of the common objects and suggested naming standards for them.

Directory Trees

Depending on your schedule for fully implementing NDS, you may be using multiple Directory trees temporarily, although this is not usually recommended. Your standards document should include a standard way of naming Directory trees. This will make it easier to refer to them when they are eventually merged. In addition, logging in to a tree outside your current Directory tree requires you to choose the correct tree name.

Typical Directory tree names include the name of the main organization followed by an identifier for the portion of the organization represented by the Directory tree: a location, subdivision, branch, or department name. For example, the STAR Corporation might use the following Directory tree names:

- STAR_Tree for the main Directory tree

- STAR_LAX for the Los Angeles branch

- STAR_NYC for the New York City branch

Usernames

Typical standards for user login names include some combination of names and initials:

First name, last initial (as in JOHNS)   For small companies, this user naming standard might be the best solution because employees know each other by first names. However, this standard can result in duplicate names (if there were two employees named John S. located in different containers) or deviation from the naming standard (if the two employees named John S. were in the same container). In addition, there may be confusion if employees are also known by nicknames.

First initial, last name (as in JSMITH)   This is another common method. The chance of duplicate names is lessened somewhat, and it's easier to determine who the name refers to.

First initial, middle initial, last name (as in JDSMITH)   More complicated schemes such as this one are often needed in larger companies. There is little chance of duplication with this naming standard.

It is also important to determine what you will do if two users have names that would produce the same username. For example, you might decide to add a middle initial, if initials are not part of your standard, or, as a last resort, a number. You should avoid these inconsistencies whenever possible.

It is good practice to limit user login names to 8 characters. Although NDS allows 64-character names, some e-mail systems require 8-character names, as do DOS and Windows 3.1 clients. If your OS and e-mail package support longer names, however, we suggest using the full name as per the naming standards you select.

In some companies, it may be acceptable to have two users called JOHNS, as long as they are in different containers. However, if usernames are used for e-mail, having two users with the same username can cause problems. In addition, no two users in bindery context containers can share the same username (if you want Bindery Services to function as expected).

Groups, Organizations, and Organizational Units

Since Organization objects and Organizational Unit objects should identify divisions, locations, or workgroups in the company, you should name them after the entity they represent. Use short and concise names, because users may need to type the name when entering a distinguished name for a user. For example, you might use MGMT for management, ACCT for accounting, AP for accounts payable, and NYC for New York City. You may want to use airport codes or other unique identifiers to name each container.

Give Group objects names that represent their functions, such as DATAENTRY for the data entry group or PROJECT1 for users working on a particular project. If the group was created to give users access to an application directory, it might be named for that application, such as WORDPROCESSING or BACKUP.

Other NDS Objects

You should also have a standard procedure for naming other types of objects in the Directory tree. Here are some examples:

Servers Often given names based on their locations, such as EAST1, NYC, or BLDG3. Since users may need to type the names of servers in order to log in to them, you should keep server names short. Server names must be unique, even if they are in different containers. Users interact frequently with servers and can browse through them in Network Neighborhood (with the appropriate client OS).

Volumes Given NDS names automatically when you create them. The name combines the server name and physical volume name, such as EAST1_SYS.

Printer agents Typically named according to the printer type and location, such as LJ4_BLDG3 or DMP_WEST.

Property Standards

In addition to object names, you should define the properties for each object that will be used. Many properties, such as a User object's Telephone property, are optional when you create the user. However, if you include values for these properties, you can provide an informational resource for users across the network and make it possible to find users with a certain attribute.

Go back through the list of objects, and determine the optional properties to include. In addition, the format of the property value is important. For example, if some phone numbers include the area code and others don't, it will be difficult to search for users in a certain area code.

Unfortunately, there is no way to force the network administrator for a branch or location to use the correct properties. For this reason, it's important to distribute a copy of the standards document to each administrator and to provide training on the importance of these standards.

Other Network Standards

It is useful to include standards for all objects and parameters in the network, even those that are not included in NDS. Here are some of the additional standards you may wish to assign:

IPX network numbers Include both the internal number that identifies a server and the external number that identifies a network segment. Using a consistent scheme for these numbers makes it easy to analyze network traffic.

IP addresses   Reserving certain host IDs for printers, servers, clients, and so on can be useful in determining IP addresses and resolving address conflicts. A standard for network IDs also makes sense.

Bindery objects   If you are using any NetWare 3 or earlier servers in the network, you should apply naming standards to the servers and the users on them also. This makes them easy to locate and aids in their migration to NDS.

Invalid Characters in Any NDS Object Name

In naming any object, you should avoid the following characters: +, =, /, \, *, ^, %, ., #, and spaces. These characters can cause some problems with various file systems as well as some utilities. Using spaces within an object name would require that you refer to that object in quotation marks. The period is used to change contexts and so is not allowed in object names (in general).

A Typical Standards Document

We've described lots of standards in this chapter. Since a picture is worth a thousand words, we'll now put all of these concepts together with an example of a standards document for a sample organization. While you can follow this format closely for your own standards documents, you should choose the format that works best for you and your client.

Table 18.1 lists object naming standards and Table 18.2 lists property and value naming standards. We've focused on the User object properties in Table 18.2, but similar lists can, and should, be created for other object types as well. The Required or Optional column in Table 18.2 is a note to administrators who will be creating the object, letting them know whether the particular property is required (by the company) or optional.

The following document is not necessarily a list of what you should include in your own standards. Follow the information in the previous sections to determine which objects and properties to include in your standards documents.

T A B L E 18.1: STAR Inc. Network Standards Document: Object Naming Standards

Object Type	Naming Standard	Examples	Notes
Directory tree	STAR_Tree for main, STAR_*location* for separate locations	STAR_Tree STAR_NYC for the New York office	Location names should be three letters, and use the local airport code where applicable.
User	First initial, last name	JSMITH	Limit to eight characters if e-mail or client OS requires. If several users have the same first initial and last name, add a middle initial.
Organization	Name of organization, all capitals	STAR	Use official company name based on corporate documents. Use only one organization for the company if possible.
Organizational Unit	Department, division or workgroup name	ACCT LEGAL CORP	Keep these names short because they will be referred to often.
Printer agent (NDPS)	Printer type plus location and printer number	LJ_NYC_1 DM_LAX_5	
Server	S plus location and unique number	S_NYC_2	Must be unique network-wide.
Print queue (non-NDPS)	Q plus location and department	Q_NYC_ACCT	
All object names	Do not use the following characters: +, =, /, \, *, ^, %, ., #, or spaces		They can cause conflicts with various utilities, file systems, and even NDS (in the case of the period). Names with spaces in them must be enclosed in quotation marks.

T A B L E 18.2: STAR Inc. Network Standards Document: Property and Value Standards

Object Type	Property Name	Required or Optional	Value Format	Examples
User	Last name	Required	Last name, first letter capitalized	Smith Johnson
	Given name	Required	First name, first letter capitalized	Robert Ashley Brianna
	Middle initial	Optional	Initial only, capitalized	E
	Telephone	Required	Phone number with area code, separated with dashes, no leading 1-	801-555-2345
	Fax number	Optional	Fax number with area code, separated with dashes, no leading 1-	801-555-2300
	Location	Required	Location code	NYC
	Description	Optional	Physical characteristics, such as eye color and height	Eyes: Brown Height: 5' 3"
	Department	Required	Name of the department, as used on organizational charts	Accounting Sales
	Other Name	Optional	User's preferred nickname, first letter capitalized	Rob
	Language	Optional	User's primary language	English

T A B L E 18.2:   STAR Inc. Network Standards Document: Property and Value Standards *(cont.)*

Object Type	Property Name	Required or Optional	Value Format	Examples
	Home directory	Required	All users get one, based on login name	DATA:USERS\ %*LOGIN_NAME*
	Password	Required	6-character minimum	BOY%FRIEND
Printer agent (NDPS)	Location	Required	Location code	NYC
Organiza-tional Unit	Description	Required	Location, department, or workgroup name	Accounting London Managers

Organizing the Upper Layers of the Tree

Now that you've defined a standard for the objects in the Directory tree, their names, and the properties that will be used, the next step is to develop the structure of the Directory tree itself. We'll start with the upper layers, working our way down from the [Root].

The upper layers are the most important part of the Directory tree when you are planning the network. While you can easily make changes at the lower levels when you need to, the upper layers define the basic structure of the Directory. To make a significant change at these levels on an existing network is a difficult task. Therefore, you should take the time to plan the best layout for the upper levels.

Fundamentally, the upper levels of the Directory tree should reflect the WAN infrastructure of the company. For example, a company might have several offices in different locations, which could be represented as branches of the Directory tree. Branches can also be created based on functions—departments of the company or groups of people who perform similar tasks. We'll explain the advantages of each of these strategies in the following sections. No matter which design you choose, however, the tree should be shaped like a pyramid for maximum efficiency. This principle gets more important as the tree gets larger.

The First Step: Country and Organization Objects

We recommend that the vast majority of companies use a single Organization object directly under the [Root], and Novell agrees. All divisions of the company are placed under this Organization object. There are exceptions to this rule, however:

- If the company has two or more major divisions (or even separate companies with a common president and management), it may be beneficial to keep the divisions in separate Organization objects. This is particularly important if one or more divisions could be sold or split off from the main company; keeping a separate Organization object for a division makes it easier to move to a new Directory tree. If the companies share any resources, though, or use a common network wiring structure, it is best to keep them under one Organization object.

- You may choose to use Country object designations, as specified by the X.500 standard. Using Country object designations may be useful for international corporations or when communicating with other types of networks that use this standard.

Novell discourages the use of the Country object, so avoid it when you can. It is included in NDS to allow compatibility with the X.500 standard. If you need this type of functionality, you may want to use the new Locality object (new with NetWare 5 and covered in Chapter 2) or the Organization or Organizational Unit objects.

You should define the name for the Organization object in the standards document, along with the name for the Directory tree itself. These names will be used when NDS is installed on the first server; be sure they are defined before you begin the installation process.

Organizing by Location

The most common, and usually the most practical, approach for organizing the Directory tree for a wide area network is to divide it into Organizational Unit objects based on locations. For example, Figure 18.1 shows a Directory tree that is divided into four locations. (Only the upper layers are pictured in Figure 18.1.)

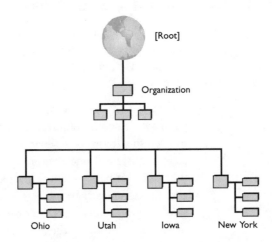

The location-based organization offers several benefits to the network and its users:

- The topology of the network wiring directly relates to the Directory tree structure. Since users in the same network segment are in the same Organizational Unit, the amount of traffic that must travel across the WAN link between locations is minimized.

- Partitioning is simplified because all of the objects at a location can be placed in a single partition. This lessens the amount of network traffic required to update replicas. (We will discuss partitioning and replicas in more detail in Chapter 20.)

- Different network administrators can manage objects for each location. Assigning rights to these administrators is a simple process if the entire location is under a single Organizational Unit.

- Granting rights needed by users is simplified. If all users in a location need access to a printer, for example, the container object can be given rights to simplify the task.

Figure 18.2 shows a Directory tree that uses the location-based organization on multiple levels. The first level of Organizational Unit objects represents the divisions of the company; the second level divides each division into regions.

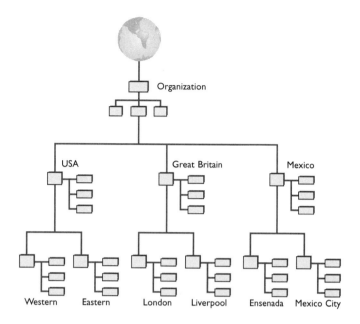

FIGURE 18.2

A location-based organization can be further subdivided into regions.

Organizing by Function

Although the location-based organization is the most common by far, an alternate choice is the functional organization. In this type of organization, Organizational Unit objects are created based on functions, rather than locations. For example, typical divisions might include a department, such as Payroll; a division, such as Corp; or a workgroup (a group of users who perform the same function or are working on a similar project). Figure 18.3 shows a Directory tree organized at the top layer into five functional divisions.

Depending on the structure and organization of the company, the functional organization might resemble the organizational chart more closely than the location-based method. However, there are some serious disadvantages to the functional approach:

- Partitioning is difficult and increases network traffic. A partition that includes a certain functional category might include users and other resources at several different locations.

- Users in the same function may be logging in from different locations. This may cause quite a bit of network traffic, and a replica will probably be needed at each location.

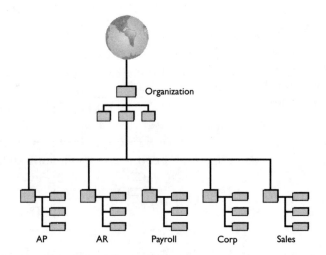

FIGURE 18.3

A Directory tree that is organized into five functional divisions

- If administrators are assigned to locations, it is difficult to assign them rights because users at their location might be at any location in the Directory tree.

- A possible concern is that the network topology is not related to the Directory tree structure. This means that if a major change is made in the network wiring, users all over the Directory tree might be affected.

Don't give up entirely on the functional organization, though. There are exceptions to every rule. Here are some situations in which the functional organization may be a better choice:

- If the network is located entirely at a single location, there is obviously little use for a location-based structure and less concern about network traffic. If plans for growth include other locations, however, you should use the location-based method described previously.

- If the network is in multiple locations but uses very high-speed links, network traffic may not be a concern.

Combining Organization Strategies

If the functional organization has so many disadvantages, why did we describe it? It may not be very useful by itself, but it shines when used in combination with the location-based strategy. In fact, the majority of large companies use some combination of the two. This type of network organization is called a *combination,* or *hybrid,* organization. It provides many of the advantages of both organization types.

Figure 18.4 shows an example of a combination organization. This Directory tree is divided first by location. Each location, in turn, is divided into several functions. This tree retains all of the advantages of the location-based organization but also allows tasks to be accomplished based on functions within the company. For example, a central AP manager might be given rights to all of the AP objects, which would simply require that you grant the user rights to three different Organizational Unit objects.

F I G U R E 18.4

An example of a combination network organization arranged by location, and then by function

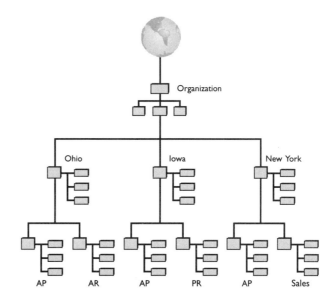

Figure 18.5 provides a slightly different example. In this Directory tree, the functional organization has been used at the first level. (This company uses high-speed links to eliminate network traffic problems.) Each functional division is further subdivided, based on the management structure of the company. While the AP division is divided into locations, the Corp container is divided into workgroups for each companywide function, such as Sales and Mgmt.

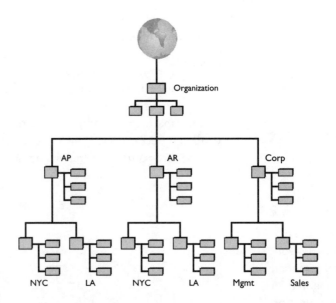

Organizing the Lower Layers of the Tree

The upper layers of the Directory tree define the basic organization. Once you've defined those, you can organize the lower layers. Since the major divisions are already in place, providing for WAN access, administration, and partitioning, the divisions in the lower layers of the Directory tree can be strictly functional. You can divide the lower layers in any way that provides a benefit without causing network problems.

You can use the location-based or functional organizations at the lower levels, dividing the tree into even smaller units. For example, a branch of the tree could be divided into regions, and each region could be divided into buildings, floors, or even rooms. You can also use departments as Organizational Units—an entire department is often on one floor or in one room.

It is tempting to divide the lower levels of the tree too much. You should keep the design as simple as possible—there is no need to create containers with only a few objects in them; use groups instead.

To determine the structure for the lower levels, consider which users will need access to the same resources. For example, all users in the Accounting department at a branch may require the use of the same printer and server. This means that you can easily serve the department's needs by creating an Organizational Unit object for the department, as shown in Figure 18.6. This OU can then be used as an effective trustee.

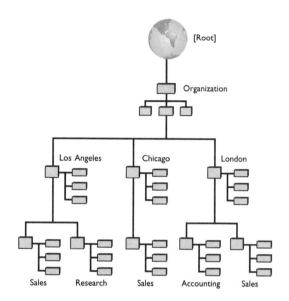

Modifying Your Design

Unless you're very lucky, the design you have created will not be the final version. Just about anything may change in the course of implementing the network—or even years later. You should be prepared to make any changes to the design that are necessary to accommodate changes in needs, resources, or configurations.

If you've planned well, you should not need to make changes at the upper levels, except to add or remove locations or functions as your company expands or downsizes. Most changes are made at the lower levels. The following sections describe some of the most common factors that may require you to change your network organization. As you fine-tune the planning of the Directory tree, consider each of these factors carefully and modify your design to take them into account.

Administration

As we discussed in Chapter 14, NetWare 5 security can use two different types of administration, summarized here:

Centralized administration   Uses a single administrator (or group of administrators) to control all objects in the Directory tree.

Distributed administration   Assigns separate administrators for portions of the Directory tree. Typically there is also some form of centralized administration as well to maintain and support the distributed administrators.

Each of these has its advantages and disadvantages. You may wish to modify the Directory tree's structure to make it simpler for the type of administration you wish to use. The following sections describe the type of Directory tree organization used for each type of administration.

Centralized Administration

In centralized administration, a single administrator (or IS department) manages the entire Directory tree. This arrangement is well suited to companies that have a central IS department that handles all network-related needs.

To make central administration convenient, it's best to minimize the amount of lower-level divisions in the Directory tree. This makes it easier for an administrator to access objects. Since the same administrator needs to manage all of the objects, there is little point in having more levels than are really needed. A Directory tree that has been designed for use with a centralized administrator is shown in Figure 18.7.

FIGURE 18.7

You can facilitate centralized administration by using fewer levels in the Directory tree.

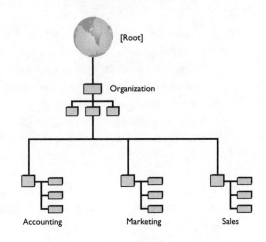

Distributed Administration

A more efficient method of managing a large Directory tree is distributed administration, also called *decentralized administration*. In this method, a separate network administrator (or department) manages each branch of the Directory tree.

The advantages of this system include the fact that an administrator at each location is often needed for other purposes anyway (such as setting up computers and troubleshooting when problems occur). In addition, the Inherited Rights Filter can be used to block the rights of Admin or other central administrators; this allows the branch administrator to be the ultimate (and only) authority for that branch of the Directory tree. This can be dangerous, however, and it's a good idea to have some form of centralized control to help when people in the field have problems, an administrator is fired and no one else knows the password, and so on. We always like to have a back door available.

The basic location-based organization provides a good foundation for distributed administration. An administrator can be assigned to each primary location. For large locations, administrators can be assigned to departments. Figure 18.8 shows a Directory tree that is suited to distributed administration. Because a separate administrator controls each branch, you can use more levels of organization without adding confusion. In fact, the branch administrator is often made responsible for organizing objects in that branch.

Combining Servers in a Container

One twist on centralized administration is to create a separate container that will hold all of the servers. You can then assign an administrator for the server container; in addition, central administrators will be able to locate and monitor each server easily. Figure 18.9 shows an example of a Directory tree in which all servers have been placed in a single container.

Because of network traffic and partitioning considerations, this solution is truly practical only for a single network or a network with high-speed, reliable WAN links between locations. This also means all of your eggs (servers) are in one basket (container), and if anything happens to that container, you may have very serious consequences to deal with.

FIGURE 18.8
With distributed administration, you can use many layers after the basic divisions are established.

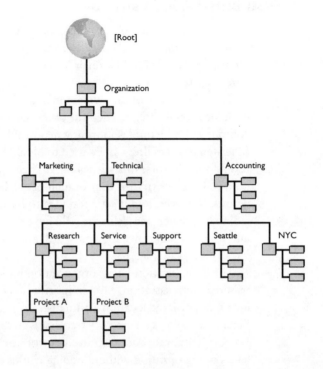

FIGURE 18.9
A separate container can be used for all servers.

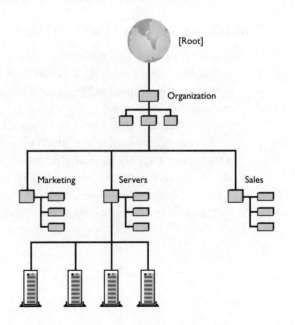

Partitioning and Replication

You should take partitioning into consideration when planning the structure of the Directory tree. Ideally, the network organization should be arranged so that partitions can be created in an efficient manner:

- Objects on opposite sides of a WAN link should not be in the same partition. Since partitions must constantly synchronize with each other (a process called *replication*), this will create traffic on the WAN and slow synchronization, increasing the possibility of errors.

- If many users (several hundred) will be in the same Organizational Unit, consider dividing it into smaller Organizational Units. This will allow you to subdivide the partition and divide the load of storing the partition between servers.

Because of network traffic considerations, the location-based design is an excellent choice for the upper layers of the Directory tree; it allows you to easily create partitions that contain objects in the same location, eliminating the need for synchronization between servers over WAN links. This section will make more sense as we move into Chapter 20, where partitioning and time synchronization are discussed in detail. However, you must consider partitioning at this phase in the design process.

Login Scripts

Although it shouldn't be a factor in the basic structure of the upper layers of the Directory tree, login scripts are something you should consider for the lowest levels. Since each User object executes only one container login script, for the object's immediate parent container, you may want to consider changing your organization in the following ways to simplify the use of login scripts:

- If users in two departments require the same login script, you may wish to create a single Organizational Unit for both departments. However, this can be impractical if the departments require different rights or access to resources.

- You may wish to subdivide an Organizational Unit if users in that Organizational Unit will require two or more different login scripts. This provides for much easier maintenance than using a profile login script, which requires setting each User object to the profile separately.

Don't take login script considerations too seriously; they should be one of the last priorities in creating your design. If necessary, it's a simple matter to copy the same login script to two containers or use an INCLUDE command to reference the same script. You can also use the IF MEMBER OF syntax to give you further control. For more information on login scripts, see Chapter 5.

Bindery Services

The next consideration in network design is Bindery Services. *Bindery Services* is a concept Novell created to provide a bridge from the bindery-based servers used in NetWare 2 and 3 to NDS, used in NetWare 4 and 5. This backward compatibility was very important in the early days of NetWare 4, when few, if any, applications were NDS-aware. The situation has changed to a large degree as NDS has matured; more and more applications have become NDS-aware, reducing the need for Bindery Services.

Each server can have a bindery context—a container whose objects are considered part of a simulated bindery for the use of older clients and applications. NetWare, before version 5, used IPX as its only protocol, so you must install either IPX or the IPX compatibility gateway for Bindery Services to work.

You can have up to 16 separate bindery contexts for any server. You should keep this limitation in mind when designing the lower levels of the Directory tree. Make a list of the container objects that will require Bindery Services. If your design leaves you with more than 16 containers that need access to Bindery Services on the same server, consider combining some of them into the same container, or spread them across servers. Fortunately, as NDS has become a more mature and proven technology, the need for Bindery Services has decreased.

Container Size

The last issue that you need to address is the optimal size for a container. For most scenarios, Novell recommends no more than 1,500 objects per container, with 3,500 as the outer practical limit. It takes a long time to find an object when you must scroll through thousands of other objects to do so.

Making container sizes smaller will be more efficient for the administrator. In addition, smaller partitions can synchronize their replicas more quickly and efficiently. Remember that this is the total number of objects, including workstations (if you are using Z.E.N.works), users, groups, and all other objects. On the other end of the spectrum, creating a container with only a few objects isn't very efficient either, as users may have many partitions to track and lots of layers to drill through before they can find the desired object.

Review

In this chapter you learned the procedures and considerations for designing an effective NDS structure for your network. These are some of the key steps involved in designing an NDS organization:

- Developing the initial design and gathering a project team to implement it

- Creating naming standards and a standards document

- Planning the upper layers of the Directory tree

- Planning the lower layers of the Directory tree

- Modifying the design, if needed, to account for other factors

Project Team Members

The following primary roles will need to be filled in order for you to efficiently design and implement NetWare 5:

Project manager   Acts as the company liaison and has access to the money

NDS expert   Coordinates with all other team members, designs the tree (with input from the other team members), and documents the design

Server administrator   Handles day-to-day server administration and deals with issues revolving around server migration, coexistence, management, and so on

Connectivity specialist   Primarily concerned with bandwidth issues, both on the LAN and the WAN

For large projects, the following secondary roles will be useful as well:

Workstation specialist   Concerned with workstation connectivity issues; responsible for client software upgrades on the workstations and login scripts

Application specialist   Responsible for application support on the new Network Operating System (NOS) and for filling the need (if any) for Bindery Services

Printing specialist   Responsible for resolving all printing-related decisions, such as NDPS versus queue-based printing, driver issues, and so on

The Standards Document

Naming standards make it easier to find a user, printer, or other resource on the network. As the network grows, finding network resources is an important consideration. The standards document should include the following specifications:

- Naming standards for each container object

- Naming standards for each type of leaf object

- A list of properties that you will implement for each object type and the format for their values

In addition to object names, you should define the properties for each object. Many properties, such as a User object's Telephone Number property, are optional when you create the user. However, if you include values for these properties, you can provide an informational resource for users across the network and make it possible to search for users with a certain attribute.

Planning the Upper Layers

When planning the network, you should take the time to determine the best layout for the upper layers; this is the most important part of the Directory tree. While you can easily make changes at the lower levels when you need to, the upper layers define the basic structure of the Directory. To make a significant change at these levels on an existing network is a difficult task.

Fundamentally, the upper levels of the Directory tree should reflect the organization of the company. Under the [Root] will be one or more Organization objects. Most companies use a single Organization object, but if the network covers two or more major divisions, or separate companies, you may wish to use multiple Organizations.

There are three approaches for organizing the remaining part of the upper layers:

- The location-based design uses separate Organizational Units for each major location of the company.

- The functional design uses separate Organizational Units for functional divisions of the company, such as departments or workgroups.

- A combined organization uses features of both types.

Planning the Lower Layers

Since the major divisions are already in place, providing for WAN access, administration, and partitioning, the divisions in the lower layers of the Directory tree can be strictly functional. You can divide the lower layers in any way that provides a benefit without causing network problems. You can use the location-based or functional designs at the lower levels, dividing the tree into even smaller units. Creating very small containers can be inefficient, however.

To determine the structure for the lower levels, consider which users will need access to the same resources.

Modifying the Basic Design

If you've planned correctly, you should not need to make changes at the upper levels of the Directory tree. Most changes are made at the lower levels. You may need to change your design based on the following factors:

Administration Depending on whether the network uses central or distributed administration, the lower levels can be set up differently.

Partitioning and replication Organizational Units may be further subdivided to allow for more efficient partitions. The basic location-based structure provides an easy way to set up partitions based on locations.

Login scripts You may wish to combine users who will require the same login script into a container, or to subdivide a container to allow for two different container login scripts.

Bindery Services   You must be careful to include no more than 16 containers that will require access to Bindery Services on a server.

Container size   You should limit containers to no more than 3,500 objects, with 1,500 a more practical limit for the best performance.

CNE Practice Test Questions

1. The two basic types of Directory tree organizations are:

    A. Location-based and divisional

    B. Location-based and functional

    C. Organization and Organizational Unit

    D. Centralized and distributed

2. A network consultant is responsible for:

    A. A single network

    B. A certain branch of a network

    C. Networks belonging to several clients

    D. Designing networks only

3. Time synchronization planning is part of which phase of NDS design?

    A. The project approach phase

    B. The design phase

    C. The implementation phase

    D. The manage and monitor phase

4. The responsibilities of the project manager do *not* include:

    A. Communicating with company executives

    B. Estimating times and costs

C. Planning time synchronization

D. Scheduling meetings

5. Which team member usually leads the project team?

A. NDS expert

B. Project manager

C. Server specialist

D. Applications specialist

6. A standards document should *not* include:

A. Naming standards for User objects

B. Number of users on the network

C. Properties to be used

D. Formats for property values

7. Which type of username is not efficient for large networks?

A. First name, last name

B. First initial, last name

C. First name

D. Last name, first initial

8. The most practical organization for a multiple location network is:

A. Functional

B. Divisional

C. Correctional

D. Location-based

9. Which object type is seldom used in a Directory tree?

   A. Organizational Unit

   B. Organization

   C. Country

   D. User

10. The advantages of the location-based design do *not* include:

   A. Ease of partitioning

   B. Minimizing WAN traffic

   C. Matching network topology

   D. Any of the above

11. The functional organization is best suited for:

   A. Multinational corporations

   B. Single-location networks

   C. Poorly organized networks

   D. WAN links

12. The area of the Directory tree you should not have to change often is:

   A. Upper layers

   B. Lower layers

   C. Server container

   D. Central administration

CHAPTER

19

Planning Network Access

Roadmap

This chapter covers some of the file system, security, login script, and client issues that must be faced in implementing a new network. We will also review issues that must be addressed when mobile users need access to the tree. This information is part of the CNE core requirement "NetWare 5 Design and Implementation."

Topics Covered

- File System Issues
- Security Matters
- Administration Considerations
- Client Access

Skills You'll Learn

- Explain the file system issues that must be taken into account, including backup planning
- List the security-related issues
- List the administrative styles that can be implemented and the strengths and weaknesses of each
- List login script options
- Describe client access considerations, including access from various operating systems and access for mobile users

A Directory tree doesn't do much good unless it manages an efficient, running network. In this chapter, we'll explore some areas you will need to plan and consider in addition to the structure of the NDS tree. As a network consultant (or member of an IS staff), you will have to understand the needs of the client in each of the following areas:

- The file system structure, network applications, and drive mappings

- Security issues and how they affect user rights and administrators
- Login scripts
- Access from a variety of clients—DOS, Windows 3.1, Windows 95/98, OS/2, Macintosh, and Unix
- Considerations for mobile users—users who travel between physical locations of the company or who access the network remotely via modem

We'll explore these areas in detail in this chapter. The purpose of this information is not to tell you how to actually set up the network—that is explained elsewhere in the book. Instead, this chapter is meant to provide a comprehensive list of the items you and your consulting client or company will need to consider in the process of planning and implementing a network.

Planning the File System

Next to NDS, the most important component of a functioning network is the file system, which includes all files and directories in all volumes on all NetWare servers. While NDS controls the users and other objects on the network, the file system is concerned with applications and data. Your network plan should include the basic file structure, the location of data files and application files, and the drive mappings that will be needed.

When you install applications on the network or provide a location for data files, you should keep the following points in mind:

Accessibility   Keep the directory structure simple so that users will be able to find files easily.

Security   Position the directories so that it will be easy to assign security. Take advantage of the fact that rights are inherited from parent directories by child directories. Thus, you can create a single directory for spreadsheet data and subdivide the directory for particular projects. Giving a user access to the data directory allows him or her access to all of the projects.

Backups   A useful strategy is to keep program and data files separate. Separating these files makes it easy to perform backups because the data files, which are the ones that need to be backed up, are always in the same place.

Planning the File Structure

First, you should plan how the volume or volumes will be used, which relates to the organization of the NDS Directory tree. Typically, each location will have at least one server; to provide quick access to files and minimize traffic on the WAN, you should place applications and data on the server for users in that location. Ideally, the only files accessed over WAN links should be files that are shared between locations, for example, a global company database or an e-mail system.

Your network plan should define a standard set of directories to be placed on file server volumes. For example, an APPS directory might be used to hold applications, and a DATA directory can be used for data files. By standardizing this information on all servers and volumes, you make it easy for the administrator to control access to files and data and facilitate backups and data migration. An example of a standard file structure is shown in Figure 19.1.

F I G U R E   19.1

A standard file
structure

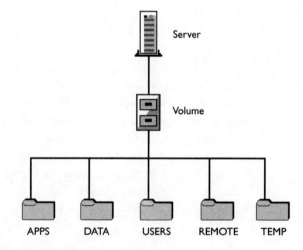

Planning Network Applications

Although all users in all of the company's locations may use a certain program, such as a word processor, it is very important to keep a local copy of the program. In addition, data files should be stored locally. You may wish to create a directory on a volume that can be used by users in multiple locations for data files, but this should be treated as a special case; users should write files to this area only if they are needed by users in other locations. By planning your network this way, you ensure that network bandwidth is used efficiently.

Although you should keep separate copies of applications for each location, it is important to create a standard for the Directory structure. This will make it easy to support users in any location and for administrators to manage their branches in a similar manner. It will also make it easier to upgrade applications in the future.

Mapping Drives

For any application or data that is used by users across the network, you should define a set of default drive mappings. This lets users know what to expect no matter what location they are in and gives them ready access to applications and data. Here are some examples of useful drive mappings:

Drive W for a word processing program   This mapping would point to the copy of the program on a local server.

Drive G for a global directory   This directory would be on one server only and would be used for files that would be shared or traded between multiple locations.

Drive H for a home directory   This drive mapping would point to the user's personal information and should be placed on a server in the user's physical location.

You should also define search mappings. All of these mappings are set up using login scripts. In addition, you may wish to use Directory Map objects to simplify the process of mapping drives and to make it easy to move an application, or far more often data, to a different directory or server when needed. The steps for setting up a Directory Map object using NetWare Administrator are covered in Procedure 19.1.

PROCEDURE 19.1

Creating a Directory Map Object

To create a Directory Map object, follow these steps:

1. Open NetWare Administrator and go to the container you want to create the object in. Usually, this is the same container that contains the users who require the mapping.

2. Create a Directory Map object. (Refer to Chapter 3 for information on creating objects.)

3. Change the Directory Map's Directory property to point to the correct directory.

4. Refer to the Directory Map in the login script.

The following command refers to a Directory Map object called WP:

```
MAP J:=WP
```

When referring to a Directory Map object in the MAP command, do not use a colon as you would with a volume name.

For more information on Directory Map objects, refer to Chapter 3; login scripts are discussed in Chapter 5.

Devising a Backup Strategy

Each location should have a person responsible for backing up the data on the server volumes in that location. Backup software should be selected and used consistently in all locations. This is one of the most important aspects of network planning: *No network should be without a solid backup plan.*

Along with a list of users who are responsible for backups, the backup plan should specify which files will be backed up and how often backups are performed. For a corporate network, backups once a day (at the very least) are a necessity. Modern backup software allows the backup procedure to be run when no users are logged in. You should also make provisions to store a copy of the backup at a separate site, such as in a safe-deposit box or even at a separate location of the company.

The easiest way to assign a user the privileges needed to run backups is by using an Organizational Role. Create the Organizational Role object in the same container as the file server and give it rights to all volumes on the server. Then assign the user as the occupant of the Organizational Role. For more information on backup issues, refer to Chapter 10.

Planning Network Security and Administration

The basics of file system and NDS security are explained in Chapter 4. You should plan a consistent strategy for security in each location. Keep rights between locations as consistent as possible. In this section we will also look at the different types of administrators—central (also know as an enterprise-wide), container, backup, password, server, and special use—and how they affect the network's configuration.

In addition to securing the network, it's important to make a security plan. This document can be given to each administrator to ensure that each one manages security in a consistent way.

File System Security

Rights to the file system should be assigned as consistently as possible. You can assign rights in many ways, each with advantages and disadvantages:

User objects   Although this method is direct, assigning rights to User objects directly should be avoided whenever possible. Alternatives include assigning rights to Group, Organizational Role, and container objects.

Organizational Roles   These should be used for situations when one or more users will be given rights to perform a certain task, such as running backup software or administering a branch of the tree.

Groups   Groups serve two major purposes—to give rights to a select set of users within a container, and to give rights to a set of users who may not be in the same container. Groups are often used for application and data directory rights. For example, making a user a member of the word processing group might give him or her access to both the word processing application and the data file directory.

Containers   If you have chosen container objects carefully, you should be able to assign many of the rights using container objects. Be careful not to use an object too high in the Directory tree, such as the entire Organization, unless you're sure you want everyone to have access to the files. A well-designed tree often uses container objects as trustees.

Centralized Administration

In the previous chapter, we looked at some ways of structuring the Directory tree to make it easy for a central administrator to manage. If you are using central administration, you should assign one or more users as the administrator. Ideally, you should do this with an Organizational Role object, because it allows you to assign the administrative rights to a varying group of users. Be sure to give administrative rights explicitly to at least two objects, in case one is accidentally deleted, corrupted, or otherwise made unusable. You may want to grant rights to an Organizational Role and to a specific user, such as Admin.

It's also possible to define administrators with limited rights. For example, if the entire Directory tree is managed by an IS department, the IS manager's account might have full rights to [Root], thus allowing complete access. An assistant administrator might be limited to Browse, Create, and Rename rights and might be locked out of one or more containers using an explicit assignment to override inherited rights. We will look at other rights-limited administrators in several of the sections below.

Note that central administration can be combined with distributed administration. Here are two possible scenarios:

- A central administrator is used, but one branch has its own administrator. The IRF is used to lock the central administrator out of that branch's container object. Be very careful with this situation, because if the administrator has trouble, you may not have the rights to get in and fix the problem. We don't recommend this approach.

- A central administrator retains full rights, but one or more branch administrators are given rights to manage containers. The central administrator can still override the actions of the branch administrators. We prefer to use this approach, with the central administrator staying out of the way of the distributed administrators unless needed.

Administrative Approaches

As mentioned above, there are many approaches that may be taken in designing the administration of your network. Some of the more common administrative roles are discussed in this section. You may add to this list or implement only some of them, depending on the network you are designing.

Container Administrators

You can create a container administrator by giving a certain User object rights to a container, but this is not the best arrangement. Once again, creating an Organizational Role object is an ideal way of doing this. Choose a standard that will be used for all container administrators: For example, an Organizational Role called CONTAINER_ADMIN could be created in each container and given rights to the container object. You could then easily assign a user as the occupant of the Organizational Role to make him or her the container administrator. This arrangement is illustrated in Figure 19.2.

FIGURE 19.2

Container administrators can be assigned using Organizational Roles.

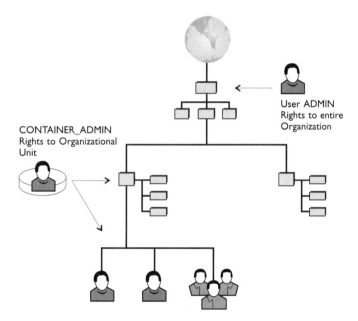

We prefer not to grant all object rights ([SBCDR]) to a container administrator, but only ([BCDR]). This gives the user authority over all of the objects he or she creates, including renaming or deleting them, but does not let the user lock out the central administrator, as that would require the Supervisor object right. Be careful in deciding what property rights to assign as well. Remember, if you have the Write right to the ACL of a *server* object, you have *all* file system rights to all files on all volumes on the server.

Exclusive Container Administrators

An exclusive container administrator is created in the same manner as the container administrator described in the previous section. Additionally, the IRF is used to block the rights of the central administrator. This arrangement gives complete control to the container administrator.

It's possible to have the best of both worlds. Create an exclusive container administrator by creating an IRF that filters the Supervisor right. The normal central administrator, given the Supervisor right to [Root], will have no rights in the container. However, you can create a central administrator with full rights ([SBCDRI] (object) and [SCRWAI] (property)) to the [Root] object. Since this administrator does not rely on the Supervisor right to get all of the other rights, he or she will have all of the remaining rights [BCDR]. In the truest sense of the term, this is not an exclusive container administrator, since others have some rights from above, but it is in a sense an exclusive role, since only that container administrator has all rights in the container.

Backup Administrators

Backup administrators facilitate backups and install new servers. They often have the ability to install servers, and are given all rights to all files and directories on all volumes on all servers in a container or branch of the tree. The simplest way to implement this type of administrator is through Organizational Roles. Backup administrators have no object rights to anything but servers in a container or branch of the tree.

Server Administrators

The purpose of this administrator is to facilitate upgrading software, helping users with data file issues, and fixing basic problems with core NDS objects. They should have Browse and Delete object rights and all property rights, allowing them to maintain passwords, login scripts, group memberships, and so on. They should also have all file system rights to the following directories: PUBLIC (to install new clients, upgrade some utilities, and so on), APPS (to install and upgrade applications), and USERS (to help users on the server administrator's server resolve file issues). The simplest way to assign this role is with Organizational Role objects.

Password Administrators

This type of administrator will quickly become your friend in a large network. In small networks, a single administrator can take care of all of the needs for the network. As it grows, however, specialization can help keep things more organized and keep costs reasonable. (Would you want to pay someone $80,000 to change passwords?)

To create this type of administrator, create an Organizational Role object and add the appropriate users as occupants. The only object right they need is Browse, so the users can be found. As for property rights, they only need the Read and Write rights to the properties you want them to maintain, such as passwords or phone numbers. They need no special file system rights, as they only maintain limited NDS information.

Special-Use Administrators

An administrator can be assigned to the file system on specialized servers, typically not under the IS department's control. You may need to include this arrangement in your network plan. Here are two ways you can assign an administrator to the file system on a server:

- A central file system administrator could be given rights to all servers' file systems. This happens by default, unless IRFs block some of the rights. This makes it easy, for example, to install a new version of a software program on all branches.

- A container administrator could delegate file system responsibilities to another user using an Organizational Role.

Remember, rights to the file system can be given two ways:

- By assigning the Supervisor [S] file system right to the root of each volume on each server

- By assigning (or inheriting) the Write right to the *server's* ACL.

The NDS rights required are only the default rights, with the possible exception of some limited property rights to control such things as group memberships (for controlling access to the file system) and login scripts (to add any necessary drive mappings).

Defining Default Restrictions

Other aspects of security you should include in your plan are the default restrictions, expiration dates, required password changes, and so forth, that will be applied to a new User object. You might also make this a part of your naming standards document (described in Chapter 18) so that this information is at hand when new users are created. You can assign these defaults by creating Template objects. You should define the properties of the Template object so that all administrators will use the same defaults for their branch of the Directory tree. If different branches require different defaults, you can create multiple Template objects. These defaults are stored in the properties of the Template object, as shown in Figure 19.3.

F I G U R E 19.3

The Template object's properties include default restrictions.

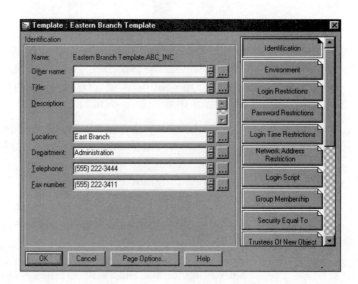

Here is an example of a standard for login restrictions:

Restriction	Value
Account Has Expiration Date	No
Limit Concurrent Connections	Yes
Maximum Connections	2
Require Password	Yes
Minimum Password Length	5
Force Periodic Password Changes	Yes
Days Between Changes	90

Restriction	Value
Require Unique Passwords	Yes
Limit Grace Logins	Yes
Grace Logins Allowed	3
Intruder Detection	Yes
Incorrect Login Attempts	5
Bad Login Count Retention	20 minutes
Lock Account After Detection	Yes
Length of Lockout	20 minutes

Physical Device Considerations

No, the network doesn't need an exercise program—this section is concerned with the physical devices on the network. In addition to creating objects for printers and other network resources, you must, of course, plan the location and accessibility of the printer (or other resources).

You will need to know certain information about each device. Be sure you have this information before you begin to formulate the network plan. Who will require access to the device? You will provide access to the device in NDS and also by physically wiring it to the network. Here are some guidelines for providing NDS access to devices:

- If the device will be accessed by all users on the network, consider giving rights to the [Root] object or to the main Organization object. This will allow all users to access the object.

- If the device will be used only by users within a particular container, place the device object inside that container. Users in the container will receive rights automatically.

- If the device will be used by users from several different containers, you will need to either grant rights individually or create a Group object to assign rights to the list of users.

Planning Login Scripts

Another aspect of planning the network is planning login scripts. Along with defining the actual scripts, you should decide which types of login scripts should be used, which containers will have container login scripts, and so on. Follow these guidelines to decide which types of login scripts to implement:

- If all or most of the users in a container require the same or a very similar configuration, use a container login script.

- If certain users in a container or in separate containers require the same settings (for example, a drive mapping to run backup software), use a profile login script.

- If a user needs a unique setting, use a user login script.

You may use all three of the options above, and the same user might execute container, profile, and user login scripts. Often, the settings in the user and profile scripts are used to override defaults in the container script. For example, most users might use LPT3 to capture to a network laser printer, so you could place the CAPTURE command in the container login script:

```
CAPTURE L=3 Q=LASER_Q
```

If a particular user wishes to use a local laser printer instead of the network printer, you can simply add this command to the user login script to end the capture:

```
CAPTURE L=3 /EC
```

Finally, if an entire group of users prints to its own laser printer, you could add this command to a profile login script:

```
CAPTURE L=3 Q=LASER_WEST
```

As you can see, this allows a wide variety of options, and a well-planned system of login scripts can help make network administration an easier task.

Planning for Client Access

Another thing you should consider when planning the network is what type of client support will be required. You should plan to install the necessary software on the server to support the various clients that will be used on your network. The types of clients supported by NetWare 5 include DOS, Windows 3.1, Windows 95/98, OS/2, Macintosh, and Unix. The following sections explain the extra setup (if any) needed for each client and any special considerations. Remember, the simplest way to set up and maintain client access for Windows-based clients is through Z.E.N.works, which will be discussed below.

DOS and Windows Clients

The most basic (and most common) clients for a NetWare 5 network are DOS and Windows clients. In fact, DOS and Windows clients are the only type that ship with NetWare 5. Support for these clients is built-in, and you do not have to install any software on the server. You can, however, copy the clients to the server to make installation simpler. However, in order to take advantage of all of the features of NDS, you should plan to install the latest DOS and Windows client software, the Novell Client, on each workstation. The procedure for installing client software is described in Chapter 2.

If some workstations are running older client software and cannot be upgraded—for example, 286 or lower computers, those with insufficient memory, or those using a network card that does not support the ODI (or NDIS for Windows 95/98 and Windows NT) specification—they will have to log in using Bindery Services. You must carefully plan the containers that will be used as bindery contexts and which server Bindery Services will be configured on for each location.

OS/2 Clients

The Novell Client for OS/2 provides the same benefits to OS/2 as the DOS and Windows clients mentioned above, except that there is no support for Z.E.N.works nor native IP. The current version of the client can be found by searching on Novell's Web site (`http://www.novell.com`) for the Novell Client for OS/2. It does not ship with NetWare 5, so you will need to either order it (for a nominal charge) or download it from their Web site.

Macintosh Clients

Macintosh workstations can log in to NDS. The Macintosh Requester (MacNDS) provides full access to the network through NDS. NetWare 5 does not ship with a client for Macintosh. The NetWare 4.11 client can still be used if the server supports IPX. Support for Macintosh clients is no longer provided by Novell, but rather by Prosoft Engineering (`http://www.prosofteng.com/nw4mac`). They are writing an IP-capable version of the client slated for release sometime in 1999.

608 Chapter 19 · Planning Network Access

There are several considerations to remember if you have Macintosh clients:

- Before Macintosh clients can access the network, you must configure the AppleTalk protocol on the server they will attach to.

- In order to store files that use Macintosh-style filenames on a volume, you must install the Macintosh name space module on the file server that holds the volume.

- There is no version of NetWare Administrator for the Macintosh.

- Macintosh workstations do not execute any login script.

For the latest information on Macintosh client support, refer to Prosoft Engineering's Web site.

Unix Clients

The software required for Unix clients to attach to the network is not provided with NetWare 5 and must be purchased separately. In addition, be aware of the following limitations:

- Unix users have limited NDS support.

- Unix workstations do not execute any login script.

- You cannot run NetWare Administrator or other NDS management utilities from Unix, but ConsoleOne should work if Java is implemented properly on the Unix machine, offering limited administrative control.

- You will need TCP/IP on the server to allow access by Unix clients. TCP/IP is the standard protocol for Unix systems.

Z.E.N.works and Object Placement

As discussed in Chapter 5, Z.E.N.works adds several new types of leaf objects. The new object types can be divided into three categories: Container, User, and Workstation Policy Packages.

Container Policy Package objects are used to specify where NDS will search in determining effective policies for users and workstations. As such, you want to place these objects as high in the tree as possible, while keeping the object within a single geographic location.

User and Workstation Policy Package objects should be placed in the same container as the user who uses them.

Application objects and the files related to them should be located near the users who will be accessing them. If you have a WAN, you should place these objects in containers at each physical location. If you have multiple servers in a location that have the same application, you should create Application objects for each server that has the application. You will need to make sure the objects you create point to the correct copy of the files. You may also want to enable the load balancing and fault tolerance capabilities of Application objects to further maximize their usefulness.

More information on Z.E.N.works and the objects discussed here can be found in Chapter 5.

Allowing Access for Mobile Users

NetWare 5 makes it easy to provide access to a special type of user: the mobile user who frequently visits different locations. Because mobile users log in from different locations, you must make special arrangements for them. There are two questions you should ask the client company about a mobile user:

- Does he or she use a notebook computer?

- Does the user access data at each location or simply log in to his or her home location?

Depending on the type of mobile user you are accommodating, you will make the provisions described in one of the following sections.

Mobile Users with Mobile Computers

It's easier to accommodate a mobile user who carries a notebook computer. You have to plan several steps to configure things for this user. First, you may have to install applications, such as a word processing program, on the notebook computer.

If the user accesses the same data (at the home location) regardless of his or her location, place a line such as the following in the NET.CFG file or the equivalent context information in the Novell Client's properties:

```
Name Context = .OU=SALES.OU=NYC.O=STAR_INC
```

This command specifies the complete context for the User object the user will log in as. No matter where the user is or which server he or she attaches to, the user will be able to log in and access data and programs (although access over the WAN may be slow).

If, on the other hand, the user needs to log in to the local container for the branch, omit the command. You will have to create a User object for the user in each container he or she will attempt to access, create alias objects to the original user, or teach the user about distinguished names. (Yuck!)

Mobile Users without Mobile Computers

A mobile user may simply use one of the computers at a location he or she visits. The login process is simple and can be set up several different ways, depending on the user's needs:

- Create a User object at each container the user will access. Make each User object security equivalent to the "home" user object.

- Create alias objects in each container to the original user. This is by far simpler than the first approach. Alias objects were covered in Chapter 3.

- If Catalog Services are installed and configured, you can allow context-less login, in which the user needs to know only his or her username and tree (and if you followed the recommendations above, you only have one tree in most cases, so this isn't a factor) to log in. If you chose to allow duplicate usernames in different contexts, the user will need to be able to pick from a list the correct context; otherwise, login will be automatic. This is probably the simplest approach, and the one we recommend. For more information on Catalog Services, refer to the online documentation.

- If the user always accesses data at his or her home location, be sure to provide a drive mapping to the needed directories.

Of course, if you're ready for a challenge, there is one more way to provide access for mobile users without mobile computers: Teach the user the basics of NDS and how to change contexts when he or she needs to. Educated and informed users can make network administration much easier for you in the long run, but you have to invest time and effort to teaching them during the short term, which is not always an easy task.

Review

In addition to planning the structure of the Directory tree, you'll also need to consider, and confer with your client about, several aspects of the network, including the following:

- The file system structure, network applications, and drive mappings

- Security issues and how they affect user rights and administrators

- Login scripts

- Access for a variety of clients—DOS, Windows, OS/2, Macintosh, and Unix

- Considerations for mobile users, who travel between physical locations of the company or access the network remotely via modem

The File System

Next to NDS, the most important component of a functioning network is the file system. The file system includes all files and directories in all volumes on all NetWare servers. While NDS controls the users and other objects on the network, the file system is concerned with applications and data. Your network plan should include the basic file structure, the location of data files and application files, and the drive mappings that will be required.

When you install applications on the network or provide a location for data files, you should keep the following in mind:

Accessibility Keep the directory structure simple so that users will be able to find files easily.

Security Position the directories so that it will be easy to assign security. Take advantage of the fact that rights are inherited from parent directories by their children. For example, you can create a single directory for spreadsheet data and then subdivide the directory for particular projects. Giving a user access to the data directory will allow access to all of the projects.

Backups Keep program and data files separate. This arrangement makes it easy to perform backups, because the data files—the ones that need to be backed up—are always in the same place.

Your network plan should define a standard set of directories to be placed on file server volumes. For example, an APPS directory might be used to hold applications, and a DATA directory can be used for data files. By standardizing this information on all servers and volumes, you make it easy for the administrator to control access to files and data and to facilitate backups and data migration.

These are some other file system considerations:

- Installing network applications
- Creating consistent drive mappings
- Devising a backup strategy

Security

You should plan a strategy for security in each location. Keep rights between locations as consistent as possible. In addition to securing the network, it's important to make a security plan. This document can be given to each administrator to ensure that each one controls security consistently. Security considerations include the following:

- File system security
- Centralized administration
- Distributed administration
- File system administration
- Default restrictions
- Physical security

Login Scripts

Another aspect of planning the network is writing login scripts. Along with defining the actual scripts, you should decide which types of login scripts should be used, which containers will have container login scripts, and so on. Follow these guidelines to decide which types of login scripts to implement:

- If all of the users in a container require the same configuration, use a container login script.

- If certain users in a container, or in separate containers, need the same settings (for example, a drive mapping to run backup software), use a profile login script.

- If a user needs a unique setting, use a user login script.

Client Access

You should plan a network setup to support different clients by installing the needed software on the server. The types of clients supported by NetWare 5 include DOS, Windows 3.1, Windows 95/98, OS/2, Macintosh, and Unix, and these are some of the considerations for each:

- Support for DOS and Windows clients is built into NetWare, and you do not have to install any software for these clients on the server. However, in order to take advantage of all of the features of NDS, you should plan to install the latest DOS and Windows client software, including the DOS Requester (VLM), on each workstation.

- OS/2 clients are supported and can access NDS. They can also run administrative programs. OS/2 runs either a user login script or a default OS/2 login script and does not execute container login scripts. You must verify that the long name space module is installed on the volumes that store long filenames.

- Macintosh clients can access the network through NDS. However, they cannot run administrative software and do not run any login script. You must install the AppleTalk protocol, and you may need to install the Macintosh name space module to support extended filenames.

- Unix clients require additional software and TCP/IP. They cannot run administrative utilities and do not execute any login script. They attach to the network through Bindery Services.

- Clients for Windows NT and Windows 95/98 provide the same features as the DOS Requester for these platforms. Neither currently supports login scripts.

Mobile Users

A mobile user is one who frequently visits and logs in from different locations. You must make special considerations for these users, which will vary depending on whether the mobile user is using a mobile computer and what his or her access needs are.

CNE Practice Test Questions

1. Which component is the most important in NetWare 5, besides NDS?

   A. Bindery Services

   B. The file system

   C. TCP/IP

   D. Mobile use

2. To minimize WAN traffic, applications:

   A. Should be installed on one server only

   B. Should be installed on every server in the network

   C. Should be installed on each local PC

   D. Should be installed on at least one server per location

3. The object best used to assign rights for backups is:

   A. Organization

   B. Organizational Unit

   C. Organizational Role

   D. Group

4. Which type of object should you generally avoid assigning rights to?

   A. [Root], User

   B. Group

   C. Organizational Role

   D. Container

5. Which is not a possible security configuration?

   A. Central administrator only

   B. Central administrator and exclusive container administrators

   C. Container administrators only

   D. Special-use administrator only

6. Which type of object can be used to assign the same rights to users in different containers?

   A. Organization

   B. Organizational Unit

   C. Group

   D. Profile

7. Which client operating system does *not* support NDS?

   A. DOS

   B. Macintosh

   C. OS/2

   D. Unix

8. Which client or clients is/are not supported without additional software that must be purchased? (Choose all correct answers.)

   A. Unix

   B. OS/2

   C. DOS

   D. Macintosh

9. Which operating systems can run most of the administration utilities? (Select two.)

   A. Windows

   B. Unix

   C. Macintosh

   D. OS/2

10. The best type of object to use to assign an administrator is:

   A. User

   B. Group

   C. Organizational Unit

   D. Organizational Role

CHAPTER

20

Advanced NDS Design

Roadmap

This chapter covers NDS design concepts, including partitioning, time synchronization, and time servers, which are part of the CNE core requirement "NDS Design and Implementation."

Topics Covered

- Partitioning Concepts and Terminology

- Partitioning Guidelines

- The Components and Process of Time Synchronization

- Time Synchronization Guidelines

Skills You'll Learn

- Explain the concepts and terminology used in partitioning the NDS tree

- List the guidelines for partitioning your tree well

- Describe the time synchronization process

- List the types of time servers and when to use each

- List the guidelines used in setting up time synchronization

In previous chapters, you learned how to plan the structure of the Directory tree and how to provide network access for a variety of users, client workstations, and applications. Now we'll look at some more advanced aspects of NDS planning: partitioning, replication, and time synchronization. You should create a detailed plan for each of these areas. In this chapter we'll explain the procedures involved in planning these aspects of the network, and the factors you should consider along the way.

NDS Partitioning Concepts

The basics of NDS partitioning and replication were introduced in Chapter 15. This section provides a summary of the basic concepts involved, along with a more detailed look at the inner workings of NDS and the process it uses to manage data: object name resolution and synchronization.

Partitions and Replication

The Directory can be physically divided into smaller units called *partitions*, which consist of container objects and the objects within them. Remember, however, that no matter how you *physically* divide up the database, *logically* it is one big database. A partition is given the name of the container closest to the [Root]. That container is also known as the *partition root*, which should not be confused with the [Root] object. The [Root] partition is the only partition that is created by default, and it is created when the first server in a tree is installed.

Each partition can be copied and stored, or *replicated*, on one or more servers. There are four types of replicas:

- *A master replica* is created when a partition is defined. There is only one master replica per partition.

- *Read/write replicas* contain the same data as the master replica, and there can be more than one of them. If changes are made to a read/write replica, they will be copied to the master replica and all other read/write replicas.

- *Read-only replicas* allow access to NDS data, but do not allow changes.

- *Subordinate references* are created automatically to point to children of a partition that are not located on the server. The easiest way to remember this is with the phrase "where there is a parent replica, but not its children."

There is always at least one replica of each partition, the master replica. Other replicas can be created if desired.

Table 20.1 lists the characteristics of each of the partition types.

T A B L E 20.1:   Characteristics of the Four Replica Types

Characteristic	Master	Read/ Write	Read- only	Subordinate Reference
Keeps list of all other replicas	Yes	Yes	Yes	Yes
Created by the administrator	Yes	Yes	Yes	No
Created and deleted by the system	No	No	No	Yes
Contains pointer information only	No	No	No	Yes
Contains all object information	Yes	Yes	Yes	No
Allows changes to objects, properties, and so on	Yes	Yes	No	No
Used in partition boundary changes	Yes	No	No	No
Supports user authentication process	Yes	Yes	No	No
Can be converted into a master replica	No	Yes	Yes	No
Can be converted into a read/write replica	No	No	Yes	No
Can be used for Bindery Services	Yes	Yes	No	No
Can have multiple replicas of this type for any given partition	No	Yes	Yes	Yes

To make changes to NDS objects, you must access either a master or read/write replica. These types of replicas are called *writable* replicas. When a change is made to these replicas, it is sent to all other replicas. A read-only replica receives updates from other servers as changes are made, but it cannot send any updates or receive updates from users.

A partition that has a container below it in another partition is said to be a *parent* partition. A partition that comes from a partition above it is called a *child* partition. Any given partition can be a parent, a child, or both. The only partition that can be a parent but not a child is the [Root] partition.

The Directory Synchronization Process

Since you can make a change to an NDS object from any master or read/write replica on the network, NetWare 5 needs to be sure all of the replicas have the same information. Each replica communicates changes to the other replicas so they can be duplicated. This process is called *Directory synchronization*.

Don't confuse the Directory synchronization process used to update replicas with time synchronization. Note, however, that time synchronization is a crucial component of the Directory synchronization process. Also, don't confuse Directory synchronization with file and directory synchronization, which requires another Novell product called Novell Replication Services (NRS).

As you have learned, NDS is a global, distributed database. When you make a change to an NDS object, the change is made to the master or read/write replica on the server to which you are attached. The NetWare 5 Directory synchronization process is then used to make sure the same change is made on all of the other replicas of the partition. This ensures that each replica is an accurate copy.

Directory synchronization doesn't happen instantaneously. It may take several minutes to disburse updates before all replicas have the same data. Because of this, NDS is called a *loosely consistent* database. In other words, it is not crucial that two replicas have exactly the same information at a particular instant. NetWare 5 takes this into account, and these inconsistencies do not produce errors.

In addition, when you make a change to an NDS object on one replica, NetWare does not update the entire replica; it's smart enough to only send updates for the object or objects you've changed. For example, if you change a user's password, only the new password is sent in an update to the other replicas. This minimizes network traffic and ensures that updates can be done quickly.

One critical element in the Directory synchronization process is that each replica must contact its neighboring replicas. It is important that all network links, particularly WAN links, are reliable. If a link is down for a long time, it may cause a loss of synchronization between the replicas; in addition, the replicas will continue trying to contact the lost replica for synchronization, which may increase network traffic. If you are taking a server or link down for a long time, be sure to remove any replicas on that server so this does not happen.

One new problem that may arise with NetWare 5 is related to protocols. What happens if two differently configured servers—one that has only IPX and one that has only IP—need to synchronize? They obviously can't synchronize with each other. The solution that Novell came up with is called *transitive synchronization*. With this approach, the server that has updates to send will attempt to contact each of the other servers in the replica ring. If any of the servers are unavailable due to incompatible protocols, it will stop trying to send changes. One of the servers that received the change and that has both protocols installed will then synchronize with the remaining servers. This is illustrated in Figure 20.1.

F I G U R E   20.1

The transitive synchro-
nization process

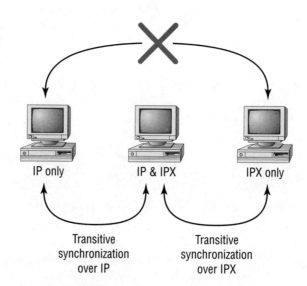

Understanding Name Resolution

Although you can access an object from any location on the network, regardless of which replica it is located on, it is important to understand the process by which NetWare 5 locates objects on the network. This process is called *name resolution*, and it involves finding an object based on its distinguished NDS name. This process is also referred to as *tree walking;* you'll understand why after reading the explanation below.

When you request access to an object, NDS first looks for a replica on the server you are attached to. If there is one, it is used. If a local replica is not available, subordinate or superior (parent or child) pointers are used to locate the replica. The server's pointers point to the servers that contain an actual replica of the partition in question.

Subordinate references can be more than one level deep. NetWare "walks" from one replica to the next, following the pointers stored in subordinate references, until it finds the resource you need.

If the replica to which a subordinate reference points is across a WAN link, name resolution can be a slow process. This is especially true if several subordinate references must be followed before NDS reaches the actual object. For this reason, it is best to place a replica on a local server for each container that will be accessed frequently by that server. This makes the name resolution process much quicker.

The process of "walking the tree" is illustrated in Figure 20.2. If a user in the Cleveland container requests a resource in the AP container, NetWare walks up and down the tree to reach it.

F I G U R E   20.2

Name resolution, or tree walking, is used by NetWare 5 to locate NDS objects.

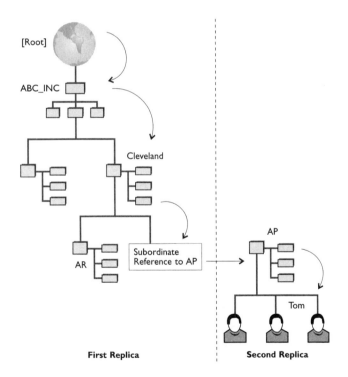

First Replica   Second Replica

Name Resolution for user:
TOM.AP.CLEVELAND.ABC_INC

Planning Partitions and Replicas

We will now look at the process of planning partitions and replicas for a large-scale network. While NetWare 5's default partitioning scheme is sufficient for small networks, an enterprise WAN network requires a carefully planned scheme of partitions and replicas. We'll start with some basic considerations for partitioning.

NetWare 5 Default Partitions and Replicas

NetWare 5 provides a default scheme of replicas and partitions—well, technically, replicas and *partition*. By default, no matter how large your network is or how many servers you are using, all objects are placed in a single [Root] partition. Needless to say, this is not the ideal solution in many cases, but it is sufficient in some situations. If a network meets the following criteria, the default scheme is probably sufficient:

- There are fewer than 15 servers with replicas.

- There are no WAN links to other locations.

- There are fewer than 3,500 objects in the network.

As you can see, these criteria are quite generous. Most small-company and single-location networks will qualify. However, in this chapter we're concerned with large-scale, enterprise-wide networks. We'll assume you've made the decision that partitioning is needed, and proceed with the details of planning partitions and replica placement.

As for replicas, servers receive the following replicas by default:

- The first server in a Directory tree receives the master replica of the [Root] partition.

- The second and third servers receive read/write replicas.

- The fourth server (and any installed thereafter) receives no replicas, unless one of the first three servers loses its replica, in which case the next server installed will get a read/write replica.

- A NetWare 3 server that is upgraded to NetWare 5 will receive a read/write replica of the partition that contains the server for Bindery Services.

This scheme is meant to provide a default setup that is effective in simple networks. However, for a large, enterprise-wide network with WAN links, you must determine the partitions and replicas you will need on each server, as the default configuration will not be efficient.

Partitioning Considerations

The following are some basic points to keep in mind when planning partitions and replicas:

WAN links   If you use these, keep each location as a separate partition.

Location   Even in a LAN, try to group replica servers near each other in a single partition.

Number of replicas   If more than 15 servers have replicas of a partition, there will be heavy network traffic when the replicas are synchronized. You should either split the partition or eliminate unnecessary replicas.

Number of partitions   You should carefully consider the number of partitions to use, as having too few or too many can cause problems.

Partition size and number of children per parent   There should be no more than 3,500 objects per partition, and there should be fewer than 35 child partitions per parent.

Keeping WAN Links Separate

If WAN links are used in your network, it is important to keep a separate partition for each location if at all possible. Network administrators call this concept "Don't span the WAN." The Directory synchronization process can take quite a bit of network traffic, and that traffic may use precious bandwidth on your WAN links.

Of course, there will still be situations when all partitions are needed and WAN links come into play, such as when you merge partitions or Directory trees. The idea is to be sure the day-to-day use of the network doesn't send large amounts of traffic over the WAN link.

Locating Replica Servers

Even if WAN links are not involved, you should keep location in mind. Place servers that are near each other (in the same room or floor) in the same partition. This provides the same benefit for the LAN backbone as this concept did for WAN links above.

In many cases, a single partition is acceptable for an entire building or location. If all of the LAN links are fast, traffic is low, and there are relatively few users, this may be an ideal situation.

A network analyzer, such as Novell's LANalyzer software, is very useful in determining the traffic level on a LAN or WAN and finding the source of the traffic.

How Many Replicas?

Of course, one way to ensure that synchronization between replicas doesn't create a network traffic problem is to minimize the number of replicas. Although a few replicas are important for reliability and redundancy, you don't want to create unnecessary replicas. If more than 15 servers have replicas of a single partition, there will be heavy network traffic when the replicas are synchronized. You should split the partition or eliminate unnecessary replicas.

A good general rule is to create two or three replicas for reliability, and replicas across WAN or LAN links to separate locations if needed. By default, NetWare creates replicas on the first three servers you install in the Directory tree. Keep the number under 15 (10 is a reasonable maximum) and you should have a fast, efficient network.

How Many Partitions?

How many partitions should you create? This depends on a large number of factors. There are disadvantages to having either too few partitions or too many. You should be able to find a number in between the two extremes that will work well.

Here are some reasons for creating additional partitions:

- A large partition can consume large amounts of disk storage on each server with a replica. By splitting the partition, you can decrease the amount of disk space used.

- You can make resources available at the server nearest the users who use them. If a partition is near the user who accesses it, the amount of network traffic required to log in or maintain NDS objects is reduced.

On the other hand, there are some good reasons *not* to create additional partitions:

- Numerous subordinate reference replicas may be created, which causes an increase in network traffic.

- Administration can take longer, since the objects you need to maintain may be stored in several different places.

- Network traffic increases, because synchronization must be performed

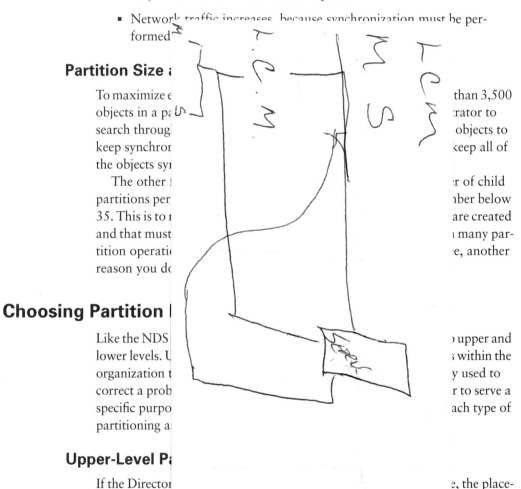

Partition Size :

To maximize e   than 3,500
objects in a pa   rator to
search throug   objects to
keep synchror   keep all of
the objects sy

The other   r of child
partitions per   ber below
35. This is to   are created
and that must   many partition operati   e, another
reason you d

Choosing Partition

Like the NDS   upper and
lower levels. U   within the
organization t   y used to
correct a prob   r to serve a
specific purpo   ach type of
partitioning a

Upper-Level Pa

If the Director   e, the place-
ment of partition boundaries is obvious. Each high-level Organizational Unit (or at least those that represent separate locations) should be made the root of a separate partition. This is particularly critical when the locations are connected with WAN links. If a partition spans a WAN link, network traffic will be a mess and the partition's replicas will almost never be properly synchronized, or you will have little available bandwidth on the link.

For example, the Directory tree in Figure 20.3 has locations in Boston, Cleveland, and Oakland. The obvious method of partitioning the upper levels would be to place each top-level Organizational Unit in its own partition, represented by the dotted lines in the figure. This keeps each partition in a single location, and provides for optimum network traffic and fast synchronization. In addition, it ensures that users will rarely have to access NDS data on a remote replica.

FIGURE 20.3

Partitioning a typical
Directory tree

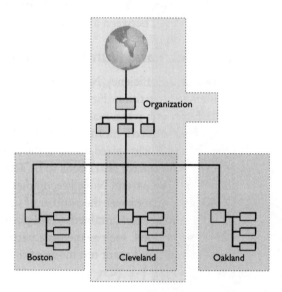

If the organization is at a single site, partitioning can be more flexible. For example, the Directory tree in Figure 20.4 is located at a single location. The top level of the NDS tree is organized by functional divisions, and the partitions follow the same scheme.

Lower-Level Partitions

For many networks, it is unnecessary to partition any further. However, if there are too many (3,500 or more) objects in a partition, you should further subdivide it. The subdivisions can follow the same boundaries as the divisions of the Directory tree; they might represent buildings within a location, departments, or workgroups.

F I G U R E 20.4

Partitioning in an NDS tree organized by function

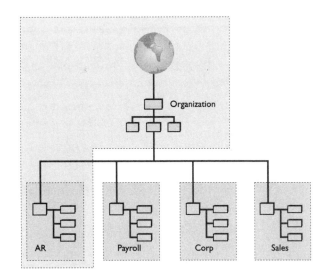

Don't partition unnecessarily. If a partition contains fewer than 300 or so objects, there is no need to partition it any further. In fact, doing so will create unnecessary subordinate references and network traffic.

General Rules for Partitioning

Here are some basic rules for partitioning:

- Partitions cannot overlap. An NDS object can be in only one partition.

- Partitions affect NDS data only; they do not divide or replicate data in the file system.

- Partitions cannot be stored on NetWare 3 or earlier servers.

- Partitions are named after the uppermost container object. The first (and only) partition created in a new Directory tree is the [Root] partition.

- The Directory tree should be divided into only a few partitions at the top level and more partitions at the lower levels, if needed.

Replica Placement Guidelines

Here are some general guidelines to follow when placing replicas. These are suggestions only; in your particular situation, things may be slightly different. These ground rules will provide a good starting point for your replica design plan:

- Create at least three replicas for each partition, if possible. This prevents any one replica from being a single point of failure.

- Make sure you replicate the [Root] partition. If it is lost, the whole Directory tree will be inaccessible.

- Create replicas close to the users who will use objects in that partition.

- Bindery Services require a writable replica of the partition containing the bindery context on each server that will be used to log into Bindery Services.

- Do not rely on subordinate references for fault tolerance. They don't contain any object data.

- For fault tolerance, be sure you have at least three replicas of each partition, including the master replica. Make sure that at least one replica is kept at a separate location; this provides an off-site backup.

- Create regional replicas if you have many locations and create partitions for them. This will help spread the load and reduce the number of subordinate references.

- Place no more than 20 replicas on an average server. You may create more if you have very powerful servers or if you are creating a server that will hold the entire NDS tree (for easy administration and faster backups).

- Keep master replicas near you, the administrator, or whoever will be responsible for partition operations, as they will be needed when it's time to merge or create new partitions.

- In planning hard drive space requirements for the SYS volume (where the tree is stored), keep in mind that the average object is 5K, with some objects, such as Z.E.N.works-related objects, requiring even more space.

- Use the WAN Traffic Manager (discussed in Chapter 21) to help control NDS usage of bandwidth.

Why Replicate a Partition?

There are three basic reasons to replicate a partition:

Fault tolerance   This is the most important reason for replication. Replicas of a partition provide a backup for the partition (but replicas should *not* be considered a replacement for tape backups).

Accessibility   Network performance is faster if a replica is available nearby for the resource being accessed.

Navigation   Having a partition nearby allows users to access resources or log in quickly. Place a replica of their User objects and any objects to which they require access on the same server to which they attach, or at least on a server at the same location.

Creating a Partitioning Plan

After you understand the partitioning and replication process and the guidelines for choosing partition boundaries, you're ready to create a document that details your plans for partitions and replicas. It's important to keep a hard copy of this information, so you (or your successor) will understand the organization when changes are needed later. In addition, a document like this can be helpful in troubleshooting a synchronization problem.

First, your document should list the partitions that will be created. This may be a simple matter of dividing the organization into three partitions based on Organizational Units. In a larger network, there may be quite a few separate partitions. After you have a list of partitions (and a diagram of their placement), you should choose where to assign replicas for each partition. Follow the guidelines given in the previous section.

Your plan should address the following questions:

- Which partitions will be used, and why?

- Where (in which location and on which server) will each replica be located, and why?

- Which replicas are to be counted on for fault tolerance?

- Are there problem areas—partitions that are growing large and that may soon need splitting?

- Where will the subordinate reference partitions be placed by NDS?

This information should be stored in a replica table. Table 20.2 shows an example, in which M represents a master replica, RW a read/write replica, and SR subordinate references. This replica table is based on the tree and partition structure shown in Figure 20.5. You may see figures and tables like those shown here on the exam, so study them carefully and be prepared to create and troubleshoot replica tables. This is also a task you should complete for your network in the field.

FIGURE 20.5

A sample NDS tree with partitions and servers listed

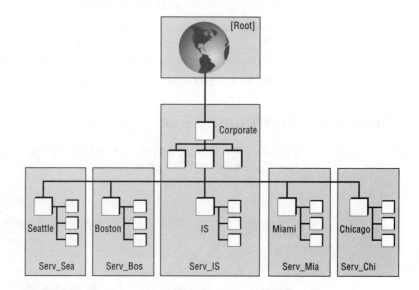

TABLE 20.2: A Sample Replica Table for the Tree Shown in Figure 20.5

Server	Partitions					
	[Root]	Corporate	Seattle	Boston	Miami	Chicago
Serv_IS	M	M	M	M	M	M
Serv_Sea	RW	SR	RW			RW
Serv_Bos	RW	RW	SR	RW	RW	
Serv_Mia		RW	SR	RW	RW	
Serv_Chi			RW			RW

Planning Time Synchronization

Your plan for a network should also include the type of time synchronization that will be used and the specific servers that will act as time servers. In this section we'll cover the concepts of time synchronization and look at the techniques you'll use in planning a time synchronization strategy for the network.

Using Time Synchronization

Because NDS is based on a database distributed across multiple servers, all the servers must keep the same time to accurately document changes to files, to order changes made to NDS objects, and to enable messaging applications such as Novell's GroupWise.

NDS uses a process called *time stamping* to assign a time to each change in the Directory tree. Changes can be made to an object in the network from any server (with a replica) at any time. Time stamping ensures that these changes are made in the correct order and that all replicas receive the correct information. You can see, for example, that it is very different to delete an object and then create a new object with the same name than it is to create and then delete the same object.

Every activity in NDS is documented with a time stamp. Time stamps use UTC time. *UTC* stands for Universal Coordinated Time (the acronym comes from the French), which is the international standard for accurate time. (UTC is the new name for Greenwich Mean Time, or GMT.)

The UTC system is independent of time zones. Because of this, the entire network can have a standard time even if servers are located in parts of the world with different time zones. When you install a server, NetWare 5 asks you to choose a *time zone*. NetWare 5 knows the offset from UTC, and uses that offset to calculate the local time from the network's UTC time. For example, the time offset for Boise, Idaho, is 7:00:00 behind, or seven hours behind, UTC. If the time in Boise is 2 A.M., UTC time is 9 A.M. NetWare also takes daylight saving time into account if necessary.

Time synchronization works differently in an IPX-only environment than in IP-only or mixed IP/IPX environments. We will begin with a discussion of how time synchronization works in an IPX environment and then turn our attention to IP and mixed environments.

Types of Time Servers in an IPX Environment

Unfortunately, clocks in computers tend to deviate slightly, so servers can end up with different times. To compensate for this problem, NDS's time synchronization feature uses *time servers* for keeping time standardized across the network. There are four types of time servers, each with a particular purpose. The next sections examine each of these types.

Single Reference Time Server

A *single reference time server* provides a single, authoritative source of time on the network. The first NetWare 5 server installed on a network defaults to this configuration.

If you use a single reference time server, you must configure all other servers as secondary time servers. Each of these must receive the time from the single reference server. This is the typical configuration for small networks. Figure 20.6 shows an example of a small network using a single reference time server.

F I G U R E   20.6

A single reference time server is the only source of time on its network.

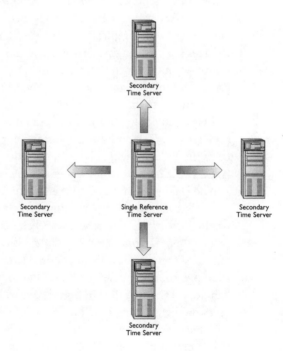

WARNING Because the single reference time server never adjusts its clock, you must be sure that its time is set correctly.

Primary Time Servers

Primary time servers negotiate, or "vote," with other primary and reference servers on the network to determine the correct time. Each primary server gets one vote when determining the correct time. If a primary server finds itself to be out of synchronization with the network time, it gradually speeds up or slows down until it is back in synchronization. Since primary time servers work by negotiation, there must be at least one other time source— a reference server or another primary server—on the network. Novell states that you should always have a reference and at least two primary time servers if you choose this strategy.

Primary time servers are frequently used on WANs, because they can provide a local time source for secondary time servers and workstations that would otherwise need to cross WAN links for a time source.

The negotiation process of primary time servers ensures that the servers agree on a time, but this time is not guaranteed to be accurate. In situations where accurate time is important (and it should always be important), you need to use a reference time server along with one or more primary servers. Figure 20.7 shows a typical primary time server arrangement, although this method (in other words, doing without a reference time server) is not usually recommended.

Reference Time Servers

A *reference time server* is the final piece of the puzzle. It is usually attached to an external time source. This could be an accurate hardware clock or a modem or radio link to a reliable time source, such as the Rugby Atomic Clock or the U.S. Naval Observatory.

Although the reference time server will adjust its time to match the external source, it does not adjust its clock in the negotiation process. When primary time servers negotiate the network time, the reference server's time is considered an accurate source, and the primary servers will eventually correct themselves to match that time. In fact, reference servers get 16 votes in the voting process. If you use a reference server, you must configure at least one primary time server, and Novell recommends at least two for fault tolerance. Figure 20.8 shows a network arrangement using primary and reference time servers.

Primary time servers negotiate with other primary and reference servers to determine the correct time.

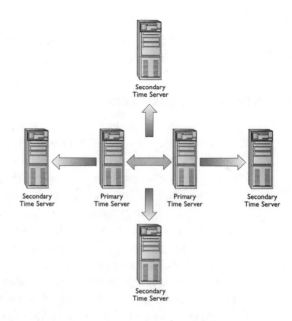

A reference time server is usually attached to an external time source.

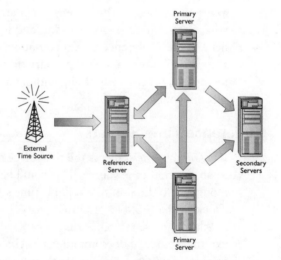

Reference, single reference, and primary time servers are called *time providers*. Secondary time servers are called *time consumers*.

Secondary Time Servers

A *secondary time server* provides the time to client workstations but not to any other servers. When you install a new server on a network that already has a NetWare 5 server, the new server will be a secondary time server by default.

Secondary time servers do not participate in the voting process to determine the correct time. They get time information from a primary or single reference time server. You must define at least one primary, reference, or single reference server before you can configure a server as a secondary time server.

Implementing and Managing Time Synchronization in an IPX Environment

In order to set up and maintain time synchronization on your network, you need to adjust settings on each server. These settings will determine what type of time server the server will act as and which server it will use as a time source.

Setting Time Synchronization Parameters

There are several SET parameters you can use to control your network's time synchronization. These SET commands can be found in the MONITOR NLM under Server Parameters ➤ Time, and the most common are described in Table 20.3. Normally these parameters are written to the server's TIMESYNC.CFG file. This happens automatically as soon as you make the change.

T A B L E   20.3:   NetWare 5 Time Synchronization SET Parameters

SET Parameter	Description
Configured Sources	This controls which type of time source is used. If set to On, you must specify a list of time sources in the TIMESYNC.CFG file. This can be done by setting the Time Sources parameter (discussed below). If set to Off, the SAP protocol is used to listen for a time source. (SAP will be discussed in the "Methods of Time Synchronization" section below.)

T A B L E   20.3:   NetWare 5 Time Synchronization SET Parameters *(continued)*

SET Parameter	Description
Directory Tree Mode	If set to On, SAP packets are ignored unless they come from the server's own Directory tree. If multiple Directory trees are used, this prevents time servers on different trees from creating conflicts. If set to Off, SAP packets from any time server on the network will be used.
Hardware Clock	Controls whether the server's hardware clock will be used for time synchronization. This should only be set to Off if the server will use an external time source. Only single reference and reference servers use this parameter; the rest set their clocks.
Polling Count	Controls how many time packets are exchanged when servers are polled. Increasing this number can create unnecessary traffic. The default is 3.
Polling Interval	Controls how often the server polls other servers. This number defaults to 600 seconds (10 minutes). If you change this, you should use the same setting for all servers on the network.
Service Advertising	If this is set to On, the SAP protocol will be used to broadcast time. If it is turned off, you must create a list of time sources in the TIMESYNC.CFG file of each server. This parameter is only used for time providers, never for time consumers (secondary time servers).
Synchronization Radius	This controls the maximum amount a server's time can be adjusted and still remain in synchronization with other servers. It defaults to 2,000 milliseconds. Increasing this parameter may prevent servers from losing synchronization. Setting it too low (below 1,000) may prevent servers from ever being synchronized. You may need to raise this parameter to compensate for slow WAN links.
Type	This determines the type of time server that the server is currently acting as. These are the available options: Reference, Primary, Secondary, or Single.
Time Sources	Lists the servers that should be contacted to determine the correct time. The servers can be referred to by physical name, IP address, or DN.

Creating the TIMESYNC.CFG Files

If you are using a custom configuration (described below), you must create a TIMESYNC.CFG file for each server. This file is located in the server's SYS:SYSTEM directory. The file consists of two parts:

Parameters   These are the parameters listed in Table 20.3.

Time Sources   This is a list of time sources for a custom configuration. The first server in the list will be polled as a time source. If it is unavailable, the other servers in the list will be tried in order.

Here is an example of a TIMESYNC.CFG file. This file is for the server CORP1, which is a primary time server. It negotiates with the servers CORP2 and CORP3 to determine the correct time.

```
#TIMESYNC.CFG for Server CORP1
# (lines beginning with # are comments)
Configured Sources = ON
Directory Tree Mode = ON
Hardware Clock = OFF
Polling Count = 3
Polling Interval = 600
Service Advertising = OFF
Synchronization Radius = 2000
Type = PRIMARY
# Time Sources
Time Source = CORP2
Time Source = CORP3
```

Since time synchronization operates at a lower level than NDS, you can't use NDS utilities to make changes to time synchronization. These changes must be made in the individual TIMESYNC.CFG files for each server.

Starting Synchronization

If you have configured time synchronization correctly, the servers should synchronize with each other as soon as they are brought online. You can verify this by entering **TIME** at each server's console. Here is the typical output of the TIME command:

```
Time zone string: "MST7MDT"
DST status: ON
```

```
DST start: Sunday, April 4, 1999 2:00:00 am MST
DST end: Sunday, October 31, 1999 2:00:00 am MDT
Time synchronization is active.
Time is synchronized to the network.
Thursday, May 6, 1999 3:35:14 am UTC
Wednesday, May 5, 1999 9:35:14 pm MDT
```

Check that the message "Time is synchronized to the network" is displayed on each server, as it is in the sample output above. If the servers are not synchronized, check the time synchronization settings.

After time synchronization is established, you should avoid changing the time on any server. If the server is a time consumer, your change will be ignored, because time is received from the other servers on the network; if it is a time provider, it will affect the network's time, which could corrupt NDS data.

Time Synchronization in an IP or Mixed IP/IPX Environment

In an IP environment or a mixed IP/IPX environment, NetWare will use Network Time Protocol (NTP) as the time synchronization protocol. This is accomplished with TIMESYNC.NLM, just as with IPX-only synchronization, with the addition of NTP.NLM, which enables NTP. This file is found in the SYS:SYSTEM directory and must be manually loaded. This should be done in AUTOEXEC.NCF. NTP is an open Internet standard, defined in RFC 1305. If this NLM is loaded, NTP will handle all time synchronization; the only time server type allowed for IPX-based computers is the secondary time server type.

More information on NTP can be found on the Internet at the following address: http://www.eecis.udel.edu/~ntp/database/html_ntp-4.0.72c/ index.htm

NTP can be configured to operate in one of two modes: server and peer. Server mode is analogous to the reference time server for IPX, in that it will update its clock from external time sources, such as an atomic clock, but will not receive updates from other time servers. In peer mode, which is similar to the primary time server, it will both send and receive time updates from other time servers, as well as receiving updates from external time sources.

To configure NTP, you must edit SYS:ETC\NTP.CFG. The contents of the default NTP.CFG read as follows:

```
The syntax for logfile is "logfile <etc\ntp.log>"
#Logging NTP messages, uncomment the line below to enable
logging
#logfile etc\ntp.log

#The syntax is SERVER IPADDRESS or server HOSTNAME
#server bitsy.mit.edu
#or
#server 18.72.0.3

#This is the local clock timer.
#Only turn it on for the primary time source or in an
isolated network.
#The primary time source is the server which acts as a time
source
#for all internal servers (or the server that has the
connection to the
#Internet or remote time source).
#Local clock timer will kick in when all outside sources
become unavailable.
#server 127.127.1.0

#Uncomment line below to point to time server at
#Lawrence Livermore National Laboratory
#serverclock.llnl.gov

#Uncomment line below to point to time server at
#NASA Ames Research Center
#server ntp.nasa.com

#Uncomment line below to point to time server at
#U.S. Naval Observatory
#server ntp2.usno.navy.mil

#MIT
server 129.7.1.66
```

```
#NIST Central Computer Facility
server 129.6.16.36

#Sony
server 198.93.3.1
```

You should notice two things in the file listed above. The first is that, even though it is commented out, the default is to use the local clock, at IP address 127.127.1.0, part of the Loopback series of IP addresses. (The Loopback series of IP addresses is for testing IP and simply loops the signal back to itself; hence the name.) The second thing of interest is that all of the time sources begin with the word *server*. This means that all of those sources are being referred to in server mode. To operate in peer mode with another server, simply use the word *peer* instead.

Methods of Time Synchronization

You can choose to install time synchronization in either the default configuration or a custom configuration. The default configuration will work well in most single-location networks. For larger networks and networks with multiple locations, a custom configuration will be more efficient.

Default Configuration

The default time synchronization configuration uses one single reference time server to provide the time to all servers on the network. The first server installed will be the single reference time server. All other servers on the network are configured as secondary time servers when they are installed.

In the default configuration, the single reference server broadcasts time information using the *Service Advertising Protocol (SAP)*, a NetWare standard. SAP is an effective means of communication. However, because SAP packets are broadcast to the entire network, using SAP will increase traffic on your network, particularly over WAN links.

NetWare 5 provides this default method to simplify installation and to enable network administrators to set up a network without necessarily understanding the complexities of the time synchronization process. This can be an effective strategy, but it has the following disadvantages:

- The single reference time server is a potential *single point of failure*. If this server goes down, all other servers will lose their source of synchronized time. One of the other servers can take over as the single reference server, but you must arrange this manually with a SET command at the server. You must always ensure that there is only one single reference time server on the network at a time.

- All servers in the network will need to contact the single reference server frequently to receive the current time. This adds traffic to the network, particularly if servers are at opposite ends of a WAN link. Worse, if a server loses its connection to the single reference server, it will also lose time synchronization.

- Because each server is not given a specific list of time servers to receive time from, any server that claims to be a single reference time server will be used. This means that if a server is accidentally configured as a time provider, there will be conflicting sources of time on the network.

Custom Configuration

Using a custom configuration, you can optimize time synchronization on your network. You'll need to plan your custom configuration, using the right combination of primary, secondary, and reference time servers to minimize network traffic.

WARNING Don't use a custom configuration unless you really need to, because it requires careful planning and maintenance, as well as a thorough understanding of the time synchronization process and the components involved. The default configuration is usually sufficient for a small company.

Custom configurations require you to create a file, TIMESYNC.CFG, at each server to specify time sources. Also, each time you add a new time source to the network, you will need to update some of those TIMESYNC .CFG files. NetWare does not provide a centralized method for maintaining these files.

Planning a Custom Configuration   When you are creating a plan for custom time synchronization, the main factors to consider are the physical location of servers and the speed of network connections between them. Here are some general rules to follow:

- Create primary time servers in major locations, along with a centrally located reference time server.

- Arrange for servers near each primary time server to receive their time from that server. That implies, of course, that you configure them as secondary time servers.

- Be sure that there are strong network links between each of the primary time servers.

- Use no more than six primary and one reference server to keep network traffic to a minimum.

In this strategy, because you use multiple primary servers and a reference server, all of which are *time sources*, there is no single point of failure. As long as network communication lines remain open, servers will have more than one available source of time. This ensures that no server will lose time synchronization.

You should avoid using more than six primary servers and one reference time server on a network, because the traffic generated by the voting process can slow down the network. For larger networks, you will want to use multiple time provider groups, as described in the next section.

Using Time Provider Groups

A *time provider group* usually consists of a reference time server, two or more primary time servers, and any number of secondary time servers. A simple time provider group was shown earlier in this chapter, in Figure 20.8.

In a large network with many servers communicating across WAN links, single time provider groups are not practical. The voting process used by primary servers will add traffic to the WAN link, creating a bottleneck. In this situation, you should use multiple time provider groups.

If you use multiple time provider groups, it is important to use some form of external time source for synchronization. If each location's reference time server communicates with the same external source (such as a radio time signal), you can keep a consistent time across all locations without adding traffic to the WAN. You also need to ensure that the two time provider groups don't communicate with each other, or you will get errors. You can do this with configured lists (so that servers only contact a predetermined list of servers to get their time) or with SAP filtering (if you choose to advertise time with SAP).

An example of a network using multiple time provider groups is shown in Figure 20.9.

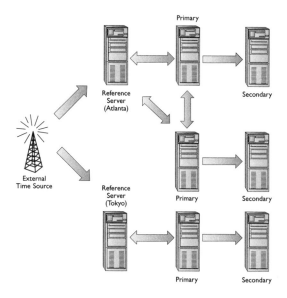

FIGURE 20.9

Multiple time provider groups should be used on a larger network.

Creating a Time Synchronization Plan

On a large-scale network, it's important not only to plan the type of time servers you will use, but also to document your plan. In the sections below, we'll describe the items you should include in the time synchronization plan and the reasons they are important. You may skip this phase of the design process if your network meets all of the following criteria:

- 30 or fewer servers
- One location
- IP is not used exclusively on any server

Defining Time Provider Groups

The first step in creating a time synchronization plan is to define your time provider groups and then list each of them. It can be helpful to include a map that relates time provider groups and time servers with physical locations.

Because time synchronization uses network traffic, it is best to keep separate time provider groups in each large geographical location of the network, such as Europe, North America, and Asia. This will keep the number of primary and secondary servers to a manageable level and minimize WAN bandwidth needs.

Defining Time Synchronization Information

Next, for each server, define the following basic time synchronization information. You will use this information to create the TIMESYNC.CFG file on the server:

- The time server type. In a large network, this is usually primary, reference, or secondary.

- The time sources that will be used to receive time.

- The time zone the server is located in.

Creating the TIMESYNC.CFG files

If you are using a custom configuration, you must create a TIMESYNC.CFG file for each server. This file is located in the server's SYS:SYSTEM directory, and consists of two parts:

Parameters   These parameters were discussed earlier in the chapter and are listed in Table 20.3.

Time sources   This is a list of time sources for a custom configuration. The first server in the list will be polled as a time source. If it is unavailable, the other servers will be tried in the order they are listed.

Here is an example of a TIMESYNC.CFG file. This file is for the server CORP1, which is a primary time server. It negotiates with the servers CORP2 and CORP3 to determine the correct time.

```
#TIMESYNC.CFG for Server CORP1
# (lines beginning with # are comments)
Configured Sources = ON
Directory Tree Mode = ON
Hardware Clock = OFF
Polling Count = 3
Polling Interval = 600
Service Advertising = OFF
Synchronization Radius = 2000
Type = PRIMARY
# Time Sources
Time Source = CORP2
Time Source = CORP3
```

Since time synchronization operates at a lower level than NDS, you can't use NDS utilities to make changes to time synchronization. You will need to make these changes in the individual TIMESYNC.CFG files for each server. The MONITOR utility provides a menu-based way to do this at the server.

Review

This chapter has given you a look at the more advanced aspects of NDS planning: partitioning, replication, and time synchronization. You should create a detailed plan for each of these areas.

The Directory can be divided into partitions. Each partition can be replicated on one or more servers. There is always at least one partition, the [Root] partition.

There are four types of replicas:

Master replica   This is created when a partition is defined. There is only one master replica per partition. This replica type supports user logins.

Read/write replicas   These contain the same data as the master replica, and there can be any number of them. Changes made to this replica will be copied to all of the other replicas. This replica type supports user logins.

Read-only replicas   These allow access to NDS data, but do not allow changes. This replica type does *not* support user logins. It is never recommended to use this type of replica.

Subordinate references   These are created automatically to point to children of a partition that are not located on the same server as the parent. They contain no data on the objects in the partition.

NDS is a global, distributed database. When you make a change to an NDS object, the change is made to the nearest master or read/write replica. The NetWare 5 synchronization process is then used to make sure the same change is made on all of the other replicas of the partition.

NDS is also a loosely consistent database. In other words, it is not crucial that two replicas have exactly the same information at a particular instant.

When you request access to an object, NDS first looks for a replica on the server you are attached to. If a local replica is not available, subordinate references can be used to locate the replica. Each subordinate reference points to a server that contains an actual replica of the partition.

Subordinate references can be more than one level deep, though they are only stored one level deep on any given server. This means that NetWare will create subordinate references for only the children (not grandchildren, great-grandchildren, and so on) of a partition that is not stored locally. NetWare "walks" from one replica to the next, following the pointers stored in subordinate references, until it finds the resource you need in either a master or read/write replica.

Default Partitions and Replicas

NetWare 5 provides a default scheme of partitions and replicas. This scheme provides basic reliability, but it is only sufficient when all of the following conditions are met:

- The number of servers used for replicas is 15 or fewer.

- There are no WAN links to other locations.

- There are 3,500 or fewer objects.

The default configuration places the entire Directory tree in a single partition. Servers receive the following replicas by default:

- The first server in a Directory tree receives the master replica of the [Root] partition.

- The second and third servers receive read/write replicas.

- The fourth server (and any that follow) receives no replicas.

- Each upgraded bindery-based server will receive a replica of the partition that contains its server object to support Bindery Services.

Creating Partitions

Here are some reasons for creating additional partitions:

- A large partition can consume large amounts of disk storage on each server with a replica. By splitting the partition, you can decrease the amount of disk space used.

- By splitting resources into partitions, you can make them available at the server nearest the users who use them. When a partition is near the user, the amount of network traffic required to log in or maintain NDS objects is reduced.

- No partition should "span the WAN," meaning that each physical location should have its own partition.

On the other hand, here are some reasons *not* to create additional partitions:

- A large amount of subordinate reference replicas may be created, which causes an increase in network traffic.

- Administration can take longer, since objects you need to maintain may be stored in several different places.

- Network traffic increases, because synchronization must be performed between all replicas.

Choosing Boundaries

Like the NDS tree itself, the partitions in the Directory tree can be divided into upper and lower levels. Upper-level partitions are generally based on locations. Lower-level partitions are usually used to split a large partition or to manage network traffic.

If the Directory tree is organized using the location-based design, each high-level Organizational Unit (representing a physical location) should be made the root of a separate partition. This is particularly critical when the locations are connected with WAN links. If a partition spans a WAN link, network traffic will be a mess and the partition's replicas will almost never be properly synchronized.

Placing Replicas

There are three basic reasons to replicate a partition:

Fault tolerance This is the most important reason for replication. Replicas of a partition provide a backup for the partition (although they should *not* be considered a replacement for tape backups).

Accessibility Network performance is faster if a replica is available nearby for the resource being accessed.

Navigation So that users can quickly access resources or log in, place a replica of their User objects and any objects they require access to at the same server that they attach to.

Follow these guidelines when placing replicas:

- Create at least three replicas for each partition. This prevents a single replica from becoming a single point of failure.

- Be certain you have replicated the [Root] partition. If it is lost, the whole Directory tree will be inaccessible.

- Create replicas close to the users who will use objects in that partition.

- Bindery Services requires a writable replica of the partition containing the bindery context on each server that will be used to support Bindery Services.

- Don't rely on subordinate references for fault tolerance. These cannot be used to restore any object data.

- You should not have more than 10 replicas (15 at most) of any given partition, due to the bandwidth required to keep them synchronized.

Time Synchronization

There are four types of time servers in an IPX environment, each with a particular purpose:

- A single reference server, when used, is the only source of time. All other servers must be secondary servers.

- Primary servers negotiate, or "vote," with other primary servers and a reference server to determine the time.

- Reference servers are used with primary servers, and are usually used with an external time source, such as an atomic clock.

- Secondary servers receive the time from a primary, reference, or single reference server and give the time to clients.

In an IP or mixed IP/IPX environment, NTP, the Network Time Protocol, is used to coordinate time. In this situation, all IPX servers must be secondary time servers. This protocol is enabled by loading NTP.NLM from SYS:SYSTEM. The configuration that controls the operation of this protocol is SYS:ETC\NTP.CFG.

The default time synchronization configuration uses one single reference time server to provide the time to all servers on the network. The first server installed will be the single reference server. All other servers on the network are configured as secondary time servers when they are installed.

Using a custom configuration, you can optimize time synchronization on your network. You'll need to plan your custom configuration, using the right combination of primary, secondary, and reference servers to minimize network traffic. Custom configurations require you to create a file, TIMESYNC .CFG, at each server to specify time sources.

CNE Practice Test Questions

1. Which is *not* one of the four types of replicas?

   A. Subordinate reference

   B. Time provider

   C. Read-only

   D. Read/write

2. Subordinate reference partitions are created:

   A. When you request them

   B. When you have the parent partition but not its child

   C. When you have the child but not the parent

   D. When you have neither the parent nor the child

3. The synchronization process in NetWare 5:

   A. Ensures that all replicas have the same information

   B. Ensures that all replicas have some of the same information (login name, password, and so on)

   C. Keeps a consistent time on the network

   D. Creates new replicas as they are needed

4. Which replicas are considered writable? (Choose two.)

   A. Master

   B. Read-only

   C. Read/write

   D. Subordinate reference

5. Name resolution is also called:

   A. Time synchronization

   B. Synchronization

   C. Tree walking

   D. Object naming

6. A single partition is practical for how many objects?

   A. 15 or fewer

   B. No more than 10

   C. 256 or fewer

   D. 3,500 or fewer

7. The default replication scheme assigns how many replicas for the [Root] partition?

   A. 1

   B. 2

   C. 3

   D. 16

8. Which is *not* a good reason to create additional partitions?

   A. To allow further subdivision of the Directory tree

   B. To make resources easily accessible

C. To minimize network traffic

D. To provide redundancy for login authentication

9. Which is *not* a disadvantage of increasing the number of partitions?

A. Network traffic may increase

B. Subordinate references may create problems

C. Time synchronization will take longer

D. Administration may take longer

10. A partition should span:

A. A single location only

B. Any number of locations

C. Nearby locations only

D. At least three locations

11. Which is *not* a benefit of replication?

A. Faster network access

B. Fault tolerance for NDS data

C. Fault tolerance for data files

D. Easy administration

12. Which of the following is not a time provider?

A. Single reference

B. Reference

C. Primary

D. Secondary

13. Which is *not* a server type found in a time provider group?

    A. Single reference

    B. Reference

    C. Primary

    D. Secondary

14. Which protocol synchronizes time in a mixed IP/IPX environment?

    A. TIMESYNC

    B. NTP

    C. DNS

    D. TCP

CHAPTER

21

Implementing an NDS Tree

Roadmap

This chapter covers several important topics related to NDS implementation, including client migration issues and methodologies, server migration issues, and how to merge two NDS trees, use WAN Traffic Manager, and schedule your NetWare 5 rollout. These topics are a part of the CNE core requirement "NDS Design and Implementation."

Topics Covered

- Client Migration Options
- Server Migration Issues
- Merging Trees with DSMERGE and Other Tools
- WAN Traffic Manager
- Scheduling the Implementation

Skills You'll Learn

- Explain the issues and benefits of upgrading to the latest Novell Client for all of the workstations on your network
- List the methods available for migrating servers and the issues involved
- Describe the process of merging two NDS trees and the effects it will have on both trees
- List the features and benefits of WAN Traffic Manager
- Describe the process of scheduling the NetWare 5 rollout

N ow that you've planned the structure of the Directory tree, arranged the objects that will be accessed, and determined the placement of partitions and replicas, it's time for the final step: planning the implementation. Here we'll show you how to plan and schedule migration to NetWare 5, for both existing clients and servers on a network; how to merge two NDS trees; how WAN traffic manager can help you manage bandwidth utilization; and how to schedule the implementation of NetWare 5 and NDS for a new network.

Planning Client Migration

To provide the full benefits of NDS throughout the network, you should plan to upgrade all clients to the latest client software: the Novell Client for DOS and Windows machines (all of which come with NetWare 5) or the appropriate software for Macintosh, Unix, or OS/2 clients (all of which you must download and/or purchase). This process is simple in an ideal situation, but can often be complicated in the real world due to software or hardware incompatibilities and other potential problems.

What You'll Need to Know

As a network consultant, you should gather as much information as possible about the existing network before planning the migration. In the following sections, we'll discuss some of the topics you must consider and some questions you should ask about DOS and Windows workstations and client software. To assess these issues, you or a member of your team may need to visit the site of the business you're consulting for, as many users are not really familiar with the concepts involved.

Current Client Software

Which client software is currently in use? If the network has been updated frequently, the Novell Client may already be configured. More likely, the workstations will be using whichever software was set up when they were first installed: the NetWare DOS Requester (VLMs) or the NetWare shell (NETX). The following sections discuss the client configurations you may find at a typical worksite.

IPX and NETX   The earlier versions of the NetWare shell used two programs: IPX, which manages the protocols, and NETX, which is the NetWare shell itself. The IPX program is not actually provided with NetWare. Instead, a program called WSGEN was used to create a version of IPX.COM for the workstation. This IPX includes the driver for the network card, the interrupt number, and other settings hard-coded into the program.

Obviously, these workstations should be upgraded if at all possible to the Novell Client or the DOS Requester.

One tip for IPX: There is a command that will display the settings for the current version of IPX. Type this command from the workstation:

```
IPX /I
```

This will display the IPX version, the network card it is designed to access, the interrupt number, and other settings, making it easy to upgrade the workstation.

There are some situations in which you will be unable to upgrade the workstation. In that case, you can continue running the current shell on the workstation and log in using Bindery Services.

NetWare Shell with ODI   The workstation may be running the NetWare shell (NETX) in combination with ODI drivers. A typical login sequence will include the following commands:

```
LSL
NE2000 (or other network board driver)
IPXODI
NETX
```

Since the NetWare DOS Requester also uses the ODI architecture, workstations that are configured to use this method can be upgraded easily. The ODI network card driver that is currently being used can, most likely, be used with the DOS Requester, if not the full Novell Client.

You should upgrade these workstations to the Novell Client, or at least the DOS Requester. Again, this may not be possible for older machines. Along with replacing NETX with the VLM.EXE program to manage the DOS Requester, the upgrade process will replace LSL and IPXODI with the latest versions. The network board driver should be replaced with a newer version if one is available.

NetWare DOS Requester   In a network that has used NetWare 3.1x or 4 in the past, the DOS Requester may be installed on clients. This was the standard client software for NetWare 3.12 and 4.1. While the Novell Client has replaced the DOS Requester in the latest version of NetWare, you are not required to use it; the DOS Requester supports NDS and can still be used, although only with IPX. The DOS Requester uses the following commands:

```
LSL
NE2000 (or other network board driver)
IPXODI
VLM
```

These commands perform the same functions as the shell with ODI described above. The final step uses VLM.EXE (the DOS Requester) rather than NETX. The DOS Requester is actually a shell that loads several programs (Virtual Loadable Modules, or VLMs) for different functions.

There are advantages to upgrading from the DOS Requester to the Novell Client (also known by its former name, Client 32). The Novell Client is a 32-bit client and is a bit more efficient with memory usage; in addition, it includes full support for Windows 95/98, including login scripts. The DOS Requester can be used with Windows 95/98, but users must go through a DOS login before Windows starts. This is slow and inefficient in terms of memory utilization.

Microsoft Clients   You can support the Novell Client if you have any of the following clients: Microsoft Client for NetWare Networks (Windows 95/98), Client Services for NetWare (CSNW for Windows NT Workstation), or Gateway Services for NetWare (GSNW for Windows NT Server). The Novell Client offers all of the new features (such as Z.E.N.works and NDPS), while the existing Microsoft client supports none of them. The only case in which you may not want to upgrade a client is with GSNW. GSNW allows the Windows NT server to act as a gateway between Microsoft clients and Novell servers. The clients don't need any client software for NetWare networks, because the server will translate the requests to and from the NetWare servers. Check with a knowledgeable Windows NT administrator before upgrading NT servers with GSNW to determine whether the upgrade is a good idea for the company's particular needs.

One more note on this subject: You can't administer NDS with any of the Microsoft clients; you must use a Novell client, preferably the Novell Client.

NetWare Client 32   If NetWare Client 32 is already set up on workstations, you're in luck—this will be an easy upgrade. You should, however, check the version of Client 32 that is installed. Several beta versions and versions for previous versions of NetWare have been available, and should be replaced with the shipping version of the Novell Client. You'll be assured of a consistent and stable network if you upgrade to the Novell Client at these workstations.

Other Considerations

Besides the version of client software that is currently running, there are several other questions you will need to ask the client to plan the migration process for workstations:

- Is bindery access needed? If users need to attach to a NetWare 3.1*x* server or use an application that requires bindery access, they can still use the Novell Client or the DOS Requester. These clients also support bindery connections.

- Should the SMS (Storage Management System) client be installed? This option is available from the client installation program, and installs the TSA (Target Service Agent) that allows backup of workstation data from the server. Ideally, you should keep all data on the network so that this is not necessary.

- Is highly sensitive information sent across the network? If so, you might want to consider turning on the NCP packet signature features provided by NetWare 5 and the client software.

- Who manages the workstations? You may need to train an administrator or other local user in the procedures for installing the client software, so that new clients will be configured consistently.

- Which protocols (IP and/or IPX) are being used? You will need to install them at the client and at the server. This also includes (for IPX) differing frame types, such as Ethernet_802.2 and Ethernet_802.3.

- Will SNMP (Simple Network Management Protocol) be used? If so, you will need to enable it when you install the Novell Client. For the DOS Requester, you'll need to install the following VLMs, which may not be installed automatically by the client install program:

  - MIB21F.VLM

  - WSASNI.VLM

  - WSREG.VLM

  - WSSNMP.VLM

> ▪ WSTRAP.VLM
>
> ▪ NMR.VLM

- Are performance enhancements needed? You may want to turn on LIP (Large Internet Packets) and Packet Burst Protocol. These protocols are supported automatically by the Novell Client and the DOS Requester; be sure you are using version 1.20 or greater of the VLM.EXE program if you are using the DOS Requester.

- Will NDPS, remote access, or remote control be used? If so, be sure the client portion of the desired options is installed during the installation of the Novell Client.

The Client Upgrade Process

Now that you understand the factors involved in upgrading clients to the latest software, Procedure 21.1 details the steps you should follow in planning and implementing the new client software.

PROCEDURE 21.1

Overview of the Client Upgrade Process

The specific details for upgrading clients are beyond the scope of this section, but these are the general steps to follow:

1. Survey the existing workstations. Make a note of the following information, which you can use in documenting the network and in determining the type of client software that is needed:

   - Operating systems: DOS, Windows, Windows 95/98, Windows NT, OS/2, etcetera. Also note the version number. You may wish to consider an operating system upgrade along with the client software upgrade.

   - Current network software: the shell, DOS Requester, or the Novell Client. Typing **NVER** at the DOS prompt will provide a quick look at version numbers for NetWare software. Note whether the ODI architecture is being used. The output of NVER is shown here.

PROCEDURE 21.1 (CONTINUED)

- The network board installed in the machine. You should be able to view the messages generated as the client software loads, or type **IPX /V** to determine the type of network card without opening the machine. For Windows 95/98, look in either Device Manager ➤ Network Adapters or Control Panel ➤ Network. For Windows NT machines, look in either Windows NT Diagnostics or Control Panel ➤ Network.

- Batch files (AUTOEXEC.BAT and STARTNET.BAT). Print a copy of both of these for future reference.

- Also print a copy of the NET.CFG file and the CONFIG.SYS file.

2. Decide upon an effective migration method. You should try migrating several workstations to determine whether there will be problems upgrading. Be sure to save a copy of the old client software first, in case you need to put it back in place. The following are some potential migration methods:

   - Run the Novell Client Setup program over the network. If you have copied the client software to the server, you may find the upgrade goes much easier. The typical path for the client files is SYS:PUBLIC\ CLIENT*platform*, where *platform* is Win95, Win31, or WinNT.

   - Create a custom batch file that upgrades the software. Again, this could be run manually or from a login script that checks whether the new client is installed already.

   - The simplest method, in many cases, is to use the Automatic Client Upgrade (ACU) feature of the Novell Client. Refer to the online documentation for details, but this is a simple process to upgrade many workstations.

PROCEDURE 21.1 (CONTINUED)

3. Edit INSTALL.CFG (DOS and Windows 3.1), NWSETUP.INI (Windows 95/98), or UNATTEND.TXT (Windows NT), if desired. If there are certain parameters you wish to include in all installations, edit the appropriate file before installing any client software. You'll find more information on these files in the online documentation.

4. Inform administrators of the results, and provide copies of software. If the administrators will be performing the client upgrade, be sure you provide them with the latest copy of the DOS Requester (if needed) and the Novell Client, or let them know where the files are on the network.

5. Plan to train users if necessary. Although client software should be transparent to the user, note the login process before and after migration on a workstation and determine whether you need to have the user perform any steps differently when logging in. Some users, for example, may be running IPX and NETX manually when they turn on the computer. You should set up their workstations to run the appropriate client automatically.

6. Perform the actual upgrade. Note that you can actually do this before you upgrade the server, since all of the clients (including the DOS Requester and the Novell Client) can be used to access bindery servers. When you perform the upgrade, keep a log of any problems you encounter.

The process of installing client software is explained in detail in Chapter 2.

Planning Server Migration

Once you've upgraded the clients, you should create a plan and schedule to migrate or upgrade existing servers to NetWare 5. This is a more complicated process, and requires careful planning. The actual server migration process is explained in Chapter 7. The following section provides a summary of the migration options you have to choose from.

Overview: Migration and Upgrade Options

Depending on the additional hardware you'll need to support a new NetWare 5 server, you may wish to consider a new machine. If you keep the existing machine, follow these guidelines:

Memory   NetWare 5 requires a minimum of 64MB of memory (128MB for Java).

Disk storage   You should have at least 35MB free on the DOS partition and 450MB free on the SYS volume.

Processor   If your processor is a 386 or a slow 486, or if it is bogged down running the current software, you may wish to consider a new machine.

Other hardware   Other necessities include a high-speed bus, high-speed network and disk controller cards, VGA video and VGA monitor, and a CD-ROM drive. You may also want to install a mouse (at least for the duration of the installation).

Types of Upgrades

The first consideration when upgrading is the type of upgrade you will use. There are actually four methods of upgrading (see Chapter 7 for more information on these upgrading methods):

Install Wizard   This is the easiest method of upgrading. You simply run the install program from the NetWare 5 installation CD-ROM. This method works for NetWare 3.1x and 4.1x servers only. The NetWare 5 files are installed over NetWare 3.1x or 4.1x files. Users, trustee rights, and all other information are converted to NetWare 5 format.

Upgrade Wizard   Here you install a brand new NetWare 5 server on a new machine, adding it to the network. You then use the Upgrade Wizard utility to copy all data, users, and trustee assignments from the old server to the new server. You can model the changes before they are committed, using a drag-and-drop interface. Once you're sure the new server is operational, you can bring the old server down and start using the new one. This utility is not installed by default; you can install it by running this file from the Novell Operating System CD (where *D* is the drive letter of your workstation's CD-ROM drive):

D:\PRODUCTS\UPGRDWZD\UPGRDWZD.EXE

What You'll Need to Know

Once again, there are a variety of questions you should ask your consulting client before you can create the migration plan. Here are items you will need information about:

- Which versions of NetWare are running on servers?

- Are other types of NOS being used on any servers, and will they also need to be migrated to NetWare 5?

- What resources are available for testing? In an ideal situation, you'll set up a dedicated network lab, with extra servers, workstations, and network wiring, where you can test the migration process in detail. This may not be practical for some companies, particularly those that are small, on a tight budget, or on a tight schedule.

- Which type of migration will be used? You should decide which one of the migration options, described in the previous section, will be best for each of the servers and discuss this with your client.

Steps in the Server Migration Process

Procedure 21.2 outlines the steps you should take to plan and perform the migration process. This is a general guideline; the specific steps will depend on the type of migration method you are using.

PROCEDURE 21.2

The Server Migration Process

To migrate a server to NetWare 5, follow these guidelines:

1. Survey the current servers. Make a note of the NOS versions they are running and the hardware they are using. Some servers may require hardware upgrades to support NetWare 5.

2. Set up a test lab if possible. You should use this lab to test migration on servers and clients, to isolate problems, and to train administrators in the migration process.

3. Schedule downtime for each department to be upgraded.

4. Choose a migration method from the choices discussed above for each server.

5. Obtain the required NetWare 5 software and licenses. You will need at least one license disk for each server. NetWare 3 and 4 licenses do not work with NetWare 5.

6. Migrate a single department as a pilot. Keep it in a separate Directory tree for now. Follow the migration procedure described below; you may wish to modify this procedure based on your findings with the pilot department. Typically you will want to migrate the IS department first.

7. Train users in the pilot department on all information they will need to know to access the new network efficiently.

8. Schedule migrations for the other departments, and perform them.

For each migration, you will perform the steps listed in Procedure 21.3. More details for the migration process are given in Chapter 7.

PROCEDURE 21.3

Migrating Servers

To upgrade a server, follow these general steps:

1. Schedule time for the people you'll need to assist in the upgrade—network administrators, assistants, and so on.

2. Clean up the bindery on NetWare 3.1*x* servers by running BINDFIX twice and deleting any unnecessary objects.

3. Back up the server and any workstations that hold critical data.

4. Perform the actual migration process. Keep a log of any problems you encounter, and modify the migration process for any future servers if necessary.

Merging NDS Trees

If you have multiple NDS trees, you may want to merge them at some point. The timing may be especially good if you can plan to do this as you upgrade to NetWare 5. In this section, we will review the process of merging two trees together, including the steps, tools involved, and NDS rights and partition issues.

Utilities Needed and Their Purpose

You will need the following tools to merge two trees:

- A backup utility, such as Enhanced SBACKUP, to back up the NDS trees on both original trees. The data should be backed up as well for greater security should something go wrong. More information on Enhanced SBACKUP can be found in Chapter 10.

- EDIT or MONITOR, to update all necessary time synchronization parameters. Information on time synchronization can be found in Chapter 20.

- NDS Manager, in particular the Schema Manager portion, to verify that the schema is the same on both trees and to update one or the other if they are not. NDS Manager was covered in Chapter 15.

- DSMERGE, to actually merge the two trees (described below).

- NetWare Administrator (along with NDS Manager), to verify that the trees were merged successfully and to reorganize and clean up the combined tree.

Steps Involved

The process of merging two trees can be divided into four phases, namely:

1. Preparation

2. Merging

3. Verification of successful merge

4. Cleanup of partitions, replicas, objects, and so on

Each of these four phases will be discussed in the following sections.

Preparation   The first phase is preparation, which is crucial for a successful outcome. The steps involved in this phase are outlined in Procedure 21.4.

Preparing to Merge Two Trees

Before you actually merge two trees, you need to complete the following steps:

1. Back up at least the two NDS trees, and preferably the data on all of the servers in the trees as well. The chances of anything going wrong are fairly small, and the chances that you would have to resort to a tape backup even smaller, but you can't be too careful when you are talking about your company's network (and your job!).

2. Make sure that time is properly synchronized on and between the two trees. You will also need to determine a combined time strategy for the two trees.

3. Verify that the same version of DS.NLM is used on all servers in both trees and that the two schemas are identical. If they are not, use NDS Manager to update the version of DS.NLM and/or synchronize the schema between the trees. Note that schema synchronization may need to take place in both directions; both trees must have the same schema before they can be merged.

4. Be sure that the top-level containers have unique names. The trees can't be merged if duplicate container names exist at this level.

5. Refer to the "Pre-merge Partitioning Guidelines" section below and make any recommended changes.

Merging   This is the phase that may be new to you; it hasn't really been covered up to this point. Merging is a simple process. Before we begin, however, you need to understand two terms, *source tree* and *target tree*. The source tree is the tree that will be going away; it is being merged into the target tree. The steps to merge two trees are described in Procedure 21.5.

Merging Two Trees

To merge the source tree into the target tree, follow these steps:

1. Begin by loading DSMERGE on the server in the source tree that has the master replica of the [Root] partition. The DSMERGE main menu will appear, as shown here.

PROCEDURE 21.5 (CONTINUED)

2. Choose Check Time Synchronization to ensure that all of the servers in both trees are in sync.

3. Choose Merge Two Trees to bring up the dialog box shown here:

4. You will see that the source tree is filled in for you. You simply need to enter the administrator's distinguished name and password. The administrator account you choose must have the Supervisor object right to the [Root] of the tree.

5. Move down to the Target Tree field using the down-arrow key, and then press Enter to select the target tree. Remember, this is the tree that will continue to exist when you have completed the process of merging the two trees.

6. You will need to enter the target tree's administrator's distinguished name and password as well. As before, this account must have the Supervisor object right to [Root].

7. When you have finished, press F10 to actually merge the trees. You will be prompted with several dialog boxes that outline the process, including one last check to make sure that everything is in order; if not, you can change your mind and halt the process. After you confirm that you want to proceed, the two trees will be merged together and, at the end of the process, the source tree will no longer exist.

Verification of Successful Merge   Now that the two trees have been merged together, you should make sure that all went well. This is a simple task, but one that is necessary to make sure that NDS has caught up before cleaning up the new tree. The simplest way to do this is to start NDS Manager, select the server that you performed the merge from in the source tree, and verify that the state is On for all of the replicas. You should repeat this process for the server that holds the master replica of the target tree as well. An example screen is shown below in Figure 21.1.

F I G U R E   21.1

NDS Manager
showing the state is
On for all replicas on
the server

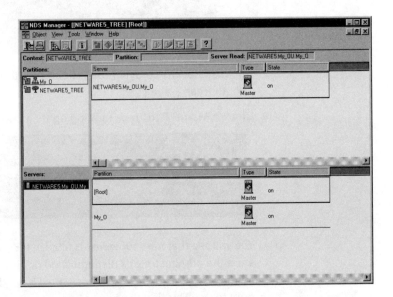

Cleanup of Partitions, Replicas, and So On   Once you have verified that the merge has been successful, you are ready to execute the last step, cleanup. This phase includes any or all of the following components (depending on your individual situation):

- Create, delete, move, and/or rename any container objects necessary to get the basic NDS structure in place. You may also want to standardize the names of objects at this point, as per the naming standards document you created early in the design phase. (The naming standards document was discussed in Chapter 18.)

- Update any login scripts, Bindery Services contexts, and so on that referred to the original tree, or any containers that were modified in any way in the previous step.

- Update the workstations to use any new context, tree, or server information necessary for the individual client. If you moved containers and you left an alias in place of the original object, they can still use the old context until you get them updated.

- Create, modify, or remove trustees from the new [Root] object as necessary. This will depend on your security guidelines and standards, as well as the administrative approach that you chose earlier in the process.

Congratulations! You have now successfully merged two trees.

Remaining Issues

Fortunately, there are only a few remaining issues to deal with at this point. The first has to do with NDS rights. The trustees of the source tree's [Root] object will be lost, except for the administrator, who will have the Supervisor object right to the [Root] of the target tree. You will need to either reassign those trustees rights in the new tree or, if you haven't merged the tree yet, you may also assign those trustees the same rights to the top-level containers directly under [Root]. All of the trustee assignments in the source tree are retained, except for trustees of the [Root] of the source tree, so if you take the latter approach, nothing will be lost.

The second issue that needs to be addressed is partition and replica placement. The following things happen when two trees are merged with regard to partitions and replicas thereof:

- All container objects under the source tree's [Root] object become partition roots. This makes the synchronization process faster and more efficient during the merging process.

- All servers in the source tree that have a replica of [Root] lose it, except for the server that holds the master replica. In exchange, however, they are given the same type of replica for each of the top-level container objects under [Root], so they still have all of the same object data.

- The source tree's server that held the master replica of [Root] will receive a read/write replica of the new [Root].

- All of the servers in the target tree that held a replica of [Root] get a copy of the new [Root] partition.

- Subordinate reference partitions are created as needed by NetWare.

Refer to the pre-merge partitioning guidelines in the next section for ways to minimize the impact of merging the two trees.

Pre-merge Partitioning Guidelines To minimize the disturbance to the network from merging the trees, follow these guidelines:

- Merge the tree that has less objects *in the [Root] partition* into the other tree. In other words, the former tree should be the source tree and the latter the target tree.

- Use the same top-level container names in both trees so that the context of objects won't change after the merge.

- Change the name of the top-level containers just before the merge.

- Move the second-level containers under the target tree's matching top-level containers, so that the context of objects doesn't change.

- Delete the temporary top-level containers that came from the source tree after the merge is complete.

Summary

All of the foregoing steps and issues to merge two trees can be summarized by looking at the before and after views of the network, as illustrated in Figures 21.2 and 21.3. The NDS rights before and after the merge, with example user .Admin.Pool (her distinguished name) performing the merge, are summarized in Table 21.1.

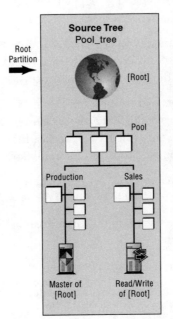
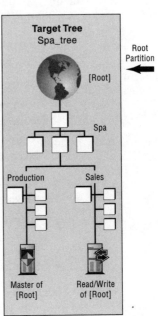

FIGURE 21.2

The two trees before they are merged

FIGURE 21.3

The final product of merging two trees

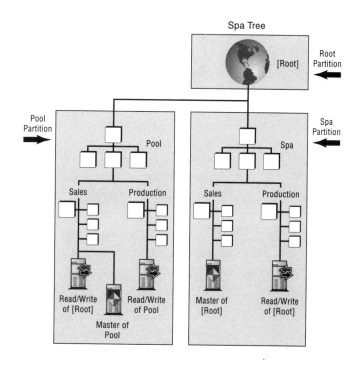

TABLE 21.1: NDS Object Rights Summary Results of Merging the Trees Depicted in Figure 21.2.

Name	NDS Object Rights Before				NDS Object Rights After		
	Pool_tree		Spa_tree		Spa_tree		
	[Root]	Pool	[Root]	Spa	[Root]	Pool	Spa
.Admin.Pool	SBCDR				S		
.Assistant.Pool	BCDR	S				S	
.Admin.Spa			SBCDR		SBCDR		
.Assistant.Spa			BR	BCDR	BR		BCDR

WAN Traffic Manager

WAN Traffic Manager is a new tool in NetWare 5. This tool allows you to control how NDS uses WAN bandwidth. It is implemented as a snap-in to NetWare Administrator, and allows you to set policies on how NetWare will use WAN bandwidth for NDS and apply those policies to servers or groups of servers of your choice. The policies that you will enforce do *not* affect traffic initiated by administrators or users, but rather housekeeping tasks by NDS and synchronization of replicas. They also do not affect data transfers or time synchronization traffic.

This section will focus on three things relating to WAN Traffic Manager: components, predefined policies, and implementation.

Components

WAN Traffic Manager has three components:

WTM.NLM   This is the NLM on each server that decides whether or not to send NDS traffic, based on various policies.

WAN Traffic Policies   These rules control what traffic is sent when. You may use predefined policies (described next), modify existing policies, or write your own. These policies can then be applied to servers, either directly or through LAN Area objects, which serve the same function for servers as groups do for users.

NetWare Administrator Snap-In   This is the component that lets you set and maintain all of the policies through NetWare Administrator.

Predefined Policies

Table 21.2 lists some of the predefined policies that ship with NetWare. You can use them as is or you can modify them to suit your needs. You can also use them as starting points to write your own policies. As stated previously, and which bears repeating here, the policies that you will enforce affect only traffic generated by NDS housekeeping tasks and synchronization of replicas.

T A B L E 21.2:   Some of the Predefined WAN Traffic Manager Policies

Policy Name	Purpose
1-3AM	Restricts traffic to 1 to 3 A.M. only.
7AM-6PM	Restricts traffic to 7 A.M. to 6 P.M. only.

T A B L E 21.2:   Some of the Predefined WAN Traffic Manager Policies *(continued)*

Policy Name	Purpose
CostLT20	Allows you to restrict traffic to those servers that have a cost of less than 20. You can set costs to control traffic across slow or congested WAN links. The cost can be in any units you like, as long as they are consistent throughout the network. For more information, refer to the online documentation.
IPX	Restricts traffic to IPX only.
IP	Restricts traffic to IP only.
SameArea	Restricts traffic to the same external network number as this server, to the same first three octets of the IP address of this server, or both. This policy is designed to keep traffic on the local LAN only. You would need some mechanism to get traffic out of the LAN to other sites, such as a server in the site without this restriction to act as a bridgehead server.

Implementation

This section is not intended to be a detailed description on how and why to create policies and assign them to servers, but rather a brief overview of the process. To assign the same policies to a group of servers, you will need to create LAN Area objects. You create these objects like any other object. The properties of the object can be configured using the tabs on the right side of the LAN Area dialog box, shown in Figure 21.4. The Servers Belonging to LAN Area tab is where you assign the servers that you want to have the same policies; you'll notice in Figure 21.4 that the NetWare 5 server is on this list. This tab is analogous to the Members tab for a group. The Cost tab is where you specify the cost to communicate with other networks (not individual servers). You can also specify a default cost on this tab. The final tab we'll cover here is WAN Policies. This is the tab where you can select the policies that you want to put in effect. By clicking the Advanced button on the WAN Policies page, you can modify how they behave. These same three tabs appear on each server as well. Figure 21.5 shows the NetWare Server dialog box and its object properties tabs, with the WAN Policies tab selected. This tab can be used to apply policies to individual servers.

F I G U R E 21.4

Use the buttons on the
right side of the screen
to configure LAN Area
object properties.

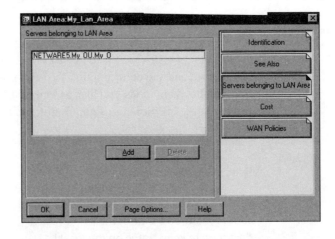

F I G U R E 21.5

The NetWare Server
dialog box with the
WAN Policies tab
selected

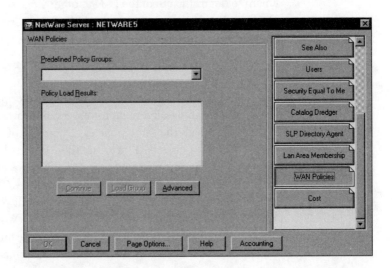

A sample policy, the 1-3AM policy, contains the following text:

```
/* This policy limits all traffic to between 1 and 3 am */

LOCAL BOOLEAN Selected;

SELECTOR
    Selected := Now.hour >= 1 AND Now.hour < 3;
```

```
    IF Selected THEN
       RETURN 50; /* between 1am and 3am this policy has a high
priority */
    ELSE
       RETURN 1;  /* return 1 instead of 0 in case there are no
other policies */
                     /* if no policies return > 0, WanMan assumes
SEND */
    END
END

PROVIDER
  IF Selected THEN
    RETURN SEND; /* between 1am and 3am, SEND */
  ELSE
    RETURN DONT_SEND; /* other times, don't */
  END
END
```

While policy modifications are beyond the scope of this book, as you can see the program code is not overly complicated. For more information on WAN Traffic Manager, refer to the online documentation.

Implementing NetWare 5

You've come a long way up to this point in the book—you've planned all aspects of the network, the Directory tree, and the file structure. The final step is to actually implement NetWare 5. In the following sections, we will discuss the various methods of implementing NetWare 5 and the process of scheduling the final implementation.

NDS Implementation Review

In a new company, it is possible to plan and create an NDS tree structure and allow it to grow with the company. For existing networks, however, it is important to plan the implementation of NDS on the network.

By choosing and planning an *implementation strategy*, you can minimize the impact on users and the network, and take advantage of the features of NDS as quickly as possible. The best implementation strategy will depend on the Directory tree structure you have chosen.

Implementing NDS by Location or Function

You can implement NDS separately for each of the upper-level divisions of the Directory tree. In this strategy, you use a separate Directory tree for each location or division. These trees should eventually be merged together so that you can have the global benefits of NDS.

You should follow these guidelines when creating Directory trees for upper-level divisions:

- Each tree should include the same Organization name at the top. This facilitates merging later. If you want to preserve the location or division name, be sure to include an Organizational Unit below the Organization for the purpose. This allows the division to be easily moved when it becomes part of a larger tree.

- Each tree must use a unique tree name (assigned during installation).

A Directory tree that was designed with these ideas in mind is shown in Figure 21.6.

When separate trees have been created for divisions, you do not necessarily need to merge them. It is possible to keep separate Directory trees on the network, as long as they have different names. However, separate trees have the following disadvantages:

- It is difficult to manage all of the trees from a central location. The administrator must log in separately to each tree to manage its resources.

- Security must be set up separately for each tree. Users who will perform administration will need a User object in each tree.

- Users who require access to resources in different trees will need to log in to a single tree, attaching to the rest through Bindery Services if using older clients, or typing in usernames and contexts in each tree with the Novell Client.

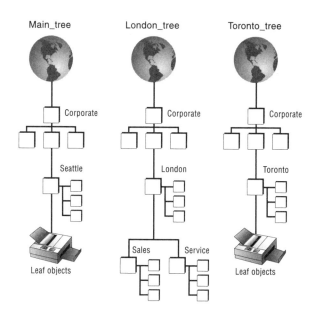

A Directory tree designed with future merging in mind

Although you lose the global advantages of NDS, multiple trees may be a practical solution for companies that have separate administrators for each location and require little communication between locations.

Implementing NDS for the Entire Organization

The *organizational* approach is the other method for implementing NDS. This method is a bit drastic—you create a tree structure for the entire organization at once. This is also referred to as the *top-down* or *all-at-once* strategy. This strategy immediately gives you the full benefits of a global Directory structure. However, it may not be practical for your purposes. In order to implement NDS across the entire organization, your network must meet the following requirements:

- There must be full connectivity between locations, via a LAN or WAN.

- All network administrators must be available to plan and implement the changes.

- The Directory tree structure for the entire organization must be planned at the same time.

Combining Implementation Strategies

When the organizational approach is not a practical solution, a combination of the two strategies may be the best solution. A central tree structure can be created for the entire organization, and individual departments or divisions can be created with their own tree. You can then merge these trees with the central tree when they are ready.

Scheduling Network Implementation

The final step before you perform the NetWare 5 installation is to schedule the implementation. This applies to new servers as well as migrated servers. You should set dates for all of the tasks involved in the project, which may include the following:

- Meet with the management and network administrators to plan the project.
- Upgrade existing clients.
- Upgrade existing servers.
- Install new servers as needed.
- Implement NDS in separate departments.
- Merge Directory trees to create a complete network structure.
- Test the network and optimize it if necessary.
- Train all users and administrators.

Depending on the specific needs of your network and users, other tasks may be required.

Conclusion

Congratulations! Now that you have come this far, all you need to do is pass the exams and get a contract. Remember, particularly for the "NDS Design and Implementation" exam, you must look at both the big picture and the minute implementation details. Refer to the Introduction for our studying recommendations and for information on registering for CNE tests.

Review

This chapter discussed how to plan and schedule migration to Net-Ware 5 for existing clients and servers on a network, and how to schedule the implementation of NetWare 5 and NDS for a new network.

Migrating Clients

You will need to answer the following questions before planning the migration of clients:

- What version of client software is currently running?
- Is bindery access needed?
- Should the SMS (Storage Management System) TSA (Target Service Agent) be installed?
- Is highly sensitive information sent across the network?
- Who manages the workstations?
- Which protocols are being used?
- Will SNMP (Simple Network Management Protocol) be used?
- Are performance enhancements needed?

The client migration process includes these steps:

1. Survey the existing workstations. Make a note of the following information, which you can use in documenting the network and in determining the type of client software that is needed:

   - Operating systems
   - Current network software
   - The network board installed in the machine
   - Batch files (AUTOEXEC.BAT and STARTNET.BAT)
   - The CONFIG.SYS file

2. Decide upon an effective migration method. You should try migrating several workstations to determine whether there will be problems upgrading.

3. Edit the appropriate automation file, if desired.

4. Inform administrators of the results, and provide them with copies of the software.

5. Plan to train users if needed.

6. Perform the actual upgrade.

Migrating Servers

After preparing the clients, you should create a plan and schedule to migrate or upgrade existing servers to NetWare 5. This is a more complicated process, and requires careful planning. You will need to choose one of the following migration options for each server:

- Install Wizard
- Upgrade Wizard

Here are the basic steps for migration:

1. Survey the current servers. Make a note of the NOS versions they are running and the hardware they are using. Some servers may require hardware upgrades to support NetWare 5.

2. Set up a test lab if possible.

3. Schedule downtime for each department that will be upgraded.

4. Choose a migration method for each server.

5. Obtain the required NetWare 5 software and licenses.

6. Migrate a single department as a pilot.

7. Train users in the pilot department on all information they will need to know to access the new network efficiently.

8. Schedule migrations for the other departments, and perform them.

Merging Two NDS Trees

You can merge two NDS trees together if needed. The source tree will become part of the target tree. There are four basic phases to the process:

1. Preparation
2. Merging
3. Verification of successful merge
4. Cleanup of partitions, replicas, objects, and so on

You will need several tools to accomplish the upgrade, including these:

- DSMERGE, the NLM that actually merges the trees
- NDS Manager to verify schemas, verify that the merge was successful, and move containers
- A backup utility capable of backing up NDS
- NetWare Administrator to clean up the tree

WAN Traffic Manager

You can use WAN Traffic Manager to manage NDS traffic on the WAN. This is not the same kind of traffic that you or users generate, but rather traffic caused by various housekeeping tasks and synchronization processes. Various policies can be applied to groups of servers via the LAN Area object or to individual servers directly through the server's properties.

Implementation

The process of implementation will depend on the strategy you use—a location-based or functional strategy, which installs separate Directory trees for each location or function, or an organizational strategy, which implements NDS across the entire network. The location-based strategy is often the most practical. Here are the basic steps for implementing NDS and NetWare 5:

- Meet with the management and network administrators to plan the project.
- Upgrade existing clients.
- Upgrade existing servers.

- Install new servers as needed.

- Implement NDS in separate locations or departments.

- Merge Directory trees to create a complete network structure.

- Test the network and optimize it if necessary.

- Train all users and administrators.

Depending on the specific needs of the users, other tasks may be needed.

CNE Practice Test Questions

1. Which of the following is *not* a client provided by Novell?

    A. NETX

    B. CSNW

    C. VLM

    D. Client 32

2. Which client *doesn't* support NDS?

    A. VLM

    B. Client 32

    C. The Novell Client

    D. NETX

3. Which of these describes the Upgrade Wizard? (Choose all that apply.)

    A. Used for upgrading from NT to Novell

    B. Lets you model what NDS will look like before you upgrade

    C. Leaves the original server intact; requires two servers

    D. Upgrades the old server directly; requires only the server to be upgraded

4. Which tools can be used to merge two NDS trees? (Choose all that apply.)

   A. DSMERGE

   B. DSCOMBINE

   C. NDS Manager

   D. NetWare Administrator

5. The purpose of WAN Traffic Manager is:

   A. To control NDS housekeeping and synchronization traffic across WAN links

   B. To control data traffic across the WAN

   C. To control all NDS traffic over WAN links

   D. To control all traffic across WAN links

6. The tools required to merge two trees together include all of the following *except*:

   A. DSMERGE

   B. NDS Manager

   C. NetWare Administrator

   D. ConsoleOne

7. Considerations when upgrading a workstation do *not* include:

   A. Bindery Services

   B. Backups

   C. Electrical hookups

   D. Security

APPENDICES

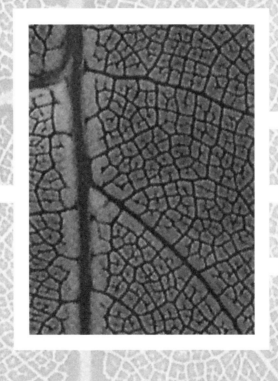

APPENDIX

A

Answers to Practice Test Questions

Chapter 1 Answers

1. The MONITOR utility:

A. Allows you to create and delete users

B. Allows you to set server parameters

C. Installs a new NetWare 5 server

D. Allows management of NDS

Answer: B

2. Network time synchronization:

A. Applies to workstations only

B. Applies to workstations and servers

C. Is used by older versions of NetWare

D. Sets the server's time from the workstation

Answer: B

3. NetWare 5 supports an IP-only implementation.

A. True

B. False

Answer: A

4. Which protocol takes priority in time synchronization across IP and IPX?

A. NTP

B. NSS

C. SLP

D. NDS

Answer: A

5. The protocol that provides the discovery of services and its registration over an IP network is called:

A. Service Advertising Protocol

B. Service Locator Protocol

C. Novell Services Protocol

D. Novell Directory Services

Answer: B

6. Remote access services for NetWare 5 is provided by:

A. RAS server

B. NIAS

C. BorderManager

D. DHCP

Answer: B

7. NetWare Peripheral Architecture (NPA):

A. Is a new method of using disk drivers

B. Controls all peripherals on the network

C. Allows expanded access to printers

D. Allows the server to use legacy peripherals

Answer: A

8. The online documentation provided with NetWare 5 is called:

A. Novell online documentation

B. DynaText

C. Netscape

D. ElectroText

Answer: A

9. The two main types of security in NetWare 5 are:

A. MHS security and NLS security

B. Hardware security and software security

C. NDS security and file system security

D. NDPS security and NCP security

Answer: C

10. The memory protection feature:

A. Protects the server's memory from errant users

B. Protects the server's core operating system files from errant NLMs

C. Protects workstation memory from NLM access

D. Protects workstation memory from power outages

Answer: B

11. The client software for DOS workstations is:

A. The NetWare DOS Controller

B. Novell DOS

C. The NetWare DOS Requester

D. Diverse client software

Answer: C

12. SCRSAVER.NLM locks the server console.

  A. True

  B. False

  Answer: A

13. _____ provides additional addressable memory space than physically available in RAM, by allocating disk space reserved for this purpose.

  A. Protected memory

  B. CACHE

  C. Compression

  D. Virtual memory

  Answer: D

14. _____ provides time synchronization in an IP-only or IP/IPX-based network.

  A. SAP

  B. NTP

  C. SNMP

  D. RIP

  Answer: B

15. _____ provides the capability for contextless logins.

  A. DHCP services

  B. DNS services

  C. Catalog services

  D. Remote Access services

  Answer: C

Chapter 2 Answers

1. Novell Directory Services (NDS):

  A. Stores information for each network resource

  B. Uses a tree-like structure

  C. Refers to each resource as an object

  D. All of the above

  Answer: D

2. Which of the following is *not* a benefit of NDS?

  A. Better organization of resources

  B. Fault tolerance

  C. An efficient file system

  D. Increased security

  Answer: C

3. The type of organization NDS uses is:

  A. Server-centric

  B. Network-centric

  C. Noncentralized

  D. Resource-centric

  Answer: B

4. The three basic types of NDS objects are:

  A. Container, Leaf, [Root]

  B. Properties, Values, Objects

  C. Organization, Organizational Unit, Country

  D. Typeless, typeful, distinguished

  Answer: A

5. The [Root] object:

  A. Can be located anywhere in the Directory

  B. Is at the top of the NDS tree and can't be modified

  C. Can be deleted when it is no longer needed

  D. All of the above

  Answer: B

6. Container objects include:

  A. Country, Group, Organization

  B. Organization, [Root], Group

  C. Country, Organization, Organizational Unit

  D. Organization and Group

  Answer: C

7. Leaf objects include:

   A. User, Group, Organization

   B. User, Printer, Resource

   C. User, Group, Profile

   D. All container objects, plus User

   Answer: C

8. NDS properties:

   A. Are the same for all objects

   B. Are used by container objects only

   C. Are all optional

   D. Can be assigned values

   Answer: D

9. An object's name along with its full context is:

   A. Its distinguished name

   B. Its relative distinguished name

   C. Its common name

   D. Its context name

   Answer: A

10. An object's context is:

   A. Any object in the same container

   B. The container object it resides in and the container's container and so on up to the [Root]

   C. Its common name

   D. The name of the Directory tree

   Answer: B

11. A relative distinguished name:

   A. Begins at the [Root] object

   B. Begins at the current context

   C. Begins with the first Organization object

   D. Uses the default system context (DSC)

   Answer: B

12. Which is an example of a *typeless* name?

   A. CN=FRED.OU=ACCT.O=ORION

   B. CN=FRED

   C. FRED.ACCT.ORION

   D. CN=FRED.ACCT.O=ORION

   Answer: C

13. The protocol(s) usually used with NetWare is/are:

   A. VLM

   B. IPXODI

   C. IPX

   D. TCP/IP

   E. Answers A and B

   F. Answers C and D

   Answer: F

14. Until you log in, the only files you can access on the network are:

   A. LOGIN.EXE and client software

   B. All files in the PUBLIC directory

   C. All files in the LOGIN directory

   D. All files on the SYS: volume

   Answer: C

15. Which is the correct order of a NetWare server's file system organization?

   A. Directory, file, volume

   B. Volume, directory, file

   C. File, volume, directory

   D. File, directory, NDS

   Answer: B

16. The NDIR utility:

   A. Must be used in place of the DOS DIR command

   B. Lists files in the current directory

   C. Lists information about NDS objects

   D. All of the above

   Answer: B

17. The NLIST utility:

   A. Can be used to list volumes or other NDS objects

   B. Displays a list of files in the current directory

   C. Is another name for NDIR

   D. Was used in NetWare 3

   Answer: A

18. Which is the correct syntax to map drive F: to the SYS:PUBLIC directory?

   A. MAP F: SYS\PUBLIC

   B. MAP SYS:PUBLIC /D=F

   C. MAP SYS:PUBLIC=F:

   D. MAP F:=SYS:PUBLIC

   Answer: D

Chapter 3 Answers

1. The two utilities used to manage NDS objects are:

   A. NetWare Administrator and NWADMN32

   B. ConsoleOne and NetWare Administrator

   C. SYSCON and NETADMIN

   D. NDSADMIN and NWMANAGE

   Answer: B

2. The Create function in NetWare Administrator is found on:

   A. The File menu

   B. The Function menu

   C. The Actions menu

   D. The Object menu

   Answer: D

3. The required properties when creating a User object are:

   A. Login name and address

   B. First name and last name

   C. Login name and last name

   D. Network address and first name

   Answer: C

4. A Template object:

   A. Is created for each user

   B. Specifies defaults for new User objects

   C. Lets you classify the context for new users created with this Template

   D. Lets you control access rights for groups

   Answer: B

5. The menu item used to display property values in NetWare Administrator is:

   A. Properties

   B. Values

   C. Attributes

   D. Details

   Answer: D

6. The Move option can move which types of objects?

   A. User, Server, and Group

   B. Container objects only

   C. Leaf objects only

   D. User objects only

   Answer: C

7. ConsoleOne can be used to manage:

   A. User objects only

   B. Only some basic NDS objects

   C. All NDS objects

   D. Bindery objects

   Answer: B

8. The Group object can group users:

   A. In the same container only

   B. In different containers only

   C. In the same or different containers

   D. In the [Root] container only

   Answer: C

9. To assign a user to an Organizational Role, you use the:

A. User's Role property

B. Organizational Role's Member property

C. User's Profile property

D. Organizational Role's Occupant property

Answer: D

10. The NetWare Server object:

A. Can be created when you wish to install a new server

B. Is created automatically when the server is installed

C. Is deleted automatically when the server is removed

D. Can be used to add logins to the server

Answer: B

11. The Alias object:

A. Represents, or points to, another object

B. Is created whenever an object is deleted

C. Can be used instead of the User object

D. All of the above

Answer: A

12. Which is a correct MAP command for the Directory Map DATA?

A. MAP F:=DATA:

B. MAP F:=DATA.MAP

C. MAP F:=DATA

D. MAP F: DATA /DM

Answer: C

13. Which objects are associated with the Novell Licensing Service (NLS)? (Choose all that apply.)

A. License Certificate

B. License Type

C. License Template

D. License Container

Answer: A and D

Chapter 4 Answers

1. The two types of NetWare 5 trustee rights are:

A. File system security and NDS security

B. File system security and object rights

C. Trustee rights and object rights

D. All Properties and Selected Properties

Answer: A

2. Which of the following cannot be a trustee?

A. Organization

B. User

C. Organizational Role

D. File

Answer: D

3. The File Scan right:

A. Allows you to copy files

B. Allows you to list files in a directory

C. Allows you to read the contents of files

D. Allows you to search for a file

Answer: B

4. The IRF affects:

A. Security equivalence

B. Inherited rights

C. Explicit assignments

D. All of the above

Answer: B

5. File attributes:

A. Are always set by NetWare itself

B. Are always set by the user

C. Cannot be changed

D. Give a file certain behaviors

Answer: D

6. You can manage file system security with:

A. NetWare Administrator

B. NETADMIN

C. SYSCON

D. SECURE

Answer: A

7. The IRF lists:

A. Rights to be blocked

B. Rights to be granted

C. Rights allowed to be inherited

D. Rights that cannot be inherited

Answer: C

8. The list of trustees for an object is stored in:

A. The Object Trustees property, also known as the ACL

B. The Trustee database

C. The Trustee file

D. Both A and B

E. Both A and C

Answer: A

9. The two types of rights in NDS are:

A. Object rights and file rights

B. Object rights and property rights

C. All Properties and Selected Properties

D. Object rights and the IRF

Answer: B

10. Inherited rights can be blocked with:

A. The IRF

B. An explicit assignment

C. Both A and B

D. None of the above

Answer: C

11. Explicit security equivalences can be granted with:

A. Container occupancy

B. Group, Organizational Role, Security Equal To

C. Group, container occupancy

D. All of the above

Answer: B

12. Which of the following does *not* have an impact on effective NDS rights?

A. Explicit rights

B. Inherited rights

C. Rights given to child objects

D. Rights given to parent objects

Answer: C

13. The [Public] trustee:

A. Assigns rights to all users when logged in

B. Assigns rights to anyone attached to the network

C. Assigns rights to Admin only

D. Assigns rights to the file system only

Answer: B

Chapter 5 Answers

1. Which is the correct order for login script execution?

A. User, container, default, profile

B. Container, user, profile or default

C. Container, profile, user or default

D. Container, default, user or profile

Answer: C

2. The container login script is executed:

A. For each container the user is in

B. For the user's parent container

C. For the profile container only

D. For the [Root] container only

Answer: B

3. Which is a properly formatted MAP command for a login script?

A. MAP F:=SYS:APPS

B. #MAP F:=SYS:APPS

C. MAP F=SYS:APPS

D. MAP F:=SYS

Answer: A

4. The INCLUDE command:

   A. Exits the login script and starts another

   B. Executes another script, then returns

   C. Adds commands to a login script

   D. Adds a login script to the Profile object

   Answer: B

5. Which of the following is *not* a valid comment?

   A. `REM Do not change this script`

   B. `***Do not change this script***`

   C. `# Do not change this script`

   D. `;Do not change this script`

   Answer: C

6. To use a DOS command in a login script:

   A. Include the name of the command only

   B. Include # and the name of the command

   C. Include a semicolon (;) and the name of the command

   D. Place the command in an INCLUDE file

   Answer: B

7. Two of the components of Application Launcher are:

   A. NAL and NAM

   B. AL and NMENU

   C. AE and Application objects

   D. AE and Windows 3.1

   Answer: C

8. AL runs under which operating systems?

   A. Windows 95

   B. Windows 3.1

   C. Windows NT

   D. All of the above

   Answer: D

9. Application objects for complex applications are created using which of the following tools?

   A. snAppShot

   B. NetWare Administrator

   C. APCONFIG

   D. Both A and B

   Answer: D

10. To give a user access to an application, modify:

   A. The User object's Application property

   B. The Application object's Association property

   C. Either A or B

   D. None of the above

   Answer: C

11. What kind of Policy Packages can be created?

   A. Container

   B. Workstation

   C. User

   D. All of the above

   Answer: D

12. User policies are *not* available for which operating systems?

   A. Windows 95

   B. Windows 3.x

   C. DOS

   D. Windows NT

   Answer: C

13. What do you have to do before you can take control of a remote workstation?

   A. Register the workstation

   B. Import the workstation

   C. Both A and B

   D. None of the above

   Answer: C

Chapter 6 Answers

1. What are the major components in NDPS Printing?

   A. Print Server, Print Queue, Printer

   B. Manager, Printer Agent, Gateway, Broker

   C. Manager, Printer Agent, Print Queue

   D. Gateway, Broker, Printer

Answer: B

2. What is the main responsibility of the NDPS Manager?

   A. Manage Printer Agents

   B. Manage printers

   C. Manage print queues

   D. None of the above

Answer: A

3. Which gateway ships with NDPS?

   A. Novell

   B. Xerox

   C. Hewlett-Packard

   D. All of the above

Answer: D

4. Which type(s) of printer can be created?

   A. Public Access

   B. Controlled Access

   C. Both of the above

   D. There is only one type of printer, simply called a printer

Answer: C

5. Which of the following is (or are) represented by an object in NDS? (Choose all correct answers.)

   A. Public Access printer

   B. Controlled Access printer

   C. Manager

   D. Broker

   E. Gateway

Answer: B, C, and D

6. The NDPS Manager Printer Agent List page lists:

   A. Public Access PAs

   B. Controlled Access PAs

   C. Both of the above

Answer: C

7. A Public Access printer is created with:

   A. NDPS Manager

   B. NetWare Administrator, as an object in the NDS tree

   C. Novell Printer Manager

   D. PCONSOLE

Answer: A

8. A new Controlled Access printer is created with:

   A. NDPS Manager

   B. NetWare Administrator, as an object in the NDS tree

   C. Novell Printer Manager

   D. PCONSOLE

Answer: B

9. Printers can be automatically installed on workstations by the administrator through:

   A. The NDPS Remote Printer Management page of printers or containers

   B. NDPS Manager

   C. Novell Printer Manager

   D. The Add Printer Wizard

Answer: A

10. Printers can be manually installed on workstations by the user through (choose all that apply):

   A. The Add Printer Wizard

   B. NDPS Manager

   C. Novell Printer Manager

   D. PCONSOLE

   E. Printers can't be installed by users

Answer: A and C

Chapter 7 Answers

1. Which item is *not* likely to need upgrading when you move to NetWare 5?

   A. The processor (CPU)

   B. Memory (RAM)

   C. Disk storage

   D. Network cabling

   Answer: D

2. Will a NetWare 5 server require more or less memory than a NetWare 3.*x* server?

   A. Less

   B. More

   C. It requires the same amount of memory

   D. It depends on the server

   Answer: B

3. Which upgrade is the most likely to require an entirely new machine?

   A. Memory

   B. Disk storage

   C. CPU

   D. Network card

   Answer: C

4. The minimum disk space for Netware 5 is approximately how much more than required for Netware 3.*x*?

   A. 180MB

   B. 100MB

   C. 75MB

   D. 32MB

   Answer: A

5. Which component does not affect the performance of the NetWare 5 server?

   A. Memory

   B. Floppy disk drive

   C. Network card

   D. Disk controller

   Answer: B

6. What speed of CPU do you need for NetWare 5?

   A. Pentium class

   B. 486 or higher

   C. 386 or higher

   D. 286 or higher

   Answer: A

7. Which software wizard is used for an across-the-wire migration?

   A. Install Wizard

   B. Upgrade Wizard

   Answer: B

8. If you were going to do a fresh install of NetWare 5 on a new machine, which wizard would you use?

   A. Install Wizard

   B. Upgrade Wizard

   Answer: A

9. All of the following should be considered when planning an upgrade, *except:*

   A. Hardware

   B. Size of the server room

   C. Software

   D. Preparing users for transition

   Answer: B

10. When installing NetWare 5 into an existing tree, you need to do which of the following to the 4.11 servers?

    A. Upgrade the DOS.NLM

    B. Upgrade the ROLLCALL.NLM

    C. Upgrade the NW32.NLM

    D. Upgrade the INSTALL.NLM

    Answer: B

11. When should you use DSRepair?

   A. When you want to repair a volume

   B. When upgrading from a version of NetWare 4.*x*

   C. When you find errors in the bindery

   D. When you want to use the BINDFIX

Answer: B

12. NetWare 5 defaults to a pure IP installation:

   A. True

   B. False

Answer: A

13. Which is the fastest method of upgrading?

   A. Install Wizard

   B. Upgrade Wizard

Answer: A

14. Using the Install Wizard involves each of the following *except:*

   A. Upgrading NDS

   B. Installing the license

   C. Selecting disk and network drivers

   D. Unloading the NLMs

Answer: D

15. To prepare a Windows 95 or Windows NT workstation to run the Upgrade Wizard, you need to do all of the following *except:*

   A. Install Client 32 version 2.2 or higher

   B. Update NLMs on the NetWare 3.*x* server

   C. Install NetWare Administrator on the workstation

   D. Reorganize the Organizational Units

Answer: D

16. Which software wizard allows for the safest installation of NetWare 5?

   A. Install Wizard

   B. Upgrade Wizard

Answer: B

17. All of the following are steps in creating an upgrade project, *except:*

   A. Launching the Upgrade Wizard

   B. Selecting protocols that you will need

   C. Choosing a project name

   D. Clicking on Create a New Upgrade Project

Answer: B

18. Which phase is *not* included in the Upgrade Wizard?

   A. Project creation

   B. Migration

   C. Verify

   D. Backup

Answer: D

Chapter 8 Answers

1. Commands you can use at the server console include:

   A. DOS commands

   B. NLMs and console commands

   C. NLMs only

   D. DOS or NLM commands

Answer: B

2. The kernel provides all of the following services *except:*

   A. Load balancing for multiple operating systems

   B. Scheduling processor time for applications

   C. Memory protection for the kernel

   D. Multi-Processor Kernel (MPK)

Answer: A

3. NLMs come from:

   A. Novell

   B. Third parties

   C. Both of the above

   D. None of the above

Answer: C

4. The two parts of an NPA disk driver are:

A. NPA and CDA

B. HAM and CAM

C. HAM and CDM

D. NPA and HDM

Answer: C

5. LAN driver modules have the extension:

A. .NLM

B. .DRV

C. .LAN

D. .MOD

Answer: C

6. The command to display configuration information is:

A. DISPLAY CONFIG

B. MODULES

C. CONFIG

D. VERSION

Answer: C

7. The command used to prevent logins is:

A. SET LOGIN = NO

B. DISABLE LOGIN

C. LOGIN OFF

D. SECURE CONSOLE

Answer: B

8. The command needed to bring down the server is:

A. DOWN

B. RESTART

C. DISMOUNT

D. UNLOAD

Answer: A

9. The key or key combination used to switch screens in RCONSOLE is:

A. F3 or F4

B. Alt+Esc

C. Ctrl+Esc

D. Alt+F3 and Alt+F4

Answer: D

10. The two modules you must load to enable remote access with RConsole are:

A. REMOTE and MONITOR

B. REMOTE and ACCESS

C. RSPX and REMOTE

D. RSPX and RCONSOLE

Answer: C

11. Utility NLMs can provide the following functions:

A. Server monitoring

B. Upgrading system files

C. Network management

D. A, B, and C

E. B and C

F. A and C

Answer: D

12. Which are the two configuration files installed with NetWare 5?

A. STARTUP.NCF and AUTOEXEC.NCF

B. RConsoleJ and RConsole

C. NWCONFIG and CONFIG

D. All of the above

E. None of the above

Answer: A

13. What new server console interface provides a user-friendly environment in NetWare 5?

A. Java applets

B. NetWare 5 GUI

C. Java AWT

D. Java Foundation classes

Answer: B

14. Which of these describes ConsoleOne?

    A. It is a server graphical utility.

    B. It allows you to do basic server and NDS administration.

    C. Its main screen has a toolbar, a menu bar, and two windowpanes.

    D. You can use it to edit server configuration files.

    E. All of the above

    F. A, C, and D

Answer: E

15. What is the *new* feature in NetWare 5 to lock the server console?

    A. SECURE CONSOLE

    B. LOCK CONSOLE

    C. LOCK SCREEN

    D. SCRSAVER.NLM

Answer: D

16. Which NLMs can generate encrypted passwords?

    A. PASSWORD.NLM and NETWORK.NLM

    B. RCONAG6.NLM and REMOTE.NLM

    C. RSPX.NLM and REMOTE.NLM

    D. EDIT and NWCONFIG

Answer: B

17. When you type the M command at the server console, it does which of the following?

    A. Loads modules currently loaded

    B. Unloads modules currently loaded

    C. Lists modules currently loaded

    D. Removes modules from the server's memory

Answer: C

18. NWCONFIG is used to do which of the following?

    A. Configure NWADMIN

    B. Install and configure SMP

    C. Configure NetWare NDS

    D. None of the above

Answer: B

19. What options does MONITOR offer?

    A. Disk cache utilization

    B. Storage devices

    C. LAN/WAN information

    D. File open/lock activity

    E. All of the above

    F. None of the above

Answer: E

Chapter 9 Answers

1. The NDS objects used for printing are:

    A. Print server, print queue, port driver

    B. Print server, print queue, printer

    C. Printer, print server, port driver

    D. CAPTURE, printer, print server

Answer: B

2. The number of printers controlled by a NetWare 5 print server:

    A. Is limited only by the server's memory

    B. Is limited to 16 printers

    C. Is limited to 256 printers

    D. Is limited to 3 parallel printers and 2 serial printers

Answer: C

3. There are three basic types of network printer:

    A. Workstation, server, queue

    B. Workstation, server, directly connected

    C. NDS, bindery, workstation

    D. Dot matrix, laser, daisy wheel

Answer: B

4. Which is the correct CAPTURE command to capture the LPT2 port to the CHECKS queue, assuming the queue is in the users' local context?

A. `CAPTURE J=2 P=CHECKS`

B. `CAPTURE L=1 B=2 Q=CHECKS`

C. `CAPTURE LPT2 P=CHECK_PRINTER`

D. `CAPTURE L=2 Q=CHECKS`

Answer: D

5. The Print Server object:

A. Is not used in NetWare 5

B. Moves jobs from the print queue to the printer

C. Moves jobs from the print queue to the port driver

D. Stores a list of jobs to be printed

Answer: C

6. To configure a workstation printer, you use the _____ program.

A. RPRINTER

B. REMOTE

C. WPRINTER

D. NPRINTER

Answer: D

7. Which is the order in which components are used when a print job is processed?

A. CAPTURE, print queue, printer

B. CAPTURE, print queue, print server, port driver, printer

C. CAPTURE, port driver, print server, print queue, printer

D. Port driver, CAPTURE, print queue, print server, printer

Answer: B

8. CAPTURE can use which LPT ports?

A. LPT 1 through 3

B. LPT 1 through 5

C. Only those you have the hardware for

D. LPT 1 through 9

Answer: D

9. The Print Server object:

A. Is created automatically when the printer is installed

B. Needs to be created for each printer

C. Can handle up to 256 printers

D. Is not needed for most printers

Answer: C

10. You can stop and continue a print job with which NWADMN32 functions?

A. Pause and play

B. Pause and resume

C. Hold and resume

D. Hold and unhold

Answer: C

11. The number of printers on the network is limited by:

A. The print server

B. The number of ports on the server

C. The number of queues

D. Disk storage available

Answer: A

12. You can use the CAPTURE command to send a print job to:

A. A printer or a print server

B. A printer only

C. A printer or a queue

D. A printer or NPRINTER

Answer: C

Chapter 10 Answers

1. Which backup strategy requires the most time for backing up data?

A. Incremental

B. Differential

C. Full

D. Partial

Answer: C

2. Which backup strategy requires the most time if you need to restore a full volume?

    A. Incremental

    B. Differential

    C. Full

    D. Partial

    Answer: A

3. What are the components of a NetWare file system?

    A. Cabinets, drawers, and folders

    B. Volumes, directories, and files

    C. Data, applications, and groups

    D. Users, groups, and administrators

    Answer: B

4. All of the NLMs provide backup functionality *except*:

    A. QMAN.NLM

    B. SBCON.NLM

    C. NWBACK32.NLM

    D. SBSC.NLM

    Answer: C

5. What are the three concepts to be familiar with in an NSS file system?

    A. Enhanced SBACKUP, TSA, and tape backup device

    B. Provider, consumer, and storage groups

    C. Full, incremental, and differential backups

    D. Print, storage, and user services

    Answer: B

6. Which is not a feature of an NSS file system?

    A. An almost unlimited number of files on the NSS volume

    B. Suballocation and file compression

    C. Improved CD-ROM support

    D. Less server memory and resources

    Answer: B

7. What is a good reason to create another volume besides the SYS volume?

    A. To provide additional volumes for user data and applications

    B. To protect your server system directories and files by having only those on the SYS

    C. To have a separate volume to hold print queues if printing levels require it

    D. All of the above

    Answer: D

8. SMS can back up the following:

    A. Unix servers

    B. Windows 95 workstations

    C. Macintosh workstations

    D. All of the above

    Answer: D

9. All of the following are TSAs *except*:

    A. TSA500

    B. TSANDS

    C. TSAPROXY

    D. TSA400

    Answer: D

10. What priorities should you follow as a guideline when designing a file system?

    A. Security, ease of administration, and user access

    B. Large SYS volume, no shared directories, and departmental printers

    C. Naming conventions, configuration of mail, and file migration

    D. Login security, printer at every workstation, and Backup/Restore

    Answer: A

11. You should create directories for which of the following to make administration of the file system easier?

   A. Print server

   B. Shared data storage

   C. Common groups of users

   D. Applications in common location

   E. A, C, D

   F. B, C, D

   Answer: F

12. Planning the NetWare file system is an important part of your overall NetWare design.

   A. True

   B. False

   Answer: A

Chapter 11 Answers

1. Which statement is true of memory allocation?

   A. Each NLM is given an allocation pool to draw memory from.

   B. Memory is allocated in 4KB pages.

   C. Memory is deallocated when it is no longer needed.

   D. All of the above.

   Answer: D

2. The garbage collection process:

   A. Returns deallocated memory to the memory pool

   B. Deallocates unused areas of memory

   C. Takes memory away from NLMs that are not currently processing

   D. All of the above

   Answer: A

3. The term *cache hit* means:

   A. Cache was successfully read instead of the disk

   B. Information is in the cache waiting to be written

   C. Data in the cache may be damaged

   D. Cache memory has run out

   Answer: A

4. Block suballocation:

   A. Allows blocks of different sizes to be used

   B. Divides blocks into 4KB sections

   C. Divides blocks into 512-byte sections

   D. Compresses files that are not in use

   Answer: C

5. File compression:

   A. Compresses all files

   B. Compresses files not in use

   C. Compresses files in the cache

   D. Allows you to compress files manually

   Answer: B

6. Which areas of server performance can be optimized?

   A. CPU, memory, video

   B. CPU, memory, disk, network

   C. Network, NIC, LIP

   D. Cache, disk, router

   Answer: B

7. For an efficient server, the Long-Term Cache Hits statistic should be:

   A. Above 50 percent

   B. Below 10 percent

   C. Above 90 percent

   D. Below 90 percent

   Answer: C

8. Packet sizes on the network:

   A. Are typically 1,514 bytes for Ethernet

   B. Can be restricted with the STARTUP.NCF file

   C. Are negotiated between the client and server

   D. All of the above

   Answer: D

9. The Large Internet Packets feature:

   A. Allows integration between NetWare and the Internet

   B. Allows large packets to be used between the client and server

   C. Allows packets to pass through a router without limiting their size

   D. All of the above

Answer: C

10. The System Resource option in MONITOR allows you to do which of the following?

   A. View the server's total allocated memory

   B. View the list of resources you can add to the server

   C. View a list of hardware resources you have installed on the server

   D. View all the SET commands for the system resources

Answer: A

11. What is the server console command to list all the SET commands?

   A. SET HELP

   B. HELP SET

   C. SET

   D. SET COMMANDS

Answer: C

12. What is the command you would use to list all the SWAP commands?

   A. SWAP HELP

   B. HELP SWAP

   C. SWAP

   D. SWAP COMMANDS

Answer: B

13. What is a thread?

   A. An NLM

   B. A portion of the CPU

   C. An application

   D. A path of code

Answer: D

14. What utility can you use to verify that the CPU is running at its proper speed?

   A. SET

   B. SPEED

   C. NWCONFIG

   D. CPU

Answer: B

15. What does SYSCALLS do?

   A. Tracks the calls the core operating system is receiving

   B. Calls the core operating system

   C. Intercepts corrupted calls and blocks them from passing calls to the core operating system

   D. Sends applications to the CPU

Answer: C

16. What is the NetWare Application group?

   A. The newest Novell software used for Java programming

   B. A group created by default when you install NetWare 5

   C. An application developed by Novell to be used with NetWare Administrator

   D. An application used for garbage collection

Answer: B

17. What is the MONITOR !H command used for?

   A. To display hidden set parameters

   B. To display HELP commands

   C. To display hot spots in the CPU

   D. To display hard drive settings

Answer: A

18. What utility can you use to enable suballocation on a volume?

   A. SET

   B. SPEED

   C. NWCONFIG

   D. CPU

   Answer: C

Chapter 12 Answers

1. Which of the following is a step in installing DNS/DHCP Services?

   A. Install network cards

   B. Install server volume

   C. Extend NDS schema

   D. None of the above

   Answer: C

2. DNS is a/an _____ name resolution protocol that maps a/an _____ address to a host _____.

   A. IP, domain, name

   B. Domain, name, IP

   C. Name, IP, domain

   D. Domain, IP, name

   Answer: D

3. You can administrate DNS/DHCP Services using NetWare Administrator.

   A. True

   B. False

   Answer: B

4. To start DNS Services once it has been installed and configured, enter this server console command:

   A. SERVER.EXE

   B. DNS.EXE

   C. DNSSRV

   D. NAMED

   Answer: D

5. DNS is a client/server protocol that provides domain name resolution services across an intranet and the Internet.

   A. True

   B. False

   Answer: A

6. DNS maps a network address to a computer name.

   A. True

   B. False

   Answer: A

7. DNS protocol standard is composed of which *two* components:

   A. Subnet range

   B. Naming conventions

   C. Mapping between IP address and name

   D. Host names

   Answer: B and C

8. DHCP provides a/an _____ with _____ configuration information.

   A. Server, IPX

   B. Client, IP

   C. Application, service

   D. Mouse, keyboard

   Answer: B

9. Snap-ins allows you to _____ DNS/DHCP objects with NetWare Administrator.

   A. Edit

   B. Configure

   C. View

   D. Start

   Answer: C

10. The following is a DNS object:

   A. Subnet object

   B. OU Object

   C. Resource Record object

D. Subnet mask

Answer: C

11. DHCP assigns IP addresses _____.

   A. Dynamically

   B. Routinely

   C. Randomly

   D. Indirectly

   Answer: A

12. DHCP allows the administrator to assign a specific address to a computer.

   A. True

   B. False

   Answer: A

13. The DNS/DHCP Management Console allows the user to:

   A. Configure and administrate DNS objects

   B. Delete user objects

   C. Edit AUTOEXEC.NCF

   D. Install DNS/DHCP Services

   Answer: A

14. After the NDS schema is extended, you can create and install DNS/DHCP objects with NetWare Admnistrator.

   A. True

   B. False

   Answer: B

15. You can install DNS/DHCP Services using:

   A. NetWare 5 GUI

   B. INSTALL.NLM

   C. ConsoleOne

   D. DNS/DHCP Console

   Answer: A

16. DHCP objects include:

   A. Subnet objects

   B. Resource Record objects

   C. Organizational objects

   D. User objects

   Answer: A

Chapter 13 Answers

1. The protocol used for Web servers is:

   A. FTP

   B. SMTP

   C. HTTP

   D. TFTP

   Answer: C

2. Web documents are typically viewed with:

   A. A Web viewer

   B. A Web browser

   C. Any word processor

   D. An HTTP server

   Answer: B

3. The language used to create hypertext Web documents is:

   A. HTTP

   B. SGML

   C. HTML

   D. NetBasic

   Answer: C

4. Which protocol must be installed on client machines for them to have access to the Web?

   A. HTTP

   B. HTML

   C. TCP/IP

   D. FTP

   Answer: C

5. By default, anonymous users have which rights to Web documents?

   A. Read and write

   B. Read only

   C. Write only

   D. Read, write, and create

   Answer: B

6. The default data directory for Web documents is:

   A. SYS:WEB\DOCS

   B. SYS:WEBDOCS

   C. SYS:\NOVONYX\SUITESPOT\DOCS

   D. SYS:WEB\SERVER\DOCS\HTML

   Answer: C

7. Which configuration file is used to restrict access to documents?

   A. CONFIG.CFG

   B. ACCESS.CFG

   C. RESTRICT.CFG

   D. None of the above

   Answer: D

8. How much RAM is required for NetWare 5 to support Web Services?

   A. 24MB

   B. 48MB

   C. 64MB

   D. 32MB

   Answer: C

9. The Netscape FastTrack Server software itself requires how much disk storage?

   A. 50MB

   B. 70MB

   C. 90MB

   D. 100MB

   Answer: D

10. Along with TCP/IP, which of the following is required to install FastTrack Server?

   A. IPX protocol

   B. A unique IP address

   C. A default gateway

   D. All of the above

   Answer: B

11. FTP is mainly used for:

   A. Logging in to remote servers

   B. Transferring files

   C. Sending files via e-mail

   D. Server management

   Answer: B

12. You can install Novell FTP Services using:

   A. SETUP program

   B. NWCONFIG utility

   C. UNICON utility

   D. CDROM utility

   Answer: B

13. FTP settings are managed with this utility:

   A. NWCONFIG

   B. INETCFG

   C. UNICON

   D. FTPCON

   Answer: C

14. The FTP Service:

   A. Starts and stops automatically when needed

   B. Can be started or stopped using UNICON

   C. Can be stopped by unloading UNICON

   D. Is always running

   Answer: B

15. Which of the following is *not* a service provided by Novell Unix Services?

    A. Unix-to-NetWare Print Server

    B. HTTP

    C. FTP Server

    D. DNS Server

    Answer: B

16. The Maximum Number of Sessions option controls:

    A. The maximum number of sessions per user

    B. The maximum number of sessions per day

    C. The maximum number of concurrent users

    D. The maximum number of configured FTP users

    Answer: C

17. If the FTP server is frequently overloaded, one solution is to adjust which parameter?

    A. Idle Time Before FTP Server Unloads

    B. Maximum Number of Sessions

    C. Maximum Bandwidth

    D. Intruder Detection

    Answer: B

18. Which of the following is an example of proper FTP URL syntax?

    A. `http://ftp.starlingtech.com/pub/novell/`

    B. `ftp://ftp.starlingtech.com\pub\novell`

    C. `ftp://ftp.starlingtech.com/pub/novell/`

    D. `ftp:ftp.starlingtech.com:pub/novell`

    Answer: C

19. Which users can log in to the FTP server?

    A. Any NDS user

    B. Users who have been given access through UNICON

    C. Administrators only

    D. Users in the FTP server's context

    Answer: B

20. Which is the correct FTP command for downloading a file?

    A. `DOWNLOAD file1.zip`

    B. `GET file1.zip`

    C. `PUT file1.zip`

    D. `MPUT file1.zip`

    Answer: B

21. If a user can connect to the FTP server but receives an error message, which is *not* a possible cause of the problem?

    A. Access is restricted

    B. FTP server is overloaded

    C. Network is down

    D. User is not set up correctly

    Answer: C

Chapter 14 Answers

1. What are the two types of administration in NetWare 5?

    A. Distributed and container

    B. Centralized and distributed

    C. Centralized and decentralized

    D. Distributed and central

    Answer: B

2. Which object is best used to assign an administrator?

    A. Organization

    B. Organizational Unit

    C. Organizational Role

    D. Group

    Answer: C

3. Who might need additional rights?

    A. Server

    B. [Public]

    C. Remote users

    D. [Root]

    Answer: C

4. Which of the following is *not* a network resource?

   A. File server

   B. [Public] object

   C. Network printer

   D. Network application

   Answer: B

5. An exclusive container administrator:

   A. Shares responsibilities with other administrators

   B. Has rights for a single container only

   C. Is the only administrator for a container

   D. Cannot control the file system

   Answer: C

6. To which property right should you change a user's login script and print job configuration property rights for better security and control?

   A. Read [R]

   B. Browse [B]

   C. Inheritable [I]

   D. Supervisor [S]

   Answer: A

7. A container administrator can do all of the following *except:*

   A. Write and maintain login scripts

   B. Move objects

   C. Create user accounts

   D. Create printer objects

   Answer: B

8. What are the two objects automatically created when you install NDS on the first server?

   A. Admin and [Root]

   B. [Root] and a print server object

   C. [Root] and a container object

   D. [Public] and an Organizational Role object

   Answer: A

9. True or False: In most cases, the default NDS rights are sufficient for administering the network.

   A. True

   B. False

   Answer: A

10. All of the following are rights *except:*

   A. Browse [B]

   B. Read [R]

   C. Inheritable [I]

   D. Configure [C]

   Answer: D

11. The following is a right of [Public]:

   A. [RW] to [Root]

   B. [C] to server

   C. [B] to [Root]

   D. [RW] to default server for user object

   Answer: C

12. NDS allows user objects to do which of the following:

   A. Change the rights assigned to them by the Admin

   B. Install their own server objects

   C. Identify and change another user object's login script

   D. Identify the default server to which the user object is assigned

   Answer: D

13. The _____ is considered a _____ administrator when it is assigned rights to add user accounts.

   A. Admin, centralized

   B. Distributed, file system

   C. Organizational Role object, container

   Answer: C

Chapter 15 Answers

1. Which factor does not need to be considered when partitioning and replicating?

A. The size of individual partitions

B. Naming standards

C. Subordinate references

D. The physical location of objects

Answer: B

2. An NDS backup:

A. Includes all data on the server

B. Can be used to install a new server if necessary

C. Includes only the NDS database

D. Includes NDS and file system information

Answer: C

3. To delete a Server object, you can use:

A. The INETCFG utility

B. NDS Manager

C. NetWare Administrator

D. The DELSERV utility

Answer: B

4. Which is *not* a good strategy for avoiding NDS problems?

A. Keep at least three replicas of each partition

B. Don't allow the SYS volume to run out of space

C. Keep at least two master replicas

D. Make frequent NDS backups

Answer: C

5. Which utility is used to check replica synchronization?

A. NDSREPAIR

B. DSCHECK

C. DSREPAIR

D. INETCFG

Answer: C

6. Which is the correct syntax for NDS TRACE?

A. `SET NDS TRACE to screen= ON`

B. `LOAD NDS TRACE`

C. `NDS TRACE BEGIN`

D. `TRACK ON`

Answer: A

7. Which option should you try first when you have found an NDS problem?

A. Reinstall NetWare 5 on the server

B. Use NDSMGR32 to send updates to all replicas

C. Restore the NDS database from a backup

D. Use DSREPAIR to check for and correct problems

Answer: D

8. How many replicas of each partition should you have?

A. 2

B. 5

C. 3

D. 1

Answer: C

9. What should you do before you remove a server from the Directory tree?

A. Down the server

B. Back up the server

C. Remove all replicas from the server

D. No preparation is necessary

Answer: C

10. Which utility is used to remove NDS from a server?

A. DSREPAIR

B. NWCONFIG

C. INETCFG

D. MONITOR

Answer: B

11. When the replica of a parent partition is placed on a server, a subordinate reference replica of the child partition is placed by NDS.

A. True

B. False

Answer: B

Chapter 16 Answers

1. Which of the following is *not* a requirement for providing a remote user access to NIAS remote access server?

A. Modem for the server

B. 5MB of additional RAM on the server

C. User account and password

D. None of the above

Answer: D

2. An important question to ask when planning for remote access services is (choose all that apply):

A. Who needs remote access?

B. Where are the users located?

C. What do they need access to?

D. How many simultaneous connections do you need to support?

Answer: A, B, C, and D

3. A dial-up connection is faster than a LAN connection.

A. True

B. False

Answer: B

4. Of the following dial-up connections, which presents you with the fastest service?

A. ISDN

B. POTS

C. xDSL

Answer: C

5. Of the following dial-up connections, which is the cheapest solution?

A. ISDN

B. POTS

C. xDSL

Answer: B

6. A consideration in the location of NIAS remote access servers is the number of remote users in a geographical area.

A. True

B. False

Answer: A

7. A critical component in optimizing performance on an NIAS is the data transmission media selected.

A. True

B. False

Answer: A

8. BRI and PRI are options within which data transmission media?

A. POTS

B. ISDN

C. HDSL

D. ADSL

Answer: B

9. Which of the following statements is true of a demilitarized zone?

A. It is used for military use *only* in their networks.

B. It makes remote connections less secure on the NIAS remote access server

C. It isolates an area, which keeps unauthorized users from going beyond the NIAS

D. It is a zone that you configure in the NIAS during installation.

Answer: C

10. Which component of the RADIUS protocol is located at the ISP?

A. RADIUS server

B. RADIUS accounting server

C. RADIUS proxy

D. None of the above

Answer: C

Chapter 17 Answers

1. Which of the following are additional network solutions offered by NetWare? (Select all that apply.)

A. NDS for NT

B. BorderManager

C. GroupWise 5

D. All of the above

Answer: D

2. Which network solution offers firewall services?

A. NDS for NT

B. BorderManager

C. GroupWise 5

D. ManageWise

Answer: B

3. Which is *not* a component of a firewall?

A. Packet-filtering routers

B. Circuit gateways

C. Application gateways

D. Application routers

Answer: D

4. Which layers of the OSI model do packet-filtering routers relate to? (Select two.)

A. Application

B. Session

C. Network

D. Transport

Answer: C and D

5. Which of these is a component of BorderManager?

A. NIAS 4.1

B. LANalyzer

C. Z.E.N.works

D. NetWare Administrator

Answer: A

6. _____ redirects requests from Windows NT domain clients to NDS.

A. MSSAMSRV.DLL

B. SAMSRV.DLL

C. PROXYSRV.DLL

D. SAMLIB.DLL

Answer: B

7. To manage GroupWise 5 components, first you need to load NetWare Administrator to access the GroupWise Administration module.

A. True

B. False

Answer: A

8. The Message Store routes messages between servers.

A. True

B. False

Answer: B

9. Which GroupWise component do the client and Message Transfer Services access?

A. Directory Store

B. Message Store

C. Document Store

D. All of the above

Answer: D

10. ManageWise can monitor network traffic as well as record, inventory, and manage network resources.

A. True

B. False

Answer: A

11. Which component of ManageWise monitors and can remotely manage workstations?

A. NetExplorer

B. LANalyzer

C. Z.E.N.works

D. NetWare Management Agent

Answer: C

Chapter 18 Answers

1. The two basic types of Directory tree organizations are:

A. Location-based and divisional

B. Location-based and functional

C. Organization and Organizational Unit

D. Centralized and distributed

Answer: B

2. A network consultant is responsible for:

A. A single network

B. A certain branch of a network

C. Networks belonging to several clients

D. Designing networks only

Answer: C

3. Time synchronization planning is part of which phase of NDS design?

A. The project approach phase

B. The design phase

C. The implementation phase

D. The manage and monitor phase

Answer: B

4. The responsibilities of the project manager do *not* include:

A. Communicating with company executives

B. Estimating times and costs

C. Planning time synchronization

D. Scheduling meetings

Answer: C

5. Which team member usually leads the project team?

A. NDS expert

B. Project manager

C. Server specialist

D. Applications specialist

Answer: A

6. A standards document should *not* include:

A. Naming standards for User objects

B. Number of users on the network

C. Properties to be used

D. Formats for property values

Answer: B

7. Which type of username is not efficient for large networks?

A. First name, last name

B. First initial, last name

C. First name

D. Last name, first initial

Answer: C

8. The most practical organization for a multiple location network is:

A. Functional

B. Divisional

C. Correctional

D. Location-based

Answer: D

9. Which object type is seldom used in a Directory tree?

A. Organizational Unit

B. Organization

C. Country

D. User

Answer: C

10. The advantages of the location-based design do *not* include:

  A. Ease of partitioning

  B. Minimizing WAN traffic

  C. Matching network topology

  D. Any of the above

  Answer: D

11. The functional organization is best suited for:

  A. Multinational corporations

  B. Single-location networks

  C. Poorly organized networks

  D. WAN links

  Answer: B

12. The area of the Directory tree you should not have to change often is:

  A. Upper layers

  B. Lower layers

  C. Server container

  D. Central administration

  Answer: A

Chapter 19 Answers

1. Which component is the most important in Net-Ware 5, besides NDS?

  A. Bindery Services

  B. The file system

  C. TCP/IP

  D. Mobile use

  Answer: B

2. To minimize WAN traffic, applications:

  A. Should be installed on one server only

  B. Should be installed on every server in the network

  C. Should be installed on each local PC

  D. Should be installed on at least one server per location

  Answer: D

3. The object best used to assign rights for backups is:

  A. Organization

  B. Organizational Unit

  C. Organizational Role

  D. Group

  Answer: C

4. Which type of object should you generally avoid assigning rights to?

  A. [Root], User

  B. Group

  C. Organizational Role

  D. Container

  Answer: A

5. Which is not a possible security configuration?

  A. Central administrator only

  B. Central administrator and exclusive container administrators

  C. Container administrators only

  D. Special-use administrator only

  Answer: D

6. Which type of object can be used to assign the same rights to users in different containers?

  A. Organization

  B. Organizational Unit

  C. Group

  D. Profile

  Answer: C

7. Which client operating system does *not* support NDS?

   A. DOS

   B. Macintosh

   C. OS/2

   D. Unix

   Answer: D

8. Which client or clients is/are not supported without additional software that must be purchased? (Choose all correct answers.)

   A. Unix

   B. OS/2

   C. DOS

   D. Macintosh

   Answer: A and D

9. Which operating systems can run most of the administration utilities? (Select two.)

   A. Windows

   B. Unix

   C. Macintosh

   D. OS/2

   Answer: A and D

10. The best type of object to use to assign an administrator is:

   A. User

   B. Group

   C. Organizational Unit

   D. Organizational Role

   Answer: D

Chapter 20 Answers

1. Which is *not* one of the four types of replicas?

   A. Subordinate reference

   B. Time provider

   C. Read-only

   D. Read/write

   Answer: B

2. Subordinate reference partitions are created:

   A. When you request them

   B. When you have the parent partition but not its child

   C. When you have the child but not the parent

   D. When you have neither the parent nor the child

   Answer: B

3. The synchronization process in NetWare 5:

   A. Ensures that all replicas have the same information

   B. Ensures that all replicas have some of the same information (login name, password, and so on)

   C. Keeps a consistent time on the network

   D. Creates new replicas as they are needed

   Answer: A

4. Which replicas are considered writable? (Choose two.)

   A. Master

   B. Read-only

   C. Read/write

   D. Subordinate reference

   Answer: A and C

5. Name resolution is also called:

   A. Time synchronization

   B. Synchronization

   C. Tree walking

   D. Object naming

   Answer: C

6. A single partition is practical for how many objects?

   A. 15 or fewer

   B. No more than 10

   C. 256 or fewer

   D. 3,500 or fewer

   Answer: D

7. The default replication scheme assigns how many replicas for the [Root] partition?

   A. 1

   B. 2

   C. 3

   D. 16

   Answer: C

8. Which is *not* a good reason to create additional partitions?

   A. To allow further subdivision of the Directory tree

   B. To make resources easily accessible

   C. To minimize network traffic

   D. To provide redundancy for login authentication

   Answer: D

9. Which is *not* a disadvantage of increasing the number of partitions?

   A. Network traffic may increase

   B. Subordinate references may create problems

   C. Time synchronization will take longer

   D. Administration may take longer

   Answer: C

10. A partition should span:

   A. A single location only

   B. Any number of locations

   C. Nearby locations only

   D. At least three locations

   Answer: A

11. Which is *not* a benefit of replication?

   A. Faster network access

   B. Fault tolerance for NDS data

   C. Fault tolerance for data files

   D. Easy administration

   Answer: C

12. Which of the following is not a time provider?

   A. Single reference

   B. Reference

   C. Primary

   D. Secondary

   Answer: D

13. Which is *not* a server type found in a time provider group?

   A. Single reference

   B. Reference

   C. Primary

   D. Secondary

   Answer: A

14. Which protocol synchronizes time in a mixed IP/IPX environment?

   A. TIMESYNC

   B. NTP

   C. DNS

   D. TCP

   Answer: B

Chapter 21 Answers

1. Which of the following is *not* a client provided by Novell?

   A. NETX

   B. CSNW

   C. VLM

   D. Client 32

   Answer: B

2. Which client *doesn't* support NDS?

  A. VLM

  B. Client 32

  C. The Novell Client

  D. NETX

  Answer: D

3. Which of these describes the Upgrade Wizard?
(Choose all that apply.)

  A. Used for upgrading from NT to Novell

  B. Lets you model what NDS will look like before
you upgrade

  C. Leaves the original server intact; requires two
servers

  D. Upgrades the old server directly; requires only
the server to be upgraded

  Answer: B and C

4. Which tools can be used to merge two NDS trees?
(Choose all that apply.)

  A. DSMERGE

  B. DSCOMBINE

  C. NDS Manager

  D. NetWare Administrator

  Answer: A, C, and D

5. The purpose of WAN Traffic Manager is:

  A. To control NDS housekeeping and synchronization traffic across WAN links

  B. To control data traffic across the WAN

  C. To control all NDS traffic over WAN links

  D. To control all traffic across WAN links

  Answer: A

6. The tools required to merge two trees together
include all of the following *except*:

  A. DSMERGE

  B. NDS Manager

  C. NetWare Administrator

  D. ConsoleOne

  Answer: D

7. Considerations when upgrading a workstation do
not include:

  A. Bindery Services

  B. Backups

  C. Electrical hookups

  D. Security

  Answer: C

APPENDIX

B

Glossary

Abend   Short for "abnormal end," this is NetWare's term for a server crash. An abend is frequently caused by an application (NLM) writing to an area of memory that belongs to the operating system.

Access Control List (ACL)   The property of an NDS object that contains the list of **trustees** or other objects that have rights to the object.

Across-the-Wire Migration   One of the two possible migration strategies from NetWare 3.*x* to NetWare 5. In the across-the-wire strategy, a new NetWare 5 server is connected to the same network as the NetWare 3.*x* server and data is copied over the network.

Additive Licensing   NetWare 5's licensing system, which allows you to add licenses when your network needs to allow more user logins. For example, you can add a 5-user license to a 25-user license for a total of 30 possible users.

Address   In TCP/IP, an IP address is a 32-bit numeric identifier assigned to a node. The address has two parts, one for the network identifier and the other for the node identifier. All nodes on the same network must share the network address and have a unique node address. For networks connected to the Internet, the Internet Activities Board (IAB) assigns network addresses.

Other types of addresses include IPX addresses—the internal network number and external network number—and the MAC address (Media Access Control) assigned to each network card or device.

Administration Server   A group of NLMs that run on the Web server, providing a single interface that helps you manage the Netscape FastTrack Server.

Alias Object   An object used to represent, or point to, another object in the NDS tree. Alias objects can be created to make a resource in a different context available in the local context. NetWare can create aliases automatically when an object or container is moved. This is very similar to a Windows shortcut.

Aliased Object   The object to which an alias refers. This is also called the *source object*.

Allocation Pool   The area of memory that NetWare 5 sets aside for server applications (NLMs). When NLMs request additional memory, it is given from this pool.

American National Standards Institute (ANSI)   A nonprofit organization responsible for creating ASCII (American Standard Code for Information Interchange), as well as numerous other voluntary standards.

Analog Data   Data that has an infinite number of possible states, rather than the simple 1s and 0s of a digital signal. Audio, video, and voice, for example, can all be represented using analog data.

ANSI   See American National Standards Institute.

AppleTalk   A networking system developed by Apple for use with Macintosh computers. The software for AppleTalk connectivity is built into the Macintosh operating system (MacOS or System 7). NetWare for Macintosh allows connectivity between AppleTalk and NetWare networks by emulating AppleTalk services on the NetWare server.

Application Launcher (AL)   A system that allows users convenient access to applications, and that allows you to manage these applications through NDS.

Applications   Composed of many threads, applications are each a path of code, like an If statement routine. NetWare 5 uses application groups to gather a number of threads and ensure that they have appropriate time on the processor.

Asynchronous   A type of communication that sends data using flow control, rather than a clock, to synchronize data between the source and destination.

Attributes   File attributes are stored for each file and directory on a server's file system. Attributes are used for security purposes and to provide status information on the file. For example, the Read-Only attribute prevents a file from being written to or erased, and the Can't Compress attribute indicates that NetWare was unable to compress the file.

Authentication   Part of the login process, during which NDS verifies that the user's password, access rights, and other settings are correct. The nearest read/write or master replica handles authentication.

AUTOEXEC.NCF   A text file with commands that are run during the server's loading sequence.

Backup Engine   Part of the NetWare Storage Management System (SMS). The backup engine is the front end, or user interface, to the backup software. Backup engines, such as Novell's Enhanced SBACKUP utility, can be run on the server and a Windows 95/98 or Windows NT 4 workstation.

Backup Strategy   A selected method of backing up data. There are three methods: full, differential, and incremental.

Bandwidth   In network communications, the volume of data that can be sent across a wire in a given amount of time. Each communication that passes along the wire decreases the amount of available bandwidth.

Base Schema   The NDS base schema defines the structure of NDS—which objects are possible, which properties an object can have, and so forth. The NDS base schema is written to the server when NDS is installed. Third-party applications can extend, or add to, this schema using the NetWare API, which is a set of programs that provide access to the network.

Batch File   A file containing a list of commands to be executed. DOS batch files have the extension .BAT. Examples include AUTOEXEC.BAT, which executes when the workstation is booted, and STARTNET.BAT, which is used to attach to the network.

Baud   An acronym for "bits of actual usable data." The baud rate in digital communication refers to the number of bits of data that can be sent per second, a speed that is usually given in Kilobits per second, or Kbps.

Binary   The numbering system used in computer memory and in digital communication. All characters are represented as a series of 1s and 0s. For example, the letter *A* might be represented as 01000001.

Bindery   The database used to store information about users, printers, and other network objects in NetWare 3.*x* and earlier versions. The bindery is a simple, flat database that is stored separately on each server. In NetWare 5 the bindery was replaced with NDS, NetWare Directory Services.

Bindery Context   The context that will be provided as a simulated bindery by Bindery Services. You can set up to 16 separate contexts to serve as bindery contexts; these will be combined into a bindery that bindery-based clients can access.

Bindery Services   A NetWare service that allows the simulation of a bindery. This allows clients using older client software, such as the NetWare DOS Shell, to access the network. A branch of the NDS tree, the bindery context, is used as a simulated bindery.

Binding   The process of connecting a communication protocol, such as TCP/IP, to a LAN board driver, such as an Ethernet driver.

Bits   In binary data, each unit of data is a bit. Each bit is represented by either a 0 or a 1, which are stored in memory to represent an On or Off state.

Block   One of the divisions of a hard disk. NetWare stores files on the volume in sets of blocks. In NetWare 3.*x* and earlier, entire blocks are always used. Block sizes are typically 4K for NetWare 3.*x* and NetWare 5.

Block Suballocation   A NetWare 5 feature that allows smaller portions of disk blocks to be used. Each block is divided into 512-byte units that can be used instead of entire blocks. This allows more efficient use of disk space.

BorderManager   Offers a comprehensive suite of services, including routing, remote access, IP gateway, proxy cache, and Virtual Private Network (VPN) encryption software.

Bridge   A device that connects two segments of a network and sends data to one or the other based on a set of criteria.

Buffer   In communications, this term means an area of memory used as temporary storage for data being sent or received. A NetWare 5 server uses packet buffers for this purpose. The term *buffer* can also be used to refer to any area of memory in a computer.

Byte   The basic unit of data storage and communication in computers. In PC systems a byte is 8 bits, or an 8-digit binary number. A single byte can represent numbers between 0 and 255, or 256 unique states.

Cache Buffer   NetWare sets aside a portion of the server's memory for cache buffers. These are used to cache information for the file system. The number of cache buffers depends on the available memory.

Cache Hit   A statistical term representing an instance when data was successfully read from the disk cache. A high percentage of cache hits indicates that the number of cache buffers is sufficient and that the server is running smoothly.

Caching   A technique used by NetWare servers to increase disk performance. Data read from the disk drive is stored in a block of RAM memory, known as a cache buffer. When clients request this data, it can be read directly from the cache, avoiding the use of the disk and speeding access. NetWare provides both read and write caching.

Carrier   A communications signal that is kept on the line at all times so that the device on the other end knows that it is connected.

CCITT   *See* Consultative Committee on International Telegraphy and Telephony.

CDM   *See* Custom Device Module.

Centralized Administration   One of the two types of administration in NetWare 5. In centralized administration, a single central administrator has rights to manage the entire NDS tree. The other type of administration is distributed administration.

Checksum   A number that is calculated based on the values of a block of data. Checksums are used in communication to ensure that the correct data was received.

Child Object   In NDS, an object that is under a container object. The container object is referred to as the *parent object*.

Child Partition   *See* Parent Partition.

Circuit Switching   A type of communication system that establishes a connection, or circuit, between two devices before communicating and that does not disconnect until all data is sent.

Client   Any device that attaches to the network server. A workstation is the most common type of client. Clients run client software to provide network access. A piece of software that accesses data on a server can also be called a client.

Client Software   Software loaded on a workstation that provides connectivity to the network in conjunction with network hardware. All network operating systems have client software. NetWare's preferred client software is the Novell Client, also called Client 32.

Client/Server Network   A server-centric network in which some network resources are stored on a file server, while processing power is distributed among workstations and the file server.

Client 32   The client software included with NetWare 5, now called by a new name, the Novell Client. (Most of the installation file directories still use the name Client 32.) Client 32 replaced the NetWare DOS Requester and DOS Shell, used in previous versions. Versions of Client 32 are available for DOS, Windows 3.1, Windows 95/98, and Windows NT.

Coaxial Cable   One of the types of cable used in network wiring. Typical coaxial cable types include RG-58 and RG-62. The 10base2 system of Ethernet networking uses coaxial cable. Coaxial cable is usually shielded. The Thicknet system uses a thicker coaxial cable.

Command-line Utilities   Utilities that run from the DOS command prompt or the server console.

Common Name   In NDS, the least significant portion of an object's name. This is the name given to the object when it is created. The common name is abbreviated CN in typeful naming.

ConsoleOne   A Java-based tool that can run on Windows 95/98 and Windows NT workstations or on a NetWare 5 server. This tool is used to manage the server and NDS.

Consultative Committee on International Telegraphy and Telephony (CCITT)   A committee, sponsored by the United Nations, that defines network standards, including X.400 and X.500. This committee has recently been renamed International Telecommunications Union/Telecommunications Standardization Sector (ITU/TSS).

Container Administrator   An administrator who is given rights to a container object and all of the objects under it. A container administrator's role can be exclusive, *meaning that no other administrator has access to the container.*

Container Object   In NDS, an object that contains other objects. Types of container objects include Organization, Organizational Unit, Country, and Locality. The [Root] object is also a specialized kind of container object. Objects within a container can be either other container objects or leaf objects, which represent network resources.

Container Security Equivalence   *See* Implied Security Equivalence.

Context   In NDS, an object's position within the Directory tree. The context is the full path to the container object in which the object resides.

Controlled Access Printer Represented as an object in the NDS tree, this type of printer must be configured with various properties, including who is allowed to use it. This printer type fully supports event notification.

Current Context The current position in the Directory tree, maintained for a workstation connection. By default, objects are assumed to be in this context, unless you specify the full distinguished name. The current context is also called the *default context*.

Custom Device Module (CDM) Part of the NetWare Peripheral Architecture (NPA) system of device drivers, the CDM provides an interface between the device and the Host Adapter Module (HAM). The HAM provides communication with the controller.

Data Migration A system in which infrequently used data is moved to a high-capacity storage device, such as a jukebox. In NetWare 5, data migration is handled by the High-Capacity Storage System (HCSS).

Data Packet A unit of data being sent over a network. A packet includes a header, addressing information, and the data itself. A packet is treated as a single unit as it is sent from device to device.

Deallocation In NetWare 5 memory management, the process of returning memory to an allocation pool when it is no longer needed.

Dedicated Line A transmission medium that is used exclusively between two locations. Dedicated lines are also known as *leased lines* or *private lines*.

Dedicated Server A server that cannot be used for another purpose, for example as a workstation. All NetWare 5 servers are dedicated.

Default Context *See* Current Context.

Default Gateway The default destination IP address to which packets are sent, when the destination host address is not on the local network. This address is the local network's router, also referred to as the *default router*. The default gateway entry is part of the configuration data for the hosts on TCP/IP networks.

Default Router *See* Default Gateway.

Demilitarized Zone An isolated area of the network between the remote access server and the internal LAN. A screening router is the main component that separates the local network from the remote access server.

Departmental Implementation One of the methods of implementing NDS, in which departments or other divisions of the company are moved to NDS one at a time, each with their own Directory tree. The trees can be merged later.

Device Driver A piece of software that allows a workstation or server to communicate with a hardware device. For example, disk drivers are used to control disk drives, and network drivers are used to communicate with network boards.

DHCP An acronym for Dynamic Host Configuration Protocol, DHCP provides dynamic or static IP address assignment to DHCP or BOOTP clients.

DHCP Objects NDS objects formed when NDS is extended, DHCP objects are used to administer and control DHCP Services.

DHCP Server Object Responsible for supplying IP configuration information to DHCP clients.

Digital Data   Data that uses 1s and 0s to store information. Digital data may have only two distinct (binary) states. *See also* Analog Data.

Directly Connected Network Printer   A type of network printer allowed by NetWare 5. This type of printer is attached to the network rather than to a workstation or server. Directly connected printers can operate in either *remote mode* or *queue server mode.*

Directory   In NDS, the database that contains information about each of the objects on the network. The Directory is organized into a tree-like structure, the Directory tree, with a [Root] object on top and leaf objects at the bottom. To distinguish it from disk directories, the name of the NDS Directory is always capitalized.

Directory Access Protocol (DAP)   *See* X.500.

Directory Map   A special NDS object that is used to map directories in the file system. The MAP command can specify the name of the Directory Map object rather than the exact directory name. The directory name is contained in a property of the Directory Map object.

Directory Store   A distributed database that provides user-addressing information to the Message Transfer agent and the GroupWise *Address Book.*

Directory Synchronization   The process by which partition data is synchronized across all its replicas. When you make a change to an NDS object or add a new one on a partition, the nearest replica is updated. Then a process starts to update all the replicas of the partition with the new information. This is called *synchronization.*

Directory Tree   *See* Directory.

Distinguished Name   In NDS, the full name of an NDS object, which includes the object's common name and its context, or location in the Directory tree. Also referred to as the *full distinguished name.*

Distributed Administration   One of the types of administration allowed by NetWare 5. In distributed administration, separate administrators are assigned for different portions of the Directory tree and file system. The other option is centralized administration.

Distributed Database   A database that is contained in multiple locations. NDS is a distributed database that is contained on multiple NetWare 5 servers.

Distributed Processing   A network model in which the computers on a network are capable of processing independently. The computers are intelligent, as opposed to the "dumb" terminals in the centralized computing model.

Divisional Implementation   One of the methods of implementing NDS in a network. Each division is moved to NDS separately, with its own Directory tree. This is similar to the *departmental* implementation.

DNS (Domain Name Service)   A client/server protocol that provides name resolution services across an intranet or the Internet. DNS resolves a host name and domain name to an IP address.

DNS Objects   Formed when the NDS schema is extended, DNS objects are used to administer and control DNS Services.

DNS Server   A server that is responsible for resolving DNS requests.

DNS Zone Object   A leaf object in the NDS tree that stores DNS zone information.

DNS/DHCP Locator Object   Maintains global default information on the location of DNS/DHCP resources such as DNS zones, IP addresses, and servers in the tree.

DNS/DHCP Management Console   A tool you can use to create and configure DNS and DHCP objects; see audit trails made by the server; see address additions and deletions; and import DNS and DHCP data to NDS.

DNS/DHCP Services   A group of NetWare applications that provides DNS and DHCP services to a NDS tree.

Document Store   A shared public library of documents and files used by a group of people who are associated or who need to share the same information.

DOS Shell   The client software used for DOS workstations in NetWare 3.*x* and earlier versions. The executable program for the DOS Shell is NETX.COM. The DOS Shell does not provide access to NDS, but can be used with NetWare 5 via Bindery Services.

DSREPAIR   A versatile utility that can be used to solve many NDS problems. You can use one of the functions of DSREPAIR to check the synchronization of replicas on the network.

DSTRACE   A special SET parameter that can be used to monitor the activities of NDS.

Effective Rights   The rights that a user (or other trustee) has in a file system directory or NDS object after all factors—explicit rights, inherited rights, the IRF, and security equivalencies—are considered.

Encrypted   When information is encrypted—typically a password, data, or a transmission—it is made unreadable from plain view by a process. This process has standards and rules so that the intended recipient can decrypt the information and read it. NetWare 5 supports encryption on many of its services and follows industry standards.

Enterprise Networking   The type of networking required to connect an entire enterprise, or a large corporation. This usually implies a wide area network (WAN). NetWare 4 was intended as an enterprise networking system, but NetWare 5 is suitable for any size of network.

Event Notification Service (ENS)   Notifies users of various events that occur in NDPS, such as a printer problem. You can configure which events trigger notification and who should receive the notification.

Exclusive Container Administrator   A special type of container administrator who is given rights to a container and the objects within it. The IRF is used to prevent other administrators from having rights in the container.

Explicit Rights   In NDS or the file system, any rights that are given directly to a user for a directory or NDS object. Explicit rights override *inherited rights*.

Explicit Security Equivalence   In NDS, a method of giving one trustee the same rights as another. Explicit security equivalence can be assigned with group membership, an Organizational Role, or the trustee's Security Equal To property.

Fault Tolerance   The capability of a system or component to withstand a crash. NDS implements fault tolerance with partition replication, which creates multiple copies of a partition. If a server crashes, the data it holds is not lost, because there is always a copy of the partitions on another server.

File Attributes   *See* Attributes.

File Compression   A NetWare feature that automatically compresses files that are not in use. A compressed file can take as little as 33 percent of the space of the original file. Compressed files are uncompressed automatically when a user accesses them.

File Transfer Protocol (FTP)   A TCP/IP protocol that permits the transferring of files between different computer systems. For example, using FTP you can transfer files between a personal computer and a minicomputer or between an FTP server and a workstation.

Firewall   A network service that protects an internal network from unauthorized external access, typically from the Internet. A firewall can be composed of a packet-filtering router, a circuit gateway, or an application gateway.

FTP   *See* File Transfer Protocol.

FTP Server   A server that allows users to transfer files via FTP (File Transfer Protocol).

Full Distinguished Name   *See* Distinguished Name.

Functional Organization   A type of NDS organization that divides the Directory tree into branches for groups that perform similar functions—such as divisions or departments. This is often a practical way to organize, since members of a department or division often require access to the same set of resources. This method is best used in a hybrid, or combined, organization.

Garbage Collection   In memory management, the process of returning memory that has been deallocated to the main memory pool, so that it can be used by other applications.

Greenwich Mean Time (GMT)   *See* Universal Coordinated Time (UTC).

Group Rights   NDS or file system rights that a user receives because of membership in a Group object. This is an example of implicit security equivalence.

GroupWise 5   A snap-in suite of network services that enables messaging together with some workgroup applications. Services include messaging, a calendar, scheduling, shared folders, a workflow system, remote access, and Internet access.

GroupWise Administration Program   An added module to NetWare Administrator, accessible through NWADMN32. This program allows you to administrate, configure, and manage users and components of GroupWise.

HAM   *See* Host Adapter Module.

Handshaking   In network communication, a process used to verify that a connection has been established correctly. Devices send signals back and forth to establish parameters for communication.

HCSS   *See* High-Capacity Storage System.

High-Capacity Storage System (HCSS)   A NetWare service that allows data to be migrated to high-capacity storage. *See* Data Migration.

Host   An addressable computer system on a TCP/IP network. Examples include endpoint systems such as workstations, servers, minicomputers, and mainframes, and immediate systems such as routers. A host is typically a system that offers resources to network nodes, similar to a NetWare server's function.

Host Adapter   A hardware device that allows communication with a peripheral, such as a disk or tape drive. The host adapter, also called a *controller*, is usually a card that is inserted into a slot on the server's motherboard.

Host Adapter Module (HAM)   One of the components of the NetWare Peripheral Architecture (NPA) device driver standard. The HAM provides communication with the host adapter.

HTML   An acronym for Hypertext Markup Language, the markup language that is used for all the documents on the World Wide Web.

HTTP   An acronym for Hypertext Transfer Protocol, the protocol that provides the request/response mechanism between a Web server and a client browser.

HTTP Accelerator   Used to accelerate access to the company web sites by requests from the Internet.

Hub   A device that connects the network to several devices at once. 10baseT and Arcnet are networking methods that use hubs.

Hybrid Organization   An NDS organization strategy that combines the two other methods—location-based and functional. A hybrid, or combination, network organization is often the most useful for larger companies.

IEEE   *See* Institute of Electronic and Electrical Engineers.

Implementation Strategy   The method used for implementing, or moving to, NDS on a network. Strategies include the departmental or divisional implementation and the organizational implementation.

Implied Security Equivalence   In NDS, an object is security equivalent to the object's parent object and its parents, leading up to the [Root] object. This is also called *container security equivalence*. The IRF does not affect this process.

Inherited Rights   In NDS or the file system, inherited rights are rights that a trustee receives for an object because of rights to the object's parent (a directory in the file system, or a parent object in NDS). Inherited rights can be blocked by an explicit assignment or by the IRF.

Inherited Rights Filter (IRF)   In the file system, the IRF is the list of rights that a user can inherit for a directory from directories above it. An IRF also exists for each NDS object, and lists the rights that a trustee can inherit from the object's parents. In NetWare 3.*x*, the IRF was called the Inherited Rights Mask (IRM) and applied only to the file system.

In-Place Migration   One of the methods for migrating (upgrading) a server from NetWare 3.*x* to NetWare 5. In this method, the server is upgraded directly to the new NOS, leaving data files on the server intact. An alternative method is across-the-wire migration.

Install Wizard   Use this method to quickly upgrade NetWare 3.*x* or 4.*x* servers to NetWare 5. This is also known as an in-place upgrade.

Institute of Electronic and Electrical Engineers (IEEE)   An international organization that sets standards. These include the IEEE 802 series, which defines standards for Ethernet and Token Ring networks.

Integrated Services Digital Network   *See* ISDN.

International Standards Organization (ISO)   The standards organization that developed the OSI model. ANSI is a member of the ISO.

Internet   A global network made up of a large number of individual networks interconnected through the use of TCP/IP protocols. The individual networks comprising the Internet are from colleges, universities, businesses, research organizations, government agencies, individuals, and other bodies. The governing body of this global network is the Internet Activities Board (IAB). When the term *Internet* is used with an uppercase *I,* it refers to the global network, but when written with a lowercase *i*, it simply means a group of interconnected networks.

Internet Protocol   *See* IP.

Internetworking   The process of connecting multiple local area networks to form a wide area network (WAN). A router handles internetworking between different types of networks.

Interoperability   In information systems, the ability to run on any operating system or network. The TCP/IP protocol suite represents an example of interoperability; it can run on Windows 95 as well as NetWare 5.

Intranet   A term for any network that makes Internet-related services, such as e-mail, FTP, and the Web, available to users of a local network.

IntranetWare   A server software package previously sold by Novell. IntranetWare included NetWare 4.11 and several intranet-related utilities: NetWare Web Server, NetWare FTP Server, NetWare Internet Access Services (NIAS), and the IPX/IP Gateway.

Intruder   Refers to anyone who attempts to log in using an invalid password and/or username. This can be someone trying to access your network via the Internet or your company intranet.

IP   An acronym for Internet Protocol. More and more companies use IP as a networking standard because of its wide use in the industry, and because they need to access the Internet.

IP Address   The logical address of a computer in a TCP/IP network. Every computer (client or server) must have a unique and registered IP address if it is connected to the Internet.

IPX   An acronym for Internetwork Packet Exchange, IPX is a connectionless network layer protocol. It is responsible for dividing data into packets and selecting routes over a multinetwork environment to deliver the data. It is part of the IPX/SPX protocol suite supported by NetWare.

IPX External Network Number   A number that is used to represent an entire network. All servers on the network must use the same external network number.

IPX Internal Network Number   A number that uniquely identifies a server to the network. Each server must have a different internal network number.

IRF   *See* Inherited Rights Filter.

ISDN   A network standard that allows high-speed communication over ordinary category 3 or 5 copper cabling. It may someday replace conventional phone systems with high-speed digital lines.

ISO   *See* International Standards Organization.

Java   A programming language developed by Sun Microsystems and modeled after C++. Java can be called from an Internet browser or executed directly. This means that a Java application can run independent of the host operating system as long as it has access to the Java virtual machine.

Java Virtual Machine   Translates the Java application's byte code, the source code for Java, into machine code, and then executes the application.

Java Applets   Short functions that run on a Java-compatible browser.

Java AWT (Abstract Windowing Toolkit)   A developer API that creates a common look and feel for all Java applications. This has become obsolete with the SWING API. See the Java Web site (http://www.javasoft.com) for more information.

Java Class   A complete Java application.

Java Foundation Classes (JFC)   A toolkit used by developers to create robust Java applications. NetWare 5 has a fully compatible implementation of the JFC.

Jukebox   A device that automatically switches optical disks, facilitating high-capacity storage on optical media. Jukeboxes are supported by NetWare 5's High-Capacity Storage System (HCSS).

Kernel   The fundamental part of the NetWare operating system that interacts directly with the hardware. The kernel acts as an interface to the hardware, and basic services provided by the operating system, for user applications.

LAN   An acronym for local area network, a LAN is a network restricted to a certain area—a single building, a group of buildings, or even a single room. A LAN often has only one server, but can have many, if desired.

LANalyzer Agent Software   An agent that gathers network traffic information and feeds that information to other utilities, such as LANalyzer Management Console or ManageWise if you have it on your network.

Large Internet Packets (LIP)   A system that NetWare 5 provides to increase the speed of network communications. Packets sent through a router are kept at their maximum possible size, rather than being reduced to 512 bytes as they were in older versions of NetWare.

Leaf Object   An object that cannot contain other objects and that represents a network resource. Types of leaf objects include User, Group, Printer, Server, Volume, and many others.

License Diskette   A disk included in the NetWare 5 package that contains licensing information. This controls the amount of users the network can have logged in at one time. Multiple licenses can be used thanks to the additive licensing feature.

Lightweight Directory Access Protocol (LDAP)   A cross-platform, scaled-down version of Directory Access Protocol. This version of Directory services is typically used in TCP/IP messaging environments. LDAP has been integrated with NetWare 5 and NDS to provide Directory services for platforms and applications that don't have native NDS support.

Load Balancing   When multiprocessors are available, this feature allows the kernel to distribute the current workload intelligently among them.

Local Area Network   *See* LAN.

Locality Object   This is a new NDS container object introduced with NetWare 5. The Locality object is used to separate sites by regions or states. It comes in two flavors, generic or state/province locality.

Location-Based Organization   A method of organizing the Directory tree that divides it into Organizational Units for each geographical location of the company. This strategy is often the best for network communication. The other organizational options are functional and hybrid.

Logical Ports   Ports used by the CAPTURE command to redirect a workstation printer port to a network print queue. The logical port has no relation to the port to which the printer is actually attached, or the physical port.

Login   The DOS command used in NetWare to access a server from a client. When you run this command, you are prompted for a username and a password. In Windows 95 or Windows NT, the Login Utility, a graphical interface, is used to log in to a NDS tree.

Login Script   A set of login script commands that are automatically executed when a user logs in. NetWare 5 includes container, profile, user, and default login scripts. Up to three of these can be executed for each user.

Login Security   The most basic form of network security. A username and password are required in order to log in to the network and access resources.

Logout   The process of terminating a session with a NetWare server. A LOGOUT command is used to run this function.

MAC Address   The six-byte address of the network interface card.

MAN   *See* Metropolitan Area Network.

ManageWise   An application package you can use with NetWare 5, ManageWise provides you with a variety of network management capabilities. With it you can track network performance, inventory assets, perform network analysis, and monitor workstations and servers.

MAP   A command-line utility used to create mapped and search drives.

Mapped Drives   Logical paths to a storage location on a server, indicated by an alphabetical character (A to Z).

Master Replica   The main replica for a partition. The master replica must be available when major changes, such as partition merging and splitting, are performed. Another replica can be assigned as the master if the original master replica is lost.

Memory Allocation   The system NetWare 5 uses to provide memory for use by applications (NLMs) on the server. Memory is allocated from an allocation pool.

Memory Protection   Allows applications to run in a separate memory area from the kernel, thus protecting the kernel from corrupted applications.

Menu Utilities   A type of NetWare utility that presents a menu of options when it executes. Menu utilities have a consistent interface. FILER and NETADMIN are two examples. Other utilities are command-line utilities, and require that all information be entered when the command is typed.

Merging Directory Trees   The process of combining two Directory trees into a single tree. The objects in the source tree are combined into the destination, or target tree. The DSMERGE utility is used to merge trees.

Merging Partitions   The process of combining an NDS partition with its parent partition, resulting in a single partition. The master replica of the partition must be available for this process.

Message File   A file used to provide prompts and messages for a NetWare workstation or server utility. Message files are provided for each supported language (English, French, Italian, German, and Spanish).

Message Store   A component of GroupWise that stores the messages clients send to each other.

Message Switching   A type of network communication that sends an entire message, or block of data, rather than a simple packet.

Message Transfer System (MTS)   Responsible for routing messages from server to server.

Metropolitan Area Network (MAN)   A network spanning a single city or metropolitan area. A MAN is larger than local area networks (LANs), which are normally restricted to a single building or neighboring buildings, but smaller than a wide area network (WAN), which can span the entire globe. (The term *MAN* is rarely used outside of Novell education courses.)

Mobile User   A user who travels from site to site and needs access to the company network.

Modem   A device used to convert the digital signals produced by a computer into the analog signals required by analog telephone lines, and vice versa. This process of conversion allows computers to communicate across telephone lines.

Modular   An approach to developing software or hardware by components. Each component runs independently but functions as part of a group. For example, NetWare 5's design is modular because it has a core component called the kernel and components that provide additional functionality (NetWare Loadable Modules, or NLMs). Each NLM can be loaded or unloaded independently of the core, but its purpose is to provide additional services to the operating system.

MONITOR   A NetWare server utility that displays server performance data and that you can use to modify server parameters. Its NLM is run on the server console.

Multi-Processor Kernel (MPK)   Can detect whether your system has one or multiple processors on the motherboard. The maximum number of processors that NetWare 5 supports for a single system is 32.

Multiprotocol Router (MPR)   The software that provides routing capabilities for a NetWare 5 server. This allows communication between different types of networks. The latest version of the MPR is included as part of the IntranetWare package.

Multi-Valued Property   In NDS, a property that can have multiple values. For example, a User object's Telephone Number property can store multiple telephone numbers.

Name Conflict   A situation in which names conflict with each other. This typically happens in Bindery Services or when using NetSync. All users in the bindery context must have unique common names.

Name Resolution   The process of locating an object in the Directory tree. NDS objects are stored in replicas, which are located throughout servers in the network. When you request a resource on the tree, NDS will locate the resource by going from one replica to another until it locates the object. This is done based on the information your default server has. This process is also called *tree walking*.

Name Space   A service that you can install on a NetWare 5 server volume to allow the use of different types of filenames. Name spaces are available for Windows 95/98 and Windows NT, OS/2, NFS, and Macintosh. The default NetWare 5 name space supports Windows 95/98, Windows NT, and DOS filenames.

NDPS (Novell Distributed Print Services)   The new printing services that come with NetWare 5. With NDPS you can print to a network printer whether it's attached to the server, to a workstation, or directly to the network. (Queue-based printing still exists, mainly for backward compatibility with clients using previous versions of NetWare.)

NDPS Broker   Supports the Gateway and the NDPS Manager, and provides three services to NDPS: Service Registry Service (SRS), Event Notification Service (ENS), and Resource Management Service (RMS).

NDPS Manager   The component of NDPS that allows you to create and manage Printer Agents.

NDS   *See* NetWare Directory Services.

NDS for NT   NetWare Directory services for Windows NT workstations and servers. This is a set of utilities used for administrating NT workstations and servers, stand-alone or in an NT domain.

NDS Manager   The Windows GUI utility used to manage partitions and to perform Directory services maintenance.

NDS Manager (NDSMGR32.EXE)   A Windows-based application used for managing partitions and replicas in NDS.

NDS Schema   Defines the structure, also referred to as a *template*, of the Directory database. The schema defines objects, their properties, and their relationships to other objects in the tree.

NDS Trace   *See* DSTRACE.

Netscape FastTrack Server   The WWW Services component that NetWare 5 uses to provide Web services for intranets and to the Internet.

NetWare Administrator   The name given to the Windows GUI utility used to manage NDS objects from a Windows workstation. The latest version is NWADMN32.EXE.

NetWare Application Group   The only application that is created by default when you install a NetWare 5 server. Some applications are created when programs load their NLMs, and those that don't are assigned to the NetWare Application group by default.

NetWare Backup/Restore   A group of NLMs and executables that provide the backup and restore services and administration utilities for NetWare servers and clients and the NDS.

NetWare Directory Services (NDS)   The system NetWare 5 uses to catalog objects on the network—users, printers, volumes, and others. NDS uses a Directory tree to store this information. All of NetWare 5's network resources can be managed through NDS.

NetWare DOS Requester   The client software that is used on a DOS workstation to access the NetWare 5 network and NDS. The VLM.EXE program is used to load the DOS Requester. The Novell Client in NetWare 5 has replaced the DOS Requester.

NetWare File System   The system that manages disk storage on the NetWare server. It uses the FAT (File Allocation Tables) file storage structure, similar to the DOS file system. The NetWare file system is designed to support DOS, Windows 95/98, and Windows NT.

NetWare Internet Access Server   *See* NIAS.

NetWare Licensing Services   A Novell product that allows you to maintain a license database for your NetWare and third-party application products.

NetWare Loadable Module (NLM)   An application or program that executes on the NetWare server. NLMs are used for device drivers, LAN drivers, and applications such as backup software. A variety of utility NLMs are provided with NetWare 5, and others are available from third-party vendors.

NetWare OS/2 Requester   The client software used to access a NetWare 5 server and NDS from an OS/2 workstation.

NetWare Peripheral Architecture (NPA)   A system NetWare 5 allows for device drivers, used to control disk and tape drives. The driver is divided into two modules: a host adapter module (HAM) and a custom device module (CDM) for each device attached to the host adapter. Older device drivers use a single program with a .DSK extension. These cannot be used in NetWare 5.

NetWare-to-Unix Print Gateway   Allows clients on the NetWare network to print to Unix machines.

Network Address   A logical address that identifies a physical network segment. This address is common for all the nodes in the segment (in contrast to the unique address that a network interface card has on each node). Only routable protocols like TCP/IP or IPX require such an address.

Network Interface Card (NIC)   A physical device that connects computers and other network equipment to the transmission medium used. When installed in a computer's expansion bus slot, a NIC allows the computer to become a workstation on the network.

Network Operating System (NOS)   The software that runs on a file server and offers file, print, and other servers to client workstations. NetWare 5 is a NOS. Other examples include NetWare 3.*x*, Banyan VINES, and IBM LAN Server.

Network Time Protocol (NTP)   An open Internet standard used to synchronize time in an IP or IP/IPX NetWare environment. NTP.NLM is located in the SYS:SYSTEM directory. The only time server allowed for IPX-based servers is a secondary server. The IP based servers using NTP are either in server mode (analogous to a reference time server) or in peer mode (analogous to a primary time server).

Network-centric   The architecture used in a NetWare 5 network, in which objects are created for the entire network, rather than for a single server. This feature is one of the benefits of NDS.

NIAS 4.1   A component of NetWare 5 and BorderManager, this software provides routing, gateway services, and remote access for dial-up clients to your network. These services include multiprotocol routing; WAN support; packet filtering; Network Address Translators (NAT, which translates private IP addresses to registered ones); an IPX mapping gateway (which translates private IPX addresses to registered IPX addresses); and inbound/outbound remote access. NIAS 4.1 also provides Virtual Private Network (VPN) tunneling and encryption services over the Internet, eliminating the need for private lines.

NIC   *See* Network Interface Card.

NIS   An acronym for Network Information Service, this is an alternate protocol for domain management, and can be used instead of, or along with, DNS.

NLM   *See* NetWare Loadable Module.

Node   In TCP/IP, an IP addressable computer system, such as workstations, servers, minicomputers, mainframes, and routers. In IPX networks, the term is usually applied to non-server devices such as workstations and printers.

Novell Client   Novell software that provides connectivity from the workstation to the server. Formerly called Client 32, the Novell Client software intercepts calls to resources to determine whether it is a local or network resource that is being requested. If it determines that a network resource is being requested, then it redirects the call to the NetWare server. The Novell Client is still often called Client 32; it was renamed with NetWare 5 but the software remains the same. The Novell Client is available for Windows 3.1, Windows 95/98, Windows NT, and DOS.

Novell Distributed Print Services   *See* NDPS.

Novell Online Documentation   An HTML document-based database that provides information on the NetWare 5 operating system, services, clients, and resources.

Novell Replication Services (NRS)   A NetWare server product that allows you to replicate and synchronize directories with their contents. This product is very useful when you want to maintain files over multiple servers to provide easy access to users, for example HR documents that need to be available to all employees.

Novell Storage Services (NSS)   A new technology developed by Novell to provide quick and unlimited access to storage devices. NSS is independent of the operating system yet compatible with NetWare 5 and the NetWare file system. NSS is not limited by FAT file system constraints as previous NetWare volumes were.

Novell's Application Programming Interface (API)   Gives software developers access to NetWare resources like NetWare Directory Services. Through Novell's API, programmers can add objects and properties to NDS so that their applications can be integrated into the Directory and take advantage of its capabilities.

NRS   *See* Novell Replication Services.

NSS   *See* Novell Storage Services.

NTP   *See* Network Time Protocol.

NTP.CFG   Located in the SYS:ETC directory, this file is used to configure NTP.

NWADMN32.EXE   The latest version of NetWare Administrator, used for managing NDS objects and the file system. This is a 32-bit version developed for Windows 95/98 and Windows NT.

NWCONFIG   A loadable module that is used to change installation parameters and to upgrade or install additional software.

Object   In NDS, any resource on the network. Users, printers, and groups are examples of leaf objects. Another type, the container object, is used to organize other objects.

Object Names   The name used when referring to a NDS object. The object name is usually the most obvious name for an object. For example, the User object name is that person's login name.

Object Trustee   *See* Trustee.

Occupant   A user who has been assigned to an Organizational Role object. Each Organizational Role can have multiple occupants, stored in the Occupants property of the object.

Open Data-Link Interface (ODI)   A specification under NetWare that allows workstations or NetWare servers to use multiple protocols on the same network card. To use ODI you need to have MLID-compliant network cards. The ODI specification is similar to Microsoft's NDIS (Network Driver Interface Specification).

Open System Interconnection (OSI)   A model defined by the ISO to conceptually organize the process of communication between computers in terms of seven layers, called *protocol stacks*. The OSI model provides a way for you to understand how communication across various protocols takes place.

Organization Object   Usually the highest-level container object used. Organizations are created under the [Root], or under the Country object if it is used. This object usually represents an entire organization or company. More than one Organization can be used in the same Directory tree.

Organizational Implementation   One of the methods of implementing NDS. In this method, the entire Organization is moved at once. This is also called the top-down approach. This method is rarely practical. The divisional or departmental implementation is the alternative.

Organizational Role Object   An object that is used to represent a role—an administrator or other specialized user—that requires access to certain NDS objects or files. This type of object is often used for container administrators. The user assigned to the Organizational Role is called the *occupant* of the role.

Organizational Unit Object   A type of container object. Organizational Units can be used to divide locations, divisions, workgroups, or smaller portions of the Directory tree. Organizational Units can be subdivided further with additional Organizational Units.

OSI   *See* Open System Interconnection.

PA   *See* Printer Agent.

Packet   The basic division of data sent over a network. Each packet contains a set amount of data along with a header that contains information about the type of packet and the network address to which it is being sent. The size and format of packets depends on the protocol and frame types used.

Packet Burst Protocol   A protocol that streamlines NetWare communications. Several packets (a burst) are sent together, and only a single acknowledgment is required from the receiving server. If there is an error, only the packets that were not received correctly need to be sent again. This eliminates most of the process of sending acknowledgments back and forth.

Packet Receive Buffers   Areas of memory that NetWare sets aside for receiving packets over the network. Packets are stored in the buffers until the server is able to process them.

Packet Switching   A type of data transmission in which data is divided into packets, each of which has a destination address. Each packet is then routed across a network in an optimal fashion. An addressed packet may travel a different route than packets related to it. Packet sequence numbers are used at the destination node to reassemble related packets.

Paging   A technique possible on the Pentium processor, and to a lesser extent on 386 and 486 processors, that allows memory to be handled in 4K blocks, or pages. NetWare 5 supports this feature for increased speed.

Parent Object   In NDS, an object that contains another object; also called a *container object*. This is a relative term; a parent object also has parent objects of its own, and is considered a child object from that perspective.

Parent Partition   The partition from which child partitions are created.

Partition (in NDS)   A branch of the NDS tree that can be replicated onto multiple servers. The partition includes a container object and the objects under it, and is named according to the name of that object. By default, a single partition—the [Root] partition—exists.

Partition (on a Disk)   NetWare uses disk partitions to divide a hard disk. A disk can contain a single NetWare partition, which is used to hold one or more NetWare volumes. In addition, it can have a DOS partition, used to boot the server and hold the SERVER.EXE program.

PDS   *See* Print Device Subsystem.

Peer Mode (in NTP)   *See* Network Time Protocol (NTP).

Peer-to-Peer Network   A local area network in which network resources are shared among workstations, without the use of a file server.

Physical Port   In printing, the port to which a printer is actually attached. This differs from the logical ports used in the CAPTURE command for printer redirection.

Ping   A TCP/IP utility used to test whether another machine is online. A ping program sends a request to the other machine, waits for a reply, and displays the time the reply took to arrive. An implementation of this utility, WinPing, is included with the IPX/IP Gateway software.

Point-to-Point   Network communication in which two devices have exclusive access to a network medium. For example, a printer connected to only one workstation would be using a point-to-point connection.

Policy Package   Contains policies that have been grouped, for ease of administration, according to the types of objects the policies can be associated with. You can use Policy Packages and NetWare Administrator to maintain Workstation objects and other NDS objects associated with workstations.

Port Driver   A component of NetWare 5 printing. The port driver accepts data from the print server and sends it to the printer. The port driver can be a hardware device, NPRINTER.EXE on a workstation, or NPRINTER.NLM on a server.

Print Device Subsystem (PDS)   An NDPS server component used by the Novell Printer Gateway, first to retrieve printer-specific information by reading Page Description Language (PDL), and second, to store it in a database.

Port Handler (PH)   The component that allows the gateway to accommodate various protocols and interfaces. It does this by abstracting the physical hardware or protocol information from the PDS.

PPP   An acronym for Point-to-Point Protocol, which allows the sending of IP packets on a dial-up (serial) connection. PPP supports compression and IP address negotiation.

PPPRNS   An acronym for Point-to-Point Protocol Remote Node Services. This service supports PPP, compression, and IP address negotiation. PPPRNS is included with the NIAS Remote Access Server, new with NetWare 5.

Preemptive Multitasking   Improves NetWare's support of applications by allowing the kernel to take over the processor at any time, without an application relinquishing control.

Primary Time Server   One of the four types of time server. A primary server communicates with other primary servers and reference servers, and negotiates or "votes" to determine the correct time.

Print Device Subsystem (PDS)   Allows the gateway to query a printer and get printer-specific information, such as whether the printer can print in color or in duplex mode.

Print Job   A file that has been sent by a client for printing. Print jobs are stored in a print queue until the print server can service them. Queues are only used in a non-NDPS printing environment.

Print Job Configuration   A set of parameters for non-NDPS network printing that is associated with the CAPTURE command. These are similar to the parameters in the CAPTURE command. Print job configurations can be set for user and container objects.

Print Queue   The area used to hold the list of print jobs, in a non-NDPS printing environment, that are waiting to print. The print queue is managed through the Print Queue object in NDS. Print jobs are sent from the print queue to the print server one at a time.

Print Server   A device that is used to manage printing in a non-NDPS print environment. The Print Server NDS object is used to manage printing. The print server itself can run on a NetWare 5 server (PSERVER.NLM) or in a hardware device.

Printer Agent (PA)   A central component of NDPS, PAs handle the functions that were previously done by Printer, Print Queue, and Print Server objects in queue-based printing.

Printer Redirection   The process of mapping a logical printer port in the workstation to a network printer. The user can then print to the port as if it was an actual printer, and the print job will be sent to the print queue. The CAPTURE utility is used to start redirection.

Profile Object   A special NDS object that is used to assign the same login script to a group of users. The profile login script is executed after the container login script and before the user login script.

Properties   In NDS, all of the possible information that can be entered for an object. The properties of a User object include Login Name, Full Name, and Telephone Number. The information in a property is called the *value* of the property.

Proprietary   A system that is defined by one vendor, and typically is not supported by others. Arcnet started as a proprietary protocol, as did Token Ring.

Protocol   A method of communicating between NetWare servers and clients. The protocol is the "language" used for sending data. Data is divided into packets specified by the protocol. NetWare 5 supports the TCP/IP and IPX protocols.

Protocol Suite   A collection of protocols that are associated with and that implement a particular communication model (such as the OSI Reference Model).

Proxy Services   An NIAS service, a proxy connects an intranet to the Internet through a single host, which makes Internet requests on behalf of the intranet hosts.

Public Access Printer   A type of NDPS printer that is available to all network users and not associated with an NDS object. These printers provide no security, and event notification is limited.

Public Switched Telephone Network (PSTN)   This includes the network we use for ordinary telephone calls and modem communications, as well as dedicated lines that are leased by customers for private, exclusive use. Commercial service providers offer numerous services that facilitate computer communication across PSTN, also known as *POTS* (plain old telephone system).

[Public] Trustee   A special NDS trustee that can be used to assign rights to all users in the network, including those that are not logged in. [Public] trustees are used to allow users to browse the Directory tree before logging in. You should avoid assigning rights to this type of trustee.

Queue-Based Printing   A printing environment supported by previous versions of NetWare, and supported by NetWare 5 for backward compatibility. *See also* Print Queue, Print Server, and Print Job.

RADIUS   An acronym for Remote Dial-In User Service, RADIUS is an access control protocol that uses a challenge response method for authentication. This is a standard implementation used to secure access over the Internet from a client to a private network.

RConsole   An application used to access the server console from a workstation. RConsole allows the administrator to run console commands and load NLMs on the server from a workstation. It is compatible with IPX installations.

RConsoleJ   A Java-based application used to access the server console from a workstation. RConsoleJ allows the administrator to run command lines and load NLMs from a workstation. It works with pure IP installations.

Read Replica   A type of replica that can be used to view partition data but cannot be updated or used for authentication.

Read/Write Replica   A type of replica that can be updated and used for authentication. This replica can also be upgraded to a master replica.

Reference Time Server   One of the four types of time server. The reference time server provides an authoritative source of time. It is often attached to an external clock or to a modem or radio link to a time source. One or more primary time servers must be used with it.

Relative Distinguished Name (RDN)   A shortened version of an object's full distinguished name that specifies the path to the object from the current context. Relative distinguished names do not begin with a period. Periods can be used at the end of the RDN to move up the Directory tree.

Remote Access   A feature of NetWare that enables remote users of Windows, Macintosh, and DOS systems to dial in to a network and access all available resources.

Remote Control   A connection mode for a workstation running Novell Client software. With remote control connections, a remote workstation can control a dedicated workstation on the network. This allows an administrator to take control of a remote workstation for support purposes. Only keystrokes and screen updates are transmitted over the communications link.

Replica Ring   A group of replicas of a NDS partition. This includes a master replica and one or more other replicas, each held on a separate NetWare 5 server. These replicas are synchronized frequently.

Replication   The process of keeping copies of the NDS information on separate servers. Each partition in NDS has a set of replicas. These include the master replica—the original partition—and, optionally, read/write and read-only replicas.

Resource Management Service (RMS)   This NDPS service keeps track of all the resources needed by NDPS clients and printers, as well as anything else that may request them.

Resource Record (RR)   Maps a host name to an IP address.

Ring   An alternate term for the domains in NetWare 5's memory protection scheme. Ring 0 is the OS domain, and ring 3 is the OS_PROTECTED domain. Applications on a ring are serviced in order by the kernel.

RMS   *See* Resource Management Service.

[Root] Object   The ultimate NDS container object. The [Root] object is created when NDS is installed, and contains all other objects. This object cannot be deleted, renamed, or moved.

RootServerInfo Zone Object   Maintains information on Internet root domain servers.

Router   A device that connects two dissimilar networks, and allows packets to be transmitted and received between them.

Scalability   A feature of NetWare 5 services, implemented through NPA (NetWare Peripheral Architecture) and the NetWare clients. Scalability means that as many of the features as are needed can be used, providing benefits for both small-scale and large-scale systems.

Scheduling Ensures that business-critical applications have adequate processor time. The kernel in NetWare 5 allows the administrator to prioritize applications through scheduling.

SCRSAVER NetWare 5 restricts access to the server console screen with the use of a screen saver. The SCRSAVR.NLM utility launches it.

Search Drives Logical paths that will be searched when an application is called. The paths are located on servers, and they are represented by an alphabetical character (A to Z).

Secondary Time Server One of the four types of time server. Secondary time servers are strictly time consumers; they do not provide time to any servers. They receive time from a primary or single reference server, and provide the time to clients.

Security Equivalence In NDS, any situation in which an object, or trustee, receives the same rights given to another object. There are two types of security equivalence: implied and explicit.

Server Console The place where you view, execute, and control server activity. This includes the monitor, keyboard, and mouse attached to the server box.

Server Manager A series of forms used by the Administration Server to configure and manage the Netscape FastTrack Server.

Server Mode (in NTP) *See* Network Time Protocol (NTP).

Server Printer One of the methods of attaching a non-NDPS printer to the network, probably the most common. The printer is attached to a printer port on the NetWare server. The port driver, NPRINTER.NLM, is used to drive the printer.

Server-centric The type of network organization used on NetWare 3.*x* networks. In this organization, each server keeps its own catalog of users and other resources (the bindery). A user who requires access to more than one server must be added to the bindery of each one. NetWare 5 provides a network-centric alternative.

Service Advertising Protocol (SAP) The protocol used for various NetWare 5, as well as 2.*x* and 3.*x*, services. Single reference time servers use this protocol to broadcast time information to the entire network at once.

Service Registry Service (SRS) Makes Public Access printers possible by providing a place for them to be registered. Then, when an administrator or user wants information on that printer or wants to use it, SRS provides a central location for obtaining the information or making the printer use possible.

Simple Network Management Protocol (SNMP) A management protocol used on many networks, particularly TCP/IP. It defines the type, format, and retrieval of management information about nodes.

Single Reference Time Server One of the four types of time server. If it's used, the single reference server is the only time provider on the network. All other servers must be configured as secondary time servers. This is the default configuration when NetWare 5 servers are installed.

SLIP An acronym for Serial Line Internet Protocol, SLIP permits the sending of IP packets on a dial-up (serial) connection but does not itself support compression or IP address negotiation.

snAppShot A tool used to create complex applications by taking a picture of a computer before and after you install an application, and then comparing the two.

SNMP   *See* Simple Network Management Protocol.

Splitting Partitions   The process of creating a new NDS partition. A container object within a current partition is specified, and that object and all objects under it are moved (split) to a new partition.

SRS   *See* Service Registry Service.

Standards Document   A document that describes the naming standards, properties, and values to be used for a network. This is a vital part of NDS planning.

Start Bit   A bit that is sent as part of a serial communication stream to signal the beginning of a byte or packet.

STARTUP.NCF   A script file used to load disk drivers when the SERVER.EXE is executed.

Stop Bit   A bit that is sent as part of a serial communication stream to signal the end of a byte or packet.

Storage Management Services (SMS)   The NetWare 5 service that allows for backup services. SMS consists of several components, ranging from the device driver that handles access to the backup device to the front end, or backup engine.

Subnet Address Range Object   A DHCP object that contains the range of IP addresses available to assign to DHCP clients in a particular subnet.

Subnet Mask   A configuration variable for the TCP/IP protocol suite that tells the source host whether the destination host is in the same local network or on a remote network.

Subnet Object   A DHCP object that represents an IP subnet assigned to a physical network segment. The subnet is the logical network address that is assigned to a physical network segment in a TCP/IP network.

Subnet Pool Object   An object that can assign IP addresses to multiple subnets in a single physical segment.

Subordinate References   Replicas that are created automatically when a server contains a replica of a parent partition but not a replica of the child partition. The subordinate reference replica points to the child partition replicas.

Synchronization   The process used by NDS to ensure that all replicas of a partition contain the same data. Synchronization is handled through replica rings.

SYSCALLS   Short for NetWare Operating System Call and Marshalling Library, SYSCALLS is an NLM that intercepts corrupted calls and blocks them from passing calls to the core operating system.

Target Service Agent (TSA)   One of the components of the NetWare 5 Storage Management System (SMS), the TSA provides an interface to the device that will be backed up. Devices include servers, workstations, and the NDS database. A separate TSA is used for each device.

TCP/IP   An acronym for Transmission Control Protocol/Internet Protocol, generally used as shorthand for the phrase *TCP/IP protocol suite*. The TCP/IP protocol suite is a set of standards for communications and services between hosts, generally referred to as the Internet.

Telnet   A TCP/IP terminal emulation protocol that permits a node, called the Telnet client, to login to a remote node, called the Telnet server. The client simply acts as a dumb terminal, displaying output from the server. The processing is done at the server.

Time Consumer A machine that receives time information but does not send time information to any other server. Secondary time servers are time consumers, as are network workstations.

Time Provider A type of time server that provides the time to other time servers, including single reference, reference, and primary time servers. Also called a *time source*.

Time Provider Group A group of time servers, usually including a reference server and one or more primary servers. In a wide area network, separate time provider groups can be used for each location.

Time Server A server that is used for time synchronization. All NetWare 5 servers are time servers of one type or another. The types of servers include primary, reference, single reference, and secondary.

Time Source *See* Time Provider.

Time Stamping A process used by databases, in particular NDS, to assign a time to each change made to the database. This process ensures that a change that was made later isn't implemented before an earlier change during the replication process. *See also* Directory Synchronization.

Time Synchronization The process NetWare 5 uses to ensure that all servers are provided with the correct time. Time synchronization is managed through time servers.

TIMESYNC.CFG A file that contains server time synchronization parameters used during the server bootup process.

Topology A type of network connection or cabling system.

Transitive Synchronization The process NetWare uses to synchronize data across incompatible servers. When replicas of a partition are on servers that support different protocols, the replica synchronization process can't complete the updates. To solve this problem, Novell allows the synchronization to be forwarded through a server that supports both protocols. This server acts as a go-between for the incompatible servers that hold the replicas, ensuring that the updates are synchronized throughout the replica ring.

Tree Walking *See* Name Resolution.

Trustee Any object that has been given rights to an NDS object or file. Trustee rights can be explicit, inherited, or effective.

Turbo FAT Indexing A NetWare 5 service that decreases disk access time for large files by keeping an index, or turbo FAT (file allocation table), of the disk blocks in use by the file. NetWare uses this system automatically for larger files.

Typeful Naming The formal method of naming NDS objects, including name types for each portion of the distinguished name. An example of a typeful name is .CN=Terry.OU=Mktg.O=QAZ_CO.

Typeless Naming The more common method of NDS object naming, which does not include name types. An example of a typeless name is .Terry.Mktg.QAZ.CO. Typeless naming is adequate for most uses within NDS utilities.

UDP An acronym for User Datagram Protocol, UDP uses a connectionless, unguaranteed packet delivery method. It works at the Transport layer as an alternative to TCP, a connection-oriented, guaranteed form of packet delivery that is part of the TCP/IP protocol suite.

UIMPORT.EXE   A utility that allows you to create multiple user objects at the same time, facilitating the process of populating the NDS tree. UIMPORT does this is by importing data from two text files, one with control parameters and the other with user account information.

UNICON (Unix Console)   The main utility for configuring FTP Services. You can use this utility to manage all aspects of FTP Services as well as the other Unix services available through NetWare.

Universal Coordinated Time (UTC)   The standard time system supported by NetWare 5. (The abbreviation is from the French.) UTC was formerly known as GMT (Greenwich Mean Time). The time zone for a NetWare server is defined in terms of the difference from UTC; for example, the mountain time zone is UTC minus 7 hours.

Unix   A multitasking operating system, created by AT&T's Bell Labs, that is used on a wide variety of computers, including Internet servers.

Unix-to-NetWare Print Server   Allows clients on a Unix network to print to NetWare printers.

Upgrade Wizard   A tool for installing NetWare 5. Use this wizard to move data and users from a NetWare 3.*x* server to a new server running NetWare 5. This is called a server-to-server upgrade.

URL (Uniform Resource Locator)   The address that defines the location of a file on the Web or any other part of the Internet. Using the URL, you can locate a Web page, FTP site, and so on. An example of a URL is http://www.sybex.com, the address for the Sybex Web site.

User Template   In NDS, a special User object that is used to assign defaults when a new user is created. A user template can be created for each NDS container, and you can change the property values of this object to provide defaults for new users in the container.

Values   The data that is stored in the properties of an NDS object. Properties can have one or more values. Some are required, and others are optional.

Virtual Loadable Module (VLM)   One of the components of the DOS Requester. The VLM.EXE program loads various VLMs, each for a certain purpose. For example, PRINT.VLM allows redirection of printers. VLMs that are not needed can be unloaded to increase available memory.

Virtual Memory   Supports applications that need more memory than available through physical RAM. NetWare provides additional RAM by using freed hard disk space, a process which is transparent to the application.

Virus Protect   Provides networkwide protection by installing elements in the workstations and the servers. Some of the services provided by Virus Protect include scanning of all resources, continuous real-time protection, workstation/mobile computer protection, and self-maintenance.

VLM   *See* Virtual Loadable Module.

Volume   A major unit of storage in a NetWare server, similar to a DOS partition.

WAN   *See* Wide Area Network.

WAN Traffic Manager   A snap-in to NetWare Administrator that allows you to manage server-to-server traffic across WAN links, reducing network costs.

Wide Area Network (WAN)   A network that extends across multiple locations. Each location typically has a local area network (LAN), and the LANs are connected together in a WAN. WANs are often used for enterprise networking.

Win2NCS   The Windows 95/NT client component of the implementation of the NSC (NetWare Asynchronous Services Interface Connection Services). The NSC makes available to the network a pool of modems. The Win2NCS on the client makes the modem pool available to the client. The NSC makes dial-out services available to your network when you implement NIAS remote access server. This software is installed separately from the Novell Client.

Windows NT Domain Controller   A domain controller that holds the account database that controls access to a domain.

Workstation Policies   Allow you to specify what a user can and can't do at his or her own workstation. For example, you could restrict a user's ability to view the Network Neighborhood in Windows 95/98 and Windows NT.

Workstation Printer   A printer that is attached to a workstation on the network. In NetWare 3.*x* these were referred to as remote printers and handled by the RPRINTER.EXE program. In NetWare 5 they are handled by the NPRINTER.EXE program.

World Wide Web (WWW)   Often called *the Web*, the World Wide Web refers to the vast collection of computers on the Internet running HTTP (Hypertext Transfer Protocol) servers. The Web allows the transmission of text, graphics, audio, video, Java programs, and more. Using a Web browser such as Netscape Navigator or Microsoft Internet Explorer, a user can link from one server to another at the click of a button.

WWW   *See* World Wide Web.

X.500   An ISO (International Standards Organization) Directory services protocol specification. NetWare uses the X.500 protocol, also known as DAP (Director Access Protocol), as a basis for its NDS implementation.

Z.E.N.works   Short for Zero Effort Networks. While they aren't truly zero effort, Z.E.N.works can make life much easier for network administrators. There are two versions of Z.E.N.works, the Starter Pack that comes for free with NetWare 5 on the Client CD and the full version, which must be purchased as a separate component. The full version offers all of the Starter Pack's functionality and adds the following features: remote control of workstations, a Help Requester application to make it easier for users to ask for help with problems, and the ability to keep a hardware inventory of each computer in NDS for troubleshooting and maintenance.

Zone   Containing DNS information pertaining to a domain name, the zone is managed and replicated throughout the Directory services.

Index

Note to the Reader: Page numbers in **bold** indicate the principal discussion of a topic or the definition of a term. Page numbers in *italic* indicate illustrations.

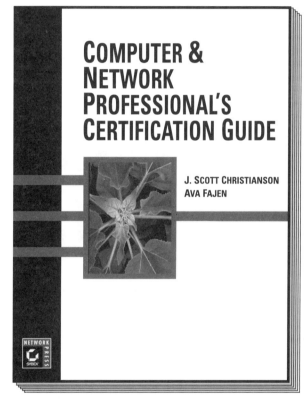

CISCO® STUDY GUIDES

FROM NETWORK PRESS®

- · Prepare for Cisco certification with the experts
- · Full coverage of each exam objective
- · Hands-on labs and hundreds of sample questions

ISBN 0-7821-2381-3
768 pp; 7½" x 9"; $49.99
Hardcover

ISBN 0-7821-2403-8
832 pp; 7½" x 9"; $49.99
Hardcover

ISBN 0-7821-2571-9
704 pp; 7½" x 9"; $49.99
Hardcover
Available April 1999

**CCDA: Cisco Certified Design
Associate Study Guide**
ISBN: 0-7821-2534-4; 800 pp; 7½" x 9"
$49.99; Hardcover; CD
Available May 1999

**CCNP: Cisco Internetwork
Troubleshooting Study Guide**
ISBN 0-7821-2536-0; 704 pp; 7½ x 9
$49.99; Hardcover; CD
Available May 1999

**CCNP: Configuring, Monitoring,
and Troubleshooting Dial-Up
Services Study Guide**
ISBN 0-7821-2544-1; 704 pp; 7½" x 9"
$49.99; Hardcover; CD
Available July 1999

SYBEX®
www.sybex.com

SYBEX BOOKS ON THE WEB

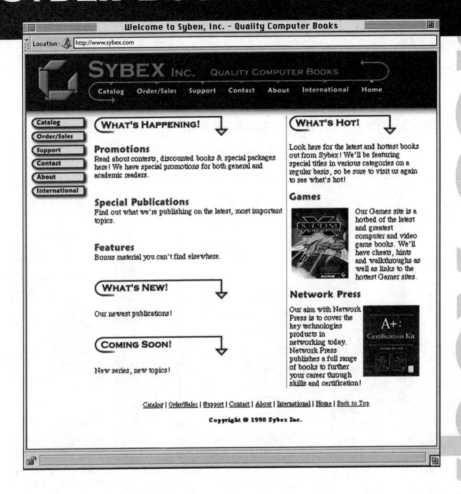

NETWARE® 5 CNE®
STUDY GUIDES FROM
NETWORK PRESS®

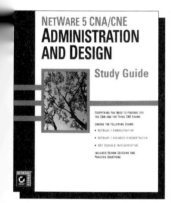

NetWare® 5 CNA℠/CNE®: Administration and Design Study Guide

ISBN: 0-7821-2387-2
864 pp.; 7 ½" X 9"
$44.99, Hardcover

Covers:

NetWare® 5 Administration
(the CNA test)

NetWare® 5 Advanced
Administration

NDS Design & Implementation

NetWare® 5 CNE®: Core Technologies Study Guide

ISBN: 0-7821-2389-9
512 pp.; 7 ½" X 9"
$44.99, Hardcover

Covers:

Networking Technologies

Service & Support

NetWare® 5 CNE®: Integrating Windows® NT® Study Guide

ISBN: 0-7821-2388-0
448 pp.; 7 ½" X 9"
$39.99, Hardcover

Covers:

Integrating Windows® NT®

NetWare® 5 CNE®: Update to NetWare® 5 Study Guide

ISBN: 0-7821-2390-2
432 pp.; 7 ½" X 9"
$39.99, Hardcover

Covers:

NetWare® 4.11 to
NetWare® 5 Update

www.sybex.com

Visit the Sybex Web Site for the NetWare 5 CNE

Go to *www.sybex.com* for additional tools and information to help you prepare for the new CNE exams. On the companion Web site for this book, you'll find:

■ Test Updates

Tests and test objectives can change. We'll provide the information you need to stay up-to-date as you prepare for the tests.

■ Online Testing Engines

Test your knowledge with our exclusive online testing program from The Edge Group. Simulate the test-taking experience with challenging questions like those you'll encounter on the NetWare 5 CNE tests.

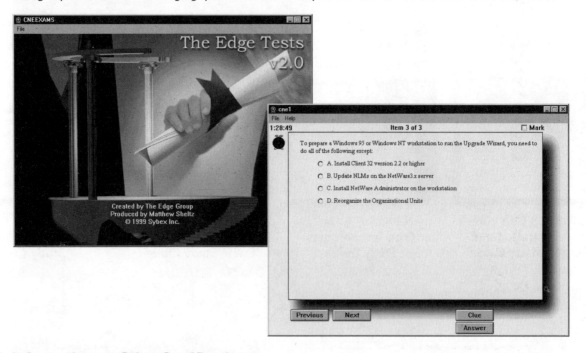

■ Information on Other Certifications

At Sybex's Web site you'll also find information on numerous other computer industry certification programs—MCSE, MCSD, A+, Java, Lotus Notes, Cisco, and more—together with details of Sybex books that will help you prepare for the certification exams.

 To get to the companion Web site for this book, click on the Catalog link on the Sybex home page (www.sybex.com), and then enter the title of the book in the keyword search box.